THE SUNDAY INDEPENDENT COMPLETE HANDBOOK OF GAELIC GAMES

Best Wishes,

Raymond Smith

GW00566732

COVER PICTURES

Front Cover: Derry captain, Henry Downey (left) in action in the 1993 All-Ireland Senior Football Final against Cork and (right) Kilkenny centre-forward, John Power, at full stretch towards the Galway goal as Gerry McInerney endeavours to curb the attack in the 1993 All-Ireland Senior Hurling Final. (Pictures: INPHO)

The Sunday Independent/ACCBANK Complete Handbook of Gaelic Games

A Comprehensive Record
of
Results and Teams
(1887-1993)

By
RAYMOND SMITH

With a Foreword by
Jack Boothman
President-elect of the GAA

DUBLIN
1993

THE SUNDAY INDEPENDENT/ACCBANK
COMPLETE HANDBOOK
OF GAELIC GAMES

First published: 1993

Published by Sporting Books Publishers, Dublin
Cover origination by The City Office, Dublin 2.
Printed in the Republic of Ireland by the
Leinster Leader Ltd., Naas, Co. Kildare.

CONTENTS

Chapter   *Page*

Acknowledgements...(vii)

Preface...(ix)

Foreword...(xi)

PART ONE – FOOTBALL: *Down's Revival and Donegal's Arrival and Derry's First Ever Title; Historic Day for Clare and Epic Meath-Dublin Series in '91.*

  1. Ulster Counties Break the Perennial Cycle of Dominence.. 3

  2. "Sam's For The Hills"... 17

  3. The Team that Refused to Die...................................... 33

  4. Down Maintain Unique Record..................................... 44

  5. Clare Bridge 75 Years Gap.. 55

  6. Cork Miss Chance of Real Immortality.......................... 66

  7. Derry's First Ever Crown – And a Hat-Trick for Ulster... 81

PART TWO – HURLING: *The Eighties – A Decade of Change – But Old Order restored in Opening Seasons of Nineties: Cork (1990), Tipperary (1991) and Kilkenny (1992-'93) farm four titles but Wexford fail in Epic Battles in '93.*

  8. Galway and Offaly Illuminate Opening Seasons of the Eighties.. 95

  9. Keating's "Babes" Attain Maturity in Epic '91 Season..108

  10. The Cycle Comes Full Circle from Centenary Year Classic..121

  11. Kilkenny's 25th Title and Second-in-a-Row....................137

RECORDS SECTION – *Hurling and Football (1887-1988), also Colleges, Camogie, Handball, Ladies Football.*

INDEX – *Quick Reference Index to Editorial Chapters and Records Section.*

ACKNOWLEDGEMENTS

MANY people co-operated in the exhaustive and demanding task of up-dating the Records Section and carrying on the effort started in 1988 to authenticate scores and also names of players that appeared incorrectly in earlier works.

We thank in particular Mick Dunne, Dublin, Jim Cronin, Cork, John Clarke, Tullamore, and Tom Ryall, Kilkenny, who bore the brunt of the enormous effort extending over many months and who made available the benefit of their own years of research in order to ensure that this book would, as far as humanly possible, satisfy the criterion of authenticity. Seamus J. King, Cashel, and Jack Mahon, Galway, gave invaluable help also in this difficult area while Seamus O'Ceallaigh, Limerick, before he died had provided us with the Railway Cup Hurling and Football teams.

There are other names listed also at the outset of the Records Section in this book and to each and everyone we express our deep appreciation.

In the editorial chapters I concentrated in the main on epic games in the hurling and football championships since the 1988 edition of *The Complete Handbook of Gaelic Games*, while recognising at the same time the impact made by outstanding teams of earlier decades.

Thus the footballers of Down (1991), Donegal (1992) and Derry (1993) merit special chapters for their All-Ireland triumphs which completed a unique three-timer for Ulster. A full chapter is devoted to the unforgettable series of four games between Dublin and Meath in 1991 and a chapter also to Clare's break-through in Munster in 1992 to win their first Provincial crown in 75 years.

In Hurling we look at what Offaly and Galway hurlers brought to the Eighties by their achievements; at the epic games too in the South between Tipperary and Cork in the 1987-'92 period while Kilkenny hurlers merit a chapter for making it two All-Ireland titles back to back by taking the '93 crown.

We express our warm thanks and appreciation to the *Sunday Independent* and ACC Bank for sponsoring this book, also to the GAA authorities for giving it their support and to the national concerns who backed the project by taking advertising space, thus helping to alleviate the heavy cost of research and ensuring at the same time that it was possible to produce a work that could cover every aspect of GAA activity.

I thank in particular Jack Boothman, President-elect of the GAA for writing the Foreword to this book and agreeing to launch it; also Liam Mulvihill, Director-General of the Association and Danny Lynch, Press Officer for their recognition of the need of an up-dated reference work for all involved in the GAA.

I extend a special word of thanks to Maurice Moore of the *Irish Independent*, who designed the cover; City Office who were responsible for print origination of the front jacket; *Sportsfile*, Inpho agencies and Tom Brett, Kilkenny, for outstanding prints and Independent Newspapers for a selection of fine pictures by staff photographers.

The book would not have met the launching deadline but for the magnificent co-operation I received from the Leinster Leader, who have printed all my recent books. A special word of thanks to my friend, Michael Kane, whose professionalism and understanding ensured that everything went smoothly from the outset.

Finaly, I express my appreciation and thanks to Terence and Annette Sweeney for providing me with facilities to get the manuscript completed on time for the printers. And during my trips to Rosslare I experienced the utmost courtest from the staff of Kelly's Strand Hotel after long hours writing. It's always a pleasure to talk to the keen sports enthusiasts among them.

Dublin,
October, 1993.   *Raymond Smith*

PREFACE

By JOHN McCLOSKEY
Chief Executive ACC Bank

OUR national games of hurling and football have entered a new era of popularity, reflected in the crowds attending key matches both at club and inter-county level, in the tremendous demand for tickets for the major all-ticket occasions and in the so-encouraging spate of activity throughout the thirty-two counties at under-age level. The future of the games is secure.

The building of the new Cusack Stand and the expansion of the accommodation for spectators in Croke Park is an indication in itself of how the Association is progressing as we move on towards the year 2,000 and the advent of a new century.

Satellite television has opened up new vistas, bringing the games to a new public around the globe, creating an awareness of their distinctiveness in Irish life and of the non-stop flowing action they provide.

The break-through achieved by Donegal in 1992 in winning their first-ever All-Ireland senior football crown and Clare's toppling of Kerry in Munster that same season as they took their first Provincial crown in seventy-five years were events that generated a tidal wave of emotion and excitement. Then in 1993 Derry, my own native county, reached the All-Ireland final for the first time since 1958, having won the National League crown in 1992.

A memorable season was crowned with Derry's name being inscribed on the Sam Maguire Cup for the first time. Taking in Down's success in 1991 and Donegal's in 1992, Ulster counties have, therefore, completed a historic three-timer.

It is against this background that ACC Bank, which has had such a long association with the GAA and its rural base, is happy to jointly sponsor with the *Sunday Independent* this new up-dated edition of *The Complete Handbook of Gaelic Games.* We were already involved, incidentally, with the *Sunday Independent* in projects like the Personalities of the Decades and the Man of the Match awards that gave fitting recognition to great players of earlier decades and men of the current era who have made a lasting imprint.

The editorial chapters in this new edition chronicle the epoch-making moments in hurling and football in recent times. In addition a vast effort has been made by a dedicated team to ensure that the GAA records have been fully authenticated and up-dated while the coverage of all aspects of GAA activity – extending to the games in the colleges and universities, Army and Garda and to camogie and handball – has been expanded from earlier record books.

We feel that all GAA followers will want to have this book on their shelves at home and we are certain that it will give great pleasure to people in different age groups, while at the same time being the book that provides the answers to the vital questions when a result or team placing has to be checked.

FOREWORD

By JACK BOOTHMAN
President-Elect of the GAA

DESPITE the phenomenal interest in the GAA and gaelic
games, I have always found it astonishing that there have
been so few publications of substance in the Records field produced over the years.

I find it even more surprising that decades passed from the
founding of the Association in 1887 without there being available
a composite and comprehensive reference publication.

This was difficult to understand as, more than any other topic,
the GAA has shown itself to be the daily subject of deliberation
by people from professional journalists, to quizmasters to bar-
room experts. Indeed, where people meet in this country, the subject of gaelic games is never far from the surface.

A few years ago Raymond Smith filled a long-standing void
through the publication of his 450-page work *The Complete Handbook of Gaelic Games.* This book was not just an account of significant and contemporary events in the world of the GAA but was also
the first major publication to contain a comprehensive record of
relevant details of games and competitions. It was a mammoth task
and an astonishing achievement that many who require a regular
authentic reference source have had reason to be grateful for.

Being the professional that he is, Raymond was never fully
happy with this publication in terms of its comprehensiveness and
its absolute accuracy. He therefore mustered a team of journalists,
GAA statisticians, sponsors and many more and co-ordinated
their efforts to produce this revised, unique, comprehensive and
valuable publication.

This particular work is a monument to the collective efforts of
a great number of people and to the vision, commitment and
energy of Raymond Smith. It has many facets and outstanding
attributes but I believe that its major significance is that it will from
now on be an invaluable and definitive reference source for
everybody interested in the GAA, but in particular, for students
of gaelic games and those associated with the GAA professionally.

I sincerely commend all those involved in the publication and
particularly Raymond. You have added significantly to the GAA
library and its chronicle easily accessible to all.

Mó bhuíochas díobh uile.

SEÁN BOOTHMAN (Uachtarán-tofa CLG)

Dedication

Dedicated to the memory of Tipperary-born Rev. Con O'Mahony, a lover of the national games, who died following a heart attack suffered during the memorable 1990 All-Ireland Final between Cork and Galway. He epitomised the spirit of deep commitment of the Holy Ghost priests who served in Nigeria during the Civil War and in other misisonary fields and still give their service unswervingly today, as do the workers of the Aid agencies in Somalia and other countries where war and famine has wrought such tragedy on millions.

PART ONE

FOOTBALL

Down's Revival and Donegal's Arrival
– and a Historic Day for Clare
in Limerick

Meath and Dublin in Epic '91
Marathon Series of Four Games
in Leinster

Derry's First Ever Title as "Sam" Goes
to Ulster for Third Successive Year

CHAPTER 1

ULSTER COUNTIES BREAK THE PERENNIAL CYCLE OF DOMINANCE

THE 1991, 1992 and 1993 seasons will be remembered for the manner in which Down, Donegal and Derry broke what seemed the perennial cycle of dominance of Munster and Leinster counties that had lasted for twenty-three years.

Indeed, if you took out that All-Ireland triumph by Down in 1968, you were talking about a dominance that had extended thirty years back from the 1991 season to 1961.

And 1992 was unique also for Clare's achievement in winning their first Munster crown in seventy-five years, a feat made more memorable for their supporters in that they beat Kerry in the Provincial decider on Sunday, July 19, in Limerick. The introduction of the open draw in Munster had the dramatic effect of ending a situation where Cork and Kerry took it almost for granted that they would contest the final each season. The doubters, who had expressed the view that the open draw would be a disaster, were made eat their words in no uncertain terms.

The seventies had been dominated to a large extent by Kerry and Dublin. These counties participated in four All-Ireland finals (1975, '76, '78 and '79) and fought out a titanic semi-final tie in 1977 that basically decided the destination of All-Ireland honours that same season. Indeed, the 1977 semi-final is generally regarded today to have developed into one of the greatest – if not THE greatest – games of gaelic football in the entire history of the All-Ireland championship. In addition Kerry (1971, '72, '73, '74 and '77) and Dublin (1976 and '78) farmed seven National League titles between them in the seventies.

Offaly had won two successive All-Ireland titles in 1971 and '72 with a powerful side. The 1971 win, in fact, represented Offaly's first time to inscribe their names on the Sam Maguire Cup.

However, the achievements of the team, led to victory by that most stylish of midfielders, Willie Bryan in 1971 and by the very accurate wing forward, Tony McTague in 1972, have tended to be completely overshadowed in retrospective debates on that decade by the intensity of the rivalry between Dublin and Kerry and all that stemmed from it.

The late Ollie Freaney described the Kerry four-in-a-row team of 1978-'81 as "one of the greatest teams that I have seen playing gaelic football and there is absolutely no doubt that it was the best side to emerge from the Kingdom."

Jimmy Barry Murphy said this Kerry combination was "the best team I have seen since I began watching games in the mid-sixties." And he added: "I have no hesitation in saying that it was the finest in football history. Not alone did they play football at all times but they were true sportsmen and outstanding ambassadors for the game."

Before I go deeper into their record and the imprint left by their battles with Dublin, let me say that I have talked to great judges of the game who have no doubt that the Down 1960-'61 side, with the penetrating half-forward line of Seán O'Neill, Jim McCartan and Paddy Doherty, was the most powerful in football history.

A streamlined combination this, with hardly a weak link, that humbled Kerry to an eight points defeat in the 1960 All-Ireland final; and if some doubts were left about the true value of that form because the Kingdom carried some "walking cripples" on the day, all arguments were settled in the following year's semi-final when the margin in the Ulster champions' favour was six points.

Even the emergence of the Dublin 1974-'78 combination, Kerry's 1978-'81 four-in-a-row team and the 1984-'86 three-in-a-row side did not cause the advocates of the supremacy of Down's 1960-'61 squad to change their allegiance.

Before 1950, Roscommon of 1944-'46 and the Murray brothers, fair-haired captain, Jimmy and Phelim, Dr Donal Keenan and the others of that fine band of footballers won many admirers. Incidentally, Jimmy Murray's pub in the little village of Knockcroghery outside Roscommon town (with the ball inscribed with the names of the men who triumphed in the 1943 All-Ireland against Cavan still hanging from the roof after surviving a fire) represents for me a veritable shrine. A shrine, I might add, to the tumultuous games Kerry and Roscommon fought out in 1944 and '46; and to study the classic old prints of those men in the pre-match parades and their high-fielding duels is akin to playing a silent film of an era in gaelic football that is gone forever, replaced today by what we writers tend to describe as "the running game".

The Cavan team of 1947-'49, led by John Joe O'Reilly and

4

including Tony Tighe and Mick Higgins, won many admirers while creating its own special niche by rallying to defeat Kerry in the thrilling Polo Grounds All-Ireland final in 1947 – the only All-Ireland played outside the country.

Mayo arrived with an outstanding team that put two All-Irelands back-to-back in 1950-'51. It is significant that two members of that side, Seán Flanagan, the left corner-back and captain, and Tom Langan, the full-forward, made the *Sunday Independent*/Irish Nationwide/GAA Football Team of the Century. And that Mayo team also included the great midfielder, Pádraic Carney, and Paddy Prendergast, the man who rates in my book as the finest full-back I have seen before the advent of the seventies and the only one who could really cope with the wiles of Kevin Heffernan, when Heffernan roamed out from the edge of the square to create the space for himself for destructive action against an opposing defence. In the period from 1975 on, Kerry's John O'Keeffe was unmatched among "modern" full-backs.

They buried Seán Flanagan in his native Mayo soil on Monday, 8 February 1993. His former team-mates, under Eamon Mongey, formed a guard of honour. They came from all the footballing strongholds to pay their final tribute. I walked from the church to the graveside in Ballaghaderreen in the company of Jack Mahon and peerless Seán Purcell.

Later in the family gathering we sat with John Nallen and Paddy Prendergast reminiscing about times past. Seán would have enjoyed the "crack". Prendergast, close friend always of Seán Flanagan – a friendship that had lasted and deepened beyond their playing days together – had been at Seán's bedside shortly before he died. He lingered longest at the graveside.

Seán Flanagan's son, Dermot, had emulated him by captaining Mayo (against Meath in the 1988 All-Ireland semi-final) but did not have the honour of holding the Sam Maguire Cup high in triumph at Croke Park. And he was again denied by Dublin in 1985 (epic drawn semi-final and replay) and by Cork in 1989 (All-Ireland final) the honour of winning an All-Ireland championship medal. When Seán Flanagan passed on, forty-two years had elapsed since he brought the Sam Maguire back to Mayo for the second successive year.

The Dublin machine of 1955 set the gaelic football scene aflame as they carried all opposition before them in their march to the

All-Ireland final. It seemed that nothing could halt them bringing the Sam Maguire Cup back to the metropolis and that in the process they would kill off the "traditional" game as espoused by Kerry.

But the media hype, claiming they were "unbeatable", got to Dublin in the end and the Ollie Freaney–Kevin Heffernan combination did not destroy the Kingdom defence as had been predicted beforehand (we had not reckoned with the brilliant covering that Micksie Palmer would produce across the full-back line).

As "Snitchy" Ferguson put it to me: "We were only a bunch of gossoons. We let the hype get to us. We didn't have a wise old head in our ranks who could have warned us from experience that there is nothing soft in an All-Ireland final, especially against Kerry when they are in the mood that they displayed in '55." ("Ours was the best display ever given by fifteen men on the one day," was how John Dowling saw it.)

The reasons, however, why Dublin lost it went deeper. As Ollie Freaney explained to me: "Marcus Wilson and Jim McGuinness, forming a fine midfield partnership, had carried us through in the replay against Mayo. Then misfortune struck us. First we lost Marcus Wilson through injury. Jim McGuinness twisted a knee in training and we had also lost Norman Allen. After being given injections, Jim McGuinness played in the final but, as everyone knows, he was only a shadow of his true self and was actually forced to retire. Kerry deserved to win on the day's play but if we had been able to field our best team, I have no doubt that we would have beaten them."

Kevin Heffernan agreed that "the chapter of injuries that crippled our midfield was a major factor in our defeat." He added that it was a disastrous decision to play Jim McGuinness when there was such a doubt about his fitness. But then Dublin had been banking on a fully-fit McGuinness as the man who would hold burly Kerry captain, John Dowling. As events turned out, Dowling was a Kingdom hero, emerging as an agent of destruction with his shoulder power, as was also Dr Jim Brosnan. Nicky Maher would admit afterwards: "We were being hit so hard and so often that we couldn't think what we should do next."

Dublin, in a word, left the All-Ireland title behind them in the titanic drawn battle and replay against a fine Mayo side, whereas Kerry looked so unimpressive in disposing of Cavan after a replay, that the Dubs were lulled into believing that the Sam Maguire Cup was theirs for the taking.

The official attendance was 87,102 but in reality it topped 90,000 as thousands flooded into the stadium free when a gate was broken down.

Never had there been such a build-up for any final. Never, I think, had there been in Croke Park itself such a clear-cut division of support. Perhaps there have been better footballing occasions but nothing like this one for the awesome atmosphere permeating the ground, for the High Noon drama of the last frenetic four minutes as Ollie Freaney goaled through a crowded goalmouth from a fourteen yards free and Dublin laid siege to the Kerry goal and everything seemed to become a blur of Blue locked in hand-to-hand combat with the Green and Gold.

And there was Jerome O'Shea, "the fair-haired wonder from Cahirciveen", making two soaring saves under the crossbar when it seemed that nothing could stop Dublin getting the equalising goal. O'Shea would confide to me later that everything else in his career after that counted for nothing really. Men talked only of those soaring leaps to the clouds and the clean catches that denied the Ollie Freaney–Kevin Heffernan axis, which had humiliated Meath (5-12 to 0-7) in the Leinster final, having already sent them plunging to defeat also in the National League final.

Methinks that it was on that Sunday in September 1955 – September 25 to be exact – that the Dublin v Kerry rivalry of modern times was forged in all its glory, a rivalry that would blossom anew in the seventies, creating bonds between the combatants that were unique. They came to respect each other so much from the confrontations they had between 1975 and '78 that they never nowadays lose an opportunity of renewing acquaintanceships, whether it is on the eve of the All-Ireland football final or its aftermath each year or at Listowel races.

Dublin were a far more mature side when they won the All-Ireland crown under the captaincy of Kevin Heffernan in 1958. And I contend that they were robbed by ill-luck and the wood-work (ask Johnny Joyce about it) from beating Kerry in the 1959 semi-final, the day Mick O'Connell gave a classic exhibition of high fielding and the cultured stylist Seán Murphy at right wing-back and Tom Long at centre-forward contributed greatly also to a victory forged against the run of the play.

Because of a weakness in fielding and in physique in certain positions in attack also and because of their dependence on the Freaney–Heffernan axis I wouldn't put the 1955 team on the same plane as the 1976-'77 combination of all the talents. Even though the magic that surrounded the 1955 team remains to this day and the revolution they brought to football.

❀ ❀ ❀

Galway's answer to the Freaney–Heffernan axis was to come with a team in 1956 powered in attack by the deadly duo of Seán Purcell–Frankie Stockwell. Purcell stands out unquestionably as one of the most natural and versatile footballers of all time. His versatility was shown in outstanding games in the Galway colours from full-back to midfield to centre-forward.

Galway in the period 1956-'59 should certainly have won more than one All-Ireland title. But my memory of that team is that, apart from Purcell and Stockwell when they were in full cry and proving themselves the wreckers of opposing defences, Galway had some terrible weaknesses up front. Leaving aside the 2-13 they ran up against Cork in the 1956 All-Ireland final when Purcell and Stockwell certainly justified the tag "The Terrible Twins", Galway failed to get a goal against Tyrone in the semi-final that season and only put 0-9 on the board when losing to Cork in the 1957 semi-final.

The Galway three-in-a-row team of 1964-'66 stands head and shoulders, to my mind, above the 1956-'58 combination as a TEAM, though in no way must that be taken as indicating that there was any individual in it who could be put ahead of Seán Purcell. Neither did it boast a full-forward with the touch of Frankie Stockwell. On its record of achievement, however, the 1964-'66 team just has to be placed ahead of the might-have-been side of 1956-'59.

Mick O'Dwyer seemed to denigrate the achievements of the 1964-'66 side when he expressed the view that the Kerry teams they beat in 1964 and '65 could in no way bear comparison with the Kingdom squad of 1978-'81. I agree that the Kerry attack in '64 and '65 must be reckoned the worst I ever saw to represent the Kingdom (they failed to score even one goal).

You cannot get away, however, from the fact that Galway put three titles back-to-back and beat all the opposition that was around in the championship over three seasons. As with the Cork 1976-'78 three-in-a-row hurling team, the stars of the Galway three-in-a-row football side – Enda Colleran, Noel Tierney, Martie Newall and Mattie McDonagh to name a quartet – stand the test of time by any standard you like to set.

Kerry owed a deep debt to Mick O'Connell for the successive

All-Ireland titles they won in 1969 and '70 – especially to his unmatched high fielding ability at midfield and the way he could kick points from a dead ball, whether it was a long-range free or "50".

There are those, even in the Kingdom, who would put Paddy Kennedy or Jack O'Shea ahead of O'Connell. In my book, however, the Man from Valentia had no equal in the two basic arts of sheer purity of fielding and controlled kicking ability. He was the total professional in the way he thought about the game and in the time he gave to his art. I saw this for myself in long summer days I spent with him on the Island and watching him in practice on the Cahirciveen pitch (he would get a young lad to stand fifty yards away from him and place the ball with uncanny accuracy almost dead at his feet, just like Sam Snead in his prime rifling iron shots to a caddy in practice sessions out in Portmarnock).

No, there was only ONE Mick O'Connell as there was only ONE Christy Ring.

We shall not see again two players with their awesome dedication and 100% commitment. O'Connell, when Captain of Kerry, left the Sam Maguire Cup behind him in the dressing-room in Croke Park in 1959.

Medals and trophies as such never meant anything to him. Art was all. And no one, I know, has been more true to himself in spurning everything (including much that passes for "the tackle" in the modern game) that reduces gaelic football, in his eyes, from a game that can be beautiful to watch when played by artists believing in their art to a pull-and-drag and get-your-man-off-the-ball affair.

✳ ✳ ✳

Offaly with a very strong all-round side, terribly difficult to halt when turning on the power, especially when Willie Bryan and Tony McTague were on song, won successive All-Irelands in 1971 and '72. I have no doubt they could have made it a three-timer but for allowing their comitment and dedication to waver in the '73 season.

That Offaly team would have earned a more lasting image of greatness, I venture to say, but for the tactics adopted at times by certain members of the defence. I recall especially a few tackles that could easily have taken a few members of the Galway attack out in the 1972 All-Ireland final – a fact conveniently overlooked subsequently in the general euphoria at Offaly winning the Sam Maguire Cup for the first time in the county's history.

Kerry's Mick O'Connell had his own thoughts too about the tactics of a few individuals in the Offaly defence and on one occasion he acted in a way that summarily ended the harrassment he was enduring. That was that for that day, and there was no come-back either. I will not elaborate.

The All-Ireland crown in 1973 went to a very exciting Cork side, captained by Billy Morgan and including Declan Barron – what a magnificent footballer he was when the mood took him – Ray Cummins, Jimmy Barry Murphy and Denis Coughlan. I saw Barron, Cummins and Barry Murphy destroy the Kerry defence in '73 as the Leesiders put 5-13 on the scoreboard in the Munster final (against Kerry's 1-15). Cork would assuredly have put two All-Irelands back-to-back but for being caught in complacent mood by Dublin in the '74 All-Ireland semi-final (indeed, they were already looking ahead to contesting the All-Ireland final).

Remember, members of the Kerry team that made such an impact in '75 when dethroning champions Dublin were on the losing end against Cork in '73 and '74. I remember too that when Páirc Uí Chaoimh was opened in '76, the Leesiders still including a strong nucleus of the 1973-'74 team, were robbed of victory against the Kingdom because of at least two very controversial incidents. Kerry were allowed also to get away with jersey-pulling tactics on Jimmy Barry Murphy, as he went through more than once, that should never have been permitted.

Cork's 1987-'90 combination contested four successive All-Ireland finals, winning two (1989 and '90). But for running up against a powerful Meath side, it could easily have been a four-in-a-row team if not a five-in-a-row team (complacency and lack of will-to-win, as Larry Tompkins has stressed, was their downfall against Kerry in the 1991 Munster final).

In the end I come down to three teams that stand head and shoulders above all the rest in the thirty-year period from 1960 to 1990, namely Kerry 1978-'81, Dublin 1976-'77 and Down 1960-'61.

⌘ ⌘ ⌘

I could present a very strong case based on their All-Ireland final win over the Kingdom in 1976 and their great fight-back to take the 1977 semi-final – the finest game of football that I have seen in my time watching gaelic – to prove the point that on their best days Dublin were equal if not ahead of Kerry.

Indeed, for most of the first half of the 1978 All-Ireland final,

10

Dublin had Kerry going on the ropes. In fact, they were so much on top that I am afraid a certain arrogance crept in and in going for the knock-out blow, they moved too far upfield, leaving the yawning gap in defence that allowed John Egan to get the snap goal that initially changed the course of things.

I don't have to dwell on the controversy surrounding the amazing Mike Sheehy goal still being heatedly debated to this day. Suffice it to say that Dublin by exercising a little more care at the back, could have had it sewn up by the interval and they would have gone into history as a three-in-a-row side with an even greater image for posterity than they actually forged.

Dublin's weakness at times was their inability to pick off a flow of long-range points from play when right on top of the opposition. They depended on working the ball close in to round off their movements – and on the deadly "boot" of Jimmy Keaveney off placed balls.

Dublin, however, proved in 1976 and '77 that the Kerry defence was vulnerable when faced by a streamlined attack that knew how to create the gaps through the centre – and this left certain lasting doubts about Kerry's strength in defence.

There was the footballing brain of the captain, Tony Hanahoe, the skill and control of Dave Hickey as he moved down the left flank, the sheer magic of Anton (The Blue Panther) O'Toole on the other flank, the way Bobby Doyle could explode into action just when you thought he was out of things and, of course, John McCarthy was invariably overshadowed in this galaxy of big names but how Dublin would have done with him in '91.

Then you had Brian Mullins at midfield (he must be categorised unhesitatingly with the greatest midfielders in football history) and Kevin Moran at centre-back. Moran who rates the finest of modern centre-backs in my book. Two players who won respect as deep in Kerry as they did in the metropolis itself and, indeed, in every football county for their ability to rise to the big occasion and prove themselves match-winners *par excellence.*

Kevin Heffernan had brought Dublin out of the wilderness to win the 1974 All-Ireland title under Seán Doherty. Mick O'Dwyer's "Young Tigers" surprised them in 1975. Heffernan, with a real touch of genius, completely recast his half-back line, already looking ahead in the manner of a Vincent O'Brien to greater goals. He fashioned the Tommy Drumm–Kevin Moran–Pat O'Neill line.

Mick O'Dwyer had confided that Heffernan set standards in fitness and commitment from his players that caused him to reach for new horizons he never imagined possible. One was inspiring the other. Mick O'Dwyer, ironically, could so easily have been ousted at the end of the '77 season. He had Ger McKenna to thank for standing by him when others would have summarily ditched him.

In the overall *purity* of their football – and I stress the word purity – I believe that Kerry had the edge over Dublin. And I am thinking here of the footballers' footballer, Paudie Lynch, most under-estimated of players, and of Mike Sheehy and Pat Spillane to mention but three. New strength was added to the team when Eoin (The Bomber) Liston and Jack O'Shea really arrived in 1978. "The Bomber" becoming the target man at full-forward while Jack O'Shea was to become a profound influence at midfield. But in 1978 the Kerry team was being shaped into the invincible machine that would be seen in full blossom over the next three seasons.

Between 1978 and '81 Kerry reached the full peak of their powers in attack and had an unbeatable sextet up front. Granted, Dublin after 1977 were not the team they had been and Roscommon (1980) and Offaly (1981) certainly did not provide the penetration in attack that Dublin had shown in 1976 and '77; but the fact must not be denied that Kerry over four seasons, 1978-'81, were superior to all opposition in the championship.

Their glorious run continued to a September day in Croke Park in 1982 when Seamus Darby wrote himself into history by kicking the goal in the dying minutes that gave Offaly sweet revenge for 1981 and prevented Kerry becoming the first team in GAA history to record a five-timer in senior championship grade.

Incidentally, I have never subscribed to the theory that it was a tragedy for Kerry to be denied their place in history by that late, late goal of Seamus Darby's. A tragedy, perhaps, in the eyes of blinkered Kerry fans who wanted the Kingdom to go on winning until it became an embarrassment.

I believe that Offaly, on the very strenuous effort they had put in since 1979 to lift the Sam Maguire Cup, were fully deserving of the title they won at last in 1982, under the astute generalship of Eugene McGee as team manager and coach. The real tragedy, of course, would have been if Matt Connor, one of the best forwards I have seen in the period since the dawn of the eighties, had not got an All-Ireland medal before his career was cut short so prematurely. Great Kerry players of that era like Mike Sheehy are among the first to sing the prowess of Matt Connor as an attacker. He ensured by his accuracy that Offaly were poised to

12

strike when Darby got that one last chance and took it into the Hill 16 goal.

The near-total Kerry dominance of the football scene was resumed in the Centenary Year of 1984 and continued with the completion of another three-in-a-row in 1986.

Carve their names with pride, the men who wrote the greatest chapter in Kerry's footballing story between 1975 and 1987 by contesting ten All-Ireland finals in that period, winning eight and losing two.

Mike Sheehy, Captain of Kerry in the '87 championship season, Ger Power, Paudie O'Shea, Pat Spillane and "Ogie" Moran comprised the quintet who had been through it all from 1975 – an amazing achievement by the five, by any standard in any sport and Pat Spillane was still there assisting the Kingdom in winning the 1991 Munster crown.

The Kerry team collected 120 medals in eight finals ('75, '78, '79, '80, '81, '84, '85, '86) and counting substitutes, who actually played in those finals, the medals total comes to 128, that is allowing 21 medals for the panel in each All-Ireland final (and, remember, that every All-Ireland senior medal has 15 grammes of gold in it and they cost £300 apiece).

Kerry were then the dominant force in gaelic football over the ten-year span from 1978 to 1987, being out of only two All-Ireland finals – '83 and '87 – and failing in '82.

The glory that this wonderful band of footballers in the Green and Gold of the Kingdom created can never fade and the standards they set will continue to inspire others.

In many ways they were The Incomparables.

❊ ❊ ❊

Once Kerry gave way to Cork in Munster in 1987, the Leesiders along with Meath became the two dominant counties in the seasons that followed, sharing four All-Ireland titles between them.

Meath had the outstanding record of winning five of the six Leinster finals played in the period 1985-'91 and of contesting four All-Ireland finals (1981, '88, '90 and '91) and winning two of them (1987 and '88) back-to-back. But for the loss of Bobby O'Malley through injury and the fact that Colm O'Rourke could not enter the fray until the second half, it can be argued that they might well have crowned a memorable 1991 season by beating Down in the All-Ireland final – their tenth game in the championship.

For sheer grit and determination and will-to-win, for their ability to stare defeat in the face and still come back in the dying minutes of a match and force a draw or an outright win, few teams in gaelic football history could match Meath, especially the Meath of 1991. While it may be seen as entering a discordant note, the point has to be made though that unacceptable statements made by a few of their leading players in the aftermath of victory over Cork in the 1987 and '88 All-Ireland finals left a sour note in the public mind that could not be totally effaced. And there was too a tendency on the part of a few of their defenders to indulge in a softening-up approach to the opposition, as evidenced in the opening phase of the 1991 All-Ireland final against Down. It affected their lasting place in football history.

Let it be stressed, however, that Meath were much more careful of the public statements they made through the marathon 1991 season and, obviously conscious of their image, never stepped out of line in this regard. They mingled freely with the Dubs in the Lord Mayor's reception on the evening they finally beat the Metropolitans, the captain, Liam Hayes, exhorting his men in the dressingroom to show their respect for Dublin in defeat by their presence in the Mansion House. Meath, for their part, had to be applauded for that gesture and Liam Hayes for doing things the right way as captain.

And Meath were generous also in defeat when it came to acknowledging Down's achievements in the All-Ireland final. So a lot of the "unforced errors" as it were of '87 and '88 were undone and we are happy for that.

Meath, because they lacked the charismatic appeal of the Kerry 1978-'81 team, Dublin 1976-'77, Down 1960-'61 and the Dublin 1955-'59 combination will not be judged as one of the great teams of footballing history. But they have to be included in any "Top Ten" of the past forty years. You might use the adjectives "dour" and "uncompromising" in desribing them but, believe me, it took far more than footballing skill to beat this side. It demanded guts and character and resilience in abundance. You had to be able to go right down to the wire with them as they could take you out in the very last minute with a sucker punch as Dublin learned to their cost in the last grandstand battle against them in '91.

They had in Colm O'Rourke, Bernard Flynn and Brian Stafford a trio of deadly-effective forwards; two midfielders who could give the attack a winning service when they got on top in enigmatic Liam Hayes and so-determined Gerry McEntee –

McEntee who could turn a game on his own and who at thirty-five gave an amazing performance at midfield in the 1991 All-Ireland final – while in defence they had in Bobby O'Malley and Martin O'Connell two players who would have been great in any era.

⌘ ⌘ ⌘

Because of the dramatic changes in the game of football itself, it is a futile exercise now trying to make exact comparisons between the top teams of the nineties and those of earlier eras. The static has given way to the fluid. Where in my young days corner-forwards were instructed to remain "glued to the square" and players in the last line of defence had a limited area of operation, the Donegal corner-backs in the 1992 All-Ireland final could be seen up in attack quite frequently. And the running game of the team as a whole would, I believe, have left a Kerry "immortal" like Joe Keohane stranded and gasping like a whale tossed up on a beach in the Kingdom.

Yes, I'm afraid that legendary figures of the thirties and forties would have been reduced to men with feet of clay.

And the "hard man" syndrome as typified in the hoary old tale of a timid young forward being asked if he was married or single and if he had life insurance (should he contemplate entering the opposing goalmouth area) would have cut little ice as incisive forwards, trained to run as men are trained to run today, drew leaden-footed defenders well out the field and then proceeded to take them to the cleaners.

Donegal had never won an All-Ireland senior championship semi-final until they overcame Mayo in the penultimate stage of the 1992 championship campaign. Having broken the hoodoo that had dogged them in semi-finals, they were strangely free going into the final itself – much more free than they had been against the Connacht champions, when they nearly threw it away by their prodigal waste of golden opportunities.

No Ulster team had ever beaten Dublin in the All-Ireland championship. Little wonder then that the Dubs were supremely confident – so confident, in fact, that they allowed themselves to be distracted in the count-down to the match (with radio interviews and "personal appearances" etc.) in a manner that would become a cause of regret later.

Not since Kerry in 1955 has a team risen to such heights on the day – all together – as Donegal did in the '92 decider. Martin

McHugh was the first to acknowledge this. And making it even more amazing was the fact that every member of the Donegal side was playing in his first final.

The previous season had seen Down maintain their unique record of NEVER being beaten once they reached an All-Ireland final. They had won in 1960 and in '61 and again in '68.

The advances made in technique and the acquirement of knowledge of the "modern game" through skilful coaching meant that the top Ulster teams no longer felt inferior.

Indeed, the balance of power in the football championship had shifted appreciably over two seasons. Ulster had altered all our concepts and nothing could be taken for granted anymore.

Even Clare by their dethroning of reigning Provincial champions, Kerry, in 1992 had changed the scenario in Munster.

More anon about that day in Limerick when Marty Morrissey in the course of a so-vivid commentary that will live like Michael O'Hehir's on the 1947 All-Ireland football final in the Polo Grounds, New York, told the nation: "There won't be a cow milked in Clare tonight."

CHAPTER 2

"SAM'S FOR THE HILLS"

"**S**AM'S for the Hills." These were the final words of the Donegal captain, Anthony Molloy, as he finished his moving victory speech after receiving the Sam Maguire Cup on Sunday, 20 September 1992. And they said it all.

The 10,000 Donegal supporters who had flooded on to the Croke Park pitch, forming a solid phalanx in front of the Hogan Stand, responded in a manner that indicated that this was a moment they would cherish for the rest of their lives. Indeed, to be a native of Donegal on that third Sunday in September, whether you were in Croke Park or simply watching it all on television, was to see a dream realised that few could have thought possible when the side, captained by Anthony Molloy, set out in '92 to make amends for losing their Ulster crown to Down at Clones in 1991.

Now the homecoming. There were bonfires at every crossroads. The county colours flew from every vantage point. The Hills were alive and singing.

The joy of the people was unrestrained and so also the overflow of emotion. It was an unforgettable evening of celebration for everyone who shared in it.

The sign at the border of Donegal, intended, of course, to welcome visitors, had been adjusted to welcome "Sam" on his first-ever trip to Tír Conaill.

The children especially will always remember that Monday evening in September '92. Out of it there will have been those already inspired to want in time to emulate Anthony Molloy. Parents had brought them out to wait the coming of the team coach, holding up banners that read: "Almost Home Boys".

Eventually the kids, their parents also, would have their moment. They would catch a glimpse of the men who had overcome the awesome statistic that proclaimed to the gaelic world that no team from Ulster had ever beaten Dublin in the championship (in fact, Brian McEniff had confided to me in the count-down to the final that it was a statistic he tried to hide from the squad, as a father would try to hide a dark secret from his children).

First there had been the burning resolve to get over Mayo and break the hoodoo that had dogged Donegal for so long at the semi-final stage. That ambition had been achieved.

17

I find myself now in Bundoran spending a long afternoon chatting to Matt Gallagher as he rested in the sitting-room above his pub from the fierce grind of training for the final.

Evening was beginning to close in over timeless Ben Bulben's head and the last of the golfers, taking part in the Belleek GAA club's sponsored outing, were finishing their rounds when Matt turned to me and remarked: "No matter whether we win or lose against Dublin, we will be remembered as the fifteen that created history by bringing the county into its first All-Ireland final. No one can ever take that from us."

The team photograph itself, taken on All-Ireland day, would be cherished down the decades, each man a household name in Donegal. And so also the photograph of the Donegal team parading behind the Artane Boys Band.

But then Matt Gallagher articulated something deeper. He talked of the ultimate ambition that went beyond mere participation in the final. He talked of the grand design of emerging as champions, REAL undisputed champions in that they would have become the first team out of Ulster to undo the proud record that Dublin had held for so long.

He had the edge of steel in his make-up to believe that it was not only possible but that it was an ambition that was attainable if Donegal did not allow themselves to be overawed by the occasion, if they could manage to play to their full potential.

Earlier that same day over coffee in the lounge of the Great Northern Hotel, looking out over the sun-drenched sweep of Bundoran golf course, Brian McEniff had made the point that trying to smash the hoodoo of being unable to get over the obstacle presented to them by an All-Ireland semi-final tie in Croke Park had "become a millstone around the necks of successive Donegal sides, so much so that they were afraid of winning as much as losing because of the psychological barrier created down the years."

"It was as if they were handed a hot potato and wanted to drop it as quickly as possible," he added.

Brian blamed the psychological burden of the losing years for those seventeen wides against Mayo in the 1992 All-Ireland semi-final, a game that could so easily have been tossed away.

He was convinced that with that barrier finally smashed, Donegal would play with far greater freedom in Croke Park on All-Ireland final day.

His judgement in that respect was to be fully vindicated.

Later I would see the lights go on in Bundoran town where the flags flew from nearly every house and there was a banner across the main street that proclaimed: "Good Luck to Brian and the Boys".

Over dinner the great lines from W. B. Yeats about "The Sixteen" come to mind and I know that they can be adapted to "The Fifteen" – "Oh, but we talked at large before the fifteen had made the great break-through . . ."

I had seen one of the staff of the Great Northern Hotel handing a fax message to Brian McEniff.

He fell silent as he read it and the enormity of what the figure 3.12 in the message meant both for himself and Donegal. For that was going to be the moment designated by Croke Park for Donegal to emerge from the dressing-room under the Hogan Stand – into the crescendo of sound that would greet them on their first All-Ireland appearance.

⌘ ⌘ ⌘

McEniff did not bring his team to Croke Park like some starry-eyed rookie manager who had arrived there ahead of his time, thinking that victory would fall into his lap like a ripe apple.

No. He had come up the hard way.

Sacked. McEniff had become familiar with the word. Behind him the memory of not just one but three sackings over the twenty years that he had been associated with Donegal as player-manager and manager.

He can laugh now at the first. It happened in the seventies and stemmed from the fact that he played for Kerry in New York against the local Donegal team and helped to defeat them. The County Board did not take kindly to the news and he paid the price for what they saw as disloyalty.

The other two sackings, one in the seventies and the other in the mid-eighties, resulted directly from failure to deliver results in the championship satisfactory to the County Board.

But he was hurt in the mid-eighties. Donegal were beaten by Down by one point in Newcastle and he was shafted. "I wanted one more year with that side as I was convinced at the time that we would have gone places the following year," he said.

Brian McEniff had known four All-Ireland semi-final defeats in the summers of Donegal's discontent. But his critics were never more vociferous than when Donegal failed to Down in the 1991 Ulster final.

Sunday, 20 September 1992, was the culmination of everything that he dreamed of from the very first occasion that he wore the Donegal jersey. What he failed to achieve as a player himself – an All-Ireland senior championship medal – he achieved as a manager. "Yes, I would like to have done it as a player," he would say afterwards, "but I am happy that my contribution enabled the squad of '92 to go down in history and Donegal has been inscribed on the Sam Maguire Cup for the first time."

Matt Gallagher, who apart from running The Bradóg pub in Bundoran, has a wholesale business on the road that normally sees him travelling the entire county, was asked by McEniff to take two days off during the week prior to the All-Ireland final in order to rest up after the intensity of training. He immediately complied – "in the interest of Donegal football".

Matt went further. He tried to avoid as much as possible getting involved in tiring debates about the final. He would slip away from the pub, even on the days he was resting up, to achieve total relaxation and it paid off in the final itself.

Matt told me that the disappointment of the entire Donegal squad was very deep after the defeat by Down in '91. He accepted that Donegal had made the mistake of looking beyond Down to the All-Ireland semi-final and when Cork were beaten by Kerry in Munster "we were even contemplating playing in our first All-Ireland final."

"We knew coming out of Clones that we owed it to Brian and to ourselves to wipe out the memory of that defeat," he said. "And the only way we could do it was to win the Ulster title in 1992 and go on from there."

Donegal were fortunate that the main spotlight was on Down as reigning All-Ireland champions at the outset of the 1992 Ulster championship. And Derry too could not avoid the spotlight after beating Tyrone in the National League final.

After being held to a draw the first day by Cavan in Breffni Park, Donegal beat them comprehensively in the replay at Ballybofey and then slipped into the final with an easy victory over Fermanagh.

Meanwhile, as Brian McGilligan put it to me, Derry had too many peaks before they faced Donegal in the Provincial decider. "We had to peak to defeat Tyrone in the first round of the championship at Celtic Park (Derry) in what was a repeat of the League final. Then, after being held to a draw by Monaghan in the second round, we had to peak to overcome them in the replay and, of course, we had to hit a new high to oust Down in the semi-final. We had nothing left to give when we came up against

Donegal and yet we only lost by two points in the end."

Dublin were lulled into a false sense of complacency by Donegal's prodigal waste of opportunities against Mayo in the All-Ireland semi-final. But some shrewd judges noted that in shooting seventeen wides, the Ulster champions had created seventeen chances. Could they be as prodigal again?

✾ ✾ ✾

Dublin's path against Kildare in the Leinster final had been eased by the wrong tactical decision on the part of the Lily Whites to play against the wind in the first half, also the playing of Martin Lynch in attack rather than at midfield – his best position – while Keith Barr's golden goal into the Hill 16 end (recalling a similar effort by Kevin Moran in the seventies that did not bring a goal) had a vital bearing on the outcome.

Dr Pat O'Neill, a selector in 1992 and successor as team manager to Paddy Cullen, who resigned in the wake of the defeat by Donegal, said he had no doubt that if Dublin had goaled from Charlie Redmond's penalty kick at the Canal end in the ninth minute of the game, they might have gone on to add a few quick points and built up a winning lead of six points.

There is no way of knowing what the psychological effect of a goal against them would have meant to Donegal – a team appearing in their first final – but it was evident that as they slowly settled down, Dublin were all over them in that opening period of play.

One could argue that if Redmond's shot had found the target instead of going narrowly wide of goalkeeper Gary Walsh's left-hand post, Donegal's composure would have been dealt a shattering blow and that they would have been struggling to hold on.

The missing of the penalty can be looked upon as the turning point. It provided Donegal with the very fillip they needed. Inexorably, they imposed their will on the game. And in the second half they were unquestionably the better side through the field.

Charlie Redmond, I am convinced, should never have been given the task of taking that penalty. He was burdened by the memory of having sent the ball over the bar from a penalty at this same end on Sunday, 31 July 1988, when, if he had planted the ball in the back of the net two and a half minutes into injury time, Dublin would have forced a draw with Meath in the Leinster final instead of losing by two points (2-5 to 0-9).

You could see when he was detailed to take the kick that he was not at all happy about it.

If he had scored a point it would not have been too bad. There was little doubt that the miss affected his entire game afterwards.

But still Dublin had long enough after the missed penalty to win the game and win it well – if they had been good enough.

A few years back when I visited the great Jim McCartan in his home in Down, he made the point to me that to make sure of wining any All-Ireland you must have a forward line that can deliver the killer goals on the day.

"You might say that we handed Offaly the 1961 All-Ireland on a plate and they could not take it," he recalled. "We threw it away so to speak and won it back again. We gave them two gilt-edged goals in the first six minutes and lost about ten points through missed frees and wides from easy scoring positions – an advantage of at least sixteen points altogether and still they could not win."

Yet, before a crowd of 90,556, Down rallied with power to score three goals – and win it by a point.

Dublin in 1992 had nothing to compare with the axis of Jim McCartan, Seán O'Neill and Paddy Doherty. And nothing to compare either with the two-pronged effectiveness of Tony Hanahoe at centre-forward and Jimmy Keaveney at full-forward in 1977 and the men around them – Anton O'Toole, Dave Hickey, Bobby Doyle and John McCarthy.

No, the missed penalty alone was not the cause of Dublin's undoing against Donegal.

Defeat stemmed from the failure to command midfield which led in turn to Paul Curran, Keith Barr and Eamon Heery – rated beforehand the best attacking half-back line in the land – being forced back on defence when they should have been coming forward. It was obvious that they were not accustomed to this role, as frees were conceded in trying to halt the Donegal attack pouring through that were clinically punished by Manus Boyle.

Keith Barr's very penchant for attack at every opportunity meant that his defensive armour was open to be exploited by the right tactics. Martin McHugh was to have a dream All-Ireland final at centre-forward.

"It was obvious that Donegal had done their homework well. The critical analysis they had carried out of our players paid off," said Pat O'Neill to me subsequently.

The Dublin dug-out did not move quickly or decisively enough when the situation was crying out for change. One might ask: why were they so slow to spot that Barr was having a nightmare afternoon on Martin McHugh? Why did they not act to shift a man into the pivotal centre-back position who might have put the clamps on McHugh?

The Dublin selectors were very slow also to try and rectify the damage Donegal were doing at midfield. While the decision was actually taken ten minutes *before* the interval to replace Dave Foran, he was allowed on until half-time and in those vital minutes Donegal put on the points that ensured a lead at the break of three points (0-10 to 0-7) and, as matters evolved in the second half, it created the platform for victory.

A strange malaise seemed to descend on the Dublin dug-out in the final phase of the game when it could still perhaps have been snatched out of the fire. (Gary Walsh denied Vinny Murphy from close range with two minutes left.)

It was as if there was total disbelief that Dublin were going to lose – that someone would wave a magic wand and all would be right at the final whistle.

The magic wand on the day was in Brian McEniff's hand.

The strength in depth of the Donegal panel, which would become more and more evident during the National League campaign subsequently, was revealed with the announcement before the start of the match that left wing-back, Martin Shovlin, had been forced to cry off (he received a neck injury in training on the previous Thursday evening). His replacement John Joe Doherty was one of the outstanding successes of the day.

Brian McEniff found himself agonising over the demotion to the subs for the All-Ireland final of Tommy Ryan who had done so well in the Ulster championship. However, room had to be made for free-taker Manus Boyle, who was to emerge as Man of the Match, proving beyond any shadow of doubt that he was a player for the big occasion. He scored 2-1 in his first All-Ireland final – the Vocational Schools final of 1984; 0-4 in the drawn U.21 All-Ireland final in 1987 and 1-7 in the replay.

Now starting a championship game for the first time in the 1992 campaign, he finished with a tally of 0-9 in his first All-Ireland senior championship final, four of those points from play.

Brian McEniff had agonised also about leaving Barry Cunningham out of the starting fifteen but Cunningham once again showed that he was the "super sub" of '92 when he came on for the injured Brian Murray and turned in a *tour de force.*

The Anthony Molloy-Brian Murray partnership first and then the Molloy-Cunningham pairing served Donegal well on the day in the vital midfield sector. Indeed, from Matt Gallagher at full-back to Martin Gavigan at centre-back, through to Tony Boyle at full-forward, the Ulster champions had a nucleus down the centre that Dublin could not match, if one excepts Vinny Murphy at full-forward.

Incredibly quick to the ball, Tony Boyle was menace personified every time he gained possession and the way he linked with Declan Bonner and Manus Boyle and with the McHugh brothers, Martin and James, and Joyce McMullan outside, created a forward machine that ticked over in highly-impressive fashion once those early All-Ireland day nerves were overcome.

The Donegal attack eschewed the static in favour of constantly changing positions to confuse the opposition, Declan Bonner, for example, playing far out from the corner. The approach was to create as much open space as possible for Tony Boyle. It was a battle plan that worked admirably.

⌘ ⌘ ⌘

"The Donegal game is a running game," former Kerry full-back, John O'Keeffe, noted in his after-match analysis in the *Irish Times*. "That's the game that suits them because of their physique, their athleticism and their skilful ball play, they played the same possession type game as against Mayo in the semi-final, but they were more direct this time. The play seemed to go forward practically all the time, whereas against Mayo much of the play seemed to end up in corners with the ball going either sideways or backwards. There was much more penetration against Dublin."

Noel Hegarty, I felt, was the perfect example of the modern attacking corner-back, so fit that he was strong in defence one moment while the next you saw him sweeping upfield to join in onslaughts on the Dublin goal. Barry McGowan had a fine game also in the other corner while the half-backs Martin Gavigan, Donal Reid and John Joe Doherty eclipsed the Dublin half-forward line of which so much was expected in advance.

Vinny Murphy ploughed a lone furrow for much of the time as full-forward for Dublin. His ability to outjump and outfield the opposition was simply amazing. As the game progressed, Dublin resorted too much to the gambit of lofting the ball into the goalmouth. Donegal brought back plenty of bodies to support Matt Gallagher at full-back. The area was overcrowded. Dublin hadn't the wit to spread things and, as John O'Keeffe aptly summed up: "Everything seemed to be channelled down the middle and they just seemed to be bereft of ideas."

"We persisted with high balls into the Donegal square. I fielded a fair amount of them but in a static position and couldn't get a run at Matt Gallagher," said Vinny Murphy in a *Sunday Press*

24

interview with Martin Breheny. "I was hoarse from shouting to the lads out the field to feed in the quick ball so that I could get Gallagher out a bit on a run. I would have beaten him in a one-to-one situation and kicked a few points. I'm sure of that.

"You never see Tony Boyle waiting for a long, slow delivery to drop. Donegal play him into space and in some ways I'm envious of the supply he gets."

When the dust had settled on a galling defeat for Dublin, Dr Pat O'Neill did not seek to gloss over the mistakes that were made or pass the buck to Paddy Cullen. He acknowledged that *all* shared the guilt of taking the wrong approach to Donegal in the sense that "we did not look at the Ulster championship in enough depth but played the type of football that had brought us to the final, thinking it would be good enough on the day."

Tommy Carr, captain of the Dubs, recalled in a very revealing interview with Tom Humphries in the *Irish Times* that Dublin went as a team to the All-Ireland semi-final between Donegal and Mayo. "We came away with no respect or regard for Donegal. None. From there on, we were fighting a battle to be mentally right on the day.

"We were overriding favourites and no matter how much you shove that to the back of your mind, you don't forget it. There were a few incidents before the final with lads modelling clothes and doing things for local radio. They were the signs of what was going wrong. The lads involved aren't to be blamed any more than the rest of us, we thought nothing of it.

"Those things were just symptoms of what was wrong with us. We didn't have just a couple of weeks of this long climb left – we were thinking as if we'd already got there.

"On the day we went three points ahead. Then we missed a penalty. It is a matter for discussion if that was relevant or not. But we never fired as a team, nobody played well. We only had one tactic. If you only have one tactic, you are very easy to play against. In the meantime, Donegal were having a right cut."

Carr didn't go along with the suggestion of a speaker at the Mansion House reception after the All-Ireland final that Dublin had done themselves proud in defeat, just as on the occasion of another Mansion House reception (the one that followed the fourth and decisive match in the marathon series with Meath) he had said in a memorable speech that it didn't just satisfy him to have been part of an epic. "We played to win, we play football to win. There is nothing good in having lost."

And coldly he argued that Dublin were exposed that same

summer as a team with some deep psychological flaws. Meath had won a mindgame as well as a football game.

When referee, Tommy Sugrue (Kerry), blew the final whistle at the end of the '92 All-Ireland final, it was the signal for the start of ecstatic celebrations throughout Donegal from Bundoran to the Innishowen Peninsula and on the islands off the coast as well that continued unabated for a week – and much, much longer.

A picture can tell a story better than words. The picture I like best of all is that of Anthony Molloy holding the Sam Maguire Cup against the background of a typical Donegal landscape of heather, sea and scudding clouds that would inspire any painter in oils.

Yes, "Sam" was seeing the Hills of Donegal for the first time.

Amazingly, despite the celebrations, despite the trips members of the squad made to England and the States, despite the seemingly unending and so-demanding and so-tiring round, Donegal went through their group games in the 1992-'93 League unbeaten and then overcame Derry and Clare at the knock-out stage to qualify for the final and a crack at completing the Championship-League double.

✄   ✄   ✄

Donegal's record of having gone unbeaten in sixteen competitive games came to an end at Croke Park on Sunday, 9 May 1993 when they lost the Royal Liver National League final replay (0-10 to 0-6) to a fiery Dublin side that finished with fourteen men, Tommy Carr having been sent to the line by referee, Brian White (Wexford) just under five minutes after the start.

The attendance of 59,703 saw Dublin respond to this blow by fashioning what Tony Hanahoe, Captain of the 1976-'77 All-Ireland winning combination, described in the *Irish Press* that next morning as "an heroic victory for fourteen men" and he added: "I know I said that I thought Dublin had played some of their best football in years in the drawn game a week ago, but I have to say that yesterday they were superb. It was the best display by a Dublin team that I have seen in years."

The key to victory, according to Hanahoe, was the dominance Dublin exerted at midfield where Jack Sheedy and Paul Bealin controlled the game. "If I had to pick a man of the match it would definitely be Jack Sheedy."

Mick Deegan played outstandingly in the half-back line as did also centre-back Paul Curran. Paul Clarke kept his head after missing the first free and went on to make an immense contribution to this victory. His four points in the first half — two from frees and two from fifties — saw Dublin leading by 0-8 to 0-1 at the interval. No score was more vital than the free he landed eight minutes into the second half that made Dublin's tally nine points to counter Barry Cunningham's point just after half-time.

It was a very sweet success for inspiring Dublin captain, John O'Leary — ten years on from that day in 1983 when he was one of the "Defiant Dozen" that beat Galway in the All-Ireland final.

But while nothing could take from the heroic quality of Dublin's ninth League title win, it was to be noted that Donegal on the day looked a tired team both mentally and physically. It was obvious that the effort they had put into winning the '92 All-Ireland crown and maintaining an unbeaten run subsequently, at last caught up with them and, as Anthony Molloy put it: "We didn't have Dublin's hunger for victory".

In a way justice was done as Dublin should have emerged the winners of the drawn game on Sunday, 2 May. They had looked a much superior team in the first half and had forged a five-points lead early in the second. Paul Curran blotted out Martin McHugh. Dermot Deasy's play at full-back was a revelation as he held Tony Boyle scoreless and in the replay he was to give a repeat performance, getting fine assistance from the corner-backs Ciaran Walsh and Paddy Moran.

The introduction of Noel Hegarty sparked a commendable Donegal fight-back but, as I saw it, they would not have forced a draw but for some controversial decisions by referee, Brian White. To put it bluntly, he caused total frustration among the Dublin supporters in the 51,400 attendance and also among the Metropolitan players themselves.

It was not simply the fact that Donegal received 35 frees to only 12 for Dublin. What was far more puzzling and baffling was his interpretation of the "tackle" on occasions. I thought, for example, that Mick Deegan had a crucial free given against him (that brought a Donegal point) when it was his opponent who should have been whistled up for charging in possession. But then until the GAA faces up to properly defining the "tackle" in gaelic football, such anomalies will continue.

In fairness to White, he had little option but to send off Charlie Redmond after he incurred a second booking and Keith Barr for a reckless high jump into a ruck of players. Fortunately time was almost up when Barr's transgression occurred and Dublin were reduced to thirteen men. If they had been beaten, there could have been some disturbing scenes.

Coming out of Croke Park at the end of that drawn game, one was inclined to the view that Dublin might have missed the boat. But, as Tony Hanahoe summed up: "The team work and discipline they displayed after losing a man so early in the replay was really admirable."

It was a match that Dublin really needed to win to wipe away the bitter memories left by the All-Ireland defeat the previous year. Having to play with fourteen men for nearly the entire game and defeating, totally on merit, the reigning All-Ireland champions made it a victory to be cherished. Little wonder that manager, Dr. Pat O'Neill and his fellow-selectors, Jim Brogan, Fran Ryder and Bobby Doyle could not conceal their feelings of delight.

The last word came from Paul Curran in the Dublin dressingroom: "Pat O'Neill asked us at half-time whether we wanted to be remembered as the Dublin team that threw away an interval lead of seven points. He told us not just to sit on that lead but to go out and attack."

Attack they did, never letting up on a supreme effort until the final whistle.

The old buzz was back on Hill 16.

�֍ �֍ ✖

The one cruel statistic that has dogged Ulster champions since 1976 sank Donegal in the quagmire that Clones became after the "Mississipi rains" of earlier in the afternoon of 18 July '93. No county had succeeded in putting two Provincial titles back-to-back since Derry in 1975-'76. And now, ironically, it was Derry who sent Donegal crashing out of the championship (0-8 to 0-6) before an attendance of 27,500 and in the process claimed their first Ulster title since 1987.

Of course the match should never have been played on such a rain-soaked apology for a playing area on which players slid about as the water splashed up from under their feet. The decision not to go ahead with utilising Clones (where development work was in progress) as the venue should have been taken, I contend, three weeks beforehand. The game should have been switched to Casement Park or Breffni Park.

Anyway it was grossly unfair to both teams. And Donegal, who in winning the All-Ireland crown the previous year had proved themselves such outstanding exponents of the "running game", had every reason to feel aggrieved at surrendering their Ulster crown in conditions that were ludicrous when it came to expecting that they could provide the platform for a true test of footballing skills. Champions should die – if champions are to fall – on a pitch that is deemed playable by the experts. Clones was *not* playable by any criteria imaginable on this Sunday in July.

That is not meant to take in the least from the merit of Derry's victory. In the appalling conditions that prevailed, they emerged clearly as worthy Ulster champions and they had in Anthony Tohill, their towering midfielder, the Man of the Match.

He ensured, in the second half especially, a stranglehold on the midfield exchanges for the challengers and, after being led by a point (0-5 to 0-4) at the interval, it meant that the Derry attack had a sufficient supply of the ball to forge a lead that they never lost subsequently.

Tohill himself set the pattern for the winning surge by starting the second half with a beautifully-struck point from a free 60 yards out.

Donegal, who had their most productive spell of the game in the opening ten minutes, starting off as if they might swamp Derry, lost a great chance of a goal entering the final phase – with just two points between the sides – when Martin McHugh had possession in goal-scoring range. But instead of shooting himself, he elected to hand-pass to a colleague, only to see Tony Scullion, a heroic figure in the Derry defence, get in the all-important deflection. An earlier rally when a goal looked on was smothered by Derry jerseys.

Henry Downey's marking of Martin McHugh, Gary Coleman's tight play at corner back and John McGurk's tremendous work rate at left wing back contributed immensely to Derry's achievement in limiting Donegal to such a meagre score.

At the other end Matt Gallagher and John Joe Doherty stood out in the Donegal defence – but it was not the defence that lost it for the All-Ireland champions but the attack, which managed only one solitary point in the second half and that from a free. "It doesn't matter what the conditions are, you're not going to win an Ulster final that way," said Brian McEniff.

McEniff hit the nail on the head, I thought, when he added: "I suppose our injury problems came home to roost. We were missing a few of our really inspirational players and, although they were physically fit, you could see when they came on that they weren't really match fit."

He was referring, of course, to Anthony Molloy and Martin Gavigan, both of whom entered the fray in the second half and while they battled valiantly to turn the tide in their side's favour, Derry by then had the bit between their teeth and were not going to be denied.

Donal Reid (injured) and Noel Hegarty (suspended) were both unavailable for selection. No team could overcome the handicap that Donegal were asked to surmount.

Personally, I believe that it was the absence of Tony Boyle from the full-forward position that was the "injury factor" that cost Donegal dearly on the day. If two points was the margin between the two teams in the end, you could argue that Boyle in his '92 All-Ireland rampaging form was good value for two points – if not three or more. The fulcrum of the attack was missing.

In cold retrospect, I believe that Donegal threw away their chance not alone of making it two back-to-back in Ulster but of winning a second successive All-Ireland title when they allowed themselves to get too involved in the 1992-'93 League. What was the winning of a League title anyway compared to the higher goals on the horizon for a squad that, leaving aside injuries, had all the ammunition and fire-power to beat any opposition in the land at its peak.

They were tired after the endless round of celebrations following a first-ever All-Ireland title win. Desperately so. "Sam" doing the rounds and New York as familiar to Anthony Molloy as Ballybofey. It's a long winter's rest they needed, accomplishing just enough in the League to command a respectable place, rather than winning through to the final. Once they got into the knock-out stages, they could not take the Munster champions, Clare for granted but the final straw was to find themselves in a draw and replay situation with Dublin – a repeat of the '92 All-Ireland which pride alone demanded they must win. They failed. And now mental fatigue was going to be a real problem facing into the defence of their Ulster crown.

They *could* have gone out in the first round to Antrim on 6 June at Ballybofey, scrambling through by just three points (0-12 to 0-9) against a side that would probably have won it – if they had sufficient belief in themselves. Donegal were visibly lethargic.

They *should* have gone out to Armagh the first day the two counties met in the semi-final at Breffni Park. They were saved by a point by the young sub they sprang, John Duffy with the very last kick of the game. Ger Houlihan, the Armagh full-forward, gave an exhibition of forceful attacking play.

By the time they faced Donegal in the replay on 5 July, Armagh were playing their sixth match in the Ulster championship and this was actually the fourth Sunday in succession on which they were compelled to turn out. The team managed so admirably by Jim McCorry had gone a bridge too far. Little wonder that they collapsed under the strain and lost by 2-16 to 1-7.

Armagh had drawn with Fermanagh (1-9 all) on 16 May, then beat them in the replay (4-8 to 1-16) the following Sunday. They drew with Tyrone (Armagh 0-13; Tyrone 1-10) on 13 June and overcame them a week later by 2-8 to 0-12. Without any chance of a respite, they faced Donegal in the Ulster semi-final on 27 June and should have emerged victorious, the game being distinguished by the brilliant, dynamic display of Ger Houlihan at full-forward.

Donegal, inspired by Martin McHugh, the wee man from Kilcar at centre-forward, had 2-5 on the board without reply in a blistering opening fifteen-minute spell in the replay at Breffni Park on 4 July. Indeed, Armagh hardly had time to settle when they were a goal and a point down after five minutes, Martin McHugh shooting a point in twenty seconds and John Duffy blasting home a goal from twelve yards out. Mark McShane got the second goal from a long pass from McHugh, who quickly added a point.

Going in at half-time 2-7 to 0-4 in arrears, Armagh had their hopes revived somewhat when Ger Houlihan scored a superb goal eight minutes after the restart. True to form, Donegal rose to the challenge and points by Declan Bonner and Manus Boyle killed the rally.

The ease of Donegal's triumph and the impressive form of the side as a whole, especially the way the attack moved, caused a number of pundits to revise opinions formed after the defeat by Dublin in the League final replay and to conclude that Donegal might be sparking again after all – and have it in them to stop the march of Derry, the League champions of '92.

"Have you ever seen a hen die – the way it gives a last kick?" That was the comment of Bosco McDermott to me about Galway's great effort in the second half of the 1967 League (Home) final against Dublin. "We were a tired team in the first half. Then, as we came out for the second half, we looked at each other, no one said anything, but each man knew what was in the other man's mind. In face of the reality of defeat, we rose to it like one man and we achieved what we had set out to do – to get to the States once more."

It represented the dying kick of the Galway three-in-a-row combination (1964-'66).

"We played for the day. We did not set out to create records," said Bosco.

Perhaps that second half effort against Dublin should have been reserved for the championship tie against Mayo. When they crashed out to Mayo, Galway looked a tired team.

The trip to America or a fourth-in-a-row All-Ireland crown – one or the other, it could not be both.

And so with Donegal. The completion of the Championshp-League double or making it two Ulster titles back-to-back and a second successive All-Ireland title.

It had to be one or the other, it could not be both. Donegal paid the same price as Galway did for involement in the ultimate stages of the League.

CHAPTER 3

THE TEAM THAT REFUSED TO DIE

THE late Saturday sunshine slanted across the Croke Park pitch as the Dublin roar rose in anticipation of the victory at hand from the stands and terraces, the fans on The Hill dancing with joy, giving the arms-aloft salute to the heavens.

It was deep and full-throated and emotional. It seemed suddenly to spread right around the stadium in spine-tingling fashion as Meath stood on the brink of defeat at the end of one of the greatest marathons in GAA history – an epic series of four matches, two of which had gone to extra time and lasting in all 340 minutes.

This, you felt, was to be Dublin's evening of celebration – a night to savour in the metropolis when the fans would acclaim their heroes, when the hostelries around Croke Park and beyond that attract the aficionados would become the hub of intense debates, of laughter and the "crack" and Dublin wit and repartee, of spontaneous singing too as the night wore on . . . of not wanting to let go the adrenalin-pumping excitement generated by all that was packed into the 70 minutes of the decisive game.

Dublin were four points clear with just six minutes to go. Fifteen minutes into the second half the scoreboard had read 0-12 to 0-6 in their favour. Nothing, it seemed, could deny them now. Nothing, it appeared, could thwart them of the triumph they so richly deserved on the run of the play. Yes, they looked to be coasting in.

But somehow or other they just could not kill Meath off when they had them going on the ropes.

Or, more correctly, Meath refused to die.

Saturday, 6 July 1991

Everyone who was in Croke Park that evening – the official attendance was 61,543 – will never forget the fantastic Meath movement from out of defence that was rounded off by Kevin Foley scoring a killer goal into the Railway end that silenced The Hill.

Two minutes remained when, after Brian Stafford had reduced

the deficit to three points, Martin O'Connell gained possession near his own end line and released to Mick Lyons . . . on to Liam Harnan . . . then to O'Rourke . . . to Foley . . . P. J. Gillic . . . Tommy Dowd . . . O'Rourke again . . . and finally to Foley, who had ranged right up from the half-back line to join in that final do-or-die assault on the Dublin goal.

From the edge of the square Foley unleashed the shot that takes its place in GAA history as one of the truly great goals and at the same time one of the most shattering in the way it completely altered the destination of honours in this first round Leinster senior championship tie.

And Meath were not finished yet. Before Dublin had time to realise what had happened, before they could regroup. Liam Hayes caught John O'Leary's kick-out, raced for goal, found Gillic with a pass and he in turn flicked the ball to Dave Beggy and right-footed he planted it over the bar.

Dublin had one minute in which to snatch the point that would have made it yet another draw but Jack Sheedy was wide from a long-range free.

The distraught Dublin players, holding their heads in their hands in total disbelief, just did not know what had hit them in those final disastrous minutes. Con Houlihan would capture it very aptly later in his *Evening Press* column when he wrote: "I understand the Dublin players who said: 'How can you win four battles and lose the War?'."

And Con would add: "I have never known a tie so enthralling as the saga enacted by Dublin and Meath. And when at last the great drama was over, the emotional fall-out was enormous. To my ears it seemed like a death in the family: an exaggeration — but not much.

"As usual after games in Croke Park, I met up with my Dublin friends in the Shakespeare Bar in Parnell Street. It was crowded but you could hear the sound of every pint being filled. Never was a silence more eloquent."

Jimmy Keaveney was gone from his seat in the Hogan Stand almost before the final whistle sounded. He could not endure it — the way it was lost.

I caught up with him in Meagher's, to get his views for my article on the game in the next day's *Sunday Independent.*

Jimmy touched on the real turning point — Keith Barr's missed penalty at the Canal goal end eight minutes from time.

Dublin were leading at that stage by three points. Jimmy Keaveney argued that if there were twenty minutes left on the clock he would have had no hesitation in going for goal. "A goal at that point would have finished Meath off and, even if you failed to convert, you would still have had ample time to build on your three points lead. It wouldn't have been a disaster."

However, Keaveney was adamant that Keith Barr should have been instructed from the dug-out to take his point from the penalty. "I believe that a point then would have caused Meath to realise that they needed two scores to level and they would have been forced to go for a point first before endeavouring to snatch the goal that would have given them a draw. It would have been a different ball game.

"The risk in going for three points in the shape of a goal was too great just eight minutes from the end when there was a point there for the taking that could have made all the difference in the end."

Keaveney was adamant also that Meath's decisive goal should NEVER have been conceded. Any one of the Meath players in the movement could have been pulled down before Kevin Foley got the final pass at the edge of the square. "If Meath were in a similar position to Dublin, you can be certain that their defenders would not have stood on ceremony and they would not have hesitated in pulling a man down to halt a movement that looked like bringing a goal."

Paddy Cullen's response to that line of argument was: "The Meath movement, as it developed out of defence, was actually stopped momentarily around the fifty-yard mark by Mick Kennedy. Meath, having regrouped, flashed the ball out to the wing under the Hogan Stand and as they moved in on our goal in a swiftly-executed passing movement, our players stood off and Kevin Foley was allowed the space to round it off with a goal."

On the missed penalty kick, Cullen said there was no doubt that the referee should have ordered that it be retaken. A Meath player ran beside Keith Barr as he was taking the penalty kick. "The video of the game left me in no doubt that there had been a breach of the rules."

On the vexed question as to whether Barr should have taken his point, Cullen said: "I know it has been argued that a point then would have put us four points clear, whereas he was risking a lot to get the two extra points on top of that. And it was even said that the original instruction to the player to take his point was counter-manded with another instruction from the dug-out.

"I can say for definite that no instruction was sent to Keith Barr. Once the penalty was awarded, he knew it was his job to take it and obviously he was going to attempt to score a goal.

"Supposing he had taken the point and the game ended in a draw, then the same people who argued later against him shooting for goal would have asked why had he not gone for broke? As it was, Meath got a goal and a point in their final rally and I believe that it would have taken a goal from Keith Barr's effort to have broken them finally and put victory beyond their reach. No, I do not regret that he went for a goal. I do regret the missed opportunity."

Turning to the criticism voiced at the late replacement of Charlie Redmond and Paul Clarke, Cullen said: "We were criticised for replacing Charlie Redmond with Vinnie Murphy and Paul Clarke with Joe McNally. Charlie was limping and would not have seen the game out anyway. We decided that by bringing in two fresh men we would give things a lift up front and really punch home the advantage we had gained at that stage. While we had Meath on the rack, we failed to put them away and that was the story also in the earlier matches".

In the final analysis, he argued that the injury to the captain, Tommy Carr was an important turning point.

"I am not saying anything against Ray Holland's performance; indeed, he performed excellently when sent in as a sub for the captain but Carr's presence would have made a lot of difference in defence when Meath rallied to get the levelling goal and then the winning point. I would venture that if Tommy had not been forced to go off then the goal might never have come and neither would the winning point.

"When it is as close as it was between Dublin and Meath in this championship tie, then an injury to one key player can swing the balance and the injury to Tommy Carr tipped the balance in Meath's favour and put us out of the championship," said Paddy Cullen.

The marathon series had the effect of creating a new mutual respect between the Dublin and Meath players, cemented to the point that neither county had any hang-ups anymore about facing the other.

The finest example of this mutual respect lay in the way Keith Barr sought out Colm O'Rourke at the Lord Mayor's reception in the Mansion House the night of the last game in the marathon series.

Keith, you will recall, caught Colm with a good old-fashioned fair shoulder that left the Meath man on the ground receiving attention for a time but, though shaken, his immense courage and commitment saw him get up and continue playing.

Well, Keith told Colm he was glad to see that he was okay, adding jokingly: "I suppose you would have done the same thing if you were in the position to hit me with your shoulder as I went through?"

"You bet I would," responded Colm.

Territorially Dublin had a definite edge in the first three games of the series and yet failed to get the clinching score on each occasion.

Here were the final scores:

First Game: June 2: Dublin 1-12; Meath 1-12. Attendance: 51,144.

Second Game: June 9: Dublin 1-11; Meath 1-11 (after 30 minutes extra time). Attendance: 60,960.

Third Game: June 23: Dublin 1-14; Meath 2-11 (after 30 minutes extra time). Attendance: 63,736.

Fourth Game: Saturday, July 6: Meath 2-10; Dublin 0-15. Attendance: 61,543.

P. J. Gillic's last-gasp point saved Meath in the first match. Mick Deegan was in possession coming out but instead of clearing the ball quickly, he was preparing to place it in pinpointed fashion to a colleague when he was dispossessed by Gillic, who lofted the ball goalwards. John O'Leary darted out but the ball flew over his head, hopped in front of goal and went over the bar – instead of into the empty net. *Phew!*

In the second match, Vinny Murphy had a glorious chance of the winning point a minute before normal time was up. He shot for goal when he could have punched the ball over the bar and saw his effort saved by Michael McQuillan. The highlights included eight points from frees from the deadly-accurate boot of Barney Rock and a punched goal by Jack Sheedy in the first period of extra time that restored Dublin's fortunes when Meath looked like getting on top.

The introduction of Gerry McEntee at midfield in the second half of normal time saved Meath from defeat in the third match, the upshot being that the Dubs failed to score in the last quarter, a fisted goal by Bernard Flynn being crucial to Meath's fighting rally.

Into extra time and it seemed that a goal by Colm Coyle had put the Meathmen on their way to victory when Paul Clarke responded with a goal for Dublin and so the great epic drama was unresolved – until the fantastic saga finally ended on Saturday, July 6 and Meath won it from a seemingly impossible position.

⌘ ⌘ ⌘

Dog-weary tired in every bone of their bodies, Meath could be said to be flying on automatic when they faced Wicklow in the second round on July 14 at Croke Park. Bobby O'Malley confessed that this was Wicklow's big opportunity of taking them, leading as they were by a point with nine minutes left. They failed to grasp it, however, and had to be content in the end with a draw. Meath beat them by three points in the replay (1-12 to 1-9), then easily disposed of Offaly in the semi-final (2-13 to 0-7) and overcame Laois (1-11 to 0-8) in the Leinster final.

Roscommon should have beaten Meath in the All-Ireland semi-final – but didn't. Again the indominatable spirit of the Meath men carried the day when all seemed lost and they won through by the narrowest of margins (0-15 to 1-11).

Meath contested nine matches before they faced Down in the All-Ireland final. That tenth game was to prove a bridge too far.

Granted, they took the field handicapped by the absence of their outstanding right corner-back Bobby O'Malley, who had suffered a fractured leg while Colm O'Rourke, who went down with viral pneumonia in the week leading up to the final, did not enter the fray until the second half.

His arrival transformed Meath who staged an amazing fightback that might well have carried them to victory. In cold retrospect, however, I believe that all the games they had played in the championship took their toll on the Meathmen. It was noticeable that Martin O'Connell, a tower of strength right through the campaign, never touched in the All-Ireland final the heights he had shown himself capable of attaining. Likewise Brian Stafford was below his best, though in the first half it could have been due to the fact that he was missing the presence of Colm O'Rourke.

There was one other important factor. Meath had been carried forward on a high, unable to stop to think, their concentration totally on the one objective – to reach the All-Ireland final and try and round off the proudest season in the annals of Meath football by putting the county's name on the Sam Maguire Cup once again.

Suddenly, after overcoming Roscommon, they found themselves with time to think, the pattern of non-stop action broken, coming down from the high to what was for the experienced members of the side the normality of the grind of getting ready for another All-Ireland final. Once you stopped, even momentarily, it was difficult to get it going again as it had been going. In a way it might have been better if there had been no break at all but, of course, it was inevitable that there would be a lull between the semi-final and final. A fatal pause for Meath, as it evolved.

Football followers everywhere sympathised with Meath when they failed to crown the season by lifting the Sam Maguire Cup. It was a fitting gesture by the GAA's Central Council, on the recommendation of the Management Committee, to decide to give the Meath panel and key officials a set of gold medals inscribed with the dates of all the matches they had played in the championship (normally the runners-up in the All-Ireland final get silver medals).

The golden goal against Dublin will remain etched in the minds of all who were privileged to be in Croke Park as a classic of its kind – a classic in the build up of the movement that led to it and a classic in its clinical execution.

John O'Leary, captain of Dublin in 1993, maintained that no other team but Meath could have pulled it out of the fire in such a manner. The Meath men had built up such confidence from playing together for so long – that is the experienced nucleus of the side – that they considered no situation hopeless, nothing impossible.

They certainly proved the truth of the adage that is so meaningful to the experienced professional poker players you find going for broke in Las Vegas: "The opera ain't over 'till the Fat Lady sings".

We will remember the Meath team of the summer of '91 as the team that refused to die.

✠ ✠ ✠

Two years on from the climactic game in the marathon four-match series of '91, Meath and Dublin faced each other again at Croke Park before an attendance of 63,164 – this time in the Leinster semi-final.

Much had happened in the meantime. Paddy Cullen was gone as manager of the .Dublin team following the failure against Donegal in the '92 All-Ireland final. Dr. Pat O'Neill, a selector under Cullen, was now at the helm and with him in the dug-out were Jim Brogan, Fran Ryde and Bobby Doyle, all three of whom had been part of the set-up in '92.

Meath had gone out sensationally to Laois at Navan (2-11 to 1-11) in the first round of the 1992 Leinster championship but Seán Boylan was still manager and you reckoned he would be there as long as he wished to be there. Ten years in command. And the General retaining the faith of the county.

Both Dublin and Meath retained a nucleus of the men who had taken part in the epic '91 season, but you can in no way say that they were the same sides. No, Mick Lyons was no longer at full-back for Meath and Gerry Hargan was gone from the full-back berth for Dublin. Barney Rock also from the attack. And Meath were missing ace goal-scoring corner forward, Bernard Flynn who had the misfortune of suffering a fractured leg during the All-Ireland club championship.

Meath had discovered three excellent young defenders in Enda McManus, Graham Geraghty and Cormac Murphy, all three of whom would make their mark against Dublin in no uncertain fashion while the Liam Hayes-Gerry McEntee midfield pairing had given way to Colm Brady and John McDermott, a mobile duo if lacking the physical strength say of Derry's pairing of Anthony Tohill and Brian McGilligan.

Dublin had a new, orthodox full-back line in Ciaran Walsh, Dermot Deasy and Paddy Moran. Deasy had done exceptionally well against Donegal in the drawn League final and replay. Pat Gilroy partnered a revitalised Jack Sheedy at midfield while new faces in attack from '91 included Niall Guiden and Dessie Farrell.

This was a poor game when set against the best of the '91 series. That didn't worry Dr. Pat O'Neill and Dublin as long as they buried the Meath hoodoo that had afflicted them for so long.

Meath, considering the amount of possession they won, had every reason to regret this as a match thrown away and over the seventy minutes they shot twelve wides. Meath played some of their best football in a period of marked dominance before half-time when they were just 0-5 to 0-4 behind, after playing against the slight wind. They would have been ahead but for the disallowing by referee, Tommy Howard (Kildare) of what would have been a magnificent goal by right half back Graham Geraghty, after receiving an excellent pass from Colm O'Rourke. He was adjudged, however, to have over-carried the ball.

Normally immaculate free-taker Brian Stafford had an off day by his high standards and his failure to convert an easy free near the end was inexplicable. It was the attack that lost it for Meath.

Dublin made the decisive switches at the interval break that were conspicuous by their absence in '91. Paul Bealin was brought in to operate at centre-forward, a ploy that paid off. So also did the switch that brought Keith Barr back to defence.

A slimmed-down Charlie Redmond, the Finglas-based fireman, who cycles to work every day from Ashbourne in his bid to combat his weight problem, emerged as Dublin's hero with 1-7 to his name. He kicked the first two scores of the match in a tentative opening quarter. But it was after the resumption when moved to his customary left corner forward position that he did the damage that was to prove Meath's undoing.

Redmond had pointed Dublin into the lead when Paul Bealin fielded a poor kick-out from Michael McQuillan. Bealin quickly parted to Jack Sheedy, who with his pace made a lot of ground and then drew the Meath cover to set up Redmond for a goal of real vintage quality. Dublin were on a high after this and looked like marching on to a convincing triumph as they increased the lead to five points.

But Meath again refused to die. Delving deep into their resources and showing great character, they gained inspiration from the ageless veteran, 36-year-old Colm O'Rourke who once again proved himself one of the most dangerous forwards of the modern era.

Meath registered four points without reply. In a tension-laden, cliff-hanging, super-charged climax it seemed certain that it would end in a draw when O'Rourke, accepting the ball from Brian Stafford's short free, shot a mighty point into the Canal end twenty seconds into injury time.

Then in 49 seconds of the purest football drama, Dublin worked the ball upfield. Jack Sheedy, now the central link-man between midfield, defence and attack in the Dublin side, picked up a blocked shot and from 40 yards out this man, who at other times had raised groans with his wild shooting, hit the target into the Hill 16 goal. As the white flag went up, we knew that there was going to be no reprieve for Meath this time. It was at the same Hill 16 end that Meath had scored their classic winning goal in '91.

Lady Fortune, who had smiled on Meath then, now turned cruelly away. She gave her favours to Dublin in this 1993 Leinster championship.

Because of a serious knee injury Colm Brady had been out of the game for two years and had missed the epic series of '91.

Asked in the Meath dressingroom how he felt, a dejected Brady replied simply: "The knees are fine . . . it's my heart now that has been dented."

✳ ✳ ✳

John O'Leary lifted high in triumph his second trophy of the '93 season when Dublin overcame Kildare far more comprehensively than the 0-11 to 0-7 score might indicate in the Leinster final before an attendance of 59,696 at Croke Park on 25 July.

Kildare's hopes of landing their first Provincial crown since 1956 died a sad death for their supporters, who had headed for the metropolis convinced that this would be a day for celebration. Indeed, the odds in favour of the Lily Whites had shortened appreciably when Dublin were forced to field without Mick Deegan, Niall Guiden, Paul Clarke and Mick Galvin, though the latter came on as a sub.

Mick O'Dwyer had to accept the salutary truth that, after all the work he had put in since taking over at the helm to shape Kildare into a championship-winning unit, no real progress had been made by the Lily Whites, especially in the forward division, since losing the 1991 League final rather unluckily to the Dubs.

When Kildare went in at half-time only a point behind (0-3 to 0-2) after playing against the wind, it was obvious that they would never be presented with a better chance of beating their bogey team. However, as Davy Dalton admitted afterwards in the dressingroom "the task of containing Dublin in the first half, when we were facing the wind, had taken an awful lot out of us. We never looked like scoring the goal that we badly needed".

Kildare had set out from the start to show that they were not going to be intimidated in the "physical stakes". Dublin had the strength to hit and hit hard and at the same time to absorb without their game being affected. They easily came out best in the close encounters.

Kildare's ploy should have been to try and stretch Dublin to the limit on the flanks and open up the vital gaps. Ultimately, however, even when they did carve openings for points, they revealed an appalling inability to pick off scores from a distance and men avoided the responsibility by passing to a colleague. Furthermore, they were significantly lacking in goal-scoring punch in an attack in which Niall Buckley and Paul McLoughlin failed to come up to expectations and neither of them got anything from play.

Mick O'Dwyer accepted that Kildare were in an ideal position at half-time – "but unfortuntely we lost our concentration and let the game slip in the first fifteen minutes of the second half by conceding six successive points".

The Dublin forwards, who missed a number of scorable chances in the first half, now picked off some magnificent long-range points. Moving the ball speedily and accurately, they continually ran at the Kildare defence and Dessie Farrell, Charlie Redmond, Pat Gilroy, Vinny Murphy and Mick Galvin gave Dublin a 0-9 to 0-2 lead.

When Vinny Murphy, who had already been booked, was sent to the line by referee. Tommy McDermott (Cavan) for a rugby-style tackle it still made no difference. As Davy Dalton put it: "It became more difficult for us as Dublin packed their defence and used only two forwards".

The introduction of Johnny Barr, Keith's brother, was a shrewd, tactical move by Pat O'Neill and his fellow selectors as he kicked a crucial point as the game entered the final five minutes and Kildare realised that, with Dublin holding a four-points lead, even a goal would not get them out of the wood.

The wind and the rain spoiled what we had thought beforehand would be a Croke Park spectacle and, frankly, it fell far below expectations. But then Kildare's failure to mount a significant challenge for honours was at the root of the packed stadium coming away very disappointed at this Leinster final.

Dr. Pat O'Neill sumed up: "The half-time re-evaluation of our tactics worked very well for us. In the first half, we were frequently making the mistake of hitting balls in to Martin Lynch, who was sweeping up behind the half-back line.

"We identified this on the line but unfortuantely we were unable to communicate it to the players. In the first half also we often played things too tight. In the second half, we played a much sounder tactical game by running at Kildare and using the short ball very well."

The depth of the Dublin panel was shown by the contributions of newcomers Paul O'Neill, who had an outstanding game at left wing back and Johnny Barr.

CHAPTER 4

DOWN MAINTAIN UNIQUE RECORD

UNQUESTIONABLY one of the most noteworthy achievements of the 1991 season on the national plane was that of Down footballers in maintaining the Mourne County's 100% record in All-Ireland finals.

In the span of just over thirty years from 1960 to '91 Down contested four finals – and won all four. But making their record even more significant was the opposition they beat and the way they showed the footballing world that the mystique surrounding the colours of one of the great traditional strongholds of the game in Kerry held no terrors at all for them.

In their very first All-Ireland in 1960 Down came up against the reigning champions Kerry and emerged victorious by eight points. Kevin Mussen had the proud honour of being the first man to carry the Sam Maguire Cup across the Border to the "wee Six".

Down, captained then by Paddy Doherty, confirmed in the 1961 All-Ireland semi-final that their 1960 form was no fluke by beating Kerry with even more impressive authority and went on to defeat Offaly in the final before an all-time official record attendance of 90,556 (they had conquered Offaly after a replay in the 1960 semi-final).

Kerry again provided the opposition to Down in the 1968 All-Ireland final – a Down side led by Joe Lennon, a link with 1960-'61, and three other links were provided with that first great combination by Dan McCartan, Paddy Doherty and Seán O'Neill. Joe Lennon had tremendous leadership qualities; Doherty's astuteness and experience and his brilliant accuracy were immense assets to the side in its march to ultimate honours while Seán O'Neill was like a panther pouncing on the half-chances at full-forward, as typified by the way he goaled when the ball came off the upright in the All-Ireland final against Kerry.

I rate Seán O'Neill one of the most dangerous and quicksilver attackers, either as a wing forward or full forward, that I have seen in my time writing about gaelic football. Not surprising then that he got an overwhelming vote for the right half forward position on the *Sunday Independent*/Irish Nationwide/GAA Team of the Century in 1984.

The true value of Down's return to the top in 1991 was the way it changed the face of football overnight in the nineties. There had been an ever-developing tendency to rule out in dismissive fashion the Ulster representatives when it came to the final stages of the All-Ireland championship.

The cold statistics were one reason for this and, secondly, some of the teams from out of Ulster were just not good enough.

Not since Down's victory in 1968 had an Ulster team succeeded in winning the Sam Maguire Cup. Twenty-three years was a long time. Just two years short of the quarter of a century.

Now it was obvious that, stemming directly from Down's 1991 title success, a new mood had been created in Ulster. "What Down can do, we can do" would become the battle-cry of other counties – counties especially like Tyrone, Armagh, Derry and Donegal. There was no longer an invincible tag surrounding Kerry or Dublin, Meath or Cork. Derry and Tyrone would contest the National League final in 1992 as the precursor to Donegal winning the All-Ireland title.

Down, by disposing of both Kerry and Meath in the same '91 season, had shown that anything was possible. Kerry were left with a record they didn't enjoy having – they had NEVER beaten Down in the All-Ireland championship.

Down had one essential ingredient going for them when it came to facing Kerry and Meath. The county had been there before and had not been found wanting. Armagh (1977) and Tyrone (1986) had both reached the All-Ireland final in the period since 1970 and had failed at the final obstacle.

Monaghan, having won the National League in 1985, held Kerry to a draw the first day in the All-Ireland semi-final only to fail by five points in the replay. But this was a Kingdom side that would go on to complete a three-timer in 1986. Donegal, too, missed a golden opportunity in the 1990 All-Ireland semi-final.

There was this clear impression abroad that just when the Sam Maguire Cup was within their grasp, the Ulster counties, outside of Down, stalled in their moment of greatest challenge – that, in effect, they froze at the sheer enormity of the thought of winning. On the surface it might seem to come down to missed chances, like the failure to convert a crucial penalty in Tyrone's case, but you sensed it went deeper than that. It was psychological.

Down did not stall in face of a tremendous Meath rally in the 1991 All-Ireland final. I was very impressed by the manner in which they maintained their poise, especially at the back and they

45

certainly gained from the tradition surrounding the jersey that had been created in 1960-'61 and '68.

Donegal's defeat of Dublin in the 1992 All-Ireland final has to be put on a par with Down's defeat of Kerry in the 1960 final. Kerry and Dublin between them farm over half-a-century of All-Ireland senior titles. It has reached the point that a Provincial crown is no longer the primary target, as Clare were satisfied to gain Munster honours in '92 and Kildare, after being so long in the championship wilderness, would have counted it a real blessing to have beaten Dublin in the '92 Leinster final. They would have seen it as the stepping-stone to greater goals.

Donegal became true aristocrats when they left no doubt whatsoever about their superiority over Dublin in the '92 final.

Now, not just one county from Ulster, but two had proved that they were *winners* and we had to reshape our thoughts on how the pendulum of power was swinging. Derry made it three-in-a-row for Ulster when winning their first-ever title in 1993. It remained for a Connacht county to rectify the situation that has seen the Sam Maguire Cup not held high in triumph by any captain from the Province since Enda Colleran led Galway to their third successive title win in 1966.

Twenty-seven years is a long time. Too long.

Most disappointing of all was the sharp decline in Galway's fortunes, after they lost the 1974 All-Ireland final to Dublin. And, as a magnificent band of hurlers left a lasting imprint with three All-Ireland title wins in the eighties (1980, '87 and '88), there came a point where supporters seemed to turn their backs altogether on the footballers.

Their disillusionment would become sharper still when Galway went out to Leitrim in the first round of the 1993 Connacht Championship.

Roscommon (1980) and Mayo (1989) had opportunities to win the Sam Maguire but failed respectively to Kerry and Cork in deciders that could have been won.

The Connacht colours flew limply as the balance of power swung to Ulster in 1991 and '92.

⌘ ⌘ ⌘

The disappointments and frustrations of thirteen long years were wiped away for Paddy O'Rourke, captain of Down, at Croke Park on Sunday, 15 September 1991, when he received the Sam Maguire Cup from GAA President, Peter Quinn.

It was difficult for the man from the Burren to conceal his emotion in that unforgettable moment. "This is the proudest day of my life," he said.

He was pictured in the *Irish Independent* the next day with his left hand covering his eyes – the tears of joy welling up – as he tried to grasp the reality of the fact that after trying since 1978 to win an All-Ireland medal, he had succeeded at last – and it was actually his first time playing in a decider.

He had come a long road from the day he had been thrown in at the deep end when sent on as a sub against Anton O'Toole in the 1978 All-Ireland semi-final against Dublin. He had starred in the All-Ireland minor victory over Meath the previous year and was still a boy in a man's game. He performed creditably for one so green but an eleven points defeat was Down's lot against the streamlined Dublin machine, heading for the third-in-a-row.

He was thirty-two then when he played in his first All-Ireland senior football final and Paddy wouldn't have to be reminded that it was an age when many players would be contemplating retirement. Indeed, O'Rourke was giving a thought or two to hanging up his boots at the very time Peter McGrath took over as team manager in 1989.

He might have been forgiven for thinking that McGrath wouldn't see any place for him in his plans, that he might adopt a policy based almost entirely on youth. Shrewdly, however, the new team manager asked Paddy O'Rourke, Liam Austin and Ambrose Rodgers to stay on because he realised that experience was essential in the panel. He went further and appointed O'Rourke captain, a responsibility that fitted easily on his shoulders as he had held the captaincy in four previous seasons.

A three-year plan was decided upon by Peter McGrath to realise the ambition of bringing Down to an All-Ireland final. It was achieved in two and meanwhile Down contested the 1990 National League final in which they ran Meath to two points.

In Newry one evening as he prepared for the semi-final tie against Kerry, Paddy O'Rourke confessed to me that he felt like a drowning man who had been thrown a lifeline when Down defeated Donegal in the '91 Ulster final. Yes, that victory achieved against all the early season predictions of the pundits who saw Donegal not alone getting out of Ulster but reaching Croke Park on September 15, represented for him a rescue from the cold waters of despair when he was beginning to think to himself that all hope of ever winning an All-Ireland medal was gone.

After Down's failure against Dublin in 1978 he had played in a

47

second All-Ireland semi-final against Offaly in 1981 and in his third Ulster final against Tyrone in 1986.

The famine seasons with no title coming Down's way in the period from 1982 up to 1991 became all the more frustrating and galling for O'Rourke in that frequently the team would start out in Ulster with the hopes of their supporters riding high and the media painting a picture of a new era of glory. Just imagine it, they even lost to Fermanagh in the first round in 1983 – after winning the National League.

Why so many barren seasons? Why did things go wrong?

"It was a case of expectations being pitched too high when we just didn't have the right material. Bad luck too – and you need your share of the breaks to be successful at this level. And then there's the kind of refereeing that has to be accepted in Ulster, where inferior teams know they will get away with pulling and dragging tactics against better footballing sides.

"Ask Mickey Linden about that."

He talked about the burden that the 1960-'61 side had imposed on all Down teams that followed. "The media compared everything with the standards set in 1960 and '61. Young lads of promise were hardly in the team when they were discarded because they did not measure up in people's minds with the players of the sixties."

There is a real romance to the way Paddy O'Rourke came out of the Burren area of county Down to wear the county colours. He is one of a family of fifteen, nine sisters and six brothers. His father, the late Philip – a man with a small farm who also worked in the local creamery – met Margaret, his wife to be, when she came from Newport, County Tipperary, to work in Newry. (Paddy, incidentally, is a first cousin of Noel O'Gorman, the former Tipperary hurler.)

There was no footballing tradition in the O'Rourke family. "But from the moment I began to kick a ball about in the back garden I wanted to be a Seán O'Neill. I used to listen with my father to Michael O'Hehir's commentaries and they had an immense effect on me. I was set on making it to the top as a gaelic footballer."

He was fortunate that he found the right nursery in St Mark's School in Warrenpoint. Fortunate too that Colm McAlarney, the outstanding Down and Ulster midfielder, was the PT teacher there.

His father's death, when he was only fifteen, saw him leave school a year earlier than he had intended and he began to serve his time as a joiner. Into club football then with Burren, knowing the encouragement and the guiding hand of Seán Murdoch, whom he describes as the father figure, "to whom we young lads owed everything really". So many honours with the club; eight county championship medals and two All-Ireland club medals.

In the All-Ireland semi-final he was opposed by Pat Spillane ("a fine athlete and a true sportsman who has put a tremendous amount into football") and in the final itself by Tommy Dowd. He held the line with all the experience being brought into play that he had gained over thirteen seasons.

Before the Kerry game he was reflecting on the honour it would be to lead Down in the pre-match parade on All-Ireland final day.

And on the day itself, Paddy O'Rourke clinched his fists and said to himself inwardly that there could be no failure now – there MUST be no failure. At thirty-two he might never get another chance like this.

You see he had been thrown a life-line in Clones . . . and now he was going to become the captain who would steer the ship to port.

Beckoning for him in the parade was the Sam Maguire Cup and that same evening he became only the third man in the history of the GAA to bring it across the Border to the "wee Six".

Kevin Mussen was one of the first to congratulate him.

⌘ ⌘ ⌘

In the course of his commentary on the All-Ireland final, Micheál Ó Muircheartaigh – the "Voice of RTE Radio" – described D. J. Kane as "the soul of the Down defence". That tribute was certainly not misplaced. D. J. not alone curbed the threat posed by flying wing-forward Dave Beggy but made an immense contribution to his side's victory from the half-back line, both in the attacking sense and in a covering role.

Like Paddy O'Rourke he knew the lean times. And so the satisfaction of sharing with his team-mates on the '91 squad the joy of winning of the All-Ireland crown went very deep for the PE teacher in Lagan College, Belfast.

D. J., they will tell you in the heartlands of Down football, was a motivator *par excellence* in days when the promise was high at the outset of successive championship seasons, only for those hopes to be dashed because too much was expected too soon.

"It was worth waiting through the years of disappointment to reach the goal of winning an All-Ireland final," said the twenty-six year old defender."

The steely edge in D. J. Kane's play, coupled with the diamond hardness of his tackling, ensured that, until Colm O'Rourke entered the fray, Meath just could not mount flowing attacks. By the time O'Rourke changed the whole pattern of things, Down had already put enough scores on the scoreboard to see them safely home – if only just in the end.

Lagan College is set high above Belfast on the Manse Road giving one a breathtaking view of the city down below, especially on a sunny morning. It is here in the North's first integrated school that D. J. Kane is in the van of a great experiment to save a vital percentage of the rising generation in Belfast from the cancer of inbuilt attitudes born of going their separate ways in the formative years in schools with entrenched views of history.

D. J. is fostering gaelic football in the college where the ratio among the 750 pupils is 50% Catholic and 50% Protestant and, who knows, but that in time this new nursery of the game may deliver a talented player for the Down senior team. In the comparatively short time he has been based here he has broken through all the barriers, all the accepted moulds that in other times would have appeared insurmountable.

Protestant children are playing gaelic side by side with Catholics without any hang-ups. While it is a long way down the road before they can hope to compete in the Belfast Schools League with teams from rural areas that are traditional strongholds of the game, D. J. is confident he will soon be able to put together a side that can at least participate in friendly matches.

"We are looking to D. J. when it comes to gaelic football," said one of his teacher colleagues, who pointed out that soccer was the primary competitive sport in the college.

D. J. Kane has had to run a gauntlet that can be as boneshattering as running headlong into Mick Lyons. He has had to defend passionately the concept of the integrated school in debates with Catholic clergymen, satisfied with nothing less than a full Catholic instruction for Catholic children in their *own* schools. But he has the courage to believe what he is doing is right and he will not be deterred.

Now Kane, the mould-breaker, who is playing his part in Lagan College to build bridges between the communities, has an All-Ireland championship medal beside the two Sigerson Cup medals he won with Charlie Sweeney's powerful University of Ulster side in the late eighties and all the other honours he has won.

Again, as in the case of Paddy O'Rourke, it was worth the wait.

✳ ✳ ✳

The effectiveness of the Greg Blaney–Mickey Linden–James McCartan axis in attack, a throw-back to another axis in another time if not assured of the same immortality in the history books, saw Down lead by no less than eleven points (1-14 to 0-6) fifteen minutes into the second half.

Greg Blaney was the fulcrum of the line, the guiding brain at centre-forward. Corner-forwards Mickey Linden and James McCartan played wide out on the flanks, turning the Meath defence and prepared to cut in along the end line.

In fact, it was superb play from McCartan and Linden out on the Cusack Stand–Canal end wing that saw the ball transferred across to the unmarked Barry Breen who sent it home for the goal that meant that the Ulster champions had the cushion that would ensure they would not be caught.

But this was no three-man attacking outfit. Big Peter Withnell, so powerful physically, caused immense problems to Mick Lyons, who was forced to retire injured midway through the second half and with his departure something of the heart went out of the Meath last line of defence, Martin O'Connell then being forced to take over the full-back role.

Ross Carr's performance was a revelation on the right wing and he took his points from frees very well, as did Gary Mason, who contributed four in all, one from play.

This was a sextet that believed totally that they had the beating of the Meath defence and proceeded to play from the outset with that kind of belief in themselves. No other forward line has dissected the Meath defence so coldly and calculatingly.

In fairness to Meath, however, it has to be stressed that the absence of Bobby O'Malley made a world of difference to their performance at the back, as I thought his covering ability across the line was sadly missed and by no one more than Mick Lyons. Indeed, Dave Foran in the *Irish Press* next morning argued that if O'Malley had been playing James McCartan would have found it much, much harder to win all the possession he did.

Foran acknowledged also that a fully fit Colm O'Rourke, playing from the outset, would have made an immense difference to Meath's bid for the title. "His experience and scoring ability were definitely missed in the first half."

And Joe Lennon generously wrote: "Meath failed because Colm O'Rourke had the terrible misfortune to be stricken by a virus which left him unable to start. When he came on for Colm

Coyle in the second half, he began to dismantle the Down defence. It is fair to say that his entry to the game saved Meath from a whitewash and almost snatched a draw or victory from an impossible deficit."

Seán Boylan, the Meath team manager, revealed to me later that there was no way they could have started Colm O'Rourke. Even as it was they took a risk – considering the medical advice – in bringing him on as early as they did in the second half. In any other circumstances O'Rourke, whose breathing was patchy, would have been confined to bed.

The uplift his arrival on the scene gave to his team-mates, the immense contribution he made in the last grandstand rally will remain for me one of the most remarkable features of an All-Ireland final that looked over to all intents and purposes when Greg Blaney sent the ball over the bar and the scoreboard read: Down 1-14, Meath 0-6.

Now O'Rourke stepped into it and scored a point that was the signal for all that was to follow. And when Liam Hayes scored a great goal from an opening by Tommy Dowd, the deficit had been cut to 1-15 to 1-10. Was it possible, we asked ourselves, that Meath could pull it out of the fire again as they had done against Dublin? Points by Bernard Flynn and Brian Stafford would leave the margin just two points between sides as the last minutes ticked away on the clock.

Neil Collins was acclaimed for a match-winning save from Bernard Flynn. A fine save it was too. But I am convinced that if Flynn could have waited just one split second and generated full power into the shot, no one could have stopped it.

Then there was the moment when Flynn had the chance of drawing it three minutes from the end. His blistering drive from the edge of the square into the Railway end goal went over the bar.

"I knew we needed a goal to stay alive," he observed in the dressing-room afterwards. "The moment the ball came to me that was my intention but then just as I fired in the shot, I slipped ever so slightly and it flew over," said Flynn, who scored six points in all during that remarkable second-half fightback.

I will remember always too a blazing shot by Colm O'Rourke that went right across the goal – and ever so narrowly wide. A fully fit O'Rourke, sharper in his reflexes, might not have missed.

Against that, Mickey Linden had nothing to do but place the ball past Michael McQuillan – but sent it wide.

A memorable day and a thrilling final saw the honours rest in the end with Down and deservedly so.

But, as we left Croke Park, we still marvelled at the spell-binding nature of Meath's rally, the manner in which, under Colm O'Rourke's inspiration, they clawed their way back to the point where they could have snatched it from a position more impossible than from where they had won it against Dublin on a July day in the marathon series in Leinster.

We will remember Bernard Flynn and Michael McQuillan sitting on the Croke Park sod – like two soldiers finding themselves on a bridge too far in enemy territory, only that the tenth game in a marathon season had proved that bridge too far after all even for these dynamic Meath men.

Tears ran down the faces of many of the players as they headed for the dressing-room under the Hogan Stand.

"To come so close and to lose is tough to take, very tough," said Michael McQuillan.

Out there though, Meath had died gloriously, adding a special quality of courage to the jerseys they wore.

✼ ✼ ✼

Down, having failed to Derry in the 1992 Ulster semi-final (0-15 to 0-12), fielded thirteen of the side that won the '91 All-Ireland crown when they faced the '92 National League champions in the '93 Provincial quarter-final, this time in Newry on Sunday 30 May. Hopes were high among Down supporters that the glory of the '91 season might be recaptured.

But Down were comprehensively beaten in virtually every sector of the field and manager, Peter McGrath was making no excuses afterwards.

It was a Down side lacking in leadership. The margin of eleven points against them at the end (3-11 to 0-9) told it all. They finished with only fourteen men, one of their backs being sent off entering the final quarter. By that stage, however, Derry were well in control.

They clinched victory with a great move initiated by full forward, Dermot Heaney and when substitute Eamon Burns had his shot blocked down by Neil Collins, wing forward Richard Ferris followed up to crash the ball to the net.

It might be argued that the dreadful conditions – a rain sodden pitch and slippery ball – were all against Down's style, especially up front. But in actual fact, Derry totally dominated midfield as their powerful pairing of "Man of the Match" Anthony Tohill and Brian McGilligan left Barry Breen and Eamonn Burns with only scraps from the table. Furthermore, a watertight defence in which Danny Quinn, Henry Downey, John McGurk and young Karl Diamond all shone, limited Down to a single point from play in the first half and two more after the break. James McCartan was held scoreless.

Mickey Linden had the better of his duel with Tommy Scullion in the first twenty minutes but then Derry switched Gary Coleman to corner-back and this plugged the gap.

The fact remained that the Greg Blaney-Mickey Linden-James McCartan axis, on which so much depended for a winning tally, only managed one point in seventy minutes between them. Greg Blaney's performance was particularly disappointing.

Granted they were playing in front of a beaten midfield and no attack could prosper really in a situation like that, as the half-back line had its hands full trying to cope with a supremely-confident Derry attacking unit.

Derry manager, Eamonn Coleman was in bullish mood afterwards, telling the world: "I never thought for a moment coming here that we were going to be beaten".

Peter McGrath, for his part, had reason to be critical and fortright about the lack of fighting spirit and meaningful purpose which marked the performance of his side.

Down knew that Sunday evening that they could no longer live on the memories of '91 or persist with men in key positions who had become household names that season but two years on no longer had the same hunger or were found wanting when inspirational qualities were demanded in the heat of championship battle.

In a word, the building of a new team capable of regaining the Ulster title had to start with a vengeance – and with no apologies to "name" players who would be dropped.

CHAPTER 5

CLARE BRIDGE
75 YEARS GAP

WE writers are supposed to remain cool and detached. We are expected to avoid at all costs being so stirred emotionally by the great occasions that our judgement is in no way affected.

But, believe me, when you get a day like that on Sunday, 23 August 1992, when Francis McInerney led Clare footballers out on to the Croke Park sod to face Dublin, you would need to be a very cold fish, indeed, not to have been moved by the roar that echoed around the stadium.

You see, it was the Banner County's first appearance in an All-Ireland semi-final since 1917.

It was an occasion of pageantry and over-flowing excitement, of a wave of emotion erupting in a manner that filled Croke Park with sound. An occasion of colour, the blaze of Saffron and Blue dwarfing the Dublin blue banners on The Hill.

I have experienced many unforgettable moments sitting in the Press Box in the Upper Deck of the Hogan Stand. But I must admit that I have seldom known anything like the soul-stirring atmosphere that enveloped the stadium during the pre-match parade as the thousands of Clare supporters gave vent to their feelings of admiration for the men who had humbled Kerry in the Munster final. It was unique in its ecstatic quality.

We were living an afternoon when all those who had missed Limerick, all those who had failed to believe that the Kingdom could be beaten, were making Croke Park the focal point of a retrospective celebration. For, in truth, this was a CELEBRATION in bold capital letters.

Clare folk, family groups among them, knew heading for the ground that even if the team lost to Dublin (who started 1/8 favourites), nothing could take from them the magnificence of their achievement in bridging a seventy-five years gap by winning the Munster crown.

Defeat in the end would be their lot – but it was defeat with honour and pride undimmed. I have no doubt in my mind that it was a game they could have won, and possibly should have won. However, they did not carry into this All-Ireland semi-final the experience of the backbone of the Dublin team.

55

There were Dublin players who had been there against Cork in the All-Ireland semi-final in 1989 and who had participated in the epic marathon four-match series against Meath in 1991. John O'Leary had been in goal in the 1983 All-Ireland victory. Charlie Redmond had been in the attack in the 1985 All-Ireland final against Kerry.

Clare fell into elementary errors that were to prove fatal to their cause. In a way, the dethroning of champions Kerry in the South was their All-Ireland day. It would have been too much to have expected them to win through to the All-Ireland final in their first season in the big-time.

Sunday, 19 July 1992, in the Limerick Gaelic Grounds was a day of deep significance for that great veteran of the Clare side, Noel Roche from Kilrush. It meant that he saw avenged "The Miltown Massacre" – Clare's own "Battle of Wounded Knee".

On a summer's day in 1979 a Clare side, including Noel Roche, plunged to a 9-21 score against them in defeat. As Kerry came off the field, a Clare fan remarked caustically to Pat Spillane: "Ye could have eased up towards the end."

Spillane took it graciously as he responded: "Don't blame me. Look at the Kerry dug-out. We were playing for our places in the Munster final team."

And Pat, of course, was right in a way. "Ogie" Moran was only a sub that day and Mick Spillane lost his place for the Munster final as Seánie Moloney scored 1-4 on him.

"Coming off the field that day in Miltown, I was amused rather than shattered," said Noel Roche, putting the defeat into proper perspective. "You see it was so terribly one-sided that I almost found myself pinching myself to check if it was not all a bad dream.

"When I realised, however, that it wasn't a dream I could only say to myself: 'What am I doing here?' It was subsequently when Kerry beat Cork by ten points in the Munster final, then ran up a score of 5-14 against Monaghan before easily beating Dublin in the All-Ireland final that I realised that we had been shattered by the greatest combination in football history."

Noel Roche, after fifteen seasons wearing the Clare jersey in senior grade (up to 1992), had become familiar – to the moment when John Maughan took over at the helm – with a frame of mind born of continuous, demoralising defeat. He admitted that deep down Clare footballers accepted that anything better than a ten points defeat against Cork or Kerry was in a sense a victory.

"If you happened to be only four points behind with ten

minutes to go, then you felt you had done enough to maintain the honour of the county."

John Maughan changed all that," he stressed. "He concentrated on getting us to develop belief in ourselves and to go after victory from the throw-in. That, I feel, was his greatest single contribution."

Those who professed to be shocked by Clare's thoroughly-deserved victory over Kerry in the Munster final overlooked the fact that the Banner County men had won eighteen of their nineteen games, including challenge games, in the lead-up to that match in the Limerick Gaelic Grounds.

Army officer, John Maughan, the former stylish Mayo footballer, whose career was cut short because of injury, had set himself an unenviable challenge when in October 1990 he met officers of the Clare County Board in Gort and, having bought time – just forty-eight hours – agreed to guide the fortunes of what many cynics would have seen as a bunch of losers. Adopting the stepping-stone approach, he went for attainable targets as he advanced towards the grand prize of a Munster crown.

As they won in turn the All-Ireland "B" competition, gained promotion to Division One of the National League and took the McGrath Cup, the confidence of the Clare players increased to a marked degree. Suddenly, born losers had acquired the outlook of winners.

Noel Walsh, another Army officer, who had been a selector for twenty years through all the dark days for Clare football, had campaigned unremittingly for the open draw in Munster. And when at last his efforts were crowned with success, the cycle was ended whereby Cork and Kerry took it almost for granted that they would be contesting the Munster final each season.

Five minutes into the Limerick game Noel Roche would have been forgiven if he had been overwhelmed by all the old doubts, by the memory of shattering experiences like "The Miltown Massacre".

Roche was grounded in the parallelogram as he broke through the Kerry defence. The resultant penalty, taken by Gerry Killeen, was saved in fine style by Peter O'Leary. Soon the Kingdom were two points clear. Clare stood scoreless after ten minutes.

But this Banner County team would not go down the road of the teams of earlier decades; it would not suffer the psychological humiliation that had become the accepted norm.

By half-time the Clare men were one point ahead (0-7 to 0-6). Now in the dressing-room John Maughan addressed them. A speech that echoed the passion that marked the side's display through the first thirty-five minutes and the almost unthinkable that was stirring among supporters on the embankments and, indeed, in every part of the ground. Was it really possible that Kerry could fall?

"How badly do you want it lads, how bad?"

As Cliona Foley wrote next day in the *Irish Independent*: "The legacy of seventy-five years as whipping boys swelled up in them and exploded."

Exploded in a second half of unforgettable excitement and tension as Clare found new inspiration with each passing minute. Meanwhile, Kerry, discovering that their title was slipping from their grasp, fought desperately but unavailingly to regain the initiative. The Clare tide would eventually sweep over them like Atlantic rollers coming in on the beach at Lahinch, which come the Spring of '93 would be a familiar training ground for the Banner County squad.

Before half-time Jack O'Shea, on his own admission subsequently, got one clear chance which should have been put away for a goal.

Tom Morrissey was excelling at midfield, with strong support from Aidan Moloney and the Clare pair dominated for long periods against Noel O'Mahony and newcomer Seamus Moynihan. The Kerry selectors had come in for criticism for leaving out 1984 victorious All-Ireland captain, Ambrose O'Donovan, always a trojan worker, and now, seven minutes into the second half, he was introduced into the game.

However, in the forty-eighth minute Clare delivered a vital blow when Francis McInerney carved a fine opening for Colm Clancy and the Corofin man hammered a terrific shot to the roof of the Kerry net.

It was a telling piece of strategy by the Clare selectors when they brought in Martin Daly. The Lissycasey player proceeded to make a very important contribution to the fashioning of a historic triumph.

As events turned out, he made the title secure for the Banner County in the fifty-ninth minute. The way it happened was an example in itself of the fire that Clare were putting into the effort for victory. A long ball into the Kerry goalmouth looked to be rolling out wide. The Kerry full-back got it into his hands and was about to clear it when he was hit a thundering fair shoulder by Gerry Killeen, which sent him flying over the end line.

From the "45" Martin Flynn broke the ball down and Martin

Daly was on the spot to fist it to the net. That second goal was a real killer blow for Kerry. It left them trailing by five points (2-8 to 0-9).

And now the Clare fans were singing "Here we go".

But Kerry, true to tradition, made one last effort to try and save it. Points by Timmy Fleming and Connie Murphy brought it back to three. Jack O'Shea took a twenty metres free from his hands – and it rebounded off the upright.

Earlier Pa Laide unleashed a shot that looked a certain goal, but goalie James Hanrahan smothered it and this, one has to conclude in cold retrospect, was the save that really foiled Kerry.

Two beautiful points by Gerry Killeen sealed victory for Clare (2-10 to 0-12). Long remembered from that day in Limerick will be the heroic work of Man of the Match Seamus Clancy in the Clare full-back line. No player earned more the All-Star award that would come later in the year.

I listened to the radio commentary in Croke Park watching Kilkenny defeat Wexford in the Leinster senior hurling final and etched in the mind are the words of Marty Morrissey: "There won't be a cow milked in Clare tonight."

After consultation between Noel Walsh and the County Board, it was decided that the surviving members of the Clare 1949 side – the last team up to 1992 to contest a Munster final – should be invited to be present at the Limerick Gaelic Grounds. A fitting gesture this that bridged the decades between '49 and '92.

For P. J. O'Dea, the former noted Munster player, who had flown in specially from Chicago for the occasion, it was a day of great nostalgia.

He had been picked to captain the side in '49. That morning he had to admit that he played in an innocuous soccer game in Limerick and was spotted by a vigilante (days of "The Ban" and all that!).

He sat in the sideline between two of the greatest of Clare hurlers, Larry Blake and "Tull" Considine, weeping at his loss – and the broken dream of a championship medal that was never realised.

He did not constrain the tears of joy as he stood on the sideline after the final whistle had sounded and he knew that the Munster crown belonged to Clare. Making it even better was the fact that Kerry had provided the opposition in Clare's finest hour and P. J. himself during his playing career always got a special thrill out of facing Kerry, especially when Clare had to travel.

Jack O'Shea announced his retirement from the inter-county

scene, thus severing the last remaining link with the Kerry four-in-a-row side that began its glorious march in 1978 and which came so close to making it a five-timer. He had been a superstar in every sense of the term. Kevin Heffernan paid him the ultimate tribute in 1986 when he made him his choice as captain of Ireland for the tests Down Under against Australia under the compromise rules. Ireland won the series 2-1 and it was an occasion of great celebration in Adelaide when the men in green won the last test (55 points to 32 points).

Francis McInerney led the Clare team on the Monday on a tour of triumph through the Banner County, proudly displaying the Cup in all the towns, villages and hamlets that had given players to the squad. Lissycasey . . . Coolaclare . . . Kilrush . . . Kilkee . . . Doonbeg . . . Corofin . . . Rineen . . . Quilty . . . Miltown-Malbay.

In Rineen it was special. Six men wearing balaclavas sprang out from behind a wall and fired a volley of shots into the sky. A re-enactment in its own way of the Rineen Ambush. And the spirit of Rineen had become the spirit of Clare football.

Seamus Hayes of the *Clare Champion* wrote that he would never forget the scenes in Limerick when the final whistle sounded, Clare supporters standing in the stands and on the terraces not seeking to hide their tears of emotion.

And of a moment during the victory tour, he added: "I remember standing in the street in Doonbeg on that Monday night, shortly after midnight and listening to the deafening cheer that hit the night sky when the team bus came close. In front of me a man, who said he was in his seventies and who had been waiting for over two hours for a glimpse of the players, openly wept with joy when Francis McInerney and his team-mates were presented to the huge crowd."

※ ※ ※

Against Dublin it was a case of the might-have-beens, stemming most of all from the disallowing by referee Tommy McDermott (Cavan) of what many observers thought was a perfectly legitimate goal by Pádraic Conway seventeen minutes into the game. This meant that Clare were a goal behind (1-7 to 0-7) at the interval when they might have been level, after playing against the wind.

But the real turning came, I thought, in the nineteenth minute of the second half. Dublin had forged six points clear when the

Banner County men hit back with a goal and a point inside three minutes – Gerry Killeen following up to find the net after his penalty shot was stopped by John O'Leary.

Had Clare been able to keep Dublin's lead to two points at that stage it is quite conceivable that they could have rallied for victory. But a sudden lack of concentration saw Dublin, the Leinster champions, break away from the kick-out to win a free, which Keith Barr dropped into the goalmouth and Vinny Murphy rose high above everyone else to fist it to the net.

It was unquestionably the goal that broke the back of the Clare challenge. Dublin's third goal from a move involving Jack Sheedy and Paul Bealin was incidental as was Clare's second from Pádraig Conway five minutes from the end.

This All-Ireland semi-final was won and lost when Dublin responded so quickly to Gerry Killeen's goal by balancing through Vinny Murphy's effort.

"Ultimately, I'm convinced that Clare's downfall can be placed at the door of inexperience," was Jimmy Keaveney's verdict in the *Irish Independent* next day.

The Clare wing-backs, Frankie Griffin especially, and the half-forwards, Noel Roche, Francis McInerney and Gerry Killeen by running at Dublin gave an ominous signal of what would become the Dubs' achilles heel in the All-Ireland final itself. Dublin in victory, however, did not read the signs well enough and persisted in fielding an attacking defensive set-up against Donegal while they should have been warned also about a continuing problem at midfield.

In this sector Tom Morrissey had lorded the scene for two-thirds of the game until taking a heavy knock in a collision with team-mate Gerry Killeen. And Seamus Clancy had another magnificent game in the last line of defence.

❊   ❊   ❊

Clare had recovered from the bitter disappointment of that All-Ireland semi-final defeat and had gone through the 1992-'93 National League campaign unbeaten to qualify for a semi-final crack against All-Ireland champions, Donegal, when I met Tom Morrissey in Lahinch. A soaring catch of his in the second half in Castlebar the previous Sunday had set up Gerry Killeen for the point that put Clare ahead at the end of the third quarter and on the road to a famous victory.

The back problem that had made him a doubtful starter at one point against Mayo saw him now take no part that evening in the intensive training on the Lahinch sands, geared specifically for the championship and the game against Cork in Cusack Park, Ennis, on May 30.

The 6 foot 3 inch tall Tom Morrissey from out of the village of Coolaclare – affectionately known as "Pig's Elbow" because of the way its one street turns – is undoubtedly one of the great characters of the Clare team. The quick wit and gift of repartee of this player, who gains his livelihood in the building trade, contribute immeasurably to the camaraderie and relaxed family atmosphere in the Clare camp. But, more important, he has a footballing pedigree second to none. It explains why he occupies such a special place in the hearts of Clare followers.

His uncles, who won county championship medals with Coolaclare in the sixties and who went for the priesthood, were towering players. His grandfather, Seán Morrissey, was a legendary figure for the club back around 1917. But it was Pana O'Brien who went into the records as Coolaclare's pride as he was the only representative from the village on the Banner County side that lost to Wexford in the 1917 final (incidentally, the band that accompanied the team to Dublin nearly split up over the fact that five of its members allowed the "long weekend" to develop into a "lost week". Even in that era it was deemed a bit too much!).

On the Sunday night that Clare beat Mayo in the League quarter-final tie, Tom Morrissey returned from Castlebar to a big social night in Sixmilebridge. Victorious Kilkenny captain of '93, Liam Fennelly, presented the medals to the members of the side that won the Clare senior hurling crown. Morrissey did the honours in the case of the county junior "B" winners.

Mounting the stage, he took the mike and said with measured understatement: "I am a man of few words."

"He brought the house down and had the members of the audience in the palm of his hand for the rest of a very amusing address," Seamus Hayes of the *Clare Champion* told me.

And Seamus added: "When I asked him afterwards if he felt tired after his exertions against Mayo, he replied with a mischievous gleam in his eye: 'I'm tired – after the three radio interviews I had to do'."

Of course they wanted him to sing the ballad of John Williams. Of course they wanted to hear his singular rendering of his great party number, *The Chapel Gate in Coolaclare*, so evocative in its own way of his role in Clare's surge to the 1992 Munster title, and all that had evolved subsequently in the League.

Yes, Tom Morrissey – The Man from Coolaclare.

I see him now as I will always see him from this out in the mind's eye, standing at the bridge near Liscannor as dusk descended over the bay beyond, the Clare footballers in Indian file jogging towards us along the beach to their destiny. A destiny not so much bound up, I reflected, with what happened in Croke Park the following Sunday but the character Clare would reveal, as reigning champions, in the cauldron that Cusack Park would become on Sunday, May 30.

Morrissey standing tall in the fading light, a knot of local football enthusiasts around him. Talking football.

In the Claremont Hotel later, Morrissey who enjoyed more than any man every rollicking, unforgettable dawn-coming-up moment of the victory tour of Clare, said to me with total conviction in his voice: "The Munster title win and all that followed is history now. We cannot live forever on the one seventy minutes in Limerick."

Clare came back to earth with a resounding thump when their shortcomings were exposed by Donegal, who, to be brutally frank about it, won in the end without being fully extended. It could be argued perhaps that Clare should not have engaged in such heavy beach work – for close on two hours – just two days after the game against Mayo in Castlebar. But, I'm afraid, that could not be advanced as an excuse for failure to reach the League final. Donegal were just too strong for them. And it was proved once again that heart and burning enthusiasm are no substitute in the final analysis for lack of the requisite class through the field at this level.

⌘ ⌘ ⌘

"The Day The Music Died" was the heading over Cliona Foley's report in the *Irish Independent* the morning after Clare had made their exit from the 1993 Munster championship at Cusack Park, on 30 May. An attendance of 18,845 saw Cork dethrone the champions by 2-14 to 1-10.

You heard the sound of fiddles in the streets of Ennis in the morning and there was Irish dancing too as this tie coincided with the Fleadh Nua.

Intrepid young Clare supporters brought their bodhrans up on the terrace at the back of the goal to add to the cacophony of sound as Clare took a 0-4 to 0-1 lead after twelve minutes. But even the bodhrans were silent by the time referee, Paddy Russell

(Tipperary) blew the full-time whistle. A clear gap in standards had been revealed – a gap that Clare, despite all their frenetic efforts, could not bridge in the end.

And yet the Banner County followers were left to ponder the might-have-beens. Colin Corkerry, who gave Seamus Clancy quite a roasting, rounded the fair-haired corner-back from Corofin against the run of the play in the fourteenth minutes and drove a fierce shot to the net. The rot set in after this. "A killer blow, coming so early," was how John Maughan described it.

But when Cork had stretched their lead to four points in the second half, Clare struck with a great goal by Martin Daly, following a point from a free by substitute, Aidan O'Keeffe. Daly won possession of a high ball behind Mark Farr and hit it to the net under the body of John Kerins.

Two minutes later Colm Clancy placed Francis McInerney for what seemed a certain goal. But Stephen O'Brien produced a very brave and brilliant block.

A second goal for Clare coming after Martin Daly's effort would certainly have changed the entire complexion of the match. As it was, Don Davis was fouled in the square soon afterwards and Colin Corkerry goaled from the resultant penalty to put the issue beyond doubt.

Colin Corkerry, finishing with a tally of 2-5, was Cork's "Man of the Match". A fine strapping player with the confidence to take on the opposition and go for his scores, he showed himself to be a real find in the Red and White colours – emulating the lasting impression that Brian Corcoran had made when he graduated to the senior hurling team the previous season.

Niall Cahalane, who twenty days beforehand was undergoing an operation for a knee cartilage problem, was an inspiration in defence; Mark Farr and Mark O'Connor left quite an imprint on the game while Stephen O'Brien was solidness personified at centre-back.

When Tom Morrissey and Pat Murray looked to be getting a grip on the midfield exchanges, Billy Morgan shrewdly introduced Shea Fahy and Liam Honohan and they won valuable possession at moments of balance.

Clare's great veteran and spiritual leader, Noel Roche was forced to retire injured at half-time. Frankie Griffin and John Enright made some excellent runs from the wing back positions but the attack lacked the cohesion and penetration power to really upset the Cork defence.

Maintaining an unbeaten record in their section in the National

League, after all that had gone into the winning of the Munster title the previous year and the emotional return to Croke Park to face Dublin in the All-Ireland semi-final, inevitably took its toll on the Clare team. The sparkle of '92 was somehow missing on the day.

I could not eradicate from my mind the memory of that evening in Lahinch when Noel Roche and the rest of the squad were running up and down the beach for almost two hours – just a few days after beating Mayo in Castlebar. "A mistake, yes a big mistake to get involved in such heavy beach work," said someone close to the squad to me later after the defeat by Cork. You do heavy beach work with an eye to an All-Ireland semi-final. But the Munster crown had to be retained first.

The music died in Ennis on a May day in '93 – and we were left to ponder when it would sound again as it had sounded through the unforgettable season of '92 and on to the defeat of Mayo in the League quarter-final in Castlebar in '93.

There were memories left that would never die for the Clare players who were part of it all and the great band of supporters who had followed them through thick and thin.

CHAPTER 6

CORK MISS CHANCE OF
REAL IMMORTALITY

THERE is little doubt that the Cork team that put two All-Irelands back-to-back in 1989-'90 could have been a three-in-a-row side.

And it is not stretching it too far to argue that a four-timer was well within their compass, though to develop the argument further and conclude that they might have made Gaelic footballing history by achieving five-in-a-row would have demanded from them a fierce sense of commitment and continuing concentration on the target before them which, I am afraid, was sadly missing in 1991.

To be fair, Cork lost two successive All-Irelands to Meath (one after a replay in 1988) before they made it two-in-a-row. So if they had reached the final in 1991, it would have meant that they would have been contesting their fifth successive decider. In the modern era it takes a super team to stand up to the pressures involved over that span of time. Even Kerry, the greatest combination in footballing history, failed at the ultimate hurdle in 1982 to Offaly with the epoch-making five-timer within their grasp.

However, the more one examines Cork's record over the period 1987-'91, the greater the conviction grows that this squad in the Red and White missed the chance of attaining real immortality.

After beating Kerry four years running in Munster (1987-'90), the Leesiders became arrogant in concluding deep down in their hearts (though naturally they did not express it openly) that the Kingdom represented no great challenge to them. In fact, a few close to the team may well have entertained visions of going on to equal Kerry's eight-in-a-row in Munster (1975-'82) and, not alone that, but even making it nine or ten-in-a-row. Kerry were going to be the victims of "ethnic cleansing" in the footballing sense!

Cork paid dearly for their arrogance. They were caught napping in 1991 by a mainly young Kerry side, who were given little or no chance in advance by a majority of the pundits.

Cork, I believe, would have beaten Meath in the 1987 All-Ireland final, had they played Dinny Allen and Dave Barry that

66

season in their attack rather than waiting until the following year to see the error of their ways.

Mick O'Connell in his summing up of that All-Ireland final made the point to me that Cork's hopes were badly damaged by the selectors overlooking the basic law which must always operate in the choice of players for the forward line. "The basic law, I have always held, is that an attacker must be able to make a score and take a score", said the Man from Valentia.

"A player is just not fit to be in an attack if he cannot ultimately answer the basic law".

And he added: "Cork's prospects were very much diminished by the selectors persevering with at least two players who did not meet the basic law. In fact, in the final analysis they were almost totally dependent on Larry Tompkins' accuracy from frees and fifties".

When his kicking boots deserted him in the second half of the 1987 All-Ireland final – after he had landed some truly brilliant efforts in the first – Cork had no one to really compensate for his misses and in a way it was an attack flying on one wing.

Would Dave Barry have answered the Mick O'Connell dictum of being able to make a score and take a score? Remember that he scored two second-half goals against Dublin in the replay of the 1983 All-Ireland semi-final while Dinny Allen got two in the drawn game.

John O'Driscoll, for all his skill and talent and the way he could bewilder and bemuse at times in jinking runs, had not the penetrative power, as Mick O'Connell saw it, to carry the attack on his own. Perhaps too much was expected of him after his brilliance in Australia the previous autumn in the Irish jersey.

Jimmy Kerrigan, a converted defender, had the chance in the seventeenth minute of the first half to score the goal at the Hill 16 end that, to my mind, would have put Cork in an impregnable position. The Munster champions were four points in front at that stage and had been threatening to take over completely, putting the Meath defence under a lot of pressure with some delightful play and swift movements. Meath looked vulnerable then.

Kerrigan got clean through but his hastily-taken shot was blocked down by Mick Lyons.

Dinny Allen agreed that if Jimmy Kerrigan had raised the green flag it could have completely altered the trend of the match. "Cork's lead would have become seven points and that lead might well have caused Meath to panic a little. Even a point would have helped but I think Jimmy was caught in two minds. He knew that Christy Ryan was inside and, after he carried the ball in, he was torn between having a shot or trying to find Christy. Meath went on to score 1-2 in the next five minutes and that was that".

Meath certainly benefitted from the experience of being in the All-Ireland semi-final against Kerry the previous year – a game they might well have won but for the concession of a soft goal through an unfortunate mix-up in the full-back line at a crucial point in the match.

An uncanny late, late goal by Mike Sheehy, scored on the turn on the proverbial sixpence, had earned Kerry a draw against Cork in Pairc Ui Caoimh. But in the Munster final replay at Fitzgerald Stadium, Killarney on 2 August '87, before an attendance of 49,359, the Kingdom's twelve years of near-total dominance in the South was finally ended as the battle-weary veterans of the side went down to a five-points defeat (0-13 to 1-5).

Eoin (The Bomber) Liston summed up in one graphic comment the mood in the Kerry dressingroom: "I think it's time to pull down the tent and move on. The circus is over – it's time for a new act".

The Cork defence, from the eminently-sound John Kerins in goal out, excelled in the drawn game and replay against Kerry but the same level of tightness was never achieved against Meath. Colman Corrigan, later to have his career prematurely ended because of injury, starred at full-back both days against the Kingdom while Tony Davis and Denis Walsh manned the corner-back positions very efficiently. Niall Cahalane won the accolade of the Cork supporters for his performances on none less than Pat Spillane while Conor Counihan, captain and centre-back, and Tony Nation had reason to retain happy memories also of both contests against Kerry.

Unfortunately for the Leesiders, Shea Fahy, who was to give a brilliant display in the '90 All-Ireland triumphs had an off-day in 1987 against Meath, for whom Gerry McEntee and Liam Hayes confirmed that they were the best midfield pairing in the country. Cork had nothing to compare up front in '87 with the Colm O'Rourke-Brian Stafford-Bernard Flynn axis in the Meath attack and O'Rourke showed his penchant for getting killer goals by finding the corner of the net – eight minutes after Jimmy Kerrigan's miss.

"We shall be back," said Cork team manager Billy Morgan, who had accomplished an outstanding feat in bringing this comparatively young Cork side out of Munster and into the All-

Ireland final in one season. He felt that the team hadn't done full justice to themselves on the day. "There is much more in them than was revealed in this defeat."

Morgan's judgment was fully vindicated when Cork won through to the All-Ireland final again in 1988.

It is my contention that Cork, a much maturer side now, and with Dinny Allen and Dave Barry backing up Larry Tompkins the centre-forward in attack, had every reason to cry "we wuz robbed" the first day against reigning champions Meath.

In the dying seconds Brian Stafford tapped the ball over the bar from the controversial close-range free awarded by Tommy Sugrue (Kerry), who ruled that Meath right-half forward Dave Beggy had been fouled as he tried to break through a ruck of players at the Railway end.

Frankly, my own impression was that Beggy had *not* been fouled. The video recording certainly didn't reveal anything to prove otherwise, though the referee was right on the spot. The vehement protests by the Cork players – Dave Barry in particular – indicated that they were convinced that no breach of the rules had been committed.

But against that I didn't think that Dave Barry should have been awarded a free a half-a-minute earlier that gave Larry Tompkins the chance to kick what appeared to be the winning point (if I had been the referee I would have pulled up Barry for over-carrying). With a magnificent dead ball kick from almost fifty yards, Larry Tompkins sent the ball high between the posts at the Canal end – and the Cork "victory" cheers filled the stadium.

It was not to be, however. A quick Meath kick-out caught the Leesiders somewhat off guard. Shea Fahy almost had the ball safely in his grasp near the sideline on the Cusack Stand side of the field but he claimed later that, as he was passing to Tony Nation, it was knocked out of his hand into touch – by a Meath player.

And it was from that sideline kick that Dave Beggy gained possession. The rest is history.

Cork in boxing parlance should have had Meath put away long before Brian Stafford stepped up to take one of the most important frees of his career. I counted at least five easy opportunities of points missed when Cork had forged three points clear (1-8 to 0-8) twelve minutes from the end. And then to torture Cork more every time they replay the video of that game, Dave Barry missed a golden chance of a goal when he kicked the ball against the legs of Michael McQuillan from a few yards range in the fifth minute of the second half. In the first half Michael McCarthy had missed a goal when he failed unaccountably to keep control of the ball at the edge of the Meath five-yard line.

So Cork should have left Croke Park that day in September starting the three-in-a-row run that would be climaxed in 1990 with victory over the Meath men, and then in 1991 they would have been setting their sights on the four-timer.

Meath had sought in the drawn game, in the words of Colm O'Rourke, "to embellish an All-Ireland win with a commanding performance of all that is *pure* in gaelic football".

But he went on to emphasise that in doing so, they were getting away from their traditional style and for the replay reverted to their "old style". He claimed also that Cork had taken them by surprise the first day by "the intensity of their physical approach".

"This was what we had to contend with, a Cork team that did not just play good football like last year (1987) but who could hit as well. Anyone who thinks that we sat down some night in training for the replay and decided to do a hatchet job on some Cork players would be totally wrong. We were very clear on this.

"What we were going to do was at least match Cork in aggression but in a controlled way. That meant using physical strength to get to the ball first; any indiscipline or wildness would be severely punished and so it proved."

It is significant to remember that O'Rourke had been flattened in the drawn match with a "tackle" that would have resulted in a player of less tougher mettle leaving the scene of battle. But he continued. And the consequences was that after the replay he complained of persistent headaches and was hospitalised for a seven-day period. He underwent a brain scan which showed no signs of permanent injury and then he was allowed home.

Likewise Paraic Lyons, who could never be described as a moaner, was also softened up with a bone-crushing tackle. Spectators in the stands and on the embankments raised their eyebrows in amazement at Cork indicating clearly to Meath that the "Class of '88" were not to be taken for granted. In situations like that Meath *never* – repeat never – go complaining to the referee. They are not wimps. They take a mental note and remember.

And that is exactly what Meath did on the day of the drawn game. In the count-down to the replay they made it clear that they would be returning to the old aggressive tactics.

They kept their promise.

I will not dwell on all the controversy that evolved in the aftermath of the replay, culminating in a number of the Cork players staying on in Ryan's of Parkgate Street and not even bothering to attend the post All-Ireland luncheon in Kilmainham hosted by the GAA for the senior and minor teams that had contested both finals the previous day. Feelings were running so high at that point it might have been just as well that the more volatile of those in the Cork camp stayed away.

Suffice it to say that Cork looked certainties to win when Meath were reduced to 14 men with the sending off of Gerry McEntee. The Leesiders, however, failed to marshal their forces to the best advantage. They allowed themselves also to be intimidated when the champions weren't standing on ceremony this time.

Meath discovered new depths of resilience and motivation with the odds stacked against them, just as they had done against Dublin in the National League final replay.

Cork had no answer really to the surge generated by Dave Beggy, in top form on the day, Bernard Flynn, so fast and dangerous all through, Colm O'Rourke, able to kick points from distances and angles that the opposition just could not match and, of course, the immaculate boot of Brian Stafford, who finished with a tally of seven points (five from frees and one from a '45).

※ ※ ※

In 1990 the wheel turned full circle. Cork, as reigning All-Ireland champions – having beaten Mayo in a magnificent game in 1989 – and battled-hardened now after campaigning at the top from '87, finally broke the hoodoo that Meath seemed to have exerted over them. And no victory could have been sweeter for the men from the Leeside, even though it was only gained by a two points margin in the end (0-11 to 0-9).

Time at last caught up on the Meath side that had been on the go since winning the Leinster title in 1986. The veterans looked tired and weary. It would take this defeat for them to recharge the batteries during the winter break. They would return in glory for the signal triumph over Dublin in the epic four-match marathon in Leinster in '91.

The Gerry McEntee-Liam Hayes partnership was subdued for once at midfield, where Shea Fahy had a stormer for Cork, ably supported by Danny Culloty. Meath could never exert the authority they had displayed in their best moments in the '87 and

'88 victories over Cork. Only defenders Bobby O'Malley, Terry Ferguson and Martin O'Connell could look back on this All-Ireland with real satisfaction.

And Meath lost it despite the fact that they had fifteen men to Cork's fourteen for 39 minutes. Colm O'Neill was sent off for using his fist in retaliation in an incident with Mick Lyons just before the interval but it was my impression from the Press Box that he was more sinned against than sinning. Lyons might have gone earlier when the two first became entangled.

Cork displayed much greater character in this confrontation with Meath than in any of their meetings in 1987-'88. But then my own personal feeling was that the reshaping of the defence made an immense difference. Stephen O'Brien was now at full-back with Mick Slocum and Barry Coffey adding both strength and attacking qualities to the wing back positions. Tony Nation, under pressure beforehand to come up with a good performance, did just that in fine style at corner-back, while Conor Counihan was an outstanding pivot at centre-back. The fact that Meath failed to record a goal was a tribute to the work of the defence as a whole.

It was an unforgettable occasion for Teddy McCarthy, who not alone joined the select band of players who have won All-Ireland senior championship medals in both hurling and football, but went into the history books as a man who collected both – in the same season.

⌘ ⌘ ⌘

The last twenty minutes of the 1989 All-Ireland final against Mayo had seen Teddy McCarthy emerge as one of the most influential figures in the game. It was essential for the Leesiders that Teddy should scale the heights at this juncture as Mayo were threatening to prove the bookmakers, who had made Cork red-hot favourites, totally wrong. Remember too that Larry Tompkins, whose training schedule for the final had been interrupted because of a thigh injury, was clearly struggling after opening the match as if he would play Mayo on his own. His opening point from a free out on the right wing was a gem and he followed with two points from play.

This All-Ireland final was a magnificent spectacle, a game of flowing grace and passion, of extraodinary skill and redolent overall with all the things that are best in gaelic football. Missing from this encounter were the aggravating interruptions, the mean and petty fouls and the undercurrents of rancour and "needle" that so besmirched the finals we had seen between Meath and Cork.

Some of the high fielding produced by Willie Joe Padden and Teddy McCarthy made us realise what the art of "going to the clouds", when the timing is right, means to the gaelic code. I have only to recall Willie Joe Padden fielding one ball brilliantly in the tenth minute and shaking off two men before he planted it over the bar. If the art of high fielding were to be submerged in the mobile or running game, then it would be a tragedy.

Liam McHale, when I talked to him in the Manor House Hotel, Ballyhaunis in the summer of '93, was still regretting the chance that was lost four years earlier. He believes that Mayo had it there for the taking but let "Sam" slip from their grasp.

Mayo took the lead three-and-a-half minutes into the second half. Sub Anthony Finnerty, climaxing a move set up by McHale and Noel Durkin, smashed the ball to the net. Mayo, 0-10 to 0-8 in arrears at the interval, were now a point in front.

True, Cork came back to regain the lead with points by Dave Barry, who had his greatest game ever in the Red and White colours, and John Cleary (2). Mayo, however, were not finished yet. Liam McHale and Michael Fitzmaurice had points and the Connacht champions were in, we felt, with a great chance of victory.

McHale, after kniving through the Cork defence, tried to place a pass across the goalmouth but it was intercepted. Then again a drive of his was blocked by Jimmy Kerrigan and Seán Maher could not capitalise on the rebound.

But the decisive miss came when Anthony Finnerty blasted the ball wide when a goal was definitely on. Mayo were playing with such freedom and flair that if they had gone four points clear, I am sure they would not have been stopped.

Michael Fitzmaurice's point from a free in the 19th minute was in actual fact to be their last score of the game.

It was then, as Liam McHale noted, that their inexperience of the Croke Park scene on All-Ireland Day left Mayo down. "I blame myself also for not taking the game by the scruff of the neck and leading a winning surge. When I look at the video of the match, I realise I did not play all that badly but I know now that if I could have lifted my game that bit higher it could have made all the difference."

The battle-hardened edge that Cork had gained through the 1987 and '88 campaigns now stood them in good stead. Having lost two All-Irelands to Meath, they were simply not prepared to lose another. You could see it in their faces when Mayo went ahead on two occasions. They gritted their teeth and refused to give in.

The selectors too made key changes in bringing on Mick McCarthy and John O'Driscoll. Four points flowed from Paul McGrath, Teddy McCarthy and Mick McCarthy (2) to give Cork victory by 0-17 to 1-11 – but everyone in the 65,519 attendance knew that there had been a very, very thin line between winning and losing as far as Mayo were concerned. A second goal by Finnerty would have made him the hero of the day and Dinny Allen would not have enjoyed the honour of receiving the Sam Maguire Cup and Allen and Dinny Barry, it might be said, had reason to feel satisfaction deep down when they reflected on the treatment they had received from the Cork County Board.

Mick O'Dwyer summed up in the course of an interview with Tom O'Riordan in the *Irish Independent*: "It boiled down in the end to pressure and Cork were the team who responded the better. On two occasions Mayo had them almost on the ropes but I think Cork demonstrated the type of inner determination which wins All-Ireland titles. On that score, it was as good an effort as I've seen from a Cork football team.

"Cork got scores under pressure which is the hallmark of a good side. They held their heads when it appeared they might lose their third successive All-Ireland final, which would have been a true catastrophe for them."

O'Dwyer added: "Mayo played well, very well and probably better than many of us anticipated. They would have won against a side who had not learned from the experience of the past. It was anyone's game with fifteen minutes remaining. It was then that Cork were asked to show their championship credentials and came to grips with what was a very tricky situation."

"What Mayo must do now is learn from their experience which is why Cork are champions," Mick O'Dwyer noted.

⌘⌘⌘

Mayo, however, failed in the 1990 Connacht final to Roscommon, who in turn went out to Cork by seven points in the All-Ireland semi-final. Roscommon were Connacht champions again in 1991, the 19-year-old jewel Derek Duggan of the powerful kick from long-range frees and accuracy to boot, providing the vital points from frees after T. J. Kilgallon had given Mayo the lead with seven minutes remaining.

John Newton, Captain of Roscommon that season, showed the same deep sense of regret when I met him in the Abbey Hotel in Roscommon in the count-down to the '93 Connacht final, about the failure to Meath in the 1991 All-Ireland semi-final that Liam McHale had shown about Mayo's defeat by Cork in '89.

"We had them on the rack, leading as we were by five points with eight minutes to go," he said. "But we left them off the hook. We couldn't put it down to lack of experience of the big occasion in Croke Park as we had been there the previous year against Cork.

"I blame myself for not showing the leadership on the field at that point that would have ensured victory for us," he added frankly.

John Newton, in fact, had played an outstanding game at midfield in the first half, his fielding being a revelation against no less an opponent than Liam Hayes, the Meath captain. Newton was ably assisted by Seamus Killoran.

In what was unquestionably one of the most enthralling, exciting and skilful games of the 1991 championship season, Roscommon touched magnificent heights in a do-or-die bid to halt the onward march of a Meath team that by the final whistle had sealed its greatness.

The Connacht champions could easily have been 2-5 to nil ahead after eight minutes. Paul Earley blasted a goal chance wide after just two minutes and soon afterwards Michael McQuillan denied him a goal with a great save while four other scorable chances were missed.

As it was, after dominating the exchanges for the greater part of the opening 35 minutes, Roscommon turned over only 1-7 to 0-7 ahead.

The Roscommon full-back line of Des Newtown, Pat Doorey and Enon Gavin had defended tenaciously and, indeed, the defence as a whole and the midfield had far exceeded expectations.

Meath revamped their side for the second half. Martin O'Connell went right corner-back, Liam Harnan to right-half, Kevin Foley to centre-back, and P. J. Gillic to centre-forward to make room for Gerry McEntee who entered the fray as a sub.

Mick Lyons, after an unhappy opening 35 minutes, was now a rock of strength in the middle of the Meath defence with Martin O'Connell playing brilliantly beside him. One felt that if Roscommon could have broken down the barrier presented by these two stalwart figures, then nothing could prevent them winning.

In a supreme effort to notch the scores that would put them in an impregnable position, Roscommon switched the tall John Newton to full forward but this meant that his ball-winning ability was immediately lost from the midfield sector. It became a crucial factor in Meath's come-back with the wind. Tactically Roscommon failed on the sideline, as it was essential that they so deploy their forces at the moment of decision to put the clamps on Mick Lyons and Martin O'Connell.

Slowly but surely Meath of the undying spirit, got a grip on the exchanges. The amazing Brian Stafford scored five points in the last three minutes, three from play. Roscommon's only reply was a fine point by Derek Duggan from a free with virtually the last kick of the game. Meath had won through to the All-Ireland final by just one point (0-15 to 1-11).

Liam Hayes summed it up in a nutshell. "We played some great football in our winning rally but there had been times when we were hanging on for dear life. Another point or two extra from them when they were in command and they could have broken our backs".

Tommy Dowd's ball-carrying ability made him one of Meath's heroes in an epic game, marked also by a goal from a drop-kicked effort by Derek Duggan in the first half that would long be remembered.

Roscommon did not score between the 51st and 70th minute and in the same period Meath responded with seven points – a statistic that had Vincent Hogan in the *Irish Independent* next morning recalling John Newton's comment in a Sunday paper. *"Mentally a lot of teams do well for 40 minutes of an All-Ireland semi-final. The difference between them and great teams is that a great team does it for 70 minutes."*

Against any other opposition on this August Sunday, Roscommon would almost certainly have emerged the winners. But again it has to be stressed that they went down to a great team in Meath. There was no disgrace in that.

⌘⌘⌘

Mayo were back to represent Connacht in the 1992 All-Ireland semi-final but in losing to Donegal, gave the kind of inept, spiritless display overall that was in total contrast to '89. Yet, amazingly, at the final whistle they were only four points (0-13 to 0-9) behind a Donegal side that would go on to win the All-

Ireland final. However, Donegal created no less than seventeen additional scoring chances that were not availed of and if they had, Mayo's defeat would have been far more embarrassing.

The result was that former Dublin player, Brian McDonald, who is domiciled in Mayo, resigned from the helm in an episode that did not do a lot of credit to some of the members of the team, as things were said in public that should never have been said. A pity really. It could so easily have been resolved with dignity behind closed doors.

Jack O'Shea took over as manager and guided Mayo to the Connacht title in '93, Roscommon being beaten by a point (1-5 to 0-7) before a capacity crowd of 26,000 in the re-developed Dr. Hyde Park with its excellent new terracing (and plans in place for a new stand).

A wonderful goal by Ray Dempsey put Mayo on the road to victory when it seemed that Roscommon, who led 0-6 to 0-2 at half-time, would edge it. Liam McHale was sent off four minutes after the restart and John Newton – very harshly I thought – two minutes from the end.

All Star T. J. Kilgallon, who had been battling an injury in the lead-up to the final, came on as a sub in the second half for Mayo and made an immediate impact with his first-class reading of situations. It was a free-riddled game of poor quality, a total of 62 in all being awarded.

✂ ✂ ✂

One of the most sensational results for years in the Connacht championship was the point defeat of Galway (1-12 to 1-11) in the first round at Tuam Stadium on 20 May '93.

The name of corner forward Aidan Rooney will live forever in the annals of Leitrim football as he was the man who sent the ball over the bar on the call of time to give his county a famous victory.

What made this result all the more amazing was the fact that Galway had produced some very good performances in the 1992-'93 League, none better than that when running Dublin close at Croke Park. When they equalised with a minute to go, it was odds-on that they would survive to fight another day, if not winning outright – but from the kick-out Leitrim gained possession and worked the ball into Aidan Rooney, who shook off two tackles before launching the kick that would see Bosco McDermott succeed Johnny Tobin as Galway team manager.

This success was not, however, to herald a new dawn for Leitrim football. In the Connacht semi-final they faced Roscommon, who had beaten them 0-12 to 0-8 in Carrick-on-Shannon in '91 and 2-11 to 1-9 at Hyde Park in '92.

Now again Roscommon confirmed their superiority over their nearest neighbours, this time in Carrick-on-Shannon before an attendance of 14,000. The margin in the end may have been only two points (1-12 to 1-10) but Roscommon – with Dermot Earley at the helm as team manager – dominated for most of the game but they should have capitalised more on the possession won by John Newton, who was in magestic form at midfield.

Leitrim, who fought bravely to the final whistle, had reason to bemoan the might-have-beens in the shape of a Liam Conlon shot being deflected for a "50" and a blazing effort by Darcy being pushed over the bar by John Newton.

Reduced to fourteen men for the last seventeen minutes, Leitrim had players in Pádraig Kenny, Barney Breen and Liam Conlon who were prepared to run at Roscommon and it was a combined move between Kenny and Conlon that brought Leitrim's goal in the 21st minute by Liam Conlon, balancing the goal scored earlier by Paul Earley. Conlon, incidentally, also had the distinction of raising a green flag against Galway.

George Dugdale, one of Leitrim's most influential players, was closely shadowed by Tommy Grehan. Even with the limited opportunities they had up front, Leitrim were still in with a very good chance at the interval when Roscommon led by 1-7 to 1-5. The point-taking of new wing forward Tommy Ryan helped Roscommon maintain their advantage through the second half, despite Leitrim's moving of captain Mickey Quinn to midfield in a last-ditch effort to break Roscommon's stranglehold in this sector. Leitrim came very close with one goal-scoring effort in injury time when Barry Breen got a firm fist to the ball after a free had been dropped to the edge of the square. However, sharp reflexes of goalie Brian Morkan saved Roscommon, who had played a dangerous game and survived.

✂ ✂ ✂

By the end of the 1993 season, Galway, once such a power in the game, had not won an All-Ireland title since completing the three-in-a-row in 1966 and their last appearance in an All-Ireland final was in 1983 when they lost out in the end by three points to Dublin's "Defiant Dozen".

78

Connacht was seen as the poor relation of the gaelic football code because of the Province's failure to lift the Sam Maguire Cup and the poor standard of football overall in the championship. You had to go back to 1951, when Mayo won their second succesive All-Ireland crown, for the last recording of a senior title win by representatives from the Western Province. Then as Donegal took their first-ever All-Ireland title in '92 to add to Down's triumph in '91 and Derry inscribed their name on the Sam Maguire Cup for the first time in 1993, Ulster replaced Connacht in the public psyche as the Province most capable of upsetting the ambitions of Munster and Leinster. The era was gone when Kerry or Dublin, for example, indeed any champions from Munster or Leinster could enter an All-Ireland semi-final confident of beating the Ulster representatives. The old order had changed dramatically.

Dermot Earley's view was that it lay in Connacht's own hands to rectify the image Connacht football had in the eyes of the public. Only by emulating Donegal's feat in '92 and Down's return to top in '91 to win their first title since 1968 could Connacht silence the critics of the current state of football in the Province, he stressed.

✼ ✼ ✼

Connacht football sank further into the doldrums on Sunday, 15 August '92 when Mayo fell like lambs to the slaughter to a Cork side that must have been embarrassed by the ease of their victory (5-15 to 0-10) in this All-Ireland semi-final.

When John Finn, after a fine burst forward, opened the way for Ray Dempsey to shoot the levelling point (0-3 all) after twenty minutes play in the first half, there was no indication that the game would finish on such a totally one-sided note. The Mayo supporters, who far outstripped Cork's backing on the day, waved their flags and banners defiantly as if the West would have its hour.

But as the game progressed, an all-too familiar story unfolded. "There seems to be no doubt that there is a gap developing between Connacht football and the rest," said John O'Keeffe in the *Irish Times* the next day. "What can be done about it is another question. Maybe it represents a case for the open draw where Conancht teams would be tested by stronger teams and would improve as a result.

"Football in the winter time is very different to the summer and the championshiup and Mayo found that to their cost. For example, Pádraig Brogan (he was introduced as a sub in the second half) might get away with winter football but his lack of pace and mobility was found out in this game."

Yes, to put it bluntly, Mayo were outclassed by a side that beat them for pace, were far superior tactically through the field and, above all, had an attack which when in full flow and putting away the many chances created, exposed the inadequacies of the Mayo forward-line, though Kevin O'Neill stands excused.

Young O'Neill, who celebrated his 20th birthday the following day, made a big impression on his All-Ireland semi-final debut. This son of former Galway All-Ireland footballer, Liam O'Neill is undoubtedly a player with a bright future, despite his lack of physical power.

Liam McHale tried his heart out at midfield but even when he was getting the ball into P. J. Loftus, Ray Dempsey and Noel Durkin they could not break down the barrier presented by Brian Corcoran, Mark O'Connor and Niall Cahalane while the Cork half-back line, particularly the find of the season, Ciaran O'Sullivan at right-wing back and Stephen O'Brien at centre-back, were generally masters of the situation.

Here were Cork starting without Teddy McCarthy and Larry Tompkins and losing Shea Fahy through injury during the game and yet in total control because the cover they had, meant that Danny Culloty, introduced at mid-field, had a storming seventy minutes.

Where, I might ask, does that leave Mayo? And what must manager Jack O'Shea's feelings have been as he reflected on all the grinding hours of preparation put in during those intensive training sessions in Ballyhaunis . . . and Cork in the last ten minutes scoring almost at will?

Paidi O'Shea's summing up in the *Irish Independent* was cruel: "Too many Mayo players lacked the bottle and the heart to contest the game and they were given a hiding as a result".

But I would say that Mayo gave it their all until the last ten minutes and threw in the towel after the missing of two great goal chances that could have inspired them. All the bottle in the world doesn't turn a handicapper into a Derby winner. Put it down to the yawning and ever-widening gap in standards . . . and you have the real reason for this massacre.

CHAPTER 7

DERRY'S FIRST-EVER CROWN – AND A HAT-TRICK FOR ULSTER

IT was won the hard way. Indeed, Derry had every reason to claim that they beat the best – the very best – on their way to their first-ever All-Ireland senior football crown.

And when you contemplate their victories in turn over Down, the 1991 All-Ireland champions, Donegal, the 1992 champions, Dublin, the 1993 National League title-holders, and Cork, All-Ireland champons in 1989-'90, you realise just how much merit there was in Derry's achievement, as Ulster welcomed "Sam" for a third successive year.

It came down in the end to self-belief and composure – and not wilting in face of Cork's dream start which saw them put 1-2 on the board before John McGurk opened the Ulster champions' account with a fine point from play into the Hill 16 goal. Again they maintained their poise in the second half when Cork, now backed by the wind, took a point lead (2-8 to 1-10) with a classic goal by John O'Driscoll, who latched on to a superb, pinpointed through pass by Don Davis to rifle the ball to the corner of the net.

Far from faltering then, Derry responded with a power surge that saw them first level the scores through a magnificent point from out on the left wing by Enda Gormley – finding the target with his left boot – and then they went on to add three more from Anthony Tohill (free), John McGurk and Enda Gormley to win by 1-14 to 2-8.

A similar late power surge had carried them to a famous point victory (0-15 to 0-14) over Dublin in the semi-final. You were left to marvel at their stamina and their ability to run the opposition into the ground in the last ten minutes. I could only conclude on All-Ireland Day that they had attained a level of fitness more impressive – in fact, higher – than I had seen from any previous All-Ireland champions and, believe me, Donegal had set a really high standard in '92.

Little wonder then that Derry's larger than life manager, Eamonn Coleman, should assert: "Most of all we won this All-Ireland on the trianing fields around Derry, where we worked as hard as any team possibly can."

The debate will continue long by winter fires and in the hostelries where football followers gather as to whether Cork would have won their seventh All-Ireland title if the harsh sending off of Tony Davis shortly before half-time had not disrupted the working of the team.

Mick O'Dwyer concluded in the *Evening Herald* that it "was still going to be Derry's day". I am not so sure. Remember, Cork were only a point behind at that stage though playing into the wind and Davis's presence in the second half would have made a world of difference, as he is particularly good at going forward, which he proved when landing his team's first point.

To my mind, the turning point actually came in the 31st minute of play. Most of the 64,500 attendance did not see Niall Cahalane giving Enda Gormley a punch in the face off-the-ball but it was caught clearly by the television cameras.

Referee Tommy Howard (Kildare) did not spot it but he quickly consulted with his umpires and as a result Cahalane was booked when the general consensus was that he should have received marching orders.

"It proved to be one of the most costly fouls in the annals of All-Ireland finals," was the opinion expressed by Micheál Ó Muircheartaigh, the "Voice of RTE Radio", in his after-match contribution in *The Star.*

"The whole scene changed within the next three minutes," he went on. "Firstly, Gormley managed to score his first point from play. And that signalled a new resolve which contributed greatly to Derry's dominance thereafter. Equally significant was the referee's decision in the 34th minute to send off Tony Davis for a foul on Dermot Heaney. Davis never was – and isn't – a dirty player. But one felt that the referee had made up his mind to demonstrate his authority by dealing severely with the next transgressor of the rules following the booking of Cahalane. Thus Anthony Davis became the victim – and I must say that I felt sympathy for him.

"In the few minutes that remained to half-time, the now-awakened Enda Gormley scored again from play. The Ulster men held a three points lead at the break, something that would have been difficult to visualise after six minutes . . . especially after that great goal by Joe Kavanagh."

If the tackle by Tony Davis was slightly reckless, it certainly was in no way dirty. I concluded from my seat in the Press Box in the Hogan Stand that the Corkman had absolutely no intention of taking Heaney out of the game. In fact, he went to catch Heaney with his shoulder but mistimed it. Davis made the long walk across the pitch to the Cork dug-out.

The dismissal of Davis upset the pattern of Cork's team-work and unquestionably they had shaped very well up front during their sweeping opening onslaught on the Derry goal. The control that had been there at the outset vanished. Worse still, as the rain came down heavily in the second half and Derry's awesome stamina and superb fitness came into full play, Cork were unable to cope with the disadvantage of being down to fourteen men. You could see how much it was taking out of them to stay with a very physically-strong Derry side that grew in confidence the longer the game progressed and used the free man better than any side has done in recent times.

I had written in my preview in the *Sunday Independent* on the day of the final that Cork were gambling in playing three men who had been "under a cloud" – namely Teddy McCarthy (cartilege), Shea Fahy (injured shoulder) and Niall Cahalane (calf injury). It was asking a lot going into an All-Ireland final, especially against a team as fit and strong as Derry.

The gamble of starting with Shea Fahy paid off handsomely as he emerged as Cork's "Man of the Match" because of his trojan work at midfield. But in cold retrospect you have to question was it wise to play Niall Cahalane when Cork had a ready-made solution in that Tony Davis could have been switched back to left corner back and Barry Coffey to wing back, or, failing that, Mick Farr, who did so well against Kerry in the Munster final, could have been brought in.

Teddy McCarthy was clearly below his best. Two uncharacteristic errors from this great-hearted servant of the Red and White – a dropped pass from Niall Cahalane and a stray kick that was intercepted – set up Brian McGilligan and Anthony Tohill for crucial points that brought Derry back into the game when Cork were in command of proceedings.

I have no doubt in my mind that if the Cork selectors had moved quickly and replaced Teddy McCarthy with Danny Culloty fifteen minutes before half-time Cork would not have gone in three points down. It was not until the interval that the decision was taken to bring on Culloty as a substitute and he made a vital difference in the second half. I would also have brought in Conor Counihan much earlier to replace Brian Corcoran whose limitations as a corner back were cruelly exposed.

The worst error of all from Cork's viewpoint and probably the one that set Derry on the road to victory was the very soft goal that resulted from a high centre from Damien Cassidy that seemed to hang in the air and whether Mark O'Connor should have moved to field it quickly or John Kerins have shouted "it's mine", there was definitely a serious miscalculation that allowed Seamus Downey to rise unchallenged and box it home.

From being 1-2 to 0-4 behind after fifteen minutes and patently battling to take command with the wind, Derry were suddenly 1-4 to 1-2 in front and you could see that Cork had a real fight on their hands.

However, had Cahalane kept his cool and not been guilty of that off-the-ball punch, leading in turn to the ultimate sanction on Davis, the odds would have been on a fifteen-man Leeside team coming out on top, though it must be emphasised that as Larry Tompkins noted in the *Sunday Press*, Cork were "cleaned out up the left-hand side even before Tony Davis was sent off."

The softness of their passage to the All-Ireland final, in particular the annihilation of Mayo in the semi-final, was no help to Cork's cause either in the final analysis, just as Tipperary's total humiliation of Clare in the Munster hurling final inculcated the wearers of the Blue and Gold with a false belief in their own invincibility against Galway.

I am certain that if Cork had the leadership of Larry Tompkins in attack plus his accuracy off frees they would not have been denied in the second half. His absence through injury was a terrible loss.

❊   ❊   ❊

But let us observe the Sons of Derry marching proudly towards "The Sam". Let nothing take from the merit of a Championship crown forged from Newry to Clones and the silencing of The Hill when Dublin were overcome and finally that great recovery from a disastrous start to finish with an authoritative flourish that left Cork with no alibis – only the unforced errors of their own making.

The toughest game of all, as Eamonn Coleman saw it, was in the All-Ireland semi-final against Dublin and my own feeling is that if the Leinster champions had not wasted four or five good opportunities of points at the outset they would have been in an impregnable position at half-time. They could still have won it if they had plugged the yawning gap created down the left flank — stemming from Paul O'Neill's inability through inexperience to cope with Joe Brolly — by bringing back Eamonn Heery earlier.

"We were at our worst for fifteen minutes before half-time and at our best in the last fourteen minutes," observed Eamonn Coleman. "If half-time hadn't come when it did I think we'd have been beaten. And yet I didn't think we were gone at the interval, although we were five points down. When we came within two points of them in the second half I knew we would win."

It is a story that would fill a chapter in itself how Eamonn Coleman got the call from the County Board while working in construction in London, asking him if he was interested in return-ing and taking over as manager of a senior team that was languishing in Division Two of the National League and seemed to be heading nowhere fast. That was in 1991. It was player power that brought him back really, for remembered was the way he had managed the Derry minor team that beat Cork in the 1983 All-Ireland final and he then took the county's Under-21 side to the All-Ireland final of 1985 when they were beaten by Cork.

Within a year of Coleman taking over at the helm, Derry had won the 1992 National League title. His crowning achievement, of course, was to guide the team he had shaped to the Ulster title in 1993 and inscribe Derry's name on the Sam Maguire for the first time.

Standing only 5 ft. 5 ins., Coleman, who recalled for me in Maghera playing for Ballymaguigan against Castledawson in a Derry Senior Championship final when he was only 14 and weighed less than 10 stone, lives by Bill Shankly's immortal phrase: "Football is not a matter of life and death. It's more important than that!" Indeed, he readily confesses that football has always been the driving force in his life and he realises, as Harry McGee put it so aptly in a *Sunday Press* feature, that if you play football in Derry you are wearing a badge of identity. It says who you are and what you are.

A son of the soil — from the townland of Ballymaguigan — his father kept a few cattle but earned his living really working on other farms in the locality. It was inevitable that Eamonn Coleman, despite his lack of height and physique, should be bitten by the gaelic football bug as this same townland gave to the game one of the greatest midfielders and finest stylists in Jim McKeever, who failed to get an All-Ireland medal when Derry were beaten in the 1958 final by Dublin.

Coleman won an All-Ireland minor medal in 1965 when Derry beat Kerry in the final and an All-Ireland Under-21 medal in 1968 when they beat Offaly. But, like Brian McEniff, he missed out on a senior football medal, though there would be ample compensation in going into the record books as the man who built the side that won Derry's first-ever All-Ireland senior championship title and gave a new image to the colours of White with the red hoop and cuffs.

As Paddy Downey noted in the *Irish Times*, Coleman has the reputation of being a tough team "boss", acerbic with sports reporters and short-fused in his reaction to criticism.

But one fact is inescapable, he's a players' manager to his finger-tips. And nothing illustrates this better than a member of the 1993 panel telling Liam Hayes of the *Sunday Press* that Coleman would "die for us" and adding rather colourfully: "He's given us some roastings all right, right in our faces. But he would lie down in front of a truck for this team."

It wasn't easy for him to leave that great stalwart, Danny Quinn, out of the starting fifteen for the All-Ireland final or Dermot McNicholl for that matter. But he had the courage to do so, as the interests of the team as a whole and the ambition to win the All-Ireland title transcended every other consideration. McNicholl admitted in the aftermath of a historic triumph that he was very disappointed because he felt he was playing the best football of his career. "I was very angry and very annoyed but I got over it because I wasn't going to let it get to me or the players."

During the interval Coleman came up to him in the dress-ingroom and asked, "Are you ready?"

"Bloody right I am. I've been ready for the past four weeks."

Coleman sprang McNicholl at exactly the right moment, his forceful contribution in the second half proving a major factor in Derry's victory. Coleman's belief in the ability of the side to lift the Sam Maguire was infectious from the outset of the campaign. When Derry were beaten by Donegal in the Ulster final in '92, he was so crestfallen that he moped around for days and refused to go anywhere for a month.

He lived for the day – and the opportunity – to avenge that defeat, wanting at the same time to avenge the reverse suffered at hands of Down the previous year. He was convinced that if Derry had overcome Donegal in '92 they would have gone on to win the All-Ireland title.

And Dermot McNicholl noted that it was when Derry failed to Donegal in '92 that the burning ambition was born in the hearts of every member of the panel to win out in Ulster in '93 – and take it from there. They weren't bothered really about the League and weren't unduly upset when failing to Donegal in the quarter-final of the competition. "In 1993 it was the championship for us – and nothing else."

Coleman had the men for the job on hand and the big days revealed that they had the qualities to cope with pressure at the highest level. From Damien McCusker in goal to Seamus Downey, who wore the No. 14 jersey on All-Ireland day, it was a side that was strong in all departments and, as John O'Keeffe put it perceptively in the *Irish Times*: "This Derry team hasn't sprung overnight. It has been developing over the past ten years. They've had their disappointments, in particular the defeat against Donegal in the '92 Ulster final. That could have proved a blessing in disguise because they obviously learned from it. It hurt very much, particularly when they saw Donegal going on and winning the All-Ireland. It also generated self-belief and confidence because they must have felt they were every bit as good as Donegal."

O'Keeffe noted that Derry had the requisite strength in depth in their panel. "There is a great spirit and a passion in their play and they work incredibly hard for possession. At no stage did they panic. Their support play was phenomenal right through the game. Once again they showed that they could last the pace and they were at their strongest in the last ten minutes of the game."

⌘ ⌘ ⌘

Coleman beforehand had seen the Cork full forward-line of Colin Corkery, John O'Driscoll and Mick McCarthy representing the biggest single threat to Derry's aspiration. It speaks volumes for the full-back line of Kieran McKeever, Tony Scullion and Fergal McCusker that they tied them down effectively and, outside of his brilliant goal in the second half, John O'Driscoll never went to town on this day as he had done against the Mayo defence. Neither did Corkery as he had done against Clare and Kerry.

Scullion was the anchor-man again, unquestionably one of the best defenders in present-day football. Henry Downey after a nightmare opening, when Joe Kavanagh ran right through the centre for a classic goal, settled down to give what John O'Keeffe described as "a masterful display", adding: "He was an inspirational captain and his forward runs were a great boost. He's so sure and he rarely misuses the ball."

His flankers, John McGurk and Gary Coleman, were outsanding. Towering Anthony Tohill and his tough-as-teak partner Brian McGilligan, proved once again that it's really impossible to totally subdue them in the centre of the field. Jack Sheedy had a great first half in the semi-final but his efforts over those thirty-five minutes took their toll and he couldn't maintain it through the second half. While the Tohill-McGilligan partnership continues to contribute as it did in the '93 campaign, Derry are going to be an extremely difficult side to beat. They just wear you down over seventy minutes.

In the count-down to the final the pundits raised doubts about the Derry attack and argued that it couldn't compare with Cork's. Yet Derry put fifteen points on the board against Dublin (the half-back line contributing handsomely) and registered the equivalent of seventeen points (1-14) against Cork.

It lacked, I reckon, the charisma that the Greg Blaney-Mickey Linden-James McCartan axis created in the Down attacking machine in '91 and likewise the killer punch of the Martin McHugh-Manus Boyle-Tony Boyle axis in the Donegal forward line against Dublin in the '92 All-Ireland final. But on the day of the '93 final Joe Brolly and Enda Gormley eventually showed that they had the legs over their markers and always looked capable of winning ball in front. Gormley scored from the vital frees while Colin Corkery missed a few that cost Cork dearly after O'Driscoll's goal had regained the lead for them in the second half.

John O'Keeffe noted that Derry played very intelligently in attack, Seamus Downey pulling Mark O'Connor out and creating great space inside. The hard running of Dermot Heaney into space was very effective. "Relentless running and support play wore Cork down and Derry used the extra man well. I would congratulate John McGurk for that."

Above all, Derry avoided dropping high balls into the goal-mouth. Against the wind in the second half they worked the ball in hand-to-hand movements out of defence and again the extra man gave them an advantage in pursuing this policy successfully.

John O'Keeffe went on record to state that Derry "are the best Ulster team I have sene in all my time watching football."

Personally, I would not agree and must say that, while not as strong at midfield or in defence, there were aspects of Down's forward play that excited me far more in '91 while Donegal likewise had overall a much better attack on their 1992 showing against Dublin, than the Derry sextet.

If Donegal had not burned themselves out in the League and Clones had not become a quagmire on Ulster final day '93, I have a gut feeling that we might have been acclaiming Donegal for making it two titles back-to-back in Ulster rather than losing by two points in appalling conditions.

⌘ ⌘ ⌘

The moment when Henry Downey, the Man from Lavey, lifted the Sam Maguire Cup high in triumph will be the moment savoured for the rest of their lives by all Derry supporters lucky enough to be in Croke Park on Sunday, September 19, 1993.

And the memory will be cherished also by every Derry person – including those scattered around the globe – who was able to see the match on television or listen to the radio commentary.

The thousands of ecstatic supporters with their White and Red flags and banners, who gathered in front of the Hogan Stand, made it a truly unforgettable scene that conjured up memories of the day Down won their first All-Ireland title in 1960. They lingered long on the Croke Park pitch after the Derry players had made their way to the dressing-room. It seemed as if they did not want to let this precious moment go. The road to its attainment had been so long and so difficult and fraught with so many disappointments and setbacks along the way.

Next evening the homecoming. Bonfires and marching bands and cheering crowds . . . amazing scenes of excitement and overflowing enthusiasm greeting the Sons of Derry as they brought "Sam" home for the first time.

Nothing matched the euphoria of the triumphant journey over the last miles into Maghera. A sea of White and Red. Young lads and lassies who had danced in O'Connell Street the night before now danced in joy on the streets of Maghera into the early hours of the morning.

Along the way the Boys in the Bus – the team bus that is – had sung a lusty version of "I Wish I Was Back Home in Derry".

"It hasn't sunk in yet. We're still drifting along," said Eamonn Burns who had come on as a sub during the game.

Yes, drifting along on a tidal wave of celebration that would continue for days and weeks, months even, as "Sam" did his rounds into every village and hamlet of a county where gaelic football is a badge of identity.

Kevin Mussen had the distinction of being the first man to bring the Sam Maguire across the Border into the "Wee Six".

Now thirty-three years on from that season of glory for Down, Henry Downey had the honour of carrying the Cup for the first time across the Border into Derry.

Hurling had always been Henry Downey's first love. "It was the biggest decision of my life to have to give it up when Eamonn Coleman asked me to become captain of the Derry football team," the 26-years-old Lavey schoolteacher told Michael Ellard of the *Cork Examiner* as the panel reached the climax of their training schedule for the All-Ireland final in Glenullen – the Glen of the Eagles – situated at the foot of the Sperrin Mountains.

As a boy, Downey's pastime was hurling. "I very rarely kicked a football, even though this was the main sport in the parish". Consequently he played little under-age football and "never came within an ass's roar of playing with Derry at minor level".

Regarded up north as an outstanding hurler, having represented Ulster in the Railway Cup together with his brother, Seamus – who was to score the vital goal against Cork – Henry Downey did not become an established footballer until 1991. "I was playing hurling with Derry regularly but my club, Lavey, felt I had something to contribute to them on the football side of things and I decided to give it a go." Lavey went on to win the Ulster and All-Ireland Club Championship titles and Downey's contributions to those stirring victories won immediate recognition from Eamonn Coleman.

"Eamonn invited me to join the Derry squad and then, out of the blue, offered me the captaincy," recalled Henry. "To say I was shell-shocked would be an understatement. Now I found myself with two onerous tasks on my hands – first, to try and establish myself on the team and, secondly, to live up to the faith Eamonn Coleman had placed in me."

Coleman's faith was not misplaced, though, amazingly, in his proudest season, Downey still harboured a tinge of regret that he was unable to develop his hurling skill further. "I would have loved to have done that but found it impossible to play both games side by side. That is why I have so much regard for Teddy McCarthy, one of the few really great dual players."

On the day of the All-Ireland final, Derry journalist Eamonn McCann had written in the *Sunday Tribune* of Downey's inspirational quality eddying outwards through the team, noting that in the second half of the semi-final against Dublin "he seemed to be *driving* his players forward in waves as they strove to overhaul the opposition with time running out".

"He is at the hub of the powerhouse which could propel Derry to triumph this afternoon and transport Dungiven, Glenullin, Ballinderry, Bellaghy, Slaughmanus, Drumsurn and all the other enclaves of Derry GAA enthusiasm into well-deserved and long-overdue delight.

"And he himself will be near enough a god in Gulladuff."

He became just that in the eyes of the rising generations, who would make the future of Derry football secure, as he brought "Sam" into the Oak Leaf county, his destiny having been achieved not as a wielder of the camán he loved but wearing the No. 6 jersey and driving his men to glory as the rain came down over the Croke Park sod in the pulsating climactic moments of the '93 All-Ireland football final.

Such a man is Henry Downey, Captain of Derry '93.

Sportstars
do not boast on winning,
nor make excuses when
they fail.
They are cheerful losers
and quiet winners.
They play fair and enjoy
the pleasure of playing.
They give their
opponents credit where
credit is due and they
value the game itself
more highly than the
result.

For thirty-five ye
Texaco has bee
involved in the
promotion of spc
Ireland, through
Sportstars Awar
The achievemen
our Irish sports r
and women dese
recognition and w
hope that our
Sportstars Award
help to demonstra
the pride the cou
takes in our sport
people.

TEXAC
SPORTSTAF

PART TWO

HURLING

The Eighties, a Decade of Change –
But Old Order Restored in Opening
Seasons of the Nineties

Cork (1990), Tipperary (1991) and
Kilkenny (1992-'93) Farm Four Titles

But Wexford Fail in Epic Battles in '93

THE STATE OF PLAY

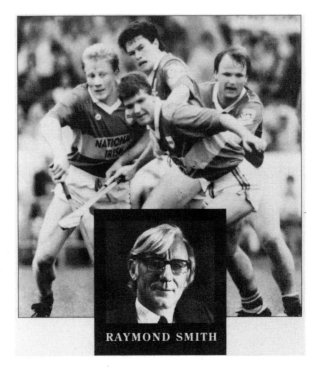

RAYMOND SMITH WRITES ON G.A.A. EVERY SUNDAY, EXCLUSIVELY IN THE SUNDAY INDEPENDENT.

Sunday Independent
IN EVERY WAY, THE COMPLETE SUNDAY.

CHAPTER 8

GALWAY AND OFFALY ILLUMINATE OPENING SEASONS OF THE EIGHTIES

THE dawn of the eighties will always be remembered for Galway's achievement in 1980 in winning their first All-Ireland crown since 1923 and also for the historic break-through by Offaly in 1981 in inscribing the County's name for the first time ever on the Liam McCarthy Cup.

Indeed the eighties saw Offaly become a real force to be reckoned with in the hurling world. Having contested – and lost to Cork – the Centenary All-Ireland final at Semple Stadium in 1984, they made amends for their defeat in a disappointing match by winning the 1985 decider against Galway, who paid a heavy price for complacency.

Offaly had some wonderful games in this decade with Kilkenny and only a point – in Offaly's favour – separated them at the end of a pulsating, thrill-a-minute Leinster final in 1980. Offaly had the unique distinction of contesting all ten Provincial finals in the decade, winning five.

They went on to make it eleven straight finals by participating in the 1990 decider as well and that same season they completed the three-in-a-row.

However, when red-hot favourites to qualify for a 12th successive Provincial final in 1991 and make a giant step at the same time towards the fourth-in-a-row, they lost by two points (0-19 to 1-14) to an under-rated Dublin side before an attendance of 31,653 in the Leinster semi-final at Croke Park on June 30 (Dublin in turn had reason to rue the manner in which they threw their chance of victory away against Kilkenny in the final, missing two close-in frees while Fortune didn't smile on them either as they hit the woodwork twice in going down by 1-13 to 1-11).

The eighties proved a decade of change also in that Cork's supremacy in Munster that had seen the Leesiders win five successive Provincial titles (1982-'86), equalling the five-in-a-row achieved in 1975-'79, was broken at last by Tipperary, who in

1987 won the crown for the first time since 1971. Christy Ring could smile somewhere in the Great Beyond for it was the Wizard from Cloyne who had said that Munster hurling without Tipperary in a position to mount a real challenge for honours was like a man without a suit.

But I believe that overall this decade belonged to Galway, who produced a team under Conor Hayes that won two All-Ireland titles back-to-back in 1987 and '88. I am convinced that they would have completed the three-in-a-row but for "The Keady Affair" in 1989. Indeed, Galway could well have equalled Cork's record of four-in-a-row (1941-'44). However, a combination of circumstances, including failure to play the "Advantage rule" when Eanna Ryan scored a smashing goal at the Railway end from a Joe Cooney pass, denied them victory against Cork in the 1990 All-Ireland final.

All right, I know it can be argued that Cork had shown themselves to be Galway's bogey team at the All-Ireland final stage for the second time in the space of five years (Galway had been beaten in 1986 when going into the game very warm favourites in the eyes of most neutrals). But such was Galway's overwhelming superiority on the general run of the play in the first half of the 1990 final – with Joe Cooney giving a display that conjured up memories of Mick Roche's *tour de force* in the first period of the 1968 All-Ireland – that there is no doubt whatsoever in my mind that the game would have been out of Cork's reach by the interval had the Eanna Ryan goal been allowed, as the lead would have been eight points instead of five.

Then to add to Galway's story of misfortune, just after Tomas Mulcahy had goaled in the second half to reduce a seven-points deficit to four, Martin Naughton broke through on a solo run. Ger Cunningham advanced to narrow the angle and cover the shot with his body. Naughton instead of trying to swerve around Cunningham or draw him in before flicking one past him elected to blast the ball to the net. It hit Cunningham on the forehead, injuring him in the process, though he was able to continue and the ball spun inches wide. The umpire waved a wide. Cunningham in true sporting fashion said to me that evening in the Burlington Hotel: "Of course, it should have been a '70' as it came off me".

Amazingly, referee John Moore instead of overruling the umpire allowed the "wide" to stand. If Galway had pointed from the '65' their lead would have been five points and had Naughton goaled it would have restored their seven-points advantage. And again I am convinced that the psychological uplift of countering

Tomas Mulcahy's goal with the raising of an immediate green flag would have carried Galway on to victory.

Shortly afterwards came another controversial incident. Tony Keady was clearly fouled and, on the ground, misdirected a hand-pass that reached Tony O'Sullivan, who scored a Cork point. Why did not the referee award a free to Galway?

Finally, John Fitzgibbon took no less than eight steps with the ball in his hand (replaying the video of the game proves this conclusively) before slamming home the second of his two goals in the 63rd minute. That goal was scored when Galway were three points behind (4-13 to 1-19). How did John Moore fail to spot Fitzgibbon's breach of the relevant rule?

✂ ✂ ✂

Conor Hayes had been full-back on the side that bridged a fifty-seven years gap by winning the 1980 All-Ireland against Limerick.

It would have been tragic if Galway, after failing in the All-Ireland finals of 1975 and '79, had not won a title before John Connolly and others like him, who had given such loyal and sterling service in the Maroon and White colours, went into retirement. That victory, in fact, was to stamp Galway's place as one of the foremost counties bidding for All-Ireland honours through subsequent seasons in the eighties.

True, they would lose finals that their supporters claim they should never have lost – the 1981 and '85 finals, for example, and even though they started very warm favourites for the 1986 final, they were well beaten in the end by a fiery and totally-committed Cork side, glorying in the tag of "under-dogs". However, they made amends for those two sucessive defeats in 1985 and '86 when they took the All-Ireland crown in 1987 – the final that marked the 100th anniversary of Galway's (Meelick) defeat by Tipperary (Thurles) in the very first All-Ireland Final in 1887.

The most important single fact about the 1980 success was that it ended for all time the apparent hoodoo that overshadowed Galway's efforts in the All-Ireland senior hurling championship. I spurn the ridiculous legend that successive defeats sprang from the famous "priest's curse" – a band of Galway hurlers heading south for the All-Ireland semi-final in Limerick on August 14, 1932 and getting Mass on the road, but leaving the Church before the end and then an angry celebrant laying on their heads the awesome curse that would ring down the decades to 1980. That was the day in '32 that "Tull" Considine went to town against the Galway defence in the second half after a new white ball had been thrown in and the cry went up, "Biddy Earley and the white ball" from those who concluded that the Witch of Feakle was conspiring too against Galway as they conceded no less than nine goals in losing a match that had appeared to be "sewn up" at one stage.

Through all the frustration heaped on frustration and narrow defeats of the forties and fifties, the shadow of the "priest's curse" remained over Galway and even sane men began to think that there must be something in it after all. The team was reported to have gone through an exorcising exercise before the 1980 All-Ireland Final – or that was the story devised by a clever reporter looking for a novel angle amid the welter of training-camp "specials" the public inevitably have to suffer before an All-Ireland Final in hurling or football.

In the end Galway laughed Fate and the priest's curse in the eye. They made their own luck in the 1980 All-Ireland final as Dame Fortune deserted Limerick in the tense moments leading up to the final whistle. But if there is any balancing out in championship games as there can be in life itself, then no county deserved to win an All-Ireland more than Galway did in that 1980 season. In the span between 1975 and '86 they contested five All-Ireland finals and had only one title to show for all their endeavours.

⌘ ⌘ ⌘

Offaly's arrival in Leinster gave a new fillip to the battle for championship honours. It meant that three counties – Wexford, Kilkenny and Offaly – were capable now of winning the Leinster crown in any given season and, of course, Dublin could not be left out of the reckoning either, even though far from being the power they were when they contested the 1961 All-Ireland against Tipperary and were most unlucky losers.

On the national plane, the fact that Galway and Offaly could compete with the best meant also that the base for All-Ireland success was broadened.

I know that traditionalists spurned pairings like Offaly v. Galway in 1981 and Cork v. Offaly in 1984. They preferred to be fed on the staple diet their fathers and grandfathers had known generally – Tipperary v. Kilkenny and Cork v. Kilkenny. But our summers, I contend, would have been much poorer if we had not been blessed with the memorable battles that Offaly provided from 1980 onwards and likewise if Galway had not become the force they did become in the eighties.

I journeyed across the Shannon with the victorious Galway team in 1980 and heard them sing *The Fields of Athenry* before it entered the charts as a very popular hit number some years later and I also heard them sing *The Galway Shawl.*

Out in the Tudor Lodge in Oranmore, amidst the company of hurling men, Martin Burns from Ahascragh took out his fiddle and played for us and someone snapped a photo of that moment. It captures for me every time I look at it, the whirl of hurling talk during that long wonderful afternoon that I would never have enjoyed if Galway had not made the big break-through. Thanks for the memory Niall and Joe.

I journeyed also with the triumphant Offaly hurlers as they returned home by rail to Tullamore to a tumultous welcome on Monday evening, September 7, 1981, and I followed them on the road to Birr and next evening again to Banagher by the banks of the Shannon.

I remember as vividly as if it was yesterday coming down to breakfast in the County Arms Hotel on Tuesday morning, September 8, 1981. Two men who had celebrated through the night and had now dropped in for breakfast left an accordion out in the hallway and I suggested that it would be a pity not to play it on a day like this when the mood of celebration was still very much in the air. They didn't need too much urging to respond. And a memorable sing-song started that carried on through the day until we departed for Banagher.

In Banagher I heard Pat Delaney sing again *The Offaly Rover* as he had sung it in Croke Park on the September Sunday that Offaly became All-Ireland senior hurling champions for the first time ("Old Kinnity I long to see when the woodbine is in bloom . . .").

We can never forget that moment in Croke Park on Sunday, September 7, 1980 when Joe McDonagh took the microphone and led the thousands of Galway supporters in front of the Hogan Stand in singing *The West's Awake* – the song that captures for me always the very spirit of the West. And prior to that there had been the never-to-be-forgotten moment when the captain of the side, Joe Connolly, held the cup high above his head and the flags and banners of the Galwaymen were raised in triumph amid scenes of unsurpassed enthusiasm.

Then he spoke unconsciously in flowing Irish – a fluency that only someone from one of the Gaeltacht areas of the Western seaboard could muster and his words touched the hearts of men who had come to Croke Park for this day from the heart of

Connemara, from the Aran Islands too and the exiles in from the United States, who had flown the Atlantic to be present and partook, as Seán Silke put it: "Of the rich harvest at last after a lot of fruitless endeavour".

We can never forget either the incredible scenes that followed the final whistle on September 6, 1981 as thousands of Offaly supporters gathered in front of the Hogan Stand to acclaim their heroes and Pat Delaney took the microphone and led the singing of *The Offaly Rover.*

To have been there on both these occasions was to realise what a break-through can mean, whether it was a county returning from a long period in the championship wilderness or one winning a first-ever title.

The songs we were accustomed to sing were *The Banks of My Own Lovely Lee, Slievenamon, The Rose of Mooncoin* and *Boolavogue.*

Now a new ballad would be associated in our minds with the season that Offaly made history while *The Fields of Athenry* would conjure up memories that would never die of our journey with the Galway hurlers across the Shannon and how we saw the dawn coming up over Galway Bay, after that fantastic welcome-home by 30,000 people in Eyre Square.

⌘ ⌘ ⌘

The Galway 1987-'90 team has got to come into the reckoning in the selection of the "Top Ten" hurling sides in GAA history. More especially so if one confines the selection to the forty years span from 1950 to 1990.

If we were to go back before 1950, two teams would stand out above all others – the Limerick side led by that most charismatic of captains, Mick Mackey, which reached the zenith of its powers in the glorious 1936 season of sweeping triumphs and also the Cork four-in-a-row team of 1941-'44 which included outstanding hurlers whose names and reputations have stood the test of time. Not forgetting either the Kilkenny team of the immortal Lory Meagher, which figured in the titanic three battles with Cork to decide the destination of honours in 1931 and over seven seasons (1931-'37) missed only one All-Ireland (1934), winning three ('32, '33 and '35) and which might well have been a three-in-a-row or a four-in-a-row side but for losing the 1934 Leinster final to Dublin after a replay.

Mick Roche rejected totally the idea that the hurlers of the sixties and subsequent decades could not be placed beside the men of Mick Mackey's and Christy Ring's earlier and middle career days. "If there was a better team in any era than the 1964-'65 Tipperary team, show it to me", was his pungent comment to me when I threw at him other powerful sides of earlier years.

Tim Flood of Wexford said to me on the eve of the 1981 All-Ireland Senior Hurling Final that the team he would have feared most of all as a member of the 1955-'56 Model County side was the Tipperary 1964-'65 combination. Why? Because that Tipperary side had an attack that left no doubts at all when recording the League-Championship-Oireachtas treble in the two seasons of its total supremacy, scoring five goals and thirteen points in beating Kilkenny in the 1964 All-Ireland and two goals and sixteen points in defeating Wexford in 1965, while overwhelming Cork in the Munster final of 1964 (3-13 to 1-5). "The really great teams had forward lines that could turn on the power when they wanted to and did not have to depend on scraping home by a point or two", he said.

The only team that came after that 1964-'65 Tipperary "machine" that could perhaps have stopped it, in my own opinion was the magnificent Kilkenny side of the 1972-'75 seasons, boasting the Eddie Keher-Paddy Delaney-Kieran Purcell axis in attack in the devastating form displayed against Wexford in the 1973 Leinster Final when Paddy Delaney maintains it reached its peak. It was one of the greatest teams of my time watching hurling.

"Babs" Keating has argued that the 1964-'65 Tipperary team would have come out "tops" against Kilkenny. He bases his argument on the contention that there were players on the 1972 Noreside panel like Pat Henderson, Pa Dillon, Martin Coogan and Eddie Keher who had played against Tipperary in the 1964 All-Ireland final and they still could not stave off overwhelming defeat.

But I would reply to that argument by making the point that Kilkenny did not have Frank Cummins at midfield in 1964 and neither was Eddie Keher supported in attack by the dynamic Paddy Delaney at centre-forward or by Kieran Purcell. Even though decimated by injuries going into the 1973 All-Ireland final (after giving one of the most power-packed performances I have ever seen from a Kilkenny side in running up 4-22 in a ten-point defeat of Wexford in the Leinster final), they pushed Limerick to the limit. They could so easily have been a four-in-a-row team (1972-'75).

Other combinations that would certainly have brought the Tipperary 1964-'65 side all the way were the Limerick team of 1936, and the Cork four-in-a-row team of 1941-'44, though I would not put the three-in-a-row side of 1976-'78 into the same category. In cold retrospect, however, some of the outstanding hurlers in that side could be placed beside the best in any era — and that is high praise indeed. I must say also that the reputation of that Cork three-in-a-row combination has gained in a strange way with the passing years because putting three All-Irelands back-to-back was an outstanding feat by any stretch of the imagination, irrespective of how carping critics endeavour to belittle the opposition that was overcome.

Clare were desperately unlucky to run up against such a talented Cork side in the 1977 and '78 Munster finals in Thurles. It was only by two points that the '78 final was lost before 54,000 spectators in Thurles, after the Banner County had looked in a winning position at half-time, having played against the wind in the first half.

This was the Clare team of the magnificent half-back line of Ger Loughnane, Seán Stack and Seán Hehir. But Clare just did not have forwards of the guile of Ray Cummins, Charlie McCarthy and Jimmy Barry Murphy.

There were times when I marvelled at the cultured grace of Seán Stack's hurling, a throw-back to the classic hurling of Mick Roche. Of course Roche was incomparable at his peak. And yet Stack left a memory behind that goes far beyond mere appreciation of individual skill to a new understanding of why no other game has the same meaning for us as hurling: the deft touch of the wrist, the beautifully-executed interception, the shortening of the grip in tight situations to outmanoeuvre an opponent in clearing and always style, the pure style of the born hurler. Eamon Cregan, I recall also, served up a classic exhibition of centre-back play on Kilkenny's tearaway centre-forward Paddy Delaney in the 1973 All-Ireland and twenty years on, as I write this chapter, still etched in the mind is a picture of his tightness and control in the rain that would have done credit to Tony Wall at his best in the pivotal position.

Seán Stack had a dream of marching behind the Artane Boys Band at Croke Park on All-Ireland Day, the terraces and stands aflame with the Saffron and Blue. A tragedy in a way that we did not see him on that stage on the first Sunday in September. An even greater tragedy for hurling overall that Clare of 1977-'78 failed to win at least one Munster crown or one All-Ireland title, even though they did win two successive League titles.

It was the same old story of high hopes dashed at the ultimate point when Clare failed to Cork once again in the 1986 Munster final in Killarney – a game, I have no doubt, they would have won if Seán Stack had not returned jet-lagged from the States just a few days beforehand and if that ridiculously soft goal by Jimmy Barry Murphy from a Kevin Hennessy pass had not been conceded at the crucial juncture in the second half.

❅ ❅ ❅

Taking the eighties and the first seasons of the nineties – the period of most relevance to the younger generation – I have to give pride of place to the Kilkenny team of 1982-'83 over the others because in beating Cork two years running in the All-Ireland final – Cork, remember, with Ray Cummins and Jimmy Barry Murphy in attack – they left no doubts, though it must be emphasised that they could never generate the invincible power-packed sweep of Tipperary 1965-'65 or Kilkenny 1972-'75 at their peak. Still I place this Kilkenny side ahead of Offaly 1981, Cork 1984 and 1986 and even of Galway 1985-'90 and Tipperary 1987-'91.

Galway come next to Kilkenny 1982-'83 because in the period 1985-90, before real change began to be made in the side, they contested five out of six All-Irelands and I have little doubt that but for the "Keady Affair" and the other setbacks of 1989, they would have contested, and won, the final that season also. They put two back-to-back in 1987 and '88, conceding no goal in either final. And they could well have become the first four-in-a-row team of hurling history since the Cork team of 1941-'44.

The question marks over the defence that cost Tipperary so dearly in 1987, '88, '90, '92 and '93 mean that there is still a point to prove, though it has to be said that the last line of Paul Delaney, Noel Sheehy and Michael Ryan performed with great credit in the winning of the 1991 All-Ireland title against Kilkenny, despite the gaps shown up in the innate half-back line, especially in the first half. This Tipperary side had great hurling talent – **hurling** being the operative word – but they knew they had to put two titles back-to-back before they could step up the rankings in the "Top Ten". Strictly on the record of achievement in the period 1987-'91, Tipperary have to be placed ahead of Limerick 1971-'74. Limerick then won two successive Munster titles (1973-74) and one All-Ireland (1973), whereas Tipperary took five of the seven Munster titles in the period 1987-'93 and

of sportsmanship in which it was contested and yet there was no holding back.

Nicky English walked off the Semple Stadium pitch knowing the numbness of defeat when he should have been carried shoulder-high by joyous and exuberant Tipperary supporters. Yes, his reputation remained all right as he finished with a tally of 1-4 from play. But a certain sense of disappointment remained, as deep down we knew that it could so easily have been 3-6 or 3-8, allowing for the quietness of his opening twenty minutes and the kicked effort saved at the post by Ger Cunningham and the opening carved so brilliantly against Denis Walsh in the second half that brought only a point instead of the goal that would have rocked the stadium.

Christy Ring's crown as the match-winner supreme of hurling history was still secure. It was on this same pitch in 1956 against Limerick in a situation far more impossible than English faced in the second half of the 1990 Munster final that the Wizard from Cloyne left no doubts on that score when he hit three amazing goals in the climactic stage of the match.

We still awaited at the end of the first season of the nineties for that kind of riveting, kill-off-the-opposition *tour de force* from Nicky English when it was Cork, Galway or Kilkenny that had to be put away – and no chance of pulling themselves up off the floor.

⌘ ⌘ ⌘

The first round Munster championship tie in Páirc Uí Chaoimh in 1992 was another bitterly-disappointing day for English. So disappointing, in fact, that afterwards he would say: "If I had ducks they would drown."

This was a reference to the very easy chances he missed in the first half – even when he had steadied himself and got the posts right in his sights. I believe that if English had been on song and in real killer mood he would have emerged as the match-winner. Beforehand he anticipated deep down having a *tour de force.* So it made it all the harder for him to accept his failure to raise even one flag against Seán O'Gorman, a pillar in a full-back line. And, as Vincent Hogan aptly put it in the *Irish Independent* next day, it was this full-back line that "cremated Tipperary's ambitions" in a 2-12 to 1-12 triumph before 42,416 spectators.

It was an inspired move by the Cork selectors to switch Brian Corcoran over on Pat Fox from the outset. Who would have bet that Fox, so deadly in Thurles the previous year, would be held to two points by the young Leeside prodigy and that Michael Cleary, who had a nightmare afternoon overall in his free-taking, would only secure one point from play?

With English, Fox and Cleary subdued the cutting edge was gone from the Tipperary attack. Cormac Bonnar was carried off, the victim of a late and heavy charge.

Mindful of how the match in Thurles the previous year had swung sharply in Tipperary's favour in the second half when Jim Cashman had his wrist fractured as a result of a wild pull that went unpunished by the referee, Cork had obviously made up their minds to hurl on this day with an edge of steel that Tipperary would have cause to remember. Cork hit in a manner that caught the reigning champions completely unaware.

The Leesiders had trained from January with only one day in mind and, as Seán O'Gorman put it, "out there we displayed a willingness to die for victory".

"You know it's much more difficult to get your motivation right when you're champions", said Jim Cashman, who with Cathal Casey, Denis Walsh, Teddy McCarthy and Tomás Mulcahy played heroically.

"We were in the same boat as Tipperary in '91 and, somehow, we found it difficult to light the fire. Having watched them take our titles it seemed natural to come back with the hunger to regain them. We couldn't wait to get at them."

Cork, ironically, gave so much in dethroning Tipperary that they would confess later – after losing to Kilkenny – that their All-Ireland Day was 7 June 1992. They were unable to peak a second time as they had peaked in Páirc Uí Chaoimh and, remember, that even though they had a comfortable win over Limerick in the Munster final in Cork they could not take the 1992 National League champions for granted after their courageous win over Tipperary in the League decider in Limerick.

✺ ✺ ✺

I rate the drawn game in Cork on 12 July 1991 one of the finest of all the Cork-Tipperary tussles in the 1987-'92 era. The hip-to-hip exchanges in the opening ten minutes were exhilarating. Tipperary played first-time hurling of a calibre that caused a tingling in the spine. On one occasion three Cork men were left sprawling on the ground after being met with shoulder power as the ball was carried on from Conal Bonnar and Bobby Ryan to the rampaging John Leahy.

Cork's full-forward line of Ger Fitzgerald (2-0), Kevin Hennessy (1-2) and John Fitzgibbon (1-2), displaying tremendous élan and panache in running up a total of 4-4, tore the Tipperary full-back line to ribbons in a dynamic eighteen-minute burst in the first half that saw them forge a seven points lead. Indeed, but for two vital saves by Ken Hogan from Mark Foley and John Fitzgibbon and a wide by Kevin Hennessy that shaved a post, the game would have been over to all intents and purposes by half-time.

John Leahy's great opportunist goal in which Nicky English had a hand revived Tipperary's fortunes and, amazingly, they recovered to go in at half-time only four points down (3-5 to 1-7) and but for six wides in a row, shared by English and Cleary, they could have been ahead against all the odds.

The drafting in of Michael Ryan of Upperchurch – making his championship debut – for the limping Conor O'Donovan at the start of the second half was no surprise. He played at left full-back with Noel Sheehy reverting to his favoured full-back position. The Paul Delaney–Noel Sheehy–Michael Ryan last line of defence stopped the rot but the Cork inside line of attack continued to pose a constant threat.

Tipperary wides were still occuring too frequently for the good of the blood pressure of supporters of the Blue and Gold. By the final whistle the total would have reached sixteen.

Cork's switching of Tony O'Sullivan to midfield was a success. When John Fitzgibbon cut a beautiful ball to the net, they were back seven points in front and the Cork victory cheers were echoing around the stadium. Fitzgibbon's leap of joy was a replica of the one he made in Thurles in 1990.

At that moment of balance Michael Ryan stepped in to vindicate the decision of "Babs" Keating and his fellow-selectors to pitch him in at the deep end. He beat one or two opponents very coolly before sending a great ball upfield. Little did we realise then but it was this stroke that was to put Tipperary on the road to the Munster and All-Ireland titles.

The ball found Pat Fox who had slipped in behind Cormac Bonnar and Richard Browne. He flashed a perfect shot low to Ger Cunningham's right. The green flag was up. Prior to that golden goal, Michael Cleary and substitute Aidan Ryan had pointed and there were only two points between the sides with nine minutes left.

Two points by Michael Cleary from frees won by Nicky English and Cormac Bonnar levelled the scores in a welter of excitement.

114

What a finish! But there was still a lot of drama to unfold. With just four minutes to go English broke through and a goal then would have wrapped it up. But the advancing Ger Cunningham parried his effort and Pat Fox could not turn the rebound into the net.

A quickly-taken puck-out by Cunningham saw the ball reach Tony O'Sullivan with oceans of space. He picked out Kevin Hennessy, who pointed to put Cork in front with just one minute left on the clock.

A third Tipperary recovery seemed too much to expect. Or was it?

Now Nicky English in a touch of sheer genius was through a gap and, after he had lost his hurley, he kicked the ball from close in over the bar. I was right behind the flight of the ball and had no doubt in my mind that it was a legitimate point but, because of the high trajectory of the ball, the umpire at the relevant side waved it wide.

English put in a frantic appeal, backed up by Pat Fox – and, even though subsequently, the slow-motion evidence on television supported the claim for a point, it goes into the records as the "point that never was".

Fortunately, in the last desperate, frenetic exchanges justice was done. There was Noel Sheehy appearing in the half-forward area, passing inside, John Leahy going on and almost getting in a shot for goal – and finally Pat Fox in possession, turning and twisting until he made an angle for himself and then hitting on the proverbial sixpence, snatching the last-gasp point in the breathless excitement of an unforgettable climax and the scoreboard read: Cork 4-10; Tipperary 2-16.

✻ ✻ ✻

On to Thurles then for the replay on July 21 – and what drama this would produce in the second half for the crowd of 55,000, who were left utterly drained at the end of a fantastic finish.

Tipperary, five points down at one stage in the first half and 1-7 (10) to 2-8 (14) behind at the interval, looked dead and buried in the 47th minute when the scoreboard read 3-13 to 1-10 in Cork's favour. First-half goals by John Fitzgibbon (18th minute) and Ger Fitzgrald (26th minute) had been followed by a brilliant Kevin Hennessy effort twenty-three minutes from the end. It was Fitzgibbon who made the opening, laying off to Hennessy. The Midleton man at first looked to be crowded out but he switched to his left and sent a screamer past Ken Hogan.

The introduction of Aidan Ryan and Joe Hayes (for Donie O'Connell and Aidan Madden) contributed largely to Tipperary's amazing fightback. John Leahy moved to midfield where he turned in a stormer, with Joe Hayes also playing his heart out in this sector.

Now the ball was beginning to flow to Pat Fox and Cormac Bonnar in the full-forward line and despite the absence of Nicky English Tipperary would before the end wreck the Cork last line of defence. It was all the more surprising considering the early dominance of half-backs Cathal Casey, Jim Cashman and Pat Hartnett and Seán O'Gorman at right full. There is little doubt that the wrist injury sustained by Cashman had an immense bearing on the eventual outcome, reflecting on the manner in which he had been lording it in the pivotal centre-back position.

Pat Fox capped his finest day in the Blue and Gold jersey by scoring a beautifully-flicked goal at the Killinan end, getting his hurley to the loose ball just before the advancing Ger Cunningham could hit it away from the danger zone. In the lead-up to that telling goal Fox (two) and Declan Ryan had pointed from play and now the gap between the sides was only three points.

With ten minutes left, Tipperary captain, Declan Carr, connected overhead on a John Leahy delivery to find the net and the scores were level. When Aidan Ryan pointed his side into the lead, young spectators in the main spilled on to the pitch in celebration.

"Babs" Keating, worried that the game might be abandoned, left the dug-out and helped in clearing the pitch – but the spectators formed a half-circle behind Ger Cunningham's goal and would invade again. It was alleged that Cunningham was struck by coins and small stones – but, as I saw it from the Press Box, this was not a concerted effort at intimidation but a case of enthusiasm and near-ecstasy running wild in the course of a winning rally.

Cork could not blame the invasion for the collapse of their defences. Tipperary just caught fire and were unstoppable as they swept all over the Leesiders and Conal Bonnar summed it up aptly when he said: "Drive, pride, anger – call it what you like. But there was something else out there. We were being driven like never before. So much yelling, so much talking among each other. It became so that we couldn't let each other down. I've never experienced anything like it."

After Tipperary had gone into the lead, it was all a blur and Semple Stadium erupted into a crescendo of sound, into a

"SAM'S FOR THE HILLS . . ."

● "SAM'S FOR THE HILLS . . ." this is how Anthony Molloy finished his acceptance speech after receiving the Sam Maguire in Croke Park and here he holds it against the background of a typical Donegal landscape of heather, sea and scudding clouds that would inspire any painter in oils.

THAT EPOCH-MAKING MOMENT

● Anthony Molloy holds the Sam Maguire high in triumph after Donegal had won their first-ever All-Ireland senior football crown on Sunday, 20 September 1992. (Photo: Sportsfile)

● AFTER THE SWEAT OF BATTLE, THE REWARD ... Anthony Molloy found that "Sam" was his constant companion as he drove through Donegal in the weeks following the All-Ireland final, people just wanting to touch the Cup to convince themselves that it wasn't just a dream that Donegal were champions after all. (Photo: INPHO)

ONEGAL SOAR TO ALL-IRELAND GLORY

● *Anthony Molloy soars high in this battle for possession with Mayo's T. J. Kilgallon as Donegal march on to their first-ever All-Ireland final and then won "SAM".*

THE EMOTION OF THE HOMECOMING

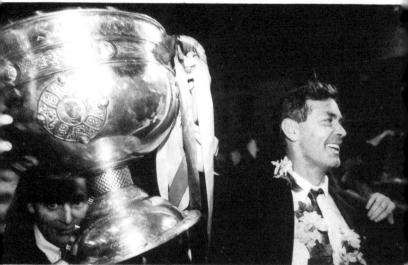

● *Brian McEniff savours the moment of unsurpassed ecstasy when the Sam Maguire Cup is brought home to Bundoran and his native Donegal for the first time. (Photo: Billy Strickland, INPHO)*

● *Gary Walsh captures the mood of joy and exultation in the homecoming celebrations. (Photo: INPHO)*

TONY BOYLE SHOWS HIS POWER

● *Tony Boyle shows the power against Mayo that was to see him help in inspiring Donegal to victory over Dublin in the '92 All-Ireland final from the full-forward position. (Photo: Irish Independent)*

● *Donegal – All-Ireland Senior Football Champions 1992. Back row: Matt Gallagher, John Joe Doherty, Noel Hegarty, Gary Walsh, Brian Murray, Barry McGowan, Declan Bonner, Donal Reid. Front row: Martin McHugh, Joyce McMullin, Manus Boyle, Tony Boyle, Anthony Molloy (captain), Martin Gavigan, James McHugh.*

THE EMOTION OF VICTORY

● *Down's Paddy O'Rourke can't believe that his dream has come true as the final whistle sounds at the end of the 1991 All-Ireland final.*

. . . THE AGONY OF DEFEAT

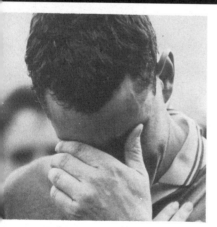 

● *Meath's Liam Harnan (left) is overcome with the disappointment of defeat and Michael McQuillan (right) can only sit on the Croke Park pitch looking totally drained at the end of the longest-ever championship marathon after the defeat by Down.*

DOWN MAINTAIN UNIQUE RECORD

● PROUDEST MOMENT
. . . Paddy O'Rourke holds
the Sam Maguire Cup high
in triumph after leading
Down to the county's
fourth All-Ireland title win
and (right) Greg Blaney
who at centre-forward was
the brains of the Down
attack through the 1991
campaign.

● Young James McCartan shows all the determination and drive of his
father, Jim McCartan, dynamic centre-forward on the 1960-'61 side, as he
heads for the Meath goal despite the attentions of Liam hayes in the 1991 All-
Ireland final.

THE SOUL OF THE DOWN DEFENCE

● *THE LESSON OF HISTORY . . . The dates on the blackboard in Lagan College, Belfast, tell it all. Down had not failed in the three previous All-Ireland finals (1960, '61 and '68) in which they appeared and D. J. Kane — "the soul of the Down defence" — would make a vital contribution to the winning of the fourth in 1991. (Photo: Irish Independent)*

● *Down — All-Ireland Senior Football Champions 1991. Back row: Eamonn Burns, Paul Higgins, Conor Deegan, Neil Collins, Barry Breen, Greg Blaney. Front row: Ross Carr, James McCartan, Gary Mason, Brendan McKernan, Mickey Linden, Paddy O'Rourke (captain), D. J. Kane, Peter Withnell, John Kelly.*

cauldron of conflicting emotions. We had lived through the heyday of Christy Ring and torrid battles in Limerick games we believed then that could never be repeated for nail-biting tension. But this was something else again. In the space of twenty minutes Tipperary turned a nine-points deficit into a five-points lead – a swing of fourteen points – before Cork came back and, finally, there was no more than a puck of a ball or two between them at the final whistle.

The Aidan Ryan point was balanced by a similar effort by substitute Pat Buckley.

Points by Cormac Bonnar and Pat Fox put Tipperary two clear. Aidan Ryan seemed to have killed off Cork finally when he pounced spectacularly for a sensational goal. Cork full-back Richard Browne was in the process of clearing his lines when Ryan made a great block down, ran on to the ball and rattled the net.

But the pulsating drama was not over yet. Referee Terence Murray was playing lost time when he awarded Cork a 20-metre free. John Fitzgibbon stood over it and crashed the ball to the net. Anything might have happened and we will always remember the snap shot from Fitzgibbon that struck the foot of the post with Hogan beaten – but instead of turning in, it turned out wide.

Tipperary, however, were not going to be denied. We saw some tigerish backs-to-the-wall defensive play and then Michael Cleary put the icing on a famous victory by scoring two points that made it 4-19 to 4-15 in what had become an eight-goal bonanza. You felt for great-hearted Teddy McCarthy, the dual All-Ireland winner of 1990, when he said later in the Anner Hotel to anyone who cared to listen: "How did it happen?"

Yes, that is all the Cork players and management team could ask themselves and Bobby Ryan, who personified Tipperary's unconquerable spirit in the last twenty minutes, gave the most fitting answer of all when he said: "We haven't played like that before in my time. This is what we've been promising for a long time but it was one hell of a long time coming.

"We were in trouble, no two ways about it. But you don't come back in games like these by accident. You come back because it's in you."

⌘⌘⌘

Tipperary, maturer now, easily overcame a Galway team in transition and in the All-Ireland final defeated a Kilkenny side which I concluded in the first half – when victory was there for the taking – had not enough conviction in themselves. Christy Heffernan and John Power caused a lot of havoc in the Tipperary defence but the Noresiders just could not get the goals that would have created the platform for the defeat of the Munster champions. Once Tipperary survived that first half when they played so badly and yet went in level at the interval (0-9 each), the writing was on the wall for the men in the Black and Amber.

And Fortune which had failed to smile on Tipperary in the '87 All-Ireland semi-final and '88 All-Ireland final, certainly favoured the Blue and Gold when referee, Willie Horgan (Cork) awarded a controversial 20-metre free for a foul on Nicky English. Michael Cleary mishit the ball but it struck the edge of Liam Walsh's hurley and flew into the net past the wrong-footed Michael Walsh and Bill Hennessy. Tipperary, from being just a point ahead after an uncertain ten minutes, were now firmly in the driving seat. And even the departure of both Cormac Bonnar and Nicky English, whose injuries had actually made their participation doubtful, could not swing matters for Kilkenny.

Paul Delaney in the first half and Noel Sheehy and Michael Ryan in the second made outstanding contributions to Tipperary's 24th All-Ireland title win and Pat Fox, with two fine points after that Michael Cleary goal, stamped his image on the occasion in no uncertain fashion, as did Michael Cleary with 1-6 to his credit (1-5 from frees). John Leahy was again a trump card in the way he ranged all over the field, whether operating from wing-back or midfield.

The experience Kilkenny gained in defeat would stand them in good stead against Cork in the 1992 All-Ireland final. This time they would make no mistake and they could appreciate the wisdom of the old adage: "You have got to win one to lose one."

On a day of rain and wind and on a pitch not suited to classical fare, the men in the Black and Amber beat the favourites Cork (3-10 to 1-12) in the 1992 All-Ireland final. Liam Fennelly had the honour of leading his county to its 24th title and later he announced his retirement. He had been captain back in 1982 when Kilkenny made it two All-Irelands back-to-back by defeating Cork for the second year running.

Fennelly elected to play against the wind in the first half. Cork were contained by a magnificent defence, the sharp "teeth" of their full-forward line of Gerry Fitzgerald, Kevin Hennessy and John Fitzgibbon – so deadly on its peak days – being blunted by

Eddie O'Connor, Pat Dwyer and Liam Simpson, a trio who comprised a powerful bulwark.

Indeed, Fitzgerald, Hennessy and Fitzgibbon only put one point on the board between them. Herein lay one of the main reasons − if not the principal one − for the downfall of the Munster champions.

Liam Walsh and Willie O'Connor showed up extremely well in the wing back positions for Kilkenny while centre-back Pat O'Neill hurled in insipred fashion in the second half after receiving a bloodied brow. The bandage became the badge of his courage in the rain.

The writing was on the wall for Cork when they led by only two points (0-7 to 1-2) at half-time, after a smart opening flourish that saw them 0-5 to 0-2 ahead after 20 minutes, Tony O'Sullivan and Tomas Mulcahy playing prominently at this stage. Brian Corcoran, making his All-Ireland debut, won his duel hands-down with Eamonn Morrissey, who was replaced late in the game.

The crucial blow for Kilkenny was struck four minutes before half-time by D. J. Carey when he goaled with a beautifully-struck penalty, foolishly concerned by Denis Walsh when Jamesie Brennan was already grounded.

Cork had squandered chances that they would live to regret. Brian Corcoran, so immaculate through the Munster campaign, drove four long-range frees wide and there were misses also by Tony O'Sullivan and Cathal Casey. Most galling of all, Kevin Hennessy when he got inside Pat Dwyer for the one and only time kicked the ball over the bar when one step more and a shortened grip might have brought the award of a certain goal.

Four minutes after the restart ginger-haired John Power showed true tenacity when he broke through four defenders to kick Kilkenny's second goal. Growing in stature all the time, Power knew how to spray the ball from the centre-forward position low to the corners and when he elected to go himself, he invariably drew enough defenders to pave the way for vital scores.

On this day, however, Ollie Walsh and his fellow-selectors moved Power to midfield in the second half to partner Billy Hennessy in order to counter Cork's introduction of Pat Hartnett and the switching of Cathal Casey to partner the Midleton man in this sector. In fact, Casey was beginning to win control for Cork until Kilkenny decided to act.

The Noreside switches paid off as Michael Phelan's move to full-forward saw him set up Liam McCarthy for the third − and what was to prove the decisive – goal in the 22nd minute of this half, and he added two valuable points into the bargain.

Ger Manly got through for a goal for Cork in the 31st minute and there was a glimmer of light for the Leesiders at the end of the tunnel. Adrian Ronan, who had come on as a sub, closed the door finally, however, when he sent over the bar for the insurance point from a difficult angle on the right wing, leaving Kilkenny victorious by four points.

The previous Tuesday his world had fallen in on Ronan when he was told that he would not be one of the starting fifteen.

He even contemplated fleetingly packing the game in altogether after the All-Ireland final. "I was shattered not to be on, absolutely devastated," he said.

Then thirteen minutes from the end he was handed the slip of paper that he would transfer in turn to the referee and which indicated that he was replacing Eamonn Morrissey. He fought ananymously until a ball reached him in front of the Cusack Stand with just three minutes to go. He seemed off-balance as he struck but he found the target all the same. The rest is history.

The hunger Kilkenny had as a result of failing against Tipperary the previous year proved too much in the end for Cork.

Cork's fierce hunger to avenge the Semple Stadium reverse by Tipperary in '91 had been satiated by the Lee in June. Three months on the same hunger was no longer there.

That's it in a nutshell.

120

CHAPTER 10

THE CYCLE COMES FULL CIRCLE FROM CENTENARY YEAR CLASSIC

THE Semple Stadium epic between Cork and Tipperary in 1991 saw the cycle of games that had started with the 1984 Centenary Year classic come full circle.

It was into the Killinan end goal that Tipperary staged the '91 replay rally that will live forever in the annals of Munster hurling and in the history of Tipperary-Cork confrontations.

And it was at this same Killinan end goal in the 1984 Munster final — a game of sheer grandeur and nobiliity, of total commitment from both sides through a second half that was on par with Killarney '71 — that fortune deserted Tipperary when a seemingly "safe" lead of four points had been forged with six minutes to go.

But before the moment of decision John Fenton had pointed a free and Cork equalised (3-14 all) when Tony O'Sullivan goaled after John Sheedy parried a seemingly unstoppable drive.

Then Michael Doyle soloed his way through the Cork defence with time running out. Edged out towards the left, he had got ahead of John Hodgins and John Blake. The argument rages in the homes of Tipperary to this day as to whether he might have gone for a point either with the stick or eassayed a palmed effort; even if he had kept going in along the end line, he might have been fouled. A free would have guaranteed a point — almost certainly the winning one. Even if he had shot wide, the puck-out would have come to the defence — *facing* it. And ready.

As it was, Michael Doyle elected to palm the ball across the goal towards Nicky English racing in and with Noel O'Dwyer lurking also in the vicinity of the square. English jumped to grab the ball. Denis Mulcahy, however, managed to intercept, drove the ball upfield, finding the unmarked Tony O'Sullivan. As he shot for a point, John Sheedy brought the ball down but unfortuantely for Tipperary he could not kill it dead on the stick as a Tony Reddan could. It bounced away. In nipped veteran corner-forward, Seanie O'Leary and he had no difficulty in raising the green flag. Where was the Tipperary cover?

121

John Fenton pointed a free and the turnover in Cork's favour in those six minutes had been eight points. The Leesiders could hardly believe how the tide had turned as they snatched victory (4-15 to 3-14) from the jaws of defeat.

A young girl sporting the Blue and Gold colours wept below me in the stand. She wept, like others, for the shattering of a dream − so real with six minutes remaining − of Tipperary reaching the Centenary All-Ireland final. Secretely, I suppose, the final we all wanted was a Tipperary v. Kilkenny or a Cork v. Kilkenny pairing, a throw-back to the days when the foundations were laid for lasting traditions.

It was into the Killinan goal once again − after sixteen minutes of the second half had elapsed in the 1987 Munster final − that Nicky English struck what seemed the decisive blow. Operating now as full forward, he got in behind the Cork full-back, Richard Browne and, despite losing his hurely, had the composure to steady himself before kicking the ball with the side of his boot Georgie Best-like to the roof of the net. This goal − one of the great goals of modern times − was greeted by a "Tipperary roar" that swamped the stadium. The scoreboard read: Tipperary 1-14; Cork 0-10.

Cork, instead of folding in face of a seven points lead, thundered back into the game in the manner of real champions, who were bidding for their sixth-in-a-row Provincial crown and a fourth-in-a-row All-Ireland title, that same season. In the next ten minutes they scored six points to Tipperary's one. With ten minutes left, the challengers' lead had been cut to two points.

Then Kieran Kingston blazed home a goal. On to the pitch at the town end swarmed red-bedecked Cork followers, dancing with the joy of impending victory. John Fenton, whose immaculate free-taking had kept Cork in touch when it seemed that the game would slip away from them (he scored a total of twelve points in all that day, nine from frees and one from a "70" while contributing thirteen points, ten from frees and three from seventies in the replay), now sent over a magnificent, sweeping long-range point, dead between the posts at the town end.

No wonder "Babs" Keating would say subsequently: "John Fenton is *The Man*, adding this tribute to the Midleton player: "If only we had a John Fenton today, how much would we have won by?"

Keating said that not since Theo English was in his prime had they seen a player able to take a line ball like Fenton. "In fact, every time he steps up to hit a line ball, it is like a free to Cork and particularly dangerous for the opposing defence when he is striking within range of goal."

Of course, this was said before Cork produced another superb line ball specialist in Cathal Casey in the early seasons of the nineties.

Now Cork stood two points clear. Just when it seemed that they had no hope of saving it, "Babs' Babes" fought back with a ferocity that restored the old glory in the Blue and Gold. As Richard Stakelum put it later: "what was born through the long grind of winter evenings of training, through all that 'Babs', Theo and Donie had inclulcated into us surfaced now in a last grandstand rally".

Pat Fox pointed a 50-yards free. Normal time was up when English won a free. Many Tipperary supporters could not bear to look as Fox bent, lifted and hit. His shot, dead on target, brought the balancing point – yes, into the Killinan end goal.

In cold restospect, I would question whether one at least of those two frees – if not both – should have been awarded. But it had been such an exhilarating game that Cork, being the supreme sportsmen they are, took it all with good grace. This day had been so memorable that we were all happy at the thought of a repeat.

Killarney, Sunday, 19 July 1987.

A replay that outstripped the Thurles tie for sheer drama and spine-tingling action and which went to thirty minutes extra time before a conclusion was finally reached, conjuring up memories of the Limerick marathon between these same rivals in 1949.

To have lived through the two games, through a marathon, extending to 170 minutes in all, was to have experienced all that is great in the national game – to have been stirred to the very marrow of one's bones by a confrontation of such rare splendour that one was left to wonder whether one would ever again witness anything as deeply compelling as these two great contests.

Tipperary went in at half-time in the replay looking a beaten side, as Cork led by 1-10 to 1-5. In fact, it could have been all over at the interval but for the genius of one player – Nicholas English. The All-Ireland champions were leading at one stage of the half by six points, though playing against the breeze, and were in command in most sectors, as Tipperary struggled, almost pathetically at times.

Then in the 26th minute of the first half English struck. Aidan Ryan kicked the ball through to him behind the Cork full-back line. English, finding himself on his own to the left of the Cork goal, rose the ball on to his stick and without ever attempting to get it into the hand, hit it all in the same movement, a powerful shot that beat Ger Cunningham going away on the right-hand and more open side of his goal.

It was a beauty – a goal of such unsurpassed brilliance in the way it was executed that I place it firmly among the greatest scores I have seen in my time writing about the game.

Although this score was quickly nullified by a fine goal for Cork by Tomas Mulcahy, Tipperary had got the boost they needed and as the Captain, Richard Stakelum said afterwards: "That goal by Nicky English really settled us and I felt much more confident of the outcome after the green flag had gone up".

Looking back on it now, I believe that English's goal was the one that inspired the Premier County to a first Provincial title win in sixteen years.

In the little village of Lattin on the Tipperary-Limerick border a lad of nine dreamed a dream when Tipperary won the All-Ireland crown in 1971. Now in the summer of '87 that same lad was a star in his own right, acknowledged by Jimmy Barry Murphy, in fact, as one of the finest forwards to grace the scene in the eighties, though a continuing battle with injury problems would dim his effectiveness as we progressed into the nineties.

✣ ✣ ✣

During the interval break, Donie Nealon told the Tipperary players that the position in Killarney in 1971 against Limerick was somewhat similar but that Tipperary had rallied to win it. "Go out there and throw caution to the winds and have a real go at Cork," he exhorted them.

Though Cork again held a six-points lead five minutes into the second half, Tipperary now, gathering momentum with each passing minute, started a tremendous rally that had the 45,000 crowd on its feet. And Paddy Delaney, the great Kilkenny centre-forward of the 1969-'75 era, who was a spectator at the match, said that in that second half and in the extra-time period he saw the best hurling he had ever seen in a Munster Final. "It was tremendous stuff," he said.

124

Point by point Tipperary inched their way back and then Nicky English set up Pat Fox for what seemed a vital goal. I was right behind the flight of the ball as it left his stick and have no doubt that it entered the net. But it struck the stanchion behind the Cork goalie, bounced back on to the goal-line and Ger Cunningham sent it clear.

Shades of the Christy Ring goal that never was!

Pat Fitzelle returned the ball over the bar and Tipperary drew level to a mighty roar from their supporters when Pat Fox pointed in the 23rd minute. Cork had reason to cry "we wuz robbed" when Tony O'Sullivan got a touch to a Teddy McCarthy centre (after McCarthy had gone high to catch the ball with his hand in exciting style) in the 25th minute but the umpires never hesitated as the flags were crossed for an "inside the square" infringement.

It could be contended that O'Sullivan was moving in on the ball and that the goal was perfectly legitimate. Personally, I didn't see all that much wrong with it, and replaying the video has convinced me that it should have been allowed. However, justice was done, I suppose, in that Pat Fox had failed to get a perfectly legitimate goal also when his shot rebounded off the stanchion.

John Fenton had edged Cork in front in the closing minutes when Ken Hogan's long puck-out, quickly taken, was grabbed by Nicky English, who slipped the defence. Initially, although hotly pursued by three Cork players and with his angle narrowing, he thought of going for goal. But, as he said to me afterwards, if the shot had been saved by Ger Cunningham, he would never have been forgiven for not taking the point.

He elected to palm the ball over the bar for the equaliser and, as subsequent events were to show, he took the right decision.

Both teams went to their dressingrooms at the end of the normal time (70 minutes) to a standing ovation.

The concensus was that in the energy-sapping heat Tipperary, with youth on their side, would stay the pace better during the thirty minutes extra-time period.

Cork, however, were in front through most of the first half of extra time and at the interval led by 1-21 to 1-20. And this despite the fact that they had lost Tom Cashman five minutes from the end of normal time – a cruel blow, as he had been hurling extremely well in the midfield sector. Jim Cashman, another key figure, went off injured at the start of extra time but when John Fenton was seen to be hobbling from a leg injury and moved in corner forward, the realisation dawned that Cork in the last fifteen minutes of extra time, were facing a desperate rearguard action to stay the mounting tide of Tipperary attacks.

⌘⌘⌘

Four minutes into the second period of extra time, Donie O'Connell put Tipperary ahead for the first time in this marathon contest with a magnificent point after a great run. Pat Fox had earlier levelled from a free and he was to finish with a tally of eleven points, seven from frees.

The balance of matters had swung in Tipperary's favour. John Crowley, who had battled so bravely for so long in the full-back line, now clearly began to feel the pace and he eventually went off with a fractured nose, to be replaced by Dermot McCurtain.

Aidan Ryan was hurling brilliantly for Tipperary with Colm Bonnar dominated at midfield, ably supported by Pat Fitzelle. Donie O'Connell was enjoying his best game ever in the Blue and Gold.

This battle of titanic proportions was taking its toll on both sides and Tipperary lost classy Paul Delaney and also Conor O'Donovan, while Richard Stakelum was showing enough blood from a cut near his eye that it would have been a case of the fight being stopped if it was a world title bout in boxing. Cramp claimed its victims on top of injuries.

Michael Doyle came on as a sub for Paul Delaney and went into the full line of attack, as Bobby Ryan switched to centre-back.

Colm Bonnar now came away with the ball on a driving, pulsating solo-run and, brushing tackles aside, passed to Donie O'Connell, who carried the attack forward into the Cork half of the field. Richard Browne, seeing the danger, moved out from the goal area and as Donie O'Connell sent in a low shot, the ball deflected off the Cork full-back's boot. Ger Cunningham, dived to try to turn it away but it had fallen right into the path of Michael Doyle and he showed great coolness in steering it around the helpless Cork goalie and into the net.

Then soon afterwards Richard Browne burst out with the ball from the Cork square but was followed by Nicholas English, who kept harrying him from behind, trying to flick the ball, without fouling, off his stick. Eventually he managed to do this and in stepped Pat Fitzelle to grab possesison and in a twinkling had sent one in to Michael Doyle standing unmarked at the edge of the square. As he was overwhelmend – it would have been a penalty anyway – he handpassed the ball to the net.

Six minutes remaining and Tipperary six points clear. "Babs", Theo and Donie are out of the dug-out on the sideline now and already enthusiastic supporters are embracing them. You can sense a moment of history in the making.

But a minute later a hush falls on the Tipperary crowd as Ken Hogan concedes a penalty in a goalmouth scramble. Seldom, we knew, had John Fenton missed with such a chance. But now his low shot is stopped by the trio manning the Tipperary goal line. It's all over.

Three minutes from the end Pat Fox, who had a wonderful game, robs Denis Walsh near the end line and passes to Donie O'Connell, who palms the ball to the net and then finds himself literally swamped at the back of the Cork goal by Tipperary followers who have run on to the pitch.

In the Tipperary dressingroom, Nicholas English looked up at Michael Doyle and mischievously wondered − "did you really get two goals".

The replay from John Doyle's son was accompanied by a defiant grin. "I sure did. I went mad out there today."

Later Michael Doyle would say to me: "This makes up for all the disappointments. Thurles '84 is history now."

Everyone was glad for him that the bitter memories left from the Centenary Year Munster decider had been erased at last.

Richard Stakleum mounted the podium to receive the trophy and I don't think Tipperary supporters have ever given vent to such an emotional response as when they cheered his words − "the famine is over − your ain't seen nothin' yet".

And then he took the microphone and led the singing of "Slievenamon", as the blood streamed down from that deep cut below his right eye.

The wound, he said, was a small price to pay for the honour of being Captain of Tipperary on this day. "We grew up and became men overnight."

✄ ✄ ✄

We were convinced that the epic Tipperary-Cork cycle of recent times that started in 1987 would be claimaxed by another memorable Munster final in Semple Stadium in 1993 − and that it would represent the Last Hurrah in the South for a number of the veterans on both sides.

But sadly it was not to be.

We saw the meeting of the two counties in the Royal Liver

127

National League semi-final in Thurles on Sunday, 26 April 1993 as simply a dress rehearsal for the real thing in July. Cork, reduced to fourteen men, snatched victory by a point (2-11 to 1-13) in dramatic fashion during the injury time period (extending to four and a half minutes) when Tomas Mulcahy ended a three-man movement with a sensational goal at the town end.

Cork then got involved in a three-match series with Wexford (conquerors of Limerick in the other semi-final by 3-14 to 1-11) to decide the destination of League honours. Cork had not won a League crown since 1981, so the incentive was there to really go for the title. But subsequently they would have reason to regret the toll of this marathon on their championship aspirations. Teddy McCarthy summed it up aptly when he remarked to me: "We left our prospects of winning the Munster and All-Ireland titles behind us in Thurles."

That was the day of the second replay – Saturday, 22 May, to be exact.

They had drawn the first day in Thurles (2-11 all), Larry Murphy levelling for Wexford with just one minute to go and John O'Connor driving wide from a forty-five yards free with the last puck of the game.

The second game, again in Thurles, went to extra time and captivated the attendance of 22,728, despite being played in a downpour. With the scores level (1-8 to 0-11) in the last second of normal time, Wexford were awarded a "70". The chance was there of taking a title which had eluded them since 1973. John O'Connor, however, mishit the ball and it dropped to the ground 30 yards in front of him.

Wexford forged a three points lead in the extra time period. Cork, never beaten until the final whistle, had points by Pat Buckley and Barry Egan and then in the last minute Jim Cashman gained possession some seventy yards out from a badly-directed ground clearance and drove the ball over the bar for the equaliser (Wexford 3-9; Cork 0-18).

And so to the last chapter at Semple Stadium. Wexford, after generating so much optimism among their supporters, lost the decisive game in the first half when they had the wind at their backs and failed to make the best use of their opportunities, shooting no less than nine wides, as they went in only level at half-time.

Cork, down to 14 men ten minutes after the start, had the ability to get killer goals at vital stages, their three goals coming from Barry Egan, Tomas Mulcahy and John Fitzgibbon. One could not but admire the spirit Wexford displayed when playing against the wind in the second half and, indeed, in one glorious seven-minute spell they actually took a 1-11 to 2-5 lead with 18 minutes remaining.

Tony O'Sullivan, who had announced his retirement after the '92 All-Ireland final, now made his come-back appearance in the Cork colours and in the 50th minute John Fitzgibbon would come on as a sub and three minutes later score the deciding goal. Yes, these two played crucial roles as the Leesiders dug deep into their resources and in a magnificent surging display of all that is best in Cork hurling, they turned a three-point deficit into a 3-11 to 1-12 victory.

As Brian Corcoran received the Cup and the 13th League crown was stitched into the record books, we could not but help conclude in our hearts that it was going to be very difficult to stop the Leesiders completing the League-Championship double.

❧ ❧ ❧

Fielding without Tomas Mulcahy and Teddy McCarthy and losing Timmy Kelleher (dislocated finger), and certainly not helped by the sodden pitch and downpour of rain, Cork fell sensationally in the Munster semi-final at the Limerick Gaelic Grounds on 13 June 1993 to Len Gaynor's battling Clare side that had ousted Limerick (3-16 to 3-12) on 23 May at Cusack Park, Ennis.

The Banner County had acclaimed Gerard ("The Sparrow") O'Loughlin following the triumph over Limerick. He was handed a No. 21 jersey in the dressingroom beforehand and didn't think he'd see action. But after three minutes he was introduced as a sub for the injured Alan Neville and left his imprint on the gmae by delivering a real Man of the Match performance in scoring 1-5.

At one stage of the second half, Clare led by fourteen points. Limerick reduced it to three, but it was super sub McLoughlin's point that made victory secure.

Against Cork "The Sparrow" emerged with three fine points to his name but the real hero this time was his Clarecastle club-mate Anthon Daly.

The turning point came in the 60th minute when the Clare goalie turned a well-struck shot for goal by Mark Mullins over the bar. A goal then for Cork and it might have been a different story.

I had written in the *Sunday Independent* on the day of this match that I would not travel to Limerick to witness "a massacre of the innocents". Those words of mine (which I was forced to eat on Clare Radio the next morning?) were used to telling effect in the Clare dressingroom before the game commenced. The "troops" went out ready to die for flag and county.

There was a graphic picture by David Maher in the *Irish Times* next morning of Banner County manager, Len Gaynor dancing a Clare jig of triumph on the sideline as the final whistle sounded and joyous Clare supporters flooded on to the pitch.

The cynics coming out of the Limerick Gaelic Grounds on Sunday, 1 July 1993 commented that what I had penned in the *Sunday Independent* had been written some weeks too soon!

This time Clare were literally lambs to the slaughter. Tipperary destroyed them in a manner that was embarrasing for all neutrals in the crowd of 41,557. The final score read 3-27 to 2-12 in favour of the men in the Blue and Gold and in reality it was all over as a contest after 24 minutes when Tipperary led by 2-11 to 0-3.

When referee Terence Murray (Limerick) sounded the full-time whistle to bring Clare's agony to an end, we could only reflect that it was the most one-sided Provincial decider in the South that we had seen since Cork beat Waterford by 3-33 to 0-12 in the 1983 Munster final, having hammered them by a cricket score (5-31 to 3-6) also the previous year.

In winning their 35th Munster crown and defeating Clare by double scores (as they had done when the counties last met in a Munster final in 1967), Tipperary gave one of the most immaculate displays ever produced by a team from the county but then it had to be set against the pathetic weakness of the opposition on the day, the looseness of the Clare defence and the space and freedom of movement they allowed the Tipperary attack. In a word, this was not the kind of opposition on which lasting judgments are made.

In the end, it was all a mere formality bearing no comparison to any of the great games between Tipperary and Cork in the 1987-'92 period.

⌘⌘⌘

The 1993 Munster championship had certainly been a topsy-turvey affair. Kerry produced an even bigger shock than Clare's overcoming of Limerick and Cork in the turn when they knocked Waterford out of contention for Provincial honours at Walsh Park on 23 May (4-13 to 3-13). You had to go all the way back to 1891 to the barefoot hurlers of Ballyduff to find the one-and-only-occasion that the Kingdom won Munster and All-Ireland honours.

John Meyler, a native of Wexford and a former Cork hurler, took charge of the Kerry squad in September '92 and, despite their good run in the League, no one could really see them toppling Waterford, who had won the All-Ireland under-21 in '92 and assuredly should have had enough talent coming on stream to withstand the challenge of the Kingdom.

Kerry's giant-killing act in Walsh Park cut no ice with Tipperary, who demolished them (4-21 to 2-9) at Semple Stadium in the Munster semi-final on Sunday, 6 June, Michael Cleary finishing with 3-2 (one goal from a penalty). And Tipperary were without Pat Fox and Nicky English.

The cold statistics at the end of the 1993 season showed that the dominance of Tipperary and Cork in the South was continuing. True, Limerick had achieved a well-merited victory over Tipperary in the National League final in Limerick in '92 but on the day that mattered – the Munster final – they disappointed against Cork in Pairc Uí Chaoimh.

They had not beaten Cork in a Munster final since 1980 and their last Provincial title win was in '81. You had to go back to 1963 – that is thirty years – to find Waterford's last Munster title success while Clare had not won since 1932 – a gap of over sixty years.

Tipperary and Cork had farmed all the titles between them in the period 1982-'93 (seven to Cork and five to Tipperary). We could only ask ourselves the very pertinent question: When will the dominance by the Big Two be broken?

And we might add: Is it good for the health or the future of the national game?

⌘⌘⌘

Sixty-four minutes into the Leinster championship first round game at Croke Park on 30 May 1993 – a classic in the rain – Offaly were leading Kilkenny by two points (0-14 to 1-9) and defeat was staring the All-Ireland champions in the face.

Then John Power, after receiving a defence-splitting pass from D. J. Carey came down as he headed into the Offaly goal area. He was awarded a penalty, which Carey netted and a minute later the same player pointed a long-range free and Kilkenny were through to the Provincial semi-final by 0-14 to 2-10.

Controversy raged over the awarding of the penalty by referee

Pat Delaney (Offaly) as it was claimed that not alone did Power carry the ball more than the number of steps allowed by the rules but that he came down as he was forcing his way through – rather than being blatantly brought down in the manner that would automatically merit a penalty.

Then too Offaly suffered a body-blow eight minutes from time when defender, Roy Mannion was sent off for a high tackle on Adrian Ronan. It did not appear to me from my seat in the Press Box in the Hogan Stand to be a malicious tackle. Ronan sportingly jumped up immediatley to clearly indicate that he was not injured. It was two minutes after the sending off that Kilkenny got their life-saving goal.

In fairness to Kilkenny, who fielded without Liam Simpson, it must be stressed that they kept their heads with time ebbing away and hurled with the controlled power and assurance of champions, the backs – particularly Pat O'Neill – making some great clearances under pressure.

But Offaly would have been in a winning position at the interval had not D. J. Carey scored one of the finest individualistic goals I have seen in Croke Park in recent years. Collecting a well-delivered pass by Liam McCarthy, he seemed initially to be well covered by two Offaly defenders but beat them for speed as he went through the gap and cutting right in close to the left-hand post he unleashed a bullet-like shot to the back of the net at the Hill 16 end.

Instead of leading by 0-10 to 0-5 at the break, Offaly had to be content with a two points lead (0-10 to 1-5) and they had reason to bemoan also the fact that a shot for goal by Gary Cahill in the ninth minute was brilliantly saved by Michael Walsh.

We saw some magnificent long-range points in that first half by Offaly midfielders, Michael Conneely and elegant sticksman Johnny Pilkington (between them they scored nine in all) but I could not understand why Offaly retained Rigney at full-forward for so long when he was making no headway on Pat Dwyer.

Offaly, to their credit, left their dismal League form far behind and manager Eamon Cregan came very close to guiding the Midland county to a famous victory over the All-Ireland champions.

When I reflect on some of the fine hurling Offaly produced in this enthralling contest in a veritable downpour – matching the innate class and beautiful touches of the Kilkenny men – I have no fear for the immediat future of the game in that county. Players like Johnny Pilkington could hold their own in any company.

Ultimately the difference between Kilkenny and Offaly on the day came down to the genius of one man – D. J. Carey – and his penchant for scoring the kind of killer goal that changes the course of a championship contest dramatically. His first-half effort was a gem of its kind and came at a time when Offaly were firmly in the driving seat and looking good.

Carey finished with a tally of 2-4, three of his points coming from frees.

He has unquestionably developed into one of the most effective match-winners of the current decade and into the bargain he is an outstanding sportsman.

※ ※ ※

Carey again left his imprint in no uncertain fashion on the replayed Leinster final against Wexford before a crowd of 41,833 on 18 July 1993.

Twenty-two minutes into the game with Wexford just one point behind, Carey scored his side's second goal with delightful timing when he connected on Eamonn Morrissey's long, diagonal centre close to the left hand post at the Canal end.

By the interval when Kilkenny led by 2-5 to 0-7 we knew it was all over and Carey finished with a tally of 1-5 (four points from frees) as the Noresiders coasted to the All-Ireland semi-final by 2-12 to 0-11.

Yet Wexford had reason to bemoan the might-have-beens, as they had dominated to a far greater extent in the drawn match. Before any score had been put on the scoreboard by either side in the replay, Eamonn Scallon missed a great chance of a goal when, on the edge of the square, he failed to generate any power into his shot and Michael Walsh saved at the expense of a "70". And even before the ball went over the line, Martin Storey running in might well have turned it into the net – but he missed out connecting with it.

Wexford captain, Tom Dempsey scored a point from the "70" but it was poor consolation as three minutes later, P. J. Delaney, a son of Pat Delaney, scored a great goal from close in, rounding off a move which began with a clearance form Liam Keoghan of Tullaroan and continued by John Power.

Power gave a devastating performance at centre-forward on no less a defender than Liam Dunne, who had lit the Croke Park scene with a superb display in the drawn game. Not since Pat Delaney was in his prime have I seen a player better able to take the straight line to goal with the ball on his stick than John Power and when he is on the burst like this, the opposing defence hits the emergency buttons.

But for a fine save by goalie Martin Fitzhenry just after half-time from a piledriver by Power, it would have been a worse result for Wexford, who did not help their cause either by shooting nine wides in the first half.

In the final analysis Wexford were outhurled by a Kilkenny combination that hit impressive form in all sectors, from mid-fielders Michael Phelan and Billy Hennessy to the quartet of Power-Carey-Morrissey-Delaney in attack with Adrian Ronan another thorn in the Wexford defence.

The fact that no goal was conceded proved the tight control of the full back line of Eddie O'Connor, the captain, Pat Dwyer and Liam Simpson and outside this trio Liam Keoghan, Pat O'Neill and Willie O'Connor played so consistently throughout that Wexford's attack just could not make the openings for the goals that would have made all the difference. And Wexford too, of course, were facing an outstanding goalie in Michael Walsh.

❋ ❋ ❋

Yes, the more you analyse the drawn Leinster final of '93 and the replay, the more you come to conclude that it was on Sunday, 11 July that Wexford let slip their chance of winning their first Provincial crown since 1977.

The only consolation they had was they were part with Kilkenny of one of the finest games of hurling I have seen at Croke Park. It was a match so engrossing for the attendance of 37,715 that it must stand assuredly as an advertisement for all that makes hurling the finest field game in the world. And this one was played at such a pace by two sides at the very peak of fitness that new vistas were opened up as to what can be achieved in the "modern game". Gaelic football, with its failure to properly define the "tackle", had to take a back seat compared with it.

The bottom line, as far as Wexford supporters were concerned, was that they were four points ahead with seven minutes to go. They had started with such fire and passion and such total com-mitment that they dominated Kilkenny for 25 minutes.

And but for two crucial incidents I am convinced they would have been in a winning position at the interval. First there was Michael Walsh's brilliant fourth minute parry of a shot from Billy Byrne at the Canal end and, secondly, there was the goal by

Eamonn Morrissey just before half-time that saw Wexford go in leading 0-10 to 1-3 instead of 0-10 to 0-3 – if not 1-10 (13) to 0-3 (assuming Billy Byrne's shot had found the net).

Early in the second half a kicked goal by Eamonn Morrissey helped put Kilkenny on the road to a 2-9 to 0-14 lead by the eighteenth minute. But Wexford were not done with. Larry Murphy levelled. Eamonn Scallan goaled and soon the lead was stretched to four points.

Two points from play by Eamonn Morrissey and a point from a free by D. J. Carey left a point between the sides.

Martin Storey, who had shown that he could be deadly in pointing with sideline pucks, got one under the Cusack Stand. This time he was wide and it meant that Michael Walsh had the puck-out (my own view was that Storey might have dropped that one in the square, though others, I know will disagree with me on the basis that what he had done more than once he coud assuredly do again).

Wexford, I am afraid, at the vital juncture failed to keep the ball in play in the Kilkenny half, failed to dictate the terms of the flow of the action in the Kilkenny defensive area.

The ball was cleared by Liam Simpson and the move was carried on by Adrian Ronan, who found Morrissey in space with a sweetly-timed pass and he picked off a fine equaliser. What a magnificent movement it was down the Cusack Stand side of the field.

Fourteen seconds remained from normal time. Wexford had come as close as that to victory.

All the magnificent work of Larry O'Gorman, Seán Flood and Liam Dunne had been for nought, also the efforts of John O'Connor and verteran George O'Connor and Ray Dempsey's accuracy from frees and seventies (he landed nine points in all, five from frees and two from seventies).

John O'Connor, who had been curbing Eamonn Morrissey well, should have been switched from corner-back when Morrissey went in full-forward, as Ger Cush could not cope with Morrissey's swerve. The situation was crying out for the kind of action that would nullify Morrissey's constant goal-scoring threat and he was to finish with a tally of 2-3.

Twelve months previously Morrissey had been one of the hottest properties in the game as a corner-forward but knew the ignominy of being taken off in the All-Ireland final when failing to master young prodigy Brian Corcoran. His form nose-dived further in the autumn and he was down with a kidney infection through the winter.

"You can take it I'm a hungry man this campaign," he told colleague Vincent Hogan.

Wexford were made suffer for the satisfying of that hunger.

Eddie O'Connor showed real leadership as he captained Kilkenny from the right corner back position despite an ankle that needed two pain-killing injections before the throw-in. "You wouldn't have thrown a marble between the Kilkenny backs at the end," said Martin Storey in a tribute to their tightness and tenacity in the dying moments.

⌘ ⌘ ⌘

"I don't know what kind of hurling we have to do to win something," said Wexford team manager Christy Keogh after the replay had been lost. "It becomes very frustrating and you can get tired of it all. We have played ten important matches in three months. If only we could get over that hurdle and win something . . . .".

"No prizes for second best," said John O'Connor. "Nobody could have begrudged us if we were League and Leinster champions – and yet we have nothing to show for all our efforts in three games against Cork and in two against Kilkenny."

Martin Storey concurred. "It's awful hard to keep coming back," he sighed. "I mean we have nothing, absolutely nothing to show for all that has gone into training since January. Kilkenny are still the Leinster champions. We're nothing. We're just memories."

And yet, ironically, they were part of an epic three-match series with Cork to decide the destination of League honours and part of the best of the summer wine, a chateau wine of rare vintage in the drawn Leinster final against Kilkenny.

They hurled heroically and with flair in their finest moments. But the inherent weaknesses that dog Wexford hurling today, especially the lack of sure-fire craft and goal-scoring power in attack, killed their hopes of winning meaningful honours.

What would they not give for a D. J. Carey.

CHAPTER 11

KILKENNY'S 25th TITLE AND SECOND IN A ROW

WHO are those guys out there? The immortal line from *Butch Cassidy and the Sundance Kid* springs to mind as I sit at my typewriter and reflect on the relentless late surge that carried Kilkenny to victory over Galway (2-17 to 1-15) in the 1993 All-Ireland final and won for the Noreside county its 25th crown.

In making it two All-Irelands back-to-back the wearers of the Black and Amber withstood a gallant and courageous Galway challenge, the goal that finally clinched it being scored three minutes from the end by 20-years-old student P. J. Delaney, a son of the great Pat Delaney of Johnstown, who won four All-Ireland medals in the period 1969-'75.

Fighting back from a disastrous start that saw them fall 1-5 to 0-3 behind after fifteen minutes, Galway not alone levelled the scores but actually edged a point ahead entering the final quarter.

The 63,460 spectators were enthralled by a magnificent contest of great intensity played out in true sporting spirit. We left Croke Park saying to ourselves that there is no game like hurling after all for non-stop action and thrills and happy that a match of such splendour was being carried by satellite television to a global audience.

An All-Ireland can swing on one missed chance or one stray pass. And this was the case with the 1993 final.

Galway had reason to bemoan the might-have-beens, especially the great opportunity of a goal let slip by Liam Burke at the Cnal end when he had only Michael Walsh to beat – and the sides were level – and his rather weak effort was easily saved by the Kilkenny goalie.

Then later when Galway were just one point in arrears and Croke Park had become a seething cauldron of tension and excitement, Joe Cooney missed a relatively easy free. With time ticking away and coming up to three minutes from full-time, Galway are attacking again. Joe Cooney in possession is tackled and delivers a clever pass to a colleague inside midfield under the Hogan Stand – but a great groan arises from the Galway supporters all around the ground when the ball does not come to hand but rolls over the sideline.

137

The sideline puck is collected by Adrian Ronan and his drive soared in to the right of the Galway posts at the Railway end. It was read expertly by P. J. Delaney who was on the turn when the ball fell to the ground. He rounded Seán Treacy and Murt Killilea and struck it perfectly to the net past goalkeeper Richie Burke. The champions finished with a flourish to add further points by Delaney and D. J. Carey to which Galway's only reply was a point by Michael McGrath. The All-Ireland final of '93 was won and lost with that Delaney goal for Kilkenny.

Eddie O'Connor, the Kilkenny captain, said to me on the Monday in the Burlington Hotel that if Liam Burke had goaled in the moment of balance in the second half, the reigning champions would have found it extremely difficult to retain their title. Why? They had done their finest hurling in an opening spell of wonderfully-controlled skilful play that had Galway on the rack and heading, it appeared, for a real drubbing. My own view was that Kilkenny were not going to be beaten in a tit-for-tat exchange of points in the climactic stages.

Overall their forward-line was far more potent than Galway's and displayed much more craft. Galway badly needed a goal in that second half to crack Kilkenny's composure – the kind of composure that had seen them snatch a late, late victory over Offaly and grab a draw from a raging hot fire the first day against Wexford.

Kilkenny, I believe, would have gone on for a decisive victory from the platform of their brilliant opening spell but for Lady Fortune stepping in to provide Galway with a very lucky goal right out of the blue and completely against the run of the play.

A harmless-looking ball hit by Liam Burke from fifty yards range was fumbled by Michael Walsh, the normally so-cool and reliable Kilkenny goalie and Galway were suddenly right back in the game, with the scoreboard now reading 1-5 to 1-3 in Galway's favour.

It was an exact replica – and at the same Hill 16 end – of the soft goal conceded by Ken Hogan in the All-Ireland semi-final but whereas it killed Tipperary's chance of victory, it didn't set Kilkenny back quite so dramatically. They still led by 1-8 to 1-6 at half-time and Walsh, let it be said, made ample amends in the second half, making a thrilling full-length dive to stop Liam Burke goaling and later when Burke had his golden chance, he failed to generate the necessary power into his shot and Walsh turned the ball out for a '70.

It can be argued perhaps that Galway failed to get one break in the shape of a goal when they most needed it during their second-half rally but at All-Ireland level you must make your own breaks. Beforehand, if one was asked to bet on who would emerge as the Kilkenny match-winners in attack, the money would almost certainly have gone on D. J. Carey, John Power and Eamonn Morrissey. Yet, amazingly, this trio, who had been the kingpins on the way to the final, mustered only four points between them from play while P. J. Delaney, Adrian Ronan and Liam McCarthy compiled a tally of 2-9.

This in itself reveals the real difference between the Kilkenny and Galway attacks. Ultimately, Kilkenny did not have to depend on any three players. Others emerged from the sextet on the day to convert the opportunities they had into the goals and points that retained the crown for the Noresiders.

In the final analysis, Galway were looking to big Joe Rabbitte to become the wrecker of the Kilkenny defence. Well as he performed on the day, he didn't have around him wing forwards or corner forwards who could pounce on the half-chance as Eanna Ryan or Noel Lane could in the heyday of the 1987-'90 team and thus the chances went abegging in the second half in particular that could have brought Galway a dramatic victory, considering that the Liam McCarthy Cup appeared totally beyond their grasp during Kilkenny's opening twenty-minute phase of complete dominance.

D. J. Carey suffered damaged ribs very early in the game and it obviously affected his performance, though he wouldn't advance it as an excuse when I talked to him next day. He simply noted that he had been fortunate enough to get goals when they were needed in earlier matches in the Championship campaign — "and you cannot expect that things will go just as you would like them every day".

But still all the same he was in like a flash at the post at one stage in the first half, being just thwarted of a goal by the so-alert Gerry McInerney as the ball hit the side netting. Remembered will be the beautiful long-range angled free he scored from under the Hogan Stand in the 62nd minute that brought Kilkenny level and a second one six minutes later from fully sixty yards that put the Noresiders ahead after Padraic Kelly had balanced his first effort when raising the white flag from play from 65 yards out.

John Power didn't take the Galway half-back line apart as some diehard Kilkenny supporters expected he would. Gerry McInerney, so brilliant in the pivotal position against Tipperary, had another fine game. However, it was a duel between the two well worthy of the occasion. Power with his strength and driving play prevented McInerney from storming through in the exhilarating runs that have become his hall-mark. The honours of the day, however, rested with McInerney for curbing the Kilkenny centre-forward.

One of the great strengths of this Kilkenny side and the one that makes them so difficult to beat – as Wexford learned to their cost in '93 – is the all-round brilliance and balance of the defence.

Pat O'Neill was once again a towering figure at centre-back though my own "Man of the Match" for the Noresiders was left corner-back Liam Simpson, so good when Galway made their big bid in the second half and whose clearances have the length to give immediate relief when the pressure is greatest.

Pat Dwyer, who had been so doubtful beforehand because of a serious groin injury and who had even made a much-publicised trip to Old Trafford, did enough at full-back to fully merit the gamble Ollie Walsh and fellow-selectors took in playing him. But then Dwyer is a "hurling" full-back in the fullest sense of the term, ideal for the modern game which can cruelly expose the stopper. Liam Simpson is the same – a hurler through and through. So this duo along with captain Eddie O'Connor, a human dynamo and a born leader, formed a last line of defence that was a rock-solid foundation for the defensive screen as a unit.

Outside them Pat O'Neill had two flankers in Liam Keoghan and Willie O'Connor, who gave nothing away easily. Kilkenny did not face in '93 an attack with the kind of penetration required to get the goals that would have upset their composure.

Bill Hennessy, a beautiful mover on the ball, said afterwards that "it must have been one of the greatest games I was ever involved in", it was so fast and full of exciting incidents. His midfield partner, Michael Phelan, while not putting it down as an excuse, said he got a dig in the stomach that knocked the stuffing out of him in the second half. The Kilkenny pair have known greater days but still it is a measure of the way the side combines as a unit from defence, through midfield to an attack with so much talent that you are not inclined to notice if the opposition are momentarily on top in the centre.

Hard to believe that the forward line ended up shooting fifteen wides and still put 2-17 on the scoreboard.

As with the Tipperary 1964-'65 attack, you cannot predict in advance who will hit the target with greater accuracy on the day – and nip in for the killer goals.

Adrian Ronan had been a brilliant member of the minor team, along side D. J. Carey, that won the 1988 All-Ireland title. A serious groin injury forced him out of action for a year. He came on as a sub in the 1991 All-Ireland final against Tipperary and again in the 1992 decider against Cork. It seemed that the golden peaks of his under-age career would never be attained in senior ranks.

Now in 1993 with two All-Ireland medals already won as a sub, he was in the team from the outset and finally came good. After ten minutes P. J. Delaney collected a good clearance out of defence by Pat O'Neill. His searing shot was saved by Richie Burke, who pushed it out to the right – but unfortunately for him right into the path of Adrian Ronan with the cover missing. Ronan had no difficulty in slotting the first Kilkenny goal from close range. He would finish with 1-2.

Liam McCarthy, the most under-rated member of the Kilkenny attack before the All-Ireland final, caused a lot of problems for the Galway defence, especially in the first half and scored three points. Eamonn Morrissey had his moments but did not make the kind of shattering impact he had made in the Leinster Championships two years running and, as in the '92 final, was again substituted. But he could say philosophically afterwards that it was "one of the finest games I was involved in in my whole life", adding: "The way we used the ball during most of the first half was top class. It was thrown around all over the park. Liam McCarthy's point was a good example of that. I think it was John Power who flicked the ball out to him. Galway didn't know where they were. The ball was over the bar before they knew anything about it. It is hard to know how good this team is. It has achieved something big by putting two All-Ireland titles back-to-back."

Yes, Kilkenny were unquestionably the better hurling team on the day and no Galway supporter could crib with that. Paddy Downey summed it up well in one cryptic sentence in his *Irish Times* report when he said: "Kilkenny's performance seemed to encapsulate all of the skill of all of the Kilkenny teams of the century." He was referring especially to the splendour of their opening spell of hurling to delight the heart of every purist in the stadium.

Galway had their heroes, none more so than left wing back Padraic Kelly, who after a very shaky start on Liam Walsh, went on to emerge as the shining star of the second half and no matter who Kilkenny tried on him during those thirty-five minutes they could not curb him. Deservedly he was voted the "Man of the Match" by the consensus view of hurling followers.

Tom Helebert hurled well on the right flank and Pat Malone, rated a very doubtful starter on the eve of the match, had an outstanding game at midfield.

I would fault the Galway selectors badly for persisting so long with Brendan Keogh at right wing forward, when he was clearly not suited to the position and made little or no impresison. Justin Campbell did much better when he came on as a sub in the second half. At least he is a natural forward. Liam Burke is not a natural attacker – so Galway were carrying up front two players in Keogh and Burke who when contrasted with their opposite numbers in the Kilkenny forward line, just did not come into the same category.

Joe Cooney played his heart out, especially when he moved to midfield and was right in the van of the Galway rally that carried them a point ahead of the champions. But it has to be said that the edge of speed is gone and he was relying very much on experience and know-how in the climactic stages of an energy-sapping contest.

Surely the Galway selectors might have introduced Anthony Cunningham into the attack in the second half. I mean he had the experience of five All-Irelands behind him and surely he could have contributed something of note at the moment of balance. Why have him on the subs' bench if there was no intention of using him?

✖ ✖ ✖

Tipperary started off in the All-Ireland semi-final as if Galway would suffer the same fate as Clare. They looked well in command of the proceedings and were moving along unruffled by a Galway side that seemed unable to find any rhythm. Then it happened. Michael McGrath mishit a strike at goal from 45 yards. It was deflected off the stick of Ramie Ryan and spun wickedly at Ken Hogan. The keeper did not get his body behind the ball and it skipped from his hurley to the net.

Soon Galway were leading by 1-6 to 0-4 and, with the wind at their backs, had increased this to 1-9 to 0-5 by the interval.

In retrospect the leg injury that initially forced Declan Ryan to move from centre-forward to corner forward and then to leave the field had a major effect on Tipperary's effort overall. It meant that Gerry McInerney turned in a *tour de force* at centre-back with no one able to keep him in check, not even Nicky English when he moved out on him.

Inexplicably, when replacing Declan Ryan with Pat Fox, the Tipperary selectors brought in Conor Stakelum at the same time for Colm Bonnar. The duel substitution had all the signs of a panic move when there was no need for desperate measures of that extent.

Then in the 10th minute of the second half worse was to befall Tipperary. Ramie Ryan clashed with team-mate Paul Delaney. The game was held up for six minutes as the medics properly took great care of Ryan who was stretchered off. Michael O'Meara, who came on as a sub, played very well and contributed to a Tipperary rally that brought the Munster champions to within three points (1-10 to 0-10) of Galway.

Galway in an inspired move switched Joe Rabbitte to centre-forward and Joe Cooney to the left corner. Rabbitte won a great deal of possession and sought Cooney each time. He held the ball, moved it around the line and kept the Tipperary defence at full stretch.

Going forward Tipperary just could not overcome the inspired play of Gerry McInerney, who over the seventy minutes had faced Declan Ryan (before he went off), Nicky English, John Leahy and Anthony Crosse.

Padraic Kelly had a wonderful All-Ireland semi-final debut while Paul Cooney, Seán Treacy and Murt Killilea formed a barrier in the last line of defence that frustrated Tipperary's best efforts to get the winning scores. It was into injury time when Pat Fox raised the green flag after goalkeeper Richie Burke had parried Aidan Ryan's effort. It was too late and Galway triumphed by 1-16 to 1-14.

"Controlled aggression" was the new phrase that entered the vocabulary of hurling men after this day. That was the way the Galway mentors described their hard-hitting approach to the task on hand and it certainly caught completely off guard a Tipperary side that had it far too soft against the Banner County. Some of the "controlled aggression", I must admit, wasn't in keeping with the canons of true sportsmanship but then Tipperary players of earlier decades would not have crumbled as meekly in face of it as some of the wearers of the Blue and Gold jerseys did on this August afternoon.

The biggest mistake of all made by the Tipperary selectors was to start Bobby Ryan instead of Michael O'Meara. Obviously they were influenced in their decision by the fact that he had not been playing well for his club, Toomevara, but he had done nothing wrong against Cork in the National League semi-final in Semple

Stadium. It was a far bigger risk to play Bobby Ryan when it was generally accepted by those who know the game that he can no longer go the pace at centre-back at this level of inter-county competition, though no one would ever question the Borris-Ileigh man's undying spirit or commitment to the colours. It back-fired badly and it is a decision that the Tipperary selectors had every cause to regret.

Be that as it may, it was probably all immaterial in the end. I have no doubt in my mind that if Tipperary had beaten Galway, they would have fallen to Kilkenny.

Tipperary wanted Kilkenny and Kilkenny wanted Tipperary just as badly in the All-Ireland final. It promised to be the mother of all battles between great trditional rivals.

Kilkenny felt that they had a score to settle since the 1991 All-Ireland final when they lost it because they did not believe enough in themselves, and failed to put Tipperary away when they had them going in the first half. They didn't make the same mistake against Cork in '92.

The maturity that was missing in '91 was there through the '93 campaign — and the belief to back it.

Kilkenny had contested three All-Irelands in a row and could so easily have been completing the three-timer on the first Sunday in September '93.

No one will cavil with my assertion that they had proved themselves beyond any doubt the finest hurling team in the land — and *hurling* is the operative word. A team for the connoisseurs like a wine of classic vintage.

An outstanding team, yes. As I finish this chapter in late September '93 the question uppermost in my mind is: Can this side go on now to even greater things and will 1994 see them achieve what both the 1972-'75 side and the 1982-'83 team failed to achieve . . . the completion of three-in-a-row?

And one final thought — its "Babs" Keating and Tipperary they would like in the 1994 All-Ireland final — assuming they get that far and Tipperary win out in Munster.

Then '91 could be avenged and they would have answered every question.

RECORDS SECTION

HURLING AND FOOTBALL RECORDS (1887-1993)

EDITED
by
RAYMOND SMITH

RAYMOND SMITH

with

DONAL KEENAN   MICK DUNNE

(**NOTE:** Raymond Smith, as Editor, oversaw the immense task by the editorial team of compiling the records of results and teams. Donal Keenan played a vital role in co-ordinating this effort for the 1988 edition. Mick Dunne brought to the 1993 revised edition his superb reference library and has contributed immensely not alone to bringing the records up to date for the past five years but also making very important changes. He deserves special thanks for his invaluable contribution.)

They helped authenticate the records . . .

JIM CRONIN   JOHN CLARKE   TOM RYALL

GAA historians, Jim Cronin, Cork; John Clarke, Tullamore; and Tom Ryall, Kilkenny; author of the highly-acclaimed 420-page book *Kilkenny: The GAA Story 1884-1984*, were key figures in laying the groundwork for ensuring that the 1988 edition was the most comprehensive Records Book of its kind produced up to that time. Now for the 1993 edition they worked for months with Mick Dunne checking and cross-checking the records of results and teams going back to the early days of the Association. A new authenticity has been achieved that must mean that this Handbook will replace all previous publications as THE authoritative reference work for GAA followers and media representatives.

Three others made notable contributions, namely Seamus J. King, Cashel, author of the 727-page *Tipperary's GAA Story* (he came in with special assistance from his own research to correct teams from pre-1900 days in particular) while Jack Mahon, Galway, was extremely helpful on Connacht records and in supplying up-dated Vocational Schools records. The late Seamus Ó Ceallaigh, Limerick,

SEAMUS J. KING   SEAMUS O'CEALLAIGH   JACK MAHON
                          R.I.P.

LIAM MULVIHILL

DANNY LYNCH

*. . . full support from GAA Headquarters for the concept
of a Handbook of Gaelic Games.*

—continued from page 146

such a prolific writer in his day, had provided revised sets of the Railway Cup teams in hurling and football for the 1988 edition before his death and also the Captains.

We acknowledge also the valued input of sports writers Cliona Foley and Noel Fallon in important areas of the records (Colleges, Universities, Army and Garda), while Sheila Wallace, Camogie Officer at GAA Headquarters in Croke Park, ensured that the Camogie records were fully up-dated.

Seamus O'Doherty, Roscrea, Co. Tipperary, was very co-operative in acquainting us of some players' names incorrectly spelt and of other errors in earlier record books and, as a result, important corrections have been made for the '93 edition.

We acknowledge again our deep dept of gratitude to Con Short, Ulster GAA; Michael Ó Ruairc, Tralee; Paddy Flanagan, Mullingar; Teddy Fennelly, *Leinster Express*; John O'Shaughnessy, *Limerick Leader*; Rev. Seamus Gardiner of the Munster Council GAA. Their efforts for the '88 edition have been carried forward to the new up-dated edition.

We acknowledge also the overall assistance of GAA Head-quarters, Provincial Council officers and various County Board officials and PROs and GAA writers and recognised historians and others. The need for an authentic set of records was recognised from the moment work commenced on the 1988 edition of *The Complete Handbook of Gaelic Games* (now out of print) and the very for-midable task of revision and up-dating has been continued on into this expanded '93 edition. The result is that where at one stage there was no proper set of records, the GAA now has its own "Wisden" – a reference work that meets essential demands.

Finally, we thank Liam Mulvihill, Director General of the GAA, and Danny Lynch, Press Officer of the Association, for their recogni-tion of the need for ensuring that the Association has an authoritative up-dated Handbook and for giving their full support to the editorial team.

G.A.A. HURLING RECORDS

RESULTS AND TEAMS

ALL-IRELAND CHAMPIONSHIPS 1887 – 1993

The distribution of Championship Honours to date is as follows:

ROLL OF HONOUR

SENIOR HURLING

Cork (27)—1890, 1892, 1893, 1894, 1902, 1903, 1919, 1926, 1928, 1929, 1931, 1941, 1942, 1943, 1944, 1946, 1952, 1953, 1954, 1966, 1970, 1976, 1977, 1978, 1984, 1986, 1990.

Kilkenny (25)—1904, 1905, 1907, 1909, 1911, 1912, 1913, 1922, 1932, 1933, 1935, 1939, 1947, 1957, 1963, 1967, 1969, 1972, 1974, 1975, 1979, 1982, 1983, 1992, 1993.

Tipperary (24)—1887, 1895, 1896, 1898, 1899, 1900, 1906, 1908, 1916, 1925, 1930, 1937, 1945, 1949, 1950, 1951, 1958, 1961, 1962, 1964, 1965, 1971, 1989, 1991.

Limerick (7)—1897, 1918, 1921, 1934, 1936, 1940, 1973.

Dublin (6)—1889, 1917, 1920, 1924, 1927, 1938.

Wexford (5)—1910, 1955, 1956, 1960, 1968.

Galway (4)—1923, 1980, 1987, 1988.

Waterford (2)—1948, 1959.

Offaly (2)—1981, 1985.

Clare (1)—1914.

Kerry (1)—1891.

Laois (1)—1915.

London (1)—1901 (Home champions: Cork).

MINOR HURLING

Kilkenny (16)—1931, 1935, 1936, 1950, 1960, 1961, 1962, 1972, 1973, 1975, 1977, 1981, 1988, 1990, 1991, 1993.

Cork (15)—1928, 1937, 1938, 1939, 1941, 1951, 1964, 1967, 1969, 1970, 1971, 1974, 1978, 1979, 1985.

Tipperary (15)—1930, 1932, 1933, 1934, 1947, 1949, 1952, 1953, 1955, 1956, 1957, 1959, 1976, 1980, 1982.

Dublin (4)—1945, 1946, 1954, 1965.

Wexford (3)—1963, 1966, 1968.

Limerick (3)—1940, 1958, 1984.

Offaly (3)—1986, 1987, 1989.

Waterford (2)—1929, 1948.

Galway (2)—1983, 1992.

(Note: Suspended 1942-'44 inclusive)

UNDER—21 HURLING

Cork (9)—1966, 1968, 1969, 1970, 1971, 1973, 1976, 1982, 1988.
Tipperary (7)—1964, 1967, 1979, 1980, 1981, 1985, 1989.
Galway (6)—1972, 1978, 1983, 1986, 1991, 1993.
Kilkenny (5)—1974, 1975, 1977, 1984, 1990.
Wexford (1)—1965.
Limerick (1)—1987.
Waterford (1)—1992.

JUNIOR HURLING

Cork (10)—1912, 1916, 1925, 1940, 1947, 1950, 1955, 1958, 1983, 1987.
Tipperary (9)—1913, 1915, 1924, 1926, 1930, 1933, 1953, 1989, 1991.
Kilkenny (8)—1928, 1946, 1951, 1956, 1984, 1986, 1988, 1990.
London (5)—1938, 1949, 1959, 1960, 1963.
Limerick (4)—1935, 1941, 1954, 1957.
Dublin (3)—1932, 1937, 1952.
Meath (3)—1927, 1948, 1970.
Warwickshire (3)—1968, 1969, 1973.
Wexford (2)—1985, 1992.

Offaly (2)—1923, 1929.	*Mayo* (2)—1980, 1981.
Kerry (2)—1961, 1972	*Louth* (2)—1976, 1977.
Waterford (2)—1931, 1934.	**Derry (2)—1975, 1982.**
Kildare (2)—1962, 1966.	*Clare* (2)—1914, 1993.
Roscommon (2)—1965, 1974.	*Down* (1)—1964.
Wicklow (2)—1967, 1971	*Galway* (1)—1939
Armagh (2)—1978, 1979	*Westmeath* (1)—1936.

[Note: Discontinued after 1973 in original format and run in conjunction with National League Division 3 as new-style Junior Championship. Limited number of counties competed. Original format restored 1983. No competition 1917-'22 and 1942-'45.].

INTERMEDIATE HURLING

Tipperary (4)—1963, 1966, 1971, 1972.

Wexford (2)—1961, 1964.	*Kildare* (1)—1969.
London (2)—1967, 1968.	*Antrim* (1)—1970.
Carlow (1)—1962.	*Kilkenny* (1)—1973.
Cork (1)—1965.	[Note: Discontinued after 1973].

SENIOR HURLING CHAMPIONSHIP

1887—Birr, April 1, 1888 (21 aside). *Tipperary* (Thurles), 1-1 Galway (Meelick), nil. Actual score — Tipperary, 1 goal 1 point and 1 forfeit point.

1888—Unfinished owing to U.S.A. Invasion by G.A.A. Athletes

1889—Inchicore, November 3, 1889. *Dublin* (Kickhams), 5-1; Clare (Tulla), 1-6.
1890—Clonturk, November 16, 1890. *Cork* (Aghabullogue) 1-6; Wexford (Castlebridge), 2-2. Unfinished, Cork awarded match.
1891—Clonturk, February 28, 1892. *Kerry* (Ballyduff), 2-3; Wexford (Crossbeg), 1-5. An extra half hour was played.
1892—Clonturk, March 26, 1893. *Cork* (Redmonds), 2-4; Dublin (Flag-Davitts), 1-1. Unfinished; Dublin withdrew after 50 minutes' play.
1893—Phoenix Park, June 24, 1894. *Cork* (Blackrock), 6-8; Kilkenny (Confederation), 0-2.
1894—Clonturk, March 24, 1895. *Cork* (Blackrock), 5-20; Dublin (Rapparees), 2-0.
1895—Jones's Road, March 15, 1896. *Tipperary* (Tubberadora), 6-8; Kilkenny (Tullaroan), 1-0.
1896—Jones's Road, March 27, 1898. *Tipperary* (Tubberadora), 8-14; Dublin (Commercials), 0-4.
1897—Tipperary, November 20, 1898. *Limerick* (Kilfinane), 3-4; Kilkenny (Tullaroan), 2-4.
1898—Jones's Road, March 25, 1900. *Tipperary* (Tubberadora), 7-13; Kilkenny (Threecastles), 3-10.
1899—Jones's Road, March 24, 1901. *Tipperary* (Moycarkey), 3-12; Wexford (Blackwater), 1-4.
1900—Jones's Road, October 26, 1902 . *Tipperary* (Two-Mile-Borris), 2-5; London (Desmonds), 0-6.
Home Final – Terenure, September 21, 1902. TIpperary, 6-3; Galway (Ardrahan), 1-5.
1901—Jones's Road, August 2, 1903. *London* (Selection), 1-5; Cork (Redmonds), 0-4.
Home Final—Carrick-on-Suir, June 14, 1903. Cork, 2-8! Wexford (Blackwater), 0-6.
1902—Cork, September 11, 1904. *Cork* (Dungourney), 3-13; London (Brian Boru), nil.
Home Final—Tipperary, July 17, 1904. Cork, 2-6; Dublin (Faughs), 0-1. On July 3 these teams drew at Tipperary, 1-7 each.
1903—Jones's Road, November 12, 1905. *Cork* (Blackrock), 3-16; London (Hibernians), 1-1.
Home Final—Dungarvan, July 16, 1905. Cork, 8-9; Kilkenny (Threecastles), 0-8.
1904—Carrick-on-Suir, June 24, 1906. *Kilkenny* (Tullaroan),

1-9; Cork (St. Finbar's), 1-8.

1905—Dungarvan, June 30, 1907. Replay: *Kilkenny* (Erin's Own), 7-7; Cork (St. Finbar's), 2-9. In a disputed match in Tipperary on April 14, 1907, the score was Cork, 5-10; Kilkenny, 3-13.

1906—Kilkenny, October 27, 1907. *Tipperary* (Thurles), 3-16; Dublin (Faughs), 3-8.

1907—Dungarvan, June 21, 1908. *Kilkenny* (Mooncoin), 3-12; Cork (Dungourney), 4-8.

1908—Athy, June 27, 1909. *Tipperary* (Thurles), 3-15; Dublin (Kickhams), 1-5. On April 25, at Jones's Road, they drew: Tipperary, 2-5; Dublin, 1-8.

1909—Cork, December 12, 1909. *Kilkenny* (Mooncoin), 4-6; Tipperary (Thurles), 0-12.

1910—Jones's Road, November 20, 1910. *Wexford* (Castlebridge), 7-0; Limerick (Castleconnell), 6-2.

1911—*Kilkenny.* Limerick, Munster champions, refused to replay the final match (not played at Cork) in Thurles on April 21st, 1912. In a substitute contest, played on July 28 at Dungarvan, Kilkenny beat Tipperary (nominated by Munster Council) by 3-3 to 2-1, and were awarded the championship.

1912—Jones' Road, November 17, 1912. *Kilkenny* (Tullaroan), 2-1; Cork (Blackrock), 1-3.

1913—Jones' Road, November 2, 1913. (15 aside). *Kilkenny* (Mooncoin), 2-4; Tipperary (Toomevara), 1-2.

1914—Croke Park, October 18, 1914. *Clare* (Quin), 5-1; Laois (Kilcotton), 1-0.

1915—Croke Park, October 24, 1915. *Laois* (Ballygeehan), 6-2; Cork (Redmonds), 4-1.

1916—Croke Park, January 21, 1917. *Tipperary* (Boherlahan), 5-4; Kilkenny (Tullaroan), 3-2.

1917—Croke Park, October 28, 1917. *Dublin* (Collegians), 5-4; Tipperary (Boherlahan), 4-2.

1918—Croke Park, January 26, 1919. *Limerick* (Newcastle West), 9-5; Wexford (Selection), 1-3.

1919—Croke Park, September 21, 1919. *Cork* (Selection), 6-4; Dublin (Collegians), 2-4.

1920—Croke Park, May 14, 1922. *Dublin* (Faughs), 4-9; Cork (Selection), 4-3.

1921—Croke Park, March 4, 1923. *Limerick*, 8-5; Dublin (Faughs), 3-2.

1922—Croke Park, September 9, 1923. *Kilkenny,* 4-2;
Tipperary, 2-6.
1923—Croke Park, April 27, 1924. Limerick, 7-4; Donegal, 0-1.
Croke Park, May 18. Galway, 5-4; Kilkenny, 2-0.
Croke Park, September 14. Final: *Galway,* 7-3; Limerick,
4-5.
1924—Croke Park, November 9. Dublin, 8-4; Antrim, 3-1.
Croke Park, November 23. Galway, 3-1; Tipperary, 2-3.
Croke Park, December 14. Final: *Dublin,* 5-3; Galway,
2-6.
1925—Croke Park, August 9. Semi-final: Galway, 9-4;
Kilkenny, 6-0.
Croke Park, September 6. Final: *Tipperary,* 5-6; Galway,
1-5.
1926—Croke Park, August 29. Semi-final: Kilkenny, 6-2;
Galway, 5-1.
Croke Park, October 24. Final: *Cork,* 4-6; Kilkenny, 2-0.
1927—Thurles, August 21. Semi-final: Cork, 5-6; Galway, 0-2.
Croke Park, September 4. Final: *Dublin,* 4-8; Cork, 1-3.
1928—Kilkenny, August 26. Semi-final: Cork, 5-3; Dublin, 0-2.
Croke Park, September 9. Final: *Cork,* 6-12; Galway, 1-0.
1929—Birr, August 11. Semi-final: Galway, 7-7; Kilkenny, 7-1.
Croke Park, September 1. Final: *Cork,* 4-9; Galway, 1-3.
1930—Birr, August 17. Semi-final: Tipperary, 6-8; Galway, 2-2.
Croke Park, September 7. Final: *Tipperary,* 2-7; Dublin,
1-3.
1931—Croke Park, August 16. Semi-final: Kilkenny, 7-2;
Galway, 3-1.
Croke Park, September 6. Final: Cork, 1-6; Kilkenny, 1-6.
October 11. Replay: Cork, 2-5; Kilkenny, 2-5.
November 1. Replay: *Cork,* 5-8; Kilkenny, 3-4.
1932—Limerick, August 14, Semi-final: Clare, 9-4; Galway, 4-14.
Croke Park, September 4, Final: *Kilkenny,* 3-3; Clare,
2-3.
1933—Birr, August 13. Semi-final: Kilkenny, 5-10; Galway, 3-8.
Croke Park, September 3. Final: *Kilkenny,* 1-7; Limerick,
0-6.
1934—Roscrea, August 5, Semi-final: Limerick, 4-4; Galway,
2-4.
Croke Park, September 2. Final: *Limerick,* 2-7; Dublin,
3-4.

THE GOAT

Dublin's Sporting Pub

A tribute to the great achievements of Ireland's
sporting stars throughout the 1980s

In a series of Fine Hand-crafted Sculptures
by Paul Ferriter
(unveiled in September 1990)

Hurling's Standard-bearer is NICHOLAS ENGLISH

Football's Standard-bearer is JACK O'SHEA

THE DECADE OF EXCELLENCE

THE GOAT: Dublin's Sporting Pub

THE ANVIL: Restaurant

THE TANEY ROOM: Weddings and Functions

Proprietor: Charlie Chawke

Croke Park, September 30. Replay: *Limerick,* 5-2; Dublin, 2-6.

1935—Birr, August 4. Semi-final: Kilkenny, 6-10; Galway, 1.8. Croke Park, September 1. Final: *Kilkenny,* 2-5; Limerick, 2-4.

1936—Roscrea, August 16. Semi-final: Limerick, 4-9; Galway, 2-4. (Match Unfinished). Croke Park, September 6. Final: *Limerick,* 5-6; Kilkenny, 1-5.

1937—Birr, August 8. Semi-final: Kilkenny, 0-8; Galway, 0-6. Killarney, September 5. Final: *Tipperary,* 3-11; Kilkenny, 0-3.

1938—Ennis, August 7. Semi-final: Waterford, 4-8; Galway, 3-1. Croke Park, September 4. Final: *Dublin,* 2-5; Waterford, 1-6.

1939—Roscrea, August 6. Semi-final: Kilkenny, 1-16; Galway, 3-1. Croke Park, September 3. Final: *Kilkenny,* 2-7; Cork, 3-3.

1940—Ennis, August 11. Semi-final: Limerick, 3-6; Galway, 0-5. Croke Park, September 1. Final: *Limerick,* 3-7, Kilkenny, 1-7.

1941—Roscrea, September 14, Semi-final: Dublin, 2-4; Galway, 2-2.

Croke Park, September 28. Final: *Cork,* 5-11; Dublin, 0-6.

1942—Limerick, July 26. Semi-final: Cork, 6-8; Galway, 2-4.

Croke Park, September 6. Final: *Cork,* 2-14; Dublin, 3-4.

1943—Corrigan Park, Belfast, August 1. Semi-final: Antrim, 3-3; Kilkenny, 1-6. Croke Park, September 5. Final: *Cork,* 5-16; Antrim, 0-4.

1944—Ennis, August 13. Semi-final: Cork, 1-10; Galway, 3-3. Belfast, August 13. Semi-final: Dublin, 6-12; Antrim, 3-1. Croke Park, September 3. Final: *Cork,* 2-13; Dublin, 1-2.

1945—Birr, July 29. Semi-final: Kilkenny, 5-3; Galway, 2-11. Croke Park, August 5. Semi-final: Tipperary, 5-9; Antrim, 1-6. Croke Park, September 2. Final: *Tipperary,* 5-6; Kilkenny, 3-6.

1946—Birr, July 28. Semi-final: Cork, 2-10; Galway, 0-3. Croke Park, August 4. Semi-final: Kilkenny, 7-11; Antrim, 0-7. Croke Park, September 1. Final: *Cork,* 7-5; Kilkenny, 3-8.

1947—Birr, July 27. Semi-final: Kilkenny, 2-9; Galway, 1-11.
Croke Park, August 3. Semi-final: Cork, 7-10; Antrim.
0-5.

Croke Park, September 7. Final: *Kilkenny, 0-14; Cork,*
2-7.
1948—Croke Park, August 1. Semi-final: Dublin 8-13; Antrim,
2-6.
Croke Park, August, 15. Semi-final: Waterford, 3-7;
Galway, 1-6.
Croke Park, September 5. Final: *Waterford, 6-7;* Dublin,
4-2.
1949—Croke Park, July 31. Semi-final: Tipperary, 6-18;
Antrim, 1-4.
Croke Park, August 7. Semi-final: Laois, 4-6; Galway,
3-5.
Croke Park, September 4. Final: *Tipperary,* 3-11; Laois,
0-3.
1950—Tuam, August 13. Semi-final: Tipperary, 4-7; Galway,
2-6.
Croke Park, September 3. Final: *Tipperary,* 1-9;
Kilkenny, 1-8.
1951—Croke Park, July 29. Semi-final: Wexford, 3-11; Galway,
2-9.
Croke Park, September 2. Final: *Tipperary,* 7-7;
Wexford, 3-9.
1952—Limerick, July 27. Semi-final: Cork, 1-5; Galway, 0-6.
Croke Park, September 7. Final: *Cork,* 2-14; Dublin, 0-7.
1953—Croke Park, August 16. Semi-final: Galway, 3-5;
Kilkenny, 1-10.
Croke Park, September 6. Final: *Cork,* 3-3; Galway, 0-8.
1954—Croke Park, August 8, Semi-finals: Wexford, 12-17
Antrim, 2-3. Cork, 4-13; Galway, 2-1.
Croke Park, September 5. Final: *Cork,* 1-9; Wexford, 1-6.
1955—Croke Park, August 7. Semi-final: Wexford, 2-12;
Limerick, 2-3.
Croke Park, September 4. Final: *Wexford,* 3-13; Galway,
2-8.
1956—Croke Park, July 29. Semi-final: Wexford, 5-13; Galway,
1-8.
Croke Park, September 23. Final: *Wexford,* 2-14; Cork,
2-8.
1957—Croke Park, July 28. Semi-final: Waterford, 4-12;

156

Galway, 0-11.
Croke Park, September 1. Final: *Kilkenny,* **4-10;**
Waterford, 3-12.

1958—Croke Park, August 10. Semi-final: Tipperary, 1-13,
Kilkenny; 1-8.
Croke Park, September 7. Final: *Tipperary,* 4-9; Galway,
2-5.

1959—Croke Park, September 6. Final: Waterford, 1-17;
Kilkenny, 5-5.
Croke Park, October 4. Replay: *Waterford,* 3-12;
Kilkenny, 1-10.

1960—Croke Park, September 4. Final: *Wexford,* 2-15;
Tipperary, 0-11.

1961—Croke Park, September 3. Final: *Tipperary,* 0-16;
Dublin, 1-12.

1962—Croke Park, September 2. Final: *Tipperary,* 3-10;
Wexford, 2-11.

1963—Croke Park, September 1. Final: *Kilkenny,* 4-17;
Waterford, 6-8.

1964—Croke Park, September 6. Final: *Tipperary,* 5-13;
Kilkenny, 2-8.

1965—Croke Park, September 5. Final: *Tipperary,* 2-16;
Wexford, 0-10.

1966—Croke Park, September 4. Final: *Cork,* 3-9; *Kilkenny,*
1-10.

1967—Croke Park, September 3. Final: *Kilkenny,* 3-8;
Tipperary, 2-7.

1968—Croke Park, September 1. Final: *Wexford* 5-8, *Tipperary,*
3-12.

1969—Croke Park, August 17. Semi-final: *Kilkenny,* 3-22;
London, 1-10.
Croke Park, September 7. Final: *Kilkenny,* 2-15; Cork
2-9.

1970—Limerick, August 16. Semi-final: *Cork,* 4-20; *London,* 2-9.
Athlone, August 16. Semi-final: *Wexford,* 3-17; *Galway,*
5-9.
Croke Park, September 6. Final: *Cork,* 6-21; *Wexford,*
5-10.

(Note: First 80-minute Final).

1971—Croke Park, August 15. Semi-final: *Kilkenny,* 2-23;
London, 2-8.
Birr, August 15. Semi-final: *Tipperary,* 3-26; *Galway,* 6-8.
Croke Park, September 5. Final: *Tipperary,* 5-17; *Kil-*
kenny, 5-14.

157

1972—Croke Park, August 6. Semi-final: Kilkenny, 5-28; Galway, 3-7.

Cork, August 6. Semi-final: Cork, 7-20; London, 1-12.

Croke Park, September 3. Final: Kilkenny, 3-24; Cork 5-11.

1973—Ennis, August 5. Semi-final: Limerick, 1-15; London, 0-7.

Croke Park, September 2. Final: Limerick, 1-21; Kilkenny, 1-14.

1974—Birr, August 4. Semi-final: Kilkenny, 2-32; Galway, 3-17.

Croke Park, September 1. Final: Kilkenny, 3-19, Limerick, 1-13.

1975—Croke Park, August 17. Semi-final: Galway, 4-15 (27); Cork, 2-19 (25).

Croke Park, September 7. Final: Kilkenny, 2-22; Galway, 2-10.

[Note: The 70-minute Final was introduced in 1975]

1976—Pairc Uí Chaoimh, August 22. Semi-final: Wexford, 3-14; Galway, 2-14 (replay)

Pairc Uí Chaoimh, August 15. Semi-final: Wexford, 5-14; Galway 2-23 (Draw).

Croke Park, September 5. Final: Cork, 2-21 (27); Wexford, 4-11 (23).

1977—Croke Park, August 7. Semi-final: Cork, 3-14 (23); Galway, 1-15 (18).

Croke Park, September 4. Final: Cork, 1-17 (20); Wexford, 3-8 (17).

1978—Croke Park, August 6. Semi-final: Kilkenny, 4-20; Galway, 4-13.

Croke Park, September 3. Final: Cork, 1-15; Kilkenny, 2-8.

1979—Croke Park, August 5. Semi-final: Galway, 2-14; Cork, 1-13.

Croke Park, September 2. Final: Kilkenny, 2-12; Galway, 1-8.

1980—Croke Park, August 3. Semi-final: Galway 4-9 (21); Offaly, 3-10 (19).

Croke Park, September 7. Final: Galway, 2-15 (21); Limerick, 3-9 (18).

1981—Croke Park, August 2. Semi-final: Galway, 1-8; Limerick 0-11 (Draw). August 16. Galway 4-16; Limerick, 2-17 (Replay).

Croke Park, September 6. Final: Offaly, 2-12; Galway, 0-15.

1982—Croke Park, August 8. Semi-final: Kilkenny, 2-20; Galway, 2-10.

Croke Park, September 5. Final: Kilkenny, 3-18; Cork, 1-13.

158

1983—Croke Park, August 7. Semi-final: Cork, 5-14; Galway 1-16.

Croke Park, September 4. Final: Kilkenny, 2-14; Cork, 2-12.

1984—Thurles, August 5. Semi-final: Offaly, 4-15; Galway 1-10.

Croke Park, August 5. Semi-final: Cork, 3-26; Antrim 2-5.

Thurles, September 2. Final: Cork, 3-16; Offaly, 1-12.

1985—Croke Park, August 4. Semi-final: Galway, 4-12; Cork, 5-5.

Armagh, August 4. Semi-final: Offaly, 3-17; Antrim, 0-12.

Croke Park, September 1. Final: Offaly, 2-11; Galway, 1-12.

1986—Thurles, August 10. Semi-final: Galway, 4-12; Kilkenny 0-13.

Croke Park, August 10. Semi-final: Cork, 7-11; Antrim, 1-24.

Croke Park, September 7. Final: Cork, 4-13; Galway 2-15.

1987—Croke Park, August 9. Semi-final: Galway, 3-20; Tipperary, 2-17.

Dundalk, August 16. Semi-final. Kilkenny, 2-18; Antrim, 2-11.

Croke Park, September 6. Final: Galway, 1-12; Kilkenny, 0-9.

1988—Croke Park, August 7. Semi-final: Tipperary 3-15; Antrim 2-10.

Croke Park, August 7. Semi-final: Galway 3-18; Offaly 3-11.

Croke Park, September 4. Final: Galway 1-15; Tipperary 0-14.

1989—Croke Park, August 6. Semi-final: Antrim 4-15, Offaly 1-15.

Croke Park, August 6. Semi-final: Tipperary 1-17, Galway 2-11.

Croke Park, September 3. Final: Tipperary 4-24, Antrim 3-9.

1990—Croke Park, August 5. Semi-final: Cork 2-20, Antrim 1-13.

Croke Park, August 5. Semi-final: Galway 1-16, Offaly 2-7.

Croke Park, September 2. Final: Cork 5-15, Galway 2-21.

1991—Croke Park, August 4. Semi-final: Tipperary 3-13, Galway 1-9.
Croke Park, August 4. Semi-final: Kilkenny 2-18, Antrim 1-19.
Croke Park, September 1. Final: Tipperary 1-16, Kilkenny 0-15.
1992—Croke Park, August 9. Semi-final: Cork 2-17, Down 1-11.
Croke Park, August 9. Semi-final: Kilkenny 2-13, Galway 1-12.
Croke Park, September 6. Final: Kilkenny 3-10, Cork 1-12.
1993—Croke Park, August 8. Semi-final: Galway 1-16, Tipperary 1-14.
Croke Park, August 8. Semi-final: Kilkenny 4-18, Antrim 1-9.
Croke Park, September 5. Final: Kilkenny 2-17, Galway 1-15.

Comhairle na Mumhan CLG

Le Gach Dea-Mhéin

do

The Complete Handbook of Gaelic Games

Dónal Ó Niallain (Rúnaí

ALL-IRELAND FINALISTS

AUTHOR'S NOTE:— Despite checking with a number of sources, allowances must still be made for possible errors in early teams, as records are not reliable from these times. It must be noted too that teams were not given in line-out order until the thirties.

1887

Tipperary—J. Stapleton (capt.), M. Maher, T. Maher, A. Maher, T. Burke, Martin McNamara, Ed. Murphy, Jer. Dwyer, Tom Stapleton, Ned Bowe, Tom Healy, Dan Ryan, Jer. Ryan, Pat Leahy, Tim Dwyer, Jack Mockler, Jack Dunne, Tom Carroll, John Leahy, M. Carroll, P. Lambe.

Galway—Patk. Larkin, John Mannion, Owen Griffin, John Saunders, Thos Foley, Ml. Conway, Ml. Kelly, John Mannion, Darby Mannion, Pat Haverty, James Haverty, Martin Griffin, Owen Griffin, John Cosgrave, A. Cosgrave, Ml. Culleen, Thos. Hanly, P. Madden, Ml. Kelly, Ml. Mannion, John Mannion. Non-playing Captain: Jas. Lynam.

1888

No final played owing to visit of a team of hurlers and athletes to the U.S.A.

1889

Dublin—N. O'Shea (capt.), Frank Coughlan, P. Butler, John Lambe, Dan Kerwick, J. D. O'Byrne, Thos. McKenna, W. J. Spain, James Harper, Chas. Hackett, Thos. Maher, J. Bishop, T. Belton, Patk. Ryan, J. Cahill, Ed. Gilligan, F. Palmer, S. Riordan, Patk. O'Shea, Patk. Riordan, Ml. Madigan.

Clare—Thos. Coughlan, D. McKenna, Daniel McNamara, John McNamara, D. Quigley, Daniel Moroney, M. O'Dea, Wm. Moroney, Ml. Corry, Ed. Corry, Patk. O'Neill, T. O'Connell, Ml. Flynn, P. Vaughan, John McKenna, Martin Russell, Patk. McGrath, T. Donnellan, J. Moloney, J. King, M. Kinnery. Non-playing Captain: John Considine.

1890

Cork—Dan Lane (capt.), J. Henchion, John Buckley, D. Lenihan, Dan Looney, Dan Drew, Tim O'Connor, Tom Twomey,

161

M. Horgan, Pat Buckley, J. Reilly, Tim Kelleher, John Kelleher,
P. O'Riordan, Dan O'Sullivan, Tom Good, D. Horgan, John
Lenihan, Jer O'Sullivan, E. Reilly, Pad O'Riordan.

Wexford—Nick Daly (capt.), E. Leary, L. Leacy, T.
Devereaux, O. Daly, J. Murphy, W. Neville, J. Murphy, P.
McDonald, J. Rossiter, W. Furlong, J. O'Leary, W. Doran, G.
Sinnott, P. Furlong, P. Devereaux, W. Fortune, J. Browne, M.
Browne, J. Fogarty, W. O'Leary.

1891

Kerry—J. Mahony (capt.), M. Kelly, J. Pierce, P. Carroll, M.
Wynne, M. J. O'Sulivan, R. Kissane, F. Crowley, J. Crowley, J.
O'Sullivan, T. Dunne, J. Murphy, M. Fitzmaurice, J. McDonnell,
T. D. McCarthy, T. E. McCarthy, M. Riordan, P. Quane, J.
Quane, P. Rourke, P. Kirby.

Wexford—N. Daly (capt.), J. Leary, E. Leary, L. Lacy, M.
Lacy, James Murphy, John Murphy, T. Murphy, N. Murphy, M.
Browne, G. Browne, P. Quirke, P. Byrne, M. Kirwan, M.
Redmond, P. Harpur, N. Maher, O. Daly, P. McDonnell, T.
Devereaux, M. Harpur.

1892

(Teams reduced to 17 a side)

Cork—W. O'Callaghan (capt.), J. Kenneally, M Casserly,
J. Keegan, J. Leahy, M. Sheehan, C. O'Callaghan, D. Halloran,
T. Irwin, J. Conway, J. O'Connor, W. O'Connor, D. Scannell,
J. Cashman, D. Coughlan, D. Drew, P. Buckley.

Dublin—P. Egan (capt.), A. Carroll, J. Dooley, A. Maher,
T. Meagher, C. Kennedy, W. Hinton, J. Kavanagh, T. Belton, R.
Stakelum, M. Kennedy, E. Gilligan, J. Ryan, P. Whelan, D.
Murphy, N. Murphy, D. Healy.

1893

Cork—John Murphy (capt.), Jer. Norbeg, D. Scannell, Ml.
Murphy, D. Hayes, P. Coughlan, Jas. Young, S. Hegarty, Ml.
Cronin, Patk. O'Keeffe, J. Cullinane, John O'Leary, Jas. Delea,
M. O'Connor, John Cashman, W. J. O'Connell, Patk. Flaherty.

Kilkenny—D. Whelan (capt.), J. Delany, J. Grace, J. Lalor,
P. Maher, E. Teehan, J. Walsh, M. Coogan, M. Berry, M.
Morrissey, J. McCarthy, R. Grace, J. King, J. Doheny, P.
Brennan, J. De Loughrey, P. Malone.

1894

Cork—S. Hayes (capt.), D. Hayes, P. Coughlan, J. O'Leary, M. Murphy, J. Cashman, J. Kidney, J. Delea, M. Cronin, D. Coughlan, J. Kelleher, J. Norberg, S. Hegarty, J. Cullinane, J. O'Connor, J. Young, W. O'Connell.

Dublin—John McCabe (capt.), John Greene, M. Brady, L. Byrne, M. Connor, J. Lawler, L. Lawler, Dan Gillis, S. Donovan, J. Quigley, D. Cregan, Ed. McCabe, P. Kelly,, N. Harding, P. O'Toole, P. Lawlor, J. O'Mullane.

1895

Tipperary—M. Maher (capt.), E. Maher, Phil Byrne, W. Kerwick, John Maher, D. Walsh, John Walsh, Peter Maher, T. Flanagan, Jas. Flanagan,. P. Riordan, Jas. Gleeson, Fergus Moriarty, John Connolly, J. Maher, E. Brennan, W. Devane.

Kilkenny—M. Dalton (capt.), P. Maher, J. Lalor, E. Teehan, E. Dunne, P. Egan, P. Ryan, M. Coogan, M. Meagher, J. Walsh, W. Walsh, J. Dunne, P. Malone, J. Grace, J. Doheny, T. Grace, J. Doheny.

1896

Tipperary—M. Maher (capt.), J. Maher (F), P. Byrne, W. Devane, M. Wall, E. Maher, E. Brennan, J. Walsh, T. Condon, J. Connolly, J. Flanagan, T. Ryan, P. Scanlon, T. Flanagan, E. Ryan, P. Doherty, D. Walsh.

Dublin—P. Buckley (capt.), W. Carroll, P. Egan, J. Hill, D. Ryan, J. O'Dwyer, J. Donohue, M. Hackett, E. Hackett, J. Delany, Joseph Ryan, D. Ryan, Jerry Ryan, John Eviston, T. O'Dwyer, P. Purcell, W. O'Connell.

1897

Limerick—D. Grimes (capt.), J. ("Sean Oge") Hanly, M. Flynn, P. Flynn, M. Finn, P. O'Brien, T. Brazill, J. Condon, J. Catterall, J. Hynes, P. Butler, J. Flood, P. Mulcahy, M. Downes, J. Reidy, John Finn, P. Buskin.

Kilkenny—J. Walsh (capt.), J. Doheny, P. Maher, M. Dalton, E. Teehan, M. Lawlor, John Lawlor, James Lawlor, John Grace, M. Malone, J. Walsh, M. Merry, J. Quinn, P. Fielding, P. Ryan, E. Dunne, P. Malone.

1898

Tipperary—M. Maher (capt.), E. Maher, E. Brennan, J.

163

Walsh, J. Connolly, T. Ryan, W. Devane, E. Ryan, P. Byrne, W. Dunne, T. Condon, J. O'Keeffe, J. Maher (M.), D. Walsh, J. Maher (F.), Dick O'Keeffe.

Kilkenny—E. Hennessy (capt.), J. Ryan, John Lawlor, M. Dalton, T. Murphy, P. Maher, T. Grace, Jer. Doheny, P. Malone, M. Malone, P. Young, E. Teehan, Jas. Lawlor (2), John Quinn, Martin Lawlor, Jas. Quinn.

1899

Tipperary—T. Condon (capt.), Joe O'Keeffe, "Big Bill" Gleeson, J. Gleeson, R. O'Keeffe, Jas. O'Keeffe, D. Walsh, M. Maher, J. Walsh, J. Flanagan, J. Ryan, M. Wall, W. Dunne, P. Byrne, J. Maher, "Little Bill" Gleeson, T. Ryan.

Wexford—Jas. Furlong (capt.), J. Corrigan, T. Byrne, John Shiel, Martin Murphy, T. Cullen, A. Dempsey, Wal. Dempsey, M. Byrne, M. Brien, D. Whelan (snr.), D. Whelan (jnr.), J. Shiel (jnr.), M. Coughlan, A. Delaney, M. Murphy, Jack Shiel.

1900

Tipperary—E. Hayes, (capt.), P. Hayes, M. Ryan, M. Purcell, T. Allen, P. Maher, W. Maher, M. Maher, J. Walsh, T. Ryan, E. Maher, "Big Bill" Gleeson, "Little Bill" Gleeson, J. O'Keeffe, M. Wall, T. Semple, Jack Gleeson.

London—Dan Horgan (capt.), M. Horgan, Jer. Connell, J. Lynch, Jer. Healy, Tim Doody, James Hanly, James Grimes, D. Roche, John Coughlan, James Keogh, M. L. McMahon, John O'Brien, Patrick McNamara, Denis McNamara, John Leary, Michael Cotter.

Home Final. *Tipperary*—E. Hayes (capt.), P. Hayes, M. Ryan, M. Purcell, T. Allen, W. Maher, J. Walsh, T. Ryan, E. Maher, W. Gleeson (2), M. Wall, J. O'Keeffe, P. Maher, J. Gleeson, T. Semple, M. Maher.

Galway—J. Mitchel (capt.), M. Keighery, J. Coy, M. Cunningham, M. Stankard, J. Sylver, M. Holland, T. Leary, T. Connors, P. Taylor, M. Leary, T. Larkin, P. Burke, J. Larkin, W. Fallon, J. Quinn, D. Farrell.

1901

London—J. Coughlan (capt.), P. King, J. King, P. Crowe, J. Fitzgerald, J. O'Brien, T. Barry, Jas. Barry, Jer. Connell, D. Horgan, M. Horgan, Seamus Lynch, Tim Doody, M. McMahon, E. Barrett, Jer. Kelleher, J. Crowley.

Cork—P. Cantillon (capt.), J. Ronayne, J. Leonard, D. McGrath, J. Kelleher, J. Hallinan, J. O'Neill, D. O'Keeffe, T.

Powell, W. O'Reilly, J. Barrett, W. Sheehan, P. Sullivan, J.
O'Leary, D. Daly, C. Young, J. Delea.

Home Final. Cork—P. Cantillon (capt.), J. Delea, D.
McGrath, T. Irwin, J. Leonard, D. O'Keeffe, T. Powell, J.
Kelleher, J. Ronayne, J. O'Neill, T. Hallinan, C. Young, P.
Sullivan, J. O'Leary, D. Daly, W. Sheehan, M. O'Reilly.

Wexford—J. Furlong (capt.), J. Corrigan, J. Murphy, M.
O'Brien, Ml. O'Brien, M. Cummins, T. Dempsey, Con Dempsey,
S. Donohue, T. Byrne, M. Byrne, P. Rath, O. Synnott, D.
Crean, B. Murphy, J. Shiel, T. Cullen.

1902

Cork—J. Kelleher (capt.), J. Ronayne, J. Desmond, J. O'Shea, W.
Daly, J. Daly, T. Mahony, T. Lynch, J. Leahy, T. Coughlan, W.
Moloney, C. Young, W. Parfrey, P. Cantillon, D. McGrath, D.
O'Keeffe, W. O'Neill.

London—J. Nestor, J. Herbert, M. McMahon, J. Burke, T. Doody,
P. Flanagan, T. Barry, J. Barry, T. Ryan, C. Sugrue, J. O'Leary, T.
Donohue, T. Cummins, E. Barrett, P. Mehigan, J. Crowley, P.
Clancy.

Home Final Replay, Cork—J. Kelleher (capt.), J. Ronayne, J. Des-
mond, J. O'Shea, W. Daly, J. Daly, T. Mahony, M. O'Shea, J. Leahy,
T. Coughlan, D. Coughlan, S. Riordan, W. Parfey, W. Fitzgibbon, D.
McGrath, D. O'Keeffe, W. O'Neill.

Note: W. Moloney, C. Young, T. Lynch and P. Cantillon played in
drawn game instead of M. O'Shea, D. Coughlan, S. Riordan and W.
Fitzgibbon.

Dublin—D. McCormack (capt.), J. O'Brien, J. Cleary, P. Mahony,
A. Harty, M. Callaghan, J. Callaghan, J. Conway, C. Dillon, W. P.
Allen, J. Quinlan, P. Flynn, J. Kennedy, J. Grace, W. Connolly, J.
Delaney, T. Gleeson, P. Purcell.

Note: P. Mulcahy, J. Gleeson and W. Scanlon played for Dublin in
the drawn game instaed of P. Mahony, P. Flynn and J. Delaney.

Dublin—D. McCormack (capt.), J. O'Brien, J. Cleary, W.
Scanlon, A. Harty, M. Callaghan, J. Callaghan, J. Conway, C.
Dillon, W. P. Allen, J. Quinlan, P. Mulcahy, J. Kennedy, J.
Grace, W. Connolly, J. Gleeson, T. Gleeson, P. Purcell.

1903

Cork—S. Riordan (capt.), T. Coughlan, J. Coughlan, D.
Kidney, L. Flaherty, J. Kelleher, J. Desmond, J. O'Leary, W.
Mackessy, A. Buckley, D. Buckley, W. Hennessy, W. O'Neill,

165

P. O'Sullivan, M. O'Leary, D. O'Keeffe, D. McGrath.

London—P. King (capt.), J. Nestor, C. Sugrue, W. Power, D. Roche, P. J. Crotty, J. Kelleher, D. Horgan, J. O'Brien, J. Barry, M. J. O'Halloran, Sean Og Hanly, P. McMahon, J. Bleech, J. O'Farrell, T. Doody, M. Larkin.

Home Final: Cork—Same as above, except J. Leary in place of J. Coughlan.

Kilkenny—M. Dalton (capt.), Jas Lalor, T. Murphy, M. Shortall, D. Grace. P. Maher, J. Doheny, S. Walton, J. Hoyne, P. Saunders, J. Kerwick, J. Fielding, P. Fielding, E. Doyle, J. Synnott, J. Quinn, J. Rochford.

1904

Kilkenny—J. Doheny (capt.), P. Maher, S. Walton, J. Hoyne, P. Saunders, J. Lawlor, R. Doyle, E. Doyle, P. Fielding. R. Walsh, J. Rochford, D. Grace, R. Brennan, D. Stapleton, P. Lanigan, J. Anthony, M. Lawlor. Sub: Jim Dunne.

Cork—D. Harrington (capt.), J. Harrington, D. Sheehan, M. O'Leary, D. Linehan, W. Moloney, P. O'Sullivan, J. Kelly, J. Kelleher, W. Hennessy, J. Desmond, J. Ronayne, T. Coughlan, S. Riordan, D. O'Keeffe, D. McGrath, W. Sheehan.

1905

Kilkenny—D. J. Stapleton (capt.), J. Hoyne, T. Kenny, D. Kennedy, J. Anthony, J. J. Brennan, R. Walsh, J. Glennon, M. Gargan, S. Walton, J. Kelly, P. Lanigan, E. Doyle, J. Lawlor, R. Doyle, J. Rochford, M. Lawlor. Sub.: T. Murphy.

Cork—Jas. Kelleher (capt.), W. Hennessy, J. Ronayne, W. Mackessy, A. Buckley, D. McGrath, M. O'Leary, J. A. Beckett, W. Moloney, John Kelly, D. O'Leary, Chris Nolan, J. Harrington, D. McCarthy, P. O'Sullivan, W. O'Neill, "Sonny" Jim McCarthy. Sub.: C. Young.

Note: The above teams took part in disputed final on 14/4/1907. The following teams contested the refixed final on 30/6/1907:

Kilkenny—D. J. Stapleton (capt.), J. Hoyne, T. Kenny, D. Kennedy, J. Anthony, J. J. Brennan, R. Walsh, E. Teehan, Dan Grace, S. Walton, J. Kelly, P. Lanigan, E. Doyle, M. Lawlor, J. Lawlor, R. Doyle, J. Rochford.

Cork—J. Kelleher, W. Hennessy, J. Ronayne, W. Mackessy, A. Buckley, D. McGrath, M. O'Leary, J. A. Beckett, W. Moloney, C. Young (capt.), John Kelly, D. O'Leary, Chris Nolan, P. D. Mehigan, ("Carbery"), D. Linehan, P. Leahy, W. O'Neill.

1906

Tipperary—Tom Semple (capt.), J. Hayes, J. O'Brien, P. Burke, M. O'Brien, T. Kerwick, P. Brolan, H. Shelley, J. Mockler, T. Kenna, P. Riordan, T. Allen, P. Maher, J. Burke, J. Gleeson, J. O'Keeffe, T. Gleeson.

Dublin—D. McCormack (capt.), A. C. Harty, P. Hogan, J. Cleary, J. O'Riordan, M. Murphy, J. Quinlan, J. O'Dwyer, P. Kennedy, W. Leonard, W. Murphy, T. Warner, B. O'Brien, M. O'Callaghan, J. Grace, M. Quinn, W. O'Callaghan.

1907

Kilkenny—R. "Drug" Walsh (capt.), R. Doyle, M. Doyle, E. Doyle, R. Doherty, J. Kelly, T. Kenny, M. Gargan, D. Stapleton, D. Kennedy, J. Keoghan, J. Rochford, D. Grace, P. Lanigan, J. Power, J. Anthony, S. Walton.

Cork—Jim Kelleher (capt.), J. Roynane, J. Desmond, W. Hennessy, T. Mahony, P. Leahy, J. O'Shea, P. Lynch, A. Buckley, J. Kelleher, T. Coughlan, S. Riordan, W. Parfrey, W. Kidney, D. O'Keeffe, J. A. Beckett, W. O'Neill.

1908

Tipperary—Tom Semple (capt.), T. Kerwick, J. Mockler, J O'Brien, H. Shelley, A. Carew, J. Mooney, T. Kenna, P. Burke, P. Brolan, J. Moloughney, J. Burke, T. Gleeson, M. O'Dwyer, J. Fitzgerald, P. Fitzgerald, Martin O'Brien.

Note: Jack Gleeson, Joe O'Keeffe, Bob Mockler and William Herns played in drawn game for Tipperary. Michael O'Dwyer, John Fitzgerald, Pat Fitzgerald and Jimmy Burke came on for replay.

Dublin—J. Grace, A. Fitzgerald, D. McCormack, W. Connolly, W. O'Callaghan, W. Leonard, R. O'Brien, J. O'Brien, J. Callaghan, D. Kelleher, P. Grace, J. Lynch, M. Quinn, T. Quane, J. McDonald, D. Doyle, J. Nolan. Sub.—P. Neville.

1909

Kilkenny—R. "Drug" Walsh (capt.), E. Doyle, M. Doyle, R. Doherty, J. Kelly, W. Henebery, J. Delahunty, J. Dunphy, D. Kennedy, J. Keoghan, S. Walton, J. Rochford, M. Gargan, M. Shortall, J. Ryan, P. Lanigan, R. Doyle, Sub.: R. Grace.

Tipperary—Tom Semple (capt.), J. O'Brien, T. Kerwick, P. P. Burke, J. Fitzgerald, J. Mockler, J. Moloughney, A. Carew, M. O'Brien, P. Fitzgerald, J. Mooney, R. Mockler, H. Shelly, T. Gleeson, J. Burke, P. Brolan, J. Hackett. Sub.: E. Hayes.

167

1910

Wexford—R. Doyle (capt.), R. Fortune, M. Cummins, P. Mackey, M. Parker, J. Mythen, A. Kehoe, J. Shortall, J. Kennedy, S. Donohue, P. Roche, D. Kavanagh, J. Fortune, W. McHugh, P. Corcoran, M. Neville, W. Devereux.

Limerick—J. Mackey (capt.), J. Burke, M. Mangan, M. Fehilly, T. Mangan, C. Scanlon, M. Harrington, Egan Clancy, E. Treacy, T. O'Brien, T. Hayes, J. Madden, P. Flaherty, M. Danagher, J. Carroll, D. Conway, M. Sweeney.

1911

No Final: *Kilkenny* awarded walk-over from Limerick. The Kilkenny team that played Tipperary in lieu of Final was the same team as played in 1912, so effectively comprised the 1911 All-Ireland champion side.

1912

Kilkenny—S. Walton (capt.), J. T. Power, P. Grace, D. Kennedy, J. J. Brennan, P. Lanigan, J. Keoghan, R. Walsh, R. Grace, J. Rochford, E. Doyle, T. McCormack, R. Doyle, M. Doyle, M. Gargan, J. Kelly, R. Doherty.

Cork—A. Fitzgerald, D. Barry, P. Mahony, W. Mackessy, B. Murphy (capt.), M. Dorney, D. Kennefick, C. Sheehan, J. Murphy, M. Kidney, J. Kelleher, M. Byrne, J. Kennedy, W. Walsh, P. O'Brien, L. Flaherty, T. Nagle.

1913

(*Teams reduced to 15 aside*)

Kilkenny—R. "Drug" Walsh (cap.), J. Power, J. Keoghan, J. Rochford, J. Lennon, D. Kennedy, R. Grace, M. Gargan, J. J. Brennan, P. Grace, R. Doherty, R. Doyle, S. Walton, M. Doyle, J. Kelly.

Tipperary—P. "Wedger" Meagher (capt.), J. O'Meara, F. McGrath, S. Hackett, B. Mockler, J. Raleigh, T. Gleeson, J. Harty, E. Gilmartin, E. Cawley, P. Brolan, H. Shelley, J. Murphy, W. Kelly, E. O'Keeffe.

1914

Clare—A. Power (capt.), J. Power, M. Flanagan, E. Grace, T. McGrath, P. McInerney, J. Shalloo, W. Considine, B. Considine, M. Moloney, R. Doherty, J. Fox, J. Clancy, J. Guerin, J. Spellisey.

Laois—J. Carroll (capt.), R. O'Keeffe, J. S. Carroll, W. Lenihan, J. Jones, T. Hyland, R. Reilly, T. Higgins, P. Goulding, J. Daly, E. P. McEvoy, F. Killeen, T. Jones, J. Hiney, T. Finlay.

1915

Laois—J. Finlay (capt.), J. Walsh, T. Finlay, Jas. Carroll, John Carroll, Jos. Carroll, J. Daly, P. Campion, J. Phelan, J. Hiney, John Phelan, E. McEvoy, R. O'Keeffe, J. Dunphy, P. Ryan.

Cork—C. Sheehan (capt.), "Bowler" Walsh, L. Flaherty, W. Fitzgerald, Sean Hyde, J. Ramsell, M. Byrne, F. Buckley, J. Kennedy, T. O'Riordan, P. Halloran, T. Nagle, Sean Og Murphy, J. Murphy, B. Murphy.

1916

Tipperary—J. Leahy (capt.), T. Dwan, J. Doherty, W. Dwyer, T. Shanahan, J. Power, J. Fitzpatrick, J. Collison, P. Leahy, H. Shelly, J. Murphy, R. Walsh, D. Walsh, W. Dwyer, A. O'Donnell.

Kilkenny—S. Walton (capt.), J. Kerwick, J. Walsh, T. Hanrahan, J. Ryan, D. Kennedy, J. Holohan, R. Grace, J. Whelan, P. Clohosey, J. Byrne, W. Finn, R. Tobin, M. Kennedy, P. Walsh.

1917

Dublin—T. Daly, John Ryan (capt.), Sean Hyde, Sean O'Donovan, H. Burke, C. Stuart, J. Phelan, R. Mockler, T. Moore, J. Cleary, F. Burke, M. Neville, M. Hackett, M. Hayes, P. Kenefick. Sub.—B. Considine, came on shortly after start of match.

Tipperary—J. Leahy (capt.), J. Power, W. Dwyer, J. Nagle, P. Leahy, J. Doherty, R. Walsh,, W. Dwyer, H. Shelly, M. Leahy, T. Shanahan, S. Hackett, J. O'Meara, J. Collison, J. Fitzpatrick.

1918

Limerick—W. Hough (capt.), P. McInerney, D. Lanigan, R. McConkey, W. Gleeson, J. Keane, M. Rochford, D. Troy, T. McGrath, M. Murphy, P. Barry, W. Ryan, R. Ryan, J. Humpheries, P. Kennedy.

Wexford—M. Cummins (capt.), M. Stafford, C. Hyland, D. Kavanagh, P. Roche, L. Leary, J. Fortune, R. Walsh, N. Leary, J. Synnott, J. Fogarty, M. Neville, M. Murphy, P. Fagan, R. Lambert.

1919

Cork—J. Kennedy (capt.), E. Gray, J. O'Keeffe, S. Og Murphy, P. Aherne, C. Lucy, J. J. Hassett, T. Nagle, P. O'Halloran, M. Murphy, F. Kelleher, D. Ring, C. Sheehan, R. Gorman, J. B. Murphy.

Dublin—C. Stuart (capt.), R. Mockler, Sean Hyde, F. Burke, B. Considine, M. Murphy, M. Hayes, T. Moore, T. Daly, J. Ryan, J. Cleary, J. Phelan, M. Neville, T. Hayes, Dr. J. Ryan.

1920

Dublin—R. Mockler (capt.), M. Hayes, M. Neville, T. Moore, T. Hayes, Jas. Cleary, E. Tobin, R. Doherty, Jas. Walsh, T. Daly (goal), F. Burke, J. J. Callanan, Joseph Phelan, John Ryan, J. Clune.

Cork—R. O'Gorman (capt.), J. Kennedy, E. Gray, J. O'Keeffe, J. Hassett, C. Lucey, P. Halloran, P. ("Balty") Ahearne, Sean Og Murphy, E. Coughlan, M. Murphy, F. Kelleher, C. Sheehan, Denis Ring, Dan Ring.

1921

Limerick—R. McConkey (capt.), M. Murphy (goal), W. Gleeson, J. Humphreys, D. Lanigan, D. Murnane, W. Hough, J. Keane, W. Ryan, G. Howard, P. McInerney, T. Mangan, M. Mullane, C. Ryan, T. McGrath.

Dublin—R. Mockler (capt.), Martin Hayes, Tom Hayes, M. Neville, Tom Moore, Jas. Walsh, R. Doherty, P. Clune, F. Burke, J. J. Callanan, T. Daly (goal), E. Tobin, J. Darcy, J. Cleary, Jos. Bannon. Sub: J. Kennedy.

1922

Kilkenny — Walter Dunphy (capt.), Ed. Dunphy, M. McDonald (goal), John Holohan, Jas. Tobin, Thos. Carroll, Richard Grace, Wm. Kenny, Patk. Glendon, Pat Aylward, Martin Lawlor, John Roberts, Pat Donohoe, Matty Power, Richard Tobin.

Tipperary — J. Leahy, (capt.), J. Power, A. O'Donnell, P. Power, P. Browne, J. Cleary, M. Kennedy, S. Hackett, J. O'Meara, J. J. Hayes, P. Spillane, J. Fitzpatrick, T. Dwan, W. Dwan, J. Darcy.

1923

Galway—M. Kenny (capt.), J. Mahony (goal), M. Derivan, Ignatius Harney, J. Power, A. Kelly, B. Gibbs, E. Gilmartin, J. Morris, M. King, T. Fleming, R. Morrissey, L. McGrath, M. Gill, J. Garvey.

Limerick—P. McInerney (capt.), J. Hanley (goal), D. Murnane, W. Hough, D. Lanigan, W. Gleeson, Jas. Humphries, M. Neville, J. Kinnane, J. Keane, T. McGrath, M. Cross, R. McConkey, J. O'Grady, M. Fitzgibbons.

170

1924

Dublin—T. Daly (goal), Joe Bannon. W. Small, T. Kelly, M. Gill, Jas. Walsh, R. Mockler, P. Aylward, R. Doherty, M. Holland, D. O'Neill, G. Howard, Tom Barry, W. Banim, T. Finlay. Note: Frank Wall, non-playing captain.

Galway—M. Kenny (capt.), J. Mahony (goal), M. Derivan, Ignatius Harney, J. Power, A. Kelly, B. Gibbs, E. Gilmartin, J. Morris, M. King, T. Fleming, R. Morrissey, L. McGrath, J. Garvey, J. Keogh.

1925

Tipperary—Johnny Leahy (capt.), A. O'Donnell (goal), M. Mockler, M. D'Arcy, J. J. Hayes, M. Kennedy, S. Hackett, J. Power, P. Leahy, P. Cahill, T. Duffy, J. D'Arcy, W. Ryan, P. Power, P. O'Dwyer.

Galway—A. Kelly (capt.), J. Mahony (goal), J. Stanford, J. Fallon, M. Derivan, M. Broderick. P. J. Morrissey, I. Harney, Ml. King, P. O'Donnell, M. Connaire, M. Houlihan, Richard Morrissey, J. Shaughnessy, P. Rooney. Subs: T. Cogavin, T. O'Dea.

1926

Cork—Sean Og Murphy (capt.), J. Coughlan (goal), Mce. Murphy, E. O'Connell, D. B. Murphy, Ml. Murphy, J. O'Regan, J. Hurley, Eugene Coughlan, Wm. Higgins, P. Delea, J. Kearney, Matt Murphy, M. Ahearne, P. Ahearne.

Kilkenny—Richard Grace (capt.), R. Cantwell (goal), Wm. Meagher, P. O'Reilly, T. Carroll, E. Doyle, W. Barry, W. Dunphy, Martin Power, L. Meagher, J. Carroll, Martin Brennan, E. Dunphy, H. Meagher, J. Roberts.

1927

Dublin—M. Gill (capt.), P. McInerney, W. Phelan, E. Tobin, J. Gleeson, T. O'Rourke, G. Howard, M. Power, E. Fahy, T. Daly, T. Barry, J. Walsh, D. O'Neill, J. Bannon, M. Hayes.

Cork—Sean Og Murphy (capt.), E. O'Connell, D. B. Murphy, M. Murphy, J. Hurley, E. Coughlan, M. Leahy, P. Ahearne, M. Ahearne, P. Delea, J. O'Regan, P. Daly, Maurice Murphy, W. Higgins, J. Burke (goal).

171

● *Jack Sheedy (left), hero of Dublin's 1993 National League title triumph in action against Donegal.*

Comhairle na Laighean CLG

Le Gach Dea-Mhéin

do

The Complete Handbook of Gaelic Games

Micheál Ó Dubhsláine (Rúnaí

1928

Cork—Sean Og Murphy (capt.), E. O'Connell, J. Hurley, E. Coughlan, P. Ahearne, P. Delea, M. Ahearne, M. Leahy, M. Burke, M. Madden, D. B. Murphy, J. O'Regan, T. Barry, P. O'Grady, M. O'Connell.

Galway—J. Power (capt.), M. Derivan, I. Harney, J. Mahony, P. Green, R. McCann, J. Shaughnessy, R. Morrissey, P. Gilligan, M. Broderick, F. Kealy, M. Cunningham, W. Curran, M. King, T. Mullins. Sub.—J. Dealy.

1929

Cork—D. Barry Murphy (capt.), J. Burke (goal), M. Madden, P. Collins, T. Barry, J. O'Regan, M. O'Connell, J. Kenneally, M. Ahearne, P. Ahearne, P. Delea, J. Hurley, E. Coughlan, P. O'Grady, E. O'Connell. Subs.—D. McCarthy.

Galway—J. Mahony (goal), D. Clarke, T. Fleming, J. Shaughnessy, W. Keane, L. Geoghegan, F. Keely, M. Cunningham, Ignatius Harney, C. Cooney, P. Corcoran, J. Derivan, R. Morrissey, W. Derivan, J. Deely. Subs.—M. Broderick, T. Furey.

1930

Tipperary—J. J. Callanan (capt.), J. O'Loughlin, J. Maher, M. Ryan, J. Harney, J. Lanigan, T. O'Meara (goal), M. Kennedy, P. McKenna, P. Purcell, P. Cahill, M. F. Cronin, T. Butler, T. Leahy, T. Treacy. Sub.—J. Heeney.

Dublin—Jas. Walsh (capt.), John Dwyer (goal), T. O'Meara, E. Campion, M. Gill, C. Griffin, C. MacMahon, P. McInerney, M. Finn, T. Quinlan, T. Burke, Matt Power, E. Byrne, T. Teehan, J. Leeson. Subs.—H. Quirke, M. Daniels.

1931

Cork—J. Coughlan, M. Madden, E. O'Connell, P. "Fox" Collins, D. Barry Murphy, J. Regan, T. Barry, J. Hurley, M. O'Connell, E. Coughlan (capt.), M. Aherne, P. O'Grady, P. Delea, P. Aherne, W. Clancy.

The above team played in all three matches. George Garret (Blackrock) came on as a sub in the first and second replay.

Kilkenny—J. Dermody, P. Phelan, P. O'Reilly, D. Treacy, T. Carroll, P. Byrne, E. Doyle, E. Byrne, Tommy Leahy, J. Duggan,

J. Leahy, Matty Power, D. Dunne, M. Larkin, P. Walsh. Sub.—
Martin Murphy.

Lory Meagher (capt.), Paddy Larkin and Billy Dalton played in
the first and second games.

Martin White and Dick Morrissey played in the first game.

Jack Duggan came on as a sub in the first game for Dick Mor-
risssey. He played in second game. Paddy Walsh played in second
game. Tommy Leahy came on as a sub in second game for Lory
Meagher.

1932

Kilkenny—J. Dermody, P. Larkin, P. O'Reilly, J. Carroll, P.
Phelan, P. Byrne, E. Doyle, E. Byrne, L. Meagher, J. Walsh
(capt.), Mar. Power, Tom Leahy, D. Dunne, M. White, Mattie
Power.

Clare—Tom Daly, J. Higgins, P. McInerney, J. J. Doyle
(capt.), J. Houlihan, J. Hogan, L. Blake, J. Gleeson, T.
McInerney, M. Falvey, M. Connery, Michael O'Rourke, J.
Mullane, T. Burnell, T. Considine.

1933

Kilkenny—E. Doyle (capt.), John Dunne, J. Dermody (goal),
L. Meagher, P. Phelan, P. Larkin, M. White, P. O'Reilly, P.
Byrne, J. Walsh, J. Fitzpatrick, E. Byrne, T. Leahy, Martin
Power, Matty Power. Subs.—J. Duggan, J. O'Connell.

Limerick—M. Fitzgibbon (capt.), P. Scanlan (goal), T. Ryan,
J. Mackey, M. Mackey, M. Cross, T. McCarthy, P. Clohessy, D.
Clohessy, E. Cregan, M. Ryan, P. Ryan, J. Roche, G. Howard,
C. O'Brien. Sub.—W. O'Donoghue.

1934 REPLY

Limerick—T. Shinny (goal), E. Cregan, T. McCarthy, M.
Kennedy, M. Cross, P. Clohessy, G. Howard, T. Ryan (capt.), M.
Ryan, J. Mackey, M. Mackey, J. Roche, J. O'Connell, D.
Clohessy, J. Close.

Note: Paddy Scanlon and Bob McConkey played in drawn
game. Tom Shinny and Jackie O'Connell came on for replay. M.
Condon came on as sub. in drawn game.

Dublin—C. Forde (goal), A. Murphy, J. Bannon, T. Teehan,
J. Walsh, D. Caniffe, P. Roche, Ed. Wade, M. Daniels, S.

174

Hegarty, T. Treacy, S. Muldowney, S. Feeney (capt.), D. O'Neill, J O'Connell. Subs.—C. McMahon, J. Culleton.

C. Boland (capt.) played in drawn game S. Feeney (capt.) came on for replay F. McCormack and J. Culleton came on as subs in drawn game.

1935

Kilkenny—J. O'Connell (goal), P. Larkin, P. O'Reilly, P. Blanchfield, E. Byrne, P. Byrne, P. Phelan, L. Meagher (capt.), T. Leahy, J. Walsh, J. Duggan, M. White, J. Dunne, L. Byrne, Matty Power. Sub.—L. Duggan for J. Dunne; J. Dunne for Duggan.

Limerick— P. Scanlan (goal), E. Cregan, T. McCarthy, M. Kennedy, M. Cross, P. Clohessy, G. Howard, T. Ryan (capt.), M. Ryan, J. Mackey, M. Mackey, J. Roche, J. O'Connell, P. McMahon, J. Close.

1936

Limerick—P. Scanlan (goal), T. McCarthy, P. O'Carroll, M. Kennedy, M. Cross, P. Clohessy, G. Howard, T. Ryan, M. Ryan, J. Mackey, M. Mackey (capt.), J. Roche, D. Clohessy, P. McMahon, J. Power.

Kilkenny—J. O'Connell (goal), P. Larkin (capt.), P. O'Reilly, P. Blanchfield, P. Byrne, E. Byrne, P. Phelan, L. Meagher, Tom Leahy, J. Walsh, M. White, J. Duggan, J. Dunne, L. Byrne, Matty Power. Sub.—W. Burke.

1937

Tipperary—T. Butler (goal), D. O'Gorman, G. Cornally, J. Lanigan, (capt.), J. Ryan, J. Maher, W. Wall, J. Cooney, J. Gleeson, Jim Coffey, T. Treacy, T. Doyle, W. O'Donnell, D. Murphy, P. "Sweeper" Ryan. Subs.—D. Mackey, T. Kennedy.

Kilkenny—J. Duggan (capt.), J. O'Connell (goal), P. Larkin, P. Byrne, P. Blanchfield, E. Byrne, W. Burke, P. Phelan, T. Leahy, V. Madigan, J. Morrissey, P. Obbins, L. Duggan, M. White, Matt Power. Sub.—L. Meagher.

175

1938

Dublin—M. Daniels (capt.), C. Forde, T. Teehan, M. Butler, C. McMahon, M. Gill, P. Farrell, J. Byrne, H. Gray, R. Ryan, M. McDonnell, P. Doody, M. Brophy, M. Flynn, W. Loughnane. Sub.—J. Gilmartin.

Waterford—M. Hickey (capt.), M. Curley, C. Ware, J. Fanning, W. Walshe, J. Keane, J. Mountain, C. Moylan, S. Feeney, W. Barron, T. Greaney, P. Sheehan, J. Halpin, L. Byrne, D. Goode.

1939

Kilkenny—J. O'Connell (goal), P. Grace, P. Larkin, P. Blanchfield, R. Hinks, W. Burke, P. Phelan, J. Walsh (capt.), J. Kelly, J. Langton, Ter. Leahy, J. Gargan, J. Mulcahy, J. O'Brien, J. Phelan. Sub.- R. Brannagan.

Cork—J. Buttimer, A. Lotty, Batt Thornhill, W. Murphy, W. Campbell, J. Quirke, J. Young, J. Lynch (capt.), J. Barrett, C. Buckley, R. Dinneen, W. Tabb, R. Ring, T. O'Sullivan, M. Brennan.

1940

Limerick—P. Scanlan, J. McCarthy, M. Hickey, M. Kennedy, T. Cooke, P. Clohessy, P. Cregan, T. Ryan, J. Roche, J. Mackey, M. Mackey (capt.), R. Stokes, E. Chawke, P. McMahon, J. Power. Sub.— T. Herbert.

Kilkenny—J. O'Connell, P. Grace, P. Larkin, P. Blanchfield, R. Hinks, W. Burke, P. Phelan, J. Walsh, J. Kelly, J. Langton (capt.), Terry Leahy, J. Gargan, J. Mulcahy, S. O'Brien, Jas. Phelan.

1941

Cork—J. Buttimer, W. Murphy, B. Thornhill, A. Lotty, W. Campbell, C. Cottrill, D. J. Buckley, S. Barrett, J. Lynch, C. Ring, C. Buckley (capt.), J. Young, J. Quirke, T. O'Sullivan, M. Brennan. Subs.—J. Ryng, P. O'Donovan.

Dublin—C. Forde, D. Nicholls, M. Connolly, C. McMahon, M. Gill (jnr.), P. Farrell, J. Byrne, H. Gray, F. White, M. McDonnell, E. Wade (capt.), G. Glenn, E. O'Boyle, P. McSweeney, C. Downes. Sub.—D. Conway.

1942

Cork—E. Porter, W. Murphy, B. Thornhill, C. Murphy, A. Lotty, D. J. Buckley, J. Young, J. Lynch (capt.), P. O'Donovan, C. Ring, Sean Condon, M. Kennefick, C. Tobin, J. Quirke, D. Beckett. Sub.—J. Buttimer (for E. Porter).

Dublin—Jim Donegan, C. O'Dwyer, M. Butler, P. McCormack, E. O'Brien, F. White, (capt.), Jim Byrne, E. Wade, H. Gray, M. Ryan, M. McDonnell, J. Roche, D. Davitt, P. Kennedy, J. Mullane. Subs.—S. Skehal (for J. Roche), M. Griffin (for S. Skehal).

1943

Cork—T. Mulcahy, W. Murphy, B. Thornhill, C. Murphy, A. Lotty, D. J. Buckley, J. Young, J. Lynch, C. Cottrell, S. Condon, C. Ring, M. Kenefick (capt.), J. Quirke, T. O'Sullivan, M. Brennan. Subs.—P. O'Donovan (for S. Condon), B. Murphy (for T. Sullivan).

Antrim—J. Hurl, J. Currie, K. Murphy, W. Graham, P. McGarry, J. Walsh (capt.), P. McKeown, J. Bateson, N. Campbell, D. McKillop, J. Butler, Joe Mullan, K. Armstrong, D. McAlister, S. Mulholland. Sub.—S. McNeill (for J. Walsh).

1944

Cork—T. Mulcahy, W. Murphy, B. Thornhill, D. J. Buckley, P. O'Donovan, C. Murphy, A. Lotty, J. Lynch, C. Cottrell, C. Ring, S. Condon (capt.), J. Young, J. Quirke, J. Morrison, J. Kelly. Sub.—P. Healy (for C. Murphy).

Dublin—Jim Donegan, J. O'Neill, M. Butler (capt.), P. McCormack, F. White, C. Flanagan, J. Egan, M. Hassett, H. Gray, T. Leahy, E. Wade, J. Byrne, P. Maher, C. Downes, M. Ryan. Sub.—M. Gill (for J. Egan).

1945

Tipperary—Jim Maher, J. Devitt, G. Cornally, F. Coffey, M. Murphy, John Maher (capt.), T. Purcell, H. Goldsboro, T. Wall, "Mutt" Ryan, T. Doyle, E. Gleeson, John Coffey, A. Brennan, P. "Sweeper" Ryan.

Kilkenny—J. Walsh, P. Grace, M. Kelly, P. Blanchfield (capt.), J. Heffernan, W. Burke, J. Maher, D. Kennedy, T. Murphy, J. Gargan, J. Langton, T. Maher, T. Walton, S. O'Brien, J. Mulcahy. Subs.—W. Walsh (for W. Burke), J. Kelly (for D. Kennedy).

1946

Cork—T. Mulcahy, W. Murphy, C. Murphy, D. J. Buckley, P. O'Donovan, A. Lotty, J. Young, J. Lynch, C. Cottrell, P. Healy, C. Ring (capt.), C. Murphy, M. O'Riordan, G. O'Riordan, J. Kelly.

Kilkenny—Jim Donegan, P. Grace, M. Butler, W. Walsh, J. Kelly, S. Downey, J. Mulcahy (capt.), D. Kennedy, T. Leahy, J. Gargan, J. Langton, L. Reidy, T. Walton, S. O'Brien, P. O'Brien. Subs.—T. Murphy, M. Kelly (Mooncoin).

1947

Kilkenny—Jim Donegan, P. Grace, P. ("Diamond") Hayden, M. Marnell, J. Kelly, P. Prendergast, J. Mulcahy, D. Kennedy (capt.), J. Heffernan, T. Walton, Terry Leahy, J. Langton, Shem Downey, W. Cahill, L. Reidy.
Sub.—E. Kavanagh for P. Prendergast.

Cork—T. Mulcahy, W. Murphy, C. Murphy, D. J. Buckley, P. Donovan, A. Lotty, J. Young, J. Lynch, C. Cottrell, S. Condon (capt.), C. Ring, C. Murphy, M. O'Riordan, G. O'Riordan, J. Kelly.

1948

Waterford—J. Ware (capt.), A. Fleming, J. Cusack, J. Goode, M. Hickey, V. Baston, M. Hayes, J. O'Connor, E. Carew, K. O'Connor, J. Keane, C. Moylan, W. Galvin, E. Daly, T. Curran.

Dublin—K. Matthews, E. Dunphy, D. Walsh, S. Cronin, A. Herbert, J. Butler, P. Donnelly, M. Hassett, L. Donnelly, J. Kennedy, D. Cantwell, S. Og O'Callaghan, M. Williams, J. Prior, F. Cummins (capt.).

1949

Tipperary—A. Reddan, M. Byrne, A. Brennan, J. Doyle, P. Stakelum (capt.), F. Coffey, T. Doyle, S. Kenny, P. Shanahan, Tommy Ryan, Mick Ryan, J. Kennedy, J. Ryan, "Sonny" Maher, S. Bannon, Sub.—P. Kenny (for F. Coffey).

Laois—T. Fitzpatrick, L. White, J. Bergin, P. McCormack, J. Murray, T. Byrne, P. Rustchitzko (capt.), J. Styles, W. Bohane, P. Hogan, H. Grey, P. O'Brien, P. Lalor, D. Forde, P. Kelly. Subs.—W. Dargan (for P. O'Brien), and A. Dunne (for P. Rustchitzko).

1950

Tipperary—A. Reddan, M. Byrne, A. Brennan, J. Doyle, J. Finn, P. Stakelum, T. Doyle, S. Bannon, P. Shanahan, E. Ryan, Mick Ryan, S. Kenny (capt.), P. Kenny, "Sonny" Maher, J. Kennedy, Sub.; Tommy Ryan (for "Sonny" Maher).

Kilkenny—R. Dowling, J. Hogan, P. "Diamond" Hayden, M. Marnell, J. Kelly, P. Prendergast, W. Walsh, D. Kennedy, Shem Downey, J. Heffernan, M. Kenny (capt.), J. Langton, W. Costigan, J. Mulcahy, L. Reidy. Sub.—T. Walton (for Costigan).

1951

Tipperary—A. Reddan, M. Byrne, A. Brennan, J. Doyle, J. Finn (capt.), P. Stakelum, T. Doyle, P. Shanahan, J. Hough, E. Ryan, Mick Ryan, Tim Ryan, P. Kenny, "Sonny" Maher, S. Bannon. Sub.—S. Kenny (for P. Kenny).

Wexford—R. Brennan, M. Byrne, N. O'Donnell, M. O'Hanlon, S. Thorpe, R. Rackard, W. Rackard, E. Wheeler, J. Morrisey, Padge Kehoe, J. Cummins, T. Russell, T. Flood, N. Rackard (capt.), Paddy Kehoe.

1952

Cork—D. Creedon, G. O'Riordan, J. Lyons, A. O'Shaughnessy, M. Fouhy, V. Twomey, S. O'Brien, J. Twomey, G. Murphy, W. Griffin, W. J. Daly, C. Ring, L. Abernethy, L. Dowling, P. Barry (capt.). Subs.—M. O'Riordan (for Griffin), J. Lynam (for Abernethy).

Dublin—K. Mathews, S. Cronin, P. Ryan, J. O'Callaghan, D. Ferguson, J. Prior (capt.), T. Fahy, C. Murphy, N. Allen, G. Kelly, R. McCarthy, S. Kennedy, J. Finan, A. O'Brien, A. Herbert. Subs.—M. Wilson (for Finan), M. Williams (for Kennedy).

1953

Cork—D. Creedon, G. O'Riordan, J. Lyons, A. O'Shaughnessy, M. Fouhy, D. Hayes, V. Twomey, J. Twomey, G. Murphy, W. J. Daly, J. Hartnett, C. Ring (capt.), T. O'Sullivan, L. Dowling, P. Barry.

Galway—S. Duggan, C. Corless, W. O'Neill, J. Brophy, M. Burke (capt.), J. Molloy, E. Quinn, J. Salmon, W. Duffy, J Duggan, H. Gordon, J. Killeen, M. McInerney, J. Gallagher, F Nolan. Subs.—M. J. Flaherty (for Nolan), P. Duggan (for J. Duggan).

1954

Cork—D. Creedon, G. O'Riordan, J. Lyons, A. O'Shaughnessy, M. Fouhy, V. Twomey, D. Hayes, G. Murphy, W. Moore, W. J. Daly, J. Hartnett, C. Ring (Capt.), J. Clifford, E. Goulding, P. Barry. Sub.—Tom O'Sullivan for Paddy Barry.

Wexford—A. Foley, W. Rackard, N. O'Donnell, M. O'Hanlon, J. English, R. Rackard, E. Wheeler, J. Morrissey, S. Hearne, Paddy Kehoe, T. Flood, Padge Kehoe (capt.), T. Ryan, N. Rackard, R. Donovan. Subs.—T. Bolger (for O'Donnell), D. Hearn (for Paddy Kehoe).

1955

Wexford—A. Foley, R. Rackard, N. O'Donnell (capt.), M. O'Hanlon, J. English, W. Rackard, M. Morrissey, J. Morrissey, S. Hearne, Paddy Kehoe, E. Wheeler, Padge Kehoe, T. Ryan, N. Rackard, T. Flood. Subs.—O. Gough (for Wheeler), Wheeler (for Gough), D. Aherne (for Ryan).

Galway—T. Boland, J. Fives, B. Power, W. O'Neill, M. Burke, J. Molloy, T. Kelly, J. Salmon, W. Duffy, J. Duggan (capt.), J. Young, P. Duggan, P. Egan, J. Burke, T. Sweeney. Subs.—H. Gordon (for Power), M. Elwood (for Sweeney).

1956

Wexford—A. Foley, R. Rackard, N. O'Donnell, M. Morrissey, J. English (capt.), W. Rackard, J. Morrissey, S. Hearne, E. Wheeler, Padge Kehoe, M. Codd, T. Flood, T. Ryan, N. Rackard, T. Dixon.

Cork—M. Cashman, J. Brohan, J. Lyons, A. O'Shaughnessy (capt.), M. Fouhy, W. J. Daly, P. Philpott, E. Goulding, P. Dowling, M. Regan, J. Hartnett, P. Barry, C. O'Shea, T. Kelly, C. Ring. Subs.—V. Twomey (for O'Shaughnessy), G. Murphy (for Hartnett).

1957

Kilkenny—O. Walsh, T. Walsh, J. Walsh, J. Maher, P. Buggy, M. Walsh, J. McGovern, M. Brophy, J. Sutton, D. Heaslip, M. Kenny, M. Kelly (capt.), R. Rockett, W. Dwyer, S. Clohessy. Sub.—W. Walsh (for Sutton).

Waterford—R. Roche, T. Cunningham, A. Flynn, J. Barron, M. O'Connor, M. Og Morrissey, S. Power, J. O'Connor, P. Grimes (capt.), M. Flannelly, T. Cheasty, L. Guinan, F. Walsh, J. Kiely, D. Whelan.

1958

Tipperary—J. O'Grady, M. Byrne, M. Maher, K. Carey, J. Finn, A. Wall (capt.), John Doyle, J. Hough, T. English, D. Nealon, T. Larkin, Jimmy Doyle, L. Keane, L. Devaney, L. Connolly.

Galway—M. Sweeney, F. Spillane, P. Burke, S. Cullinane (capt.), J. Duggan, J. Fives, F. Benson, J. Salmon, P. J. Lally, T. Sweeney, J. Young, T. Kelly, P. J. Lawless, W. O'Neill, T. Conway. Subs.—E. Derrivan (for Spillane), M. Fox (for Young).

1959 REPLAY

Waterford—E. Power, J. Harney, A. Flynn, J. Barron, M. Lacey, M. Óg Morrissey, Jackie Condon, S. Power, P. Grimes, M. Flannelly, T. Cheasty, F. Walsh (capt.), L. Guinan, T. Cunningham, J. Kiely. Subs.—M. O'Connor (for Lacey), D. Whelan (for Cunningham).

Kilkenny—O. Walsh, T. Walsh, J. Walsh, J. Maher, P. Buggy, T. Kelly, J. McGovern, P. Kelly, M. Walsh, D. Heaslip, M. Fleming, S. Clohosey (capt.), R. Carroll, W. Dwyer, T. O'Connell. Sub.—E. Keher (for McGovern), M. Kelly (for M. Fleming).

D. Whelan and C. Ware (Waterford) who played in the drawn game were replaced by T. Cunningham and M. Flannelly who retained their places for the replay, while M. Brophy (Kilkenny) was replaced by T. Kelly for replay. Tim Kelly, John Sutton and Mick Kelly came in as subs in drawn game for Kilkenny.

1960

Wexford—P. Nolan, J. Mitchell, N. O'Donnell (capt.), T. Neville, J. English, W. Rackard, J. Nolan, E. Wheeler, J. Morrissey, J. O'Brien, P. Kehoe, S. Quaid, O. McGrath, J. Harding, T. Flood. Subs.—Seán Power (for Quaid), M. Morrissey (for Power).

Tipperary—T. Moloney, M. Hassett, M. Maher, K. Carey, M. Burns, A. Wall (capt.), John Doyle, T. English, Tom Ryan (Killenaule), Jimmy Doyle, L. Devaney, D. Nealon, L. Connolly, Tom Moloughney, S. McLoughlin. Subs.—W. Moloughney (for McLoughlin), N. Murphy (for English).

1961

Tipperary—D. O'Brien, M. Hassett (capt.), M. Maher, K. Carey, M. Burns, A. Wall, John Doyle, M. O'Gara, T. English, Jimmy Doyle, L. Devaney, D. Nealon, J. McKenna, W. Moloughney, T. Moloughney. Subs.—T. Ryan (Killenaule) (for McKenna), J. Hough (for O'Gara), S. McLoughlin (for Wall).

Dublin—J. Grey, D. Ferguson, N. Drumgoole (capt.), L. Foley, L. Ferguson, C. Hayes, S. Lynch, D. Foley, F. Whelan, A. Boothman, M. Bohan, L. Shannon, B. Boothman, P. Croke, W. Jackson. Sub.—E. Malone (for Bohan).

1962

Tipperary—D. O'Brien, John Doyle, M. Maher, K. Carey, M. O'Gara, A. Wall, M. Burns, T. English, L. Devaney, Jimmy Doyle (capt.), J. McKenna, T. Ryan (Killenaule), D. Nealon, T. Moloughney, S. McLoughlin. Subs.—L. Connolly (for O'Gara), T. Ryan (Toomevara) (for Jimmy Doyle).

Wexford—P. Nolan, T. Neville, N. O'Donnell, E. Colfer, J. English, W. Rackard (capt.), J. Nolan, P. Wilson, M. Lyng, J. O'Brien, Padge Kehoe, P. Lynch, O. McGrath, E. Wheeler, T. Flood.

1963

Kilkenny—O. Walsh, P. Larkin, C. Whelan, M. Treacy, S. Cleere (capt.), T. Carroll, M. Coogan, P. Moran, S. Clohosey, D. Heaslip, J. McGovern, E. Keher, T. Walsh, W. Dwyer, T. Murphy. Sub.—O. Gough (for McGovern).

Waterford—E. Power, T. Cunningham, A. Flynn, J. Byrne, L. Guinan, M. Óg Morrissey, J. Irish, M. Dempsey, Joe Condon (capt.), M. Flannery, T. Cheasty, F. Walsh, S. Power, J. Barron. P. Grimes. Subs.—P. Flynn (for E. Power), J. Meaney (for Condon), M. Walsh (for Byrne).

1964

Tipperary—J. O'Donoghue, John Doyle, M. Maher, K. Carey, M. Burns, A. Wall, M. Murphy (capt.), T. English, M. Roche, Jimmy Doyle, L. Kiely, M. Keating, D. Nealon, J. McKenna, S. McLoughlin. Subs.—M. Lonergan (for Maher), L. Devaney (for Kiely).

Kilkenny—O. Walsh, C. Whelan, P. Dillon, P. Larkin, P. Henderson, T. Carroll, M. Coogan, P. Moran, S. Buckley (capt.), S. Cleere, J. Teehan, E. Keher, T. Walsh, T. Forrestal, T. Murphy. Subs.—W. Murphy (Carrickshock), (for Coogan), D. Heaslip (for T. Murphy).

1965

Tipperary—J. O'Donoghue. John Doyle, M. Maher, K. Carey, M. Burns, A. Wall, L. Gaynor. T. English, M. Roche, Jimmy Doyle (capt.), L. Kiely, L. Devaney, D. Nealon, J. McKenna, S. McLoughlin.

Wexford—P. Nolan, W. O'Neill, D. Quigley, E. Colfer, V. Staples, T. Neville (capt.), W. Murphy, P. Wilson, M. Byrne, J. O'Brien, J. Nolan, R. Shannon, P. Quigley, M. Codd, J. Foley. Subs.—E. Wheeler (for J. Nolan), O. McGrath (for P. Quigley).

1966

Cork—P. Barry, P. Doolan, T. O'Donoghue, D. Murphy, A. Connolly, J. O'Sullivan, P. Fitzgerald, J. McCarthy, M. Waters, S. Barry, J. O'Halloran, G. McCarthy (capt.), C. McCarthy, C. Sheehan, J. Bennett.

Kilkenny—O. Walsh, P. Henderson, J. Lynch (capt.), J. Treacy, S. Cleere, T. Carroll, M. Coogan, P. Moran, J. Teehan, E. Keher, C. Dunne, S. Buckley, J. Dunphy, P. Dillon, T. Walsh. Subs.—T. Murphy (for P. Dillon), P. Carroll (for T. Murphy).

1967

Kilkenny—O. Walsh, T. Carroll, P. Dillon, J. Treacy (capt.), S. Cleere, P. Henderson, M. Coogan, P. Moran, J. Teehan, E. Keher, T. Walsh, C. Dunne, J. Bennett, J. Lynch, Martin Brennan. Subs.—R. Blanchfield, J. Kinsella, P. Carroll.

Tipperary—J. O'Donoghue, J. Doyle, K. Carey, N. O'Gorman, M. Burns, A. Wall, L. Gaynor, T. English, M. Roche (capt.), D. Nealon, J. Flanagan, L. Devaney, Jimmy Doyle, M. Keating, S. McLoughlin. Subs.—L. Kiely, M. Lonergan, P. J. Ryan.

1968

Wexford—P. Nolan, T. Neville, E. Kelly, E. Colfer, V. Staples, D. Quigley (Capt.), W. Murphy, P. Wilson, D. Bernie,

P. Lynch, A. Doran, C. Jacob, J. O'Brien, S. Whelan, J. Berry
Sub: J. Quigley (for S. Whelan).

Tipperary—J. O'Donoghue, J. Costigan. N. O'Gorman, J.
Gleeson, M. Burns, M. Roche (Capt.), L. Gaynor, P. J. Ryan,
D. Nealon, M. Keating, J. Ryan, J. Doyle, L. Devaney, J.
McKenna, S. McLoughlin. Sub.: F. Loughnane (for Jimmy Doyle).

1969

Kilkenny—O. Walsh, T. Carroll, P. Dillon, J. Treacy, W. Mur-
phy (Rower-Inistioge), P. Henderson, M. Coogan, F. Cummins,
M. Lawler, C. Dunne, P. Delaney, E. Keher (capt.), J. Millea,
Martin Brennan, T. Murphy. Subs.: P. Kavanagh (for Dunne); P.
Moran (for Delaney); S. Buckley (for Murphy).

Cork—P. Barry, A. Maher, T. O'Donoghue, D. Murphy
(capt.), D. Clifford, W. Walsh, G. McCarthy, D. Coughlan, R.
Tuohy, T. Ryan, C. Cullinane, P. Hegarty, C. McCarthy, R.
Cummins, Eddie O'Brien. Subs.: J. O'Halloran (for O'Brien); J.
Murphy (for Tuohy); S. Looney (for Ryan).

Referee: S. O'Connor (Limerick).

1970

Cork—P. Barry (capt.), T. Maher, P. McDonnell, J. Horgan,
D. Clifford, P. Hegarty, C. Roche, G. McCarthy, S. Looney, T.
Ryan, W. Walsh, C. Cullinane, C. McCarthy, R. Cummins, Eddie
O'Brien. Subs: S. Murphy (for Clifford).

Wexford—P. Nolan, E. Colfer, M. Collins (capt.), T. Neville,
M. Browne, D. Quigley, T. O'Connor, D. Bernie, M. Jacob, M.
Quigley,P. Quigley, J. Quigley, M. Butler, A. Doran, J. Berry.
Subs: T. Byrne (for Butler); J. Russell (for Neville).

Referee: J. Hatton (Wicklow).

1971

Tipperary—P. O'Sullivan, L. King, J. Kelly, J. Gleeson, T.
O'Connor (capt.), M. Roche, L. Gaynor, P. J. Ryan, S. Hogan,
F. Loughnane, N. O'Dwyer, D. Ryan, J. Flanagan, R. Ryan, M.
Keating. Subs: Jimmy Doyle (for Hogan); P. Byrne (for
Flanagan).

Kilkenny—O. Walsh, F. Larkin, P. Dillon, J. Tracey, W. Murphy (Rower-Inistioge), P. Henderson (capt.), M. Coogan, F.
Cummins, P. Lalor, M. Murphy, P. Delaney, E. Keher, Mick

Brennan, K. Purcell, E. Byrne. Subs: P. Moran (for W. Murphy); P. Cullen (for Brennan); T. Carroll (for Larkin).
Referee: F. Murphy (Cork).

1972

Kilkenny—N. Skehan (capt.), P. Larkin, P. Dillon, J. Treacy, P. Lalor, P. Henderson, E. Morrissey, F. Cummins, L. O'Brien, M. Crotty, P. Delaney, J. Kinsella, E. Byrne, K. Purcell, E. Keher. Subs.: M. Murphy (for Byrne), M. Coogan (for Larkin), P. Moran (for Kinsella).

Cork—P. Barry, T. Maher, P. McDonnell, B. Murphy, F. Norberg (capt.), S. Looney, C. Roche, J. McCarthy, D. Coughlan, G. McCarthy, M. Malone, P. Hegarty, C. McCarthy, R. Cummins, S. O'Leary. Subs.: Ted O'Brien (for Norberg), D. Collins (for Hegarty).

Referee: M. Spain (Offaly).

1973

Limerick—S. Horgan, W. Moore, P. Hartigan, J. O'Brien, P. Bennis, E. Cregan, S. Foley, R. Bennis, E. Grimes (capt.), B. Hartigan, M. Dowling, L. O'Donoghue, F. Nolan, E. Rea, J. McKenna. Subs.: T. Ryan (for B. Hartigan).

Kilkenny—N. Skehan, F. Larkin, N. Orr, P. Cullen, P. Lalor, P. Henderson, B. Cody, F. Cummins, L. O'Brien, C. Dunne, P. Delaney (capt.), P. Broderick, M. Crotty, J. Lynch Mick Brennan. Subs.: K. Purcell (for Broderick), W. Harte (for Cummins), J. Kinsella (for Lynch).

Referee: M. Slattery (Clare).

1974

Kilkenny—N. Skehan, F. Larkin, N. Orr (capt.), J. Treacy, P. Lalor, P. Henderson, T. McCormack, L. O'Brien, F. Cummins, M. Crotty, P. Delaney, W. Fitzpatrick, Mick Brennan, K. Purcell, E. Keher.

Limerick—S. Horgan, W. Moore, P. Hartigan, J. O'Brien, T. Ryan, E. Cregan, S. Foley (capt.), B. Hartigan, E. Grimes, J. McKenna, R. Bennis, M. Ruth, L. O'Donoghue, E. Rea, F. Nolan. Subs.: P. Bennis (for Ryan), P. Kelly (for B. Hartigan), P. Fitzmaurice (for McKenna).

Referee: J. Moloney (Tipperary).

1975

Kilkenny—N. Skehan, F. Larkin, N. Orr, B. Cody, P. Lalor,

185

P. Henderson, T. McCormack, L. O'Brien, F. Cummins, M. Crotty, P. Delaney, B. Fitzpatrick (capt.), Mick Brennan, K. Purcell, E. Keher.

Galway—M. Conneely, N. McInerney, J. Clarke, P. Lally, J. McDonagh, S. Silke, I. Clarke, S. Murphy, John Connolly (capt.), G. Coone, F. Burke, P. J. Molloy, M. Barrett, P. J. Qualter, P. Fahy. Subs.: M. Connolly (for Barrett), Ted Murphy (for Lally), J. Grealish (for Murphy).

Referee: S. O'Connor (Limerick).

1976

Cork—M. Coleman, B. Murphy, P. McDonnell, M. Doherty, P. Barry, J. Crowley, D. Coughlan, G. McCarthy, P. Moylan, M. Malone, B. Cummins, J. Barry Murphy, C. McCarthy, R. Cummins (capt.), S. O'Leary. Subs.: E. O'Donoghue (for O'Leary), J. Horgan (for Barry).

Wexford—J. Nolan, T. O'Connor, W. Murphy, J. Prendergast, L. Bennett, M. Jacob, C. Doran, N. Buggy, B. Rowesome, J. Murphy, M. Quigley, J. Quigley, M. Butler, T. Doran (capt.), C. Keogh. Subs.: D. Rowesome (for Keogh), M. Casey (for B. Rowesome).

Referee: P. Johnson (Kilkenny).

1977

Cork—M. Coleman, B. Murphy, M. Doherty (capt.), J. Horgan, D. McCurtain, J. Crowley, D. Coughlan, T. Cashman, T. Crowley, M. Malone, G. McCarthy, J. Barry Murphy, C. McCarthy, R. Cummins, S. O'Leary. Subs.: P. Moylan (for Malone), Tadgh Murphy (for G. McCarthy).

Wexford—J. Nolan, T. O'Connor, W. Murphy, J. Prendergast, L. Bennett, M. Jacob, C. Doran, D. Bernie, N. Buggy, C. Keogh, M. Quigley, M. Butler, J. Quigley, T. Doran (capt.), J. Murphy. Subs.: J. Russell (for Prendergast), M. Casey (for J. Murphy), E. Walsh (for Bernie).

Referee: S. O'Grady (Limerick).

1978

Cork—M. Coleman, B. Murphy, M. O'Doherty, J. Horgan, D. McCurtain, J. Crowley, D. Coughlan, T. Cashman, P. Moylan, J. Barry Murphy, G. McCarthy, T. Crowley, C. McCarthy (capt.), R. Cummins, S. O'Leary. Subs.: J. Allen (for Cashman), E. O'Donoghue (for O'Leary).

Kilkenny—N. Skehan, P. Prendergast, P. Larkin, D. O'Hara.

186

J. Hennessy, G. Henderson (capt.), R. Reid, F. Cummins, L. O'Brien, K. Fennelly, M. Crotty, B. Fitzpatrick, Mick Brennan, B. Cody, M. Ruth. Subs.: T. Malone (for Fennelly), P. Henderson (for O'Brien).

Referee: J. Rankins (Laois).

1979

Kilkenny—N. Skehan, P. Larkin, P. Prendergast, J. Henderson, R. Reid, G. Henderson, N. Brennan, J. Hennessy, F. Cummins, G. Fennelly (capt.), B. Fitzpatrick, L. O'Brien, Mick Brennan, M. Crotty, M. Ruth. Subs.: K. Fennelly (for Crotty), D. O'Hara (for Prendergast).

Galway—S. Shinnors, N. McInerney, C. Hayes, A. Fenton, J. McDonagh (capt.), S. Silke, I. Clarke, John Connolly, S. Mahon, B. Forde, F. Burke, Joe Connolly, P. J. Molloy, N. Lane, F. Gantley. Subs.: S. Linnane (for Forde), M. Whelan (for Burke).

Referee: G. Ryan (Tipperary).

1980

Galway—M. Conneely, C. Hayes, N. McInerney, Jimmy Cooney, S. Linnane, S. Silke, S. Coen, M. Connolly, S. Mahon, F. Burke, Joe Connolly (capt.), P. J. Molloy, B. Forde, John Connolly, N. Lane. Subs.: F. Gantley (for M. Connolly), J. Ryan (for Molloy).

Limerick—T. Quaid, D. Murray, L. Enright, Dom Punch, L. O'Donoghue, M. Carroll, S. Foley (capt.), J. Carroll, David Punch, P. Fitzmaurice, J. Flanagan, W. Fitzmaurice, O. O'Connor, J. McKenna, E. Cregan. Subs.: B. Carroll (for Flanagan), P. Herbert (for M. Carroll), E. Grimes (for W. Fitzmaurice).

Referee: N. O'Donoghue (Dublin).

1981

Offaly—D. Martin, T. Donoghue, E. Coughlan, P. Fleury, A. Fogarty, P. Delaney, G. Coughlan, J. Kelly, L. Currams, P. Kirwan, B. Bermingham, M. Corrigan, P. Carroll, P. Horan (capt.), J. Flaherty. Subs.: B. Keeshan (for O'Donoghue), D. Owens (for Kirwin).

Galway—M. Conneely, S. Coen, N. McInerney, Jimmy Cooney, S. Linnane, S. Silke (capt.), I. Clarke, M. Connolly, S. Mahon, F. Gantley, Joe Connolly, P. J. Molloy, B. Forde, John Connolly, N. Lane. Subs.: F. Burke (for Gantley), P. Ryan (for Forde).

Referee: F. Murphy (Cork).

● *Kilkenny forward Liam Smith shows his delight after scoring a goal against Dublin in the 1993 Leinster final. Kilkenny went on to win the All-Ireland title. (Photo: Irish Independent)*

1982

Kilkenny—N. Skehan, J. Henderson, B. Cody (capt.), D. O'Hara; N. Brennan, G. Henderson, P. Prendergast, J. Hennessy, F. Cummins, R. Power, G. Fennelly, K. Brennan, B. Fitzpatrick, C. Heffernan, L. Fennelly.

Cork—G. Cunningham, B. Murphy, M. O'Doherty, J. Blake, J. Buckley,J. Crowley, D. MacCurtain, T. Cashman, T. Crowley T. O'Sullivan, P. Horgan, J. Barry, Murphy (capt.), S. O'Leary, R. Cummins, E. O'Donoghue. Subs: B. Óg Murphy for Buckley, K. Hennessy for O'Sullivan, F. Collins for MacCurtain.

Referee—Noel Drumgoole (Dublin).

1983

Kilkenny— N. Skehan, J. Henderson, B. Cody, D. O'Hara, J. Hennessy, G. Henderson, P. Prendergast, F. Cummins, G. Fennelly, R. Power, K. Brennan, H. Ryan, B. Fitzpatrick, C. Heffernan, L. Fennelly (capt.). Sub.: P. Lannon for Power.

Cork— G. Cunningham, B. Murphy, D. O'Grady, D. MacCurtain, P. Horgan, J. Crowley, T. Cashman, J. Buckley, J. Fenton, B. Og Murphy, K. Hennessy, T. Crowley, T. Mulcahy, J. Barry Murphy (capt.), E. O'Donoghue. Subs: F. Collins for Fenton, T. O'Sullivan for Mulcahy, S. O'Leary for B. Óg Murphy.

Referee—Neilly Duggan (Limerick).

1984

Cork—G. Cunningham, D. Mulcahy, D. O'Grady, J. Hodgins, T. Cashman, J. Crowley, D. MacCurtain, J. Fenton (capt.), P. Hartnett, K. Hennessy,T. Crowley, T. O'Sullivan, T. Mulcahy, J. Barry Murphy, S. O'Leary.

Offaly—D. Martin, L. Carroll, E. Coughlan, P. Fleury (capt.), A. Fogarty, P. Delaney, G. Coughlan, T. Conneely, J. Kelly, M. Corrigan, B. Bermingham, P. Carroll, D. Fogarty, P. Horan, J. Dooley. Subs: P. Corrigan for Bermingham, P. Kirwan for Dooley.

Referee—Pascal Long (Kilkenny).

1985

Offaly— J. Troy, A. Fogarty, E. Coughlan, P. Fleury (capt.), T. Conneely, P. Delaney, G. Coughlan, D. Owens, J. Kelly, P. Corrigan, B. Bermingham, M. Corrigan, P. Cleary, P. Horan, J. Dooley. Subs: D. Fogarty for Owens, B. Keeshan for Conneely.

Galway—P. Murphy, O. Kilkenny, C. Hayes, S. Linnane, P.

Finnerty, T. Keady, T. Kilkenny, M. Connolly (capt.), S. Mahon, M. McGrath, B. Lynskey, Joe Cooney, B. Ford, N. Lane, P. J. Molloy. Subs: J. Murphy for McGrath, A Cunningham for Ford, M. Haverty for Connolly.

Referee—George Ryan (Tipperary).

1986

Cork—G. Cunningham, D. Mulcahy, R. Brown, J. Crowley, P. Hartnett, T. Cashman (capt.), D. Walsh, J. Fenton, J. Cashman, T. McCarthy, T. Mulcahy, T. O'Sullivan, G. Fitzgerald, J. Barry Murphy, K. Hennessy. Subs: K. Kingston for Fenton.

Galway—J. Commins, C. Hayes, S. Linnane, O. Kilkenny, P. Finnerty, T. Keady, G. McInerney, S. Mahon, ''. Piggott, T. Kilkenny, B. Lynskey, M. Naughton, A. Cunningham, Joe Cooney, N. Lane (capt.). Subs: P. J. Molloy fo. Piggott, M. Connolly for Mahon, P. Murphy for Cunnningham.

Referee—John Bailey (Dublin).

1987

Galway—J. Commins, S. Linnane, C. Hayes (capt.), O. Kilkenny, P. Finnerty, T. Keady, G. McInerney, S. Mahon, P. Malone, M. McGrath, J. Cooney, M. Naughton, E. Ryan, B. Lynskey, A. Cunningham. Subs: N. Lane for Naughton, P. J. Molloy for Cunningham, T. Kilkenny for McGrath.

Kilkenny—K. Fennelly, J. Hennessy, P. Prendergast (capt.), J. Henderson, L. Walsh, G. Henderson, S. Fennelly, G. Fennelly, L. Ryan, K. Brennan, C. Heffernan, R. Power, P. Walsh, L. Fennelly, H. Ryan. Subs: T. Lennon for P. Walsh, L. McCarthy for Power.

Referee—Terence Murray (Limerick).

1988

Galway—J. Commins, S. Linnane, C. Hayes (capt.), O. Kilkenny, P. Finnerty, A. Keady, G. McInerney, M. Coleman, P. Malone, A. Cunningham, B. Lynskey, M. Naughton, M. McGrath, Joe Cooney, E. Ryan. Subs: N. Lane for Cunningham; A. Kilkenny for Naughton; G. Burke for Lynskey.

Tipperary—K. Hogan, P. Delaney, C. O'Donovan, J. Heffernan, B. Ryan, N. Sheehy, J. Kennedy, C. Bonnar, J. Hayes, D. Ryan, D. O'Connell, J. Leahy, P. Fox, N. English (capt.), A. Ryan. Sub. Cormac Bonnar for J. Hayes.

Referee: G. Kirwan (Offaly).

190

Tipperary—K. Hogan, J. Heffernan, C. O'Donovan, N. Sheehy, Conal Bonnar, B. Ryan (Capt.), J. Kennedy, Colm Bonnar, D. Carr, J. Leahy, D. Ryan, M. Cleary, P. Fox, Cormac Bonnar, N. English. Subs.: J. Hayes for Cormac Bonnar, D. O'Connell for Leahy. A. Ryan for Cleary.

Antrim—N. Patterson, G. O'Kane, T. Donnelly, D. Donnelly, J. McNaughton, D. McKinley, L. McKeegan, P. McKillen, D. McMullan, C. Barr (Capt.), A. McCarry, O. McFetridge, D. Armstrong, B. Donnelly, T. McNaughton. Subs.: D. McNaughton for McMullan, D. McKillop for O'Kane, M. Sullivan for McKinley.

Referee: P. Delaney (Laois).

Cork—G. Cunningham, J. Considine, D. Walsh, S. O'Gorman, S. McCarthy, J. Cashman, K. McGuckian, B. O'Sullivan, T. McCarthy, G. Fitzgerald, M. Foley, T. O'Sullivan, T. Mulcahy (Capt.), K. Hennessy, J. Fitzgibbon. Subs.: D. Quirke for McGuckian, C. Casey for B. O'Sullivan.

Galway—J. Commins, D. Fahy, S. Treacy, O. Kilkenny, P. Finnerty, T. Keady, G. McInerney, M. Coleman, P. Malone, A. Cunningham, J. Cooney (Capt.), M. Naughton, M. McGrath, N. Lane, E. Ryan. Subs.: T. Monaghan for Malone, B. Lynskey for Cunningham.

Referee: J. Moore (Waterford).

Tipperary—K. Hogan, P. Delaney, N. Sheedy, M. Ryan, Colm Bonnar, B. Ryan, Conal Bonnar, D. Carr (Capt.), A. Ryan, M. Cleary, D. Ryan, J. Leahy, P. Fox, Cormac Bonnar, N. English. Subs.: C. Stakelum for Cormac Bonnar. D. O'Connell for N. English.

Kilkenny—M. Walsh, B. Hennessy, J. Henderson, L. Simpson, L. Walsh, P. Dwyer, E. O'Connor, R. Power, M. Phelan, J. Power, C. Heffernan (Capt.), D. J. Carey, E. Morrissey, L. Fennelly, L. McCarthy. Subs.: A. Ronan for McCarthy, L. Ryan for Power.

1992

Kilkenny—M. Walsh, E. O'Connor, P. Dwyer, L. Simpson, L. Walsh, P. O'Neill, W. O'Connor, M. Phelan, B. Hennessy, L. McCarthy, J. Power, D. J. Carey, E. Morrissey, L. Fennelly (Capt.), J. Brennan. Subs.: C. Heffernan for Brennan, A. Ronan for Morrissey.

Cork—G. Cunningham, S. O'Gorman, D. Mulcahy, B. Corcoran, C. Casey, J. Cashman, D. Walsh, P. Buckley, S. McCarthy, T. McCarthy, T. Mulcahy, T. O'Sullivan, G. Fitzgerald (Capt.), J. Fitzgibbon, K. Hennessy. Subs: P. Hartnett for Walsh, G. Manley for Fitzgerald, M. Foley for Buckley.

Referee: D. Murphy (Wexford).

1993

Kilkenny—M. Walsh, E. O'Connor (Capt.), P. Dwyer, L. Simpson, L. Keoghan, P. O'Neill, W. O'Connor, B. Hennessy, M. Phelan, L. McCarthy, J. Power, D. J. Carey, E. Morrissey, P. J. Delaney, A. Ronan. Subs.: J. Brennan for Morrissey, T. Murphy for Phelan, C. Heffernan for Delaney.

Galway—R. Burke, P. Cooney, S. Treacy, M. Killilea, T. Helebert, G. McInerney, P. Kelly, M. Coleman, P. Malone, B. Keogh, J. McGrath, J. Cooney, M. McGrath (Capt.), J. Rabbitte, L. Burke. Subs.: J. Campbell for J. McGrath, P. Finnerty for Keogh.

Referee: T. Murray (Limerick).

1887—Open Draw.
1888—Cork/Clare (unfinished due to American "Invasion").
1889—Clare.
1890—Cork 2-0, Kerry 0-1
1891—Kerry 2-4, Limerick 0-1 (replay)
   Limerick 1-2, Kerry 1-1 (objection)
1892—Cork 5-3, Kerry 2-5
1893—Cork 5-3, Limerick 0-0
1894—Cork 3-4, Tipperary 1-2
1895—Tipperary 7-8, Limerick 0-2
1896—Tipperary 7-9, Cork 2-3 (replay)
   Tipperary 1-3, Cork 1-3 (unfinished, replay ordered).
1897—Limerick 4-9, Cork 1-6
1898—Tipperary 1-13, Cork 1-2 (replay)
   Tipperary 3-0, Cork 2-3 (draw)
   (unfinished owing to fading light)
1899—Tipperary 5-16, Clare 0-8
1900—Tipperary 6-11, Kerry 2-1
1901—Cork 3-10, Clare 2-6
1902—Cork 2-9, Limerick 1-5
1903—Cork 5-16, Waterford 1-1
1904—Cork 3-10, Tipperary 3-4
1905—Cork 7-12, Limerick 1-4
1906—Tipperary 3-4, Cork 0-9
1907—Cork 1-6, Tipperary 1-4
1908—Tipperary, w.o., Kerry, scr.
1909—Tipperary 2-10, Cork 2-6
1910—Limerick 5-1, Cork 4-2
1911—Limerick 5-3, Tipperary 4-3
1912—Cork 5-1, Tipperary 3-1
1913—Tipperary 8-2, Cork 4-3
1914—Clare 3-2, Cork 3-1
1915—Cork 8-2, Clare 2-1
1916—Tipperary 5-0, Cork 1-2
1917—Tipperary 6-4, Limerick 3-1 (replay)
   Tipperary 3-4, Limerick 3-4 (draw)
1918—Limerick 11-3, Clare 1-2
1919—Cork 3-5, Limerick 1-6
1920—Cork 3-4, Limerick 0-5
1921—Limerick 5-2, Cork 1-2
1922—Tipperary 4-2, Limerick 1-4 (replay)

Tipperary 2-2, Limerick 2-2 (draw)
1923—Limerick 2-3, Tipperary 1-0
1924—Tipperary 3-1, Limerick 2-2
1925—Tipperary 6-6, Waterford, 1-2
1926—Cork 3-6, Tipperary 2-4 (third game)
      Cork 4-1, Tipperary 3-4 (second game)
      Tipperary 1-2, Cork 0-0 (first game abandoned)
1927—Cork 5-3, Clare 3-4
1928—Cork 6-4, Clare 2-2 (replay)
      Cork 2-2, Clare 2-2 (draw)
1929—Cork 4-6, Waterford 2-3
1930—Tipperary 6-4, Clare 2-8
1931—Cork 5-4, Waterford 1-2 (replay)
      Cork 1-9, Waterford 4-0 (draw)
1932—Clare 5-2, Cork 4-1
1933—Limerick 3-7, Waterford 1-2
      (unfinished Limerick awarded game)
1934—Limerick 4-8, Waterford 2-5
1935—Limerick 5-5, Tipperary 1-4
1936—Limerick 8-5, Tipperary 4-6
1937—Tipperary 6-3, Limerick 4-3
1938—Waterford 3-5, Clare 2-5
1939—Cork 4-3, Limerick 3-4
1940—Limerick 3-3, Cork 2-4 (replay)
      Limerick 4-3, Cork 3-6 (draw)
1941—Tipperary 5-4, Cork 2-5 (played in October after
      All-Ireland Final)
1942—Cork 4-15, Tipperary 4-1
1943—Cork 2-13, Waterford 3-8
1944—Cork 4-6, Limerick 3-6 (replay)
      Limerick 4-13, Cork 6-7 (draw)
1945—Tipperary 4-3, Limerick 2-6
1946—Cork 3-8, Limerick 1-3
1947—Cork 2-6, Limerick 2-3
1948—Waterford 4-7, Cork 3-9
1949—Tipperary 1-16, Limerick 2-10
1950—Tipperary 2-17, Cork 3-11
1951—Tipperary 2-11, Cork 2-9
1952—Cork 1-11, Tipperary 2-6
1953—Cork 3-10, Tipperary 1-11
1954—Cork 2-8, Tipperary 1-8
1955—Limerick 2-16, Clare 2-6
1956—Cork 5-5, Limerick 3-5

1957—Waterford 1-11, Cork 1-6
1958—Tipperary 4-12, Waterford 1-5
1959—Waterford 3-9, Cork 2-9
1960—Tipperary 4-13, Cork 4-11
1961—Tipperary 3-6, Cork 0-7
1962—Tipperary 5-14, Waterford 2-3
1963—Waterford 0-11, Tipperary 0-8
1964—Tipperary 3-13, Cork 1-5
1965—Tipperary 4-11, Cork 0-5
1966—Cork 4-9, Waterford 2-9
1967—Tipperary 4-12, Clare 2-6
1968—Tipperary 2-13, Cork 1-7
1969—Cork 4-6, Tipperary 0-9
1970—Cork 3-10, Tipperary 3-8 (First 80-minute Final)
1971—Tipperary 4-16, Limerick 3-18
1972—Cork 6-18, Clare 2-8
1973—Limerick 6-7, Tipperary 2-18
1974—Limerick 6-14, Clare 3-9
1975—Cork 3-14, Limerick 0-12 (70-minute Final introduced)
1976—Cork 3-15, Limerick 4-5
1977—Cork 4-15, Clare 4-10
1978—Cork 0-13, Clare 0-11
1979—Cork 2-14, Limerick 0-9
1980—Limerick 2-14, Cork 2-10
1981—Limerick 3-12, Clare 2-9
1982—Cork 5-31, Waterford 3-6
1983—Cork 3-22, Waterford 0-12
1984—Cork 4-15, Tipperary 3-14
1985—Cork 4-17, Tipperary 4-11
1986—Cork 2-18, Clare 3-12
1987—Tipperary 1-18, Cork 1-18 (draw)
          Tipperary 4-22, Cork 1-22 (after extra time) (replay)
1988—Tipperary 2-19, Cork 1-13
1989—Tipperary 0-26, Waterford 2-8
1990—Cork 4-16, Tipperary 2-14
1991—Tipperary 2-16, Cork 4-10 (draw)
          Tipperary 4-19, Cork 4-15 (replay)
1992—Cork 1-22, Limerick 3-11
1993—Tipperary 3-27, Clare 2-12

1887—Open Draw
1888—Kilkenny 0-7, Dublin 0-3
1889—Dublin w.o. from Laois (Louth only other county to compete)
1890—Wexford 2-9, Laois 0-3
1891—Wexford w.o. from Laois
1892—Dublin unopposed
1893—Kilkenny w.o. from Dublin
1894—Dublin unopposed
1895—Kilkenny 1-5, Dublin 0-5
1896—Dublin 4-6, Kilkenny 0-0 (replay)
Dublin 1-8, Kilkenny 0-6 (replay ordered, objection)
1897—Kilkenny w.o. from Wexford
1898—Kilkenny 4-12, Dublin 3-2
1899—Wexford 2-12, Dublin 1-4
1900—Kilkenny 4-11 Dublin 4-10
1901—Wexford 7-6, Offaly 1-3
1902—Dublin 0-8, Kilkenny 1-4
1903—Kilkenny 1-5, Dublin 1-5 (Kilkenny awarded title; Dublin goal disputed)
1904—Kilkenny 2-8, Dublin 2-6
1905—Kilkenny 2-8, Dublin 2-2
1906—Dublin 1-14, Kilkenny 0-5
1907—Kilkenny 4-14, Dublin 1-9
1908—Dublin w.o. Kilkenny (scratched)
1909—Kilkenny 5-16, Laois 2-7
1910—Wexford 3-3, Dublin 1-1
1911—Kilkenny 4-6, Dublin 3-1
1912—Kilkenny 6-6, Laois 2-4
1913—Kilkenny 7-5, Dublin 2-1 (replay)
Kilkenny 0-3, Dublin 1-0 (draw)
1914—Laois 3-2, Kilkenny 2-4
1915—Laois 3-2, Dublin 0-5
1916—Kilkenny 11-3, Wexford 2-2
1917—Dublin 5-1, Kilkenny 4-0
1918—Wexford 2-3, Dublin 1-2
1919—Dublin 1-5, Kilkenny 1-2
1920—Dublin 4-5, Kilkenny 2-2
1921—Dublin 4-4, Kilkenny 1-5
1922—Kilkenny 3-4, Dublin 1-2
1923—Kilkenny 4-1, Dublin 1-1

1924—Dublin 4-4, Offaly 3-1
1925—Kilkenny awarded title on objection (Dublin "won" at Croke Park 6-4 to 4-7)
1926—Kilkenny 3-8, Offaly 1-4
1927—Dublin 7-7, Kilkenny 4-6
1928—Dublin 9-7, Offaly 4-3
1929—Declared void (both teams disqualified for being late on field after Kilkenny had beaten Dublin by 3-5 to 2-6 in the final)
1930—Dublin 4-7, Laois 2-2
1931—Kilkenny 4-7, Laois 4-2
1932—Kilkenny 4-6, Dublin 3-5
1933—Kilkenny 7-5, Dublin 5-5
1934—Dublin 3-5, Kilkenny 2-2 (replay)
   Dublin 2-8, Kilkenny 4-2 (draw)
1935—Kilkenny 3-8, Laois 0-6
1936—Kilkenny 4-6, Laois 2-5
1937—Kilkenny 5-3, Westmeath 2-4
1938—Dublin 4-9, Kilkenny 3-5 (replay)
   Dublin 2-3, Kilkenny 2-3 (draw)
1939—Kilkenny 2-12, Dublin 4-3
1940—Kilkenny 3-6, Dublin 2-5
1941—Dublin 2-8, Kilkenny 1-8
1942—Dublin 4-8, Kilkenny 1-4
1943—Kilkenny 3-9, Dublin 2-6
1944—Dublin 4-7, Wexford 3-3
1945—Kilkenny 5-12, Dublin 3-4
1946—Kilkenny 3-8, Dublin 1-12
1947—Kilkenny 7-10, Dublin 3-6
1948—Dublin 5-9, Laois 3-3
1949—Laois 3-8, Kilkenny 3-6
1950—Kilkenny 3-11, Wexford 2-11
1951—Wexford 3-12, Laois 4-3
1952—Dublin 7-2, Wexford 3-6
1953—Kilkenny 1-13, Wexford 3-5
1954—Wexford 8-5, Dublin 1-4
1955—Wexford 5-6, Kilkenny 3-9 (replay)
   Wexford 2-7, Kilkenny 2-7 (draw)
1956—Wexford 4-8, Kilkenny 3-10
1957—Kilkenny 6-9, Wexford 1-5
1958—Kilkenny 5-12, Wexford 4-9.
1959—Kilkenny 2-9, Dublin 1-11

1960—Wexford 3-10, Kilkenny 2-11
1961—Dublin 7-5, Wexford 4-8
1962—Wexford 3-9, Kilkenny 2-10
1963—Kilkenny 2-10, Dublin 0-9
1964—Kilkenny 4-11, Dublin 1-8
1965—Wexford 2-11, Kilkenny 3-7
1966—Kilkenny 1-15, Wexford 2-6
1967—Kilkenny 4-10, Wexford 1-12
1968—Wexford 3-13, Kilkenny 4-9
1969—Kilkenny 3-9, Offaly 0-16
1970—Wexford 4-16, Kilkenny 3-14
1971—Kilkenny 6-16, Wexford 3-16
1972—Kilkenny 3-16, Wexford 1-14 (replay)
      Kilkenny 6-13, Wexford 6-13 (draw)
1973—Kilkenny 4-22, Wexford 3-15.
1974—Kilkenny 6-13, Wexford 2-24
1975—Kilkenny 2-20, Wexford 2-14 (80 minute Final introduced)
1976—Wexford 2-20, Kilkenny 1-6
1977—Wexford 3-17, Kilkenny 3-14
1978—Kilkenny 2-16, Wexford 1-16
1979—Kilkenny 2-21, Wexford 2-17
1980—Offaly 3-17, Kilkenny 5-10
1981—Offaly 3-12, Wexford 2-13
1982—Kilkenny 1-11, Offaly 0-12
1983—Kilkenny 1-17, Offaly 0-13
1984—Offaly 1-15, Wexford 2-11
1985—Offaly 5-15, Laois 0-17
1986—Kilkenny 4-10, Offaly 1-11
1987—Kilkenny 2-14, Offaly 0-17
1988—Offaly 3-12, Wexford 1-14
1989—Offaly 3-15, Kilkenny 4-9
1990—Offaly 1-19, Dublin 2-11
1991—Kilkenny 1-13, Dublin 1-11
1992—Kilkenny 3-16, Wexford 2-9.
1993—Kilkenny 2-12, Wexford 0-11 (replay)
      Kilkenny 2-14, Wexford 1-17 (draw)

1928—Cork 7-6, Dublin 4-0 (Replay).
       Cork 1-8, Dublin 3-2 (Draw).
1929—Waterford 5-0, Meath 1-1.
1930—Tipperary 4-1, Kilkenny 2-1.
1931—Kilkenny 4-7, Galway 2-3.
1932—Tipperary 8-6, Kilkenny 5-1.
1933—Tipperary 4-6, Galway 2-3.
1934—Tipperary 4-3, Laois 3-5.
1935—Kilkenny 4-2, Tipperary 3-3.
1936—Kilkenny 2-4, Cork 2-3.
1937—Cork 8-5, Kilkenny 2-7.
1938—Cork 7-2, Dublin 5-4.
1939—Cork 5-2, Kilkenny 2-2.
1940—Limerick 6-4, Antrim 2-4.
1941—Cork 3-11, Galway 1-1.
1942—Suspended.
1943—Suspended.
1944—Suspended.
1945—Dublin 3-14, Tipperary 4-6.
1946—Dublin 1-6, Tipperary 0-7.
1947—Tipperary 9-5, Galway 1-5.
1948—Waterford 3-8, Kilkenny 4-2.
1949—Tipperary 6-5, Kilkenny 2-4.
1950—Kilkenny 3-4, Tipperary 1-5.
1951—Cork 4-5, Galway 1-8.
1952—**Tipperary 9-9, Dublin 2-3.**
1953—Tipperary 8-6, Dublin 3-6.
1954—Dublin 2-7, Tipperary 2-3.
1955—Tipperary 5-15, Galway 2-5.
1956—Tipperary 4-16, Kilkenny 1-5.
1957—Tipperary 4-7, Kilkenny 3-7.
1958—Limerick 5-8, Galway 3-10.
1959—Tipperary 2-8, Kilkenny 2-7.
1960—Kilkenny 7-12, Tipperary 1-11.
1961—Kilkenny 3-13, Tipperary 0-15.
1962—Kilkenny 3-6, Tipperary 0-9.
1963—Wexford 6-12, Limerick 5-9.
1964—Cork 10-7, Laois 1-4.
1965—Dublin 4-10, Limerick 2-7.
1966—Wexford 4-1, Cork 1-8 (Replay)
      Wexford 6-7, Cork 6-7 (draw)

1967—Cork 2-15, Wexford 5-3.
1968—Wexford 2-13, Cork 3-7.
1969—Cork 2-15, Kilkenny 3-6.
1970—Cork 5-19, Galway 2-9.
1971—Cork 2-11, Kilkenny 1-11.
1972—Kilkenny 8-7, Cork 3-9.
1973—Kilkenny 4-5, Galway 3-7.
1974—Cork 1-10, Kilkenny 1-8.
1975—Kilkenny 3-19, Cork 1-14.
1976—Tipperary 2.20, Kilkenny 1-7.
1977—Kilkenny 1-8, Cork 0-9 (Replay)
        Kilkenny 4-8, Cork 3-11 (Draw)
1978—Cork 1-15, Kilkenny 1-8.
1979—Cork 2-11, Kilkenny 1-9.
1980—Tipperary 2-15, Wexford 1-10.
1981—Kilkenny 1-20, Galway 3-9.
1982—Tipperary 2-7, Galway 0-4.
1983—Galway   0-10, Dublin 0-7
1984—Limerick 1-14, Kilkenny 3-8 (draw).
        Limerick 2-5, Kilkenny 2-4 (replay).
1985—Cork 3-10, Wexford 0-12.
1986—Offaly 3-12, Cork 3-9.
1987—Offaly 2-8, Tipperary 0-12.
1988—Kilkenny 3-13, Cork 0-12.
1989—Offaly 2-16, Clare 1-12
1990—Kilkenny 3-14, Cork 3-14 (draw)
        Kilkenny 3-16, Cork 0-11 (replay)
1991—Kilkenny 0-15, Tipperary 1-10
1992—Galway 1-13, Waterford 2-4
1993—Kilkenny 1-17, Galway 1-12

ALL-IRELAND MINOR HURLING FINAL TEAMS

1928

Cork—L. Horgan, J. Galvin, F. Cronin, D. Coughlan, C. Sheehan, J. Lee, Der Cogan, C. Murphy, Dan Lynch Denis Lynch, M. Lewis, M. Moloney, M. Finn, G. O'Connor, J. Ryng.

Note: C. Duggan, J. Mannix, J. Healy, J. O'Connor played in drawn game.

Dublin—M. Gleeson, J. Lloyd, G. Hughes, M. Kinsella, B. Reynolds, P. Melinn, R. Kavanagh, W. Kells, J. Hannon, M. Collins, G. O'Toole, F. Whelan, P. McHenry, P. Carton, K. O'Toole.

1929

Waterford—P. Rellis, F. Pinkert, L. Byrne, D. Wyse, P. Ryan, P. Donnelly, J. Butler, A. Noonan, J. Dwyer, N. Faraday, T. Sheehan, D. Goode, J. Goode, J. Houlihan, J. Murphy.

Meath—S. Ó Daláigh, M. Trabbers, S. O'Gibne, P. Ó Lionaird, P. O'Fearghaill, P. MacOireachtaig, P. Monnalain, P. Bluincead, T. Ceinnide, S. Moráin, R. MacNamee, S. Gearoid, G. O'Dare, N. de Bernett, P. Briain.

1930

Tipperary—M. Maher, J. Russell, M. Coffey, W. O'Neill, L. Burke, G. Heavey, J. Lanigan, T. Coffey, J. Dunne, J. Semple, E. Wade, P. Ryan, J. Close, T. Harney, J. Quinlan.

Kilkenny—A. Cullen, M. Tyrrell, J. Buggy, W. Burke, T. Deneiffe, Milo Kennedy, W. Ayres, J. Morrissey, J. Shortall, F. Minogue, P. Kelly, M. Byrne, J. Maher, M. Shortall, P. Leahy.

1931

Kilkenny—M. Doyle, D. Hughes, A. Cullen, M. Tyrrell, T. Shortall, M. Brennan, A. N. Other, J. Phelan, P. Kelly, J. Shortall, J. Dwyer, C. Barry, W. Walsh, B. Ayres, P. Shortall.

Galway—P. Comer, M. Tuohy, M. Kelly, M. Loughnane, R. Brogan, M. Donnellan, M. Lane, J. Moore, J. Barrett, J. Kelleher, J. Darcey, A. Strong, P. J. Walsh, M. Hanniffy, A. Burke. Sub: J. Kinlen.

1932

Tipperary—T. O'Keeffe, J. Looby, J. O'Dwyer, M. Burke, P. Leahy, C. Downes, J. Cooney, P. Bowe, Ned Barry, P. Purcell, T. Burke, J. Fletcher, D. Gorman, W. Nolan, J. Maher.

Kilkenny (selection)—M. Doyle, M. Meaney, W. Wyse, G. Dunne, M. Frisby, M. Brennan, J. McCarthy, M. Gargan, E. Bergin, E. O'Gorman, J. Giles, M. Doyle, E. Shortall, P. Larkin, M. Barry, J. Fitzparick, M. Foley, T. Kavanagh, L. Butler, S. Cleere, D. Roche.

1933

Tipperary—J. Moloney, J. Mooney, T. Doyle, Matt Ryan, M. Condon, M. Everard, P. Duggan, P. Dwyer, Tony Brennan, P. Frazer, M. Burke, J. Farrell, P Callaghan, Tim Maher, Joe Fletcher.

Galway—J. Keller, M. Loughnane, P. Brogan, F. Brogan, T. Molloy, M. Fennessy, T. Coughlan, D. Donnellan, P. J. Walshe, P. Fahy, T. B. Murphy, C. Murphy, R. Lahiffe, J. Cox, B. Noone.

1934

Tipperary—C. Maher, T. Lanigan, J. Noonan, J. Mooney, J. Moloney, Jerry Coffey, Denis Ryan, Tom English, P. O'Neill, Tony Brennan, P. Callaghan, Martin Loughnane, M. Mockler, Tom Cawley, P. O'Dwyer.

Laois—J. McCabe, P. O'Connor, W. Brophy, W. O'Neill, R. Bergin, J. Ring, H. Moloney, P. Rustchitzko, J. Kelly, T. Carroll,J. Hynan, M. Cahill, M. Delaney, P. Farrell, P. Carroll.

1935

Kilkenny—Tom Delaney, R. Hinks, P. Grace, W. Holohan, P. Boyle, P. Walsh, M. McEvoy, T. Leahy, J. Cahill, E. Tallent, B. Brannigan, J. Langton, J. Mulcahy, T. Prendergast, S. O'Brien. Sub.: P. Long.

Tipperary—P. Morris, P. O'Neill, C. Maher, T. Walsh, R. Ryan, J. O'Dwyer, T. Leahy, W. Brussels, J. Hennessy, P. Kearns, D. Ryan, M. Loughnane, T. Lanigan, P. Leahy, J. Coffey.

1936

Kilkenny—T. Delaney, R. Hinks, P. Kavanagh, E. Fitzpatrick, N. Hyland, J. O'Neill, T. Waldron, B. Brannigan, P. Giles, J. Langton, T. Mahon, E. Tallent, J. Mulcahy, M. Grace, S. O'Brien.

Cork—M. O'Donovan, M. Healy, P. Murphy, D. Coughlan, M. Goggin, C. Atkinson, P. O'Callaghan, M. Prenderville, P. J. O'Riordan, C. McSweeney, W. Campbell, M. Cahill, R. Dinneen, W. Buckley, D. McCarthy.

1937

Cork—D. Coughlan, R. Murphy, R. Dineen, D. O'Sullivan, J. Duggan, J. O'Shea, D. Lynch, J. Burrows, M. Goggin, K. McGrath, J. Hackett, J. P. Creedon, J. O'Mahony, K. McMahon, M. Emphy.

Kilkenny—E. Brett, P. Kavanagh, E. O'Connor, N. Dollard, J. O'Neill, D. Dalton, J. Hennessy, P. Savage, M. Heffernan, P. Burke, J. Dwyer, T. Larkin, J. Murphy, P. Fahy, S. O'Brien.

1938

Cork—P. J. Quinn, J. O'Mahony, A. Lotty, G. Sadlier, C. Ring, P. Hogan, W. Cummins, E. Young, J. Looney, W. Aherne, T. Foley, Luke O'Sullivan, T. Ryan, K. McGrath, Ted O'Sullivan.

Dublin—C. McCarthy, P. Collins, E. Dunphy, C. Nicholson, M. Hickey, F. Flynn, F. Fagan, P. Rafferty, D. Keane, G. Glynn, E. Walsh, M Keane, R. Molumby, J. Jenkinson, J. Bradley.

1939

Cork—T. McGrath, W. Cummins, D. O'Driscoll, W. Holton, P. Hayes, G. Sadlier, S. Murphy, E. Young, T. Crowley, M. Cody, T. Barry, J. White, P. Keohane, D. Cahalane, K. McGrath.

Kilkenny—A. Roberts, E. Quinlan, R. Dowling, P. O'Brien, J. Murphy, J. Grogan, M. Holden, P. O'Neill, J. Walsh, A. Murray, M. Andrews, K. Ruth, M. Walsh, S. Downey, J. Kelly.

1940

Limerick—P. Healy, K. O'Donoghue, J. Crotty, P. Murphy, M. Culhane, T. Hogan, T. Cregan, M. Fenton, P. McCarthy (Newcastlewest), P. McCarthy (Mungret), J. Hayes, W. Deere, A. O'Rourke, C. Birrane, J. Blackwell.

Antrim—L. Webb, E. Duke, W. Feeney, M. Flynn, J. Lougheed, F. Fleming, J. Butler, J. Corrigan, J. Quinn, W. McGowan, J. Gallagher, T. Lennon, P. Carmichael, J. McCallin, S. Mulholland.

1941

Cork—T. Mulcahy, J. Murphy, J. Looney, D. Lyons, J. Aherne, M. Murphy, C. Flaherty, P. Hill, S. Condon, D.

Twomey, M. Kennefick, P. O'Leary, J. McCarthy, J. Morrison, J. Kelly.

Galway—P. Doyle, P. Murphy, W. Fahy, P. Brady, W. Coen, C. Creane, S.Murphy, R. Beahan, V. Keane, G. McNamee, K. Kennelly, D. Solan, D. Quigley, T. Neary, M. Nestor.

1945

Dublin—S. Copeland, P. Whelan, S. McLoughlin, G. Jennings, J. Prendergast, T. McLysaght, B. Clancy, S. McEntaggert, D. Healy, P. Donnelly, L. Donnelly, N. Maher, F. Tormey, P. McCarthy, P. Lynch. Sub.: S. O'Neill.

Tipperary—N. Egan, D. Ryan, S. Bannon, T. Tynan, M. McCormack, P. Stakelum, M. Shaughnessy, J. O'Grady, W. Carroll, J. Harris, M. Maher, P. Kenny, W. Molloy, J. Byrne, M. Ryan. Sub.: W. O'Brien.

1946

Dublin—G. Sutton, P. Whelan, J. Lavin, S. McLoughlin, J. Butler, N. Fingleton, B. Clancy, J. Guinea, C. McHale, N. Maher, L. Donnelly, J. Finnan, A. Young, C. Kavanagh, W. Fletcher. Sub. S. Molumby.

Tipperary—W. O'Brien, J. Doyle, J. Nolan, H. Sheehy, C. Dalton, J. Ryan, B. McGrath, J. O'Grady, P. Shanahan, M. Ryan, M. Shaughnessy, P. Kenny, T. O'Meara, M. Maher, W. Steiglitz. Sub.: D. McNulty.

1947

Tipperary—J. O'Grady, J. Doyle, J. J. McCormack, B. Mockler, C. Keane, J. Ryan, S. Twomey, M. Ryan, J. Farrell, D. Butler, D. McNulty, P. Kenny, T. O'Meara, M. Butler, S. McDonnell.

Galway—S. Leaper, D. O'Sullivan, P. Daly, S. McGrath, M. McGrath, P. Conroy, M. Power, T. Murphy, J. Salmon, M. McKeown, P. Rooney, C. McNamee, D. Mullaly, S. Manning, S. Duggan.

1948

Waterford—S. O'Flynn, M. Morrissey, S. Hayden, M. Hogan, V. Walsh, M. Kelleher, T. Cunningham, S. Conlon, T. Gallagher, L. Conway, M. Flannelly, M. O'Connor, M. McHugh, P. O'Connor, M. Browne.

Kilkenny—S. Tobin, W. Doyle, K. Crotty, P. Dalton, T.

O'Connor, D. Galaven, H. Ryan, M. O'Loughlin, W. Maher, T. Connolly, M. Roche R. Carroll, W. Bennett, W. Ronan, R. O'Neill.

1949

Tipperary—J. O'Grady, Jim Moloney, John Moloney, S. Browne, D. Maher, J. Finn, S. McGrath, R. Holden, W. Perkins, A. McDonnell, L. Keane, T. Aherne, M. Buckley, M. Maher, J. Doyle.

Kilkenny—J. Murphy, J. Dobbyn, D. Maher, T. Walton, T. O'Connor, M. O'Shaughnessy, J. McGovern, H. Ryan, P. Fitzgerald, T. Dowling, R. O'Neill, T. Prendergast, R. Mahony, P. Horgan, M. Cuggy.

1950

Kilkenny—J. Murphy, J. Doherty, J. Maher, P. Lyng, P. Lennon, Jim Walsh, J. McGovern, P. Johnston, D. Gorey, M. Gardiner, M. Brophy, T. O'Hanrahan, S. O'Brien, J. Brennan, R. Brennan. Sub.: C. Gough.

Tipperary—G. Butler, P. Mockler, S. Power, M. Hynes, P. Croke, A. Wall, P. McGrath, S. Cunningham, G. Doyle, D. Ryan, D. Nolan, L. McDonnell, W. McLoughney, S. Keaty, D. O'Brien. Subs.: W. Quinn, S. Walsh.

1951

Cork—J. Dempsey, J. Coffey, M. Sheehan, P. Dreivers, P. Gaffney, S. O'Regan, F. O'Regan, F. O'Mahony, P. Duggan, P. Crowley, J. O'Donoghue, J. Clifford, T. Kelly, S. O'Sullivan, E. Goulding. Sub.: V. Dorgan.

Galway—D. Corrigan, B. Hoare, T. Tarpey, P. Cullinane, A. Sexton, W. Duffy, S. Larkin, E. Fallon, S. Cullinane, A. Hansberry, J. McDonagh, M. Murphy, M. Cullinane, P. Finn, S. Trayers. Sub.: A. Creaven.

1952

Tipperary—E. McLoughney, D. Quinn, E. McGrath, E. Burke, F. Dyer, W. Hayes, L. Quinn, P. Hennessy, B. Quinn, L. Devaney, T. Wall, S. McLoughlin, M. Butler, J. Browne, P. Cleary. Sub.: S. McGovern.

Dublin—S. O'Neill, S. Hall, B. Campbell, L. Horan, M. Boylan, P. Higgins, S. Doyle, C. McLaughlin, P. Feeley, P. Haughey, B. Boothman, C. Dolan, M. Doyle, M. O'Connor, V. Bell.

1953

Tipperary—T. McCormack, M. Cleary, T. Kelly, P. Barry, L. Quinn, R. Reidy, S. Kenny, B. Quinn, M. Kennedy, L. Devaney, S. Murphy, S. McLoughlin, S. Corcoran, M. Stapleton, L. Connolly. Sub.: R. Ryan.

Dublin—M. Meagher, T. Toner, T. O'Neill, S. Murphy, M. Bohane, B. Boothman, S. Dart, T. Bracken, R. Feely, A. Kavanagh, V. Bell, T. Synott, L. Rowe, E. Clarke, C. Feely.

1954

Dublin—S. O'Neill, C. Moore, T. O'Neill, M. Bohan, M. Meagher, B. Boothman, F. Whelan, T. Bracken, P. McGurk, A. Kavanagh, V. Bell, P. Delaney, P. Hyland, E. Kelly, P. Farnan. Sub.: M. Mannion.

Tipperary—J. Doyle, M. Cleary, D. O'Shea, C. Moloney, R. Ryan, R. Reidy, L. Quinn, L. Mahony, M. Burns, S. Murphy, T. Gouldsboro, L. O'Donovan, S. Kenny, C. Ahearne, L. Connolly. Subs.: K. Dermody, P. Ryan.

1955

Tipperary—S. Ryan, T. Gleeson, R. O'Donnell, M. Craddock, D. Ryan, R. Reidy, S. Warren, C. Foyle, M. Burns, J. Doyle, A. Leahy, M. Gilmartin, L. O'Grady, P. Ryan, P. Dorney. Subs.: S. Small, M. O'Gara.

Galway—K. Croke, S. Naughton, T. Broderick, S. Keane, P. Davis, A. O'Dwyer, S. Murray, M. Fox, P. Labby, N. Murray, T. Ryan, C. Marmion, T. Flanagan, E. Newell, S. Gannon. Sub.: N. O'Neill.

1956

Tipperary—A. Tierney, T. Gleeson, M. Dorney, B. Maher, M. Craddock, P. Reynolds, J. Mulooly, S. Warren, S. Mackey, J. Doyle, P. Ryan, W. O'Grady, T. Flynn, J. Scott, S. Dalton.

Kilkenny—W. Barry, J. Blanchfield, P. Dillon, H. Hickey, J. McCormack, P. Moran, T. Carroll, S. Buckley, T. Brennan, T. Molloy, P. Driscoll, B. Buckley,M. Dunne, S. Leahy, J. Cullinane. Subs.: A. Comerford, R. Dowling.

1957

Tipperary—T. Moloney, M. Craddock, M. Lonergan, P. Kearns, M. Stapleton, P. Reynolds, A. Croke, M. Murphy, P. Kennedy, S. Ryan, L. Kiely, J. Doyle, P. Doyle, M. Hogan, P. Butler. Subs.: W. Hogan, P. Woodlock.

Kilkenny—W. Barry, P. Moran, J. O'Donnell, H. Hickey, L. O'Brien, T. Carroll, N. Hanrahan, L. McCarthy, A. Comerford, P. Maher, R. Walsh, E. Kehir, T. Bowe, J. Doherty, M. Dunne. Sub.: T. O'Connell.

1958

Limerick—T. Hanley, J. McDonagh, J. Guinane, C. O'Connell, J. J. Bresnihan, J. Leonard, M. Hanrahan, B. Kelleher, P. Hartnett, P. Cobbe, L. Canty, P. Murphy, E. Carey, J. Hayes, S. Sexton. Sub.: D. Dillane.

Galway—P. Fahy, D. Robinson, A. McDonnell, S. Francis, S. Coughlan, J. Lyons, P. J. Cormican, S. Kelly, C. Stanley, J. Egan, S. Devlin, J. Spillane, P. Jordan, H. Conway, P. Glynn. Sub.: G. Loughnane.

1959

Tipperary—J. O'Donoghue, P. Griffin, G. Kinnane, M. Lonergan, J. Carroll, A. Croke, R. Slevin, T. Ryan (Killenaule), T. Ryan (Toomevara), P. Doyle, B. Carey, M. Duggan, M. Nolan, L. Kiely, J. Ryan. Sub.: S. Gleeson, P. Crampton.

Kilkenny—E. Fitzpatrick, P. Larkin, P. Brett, S. Rafferty, P. Grace, A. McGrath, N. Hanrahan, T. Barry, M. Murphy, J. Ayres, T. Brennan, E. Keher, R. Walsh, S. Nyhan, M. Walsh. Subs.: D. Lannon, E. Connolly.

1960

Kilkenny—D. Kinsella, N. Roughan, J. Ayres, P. Dempsey, R. Walsh, O. Ryan, P. Brett, T. Murphy, T. Barry, P. Freaney, W. Grace, J. Nyhan, S. O'Brien, P. Ryan, A. McGrath.

Tipperary—J. O'Donoghue, J. Kennedy, Christy O'Dwyer, M. Cummins, J. Cummins, Conor O'Dwyer, W. Greene, P. O'Connell, J. Ryan, B. Nolan, M. Keating, A. McGovern, M. O'Connor, M. Ryan, W. Ryan. Sub.: W. Burke.

1961

Kilkenny—P. Foley, J. McGrath, N. Forrestal, P. Cullen, S. O'Brien, P. Henderson, S. Hanrahan, T. Barry, J. Murphy, T. Walsh, D. Kinsella, P. Freaney, J. Dunphy, M. Aylward, J. Delaney.

Tipperary—P. O'Sullivan, J. Dillon, L. White, W. Eakins, D. Ryan, N. Lane, P. O'Dwyer, C. O'Dwyer, M. Roche, W. Nolan, M. Keating, W. Ryan, N. Hogan, G. Ryan, T. Brennan.

● **Nicholas English leads out Tipperary against Galway in the 1988 All-Ireland Final – the first appearance of the Blue and Gold in a Final in seventeen years.**

Kilkenny—N. Skehan, S. Treacy, T. Phelan, J. Walsh, S. Hanrahan, P. Drennan, W. Burke, J. Byrne, S. Muldowney, S. Cooke, T. Walsh, J. Delaney, J. Dunphy, P. Walsh, M. Aylward. Sub.: T. Ryan.

Tipperary—P. Fleming, W. Smith, P. O'Rourke, M. O'Meara, O. Killoran, L. Gaynor, E. Loughnane, P. Delaney, M. O'Brien, W. Nolan, M. Keating, F. Loughnane, D. Moloney, T. Buckley, T. Brennan. Subs.: P. Hayes, S. Dermody, S. Nash.

1963

Wexford—L. Byrne, J. Hartley, M. Nolan, E. O'Connor, J. Murphy, M. Kinsella, V. Staples, W. Bernie, C. Rafferty, C. Dowdall, T. Doran, F. Swords, W. Carley, S. Barron, P. Quigley. Sub.: B. Gaule.

Limerick—A. Dunworth, S. O'Brien, J. Egan, S. O'Shaughnessy, P. Heffernan, T. McAuliffe, P. O'Brien, A. Roche, E. Cregan, C. Danagher, B. Savage, M. Graham, S. Geary, G. Cosgrove, B. Cobbe. Subs.: E. Grimes, P. Nash, W. O'Gorman.

1964

Cork—H. O'Brien, T. Murphy, G. Aherne, P. O'Sullivan, J. O'Callaghan, B. Wylie, W. Murphy, P. O'Riordan, C. Roche, D. Clifford, L. McAuliffe, K. Cummins, C. McCarthy, A. O'Flynn, M. Kenneally.

Laois—E. Bergin, L. Moore, M. McDonnell, P. Byrne, L. Phelan, L. Purcell, L. Delaney, M. Fennell, P. Dowling, B. Delaney, P. Dillon, P. Payne, D. Conlon, S. Kavanagh, P. Keyes. Subs.: S. Sheppard, P. Kavanagh.

1965

Dublin—P. Cunningham, A. Fletcher, L. Deegan, C. Brennan, W. Markey, P. Kennedy, L. Martin, H. Dalton, F. McDonald, J. Fetherston, E. Davey, T. Grealish, T. McCann, B. Whelan, M. Kinsella. Sub.: P. Cassels.

Limerick—T. Brennan, M. O'Flaherty, D. Manning, A. Cronin, S. Toomey, E. Boland, J. O'Hehir, P. Doherty, D. Foley, E. Grimes, C. Shanahan, N. Hayes, M. Grace, B. Murnane, S. Burke. Subs.: J. Moynihan, M. Hennessy.

1966

Wexford—H. Butler, J. Quigley, E. Murphy, W. Butler, E. McDonald, E. Buggy, M. Fitzpatrick, D. Howell, T. Kavanagh,

T. Furlong, L. Bent, P. Byrne, T. Royce, M. Browne, P. Bernie. Subs.: J. Nangle, J. Ryan. M. Butler played in drawn game. T. Kavnagh came on as sub in drawn game.

Cork—B. Hurley, D. Carroll, P. Geary, N. Norberg, Joe Aherne, J. Horgan, R. Cummins, P. Moylan, W. Walsh, B. Meade, S. Murphy, P. Ring, F. Keane, G. O'Riordan, M. Curley. D. Clifford, L. Comer, C. Kelly played in drawn game. Comer and Kelly came on as subs in replay, F. Hogan came on as a sub in drawn game.

1967

Cork—W. Glavin, M. McCarthy, B. Tobin, M. Bohane, Ted O'Brien, J. Horgan, M. Aherne, P. Moylan, J. Barrett, S. Murphy, M. Malone, C. Kelly, T. Buckley, B. O'Connor, P. Ring. Subs.: M. Ryan, K. Fitzgerald.

Wexford—P. Cox, J. Quigley, J. Royce, E. McDonald, E. Walsh, L. Byrne, L. Bennett, A. Kavanagh, P. Walsh, J. Murphy, M. Butler, P. Byrne, M. Quigley, M. Casey, J. Murphy. Sub.: D. Lawlor.

1968

Wexford—P. Cox, G. O'Connor, J. Russell, P. O'Brien, A. Kerrigan, L. Byrne, L. Bennett, P. Kennedy, T. Byrne, M. Quigley, P. Walsh, J. Murphy, M. Butler, M. Casey, M. Byrne. Subs.: L. Kinsella, B. Walsh.

Cork—M. Coleman, J. Horgan, B. Cummins, M. Bohane, B. Coleman, S. Looney, T. O'Shea, K. McSweeney, G. O'Sullivan, M. Ryan, P. Ring, T. Buckley, D. McCarthy, J. Rothwell, M. Malone. Sub.: P. Kavanagh.

1969

Cork—P. Lawton, P. Casey, J. Rothwell, J. O'Sullivan, K. Murray, M. O'Doherty, S. Collins, N. Crowley, S. O'Farrell, P. Kavanagh, T. Crowley, T. Sheehan, F. Coughlan, G. Hanley, S. O'Leary. Sub.: J. Buckley.

Kilkenny—T. Condon, P. Boran, P. Butler, T. Teehan, D. McCormack, G. Burke, G. McCarthy, T. Phelan, T. Waters, P. Bollard, M. O'Shea, M. Buggy, T. Neary, M. Carroll, D. Corcoran. Subs.: R. O'Shea, J. O'Brien.

1970

Cork—D. O'Brien, B. Murphy, L. Kelly, M. Corbett, V. Twomey, M. O'Doherty, J. Buckley, P. Kavanagh, N. Crowley,

G. Hanley, S. O'Farrell, T. Sheehan, D. Relihan, T. Crowley, S. O'Leary.

Galway—E. Campbell, S. Cloonan, C. Maher, S. Fahy, I. Clarke, A. Fenton, S. Healy, S. Donoghue, S. Hynes, M. Donoghue, Joe McDonagh, D. Campbell, P. J. Molloy, C. Fitzgerald, J. Holland. Subs.: W. Cummins, B. Brennan, J. Hanniffy.

1971

Cork—F. O'Sullivan, M. Corbett, L. McNally, D. J. Foley, D. Coakley, J. Buckley, D. O'Keeffe, T. Canavan, D. O'Dwyer, P. Buckley, A. Creagh, V. Twomey (Na Piarsaigh), T. Fogarty, J. Barry Murphy, E. O'Sullivan. Subs.: S. Coughlan, B. Cotter, J. Ryan.

Kilkenny—K. Fennelly, N. Brennan, A. Teehan, S. Brophy, M. Hogan, B. Cody, T. McCormack, T. Barry, J. McCormack, P. Kearney, N. Minogue, E. Holohan, P. Butler, P. J. Butler, B. Sweeney. Sub.: W. Fitzpatrick.

1972

Kilkenny—K. Fennelly, J. Ryan, J. Burke, P. O'Brien, K. Robinson, B. Cody, J. Dowling, G. Woodcock, G. Fennelly, S. O'Brien, M. Tierney, W. Fitzpatrick, P. Butler, M. McCarthy, B. Sweeney. Sub.: J. O'Sullivan.

Cork—F. O'Sullivan, J. Kennefick, L. McNally, J. Barrett, B. Manley, F. Delaney, S. Farrell, R. Wilmot, K. Collins, R. Fitzgerald, T. O'Sullivan, B. Óg Murphy, T. Collins, J. Barry Murphy, E. O'Sullivan. Subs.: J. Norberg, B. Gallagher.

1973

Kilkenny—P. Dunphy, R. O'Hara, G. Doheny, K. Robinson, J. Hennessy, J. Marnell, O. Bergin, G. Devane, B. Waldron, P. Lannon, P. Mulhall, J. Lyng, P. Treacy, S. O'Brien, M. Lyng. Subs: J. Purcell, M. Lanigan.

Galway—F. Larkin, H. Silke, G. Maher, G. Murphy, J. Dervan, T. Murphy, G. Lohan, G. Holian, S. Linnane, M. Hanniffy, J. Donoghue, Brian Kelly, F. Power, G. Burke, E. Dooley.

1974

Cork—J. Cronin, P. Coughlan, L. Geaney, J. Crowley, C. Brassil, T. Cashman, D. McCurtain, R. O'Mahony, F. Delaney, K. O'Driscoll, D. Ryan, G. McEvoy, T. Murphy, T. Cullinane, D. Buckley. Subs.: D. Keane, D. Murphy, Pat Horgan.

Kilkenny—A. Murphy, R. O'Hara, J. Marnell, G. Stapleton, J. Hennessy, G. Devane, J. Costelloe, B. Waldron, P. Lannon, M. Lyng, J. Walsh, K. Brennan, A. Driscoll, G. Tyrell, B. Fennelly. Subs.: M. Kennedy, J. Henderson.

1975

Kilkenny—E. Mahon, R. Power, P. Prendergast, J. Henderson, H. Ryan, R. O'Hara, G. Stapleton, P. Lannon, J. O'Brien, K. Brennan, J. Wall, K. O'Shea, S. Hennessy, P. Brennan, J. Ryan.

Cork—J. Hayes, M. Cronin, F. Walsh, Jerry Murphy, B. Dinneen, T. Cashman, D. McCurtain, D. Herlihy, Padraig Crowley, Paul Crowley, P. Horgan, J. O'Sullivan, F. Tobin, John Murphy, D. Buckley. Subs.: Peter Horgan, T. Lyons.

1976

Tipperary—V. Mullins, P. Loughnane, P. J. Maxwell, T. Slattery, M. Stapleton, G. Stapleton, J. O'Dwyer, J. Hogan, P. Ryan, E. O'Shea, M. Doyle, T. Grogan, M. Murphy, J. Stone, P. Power. Sub.: P. Looby.

Kilkenny—E. Mahon, G. Stapleton, P. Holden, T. Lennon, J. Byrne, P. Prendergast, P. Murphy, S. Hennessy, J. Brennan, L. Fennelly, J. Wall, J. Heffernan, J. Ryan, P. Brennan, J. Waters. Subs.: J. Carroll, J. Power, E. Deegan.

1977

Kilkenny—L. Ryan, C. Mackey, M. Meagher, Bill O'Hara, T. Lennon, S. Fennelly, D. Connolly, G. Ryan, J. Mulcahy, E. Deegan, R. Murphy, E. Crowley, M. Nash, E. Wallace, B. McEvoy. Sub.: J. Waters (Drawn game). J. Heffernan (Replay and he also played in drawn match). R. Murphy did not play in drawn game.

Cork—J. Hegarty, J. Murphy, S. O'Mahony, S. O'Brien, W. Cashman, S. Hayes, J. Whooley, T. O'Connell, Tadgh McCarthy, J. Hartnett, R. O'Connor, J. Monaghan, S. O'Gorman, J. Keane, T. Aherne. Sub.: D. Murphy (Note: J. Walsh played in drawn game. S. O'Mahony came on as a sub in drawn game.)

1978

Cork—G. Cunningham, W. Cashman, P. Murphy, J. Hodgins, B. O'Driscoll, J. Murphy, T. McCarthy, D. Walsh, J. Hartnett, L. Lynch, Tom Aherne, G. O'Regan, D. Murphy, S. O'Gorman, S. Cashman.

Kilkenny—B. Walton, R. Maloney, B. O'Hara, P. Crowley, L.

Hennessy, P. Gannon, M. Cleere, W. Walsh, J. Moriarty, E. Crowley, B. McEvoy, J. Holland, P. Phelan, M. Heffernan, W. Purcell. Subs.: J. J. Long, P. Heffernan.

1979

Cork—G. Cunningham, W. Cashman, C. O'Connor, J. Hodgins, C. Marshall, K. O'Driscoll, C. Coughlan, D. Scanlon, D. Walsh, T. O'Sullivan, K. Hennessy, J. Greally, A. Coyne, M. O'Sullivan, T. Coakley. Sub.: R. Hegarty.

Kilkenny—M. Walsh, P. Ryan, E. Aylward, J. Holden, L. Hennessy, P. Heffernan, M. Gaffney, J. Moriarty, J. Mahon, W. Purcell, J. O'Dwyer, S. Tyrell, P. Phelan, J. Murphy, T. Moylan. Subs.: W. Walton, M. Walsh, M. Byrne.

1980

Tipperary—K. Hogan, M. Conway, P. Maher, E. Hogan, I. Conroy, J. Maher, D. Finnerty, J. Hayes, P. Kenny, G. O'Neill, M. McGrath, J. Darcy, A. Browne, W. Peters, N. English. Subs.: V. Dooley, J. Treacy.

Wexford—T. Doyle, B. Keeling, P. Gahan. D. Sheehan, J. Roche, E. Cleary, J. Grennells, G. Coady, A. Gahan, J. Byrne, J. Codd, T. Morrissey, M. Fitzhenry, J. Barnwell, E. Murphy.

1981

Kilkenny—D. Burke, G. O'Neill, E. Kennedy, E. Wall, D. Hoyne, M. Morrissey, J. O'Hara, P. Ryan, T. Bawle, J. McDonald, D. Carroll, R. Heffernan, L. McCarthy, S. Delahunty, M. Rafter. Subs.: S. Whearty, P. Cleere, J. Donnelly.

Galway—T. Coen, S. Moylan, P. Finnerty, K. Flannery, J. Grealish, G. Fallon, T. Helebert, J. Burke, P. Winters, M. McGrath, T. Keady, J. Leahy, P. Burke, E. Ryan, A. Cunningham. Subs.: M. Coleman, S. Brody.

1982

Tipperary—J. Leamy, J. Flannery, J. Bergin, C. Bonnar, B. Everard, D. Kealy, W. Hayes, J. Kennedy, G. Bradley, N. Sheehy, M. Cunningham, S. Slattery, J. Cormack, L. Stokes, M. Scully. Subs.: M. Corcoran, G. Ryan, A. Ryan.

Galway—T. Kenny, S. Murphy, P. Finnerty, P. Malone, P. Lynch, T. Helebert, G. McInerney, J. Byrne, M. Kenny, J. Noone, J. Burke, S. Connolly, G. Brehony, T. Moloney, A. Cunningham. Subs.: G. Waldron, D. Murphy.

1983

Galway—J. Commins, M. Killeen, P. Dervan, S. Treacy, P. Brehony, P. Malone, G. McInerney, D. Jennings, J. J. Broderick, T. Monaghan, T. Moloney, J. Cooney, S. Keane, A. Cunningham, P. Higgins. Subs.: M. Shiel, G. Elwood, N. Brody.

Dublin—T. O'Riordan, N. O'Carroll, E. Clancy, J. P. Byrne, D. Byrne, J. Murphy, S. Cullen, P. Williams, D. Foley, M. Hayes, B. Collins, P. Confrey, N. Quinn, S. Dalton, B. Gavin. Subs.: P. Kearns, T. Spellman.

1984

Limerick—V. Murnane, A. Madden, P. Carey, J. Fitzgerald, G. Hegarty, A. O'Riordan, A. Cunneen, A. Carmody, M. Reale, T. Byrnes, G. Kirby, G. Ryan, J. O'Neill, P. Davern, B. Stapleton. Subs.: M. O'Brien (Draw), C. Coughlan (both games), D. Flynn (played in draw). D. Marren (replay).

Kilkenny—A. McCormack, W. O'Dwyer, B. Bryan, F. Morgan, L. O'Brien, J. Power, D. Mullen, G. Drennan, P. Phelan, P. McEvoy, T. Lennon, B. Ayres, W. Purcell, M. Frisby, L. Dowling. Subs.: Drawn game: W. Purcell, P. Phelan, B. Ayres. Replay: A. Byrne, L. Egan, J. Farrell. (Note: Frisby, Purcell, Ayres and Phelan replaced Farrell, Egan, P. Fennelly and W. Cleere for replay.)

1985

Cork—T. Kingston, C. Connery, P. Cahalane, B. Coutts, C. Casey, B. Murphy, K. McGuckian, M. O'Mahony, L. Kelly, G. O'Riordan, B. Harte, J. Fitzgibbon, G. Manley, M. Foley, M. Mullins.

Wexford—P. Nolan, L. Gorman, J. Redmond, S. Flood, J. Codd, Ger Cush, V. Reddy, J. Bolger, J. O'Connor, E. Broders, V. Murphy, P. O'Callaghan, E. Synnott, B. Moran, P. Carton. Subs.: S. Wickham, J. Quirke.

1986

Offaly—J. Errity, P. Nallen, R. Mannion, D. Sherlock, J. Kilmartin, M. Hogan, B. Kelly, D. Geoghegan, A. Kelly, G. Cahill, D. Regan, R. Byrne, T. Moylan, M. Duignan, D. Pilkington. Sub.: B. Dooley.

Cork—P. Barry, N. Hackett, D. Irwin, K. Keane, R. O'Connor, P. Kenneally, Tony O'Keeffe, J. O'Mahony, J. Corcoran, R. Sheehan, J. Walsh, M. Mullins, B. Cunningham, D. O'Connell, G. Manley. Subs.: D. Walsh, P. O'Brien.

1987

Offaly—J. Troy, B. Whelehan, D. Geoghegan, B. Hennessy, J. Dooley, J. Errity, A. Cahill, J. Pilkington, T. Dooley, S. Morkam, B. Dooley, K. Egan, T. Moylan, J. Troy, D. Pilkington.

Tipperary—P. Kearns, L. Sheedy, M. O'Meara, N. Keane, M. Ryan, C. Bonnar, B. Corcoran, M. Perdue, J. Quinlan, J. Leahy, S. Bohan, G. Dealey, D. Lyons, C. Egan, B. Hogan. Sub.: S. Quinn, D. O'Meara.

1988

Kilkenny—J. Conroy, G. Henderson, P. J. O'Connor, D. Roche, P. O'Neill, P. Brophy, J. Conlon, D. Dooley, D. Bradley, W. O'Keeffe, B. Ryan, P. O'Grady, A. Ronan, C. Carter, D. J. Carey. Subs.: P. Treacy for O'Keeffe; J. Buggy for O'Grady.

Cork—I. Lynam, T. Twomey, D. Holland, L. Callinan, T. Dineen, D. Quirke, M. Noonan, T. Kelleher, B. Corcoran, T. Hurley, K. Roche, M. Sheehan, P. O'Brien, B. Cunningham, J. Dillon. Subs.: S. Guitheen for Hurley (injured); P. Murray for Dillon.

1989

Offaly—John Troy, M. Hogan, F. Cullen, H. Rigney, D. Barron, B. Whelehan, Donal Franks, A. Cahill, R. Dooley, Johnny Dooley, S. Grennan, O. O'Neill, R. McNamara, N. Hand, K. Flynn. Sub.: R. Deegan for R. Dooley.

Clare—D. Fitzgerald, D. McInerney, P. Lee, F. Corey, P. Markham, J. O'Gorman, G. Cahill, C. Chaplin, S. Power, P. O'Rourke, G. Moroney, P. Minogue, P. McNamara, C. Clancy, P. Keary. Subs.: J. O'Connor for Moroney, K. McNamara for Keary.

1990

Kilkenny—A. Behan, M. Holohan, L. Mahony, J. Carroll, D. O'Neill, C. Brennan, P. Larkin, J. McDermott, P. Long, A. Comerford, J. Shefflin, P. Farrell, P. J. Delaney, S. Ryan, D. Lawlor. Subs.: A. Cleere for Long, B. Power for O'Neill. (Note: S. Meally, D. Beirne and A. Cleere played in drawn game. B. Power, C. Brennan and J. Carroll came on as subs in drawn game).

Cork—D. O'Mahony, F. Ryan, A. Murphy, A. White, C. Buckley, P. Smith, B. Sheehan, C. Dillon, R. O'Connell, B. Egan,

B. Walsh, L. Meaney, K. Murray, M. Landers, D. Fleming. Subs.: B. Corcoran for Buckley, M. Quirke for Ryan, R. Lewis for O'Connell. (Note: N. O'Donnell, C. Walsh and B. Corcoran played in drawn game. M. Quirke, C. Dillon and D. Fleming came on as subs in drawn game).

1991

Kilkenny—M. Carey, S. Meally, L. Mahony, B. Power, A. O'Sullivan, E. Dwyer, D. O'Neill, D. Maher, J. Hickey, S. Dollard, P. J. Delaney, G. Walsh, D. Byrne, M. Owens, R. Shortall. Sub.: P. Davis for Walsh.

Tipperary—M. Ferncombe, S. O'Donoghue, M. Rabbitte, M. Gleeson, P. Shanahan, B. Gaynor, T. Gleeson, T. Shelly, M. Leonard, T. Dunne, B. O'Meara, A. Hogan, L. Barrett, T. Fogarty, G. Maguire. Sub.: C. Egan for Barrett.

1992

Galway—L. Donoghue, T. Healy, M. Spellman, C. Moore, N. Shaughnessy, C. Donovan, M. Donoghue, F. Forde, S. Walsh, M. Lynskey, D. Coen, P. Kelly, S. Corcoan, C. O'Doherty, D. Walsh. Subs.: J. Murray for Lynskey, J. Kerans for O'Doherty.

Waterford—P. Haran, T. Morrissey, P. O'Donnell, J. O'Connor, A. Kirwan, G. Harris, T. Feeney, T. Kiely, F. O'Shea, J. P. Fitzpatrick, D. McGrath, J. J. Ronayne, R. Ryan, P. Foley, P. Flynn. Sub.: B. McCarthy for Kiely.

1993

Kilkenny—O. Blanchfield, T. Hickey, S. Doyle, J. Ayres, V. O'Brien, B. Lonergan, B. Bolger, K. Grogan, S. Kealy, D. Cleere, L. Smith, E. Mackey, B. Dalton, D. Buggy, O. O'Connor. Sub.: J. Young for Kealy.

Galway—K. Broderick, J. Linnane, T. Healy, R. Fahy, G. Kennedy, C. Moore, N. Linnane, O. Canning, S. Walsh, M. Conroy, D. Coen, K. Donoghue, S. Corcoran, D. Walsh, O. Fahy. Subs.: M. Lynskey for J. Linnane, F. Healy for Corcoran, L. Madden for N. Linnane.

CAPTAINS OF WINNING ALL-IRELAND
MINOR HURLING TEAMS

1928—L. Horgan (Cork)
1929—P. Donnelly (Waterford)
1930—J. Russell (Tipperary)
1931—J. Shortall (Kilkenny)
1932—D. O'Gorman (Tipperary)
1933—J. Fletcher (Tipperary)
1934—C. Maher (Tipperary)
1935—P. Grace (Kilkenny)
1936—E. Tallent (Kilkenny)
1937—M. Goggin (Cork)
1938—K. McGrath (Cork)
1939—T. Barry (Cork)
1940—P. McCarthy (Limerick)
1941—S. Condon (Cork)
1942-44—Abandoned
1945—D. Healy (Dublin)
1946—G. Sutton (Dublin)
1947—P. Kenny (Tipperary)
1948—M. Flannelly (Waterford)
1949—J. O'Grady (Tipperary)
1950—P. Lennon (Kilkenny)
1951—J. Clifford (Cork)
1952—A. Wall (Tipperary)
1953—B. Quinn (Tipperary)
1954—B. Boothman (Dublin)
1955—R. Reidy (Tipperary)
1956—P. Ryan (Tipperary)
1957—J. Doyle (Tipperary)
1958—P. Cobbe (Limerick)
1959—L. Kiely (Tipperary)
1960—W. Grace (Kilkenny)
1961—J. Dunphy (Kilkenny)
1962—J. Dunphy (Kilkenny)
1963—L. Bernie (Wexford)
1964—K. Cummins (Cork)
1965—L. Martin (Dublin)
1966—P. Bernie (Wexford)
1967—P. Moylan (Cork)
1968—T. Byrne (Wexford)

1969—S. Collins (Cork)
1970—P. Kavanagh (Cork)
1971—J. Buckley (Cork)
1972—B. Cody (Kilkenny)
1973—K. Robinson (Kilkenny)
1974—L. Geaney (Cork)
1975—H. Ryan (Kilkenny)
1976—J. Hogan (Tipperary)
1977—S. Fennelly (Kilkenny)
1978—P. Murphy (Cork)
1979—C. Coughlan (Cork)
1980—J. Maher (Tipperary)
1981—E. Kennedy (Kilkenny)
1982—J. Kennedy (Tipperary)
1983—A. Cunningham (Galway)
1984—A. O'Riordan (Limerick)
1985—M. O'Mahony (Cork)
1986—M. Hogan (Offaly)
1987—T. Moylan (Offaly)
1988—P. Brophy (Kilkenny)
1989—B. Whelehan (Offaly)
1990—J. McDermott (Kilkenny)
1991—D. O'Neill (Kilkenny)
1992—C. Donovan (Galway)
1993—S. Doyle (Kilkenny)

LEINSTER MINOR HURLING

1928—Dublin 6-6, Offaly 3-2
1929—**Meath 10-1, Kilkenny 6-1**
1930—Kilkenny 6-3, Laois 3-5
1931—Kilkenny 4-9, Meath 0-3
1932—Kilkenny 9-6, Dublin 6-1
1933—Kilkenny 5-8, Dublin 2-6
1934—Laois 8-4, Dublin 2-0
1935—Kilkenny 7-8, Laois 1-1
1936—Kilkenny 3-13, Dublin 1-1
1937—Kilkenny 6-12, Dublin 2-4
1938—Dublin 5-4, Laois 1-3
1939—Kilkenny 3-8, Dublin 2-2
1940—Dublin 10-5, Laois 3-3
      (Laois awarded title on objection)
1941—Laois 3-5, Kilkenny 2-4
1942—Kilkenny 3-10, Dublin 0-4
1943-1944—Championship suspended.
1945—Dublin 5-4, Kilkenny 3-1
1946—Dublin 7-5, Laois 0-1
1947—Dublin 1-5, Kilkenny 2-2
      Dublin 3-2, Kilkenny 2-4 (Replay)
1948—Kilkenny 5-2, Offaly 3-6
1949—Kilkenny 4-6, Dublin 0-4
1950—Kilkenny 4-2, Offaly 3-2
1951—Kilkenny 5-11, Dublin 2-2
1952—Dublin 4-7, Kilkenny 4-5
1953—Dublin 2-6, Laois 1-4
1954—Dublin 4-12, Kilkenny 4-7
1955—Kilkenny 3-10, Wexford 5-4
      Kilkenny 0-11, Wexford 0-8 (Replay)
1956—Kilkenny 4-7, Wexford 3-7
1957—Kilkenny 5-10, Offaly 4-2
1958—Kilkenny 5-11, Laois 1-7
1959—Kilkenny 7-9, Wexford 3-4
1960—Kilkenny 6-14, Wexford 5-5
1961—Kilkenny 4-12, Dublin 0-7
1962—Kilkenny 5-7, Wexford 5-4
1963—Wexford 6-10, Kilkenny 6-8
1964—Laois 4-9, Kilkenny 3-8
1965—Dublin 4-7, Wexford 1-6
1966—Wexford 7-6, Laois 1-7

1967—Wexford 6-7, Dublin 2-3
1968—Wexford 4-11, Kilkenny 4-4
1969—Kilkenny 3-9, Dublin 2-7
1970—Wexford 3-10, Kilkenny 1-10
1971—Kilkenny 7-18, Wexford 3-5
1972—Kilkenny 7-10, Wexford 0-4
1973—Kilkenny 3-10, Wexford 2-9
1974—Kilkenny 8-19, Dublin 3-5
1975—Kilkenny 2-18, Dublin 3-4
1976—Kilkenny 2-14, Wexford 1-8
1977—Kilkenny 5-10, Wexford 3-6
1978—Kilkenny 4-19, Laois 2-6
1979—Kilkenny 5-13, Antrim 1-9
1980—Wexford 1-10, Dublin 2-6
1981—Kilkenny 3-10, Wexford 3-9
1982—Kilkenny 3-16, Offaly 3-4
1983—Dublin 5-14, Wexford 4-12
1984—Kilkenny 2-10, Wexford 1-11
1985—Wexford 0-12, Kilkenny 0-8
1986—Offaly 4-7, Wexford 1-5
1987—Offaly 2-13, Kilkenny 0-12
1988—Kilkenny 2-16, Offaly 0-6
1989—Offaly 0-14, Kilkenny 0-14 (draw)
       Offaly 4-13, Kilkenny 0-13 (replay)
1990—Kilkenny 3-15, Laois 0-15
1991—Kilkenny 1-20, Laois 0-4
1992—Kilkenny 1-9, Wexford 0-11
1993—Kilkenny 4-14, Dublin 0-11

MUNSTER MINOR HURLING FINALS

1928—Cork 3-4, Waterford 3-2
1929—Waterford 7-5, Tipperary 1-2
1930—Tipperary 4.3, Cork 3-0
1931—Tipperary 6-5, Waterford 6-2
1932—Tipperary 7-8, Clare 3-0
1933—Tipperary 3-1, Cork 2-2
1934—Tipperary 3-6, Waterford 0-6
1935—Tipperary 4-3, Cork 2-1
1936—Cork 6-5, Tipperary 1-4
1937—Cork 8-4, Limerick 3-2
1938—Cork 9-3, Kerry 0-0
1939—Cork 8-3, Clare 0-2
1940—Limerick 8-3, Clare 0-4

1941—Cork 4-6, Tipperary 3-3
1942–44 (inclusive) – no championship
1945—Tipperary 8-10, Clare 0-2
1946—Tipperary 5-6, Cork 4-2
1947—Tipperary 2-4, Waterford 1-2
1948—Waterford 3-6, Tippearry 0-3
1949—Tipperary 5-6, Clare 5-5
1950—Tipperary 12-3, Clare 2-0
1951—Cork 5-11, Limerick 1-2
1952—Tipperary 10-7, Clare 1-2
1953—Tipperary 3-11, Limerick 3-3
1954—Tipperary 3-5, Limerick 2-3
1955—Tipperary 8-11, Waterford 2-5
1956—Tipperary 10-10, Waterford 4-4
1957—Tipperary 3-8, Limerick 1-4
1958—Limerick 8-9, Waterford 2-5
1959—Tipperary 5-8, Limerick 1-4
1960—Tipperary 6-7, Galway 4-3
1961—Tipperary 7-11, Cork 1-6
1962—Tipperary 4-11, Cork 4-1
1963—Limerick 4-12, Tipperary 5-4
1964—Cork 2-14, Tipperary 2-9
1965—Limerick 5-5, Tipperary 3-9
1966—Cork 6-7, Galway 2-8
1967—Cork 4-10, Limerick 0-3
1968—Cork 7-8, Waterford 4-2
1969—Cork 1-12, Tipperary 2-4
1970—Cork 3-8, Tipperary 4-4
1971—Cork 6-13, Clare 3-5
1972—Cork 4-11, Limerick 0-3
1973—Tipperary 5-12, Limerick 5-4
1974—Cork 2-11, Tipperary 2-7 (replay)
      Cork 3-7, Tipperary 2-10 (draw)
1975—Cork 3-16, Tipperary 1-7
1976—Tipperary 5-10, Limerick 5-6
1977—Cork 2-8, Limerick 2-7
1978—Cork 1-14, Tipperary 3-6
1979—Cork 3-17, Limerick 4-4
1980—Tipperary 1-17, Limerick 1-4
1981—Clare 3-13, Tipperary 3-11
1982—Tipperary 1-10, Limerick 1-7
1983—Tipperary 3-15, Limerick 2-8

1984—Limerick 3-6, Tipperary 2-7
1985—Cork 1-13, Tipperary 1-8
1986—Cork 2-11, Tipperary 1-11 (replay)
      Cork 3-10, Tipperary 2-13 (draw)
1987—Tipperary 2-11, Cork 1-9
1988—Cork 5-7,   Tipperary 1-2
1989—Clare 2-13, Limerick 2-12
1990—Cork 1-9, Clare 0-9
1991—Tipperary 3-13, Limerick 1-5
1992—Waterford 4-7, Tipperary 3-10 (draw)
      Waterford 2-10, Tipperary 0-14 (replay)
1993—Tipperary 1-12, Cork 1-9

£1.5 Million Boost for 1993-'94 National Leagues

The GAA signed a new £1.5 million three-year sponsorship contract with Church and General for the National Leagues in hurling and football, starting with the 1993-'94 competition.

The financial arrangement will see Church and General make a straight cash contribution of £250,000 for the first year and the new sponsors will spend a similar amount in promoting and advertising.

The new sponsorship will see a continuation of bonus payments made to teams who figure prominently in the closing stages of both the hurling and football competitions, with the prospect of the winners each receiving up to £15,000.

The sponsors intend to continue with the "top team" award and they are also introducing a new "player of the division", which will be presented to those who show a high level of consistency throughout the season.

ALL-IRELAND UNDER-21 HURLING FINALS

1964—Tipperary 8-9; Wexford 3-1.
1965—Wexford 3-7; Tipperary 1-4.
1966—Cork 9-9; Wexford 5-9 (second replay).
      Cork 4-9; Wexford 4-9 (replay).
      Cork 3-12; Wexford 5-6 (first game).
1967—Tipperary 1-8; Dublin 1-7.
1968—Cork 2-18, Kilkenny 3-9
1969—Cork 5-13; Wexford 4-7.
1970—Cork 5-17; Wexford 0-8 (replay).
      Cork 3-8; Wexford 2-11 (draw).
1971—Cork 7-8; Wexford 1-11.
1972—Galway 2-9; Dublin 1-10.
1973—Cork 2-10; Wexford 4-2.
1974—Kilkenny 3-8; Waterford 3-7.
1975—Kilkenny 5-13; Cork 2-19.
1976—Cork 2-17; Kilkenny 1-8.
1977—Kilkenny 2-9; Cork 1-9.
1978—Galway 3-15; Tipperary 2-8 (replay).
      Galway 3-5; Tipperary 2-8 (draw).
1979—Tipperary 2-12; Galway 1-9.
1980—Tipperary 2-9; Kilkenny 0-14.
1981—Tipperary 2-16; Kilkenny 1-10.
1982—Cork 0-12, Galway 0-11
1983—Galway 0-12, Tipperary 1-6
1984—Kilkenny 1-12, Tipperary 0-11
1985—Tipperary 1-10, Kilkenny 2-6
1986—Galway 0-14, Wexford 2-5
1987—Limerick 2-15, Galway 3-6
1988—Cork 4-11, Kilkenny 1-5.
1989—Tipperary 4-10, Offaly 3-11
1990—Kilkenny 2-11, Tipperary 1-11
1991—Galway 2-17, Offaly 1-9
1992—Waterford 0-12, Offaly 2-3 (replay)
      Waterford 4-4, Offaly 0-16 (draw)
1993—Galway 2-9, Kilkenny 3-3 (replay)
      Galway 2-14, Kilkenny 3-11 (draw)

ALL IRELAND HURLING UNDER-21 FINALISTS

1964

Tipperary—P. O'Sullivan, J. Smith, N. O'Gorman, M. O'Meara, O. Killoran, C. O'Dwyer, L. Gaynor, M. Roche, J. Fogarty, N. Lane, M. Keating, F. Loughnane, J. Dillon, T. J. Butler, T. Brennan. Sub.: P. J. Ryan.

Wexford—M. Jacob, J. Dunne, D. Quigley, B. Doyle, V. Staples, J. Berry, W. Murphy, M. Byrne, J. Doran, C. Dowdall, C. Jacob, O. Cullen, S. Barron, T. Maher, P. Quigley. Subs.: M. Kinsella, B. Murray, P. O'Connor.

1965

Wexford—M. Jacob, W. O'Neill, D. Quigley, A. Somers, V. Staples, M. Kinsella, W. Murphy, E. Ryan, J. Doran, C. Dowdall, P. Quigley, S. Barron, T. Maher, T. Doran, J. Berry. Sub.: C. Jacob.

Tipperary—S. Shinnors, M. Flanagan, J. Costigan, D. Burke, O. Killoran, N. O'Gorman, L. Gaynor, P. J. Ryan, J. Quinlan, F. Loughnane, M. Keating, P. Ryan, T. Brennan, T. J. Butler, J. Ryan. Sub.: J. O'Meara.

1966

Cork—J. Mitchell, W. Murphy, T. Falvey, P. O'Sullivan, C. Roche, J. Russell, D. Coughlan, J. McCarthy, G. McCarthy, S. Barry, T. Browne, P. Curley, C. McCarthy, A. O'Flynn, Eddie O'Brien. Subs.: A. Maher, B. McKeown. (Note: B. Wylie played in both draws; K. Farrell, D. Mc Keown, D. Clifford, P. O'Riordan played in first draw).

Wexford—H. Butler, W. O'Neill, M. Nolan, A. Somers, W. Bowe, M. Kinsella, V. Staples, M. Jacob, C. Dowdall, S. Barron, P. Quigley, J. Quigley, M. Butler, T. Doran, E. Cousins. Sub.: M. Gardiner. (Note: J. Murphy and P. Murphy played in first draw; Sub.: B. Ronan. P. O'Brien and B. Ronan played in second draw; Sub.: N. Rochford.

1967

Tipperary—H. Condron, S. Ryan, J. Kelly, D. Grady, M. Esmonde, T. O'Connor, S. Hogan, P. J. Ryan, C. Davitt, N. O'Dwyer, J. Ryan, J. Walsh, P. O'Connor, P. Lowry, J. Flanagan. Subs.: M. Nolan, T. Delaney.

Dublin—M. Behan, M. Hannick, P. Martin, C. Brennan, W.

Markey, F. Cooney, G. O'Driscoll, H. Dalton, F. McConnell, E. McGrath, E. Davey, L. Hennebry, T. Grealish, C. Moran, N. Kinsella. Sub.: M. Kennedy.

1968

Cork—B. Hurley, W. Murphy, B. Tobin, F. Norberg, N. Dunne, W. Walsh, R. Cummins, D. Clifford, P. Moylan, B. Meade, S. Murphy, P. Hegarty, H. O'Sullivan, P. Curley, P. Ring. Subs.: M. McCarthy, R. Lehane, J. Murphy.

Kilkenny—J. Nolan, L. Byrne, C. O'Brien, M. Leahy, J. O'Shea, N. Morrissey, P. Kealy, F. Cummins, P. Lawlor, W. Harte, F. Farrell, J. Kinsella, P. Dowling, P. Keyes, B. Sullivan. Subs.: T. Grant, S. Brennan, S. Kearney.

1969

Cork—B. Hurley, M. McCarthy, B. Tobin, F. Norbert, S. Looney, D. Clifford, T. O'Brien, S. Murphy, P. Moylan, B. Meade, W. Walsh, N. Dunne, F. Keane, R. Cummins, B. Cummins. Sub.: P. McDonnell.

Wexford—P. Cox, E. McDonald, E. Murphy, B. Butler, E. Walsh, J. Russell, L. Bennett, M. Dalton, E. Buggy, T. Royce, M. Quigley, M. Browne, J. Quigley, M. Butler, C. Doran. Subs.: I. Byrne, M. Casey.

1970

Cork—M. Coleman, M. McCarthy, P. McDonnell, B. Tobin, S. Murphy, J. Horgan, T. O'Brien, S. Looney, P. Moylan, C. Kelly, B. Cummins, K. McSweeney, S. O'Leary, J. Barrett, P. Ring. (Note: M. Malone, J. Nodwell played in drawn game.)

Wexford—P. Cox, J. Pender, J. Russell, E. McDonald, G. Collins, L. Byrne, L. Bennett, T. Byrne, C. Doran, B. Murphy, M. Quigley, E. Murphy, M. Butler, M. Casey, P. Byrne. Sub.: A. Kerrigan.

1971

Cork—M. Coleman, J. Horgan, P. McDonnell, B. Murphy, Seamus O'Farrell, M. O'Doherty, B. Coleman, S. Looney, N. Crowley, E. Fitzgerald, M. Malone, K. McSweeney, B. Cummins, J. Rothwell, S. O'Leary. Subs.: P. Casey, D. Collins, P. Kavanagh.

Wexford—P. Cox, J. Higgins, G. O'Connor, P. O'Brien, A. Kerrigan, L. Kinsella, L. Bennett, M. Quigley, A. Dwyer, B. Dunne, T. Byrne, S. Kinsella, P. Flynn, M. Casey, M. Butler. Subs.: J. Russell, B. Murphy.

1972

Galway—E. Campbell, L. Glynn, G. Kelly, L. Shields, I. Clarke, F. Donoghue, T. Brehony, G. Glynn F. Burke, M. Coen, A. Fenton, M. Donoghue, M. Barrett, T. O'Donoghue, G. Holland. Subs.: P. J. Molloy, J. Duggan.

Dublin—M. Holden, M. Leonard, N. Quinn, V. Lambe, G. Ryan, J. Brennan, E. Rheinisch, P. J. Holden, M. Greally, P Lee, V. Holden, J. Kealy, C. Hennebry, B. Sweeney, J. Whelan. Sub.: G. O'Connor.

1973

Cork—F. O'Sullivan, M. Corbett, L. Kelly, B. Murphy, M. O'Doherty, J. Buckley, D. Burns, T. Crowley, B. Cotter, P. Kavanagh, Seamus O'Farrell, Tony Murphy, D. Relihan, T. Fogarty, S. O'Leary. Subs.: T. Sheehan, J. Barry Murphy.

Wexford—J. Nolan, M. Hickey, S. Byrne, P. Dempsey, J. Moloney, E. Breen, R. Lambert, R. Kinsella, P. J. Harris, J. Murphy, T. Dwyer, C. Kehoe, N. Walsh, J. Allen, S. Storey. Subs.: M. Carty, S. Murphy.

1974

Kilkenny—K. Fennelly, T. McCormack, M. Hogan, J. Dunne, G. Henderson, B. Cody, M. Tierney, J. Dowling, S. Brophy, N. Brennan, G. Woodcock, G. Fennelly, P. Kearney, Tony Teehan, B. Fitzpatrick. Subs.: Bobby Sweeney, P. Mulcahy.

Waterford—W. Ryan, F. McCarthy, M. Flynn, K. Ryan, L. O'Brien, J. Galvin, E. Ryan, P. Egan, P. McGrath, B. Mansfield, L. Power, T. Casey, B. O'Keeffe, M. McNamara, P. Moore. Subs.: L. Ahearne, E. Kehoe.

1975

Kilkenny—K. Fennelly, J. Marnell, J. Moran, Dick O'Hara, G. Henderson, B. Cody, J. Grace, J. Dowling, G. Fennelly, J. Hennessy, M. Tierney, J. Lyng, Terry Brennan, B. Sweeney, B. Fitzpatrick. Subs.: K. Robinson, J. O'Sullivan, G. Woodcock.

Cork—F. O'Sullivan, J. Kennefick, D. Hurley, J. O'Herlihy, C. Brassil, K. Murphy, J. Crowley, J. Fenton, F. Delaney, B. Óg Murphy, Seán O'Farrell, Tadhg Murphy, E. O'Sullivan, J. Barry Murphy, Tom Collins. Sub.: Tadhg O'Sullivan.

1976

Cork—J. Cronin, J. Crowley, B. Geaney, D. McCurtain, J. Fenton, T. Cashman, F. Delaney, S. O'Mahony, C. Brassil, J.

Allen, R. McDonnell, P. Horgan, Tadhg Murphy, K. Murphy, D. Buckley. Sub.: B. Reidy.

Kilkenny—K. Fennelly, J. Marnell, D. Tyrell, D. O'Hara, H. Ryan, J. Moran, R. Reid, J. Hennessy, J. Hennessy, K. Robinson, J. Lyng, M. Lyng, K. Brennan, B. Fennelly, G. Tyrell, O. Bergin. Subs.: B. Waldron, P. Dunphy, M. Kennedy.

1977

Kilkenny—E. Mahon, J. Lennon, J. Henderson, P. Prendergast, J. Hennessy, D. O'Hara, R. Reid, P. Lannon, M. Kennedy, R. Power, M. Lyng, B. Waldron, B. Fennelly, G. Tyrell, J. Wall. Sub.: K. Brennan.

Cork—J. Cronin, J. Murphy, J. Crowley, F. Delaney, C. Brassil, T. Cashman, D. McCurtain, D. O'Herlihy, J. O'Brien, P. Horgan, T. Lyons, Padraig Crowley, T. Murphy, R. McDonnell, D. Buckley. Subs.: D. Keane, G. McEvoy, D. Ryan.

1978 (replay)

Galway—G. Smith, C. Hayes, M. Headd, P. J. Burke, J. Greaney, M. Earls, S. Coen, S. Mahon, M. Kilkenny, G. Kennedy, J. Good, P. Ryan, B. Forde, M. Conneely, J. Ryan. Sub.: T. Brehony, J. Coen and S. Forde came on as subs in drawn game. G. Linnane played in drawn game. Gerry Kennedy came on for replay.

Tipperary—V. Mullins, J. Doyle, J. O'Dwyer, P. Loughnane, M. Stapleton, P. Fitzelle, G. Stapleton, J. Grace, P. Ryan, T. Walsh, M. Doyle, E. O'Shea, T. Ryan, S. Burke, T. Grogan. Subs draw K. Fox, M. Murphy, E. Hogan; replay E. Hogan, K. Fox, T. Slattery; J. Minogue played in drawn game. M. Stapleton came on for replay.

1979

Tipperary—V. Mullins, P. Loughnane, J. Ryan, E. Hogan, T. Slattery, J. O'Dwyer, G. Stapleton, G. O'Connor, P. Fox, M. Murphy, E. O'Shea, T. Grogan, B. Mannion, M. Doyle, P. Looby. Sub.: P. Ryan.

Galway—A. Carr, T. Brehony, M. Headd, C. Hayes, S. Coen, M. Earls, E. Reilly, S. Davoren, M. Donoghue, J. Coen, G. Linnane, P. Ryan, S. Dolan, D. Burke, J. Ryan. Subs.: G. Dempsey, J. Hanlon, V. Kelly.

1980

Tipperary—V. Mullins, M. Ryan, C. Bonnar, P. Fox, B . Heffernan, J. O'Dwyer, P. McGrath, M. Kennedy, P. Kennedy, M. Murphy, B. Ryan, A. Buckley, J. Kennedy, D. O'Connell, P. Power. Sub.: A. Kinsella.

Kilkenny—M. Walsh, M. Morrissey, M. Meagher, B. O'Hara, T. Lennon, B. Doherty, S. Fennelly, E. Wallace, G. Ryan, J. Mulcahy, R. Murphy, M. Nash, B. McEvoy, L. Ryan, B. Purcell. Sub.: J. Heffernan.

1981

Tipperary—J. Farrell, M. Ryan, P. Brennan, P. Fox, I. Conroy, J. McIntyre, P. McGrath, A. Kinsella, P. Kennedy, N. English, B. Ryan, M. McGrath, G. O'Neill, D. O'Connell, A. Buckley.

Kilkenny—M. Walsh, P. Ryan, E. Aylward, J. Holden, S. Norris, B. O'Hara, M. Cleere, P. Gannon, M. Byrne, B. McEvoy, M. J. Ryan, B. Walton, J. Murphy, J. O'Dwyer, B. Purcell. Subs.: S. Tyrell, E. Crowley.

1982

Cork—G. Cunningham, M. McCarthy, M. Boylan, J. Hodgins, W. Cashman, K. O'Driscoll, Colm O'Connor, K. Hennessy, D. Curtin, Tony O'Sullivan, Tony Coyne, D. Walsh, E. Brosnan, M. O'Sullivan, Ger Motherway. Subs.: P. Deasy, T. Mulcahy, Gabriel McCarthy.

Galway—T. Coen, M. Mooney, P. Casserly, D. Burke, P. Kealy, T. Nolan, O. Kilkenny, A. Staunton, J. Boland, M. Haverty, P. Pigott, P. Murphy, J. Murphy, M. Grealish, M. McGrath. Subs.: N. Morrissey, T. Keady.

1983

Galway—T. Coen, B. Derivan, P. Casserly, M. Donoghue, P. Finnerty, T. Keady, O. Kilkenny, A. Moylan, P. Healy, A. Staunton, M. Coleman, M. Costelloe, G. Burke, J. Murphy, M. McGrath. Subs.: E. Ryan, M. Kenny, C. Hennebry.

Tipperary—K. Hogan, C. Bonnar, P. Maher, E. Hogan, I. Conroy, N. English, D. Finnerty, J. Hayes, L. Bergin, P. Kenny, C. Donovan, M. McGrath, G. O'Neill, W. Peters, A. Browne. Subs.: J. Kennedy, J. Maher, V. Dooley.

1984

Kilkenny—D. Burke, E. Wall, E. O'Connor, B. Young, D. Hoyne, L. Cleere, L. Walsh, T. Phelan, R. Heffernan, D. Carroll, P. Walsh, J. McDonald, L. McCarthy, R. McCarthy,S. Delahunty. Subs.: P. Ryan, M. Rafter.

Tipperary—K. Hogan, J. McKenna, E. Hogan, C. Bonnar, R. Stakelum, D. Kealy, J. Leahy, J. Kennedy, J. Hayes, A. Ryan,

N. Sheehy, P. Kenny, A. Waters, D. Fogarty, M. Scully. Subs.:
W. Peters, M. Cuningham.

1985

Tipperary—J. Leamy, N. McDonnell, P. O'Donoghue, C.
Bonnar, M. Corcoran, D. Kealy, P. Delaney, J. Kennedy, A.
Ryan, M. Cunningham, J. McGrath, N. Sheehy, J. Cormack, L.
Stokes, M. Scully. Sub.: M. Bryan.

Kilkenny—R Dunne, K. Ryan, E. O'Connor, P. Healy, T.
Lannon, L. Cleere, L. O'Brien, T. Phelan, J. Scott, R. Moran,
S. Delahunty, E. Morrissey, M. Dunne, M. Rafter, J. Walsh.
Subs.: P. Cleere, T. Bawle, P. Barron.

1986

Galway—J. Commins, P. Dervan, M. Kelly, M. Flaherty, M.
Helebert, P. Malone, G. McInerney, T. Monaghan, D. Jennings,
M. Connolly, A. Cunningham, A. Davoren, P. Nolan, Joe
Cooney, P. Higgins. Subs.: G. Elwood, S. Keane.

Wexford—P. Nolan, J. Doyle, M. Foley, P. Bridges, L.
O'Gorman, T. Dempsey, K. Murphy, Matt Foley, P. Barden, E.
Synnott, V. Murphy, D. Prendergast, M. Morrissey, P. Carton, R.
Murphy. Subs.: N. McDonald, J. Murray, C. Whelan.

1987

Limerick—V. Murnane, A. Madden, P. Carey, D. Flynn, D.
Nash, A. O'Riordan, M. Reale, G. Hegarty, J. O'Neill, G. Kirby,
A. Carmody, G. Ryan, P. Barrett, J. O'Connor, L. O'Connor.
Sub.: D. Marren.

Galway—M. Finnerty, B. Cawley, S. Dolphin, B. Cooney, T.
Broderick, J. Burke, T. King, D. Cox, G. Coyne, M. Connolly,
K. Coen, H. Davoren, M. Greaney, E. Burke, R. Duane. Subs.:
E. Lyons, P. Killilea, B. Hurney.

1988

Cork—T. Kingston, C. Connery, D. Irwin, S. O'Leary, C.
Casey, P. Kennealy, T. O'Keeffe, L. Kelly, T. Cooney, J. Corcoran, G. Manley, F. Horgan, D. O'Connell, M. Foley, J. Fitzgibbon.

Kilkenny—T. Phelan, F. Morgan, W. O'Connor, L. Drennan,
R. Minogue, L. Keoghan, B. Hennessy, T. Fogarty, L. Egan, T.
O'Keeffe, M. Phelan, J. Feehan, P. Hoban, S. O'Mahoney, J.
Larkin. Subs.: P. Carroll for Drennan; T. Murphy for Larkin;
L. Dowling for T. Fogarty.

● *Brian Corcoran who emerged as the defensive find on the Cork senior hurling team during the 1992 season and captained his county to a League title win in 1993. He played in the All-Ireland senior football final against Derry in 1993, having added a Munster medal to the Provincial medal in hurling he won the previous year.*

1989

Tipperary—B. Bane, L. Sheedy, M. Ryan, G. Frend, J. Madden, Conal Bonnar, S. Maher, J. Leahy, Declan Ryan, P. Hogan, C. Stakelum, Dinny Ryan, M. Nolan, D. Quirke, T. Lanigan. Subs.: J. Cahill for Maher, D. Lyons for Lanigan, K. Ryan for Cahill.

Offaly—John Troy, B. Whelehan, B. Geoghegan, B. Hennessy, R. Mannion, B. Kelly, G. Cahill, J. Pilkington, A. Cahill, B. Dooley, D. Regan, Johnny Dooley, R. Byrne, D. Pilkington, M. Duignan. Sub.: J. Kilmartin for Byrne.

1990

Kilkenny—J. Conroy, J. Houlihan, P. O'Neill, D. Carroll, P. Brophy, T. Murphy, J. Conlon, J. Brennan, B. McGovern, A. Ronan, J. Lawlor, T. Shefflin, D. J. Carey, P. Treacy, C. Carter. Subs.: P. O'Grady for Shefflin, J. Walton for McGovern.

Tipperary—B. Bane, L. Fallon, M. Ryan, G. Frend, E. Maher, N. Keane, B. Corcoran, J. Leahy, Conal Bonnar, C. Egan, L. Sheedy, G. Deely, D. Lyons, P. O'Brien, A. Wall. Subs.: M. O'Meara for Egan, K. McCormack for Lyons.

1991

Galway—R. Burke, C. Helebert, B. Feeney, M. Killalea, G. McGrath, P. Hardiman, N. Power, B. Keogh, N. Larkin, L. Burke, J. Campbell, T. O'Brien, B. Larkin, J. Rabbitte, C. Moran. Subs.: P. Egan for Hardiman, M. Curtin for Larkin.

Offaly—Damien Franks, M. Hogan, K. Kinehan, Donal Franks, D. Dooley, H. Rigney, B. Whelehan, J. Pilkington, P. Temple, Johnny Dooley, S. Grennan, A. Cahill, John Troy, J. Brady, E. Mulhare. Subs.: O. O'Neill for Cahill, D. Barron for Brady.

1992

Waterford—R. Barry, K. O'Gorman, O. Dunphy, M. O'Sullivan, T. Browne, P. Fanning, F. Hartley, T. Fives, J. Brenner, A. Fitzgerald, M. Hubbard, K. McGrath, N. Dalton, S. Daly, P. Flynn. Sub.: P. Power for Dalton. (Note: P. Power played in drawn game. M. Geary and P. Flynn came on as subs in drawn game).

Offaly—Damien Franks, H. Kilmartin, K. Kinehan, Donal Franks, D. Barron, H. Rigney, B. Whelehan, S. Óg Farrell, M. Hogan, Johnny Dooley, S. Grennan, John Troy, M. Gallagher, N. Hand. O. O'Neill. Sub.: A. Cahill for Hogan. (Note: K. Martin played in drawn game. B. Gath came on as sub in drawn game).

1993

Galway—M. Darcy, T. Headd, W. Burke, D. Canning, R. Walsh, N. Shaughnessy, M. Donoghue, L. Burke, M. Kearns, F. Forde, J. McGrath, T. Kirwan, P. Kelly, D. Coleman, M. Headd. Subs.: C. O'Donovan for Coleman, C. O'Doherty for Kirwan, M. Kilkelly for P. Kelly. (Note: M. Kilkelly played in drawn game, C. O'Doherty and P. Coyne went in as subs in the drawn game.)

Kilkenny—J. Dermody, D. Beirne, M. Holohan, J. Carroll, D. O'Neill, E. Kennedy, P. Larkin, A. Comerford, C. Brennan, P. Farrell, J. McDermott, D. Maher, P. J. Delaney, S. Ryan, D. Lawlor. Subs.: M. Owens for McDermott, P. Hennessy for Ryan. (Note: J. Shefflin played in drawn game, J. McDermott, M. Dowling and M. Owens went in as subs in drawn game.)

● *John Power, Kilkenny's outstanding centre-forward, displays the classic art of the solo run as he breaks through the Wexford defence in the 1992 Leinster final.*

MUNSTER UNDER-21 HURLING FINALS

1964—Tipperary 8-9, Waterford 3-1
1965—Tipperary 4-9, Galway 3-3
1966—Cork 5-12, Limerick 2-6
1967—Tipperary 3-9, Galway 3-5
1968—Cork 4-10, Tipperary 1-13
1969—Cork 3-11, Tipperary 1-5
1970—Cork 3-11, Tipperary 2-7
1971—Cork 5-11, Tipperary 4-9
1972—Tipperary 4-10, Clare 3-10
1973—Cork 4-11, Limerick 2-7
1974—Waterford 2-5, Clare 1-3
1975—Cork 3-12, Limerick 2-6
1976—Cork 2-11, Clare 3-6
1977—Cork 5-9, Limerick 1-8
1978—Tipperary 3-8, Cork 2-9

1979—Tipperary 1-13, Cork 2-7
1980—Tipperary 4-11, Cork 2-9
1981—Tipperary 1-15, Cork 0-10
1982—Cork 1-14, Limerick 1-4
1983—Tipperary 2-17, Clare 3-8
1984—Tipperary 0-12, Limerick 1-8
1985—Tipperary 1-16, Clare 4-5
1986—Limerick 2-10, Clare 0-3
1987—Limerick 3-14, Cork 2-9
1988—Cork 4-12, Limerick 1-7
1989—Tipperary 5-16, Limerick 1-6
1990—Tipperary 2-21, Limerick 1-11
1991—Cork 0-17, Limerick 1-11
1992—Waterford 0-17, Clare 1-12
1993—Cork 1-18, Limerick 3-9

LEINSTER UNDER-21 HURLING FINALS

1964—Wexford 4-7, Laois 2-2
1965—Wexford 7-9, Dublin 1-5
1966—Wexford 7-10, Laois 2-8
1967—Dublin 2-10, Offaly 2-9
1968—Kilkenny 4-10, Dublin 5-4
1969—Wexford 3-10, Kilkenny 4-3
1970—Wexford 2-15, Kilkenny 5-4
1971—Wexford 2-16, Kilkenny 2-9
1972—Dublin 2-11, Offaly 0-15
1973—Wexford 2-13, Offaly 2-9
1974—Kilkenny 3-8, Wexford 1-5
1975—Kilkenny 3-14, Wexford 0-8
1976—Kilkenny 3-21, Wexford 0-5
1977—Kilkenny 3-11, Wexford 1-10
1978—Offaly 2-14, Laois 2-7
1979—Wexford 1-8, Kilkenny 0-10

1980—Kilkenny 2-14, Wexford 2-9
1981—Kilkenny 6-11, Wexford 2-10
1982—Kilkenny 5-20, Offaly 2-6
1983—Laois 3-14, Wexford 4-8
1984—Kilkenny 0-18, Wexford 1-10
1985—Kilkenny 4-18, Wexford 1-4
1986—Wexford 2-9, Offaly 2-9
        Replay—Wexford 1-16, Offaly 0-10
1987—Wexford 4-11, Offaly 0-5
1988—Kilkenny 3-13, Offaly 2-5
1989—Offaly 3-16, Kilkenny 3-9
1990—Kilkenny 2-9, Laois 1-10
1991—Offaly 1-15, Kilkenny 2-10
1992—Offaly 2-10, Kilkenny 0-12
1993—Kilkenny 4-13, Wexford 2-7

ULSTER UNDER-21 HURLING FINALS

1965—Antrim 4-5, Down 2-7
1966—Antrim 4-5, Down 0-8
1967—Antrim 3-8, Down 2-7
1968—Antrim unopposed
1979—Down 5-17, Antrim 2-11
1970—Antrim 6-12, Down 2-10
1971—Down 5-11, Antrim 2-9
1972—Antrim 4-9, Down 1-11

233

1973—Antrim 3-13, Down 3-3
1974—Antrim unopposed
1975—Down 3-10, Antrim 1-3
1976—Antrim 1-8, Down 0-5
1977—Down 3-7, Antrim 0-9
1978—Antrim 5-18, Down 3-9
1979—Antrim 9-13, Armagh 2-2
1980—Antrim 4-16, Down 0-9
1981—Antrim 2-9, Down 1-5
1982—Antrim 9-14, Down 4-5
1983—Down 2-7, Antrim 0-7
1984—Down 1-14, Antrim 0-15
1985—Down 1-12, Antrim 1-11
1986—Derry 2-9, Down 2-9 (draw)
        Derry 3-9, Down 1-2 (replay)
1987—Down 3-12, Derry 2-9
1988—Antrim 6-11, Down 1-4
1989—Antrim 4-18, Derry 0-4
1990—Antrim 2-9, Down 2-6
1991—Antrim 2-19, Down 2-6
1992—Antrim 3-11, Down 3-4
1993—Derry 2-13, Antrim 1-8

CAPTAINS OF WINNING ALL-IRELAND
UNDER-21 HURLING TEAMS

1964—Francis Loughnane (Tipperary)
1965—W. O'Neill (Wexford)
1966—G. McCarthy (Cork)
1967—P. J. Ryan (Tipperary)
1968—P. Hegarty (Cork)
1969—D. Clifford (Cork)
1970—T. O'Brien (Cork)
1971—P. McDonnell (Cork)
1972—I. Clarke (Galway)
1973—M. O'Doherty (Cork)
1974—G. Fennelly (Kilkenny)
1975—K. Fennelly (Kilkenny)
1976—T. Murphy (Cork)
1977—M. Lyng (Kilkenny)
1978—B. Forde (Galway)
1979—M. Doyle (Tipperary)
1980—Philip Kennedy (Tipperary)
1981—Philip Kennedy (Tipperary)
1982—M. McCarthy (Cork)
1983—P. Casserly (Galway)
1984—S. Delahunty (Kilkenny)
1985—M. Scully (Tipperary)
1986—A. Cunningham (Galway)
1987—G. Ryan (Limerick)
1988—C. Connery (Cork)
1989—Declan Ryan (Tipperary)
1990—J. Brennan (Kilkenny)
1991—B. Feeney (Galway)
1992—T. Browne (Waterford)
1993—L. Burke (Galway)

HURLING "B" CHAMPIONSHIP FINALS

1974—Croke Park, June 23. Kildare 1-26, Antrim 3-13.
1975—Croke Park, June 15. Westmeath 4-16, London 3-19.
Croke Park, June 22. Replay: Westmeath 3-23, London 2-7.
1976—Croke Park, June 27: Kerry 0-15, London 1-10.
1977—Croke Park, June 26. Laois 3-21, London 2-9.
1978—Croke Park, June 25. Antrim 1-16, London 3-7.
1979—Tullamore, June 17. Laois 2-13, London 3-10.
Athy, June 24. Replay: Laois 1-20, London 0-17.
1980—Croke Park, July 6. Kildare 2-20, London 2-14.
1981—Loughgiel, July 5. Antrim 3-17, London 3-14.
1982—Ruislip, July 4. Antrim 2-16, London 2-14.
1983—Tralee, June 26. Kerry 2-8, London 1-7.
1984—Ruislip, July 8. Westmeath 4-10, London 1-16.
1985—Trim, July 7. London 1-8, Meath 1-6.
1986—Ruislip, June 29. Kerry 3-10, London 1-9.
1987—Carlow, July 5. London 0-20, Carlow 1-15.
1988—Ruislip, July 3. London 2-6, Down 1-7.
1989—Newbridge, July 2. Kildare 1-13, London 1-12.
1990—Ruislip, July 8. London 1-15, Kildare 5-2.
1991—Mullingar, July 7. Westmeath 2-12, London 2-6.
1992—Ruislip, July 12. Carlow 2-15, London 3-10.
1993—Ruislip, July 11. Meath 2-16, London 1-16.

Note: The All-Ireland "B" winners play in the quarter-final of the Championship proper and Galway, for example, beat Carlow by 4-19 to 3-9 in 1992.

ALL-IRELAND INTERMEDIATE HURLING FINALS

1961—Wexford, September 17. Wexford 3-15, London 4-4.
1962—Croke Park, September 9. Carlow 6-15, London 3-3.
1963—Thurles, September 8, Tipperary 1-10, London 1-7.
1964—Enniscorthy, September 20, Wexford 4-7, London 1-11.
1965—Cork, September 19. Cork 2-20, London 5-5.
1966—Enniscorthy, September 18. Tipperary 4-11, Dublin 2-12.
1967—Limerick, September 17. London 1-9, Cork 1-5.
1968—Croke Park, September 29. London 4-15, Dublin 0-3.
1969—Thurles, October 12. Kildare 2-8, Cork 3-4.
1970—Croke Park, October 4. Antrim 4-18, Warwickshire 3-6.
1971—Kilkenny, September 19. Tipperary 3-16, Wicklow 3-13.
1972—Birr, September 17. Tipperary 2-13. Galway 1-9.
1973—Waterford, September 16. Kilkenny 5-15, London 2-9.
Discontinued

ALL-IRELAND JUNIOR HURLING FINALS

1912—Cork 3-6, Westmeath 2-1
1913—Tipperary 2-2, Kilkenny 0-0
1914—Clare 6-5, Laois 1-1
1915—Tipperary 1-6, Offaly 2-2
1916—Cork 4-6, Kilkenny 3-4
1917-1922—Suspended
1923—Offaly 3-4, Cork 3-2
1924—Tipperary 5-5, Galway 1-2
1925—Cork 5-6, Dublin 1-0
1926—Tipperary 6-2, Galway 2-3
1927—Meath 2-3, Britain 1-1
1928—Kilkenny 4-6, Tipperary 4-4
1929—Offaly 6-1, Cork 2-3
1930—Tipperary 6-8, Kilkenny 3-2
1931—Waterford 10-7, Lancashire 1-2
1932—Dublin 8-4, London 2-0
1933—Tipperary 10-1, London 1-4
1934—Waterford 3-5, London 3-3
1935—Limerick 4-9, London 3-3
1936—Westmeath 2-5, Waterford 3-1
1937—Dublin 7-8, London 3-6
1938—London 4-4, Cork 4-1
1939—Galway 2-6, London 2-2
1940—Cork 3-3, Galway 3-1
1941—Limerick 8-2, Galway 4-1
1942-45—Suspended
1946—Kilkenny 5-4, London 2-2
1947—Cork 3-10, London 2-3
1948—Meath 2-7, London 2-5 (replay)
　　　Meath 3-5, London 3-5 (draw)
1949—London 3-7, Clare 3-6
1950—Cork 5-5, London 1-4
1951—Kilkenny 3-9, London 3-5
1952—Dublin 3-4, London 2-6
1954—Limerick 4-6, London 2-4
1955—Cork 6-10, Warwickshire 0-5
1936—Kilkenny 5-2, London 2-8
1956—Limerick 5-12, London 2-5
1958—Cork 7-10, Warwickshire 4-2
1959—London 5-10, Antrim 2-10
1960—London 4-8, Carlow 2-11 (replay)
　　　London 2-4, Carlow 2-4 (draw)
1961—Kerry 4-14, London 2-5
1962—Kildare 4-7, London 2-4
1963—London 4-7, Antrim 3-6
1964—Down 3-2, London 1-3
1965—Roscommon 3-9,
　　　　　　Warwickshire 2-11

1966—Kildare 4-6, Warwickshire 2-9
1967—Wicklow 3-15, London 4-4
　　　(replay)
　　　Wicklow 3-15, London 6-6
　　　(draw)
1968—Warwickshire 1-14, Kerry 1-9
1969—Warwickshire 3-6, Kerry 0-11
1970—Meath 3-14, Hertfordshire 3-7
　　　(replay)
　　　Meath 1-15, Hertfordshire 4-6
　　　(draw)
1971—Wicklow 4-6, Herefordshire 3-8
　　　(second replay)
　　　Wicklow 3-9, Hertfordshire 2-12
　　　(draw)
　　　Hertfordshire 4-9, Wicklow 3-11
　　　(Dispute—replay ordered)
1972—Kerry 5-5, Warwickshire 2-9
1973—Warwickshire 6-9, Louth 3-8
*1974—Roscommon 2-11, Derry 2-9
1975—Derry 5-12, Louth 3-5
1976—Louth 6-8, Mayo 4-9.
1977—Louth 1-14, Fermanagh 2-4
1978—Armagh 5-15, Mayo 2-6
1979—Armagh 2-13, Derry 2-1
1980—Mayo 2-13, Monaghan 0-7
1981—Mayo 2-13, Louth 1-8
1982—Derry 1-10, Monaghan 0-6
**Resumed in original format
1983—Cork 3-14, Galway 2-15
1984—Kilkenny 0-13, Galway 2-5
1985—Wexford 3-9, Tipperary 1-13
1986—Kilkenny 1-17, Limerick 0-15
1987—Cork 3-11, Wexford 2-13
1988—Kilkenny 1-12, Tipperary 0-10
1989—Tipperary 0-12, Galway 0-8
1990—Kilkenny 4-21, Tipperary 2-11
1991—Tipperary 4-17, London 1-5
1992—Wexford 2-7, Cork 0-13 (draw)
　　　Wexford 0-13, Cork 1-8 (replay)
1993—Clare 3-10, Kilkenny 0-8

*From 1974-'82 the original for-
mat of the championship was
abandoned and the competition
was incorporated in Division 3 of
the N.H.L. The original format,
including the strong hurling counties, was reintroduced 'n 1983.

NATIONAL HURLING LEAGUE

1925-'26—Cork, 3-7; Dublin, 1-5.

1926-'27—None.

1927-'28—Tipperary winners on points system – 14 points (from eight games). Draws with Dublin and Laois. Runners-up: Dublin (with 11 points).

1928-'29—Dublin, 7-4; Cork, 5-5.

1929-'30—Cork, 3-5; Dublin, 3-0.

1930-'31—None.

1931-'32—Galway, 4-5; Tipperary, 4-4.

1932-'33—Kilkenny, 3-8; Limerick, 1-3 (Final at Kilkenny).

1933-'34—Limerick, 3-6; Dublin, 3-3 (Final at Limerick).

1934-'35—Limerick: winners on points system – 15 points (from eight games). Runners-up: Kilkenny (with 14 points).

1935-'36—Limerick: winners on on points system – 15 points (from eight games). Runners-up: Cork (with 12 points).

1936-'37—Limerick: winners on points system – 13 points (from eight games). Runners-up: Tipperary with 12 pts.

1937-'38—Limerick, 5-2; Tipperary, 1-1.

1938-'39—Dublin, 1-8; Waterford, 1-4.

1939-'40—Cork, 8-9; Tipperary, 6-4.

1940-'41—Cork, 4-11; Dublin, 2-7.

Suspended 1942, '43, '44, '45.

1945-'46—Clare, 2-10; Dublin, 2-5 in replay (Draw: Clare, 1-6; Dublin, 1-6).

1946-'47—Limerick, 3-8; Kilkenny, 1-7 in replay.   (Draw: Limerick, 4-5; Kilkenny, 2-11).

1947-'48—Cork, 3-3; Tipperary, 1-2.

1948-'49—Tipperary, 3-5; Cork, 3-3.

1949-'50—Tipperary, 1-12; New York, 3-4 (in New York. Home Final: Tipperary, 3-8; Kilkenny, 1-10.

1950-'51—Galway, 2-11; New York, 2-8 (in New York). Home final: Galway, 6-7; Wexford, 3-4.

1951-'52—Tipperary, 6-14; New York, 2-5 (in Croke Park) Home final: Tipperary, 4-7; Wexford, 4-6.

1952-'53—Cork, 2-10; Tipperary, 2-7.

1953-'54—Tipperary, 3-10; Kilkenny 1-4

1954-'55—Tipperary, 3-5; Wexford, 1-5.

1955-'56—Wexford, 5-9; Tipperary, 2-14.

1956-'57—Tipperary, 3-11; Kilkenny, 2-7.

1957-'58—Wexford, 5-7; Limerick, 4-8.

1958-'59—Tipperary, 0-15; Waterford, 0-7.

1959-'60—Tipperary, 2-15; Cork, 3-8.

1960-'61—Tipperary, 6-6; Waterford, 4-9.

1961-'62—Kilkenny, 1-16; Cork, 1-8.

1962-'63—Waterford, 3-10; New York, 1-10 in replay (at Kilkenny). Drawn game at Croke Park: Waterford 3-6; New York, 3-6. Home final: Waterford, 2-15; Tipperary, 4-7.

1963-'64—Tipperary, 4-16; New York, 6-6 (in New York). Home final: Tipperary, 5-12; Wexford, 1-4.

1964-'65—Tipperary, 4-10; New York, 2-11 (first leg). New York, 3-9; Tipperary, 2-9 (second leg). Aggregate: Tipperary, 6-19; New York, 5-20. Tipperary winners by two points on aggregate (both games in New York). Home final: Tipperary, 3-14; Kilkenny, 2-8

1965-'66—Kilkenny, 3-10; New York, 2-7 (first leg in Croke Park) Kilkenny, 7-5; New York 0-8 (second leg in Nowlan Park) (Aggregate: Kilkenny, 10-15; New York, 2-15 Home Final: Kilkenny, 0-9; Tipperary, 0-7

1966-'67—Wexford, 3-10; Kilkenny, 1-9.

1967-'68—New York, 2-14; Tipperary, 2-13, (First Leg). Tipperary, 4-14; New York, 2-8. (Second Leg). Aggregate: Tipperary, 6-27; New York, 4-22. (Both games in New York).

HOME FINAL—Tipperary, 3-9; Kilkenny, 1-13.

1968-'69—Cork, 3-12, Wexford, 1-14.

1969-'70—Cork, 4-11; New York, 4-8 (first leg). New York, 2-8; Cork, 1-10 (second leg). Aggregate: Cork, 5-21 (36 points); New York, 6-16 (34 points). Both games in New York. Semi-finals: April 12—Cork: Cork, 2-10; Tipperary, 2-7. April 19—Thurles: Limerick, 4-15; Offaly, 2-8. " Home " Final, May 3, at Croke Park: Cork, 2-17; Limerick, 0-7.

1970-'71—(League Re-arranged into Two Groups with promotion and relegation): Semi-finals: May 9 (Limerick): Tipperary, 2-12; Cork, 2-10. May 16 (Thurles): Limerick, 1-11; Clare, 2-6. Final, May 23 in Cork: Limerick, 3-12; Tipperary, 3-11. Division Two Promotion Play-off, August 22 (Ennis): Clare, 4-9; Kildare, 3-9.

1971-'72 — League Semi-finals: April 16, at Limerick — Cork, 5-12 (27); Tipperary, 4-8 (20) (Attendance — 15,890); April 23, at Thurles — Limerick, 3-13 (22); Kilkenny, 2-13 (19). (Attendance — 14,600).

League Final: May 7, at Thurles — Cork, 3-14 (23); Limerick, 2-14 (20). Attendance — 30,000.

1972-'73 — Semi-finals: April 15, at Kilkenny — Limerick, 2-11; Tipperary, 2-11; (draw). April 22, at Birr — Limerick, 5-10 (25); Tipperary, 3-14 (23), after extra time. April 29, at Waterford — Wexford, 2-10; Kilkenny, 2-9.

League Final: May 13, 1973, at Croke Park — Wexford, 4-13 (25); Limerick, 3-7 (16). Attendance — 20,814.

1973-'74 — Semi-finals: April 21, at Limerick — Limerick, 1-16 (19); Tipperary, 3-8 (17). (Attendance — 26,280). April 7, at Croke Park — Cork, 0-18; Dublin 1-11 (14).

League Final: May 5, 1974, at Limerick — Cork, 6-15 (33); Limerick, 1-12 (15). Attendance — 25,100.

1974-'75 — Semi-finals: April 28, at Limerick — Tipperary, 1-9, Clare, 0-10 (Attendance – 10,000). May 4, at Thurles — Galway, 1-9; Kilkenny, 1-6.

League Final: May 25, 1975, at Limerick — Galway, 4-9; Tipperary, 4-6. Attendance — 32,400.

1975-'76 — Semi-finals: April 4, at Thurles — Cork, 2-11, Kilkenny, 3-8 (Draw). April 25, at Thurles — Kilkenny, 2-17; Cork, 3-10. April 11, at Thurles — Wexford, 2-9; Clare, 3-6 (draw). April 25, at Thurles — Clare 3-24 (33); Wexford, 4-16 (28).

League Final: May 9, at Thurles — Clare, 2-10; Kilkenny, 0-16 (draw). June 20, at Thurles — Kilkenny 6-14; Clare, 1-14.

1976-'77 — Semi-finals: April 10, Thurles — Clare, 2-15; Offaly, 0-7. Kilkenny, 3-12; Tipperary 2-9.

Final: April 24, Thurles — Clare, 2-8; Kilkenny, 0-9.

1977-'78 — Semi-finals: April 9, Thurles — Clare, 2-16; Limerick, 3-6. April 9, Carlow — Kilkenny, 3-5; Wexford, 2-8 (Draw). April 16, Carlow — Kilkenny, 5-15; Wexford, 5-14 (replay after extra time). Final: April 30, Thurles — Clare, 3-10; Kilkenny, 1-10.

1978-'79 — Semi-finals: April 15, Thurles — Galway, 1-15; Limerick 4-5: April 16, Limerick — Tipperary 2-13, Clare 2-12.

Final: May 6, Limerick — Tipperary, 3-15; Galway, 0-8.

1979-'80 — Semi-finals: April 21, Limerick — Cork, 1-12; Galway, 0-12. Limerick, 2-13; Tipperary, 1-11.

Final: May 4, Cork — Cork, 2-10; Limerick, 2-10 (draw). May 18, Cork — Cork, 4-15; Limerick, 4-6 (replay).

1980-'81 — Semi-finals: April 19, Kilkenny —Offaly 2-13, Laois 4-6. April 19, Thurles — Cork 1-19, Waterford 2-10.

Final: May 3, Thurles —Cork 3-11, Offaly 2-8.

1981-'82 — Semi-finals: April 4, Thurles — Wexford, 2-17; Cork, 1-16. Kilkenny, 2-14; Waterford, 1-17 (Draw). April 11, Thurles — Kilkenny, 5-14; Waterford 4-6 (Replay).

Final: April 18, Croke Park — Kilkenny, 2-14; Wexford, 1-11.

1982-'83 — Semi-finals: April 3, Thurles — Kilkenny 5-11; Laois, 1-17. April 10, Thurles — Limerick, 3-10; Wexford, 2-6.

Final: April 24, Thurles — Kilkenny, 2-14; Limerick 2-12.

1983-'84 — Semi-finals: April 1, Thurles — Limerick, 2-10; Tipperary 1-10: Wexford 4-9, Cork 1-14.

Final: April 8, Thurles — Limerick, 3-16; Wexford, 1-9.

1984-'85 — Semi-finals: March 31, Thurles — Limerick, 0-15; Offaly 1-9. Clare, 1-14, Galway, 0-11.

Final: April 14, Thurles — Limerick, 3-12; Clare, 1-7.

1985-'86 — Semi-finals: April 27, Thurles — Kilkenny, 2-15; Cork, 1-8. Galway, 1-16; Wexford, 3-10 (Draw). May 4, Thurles — Galway, 3-11; Wexford, 2-5 (Replay).

Final: May 11, Thurles — Kilkenny, 2-10; Galway, 2-6.

1986-'87—Semi-finals: April 19, Portlaoise —Galway 5-16, Waterford 1-12. April 19, Cork — Clare 2-11, Tipperary 1-11.

Final: May 3, Thurles —Galway 3-12, Clare 3-10.

1987-88 — Semi-finals: April 10, 1988, Croke Park — Tipperary 4-19; Waterford 1-8; Offaly 2-16; Wexford 3-11.

Final: April 24, 1988, Croke Park : Tipperary 3-15; Offaly 2-9.

1988-'89—Semi-finals: April 16, 1989, at Croke Park — Tipperary 0-15, Kilkenny 1-11; Galway 2-13, Dublin 1-9.

Final: April 30, 1989, at Croke Park — Galway 2-16, Tipperary 4-8.

1989-'90—Semi-finals: April 8, 1990, at Thurles — Wexford 2-12, Cork 2-12 (draw); Kilkenny 2-16, Dublin 1-9. April 16, 1990 at Kilkenny: Wexford 1-9, Cork 0-6 (replay).

Home Final: April 22, 1990 at Croke Park — Kilkenny 3-12. Wexford 1-10.

Final: May 6, 1990 at Gaelic Park (New York) — Kilkenny 0-18, New York 0-9.

1990-'91—Semi-finals: April 28, 1991, at Croke Park — Wexford 2-12, Kilkenny 2-12 (draw): at Limerick—Offaly 1-7, Tipperary 0-7. May 5, at Thurles — Wexford 2-14, Kilkenny 1-12 (replay).

Final: May 12, 1991, at Croke Park — Offaly 2-6, Wexford 0-10.

1991-'92 — Semi-finals: April 19, 1992 at Ennis — Tipperary 1-15, Galway 1-8; April 26, 1992 at Limerick — Limerick 2-11, Cork 1-4.

Final: May 10, 1992 at Limerick — Limerick 0-14, Tipperary 0-13.

1992-'93—Semi-finals: April 25, 1993 at Thurles — Cork 2-11, Tipperary 1-13; Wexford, 3-14, Limerick 1-11.

Final: May 9, 1993 at Thurles — Cork 2-11, Wexford 2-11 (draw): May 16 1993 at Thurles — Cork 0-18, Wexford 3-9 (after extra time: 1st replay): May 22, 1993 at Thurles — Cork 3-11, Wexford 1-12 (2nd replay).

Roll of Honour — Tipperary (15), Cork (13), Limerick (10), Kilkenny (8), Galway (4), Wexford (4), Clare (3), Dublin (2), Offaly (1), Waterford (1).

●*SUPER SHANE . . . Kilkenny minor captain Shane Doyle, who playe excellently at full-back in the 1993 final against Galway, holds aloft the Al Ireland Minor Trophy at Croke Park after receiving it from the Archbisho of Cashel and Emly and Patron of the GAA, Most Rev. Dr. Clifford. (Phot Tom Brett)*

OIREACHTAS TOURNAMENT (HURLING)

1939—Limerick, 4-4; Kilkenny, 2-5
1940—Kilkenny, 7-11; Cork 1-6
1941-'43—Run as Football Tournament
  (Won by Dublin after replay with Kildare in 1941; by Dublin
  from Cavan in 1942 and by Roscommon from Louth in 1943.)
1944—Dublin, 6-6; Galway, 3-6.
1945—Tipperary, 4-6; Galway, 4-3.
1946—Antrim beat Laois in football tournament.
1947—Start of Comortas Corn Tomáis Aghas: Kilkenny, 2-12;
  Galway, 2-6.
1948—Dublin, 3-6; Waterford, 2-6.
1949—Tipperary, 2-8; Laois, 1-6.
1950—Galway, 2-9; Wexford, 2-6.
1951—Wexford, 4-7; Kilkenny, 3-7.
1952—Galway, 3-7; Wexford, 1-10.
1953—Wexford, 5-11; Clare, 4-5.
1954—Clare, 3-6; Wexford, 0-12 in replay (Draw: Clare, 2-8;
  Wexford, 2-8).
1955—Wexford, 3-11; Kilkenny, 3-4.
1956—Wexford, 0-16; Kilkenny, 1-9.
1957—Kilkenny, 4-10; Waterford, 3-5.
1958—Galway, 5-16; Wexford, 2-4.
1959—Kilkenny, 6-6; Galway, 5-8.
1960—Tipperary, 4-11; Cork, 2-10.
1961—Tipperary, 2-13; Wexford, 3-4 in replay. (Draw: Tipperary, 3-6; Wexford, 2-9).
1962—Waterford, 4-12; Tipperary, 3-9.
1963—Tipperary, 4-15; Wexford, 3-12.
1964—Tipperary 5-7; Kilkenny, 4-8.
1965—Tipperary, 2-12; Kilkenny, 2-7.
1966—Kilkenny, 4-7; Wexford, 1-7.
1967—Kilkenny, 4-4; Clare, 1-8.
1968 (at Thurles) — Tipperary, 1-9, Cork, 1-6.
1969—Kilkenny, 4-14; Cork, 3-10. (Cork beat Tipperary in semi-
  final in Cork by 3-16 to 2-14).
1970 (at Thurles)—Tipperary, 1-12; Cork, 0-8.
1971—Limerick, 4-12; Wexford, 3-8. (On way to the final
  Wexford beat Galway 3-12 to 2-12 at Galway and Limerick beat Kilkenny 3-11 to 3-10 in Limerick. Tipperary
  withdrew).

1972—Tipperary, 2-13; Wexford, 1-8 in replay (before 12,000 at Nowlan Park, Kilkenny, on November 26).

Drawn Game (at Croke Park, October 15)—Tipperary, 2-13; Wexford, 2-13.

1973—Cork, 1-8; Kilkenny, 1-6 (in Cork on December 16).

1974—Cork, 3-15; Waterford, 1-5.

1975—Cork, 3-13; Wexford, 2-7.

1976—Galway, 1-15; Cork, 2-9.

1977—Galway, 2-8; Cork, 2-8.

(There was no replay, so no outright winner declared that year.)

1978—Wexford, 0-18; Galway, 1-10.

1979—Wexford 3-17; Offaly, 5-8.

1980—Wexford, 1-19; Offaly, 3-5.

1981—Galway, 1-15; Wexford, 1-7.

1982—Clare 3-9, Limerick 2-9

1983—Clare 1-12, Kilkenny 1-11

1984—Kilkenny 1-11, Cork 1-7

1985—Cork 2-11, Galway 1-10

1986—Wexford 3-17, Galway 1-22 (after extra time).

1987—No competition.

1988—Galway 4-15, Wexford 3-11.

1989—Galway 1-19, Tipperary 0-8

1990—Tipperary 1-15, Galway 0-7

1991—Galway 2-12, Wexford 3-5

1992—Galway 1-13, Waterford 0-10

LIAM FENNELLY'S FAREWELL

● Liam Fennelly, the Kilkenny captain, in the moment that he held the Liam McCarthy Cup high in triumph was actually saying farewell to Croke Park as he announced his retirement soon after the victory over Cork in the 1992 All-Ireland final.

THE MAGIC OF D. J. CAREY

● *D. J. Carey is on the ball and it spells danger for Wexford who suffered at the hands of his brilliance in the 1992 Leinster final.*

GAILLIMH 1-3
CILL CHAINNIGH 1-5

● *Carey (right) although he suffered fractured ribs early in the 1993 All-Ireland final, still has Galway defenders Murty Kelly (left) and Paul Cooney at full stretch as team-mate P. J. Delaney awaits developments (Photo: Tom Brett).*

THE POINT THAT NEVER WAS

● *Nicky English (top) kicks the "point-that-never-was" in the titanic drawn 1991 Munster final against Cork in Páirc Uí Chaoimh as time ebbed away and (below) he avoids the tackles of two Waterford defenders in the 1988 National League semi-final at Croke Park, one of his finest games in the Blue and Gold.*

FOX AND FITZGIBBON SPELL DANGER

● *Pat Fox bursts past Galway corner-back Ollie Kilkenny before going on to find the net for the brilliantly-taken goal that put Tipperary on the road to victory in the 1989 All-Ireland semi-final.*

● *John Fitzgibbon (centre) hits an ecstatic high after raising the green flag against Tipperary in the 1990 Munster final at Semple Stadium, the men in the Red and White thus preventing the men in the Blue and Gold from recording their first-ever four-timer in the Province.*

THE CUP THAT GOT AWAY

● *The width of a post at the town end denied John Fitzgibbon what could have been the winning goal in the 1991 Munster final replay at Semple Stadium. Declan Carr went on to know the joy of bringing the Liam McCarthy Cup back to Tipperary.*

● *Borris-Ileigh stalwart, Bobby Ryan, after leading Tipperary to victory in the 1989 All-Ireland final, allows a young supporter to hold the Liam McCarthy Cup high in triumph.*

THE VIKING

• *THE WARRIOR KING . . . Cormac Bonnar is chaired off the field by delighted Tipperary supporters on the day of the 1991 All-Ireland final against Kilkenny. Although he did not finish the match they were only too aware of his contribution to the winning of the 24th All-Ireland title, especially in the epic replay against Cork in Thurles.*

• *Cormac's brothers, Colm (left) and Conal (right) who made vital contributions during the 1991 Championship campaign.*

● *A FACE IN THE CROWD . . . John Doyle, a legend in his own lifetime, who shares with Christy Ring the honour of having won eight All-Ireland medals on the field of play, pictured at the 1991 All-Ireland final.*

● *"Babs" Keating, Donie Nealon and John O'Donoghue, comprising the "Three Wise Men", team-mates on the great 1964 team, celebrate as the final whistle sounds at the end of the 1991 final.*

● *STONEWALL WILLIE*
. . . Kilkenny wing-back,
Willie O'Connor, gets away
a good clearance in this
clash with Joe Rabbitte
(Galway) in the 1993 All-
Ireland final.

● *DYNAMIC EDDIE . . . Kilkenny captain of 1993, Eddie O'Connor,*
gathers the ball neatly under the flying John Carson (Antrim) in the 1991 All-
Ireland semi-final.

CLUBMAN OF THE YEAR AWARDS

● *Former Taoiseach and Cork hurling great, Jack Lynch, on the night he launched "The Greatest Hurlers of Our Time" in Cork, took the opportunity to congratulate Dick Hickey, Managing Director of CIBA-GEIGY, second from left, on the success of the Clubman of the Year Awards scheme. Also in picture (left to right), Michael Maher, then Chairman of the Munster Council, Raymond Smith, the author, and John Fenton, the former brilliant Cork midfielder.*

● *In the GAA's Centenary Year, Dick Hickey, the Managing Director of one of the country's leading agri-chemicals, animal health and pharmaceutical groups, CIBA-GEIGY, decided that his company should mark the event by forging a link with the Association.*

As a strong GAA and Tipperary supporter, Dick Hickey observed that the only people in the GAA who did not get due public recognition of their contribution were the club workers. His view was that the strength of the GAA lay in the huge volume of voluntary work done at club level. He also believed that in an increasingly competitive environment, the GAA would be more reliant on its clubs to attract young people to choose Gaelic games rather than other sports.

His views led to the sponsorship of the CIBA-GEIGY GAA Clubman of the Year Awards which were warmly welcomed by the GAA President Mick Loftus. In fact, at the Centenary Year presentation of awards the GAA President stressed that he regarded the CIBA-GEIGY sponsorship as the most important of any connected to the GAA affairs.

"CIBA-GEIGY sponsored these awards as a recognition of the very important role which the GAA plays in the community which we service," stressed Dick Hickey.

CLUBMAN OF THE YEAR AWARDS

● *Michael Lee of Tubber GAA club in Co. Clare, National Clubman of the Year winner in 1987, being congratulated by Dick Hickey, managing director of CIBA-GEIGY (Ireland) Ltd., after receiving his magnificent inscribed trophy. John Dowling, then GAA President, adds his tribute.*

● *The success of Galway teams in recent times owes much to people like Jarleth McDonagh of Turloughmore GAA club, pictured here receiving his award (1987).*

DAYS OF GALWAY GREATNESS

● *Conor Hayes (left), who captained Galway to successive All-Ireland wins in 1987-88 and was also a member of the victorious 1980 side; Joe Cooney (centre), an outstanding servant to his county over a decade (1984-93), and Eanna Ryan (right), brilliant forward who retired prematurely as a result of an accidental stroke in a club game.*

● *During the memorable homecoming celebrations after Galway's triumph in 1980 Martin Burns from Ahascragh took out his fiddle amidst the company of hurling men, Mickie Burke and John Connolly included, and helped while away a long wonderful afternoon in the Tudor Lounge out in Oranmore, recalls Raymond Smith.*

THE MEN FOR THE OCCASION

● *Galway, who made it two All-Ireland titles back-to-back in 1988: Back row (from left): Brendan Lynskey, Peter Finnerty, Michael Coleman, Anthony Cunningham, John Commins, Tony Keady, Martin Naughton, Pat Malone. Front row (from left): Michael McGrath, Joe Cooney, Conor Hayes (captain), Sylvie Linnane, Gerry McInerney, Ollie Kilkenny, Eanna Ryan.*

● *Kilkenny, who made it two All-Ireland titles back-to-back in 1993: Back row (from left): Michael Phelan, John Power, Pat Dwyer, Liam Simpson, Eamonn Morrissey, Pat O'Neill. Front row (from left): Adrian Ronan, Liam Keoghan, P. J. Delaney, Willie O'Connor, Eddie O'Connor (captain), Michael Walsh, D. J. Carey, Bill Hennessy, Liam McCarthy.*

CLARE'S BREAK-THROUGH IN MUNSTER

● *BRIDGING A SEVENTY-FIVE YEAR GAP . . . Francis McInerney holds the Munster football champion-ship trophy high in triumph after Clare had won their first crown since 1917 by defeating Kerry in the 1992 Provincial final in Limerick.*

● *It will live forever in the annals of Clare football . . . the moment that Francis McInerney was chaired from the field of battle after the Kingdom had been beaten.*

● *Gerry Killeen ... one of the Doonbeg five.*

● *Noel Roche ... a legend in his own lifetime in Kilrush.*

● *P. J. O'Dea ... Munster final day in Limerick was an occasion of great nostalgia for the former Clare and Munster stalwart.*

● *Marty Morrissey ... a commentary that will live like Michael O'Hehir's on the 1947 All-ireland football final in the Polo Grounds, New York.*

THE END OF THE DAY

● *A GOAL OUT OF THE TOP DRAWER . . . Kevin Foley rounds off a fantastic Meath movement by scoring the goal that silenced The Hill and saw Meath defeat Dublin in the fourth match of their first-round marathon tie.*

● *END OF AN EPIC MARATHON . . . the marathon between Meath and Dublin is finally concluded and joyous supporters embrace the Meath captain, Liam Hayes. In the background the lonely figure of Dublin skipper, Tommy Carr, trudges towards the losers' dressingroom holding one boot in his hand.*

● *DECISIVE . . . As Michael McQuillan dives to his right, Keith Barr, with a Meath player running right beside him, blasts the ball wide of the post at the Canal end and Dublin have lost their chance of putting Meath away. There was a blatant breach of the rules and the penalty should have been retaken, asserts Paddy Cullen.*

● *UNFORGETTABLE . . . Meath's Dave Beggy cannot contain his sense of jubilation after Dublin had been beaten at the end of the epic marathon.*

RAILWAY CUP HURLING
INTER-PROVINCIAL CHAMPIONSHIP 1927-1992
ROLL OF HONOUR

Munster (38)—1928, 1929, 1930, 1931, 1934, 1935, 1937, 1938, 1939, 1940, 1942, 1943, 1944, 1945, 1946, 1948, 1949, 1950, 1951, 1952, 1953, 1955, 1957, 1958, 1959, 1960, 1961, 1963, 1966, 1968, 1969, 1970, 1976, 1978, 1981, 1984, 1985, 1992.

Leinster (19)—1927, 1932, 1933, 1936, 1941, 1954, 1956, 1962, 1964, 1965, 1967, 1971, 1972, 1973, 1974, 1975, 1977, 1979, 1988.

Connacht (8)—1947, 1980, 1982, 1983, 1986, 1987, 1989, 1991.

1927—November, 21 1926, Portlaoise: Leinster, 7-6; Connacht, 3-5.

Final, March 17, 1927, Croke Park, *Leinster,* 1-11; Munster, 2-6.

1928—February 12, Tuam: Munster, 7-3 Connacht, 2-4.

Final March 17, Croke Park: *Munster,* 2-2; Leinster, 1-2.

1929—(Ulster not competing, Leinster had a bye, and Connacht being struck out, Munster got a walk-over.

Final, March 17, Croke Park: *Munster,* 5-3; Leinster, 3-1.

1930—Final, March 17, Croke Park: *Munster,* 4-6; Leinster, 2-7.

1931—Semi-final, February 8, Birr: Munster, 10-9; Connacht, 1-2.

Final, March 17, Croke Park: *Munster,* 1-12; Leinster, 2-6.

1932—Semi-final, February 28, Birr: Leinster, 6-8; Connacht, 2-4.

Final, March 17, Croke Park: *Leinster,* 6-8; Munster, 4-4.

1933—February 19, Portumna: Munster 5-5; Connacht, 3-7.

Final, March 17, Croke Park: *Leinster,* 4-6; Munster, 3-6.

1934—February 25, Roscrea: Leinster, 7-6; Connacht, 4-6.

Final, March 17, Croke Park: *Munster,* 6-3; Leinster, 3-2.

1935—February 24, Portumna: Munster, 7-5; Connacht, 4-4.

Final, March 17, Croke Park: *Munster,* 3-4; Leinster, 3-0.

1936—February 16, Roscrea: Leinster, 2-7; Connacht, 2-4.

Final, March 17, Croke Park: *Leinster,* 2-8; Munster, 3-4.

1937—February 14, Ennis: Munster, 4-5; Connacht, 3-1.

Final, March 17, Croke Park: *Munster,* 1-9; Leinster, 3-1.

1938—February 20, Ballinasloe: Connacht, 3-6; Leinster, 3-6.

Replay, February 27, Tullamore: Leinster, 4-5; Connacht, 0-3.

Final, March 17, Croke Park: *Munster,* 6-2; Leinster, 4-3.

245

1939—February 26, Birr: Munster, 8-5; Connacht, 0-2.
Final, March 17, Croke Park: *Munster,* 4-4; Leinster, 1-6.
1940—February 25, Birr: Leinster, 4-5; Connacht, 1-4.
Final, March 17, Croke Park: *Munster,* 4-9; Leinster, 5-4.
1941—February 16, Galway: Munster, 7-5; Connacht, 0-6.
Final, March 16, Croke Park: *Leinster,* 2-5; Munster, 2-4.
1942—February 15, Ballinasloe: Leinster, 7-8; Connacht, 4-7.
Final, March 17, Croke Park: *Munster,* 4-9; Leinster, 4-5.
1943—February 14, Nenagh: Munster, 3-5; Connacht, 3-2.
Final, March 17, Croke Park: *Munster,* 4-3; Leinster, 3-5.
1944—February 13, Birr: Connacht, 4-5; Leinster, 1-5.
February 20, Croke Park: Munster, 9-3; Ulster, 3-1.
Final, March 17, Croke Park: *Munster* 4-10; Connacht,
4-4.
1945—February 11, Belfast: Ulster, 3-1; Leinster, 2-3.
February 11, Galway: Munster, 2-5; Connacht, 2-5
Replay, March 4, Limerick: Munster, 4-8, Connacht, 3-7.
Final, March 17, Croke Park: *Munster* 6-8; Ulster, 2-0.
1946—**February 17, Croke Park: Connacht, 4-14; Ulster, 1-7.**
February 17, Waterford: Munster, 0-6; Leinster, 1-2.
Final, March 17, Croke Park: *Munster,* 3-12; Connacht,
4-8.
1947—March 9, Croke Park: Connacht, 2-6; Leinster, 2-5.
March 16, Croke Park: Munster, 9-7; Ulster, 0-0.
Final, April 6, Croke Park: *Connacht,* 2-5; Munster, 1-1.

1948—February 15, Lurgan: Leinster, 5-5; Ulster, 4-2.
February 15, Ballinasloe: Munster, 6-5; Connacht, 1-4.
Final, March 17, Croke Park: *Munster,* 3-5; Leinster, 2-5.
1949—February 13, Croke Park: Munster, 2-8; Leinster, 1-8.
Connacht, 5-7; Ulster, 2-7.
Final, March 17, Croke Park: *Munster,* 5-3; Connacht,
2-9.
1950—February 12, Croke Park: Munster, 9-4; Ulster, 3-2.
February 12, Ballinasloe: Leinster, 3-10; Connacht, 2-6.
Final, March 17, Croke Park: *Munster,* 0-9; Leinster, 1-3.
1951—February 18, Croke Park: Leinster, 7-9; Ulster, 0-2.
Munster, 6-7; Connacht, 2-7.
Final, March 17, Croke Park: *Munster,* 4-9; Leinster, 3-6.
1952—February 17, Cork: Munster, 4-8; Leinster, 3-5.
February 17, Corrigan Park: Connacht 7-6; Ulster, 3-0.
Final, March 17, Croke Park: *Munster,* 5-11; Connacht,
4-2.

1953—February 8, Croke Park: Munster, 8-6; Ulster, 1-5.
February 22, Croke Park: Leinster, 7-9; Connacht, 4-3.
Final, March 17, Croke Park: *Munster,* 5-7; Leinster, 5-5.
1954—February 21, Croke Park: Munster, 4-12; Connacht, 3-7.
Leinster, 8-7; Ulster, 1-1.
Final, March 17, Croke Park: *Leinster,* 0-9; Munster, 0-5.
1955—March 13, Casement Park: Connacht, 5-10; Ulster, 2-4.
March 17, Croke Park: Munster, 3-10; Leinster, 2-9.
Final, April 3, Croke Park: *Munster,* 6-8; Connacht, 3-4.
1956—February 19, Casement Park: Munster, 5-13; Ulster, 2-6.
February 26, Ballinasloe: Leinster, 5-7; Connacht, 2-9.
Final, March 17, Croke Park: *Leinster,* 5-11; Munster,
1-7.
1957—February 17, Limerick: Munster, 3-11; Connacht, 3-11 (draw).
Replay: March 3, Limerick: Munster, 6-6; Connacht, 0-10.

February 17, Casement Park: Leinster, 7-7; Ulster, 2-5.
Final, March 17, Croke Park: *Munster,* 5-7; Leinster, 2-5.
1958—February 16, Belfast: Leinster, 8-10; Ulster, 3-3.
March 2, Galway: Munster, 2-15; Connacht, 1-8.
Final, March 17, Croke Park: *Munster,* 3-7; Leinster, 3-5.
1959—March 17, Croke Park: Connacht, 2-14; Leinster, 3-7.
Final, June 7, Croke Park: *Munster,* 7-11; Connacht,
2-6. Note: Ulster did not compete.
1960—February 21, Limerick: Munster, 5-12; Connacht, 1-9.
February 21, Croke Park: Leinster, 8-6; Ulster, 5-3.
Final, March 17, Croke Park: *Munster,* 6-6; Leinster, 2-7.
1961—February 19, Ballinasloe: Leinster, 5-8; Connacht, 3-7.
February 19; Belfast: Munster, 3-13; Ulster, 1-2.
Final, March 17, Croke Park: *Munster,* 4-12; Leinster,
3-9.
1962—February 18, Ballinsaloe: Munster, 6-11; Connacht, 1-3.
February 25, Cavan: Leinster 11-4; Ulster 6-3.
Final, March 17, Croke Park: *Leinster,* 1-11; Munster,
1-9.
1963—February 24, Croke Park: Munster, 9-7; Ulster, 3-5.
February 24, Croke Park: Leinster, 5-14; Connacht, 3-3.
Final, March 17, Croke Park: Munster, 5-5, Leinster, 5-5.
Replay, 14 April 1964, Croke Park: *Munster,* 2-8; Leinster 2-7.
1964—February 16, Limerick: Munster, 4-9; Connacht, 3-5.
February 16, Croke Park: Leinster, 8-9; Ulster, 1-4.
Final, March 17, Croke Park: *Leinster,* 3-7; Munster, 2-9.
1965—February 28, Belfast: Munster, 3-11; Ulster, 3-2.
February 21, Galway: Leinster, 4-9; Connacht, 2-3.
Final, March 17, Croke Park: *Leinster,* 3-11; Munster, 0-9.

1966—February, 27, Ballinasloe: Munster, 6-10; Connacht, 3-3.
March 7, Ballybay: Leinster, 6-14; Ulster, 3-7.
Final, March 17, Croke Park: Munster, 3-13; Leinster,
3-11.
1967—February 26, Croke Park: Leinster, 10-10; Connacht, 3-2.
Munster, 6-11; Ulster, 2-6.
Final, March 17, Croke Park: Leinster, 2-14; Munster,
3-5.
1968—February 25, Thurles: Munster, 3-15; Connacht, 1-5.
An Uaimh: Leinster, 5-10; Ulster, 3-8.
Final, March 17, Croke Park: Munster, 0-14, Leinster,
0-10.
1969—February 23, Casement Park (Preliminary Round): Connacht,
3-9; Ulster, 3-8.
1969—March 2, Ballinasloe: Connacht, 1-11; Leinster, 2-6.
Final, March 17, Croke Park: Connacht, 2-9; Munster,
2-9.
Replay, April 6, Galway: Munster 3-13; Connacht, 4-4.
1970—February 8, Galway (Preliminary Round): Ulster, 3-6;
Connacht, 2-6.
February 22, Croke Park: Semi-final: Munster, 6-14;
Ulster, 3-6.
Final, March 17, Croke Park: Munster, 2-15; Leinster, 0-9.
1971·—February 21, Casement Park, Belfast (Preliminary Round):
Connacht, 4-11; Ulster, 1-4.
February 28, Athlone: Semi-final: Leinster, 5-13; Con-
nacht, 4-14.
Final, March 17, Croke Park: Leinster, 2-17; Munster,
2-12.
1972—January 30, Croke Park (Preliminary Round): Combined
Universities, 0-5; Ulster, 1-1. Abandoned owing to snow.
February 6, Croke Park, Refixture: Combined Universities,
0-14; Ulster, 1-7.
1972—February 20, Croke Park: Semi-final: Leinster, 3-12;
Universities of Ireland, 2-13.
February 20, Portumna: Semi-final: Munster, 2-10; Con·
nacht, 2-8.
Final, March 17, Croke Park: Leinster, 3-12 (21);
Munster, 1-10 (13).
1973—January 28, Croke Park (Preliminary Round): Combined
Universities, 6-13; Ulster, 1-7.

248

1973—February 18, Croke Park: Semi-final: Leinster, 4-13; Combined Universities, 0-9.

February 18, Cork: Semi-final: Munster, 3-10; Connacht, 2-7.

Final—March 17, Croke Park: Leinster, 1-13 (16); Munster, 2-8 (14).

1974—February 17, Kilkenny: Semi-final: Leinster, 3-13; Connacht, 3-6.

February 17, Limerick: Semi-final: Munster, 5-11; Combined Universities, 2-7.

Final, March 18, Croke Park: Leinster, 2-15 (21); Munster, 1-11 (14).

1975— February 16, Parnell Park: Semi-final: Munster, 4-16; Ulster, 2-5.

February 16, Ballinasloe: Semi-final: Leinster, 1-11; Connacht, 1-7.

Final, March 17, Croke Park: Leinster, 2-9; Munster, 1-11.

1976— February 15, Croke Park: Semi-final: Leinster, 6-15; Ulster, 0-12.

February 15, Ballinasloe: Semi-final: Munster, 2-10; Connacht, 3-6.

Final: March 17, Croke Park: Munster, 4-9; Leinster, 4-8.

1977— February 13, Enniscorthy; Semi-final: Leinster, 1-12; Connacht, 2-5.

February 13, Croke Park: Semi-final: Munster, 3-17; Ulster, 3-6.

Final: March 17, Croke Park: Leinster, 2-17; Munster, 1-13.

1978—April 16, Cork: Semi-final: Munster, 0-20; Connacht, 1-11.

April 23, Belfast: Semi-final: Leinster, 3-17; Ulster, 1-13.

Final: May 7, Cork: Munster, 2-13; Leinster, 1-11.

1979—March 11, Ballinasloe: Semi-final: Connacht, 4-9; Munster, 2-7.

March 11, Croke Park, Semi-final: Leinster 1-19; Ulster, 0-11.

Final, April 1, Thurles: Leinster, 1-13; Connacht, 1-9.

1980—February 17, Ballinsaloe: Semi-final: Connacht, 1-13; Leinster, 1-10 (after extra time).

February 17, Croke Park: Semi-final: Munster, 4-16; Ulster, 1-10.

Final: March 17, Croke Park: Connacht, 1-5; Munster, 0-7.

249

1981—March 1, Birr: Semi-final: Leinster, 0-11; Connacht, 0-6.
Newbridge: Semi-final: Munster, 5-13; Ulster, 1-8.
Final: March 17, Ennis: Munster, 2-16; Leinster, 2-6.

1982—February 14, Galway: Semi-final: Connacht 1-13, Munster 2-8

February 14, Casement Park: Semi-final: Leinster 3-15, Ulster 2-5.

Final, March 17, Tullamore: Connacht 3-8, Leinster 2-9.

1983—February 6, Croke Park, Semi-final: Leinster 3-16, Ulster 1-8.

February 6, Limerick, Semi-final: Connacht 1-9, Munster 0-9

Final: March 17, Cavan: Connacht 0-10, Leinster 1-5

1984—March 17, Ballinasloe, Semi-final: Leinster 2-10, Connacht 0-5.

March 17, Limerick, Semi-final: Munster 3-21, Ulster 1-7

Final: March 18, Ennis: Munster 1-18, Leinster 2-9

1985—January 27, Birr, Semi-final: Connacht 1-12, Leinster 2-6

January 27, Newcastle, Semi-final: Munster 3-16, Ulster 2-6

Final: March 18: Thurles: Munster 3-6, Connacht 1-11

1986—February 16, Galway, Semi-final: Connacht 1-10, Leinster 1-9

February 16, Croke Park, Semi-final: Munster 1-19, Ulster 0-11

Final: March 17, Ballinasloe: Connacht 3-11, Munster 0-11

1987—October 3, Ennis, Semi-finals: Connacht 5-13, Ulster 0-15 Leinster 1-16, Munster 1-11

Final: October 4, Ennis: Connacht 2-14, Leinster 1-14.

1988—October 15, Belfast, Semi-finals: Connacht 4-13, Munster 2-11. Leinster 1-13, Ulster 1-8.

Final: October 16, Casement Park: Leinster 2-14, Connacht 1-12

1989—October 7, Wexford: Semi-final: Munster 3-31, Ulster 1-22 (after extra time).

October 7, Wexford. Semi-final: Connacht 1-19, Leinster 2-15.

October 8, Wexford. Final: Connacht 4-16, Munster 3-17.

1990—No competition.

1991—March 10, Pairc Ui Chaoimh. Semi-final: Munster 2-19, Leinster 1-10.

March 10, Athenry, Semi-final: Connacht 1-11, Ulster 1-6.

April 7, Croke Park, Final: Connacht 1-13, Munster 0-12.

1992— March 14, Kilkenny. Semi-final: Munster 1-12, Leinster 0-10.

March 14, Kilkenny. Semi-final: Ulster 2-6, Connacht 0-7.

March 15, Kilkenny. Final: Munster 3-12, Ulster 1-8.

Note: The 1993 competition was not completed by the time we went to press. However, here are the semi-final results:

1993—October 10, Tullamore. Semi-final: Leinster 3-14, Connacht 1-9.

October 10, Casement Park. Semi-final: Ulster 0-21, Munster 0-18.

RAILWAY CUP HURLING TEAMS

1927

Leinster—Dr. T. Daly (goal), Ed. Tobin, P. McInerney, G. Howard, M. Gill, D. O'Neill, E. Fahy, Jas. Walsh, M. Power (Dublin), J. Byrne (Laois), W. Dunphy, E. Doyle, L. Meagher, J. Roberts, H. Meagher (Kilkenny).

Munster—Seán Óge Murphy, E. Coughlan, E. O'Connell, M. Murphy, J. Regan, J. Hurley, P. Aherne, M. Aherne (Cork), M. Murphy (goal), J. J. Kinnane, M. Cross, W. Gleeson (Limerick), M. D'Arcy, P. Cahill, M. Kennedy (Tipperary).

1928

Munster—Seán Óg Murphy, E. O'Connell, D. B. Murphy, J. Hurley, E. Coughlan (Cork), T. Shinny (goal), J. J. Kinnane, M. Fitzgibbon, T. Conway (Limerick), P. Cahill, M. Kennedy, J. J. Callanan, P. Purcell, M. Cronin (Tipperary), T. Considine (Clare). Sub.: M. Leahy (Cork).

Leinster—M. Gill, T. Daly (goal), P. McInerney, J. Walsh, E. Tobin, G. Howard, D. O'Neill, M. Power, E. Fahey, T. Barry (Dublin), W. Dunphy, E. Doyle, L. Meagher (Kilkenny), J. Byrne, P. Kelly (Laois).

1929

Munster—Seán Óg Murphy, D. B. Murphy, J. O'Regan, M. O'Connell, E. Coughlan, M. Aherne (Cork), T. Shinny (goal), M. Fitzgibbon, T. Conway, M. Cross (Limerick), J. Doyle, T. Considine (Clare), P. Purcell, P. Cahill, M. Kennedy (Tipperary). Sub.: C. Keane (Tipperary).

Leinster—M. Gill, G. Howard, T. Barry, P. McInerney, J. Walsh, M. Power (Dublin), R. Collins (goal) (Meath), J. Byrne, E. Tobin, D. O'Neill, J. Murphy (Laois), J. Byrne, P. Kealy, L. Meagher (Kilkenny), W. Cordial (Offaly).

1930

Munster—D. B. Murphy, J. O'Regan, J. Hurley, M. O'Connell (Cork), T. Shinny (goal), M. Cross, M. Fitzgibbon, T. Conway (Limerick), P. Cahill, P. Purcell, M. Kennedy, T. Treacy (Tipperary), J. J. Doyle, T. Considine (Clare), C. Ware (Waterford).

Leinster—W. Dunphy, P. Phelan (goal), Martin Power, P. Byrne, L. Meagher, P. Walsh (Kilkenny), T. Burke, C. McMahon, E. Byrne, Jim Walsh, M. Gill, M. Power, M. Finn, S. Tumpane (Dublin), E. Giles (Meath). Sub.: P. Kelly (Laois).

1931

Munster—T. O'Meara, P. Purcell, P. Cahill, T. Treacy, M. Kennedy (Tipperary), C. Ware (Waterford), J. J. Doyle, T. Considine (Clare), P. Collins, J. Hurley, D. B. Murphy, E. Coughlan, P. Aherne (Cork), M. Cross, G. Howard (Limerick).

Leinster—Jas. Walsh, John O'Dwyer (goal), P. McInerney, Chas. McMahon, T. Teehan, M. Gill, S. Tumpane, T. Quinlan, S. Hegarty, M. Power (Dublin), P. Byrne, E. Doyle, P. Phelan, J. Roberts, Ed. Byrne (Kilkenny).

1932

Leinster—J. Dermody (goal), P. O'Reilly, P. Larkin, P. Phelan, D. Dunne, T. Leahy, M. Power, E. Byrne (Kilkenny), T. Teehan, C. McMahon, J. Walsh, S. Hegarty, D. O'Neill (Dublin), P. Drennan, E. Tobin (Laois). Sub.: Jim Grace (Kilkenny).

Munster—E. Coughlan, P. Collins, G. Garrett, W. Clancy, D. B. Murphy, M. Aherne (Cork), T. O'Meara (goal), P. Purcell, T. Treacy, P. Cahill, M. Kennedy (Tipperary), J. J. Doyle (Clare), C. Ware, P. Browne (Waterford), M. Cross (Limerick). Sub.: P. Clohessy (Limerick).

1933

Leinster—J. Dermody, P. Larkin, P. O'Reilly, P. Phelan, P. Byrne, E. Doyle, E. Byrne, L. Meagher, J. Walsh, D. Dunne, M. Power (Kilkenny), C. McMahon, E. Wade, J. Walsh, D. O'Neill (Dublin). Subs.: Tommy Leahy and Johnny Dunne (Kilkenny).

Munster—Tom Daly, J. J. Doyle, J. Houlihan, L. Blake (Clare), G. Garrett, P. Collins, D. B. Murphy, T. McCarthy, W. Clancy (Cork), T. McCarthy, P. Clohessy, Tim Ryan (Limerick), P. Purcell, M. Kennedy (Tipperary), D. Wyse (Waterford). Sub.: M. Cross (Limerick).

1934

Munster—P. Scanlan, E. Cregan, T. McCarthy, M. Cross, P. Clohessy, Tim Ryan, Ml. Mackey (Limerick), G. Garrett, D. B. Murphy, J. Kennedy (Cork), P. Purcell, T. Treacy, M. Kennedy (Tipperary), L. Blake (Clare), D. Wyse (Waterford).

Leinster—C. Forde, C. McMahon, Ed. Wade, S. Hegarty (Dublin), P. Larkin, P. Byrne, P. Phelan, E. Byrne, T. Leahy, L. Meagher, Martin Power, J. Walsh, J. Fitzpatrick, J. Dunne, Matty Power (Kilkenny).

1935

Munster—T. Ryan, P. Scanlan (goal), T. McCarthy, M. Kennedy, John Mackey, M. Mackey, P. Clohessy (Limerick), C. Ware (Waterford), G. Garrett, J. Barrett, M. Brennan (Cork), L. Blake, M. Hennessy, J. Harrington (Clare), M. Kennedy (Tipperary).

Leinster—C. McMahon, C. Forde (goal), A. Murphy, D. Canniffe, S. Hegarty, E. Wade, J. O'Connell (Dublin), P. Larkin, P. Phelan, T. Leahy, E. Byrne, L. Meagher, Matt Power, L. Byrne, J. Dunne (Kilkenny). Subs.: T. Treacy (Dublin), J. Walsh (Kilkenny).

1936

Leinster—J. O'Connell (goal), P. Larkin, P. Byrne, P. Blanchfield, T. Leahy, Ed. Byrne, P. Phelan, J. Walsh, J. Dunne, M. Power (Kilkenny), T. Teehan, D. Canniffe, C. McMahon, M. Daniels, Ed. Wade (Dublin).

Munster—P. Scanlan (goal), T. McCarthy, M. Kennedy, M. Cross, P. Clohessy, T. Ryan, J. Mackey, M. Mackey, P. McMahon (Limerick), J. Maher, P. Purcell (Tipperary), S. Barrett, M. Brennan (Cork), L. Blake, M. Hennessy (Clare). Subs.: J. Cooney (Tipperary), J. Quirke (Cork).

1937

Munster—M. Mackey, P. Scanlan (goal), T. McCarthy, M. Kennedy, P. Clohessy, T. Ryan, J. Mackey, P. McMahon (Limerick), J. Maher, J. Cooney, (Tipperary), J. Keane, C. Moylan (Waterford), J. Quirke, M. Brennan (Cork), L. Blake (Clare).

Leinster—J. O'Connell (goal), P. Larkin, P. Byrne, T. Leahy, E. Byrne, P. Phelan, M. White (Kilkenny), T. Teehan, C. McMahon, E. Wade, C. Downes, D. Canniffe (Dublin), A. Bergin, H. Gray, P. Farrell (Laois).

1938

Munster—J. Lanigan, J. Coffey, D. O'Gorman, W. O'Donnell (Tipperary), P. Scanlan (goal), T. McCarthy, P. Clohessy, T. Ryan, M. Mackey, J. Mackey (Limerick), J. Keane, C. Moylan (Waterford), L. Blake (Clare), S. Barrett, J. Quirke (Cork). Sub.: J. Lynch (Cork).

Leinster—P. Larkin, J. O'Connell (goal), W. Burke, P. Blanchfield, T. Leahy, P. Phelan (Kilkenny), T. Teehan, P. Farrell, C. McMahon, E. Wade, P. MacCormack, M. Daniels, W. Brophy (Dublin), F. Monaghan (Westmeath), W. Delaney (Laois). Subs.: A. Bergin (Laois), C. Boland (Westmeath).

1939

Munster—M. Curley, J. Keane, C. Moylan, L. Byrne (Waterford), P. Carroll, P. Clohessy, T. Ryan, J. Mackey, M. Mackey (Limerick), S. Barrett, M. Brennan (Cork), D. O'Gorman, E. Wade (Tipperary), T. Loughnane, J. Mullane (Clare).

Leinster—J. O'Connell, P. Larkin, W. Burke, P. Blanchfield, T. Leahy, P. Phelan, J. Walsh (Kilkenny), M. Gill, P. Farrell, J. Byrne, H. Gray, M. McDonnell, M. Flynn, P. Doody (Dublin), F. White (Westmeath).

1940

Munster—P. Scanlan (goal), P. Clohessy, J. Power, J. Mackey, M. Mackey, P. McMahon (Limerick), W. Murphy, W. Campbell, Seán Barrett, J. Quirke, M. Brennan (Cork), G. Cornally, W. O'Donnell (Tipperary), J. Mullane (Clare), C. Moylan (Waterford). Sub.: J. Keane (Waterford).

Leinster—J. O'Connell (goal), P. Grace, W. Burke, P. Blanchfield, R. Hinks, J. Walsh, J. Langton, P. Phelan, J. Kelly, J. Phelan (Kilkenny), A. Bergin, P. Farrell (Laois), M. Gill, H. Gray, M. Brophy (Dublin). Subs.: J. Byrne (Dublin), F. White (Westmeath), Seán O'Brien (Kilkenny).

1941

Leinster—J. O'Connell, P. Grace (Kilkenny), M. Butler (Dublin), P. Blanchfield, R. Hinks (Kilkenny), F. White (Westmeath), P. Phelan (Kilkenny), E. Wade, H. Gray, (Dublin), J. Langton (Kilkenny), P. McSweeney, M. McDonnell (Dublin), J. Mulcahy, S. O'Brien (Kilkenny), J. Phelan (Kilkenny). Sub.: J. Kelly (Kilkenny) for M. McDonnell.

Munster—P. Scanlan (Limerick), W. Murphy (Cork), J. Maher (Tipperary), A. Lotty, W. Campbell (Cork), J. Keane (Waterford), P. Cregan, T. Ryan (Limerick), C. Buckley (Cork), J. Power (Limerick), J. Lynch (Cork), R. Stokes (Limerick), J. Mullane (Clare), J. Quirke (Cork), P. Flanagan (Tipperary).

1942

Munster—J. McCarthy (Limerick), D. O'Gorman (Tipperary), B. Thornhill, W. Murphy (Cork), J. Ryan (Tipperary), J. Keane (Waterford), P. Cregan (Limerick), J. Lynch (Cork), C. Moylan (Waterford), W. Barron (Waterford), C. Ring (Cork), R. Stokes

(Limerick), J. Quirke (Cork), W. O'Donnell (Tipperary), J. Power (Limerick).

Leinster—D. Conway (Dublin), P. Larkin (Kilkenny), M. Butler (Dublin), P. Blanchfield (Kilkenny), F. White (Westmeath), J. Byrne (Dublin), P. Grace, J. Langton (Kilkenny), W. Burke, P. Phelan, J. Walsh (Kilkenny), H. Gray (Dublin), J. Mulcahy, J. J. Phelan (Kilkenny), C. Downes (Dublin).

1943

Munster—J. Maher (Tipperary), W. Murphy, B. Thornhill (Cork), P. Cregan (Limerick), A. Fleming, J. Keane (Waterford), J. Young, J. Lynch (Cork), R. Stokes (Limerick), C. Ring (Cork), J. Power (Limerick), T. Doyle (Tipperary), J. Quirke (Cork), W. O'Donnell (Tipperary), M. Mackey (Limerick). Sub.: J. Mackey (Limerick) for W. O'Donnell.

Leinster—J. Donegan (Dublin), P. Grace (Kilkenny), M. Butler (Dublin), Joe Bailey (Wexford), F. White (Dublin), W. Burke (Kilkenny), J. Byrne (Dublin). J. Kelly (Kilkenny), D. Dooley (Offaly), M. Ryan (Dublin), N. Rackard (Wexford), J. Farrell (Laois), J. Langton, J. Walsh, J. Phelan (Kilkenny).

1944

Munster—J. Ware (Waterford), W. Murphy, B. Thornhill (Cork), P. Cregan (Limerick), A. Fleming (Waterford), J. Power (Limerick), C. Cottrell, J. Lynch, S. Condon (Cork), R. Stokes (Limerick), C. Ring, J. Young, J. Quirke (Cork), J. Mackey (Limerick), P. J. Quane (Clare).

Connacht—(All Galway). S. Duggan, P. Forde, M. Forde, M. Brogan, M. Lynch, J. Brophy, D. Flynn, P. Thornton, R. Forde, T. Ryan, M. J. Flaherty, J. Gallagher, M. Nestor, A. Brennan, M. Fennessy. Subs.: R. Quinn for M. Brogan, W. Fahy for J. Gallagher.

1945

Munster—J. Ware, A. Fleming (Waterford), W. Murphy (Cork), P. Cregan (Limerick), P. O'Donovan (Cork), J. Power (Limerick), J. Young (Cork), P. McCarthy (Limerick), C. Cottrell (Cork), T. Purcell (Tipperary), C. Ring (Cork), R. Stokes

(Limerick), M. Mackey (Limerick), J. Quirke (Cork), P. J. Quane (Clare).

Ulster—M. McKeown, W. Feeney (Antrim), J. Butler, E. O'Toole (Monaghan), P. McKeown (Antrim), B. Denvir (Down), M. Butler (Antrim), O. Keenan (Down), N. Campbell, D. Cormichan, K. Armstrong, L. McGrady (Antrim), J. White (Down), C. Mullan, S. Mulholland (Antrim). Subs.: T. McAllister for E. O'Toole, J. Butler for J. White.

1946

Munster—J. Maher (Tipperary), W. Murphy (Cork), G. Cornally (Tipperary), A. Fleming (Waterford), J. Devitt (Tipperary), P. Lyons (Clare), M. Hayes (Waterford), R. Stokes, J. Power, S. Herbert (Limerick), C. Ring, J. Young (Cork), P. Fitzgerald (Limerick), A. O'Brien (Clare), T. Doyle (Tipperary).

Connacht—(All Galway). S. Duggan, J. Killeen, R. Quinn, D. Flynn, M. J. Flaherty, J. Brophy, W. Fahy, J. Killeen, P. Gantley, J. Gallagher, P. Jordan, S. Gallagher, M. Doyle, T. Flynn, M. Nestor. Sub.: T. Doyle for M. Doyle).

1947

Connacht—(All Galway). S. Duggan, D. Flynn, P. Forde, W. Fahy, M. J. Flaherty, J. Brophy, B. Power, J. Killeen, P. Gantley, J. Gallagher, H. Gordon, P. Jordan, M. Nestor, T. Kelly, S. Gallagher.

Munster—T. Mulcahy, W. Murphy (Cork), J. Keane (Waterford), P. Cregan (Limerick), M. Maher (Tipperary), A. Lotty (Cork), A. Fleming, V. Baston, M. Hayes (Waterford), C. Ring (Cork), J. Power (Limerick), J. Young, M. O'Riordan, G. O'Riordan (Cork), T. Doyle (Tipperary). Subs.: M. Ryan (Limerick) for M. Hayes and D. Solon (Clare for A. Lotty.

1948

Munster—T. Mulcahy, W. Murphy, C. Murphy (Cork) J. Goode (Waterford), J. Devitt (Tipperary), P. Donovan (Cork), D. Solon (Clare), V. Baston, M. Hayes (Waterford), S. Herbert, J. Power (Limerick), C. Ring (Cork), M. Daly (Clare), E. Daly (Waterford), T. Doyle (Tipperary). Sub.: M. Riordan (Cork) for S. Herbert; G. Sadlier (Limerick) for D. Solon.

Leinster—R. Dowling, P. Grace, P. Hayden M. Marnell, J. Kelly (Kilkenny), J. Brennan (Dublin), J. Mulcahy (Kilkenny),

258

M. Hassett (Dublin), J. Heffernan, J. Langton, T. Leahy (Kilkenny), A. Herbert (Dublin), N. Rackard (Wexford), J. Prior (Dublin), S. Downey (Kilkenny).

1949
Munster—J. Ware, A. Fleming (Waterford), C. Murphy (Cork), T. Cregan (Limerick), J. Devitt (Tipperary), P. Donovan (Cork), T. Purcell (Tipperary), V. Baston (Waterford), M. Ryan (Limerick), C. Ring (Cork), J. Keane (Waterford), S. Herbert (Limerick), M. Daly (Clare) E. Daly (Waterford), W. O'Carroll (Tipperary). Sub.: P. Fitzgerald (Limerick) for W. O'Carroll.

Connacht—S. Duggan, M. Badger, R. Quinn, W. Fahy, M. McInerney, C. Corless, M. J. Flaherty, T. Boyle, J. Killeen, F. Duignan, H. Gordon, T. Moroney, T. Kelly, B. Power, J. Gallagher. Sub.: J. Salmon for W. Fahy.
Note: All Galway with exception of T. Boyle (Roscommon).

1950
Munster—A. Reddan (Tipperary), A. Fleming (Waterford), G. O'Riordan (Cork), J. Sadlier (Limerick), P. Stakelum, (Tipperary), V. Baston (Waterford), M. Fouhy (Cork), S. Bannon, P. Shanahan, J. Kennedy, M. Ryan, S. Kenny (Tipperary), M. Riordan (Cork), W. McAllister (Clare), C. Ring (Cork).

Leinster—T. Fitzpatrick (Laois), S. Cronin (Dublin), P. Hayden, M. Marnell (Kilkenny), J. Murray, T. Byrne (Laois), R. Rackard (Wexford), J. Styles (Laois), W. Walsh (Kilkenny), A. Dunne (Laois), A. Herbert (Dublin), J. Langton, S. Downey (Kilkenny), N. Rackard (Wexford), L. Reidy (Kilkenny). Subs.: P. Prendergast (Kilkenny) for J. Murray, M. Lyons (Dublin) for N. Rackard.

1951
Munster—A. Reddan (Tipperary), A. Fleming, D. Walsh (Waterford), D. McInerney (Clare), S. Bannon, P. Stakelum (Tipperary), J. Goode (Waerford), M. Fouhy (Cork), S. Kenny, (Tipperary), M. Nugent (Clare), M. Ryan (Tipperary), E. Stokes (Limerick), P. Kenny (Tipperary), D. McCarthy (Limerick), C. Ring (Cork). Subs.: John Doyle, P. Shanahan (Tipperary), W. J. Daly (Cork).

Leinster—R. Dowling (Kilkenny), S. Cronin (Dublin), P. Hayden, M. Marnell (Kilkenny), R. Rackard (Wexford), P. Prendergast, W. Walsh, D. Kennedy (Kilkenny), J. Morrissey, P.

Kehoe (Wexford), J. Prior (Dublin), J. Langton, S. Downey (Kilkenny), N. Rackard, T. Flood (Wexford). Subs.: N. Allen and P. Donnelly (Dublin) and J. Hogan (Kilkenny).

1952

Munster—A. Reddan (Tipperary), J. Goode, D. Walsh (Waterford), J. Doyle (Tipperary), S. Herbert (Limerick), P. Stakelum (Tipperary), M. Fouhy (Cork), P. Shanahan (Tipperary), J. Kiely (Waterford), M. Nugent (Clare), M. Ryan, S. Bannon, P. Kenny (Tipperary), D. McCarthy (Limerick), C. Ring (Cork).

Connacht—(All Galway). S. Duggan, C. Corless, F. Flynn, J. Brophy, J. Molloy, T. Kelly, H. Gordon, J. Salmon, J. Killeen, F. Duignan, M. Burke, P. Nolan, P. Manton, M. J. Flaherty, J. Gallagher. Subs.: T. Moroney, M. Glynn.

1953

Munster—A. Reddan (Tipperary), J. Goode (Waterford), J. Doyle (Tipperary), A. O'Shaughnessy (Cork), S. Herbert (Limerick), P. Stakelum (Tipperary), D. O'Grady (Clare), G. Murphy (Cork), P. Shanahan (Tipperary), M. Nugent (Clare), W. J. Daly (Cork), S. Bannon, P. Kenny (Tipperary), D. McCarthy (Limerick), C. Ring (Cork). Subs: M. Queally (Waterford) for A. O'Shaughnessy, P. Barry (Cork) for C. Ring.

Leinster—K. Matthews (Dublin), J. Hogan, P. Hayden, M. Marnell (Kilkenny), D. Ferguson (Dublin), R. Rackard (Wexford), W. Walsh (Kilkenny), C. Murphy, N. Allen (Dublin), Paddy Kehoe, E. Wheeler (Wexford), T. Maher (Laois), M. Kelly (Kilkenny), N. Rackard, T. Flood (Wexford). Sub: W. Rackard (Wexford) for Tim Maher, Jim Prior (Dublin) for M. Kelly.

1954

Leinster—K. Matthews (Dublin), J. Hogan, P. Hayden (Kilkenny), M. Hanlon (Wexford), P. Buggy (Kilkenny), E. Wheeler (Wexford), J. McGovern (Kilkenny), N. Allen (Dublin), J. Sutton (Kilkenny), M. Ryan (Dublin), D. Carroll (Kilkenny), T. Flood (Wexford), J. Langton, P. Fitzgerald, M. Kelly (Kilkenny). Subs.: J. Morrissey, W. Rackard (Wexford).

Munster—A. Reddan (Tipperary), G. O'Riordan, J. Lyons (Cork), J. Doyle, J. Finn, P. Stakelum (Tipperary), M. Fouhy (Cork), J. Hough (Tipperary), J. Kiely (Waterford), W. J. Daly (Cork), J. Harnett (Cork), S. Bannon (Tipperary), J. Smith (Clare), D. McCarthy (Limerick), C. Ring (Cork).

1955

Munster—A. Reddan (Tipperary), G. O'Riordan, J. Lyons (Cork), J. Doyle, P. Stakelum (Tipperary), D. O'Grady (Clare), V. Twomey (Cork), J. Smith (Clare), J. Hough (Tipperary), W. J. Daly (Cork), D. Dillon (Clare), J. Hartnett (Cork), S. Power (Waterford), J. Greene (Clare), C. Ring (Cork).

Connacht—(All Galway). T. Boland, F. Spillane, B. Power, H. Gordon, M. Murphy, W. Duffy, T. Kelly, J. Salmon, J. Duggan, P. Duggan, E. Monahan, M. Cullinane, P. Manton, M. Elwood, J. Fives. Subs.: S. Cullinane for Boland, T. Glynn for Murphy.

1956

Leinster—A. Foley (Wexford) D. Ferguson (Dublin), N. O'Donnell, R. Rackard, J. English, W. Rackard (Wexford), W. Walsh (Kilkenny), J. Morrisey (Wexford), J. McGrath (Westmeath), S. Clohosey (Kilkenny), E. Wheeler, T. Flood (Wexford), L. Cashin (Dublin), N. Rackard (Wexford), R. Rockett (Kilkenny). Sub.: S. Hearne (Wexford) for McGrath.

Munster—A. Reddan, M. Byrne (Tipperary), J. Lyons, A. O'Shaughnessy, V. Twomey (Cork), J. Finn, J. Doyle, P. Stakelum (Tipperary), J. O'Connor (Waterford), J. Carney (Clare), D. Kelly (Limerick), J. Smith (Clare), S. Power (Waterford), J. Hartnett, C. Ring (Cork). Sub: T. Casey (Limerick) for O'Shaughnessy.

1957

Munster—M. Cashman, J. Brohan, J. Lyons, A. O'Shaughnessy (Cork), M. O'Connor (Waterford), J. Finn (Tipperary), P. Philpott (Cork), M. Ryan (Tipperary), J. O'Connor (Waterford), D. Kelly (Limerick), T. Kelly (Cork), F. Walsh (Waterford), P. Kenny (Tipperary), C. Ring, P. Barry (Cork).

Leinster—A. Foley, R. Rackard, N. O'Donnell (Wexford), D. Ferguson (Dublin), J. English, W. Rackard (Wexford), J. McGovern, W. Walsh (Kilkenny), E. Wheeler (Wexford), S. Clohosey, M. Kenny (Kilkenny), T. Flood (Wexford), R. Rockett (Kilkenny), N. Rackard (Wexford), W. Dwyer (Kilkenny). Subs.: O. Walsh (Kilkenny) for Foley, L. Cashin (Dublin) for Rockett.

1958

Munster—M. Cashman (Cork), J. Finn (Tipperary), J. Lyons (Cork), J. Barron (Waterford), T. McGarry (Limerick), M. Óg Morrissey (Waterford), A. Wall (Tipperary), S. Power, P. Grimes (Waterford), J. Smith (Clare), L. Moloney (Limerick), J. Doyle (Tipperary), P. Barry, C. Ring (Cork), D. Whelan (Waterford. Subs.: M. Maher (Tipperary) for Finn, T. Cheasty (Waterford) for Moloney.

Leinster—O. Walsh (Kilkenny) N. Drumgoole (Dublin), N. O'Donnell (Wexford), J. Maher (Kilkenny), J. English (Wexford), P. Buggy, J. McGovern, M. Brophy, J. Sutton, D. Heaslip (Kilkenny), E. Wheeler (Wexford), C. O'Brien (Laois), M. Kenny, W. Dwyer, S. Clohosey (Kilkenny). Sub.: W. Rackard (Wexford) for Buggy.

1959

Munster—M. Cashman, J. Brohan (Cork). M. Maher (Tipperary), J. Barron (Waterford), T. McGarry (Limerick), A. Wall (Tipperary), M. Óg Morrisey (Waterford), T. English (Tipperary), T. Casey (Limerick), D. Nealon (Tipperary), S. Power (Waterford), J. Doyle (Tipperary), J. Smith (Clare), C. Ring (Cork), L. Guinan (Waterford). Sub.: T. Kelly (Cork) for Power.

Connacht—All Galway). F. Benson, R. Stanley, P. Burke, S. Cullinane, J. Duggan, J. Fives, M. Sweeney, T. Kelly, P. J. Lally, T. Sweeney, P. J. Lawless, S. Gohery, P. Egan, T. Conway, M. Fox. Subs.: J. Lyons for Fives, G. Cahill for Kelly.

1960

Munster—M. Cashman, J. Brohan (Cork), A. Flynn, J. Barron (Waterford), T. McGarry (Limerick), M. Óg Morrissey (Waterford), John Doyle (Tipperary), S. Power, P. Grimes (Waterford), Jimmy Doyle (Tipperary), T. Cheasty, F. Walsh (Waterford), J. Smith (Clare). C. Ring, P. Barry (Cork). Sub. D. Kelly (Limerick) for McGarry.

Leinster—O. Walsh, T. Walsh (Kilkenny), N. O'Donnell (Wexford), P. Croke (Dublin), J. English (Wexford), M. Bohan (Dublin), J. McGovern (Kilkenny), L. Shannon (Dublin), E. Wheeler (Wexford) D. Heaslip, S. Clohosey (Kilkenny), Padge Kehoe (Wexford), C. O'Brien (Laois), W. Dwyer, T. O'Connell (Kilkenny). Subs.: J. Byrne (Dublin) for O'Connell, R. Carroll (Kilkenny) for Byrne.

1961

Munster—M. Cashman, J. Brohan (Cork), M. Maher (Tipperary), J. Barron (Waterford), T. McGarry (Limerick), A. Wall (Tipperary), M. Morrissey (Waterford), T. English (Tipperary), S. Power (Waterford), Jimmy Doyle (Tipperary), T. Kelly (Cork), F. Walsh (Waterford), J. Smith (Clare), C. Ring (Cork), L. Devaney (Tipperary). Subs.: T. Cheasty (Waterford) for Ring, P. Duggan (Cork) for Morrissey.

Leinster—O. Walsh, T. Walsh (Kilkenny), N. O'Donnell, T. Neville, J. English, E. Wheeler, J. Nolan (Wexford), D. Foley (Dublin), S. Clohosey (Kilkenny), J. O'Brien, P. Kehoe (Wexford), E. Keher (Kilkenny), O. McGrath (Wexford), W. Dwyer (Kilkenny), T. Flood (Wexford). Subs.: M. Walsh (Kilkenny) for Keher, S. Quaid (Wexford) for Dwyer, O. Fennell (Laois) for Clohosey.

1962

Leinster—O. Walsh (Kilkenny), D. Ferguson, N. Drumgoole, L. Foley (Dublin), J. English, W. Rackard (Wexford), O. Fennell (Laois), D. Foley, M. Kennedy, A. Boothman (Dublin), C. O'Brien (Laois), F. Whelan (Dublin), O. McGrath (Wexford), W. Dwyer (Kilkenny), W. Jackson (Dublin). Sub.: D. Heaslip (Kilkenny) for Jackson.

Munster—M. Cashman, J. Brohan (Cork), M. Maher, K. Carey (Tipperary), J. O'Sullivan (Cork), M. Óg Morrissey (Waterford), M. Burns, T. English, L. Devaney, Jimmy Doyle (Tipperary), T. Kelly (Cork), D. Nealon (Tipperary), J. Smith (Clare), C. Ring (Cork), S. Power (Waterford). Subs.: P. J. Keane (Limerick) for Kelly, A. Wall (Tipperary) for English, F. Walsh (Waterford) for Devaney.

1963 REPLAY

Munster—M. Cashman, J. Brohan (Cork), M. Maher, John Doyle (Tipperary), T. McGarry (Limerick), A. Wall (Tipperary), J. Byrne (Waterford), P. J. Keane (Limerick), J. Condon (Waterford), Jimmy Doyle (Tipperary), T. Cheasty (Waterford) D. Nealon (Tipperary), J. Smith (Clare), C. Ring (Cork), L. Devaney (Tipperary). Subs.: F. Walsh (Waterford) for Ring, T. English (Tipperary) for Walsh.

[Note: T. English (Tipperary) played in drawn game. M. Burns and Tom Ryan (Tipperary) came on as subs in drawn game.]

Leinster—O. Walsh (Kilkenny), T. Neville (Wexford), J. Walsh (Kilkenny), L. Foley (Dublin), S. Cleere (Kilkenny), W.

263

Rackard, J. Nolan (Wexford), D. Foley (Dublin), P. Wilson, J. O'Brien (Wexford), C. O'Brien (Laois), F. Whelan (Dublin), W. Hogan (Carlow), E. Wheeler (Wexford), D. Heaslip (Kilkenny). Subs.: J. English (Wexford), for Cleere, E. Keher (Kilkenny) for Hogan, O. McGrath (Wexford) for Heaslip.

[Note: E. Keher (Kilkenny) and M. Kennedy (Dublin) played in drawn game. O. McGrath (Wexford), O. Fennell (Laois) and M. Coogan (Kilkenny) came on as subs in drawn game.]

1964

Leinster—O. Walsh (Kilkenny), T. Neville, D. Quigley (Wexford), L. Foley (Dublin), S. Cleere (Kilkenny), W. Rackard (Wexford), O. Fennell (Laois), P. Wilson (Wexford), P. Moran (Kilkenny), F. Whelan (Dublin), E. Wheeler (Wexford), E. Keher, T. Walsh (Kilkenny), C. O' Brien (Laois), M. Bermingham (Dublin). Subs.: M. Coogan (Kilkenny) for Fennell, Martin Hogan (Carlow) for Foley, D. Foley (Dublin) for Bermingham.

Munster—J. Hogan (Limerick), John Doyle (Tipperary), A. Flynn (Waterford), D. Murphy (Cork), L. Guinan (Waterford), A. Wall (Tipperary), P. Fitzgerald, J. O'Sullivan (Cork), T. English, Jimmy Doyle (Tipperary), T. Cunningham (Waterford), P. Cronin (Clare), L. Devaney (Tipperary), J. Smith (Clare), P. Grimes (Waterford). Sub.: A. O'Brien (Limerick) for Wall.

1965

Leinster—O. Walsh (Kilkenny), T. Neville (Wexford), P. Dillon (Kilkenny), E. Colfer (Wexford), S. Cleere, T. Carroll (Kilkenny), P. Molloy (Offaly), P. Wilson (Wexford), P. Moran (Kilkenny), J. O'Brien (Wexford), D. Foley (Dublin), E. Keher, T. Walsh (Kilkenny) C. O'Brien (Laois), M. Bermingham (Dublin).

Munster—J. O'Donoghue, John Doyle (Tipperary), A. Flynn (Waterford), K. Carey (Tipperary), L. Guinan (Waterford), A. Wall (Tipperary), P. Fitzgerald (Cork), T. English, M. Roche, Jimmy Doyle (Tipperary), P. J. Keane (Limerick), M. Keating (Tipperary), J. Bennett (Cork), L. Devaney, S. McLoughlin (Tipperary). Subs.: N. Gallagher (Cork) for English, K. Long (Limerick) for Carey.

1966

Munster—E. Power (Waterford), A. O'Brien (Limerick), A. Flynn (Waterford), D. Murphy, D. O'Riordan (Cork), A. Wall (Tipperary), L. Guinan (Waterford), M. Roche (Tipperary), B. Hartigan (Limerick), L. Danaher (Clare), L. Kiely (Tipperary), F. Walsh (Waterford), D. Nealon, J. McKenna, Jimmy Doyle (Tipperary). Subs.: P. Fitzgerald (Cork) for O'Riordan, L. Devaney (Tipperary), for Danagher, P. Cronin (Clare) for Nealon.

Leinster—O. Walsh (Kilkenny), T. Neville (Wexford), J. Lynch (Kilkenny), E. Colfer (Wexford), S. Cleere (Kilkenny), D. Quigley, W. Murphy (Wexford), B. Cooney (Dublin), P. Molloy (Offaly), W. Walsh (Carlow), T. Forrestal, E. Keher, T. Walsh, P. Dillon (Kilkenny), J. O'Brien (Wexford). Subs P. Moran (Kilkenny) for Quigley, J. Foley (Wexford) for Molloy.

1967

Leinster—O. Walsh (Kilkenny), D. Quigley, T. Neville, E. Colfer (Wexford), S. Cleere, P. Henderson, M. Coogan, P. Moran (Kilkenny), H. Dalton (Dublin), E. Keher, J. Teehan, C. Dunne (Kilkenny), P. Molloy (Offaly), J. Bennett, T. Walsh (Kilkenny). Subs.: N. Kinsella (Dublin) for Teehan, M. Browne (Wexford) for Dunne.

Munster—P. Barry (Cork), V. Loftus (Clare), A. Flynn (Waterford), D. Murphy (Cork), A. O'Brien, K. Long (Limerick), P. Fitzgerald (Cork), M. Roche (Tipperary), B. Hartigan (Limerick), S. Barry, J. O'Halloran (Cork), P. Cronin (Clare), D. Nealon, J. McKenna (Tipperary), T. Bluett (Limerick).

1968

Munster—M. Foley (Waterford), P. Doolin, T. O'Donoghue (Cork), N. O'Gorman (Tipperary), A. O'Brien (Limerick), J. Cullinane (Clare), L. Gaynor, M. Roche (Tipperary), J. McCarthy (Cork), B. Hartigan (Limerick), L. Guinan (Waterford), E. Cregan (Limerick), S. Barry (Cork), M. Keating, D. Nealon (Tipperary). Subs.: C. McCarthy (Cork) for Nealon, P. Cronin (Clare) for Cregan.

Leinster—O. Walsh (Kilkenny), D. Quigley (Wexford), P. Dillon, J. Treacy, S. Cleere, P. Henderson (Kilkenny), W. Murphy (Wexford), P. Moran (Kilkenny), D. Foley (Dublin), E. Keher, C. Dunne (Kilkenny), P. Wilson, J. O'Brien, A. Doran (Wexford), P. Molloy (Offaly). Subs.: P. Lynch (Wexford) for Wilson, T. Carroll (Kilkenny) for Murphy.

1969 REPLAY

Munster—J. O'Donoghue (Tipperary), A. O'Brien (Limerick), T. O'Donoghue, D. Murphy (Cork), J. Cullinane (Clare), J. McCarthy (Cork), L. Gaynor, P. J. Ryan (Tipperary), E. Cregan (Limerick), N. Pyne (Clare), N. O'Dwyer (Tipperary), G. McCarthy (Cork), Jimmy Doyle (Tipperary), C. Cullinane (Cork), J. Flanagan (Tipperary).

[Note: J. Kirwan (Waterford) and N. O'Gorman (Tipperary) played in drawn game. C. Cullinane (Cork) came in as a sub.]

Connacht—(All Galway unless stated). A. Gavin, M. Howley, T. Bohan, S. Francis, M. Burke (Sligo), M. McTigue, T. Murphy, J. Connolly, S. Stanley, P. Fahy, B. O'Connor, P. Mitchell, W. Murphy (Sligo), M. O'Connor, D. Coen. Subs.: B. Mitchell (Roscommon) for P. Mitchell, C. Muldoon for W. Murphy.

[Note: B. Mitchell (Roscommon) played in drawn game. Paddy Fahy (Galway) came on as sub.]

1970

Munster—J. O'Donoghue (Tipperary), A. Maher (Cork), M. Considine (Clare), J. O'Brien (Limerick), D. Clifford (Cork), M. Roche, L. Gaynor (Tipperary), G. McCarthy (Cork), B. Hartigan (Limerick), N. O'Dwyer (Tipperary), W. Walsh (Cork), P. Enright (Waterford), Jimmy Doyle (Tipperary), R. Cummins (Cork), M. Keating (Tipperary). Sub.: A. O'Brien (Limerick) for Roche.

Leinster—O. Walsh, T. Carroll, P. Dillon (Kilkenny), P. Spellman (Offaly), P. Henderson (Kilkenny), D. Quigley (Wexford), M. Coogan, P. Moran (Kilkenny), D. Haniffy, J. J. Healion (Offaly), P. Wilson (Wexford), E. Keher (Kilkenny), P. Molloy (Offaly), L. Lawlor (Dublin), A. Doran (Wexford). Subs.: P. Delaney (Kilkenny) for Healion, F. Cummins (Kilkenny) for Haniffy.

1971

Leinster—P. Nolan, D. Quigley, P. Kavanagh (Wexford), J. Treacy (Kilkenny), M. Browne (Wexford), P. Dunny (Kildare), H. Dalton (Dublin), D. Bernie (Wexford), F. Cummins (Kilkenny), J. Quigley (Wexford), P. Delaney, E. Keher, J. Millea (Kilkenny), A. Doran (Wexford), M. Bermingham (Dublin). Subs.: D. Martin (Offaly) for Nolan, P. Henderson (Kilkenny) for Dunny.

Munster—P. O'Brien (Clare), T. Maher (Cork), J. Kelly (Tip-

266

perary), J. Horgan, C. Roche (Cork), M. Roche, L. Gaynor (Tipperary), B. Hartigan (Limerick), P. J. Ryan, F. Loughnane, N. O'Dwyer (Tipperary), P. Hegarty (Cork), J. Flanagan (Tipperary), R. Cummins (Cork), E. Cregan (Limerick). Subs.: G. McCarthy (Cork) for P. J. Ryan; Ryan for Loughnane.

1972

Leinster—D. Martin (Offaly), F. Larkin, P. Dillon, J. Treacy (Kilkenny), M. Browne (Wexford), P. Dunny (Kildare), M. Coogan, F. Cummins (Kilkenny), H. Dalton (Dublin), B. Moylan (Offaly), P. Delaney, E. Keher, M. Brennan (Kilkenny), A. Doran (Wexford), K. Purcell (Kilkenny). Subs.: M. Bermingham (Dublin) for Brennan, P. Wilson (Wexford) for Dalton.

Munster—P. O'Sullivan, L. King (Tipperary), P. Hartigan, J. O'Brien (Limerick), C. Roche (Cork), J. Kirwan (Waterford), J. O'Gorman (Clare), M. Roche (Tipperary), S. Foley (Limerick), F. Loughnane, N. O'Dwyer (Tipperary), P. Hegarty (Cork), E. Grimes (Limerick), R. Ryan (Tipperary), E. Cregan (Limerick). Subs.: J. Flanagan (Tipperary) for Grimes, C. McCarthy (Cork) for Hegarty.

1973

Leinster—N. Skehan (Kilkenny), T. O'Connor (Wexford), P. Horan (Offaly), J. Treacy, P. Lalor, P. Henderson (Kilkenny), M. Mahon (Laois), F. Cummins (Kilkenny), M. Jacob, M. Quigley (Wexford), P. Delaney, K. Purcell (Kilkenny), M. Bermingham (Dublin), A. Doran (Wexford), E. Keher (Kilkenny). Subs.: L. O'Brien (Kilkenny) for Cummins, B. Moylan (Offaly) for Bermingham.

Munster—S. Durack (Clare), A. Maher (Cork), P. Hartigan (Limerick), J. Gleeson (Tipperary), S. Foley (Limerick), T. O'Connor, L. Gaynor (Tipperary), D. Coughlan (Cork), E. Grimes (Limerick), F. Loughnane, J. Flanagan, N. O'Dwyer (Tipperary), M. Malone, R. Cummins, S. O'Leary (Cork). Subs.: J. O'Brien (Limerick) for Grimes, C. McCarthy for O'Dwyer.

1974

Leinster—N. Skehan, F. Larkin (Kilkenny), P. Horan (Offaly), P. Dunny (Kildare), P. Lawlor, P. Henderson (Kilkenny), C. Doran, C. Kehoe (Wexford), F. Cummins (Kilkenny), M. Quigley (Wexford), P. Delaney (Kilkenny), P.

Quigley (Dublin), K. Purcell (Kilkenny), A. Doran (Wexford), E. Keher (Kilkenny).

Munster—S. Durack (Clare), B. Murphy (Cork), P. Hartigan, J. O'Brien (Limerick), T. O'Connor (Tipperary), E. Cregan (Limerick), C. Roche (Cork), S. Hogan (Tipperary), S. Foley (Limerick), F. Loughnane (Tipperary), A. Heffernan (Waterford), E. Grimes, L. O'Donoghue, E. Rea, F. Nolan (Limerick). Subs.: G. McCarthy (Cork) for Heffernan, M. Hickey (Waterford) for Nolan, P. McGrath (Waterford) for Rea.

1975

Leinster—N. Skehan, P. Larkin (Kilkenny), P. Horan (Offaly), P. Dunny (Kildare), P. Lalor, P. Henderson (Kilkenny), M. Jacob (Wexford), L. O'Brien, F. Cummins (Kilkenny), M. Quigley (Wexford), P. Delaney (Kilkenny), P. Quigley (Dublin), K. Purcell (Kilkenny), A. Doran (Wexford), E. Keher (Kilkenny). Subs.: C. Doran (Wexford) for Jacob, J. Quigley (Wexford) for P. Quigley.

Munster—S. Durack (Clare), L. King (Tipperary), P. Hartigan (Limerick), S. Hannon (Waterford), G. Loughnane (Clare), E. Cregan (Limerick), P. McGrath (Waterford), G. McCarthy (Cork), S. Hogan, F. Loughnane, N. O'Dwyer, J. Kehoe (Tipperary), E. O'Connor (Clare), W. Walsh (Cork), J. McKenna (Limerick). Sub.: J. Barry-Murphy (Cork) for McKenna.

1976

Munster—S. Shinnors (Tipperary), P. McDonnell (Cork), P. Hartigan (Limerick), S. Hannon (Waterford), T. O'Connor, N. O'Dwyer (Tipperary), P. McGrath (Waterford), G. McCarthy (Cork), J. McKenna (Limerick), F. Loughnane (Tipperary), M. Hickey (Waterford), J. Callinan (Clare), L. O'Donoghue (Limerick), R. Cummins, E. O'Donoghue (Cork). Sub.: G. Loughnane (Clare) for O'Connor.

Leinster—N. Skehan, P. Larkin (Kilkenny), P. Horan (Offaly), P. Dunny (Kildare), P. Lalor, P. Henderson (Kilkenny), C. Doran, M. Quigley (Wexford), F. Cummins, M. Crotty, M. Ruth (Kilkenny), J. Quigley (Wexford), M. Brennan (Kilkenny), A. Doran (Wexford), E. Keher (Kilkenny). Subs.: B. Cody (Kilkenny) for Dunny. M. Holden (Dublin) for J. Quigley.

1977

Leinster—J. Nolan (Wexford), P. Larkin (Kilkenny), W. Murphy (Wexford), P. Henderson, P. Lalor (Kilkenny), M. Jacob, C. Doran (Wexford), F. Cummins (Kilkenny), N. Buggy (Wexford), L. O'Brien (Kilkenny), M. Quigley (Wexford), M. Ruth, M. Brennan (Kilkenny), T. Doran (Wexford), E. Keher (Kilkenny).

Munster—S. Durack (Clare), N. Cashin (Waterford), P. Hartigan (Limerick), J. Horgan (Cork), G. Loughnane (Clare), N. O'Dwyer (Tipperary), D. Coughlan, G. McCarthy, P. Moylan (Cork), E. O'Connor (Clare), J. Kehoe (Tipperary), J. Callinan (Clare), L. O'Donoghue (Limerick), N. Casey (Clare), P. Moriarty (Kerry). Subs.: C. Honan (Clare) for Moriarty, M. Hickey (Waterford) for O'Donoghue.

1978

Munster— S. Durack (Clare), N. Cashin (Waterford), M. Doherty, J. Horgan (Cork), G. Loughnane (Clare), P. Hartigan (Limerick), P. McGrath (Waterford), J. Callanan (Clare), T. Cashman (Cork), T. Butler (Tipperary), G. McCarthy (Cork), C. Honan (Clare), C. McCarthy (Cork), J. McKenna (Limerick), N. Casey (Clare).

Leinster—N. Skehan, P. Larkin, R. O'Hara (Kilkenny), W. Murphy (Wexford), G. Henderson (Kilkenny), M. Jacob, C. Doran, E. Buggy (Wexford), F. Cummins (Kilkenny), M. Walsh (Laois), M. Quigley, M. Butler (Wexford), W. Fitzpatrick (Kilkenny), A. Doran (Wexford), M. Ruth (Kilkenny). Subs: L. O'Brien (Kilkenny), C. Keogh (Wexford).

1979

Leinster—N. Skehan. P. Larkin (Kilkenny), W. Murphy, J. Prendergast (Wexford), J. Hennessy (Kilkenny), P. Carton (Dublin), C. Doran (Wexford), G. Henderson (Kilkenny) P. Quirke (Carlow), J. Kelly (Offaly), M. Holden (Dublin), M. Walsh (Laois), B. FItzpatrick (Kilkenny), T. Doran, N. Buggy (Wexford).

Connacht—(All Galway, except where stated) F. Larkin, N. McInerney, J. McDonagh, J. Lucas, J. Greaney, C. Hayes, J. Cooney, S. Mahon, John Connolly, N. Lane, Joe Connolly, P. J. Molloy, A. Fenton, F. Gantley, J. Henry (Mayo). Subs.: M. Coen for Molloy, F. Burke for Gantley, Molloy for Lucas.

1980

Connacht—(All Galway), S. Shinnors, N. McInerney,C. Hayes, J. Cooney, S. Linnane, S. Silke, I. Clarke, S. Mahon, John Connolly, M. Kilkenny, Joe Connolly, P. J. Molloy, N. Lane, G. Curtin, F. Gantley.

Munster—P. Moloughney (Tipperary), B. Murphy (Cork), J. Keogh, T. O'Connor (Tipperary), D. McCurtain (Cork), M. Carroll (Limerick), G. Loughnane (Clare), T. Cashman (Cork), P. McGrath, M. Walsh (Waterford), J. McKenna (Limerick), J. Callinan (Clare), J. Barry-Murphy, R. Cummins (Cork), P. O'Connor (Clare.). Subs.: O. O'Connor (Limerick) for Barry-Murphy, E. O'Donoghue (Cork) for P. O'Connor, T. Crowley (Cork) for McGrath.

1981

Munster—P. Moloughney (Tipperary), G. Loughnane (Clare), B. Murphy (Cork), T. O'Connor (Tipperary), D. McCurtain (Cork), S. Hehir (Clare), L. O'Donoghue (Limerick), J. Fenton, T. Cashman (Cork), J. Callinan (Clare), P. Horgan (Cork), M. Walsh (Waterford), E. O'Donoghue (Cork), J. McKenna, E. Cregan (Limerick). Subs.: O. O'Connor (Limerick) for E. O'Donoghue, T. Crowley (Cork) for O'Connor.

Leinster—N. Skehan (Kilkenny), C. Doran (Wexford), E. Coughlan, P. Fleury (Offaly), P. Carton (Dublin), P. Delaney (Offaly), C. Jones (Laois), J. Murphy (Wexford), J. Kelly, M. Corrigan (Offaly), P. Quirke (Carlow), P. Carroll (Offaly), Martin Cuddy (Laois), P. Horan (Offaly), M. Walsh (Laois). Subs.: J. Hennessy (Kilkenny) for M. Walsh.

1982

Connacht—(All Galway except where stated): D. Synnott (Mayo), S. Coen, N. McInerney, J. McDonagh, S. Linnane, S. Silke, I. Clarke, M. Connolly, S. Mahon, J. Henry (Mayo), Joe Connolly, P. Piggott, F. Gantley, B. Lynskey, P. J. Molloy. Subs.: Jimmy Cooney for McDonagh, B. Forde for Gantley, N. Lane for Piggott.

Leinster—J. Nolan, L. Bennett (Wexford), J. Bohane (Laois), P. Fleury, A. Fogarty, P. Delaney (Offaly), J. Hennessy (Kilkenny), G. O'Connor (Wexford), G. Henderson (Kilkenny), M. Brophy (Laois), B. Bermingham, M. Corrigan, P. Carroll (Offaly), P. J. Cuddy (Laois), B. Fitzpatrick (Kilkenny).

270

Connacht—(All Galway, except where stated). D. Synnott (Mayo), N. McInerney, C. Hayes, S. Coen, S. Linnane, S. Mahon, J. McDonagh, M. Connolly, I. Clarke, A. Staunton, F. Burke, B. Lynskey, B. Forde, N. Lane. P. J. Molloy.

Leinster—N. Skehan, J. Henderson (Kilkenny), E. Coughlan (Offaly), L. Bennett (Wexford), A. Fogarty, P. Delaney (Offaly), G. Henderson, G. Fennelly (Kilkenny), J. Kelly, P. Carroll (Offaly), M. Cuddy (Laois), L. Fennelly, B. Fitzpatrick, C. Heffernan (Kilkenny), S. Kinsella (Wexford). Subs.: F. Cummins (Kilkenny) for G. Fennelly, J. Conran (Wexford) for Delaney.

1984

Munster—G. Cunningham (Cork), S. Hehir (Clare), L. Enright, P. Herbert, L. O'Donoghue (Limerick), S. Stack (Clare), P. Ryan (Waterford), J. Fenton (Cork), J. Carroll (Limerick), N. English (Tipperary), D. Fitzgerald (Limerick), B. Ryan (Tipperary), K. Hennessy (Cork), J. McKenna (Limerick), G. McInerney (Clare). Sub.: T. Mulcahy (Cork) for Hennessy.

Leinster—N. Skehan, J. Henderson (Kilkenny), E. Coughlan, P. Fleury (Offaly), J. Conran (Wexford), J. Delaney (Laois), A. Fogarty (Offaly), F. Cummins, J. Hennessy (Kilkenny), P. Critchley , M. Cuddy (Laois), G. Fennelly (Kilkenny), P. J. Cuddy (Laois), C. Heffernan, B. Fitzpatrick (Kilkenny). Subs.: P. Courtney (Wexford) for Critchley, M. Cosgrove (Westmeath) for Fitzpatrick.

1985

Munster—G. Cunningham, (Cork), S. Hehir (Clare), L. Enright, P. Herbert (Limerick), T. Cashman (Cork), S. Stack (Clare), D. MacCurtain (Cork), J. Carroll (Limerick), P. Hartnett (Cork), N. English, D. O'Connell (Tipperary), J. Fenton, T. Mulcahy, K. Hennessy, T. O'Sullivan (Cork). Subs.: J. Callinen (Clare), S. Power, R. Ryan (Tipperary).

Connacht—(All Galway): P. Murphy, P. Finnerty, C. Hayes, S. Linnane, T. Keady, M. Mooney, Ollie. Kilkenny, S. Mahon, T. Kilkenny, M. Haverty, P. Piggott, Joe Cooney, M. McGrath, N. Lane, A. Cunningham. Subs.: A. Staunton, B. Forde.

272

1986

Connacht—(All Galway): P. Murphy, A. Kilkenny, C. Hayes, S. Linnane, P. Finnerty, T. Keady, A. Kilkenny, P. Malone, S. Mahon, M. McGrath, A. Cunningham, Joe Cooney, P. J. Molloy, M. Connolly, N. Lane.

Munster—G. Cunningham (Cork), P. Fitzmaurice (Limerick), D. Mulcahy (Cork), T. Keane (Clare), D. Foran (Waterford), J. Carroll (Limerick), B. Ryan (Tipperary), J. Fenton, P. Hartnett (Cork), N. English (Tipperary), K. Hennessy (Cork), C. Lyons (Clare), D. Fitzgerald, P. McCarthy (Limerick), D. O'Connell (Tipperary). Subs.: P. Kelly, L. O'Donoghue (Limerick).

1987

Connacht (all Galway)— J. Commins, S. Linnane, C. Hayes, O. Kilkenny, P. Malone, P. Piggott, T. Monaghan, S. Mahon, A. Kilkenny, M. Naughton, A. Cunningham, Joe Cooney, M. McGrath, B. Lynskey, E. Ryan. Subs.: P. J. Molloy for Naughton; N. Lane for Mahon.

Leinster—J. Troy (Offaly), J. Bohane (Laois), P. Prendergast (Kilkenny), J. Henderson (Kilkenny), B. Keeshan (Offaly), G. Henderson (Kilkenny), J. Taylor (Laois), G. Fennelly (Kilkenny), J. Kelly (Offaly), P. Critchley (Laois), W. Byrne (Wexford), L. Ryan (Kilkenny), P. Cleary (Offaly), H. Ryan (Kilkenny), D. Fogarty (Offaly). Subs.: R. Power (Kilkenny) for Kelly; T. Dempsey (Wexford) for W. Byrne.

1988

Leinster—J. Troy (Offaly), E. Cleary (Wexford), A. Fogarty (Offaly), J. Henderson (Kilkenny), J. O'Connor (Wexford), M. Cleere (Kilkenny), J. Power (Kilkenny), L. Ryan (Kilkenny), S. Dalton (Dublin), V. Teehan (Offaly), B. McMahon (Dublin), M. Corrigan (Offaly), P. J. Cuddy (Laois), C. Heffernan (Kilkenny), D. Kilcoyne (Westmeath).

Connacht (all Galway)—J. Commins, S. Linnane, C. Hayes, M. Helebert, R. Duane, B. Lynskey, T. Monaghan, P. Malone, J. Cooney, M. Connolly, A. Cunningham, M. Naughton, M. McGrath, E. Dervan, G. Burke, Subs.: P. Nolan for Burke (45th minute).

1989

Connacht (all Galway)—J. Commins; D. Fahy, S. Treacy, S. Dolphin; P. Finnerty, M. Coleman, P. Higgins; J. Hardiman, T. Monaghan; A. Cunningham, J. Cooney, M. Kenny; G. Burke, S. Dolan, E. Ryan. Subs.: P. Malone for Hardiman, R. Duane for Monaghan.

Munster—T. Quaid (Limerick); G. Fitzpatrick (Water-O'Donovan (Tipperary), J. Heffernan (Tipperary); Conal Bonnar (Tipperary), L. O'Connor (Waterford), B. Finn (Limerick); S. Ahearne (Waterford), T. O'Sullivan (Cork); S. Fitzgibbon (Limerick), G. Kirby (Limerick), M. Cleary (Tipperary); T. Guilfoyle (Clare), Cormac Bonnar (Tipperary), N. English (Tipperary). Subs.: C. Stakelum (Tipperary) for O'Sullivan, Colm Bonnar (Tipperary) for Fitzpatrick.

1990

No competition

1991

Connacht (all Galway)—R. Burke; B. Dervan, P. Finnerty, D. Fahy; T. Keady, M. Coleman, G. Keane; A. Cunningham, P. Malone; M. McGrath, J. Cooney, M. Naughton; G. Burke, B. Lynskey, J. Rabbitte. Subs.: D. Curley for Burke, P. Higgins for Cunningham.

Munster—G. Cunningham (Cork); D. Byrne (Waterford), P. Carey (Limerick), J. O'Connell (Clare): J. Cashman (Cork), D. Ryan (Tipperary); B. Ryan (Tipperary); M. Houlihan (Limerick), G. Hegarty (Limerick); C. Carey (Limerick), T. Guilfoyle (Clare), J. Leahy (Tipperary); B. O'Sullivan (Waterford), G. Fitzgerald (Cork); M. Cleary (Tipperary). Subs.: C. Casey (Cork) for Hegarty, Conal Bonnar (Tipperary) for Cashman, C. Stakelum (Tipperary) for Guilfoyle.

1992

Munster—G. Cunningham (Cork); D. Byrne (Waterford), N. Sheehy (Tipperary), P. Delaney (Tipperary); J. O'Connell (Clare), J. Cashman (Cork), D. Walsh (Cork); M. Houlihan (Limerick), D. Carr (Tipperary); M. Cleary Tipperary), J. Leahy (Tipperary), A. Ryan (Tipperary); B. O'Sullivan (Waterford), G. Kirby (Limerick), C. Carey (Limerick). Subs: C. Walsh (Kerry) for Leahy, B. Ryan (Tipperary) for Delaney, L. Garvey (Limerick) for Cleary.

Ulster—P. Gallagher (Antrim); K. Coulter (Down), D.

274

McKinley (Antrim), P. Braniff (Down); M. Mallon (Down), P. Jennings (Antrim), P. McMullan (Down); D. Hughes (Down), C. Mageean (Down); J. Carson (Antrim), A. McCarry (Antrim), S. Downey (Derry); O. McFetridge (Antrim), C. Barr (Antrim), N. Sands (Down). Subs.: N. Keith (Down) for Gallagher, M. Baillie (Down) for Carson, G. O'Kane (Antrim) for Coulter, D. McKillop (Antrim) for McCarry.

CAPTAINS OF WINNING RAILWAY CUP HURLING TEAMS

1927—Watty Dumphy (Kilkenny)
1928—Seán Óg Murphy (Cork)
1929—Seán Óg Murphy (Cork)
1930—Dinny Barry Murphy (Cork)
1931—Philip Purcell (Tipperary)
1932—Jim Dermody (Kilkenny)
1933—Eddie Doyle (Kilkenny)
1934—Timmy Ryan (Limerick)
1935—Timmy Ryan (Limerick)
1936—Paddy Larkin (Kilkenny)
1937—Mick Mackey (Limerick)
1938—Jim Lanigan (Tipperary)
1939—John Keane (Waterford)
1940—Seán Barrett (Cork)
1941—Bobby Hinks (Kilkenny)
1942—Willie O'Donnell (Tipperary)
1943—Jack Lynch (Cork)
1944—Seán Condon (Cork)
1945—Johnny Quirke (Cork)
1946—Ger Cornally (Tipperary)
1947—Seán Duggan (Galway)
1948—Willie Murphy (Cork)
1949—Jim Ware (Waterford)
1950—Pat Stakelum (Tipperary)
1951—Seán Kenny (Tipperary)
1952—Pat Stakelum (Tipperary)
1953—Christy Ring (Cork)
1954—Johnny McGovern (Kilkenny)
1955—Christy Ring (Cork)
1956—Nick O'Donnell (Wexford)

1957—Mick Cashman (Cork)
1958—Phil Grimes (Waterford)
1959—Tony Wall (Tipperary)
1960—Frankie Walsh (Waterford)
1961—Tony Wall (Tipperary)
1962—Noel Dromgoole (Dublin)
1963—Jimmie Doyle (Tipperary)
1964—Seamus Cleere (Kilkenny)
1965—Paddy Moran (Kilkenny)
1966—Jimmy Doyle (Tipperary)
1967—Ollie Walsh (Kilkenny)
1968—Mick Roche (Tipperary)
1969—Len Gaynor (Tipperary)
1970—Gerald McCarthy (Cork)
1971—Dan Quigley (Wexford)
1971—Tony Doran (Wexford)
1972—Jim Treacy (Kilkenny)
1973—Pat Delaney (Kilkenny)
1974—Pat Henderson (Kilkenny)
1976—Eamon O'Donoghue (Cork)
1977—Tony Doran (Wexford)
1978—Martin O'Doherty (Cork)
1979—Phil "Fan" Larkin (Kilkenny)
1980—Joe Connolly (Galway)
1981—Joe McKenna (Limerick)
1982—Seán Silke (Galway)
1983—Sylvie Linnane (Galway)
1984—John Fenton (Cork)
1985—Ger Cunningham (Cork)
1986—Noel Lane (Galway)
1987—Conor Hayes (Galway)
1988—Aidan Fogarty (Offaly)
1989—Joe Cooney (Galway)
1990—No competition
1991—Pete Finnerty (Galway)
1992—Declan Carr (Tipperary)

ATTENDANCE FIGURES—ALL-IRELAND FINALS

1993—Kilkenny v. Galway 63,460
1992—Kilkenny v. Cork 64,354
1991—Tipperary v. Kilkenny 64,500
1990—Cork v. Galway 63,954
1989—Tipperary v. Antrim 65,496
1988—Galway v. Tipperary 63,545
1987—Galway v. Kilkenny 59,550
1986—Cork v. Galway 63,451
1985—Offaly v. Galway 61,814
1984—Cork v. Offaly 59,814
1983—Kilkenny v. Cork 58,381
1982—Kilkenny v. Cork 59,550
1981—Offaly v. Galway 71,384
1980—Galway v. Limerick 64,384
1979—Kilkenny v. Galway 53,535
1978—Cork v. Kilkenny 64,155
1977—Cork v. Wexford 63,168
1876—Cork v. Wexford 62,684
1975—Kilkenny v. Galway 63,711
1974—Kilkenny v. Limerick 62,071
1973—Limerick v. Kilkenny 58,009
1972—Kilkenny v. Cork 66,135
1971—Tipperary v. Kilkenny 61,393
1970—Cork v. Wexford .....'.. 65.062
1969—Kilkenny v. Cork 66,844
1968—Tipperary v. Wexford 63,461
1967—Tipperary v. Kilkenny 64,241
1966—Cork c. Kilkenny 68,249
1965—Tipperary v. Wexford 67,498
1964—Tipperary v. Kilkenny 71,282
1963—Kilkenny v. Waterford 73,123
1962—Tipperary v. Wexford 75,039
1961—Tipperary v. Dublin 67,866
1960—Wexford v. Tipperary 77,154
1959—Waterford v. Kilkenny 73,707
1959—Waterford v. Kilkenny (replay) 77,285
1958—Tipperary v. Galway 47,276
1957—Kilkenny v. Waterford 70, 594
1956—Wexford v. Cork 83,096
1955—Wexford v. Galway 77, 854
1954—Cork v. Wexford 84,856

```
1953—Cork v. Galway .................................................... 71,195
1952—Cork v. Dublin .................................................... 64,332
1951—Tipperary v. Wexford ............................................ 68,515
1950—Tipperary v. Kilkenny .......................................... 67,629
1949—Tipperary v. Laois .............................................. 67,168
1947—Kilkenny v. Cork ................................................ 61,510
1946—Cork v. Kilkenny ................................................ 64,415
1945—Tipperary v. Kilkenny .......................................... 69,459
1944—Cork v. Dublin .................................................. 26,896
1943—Cork v. Antrim .................................................. 48,843
1942—Cork v. Dublin .................................................. 27,313
1941—Cork v. Dublin .................................................. 26,150
1940—Limerick v. Kilkenny ........................................... 39,260
1939—Kilkenny v. Cork ................................................ 39,302
1938—Dublin v. Waterford ............................................ 37,129
1937—Tipperary v. Kilkenny .......................................... 43,638
1936—Limerick v. Kilkenny ........................................... 51,235
1935—Kilkenny v. Limerick ........................................... 46,591
1934—Limerick v. Dublin .............................................. 34,867
1934—Limerick v. Dublin (replay) .................................... 30,250
1933—Kilkenny v. Limerick ............................................45,176
1932—Kilkenny v. Clare ............................................... 34,372
1931—Cork v. Kilkenny ................................................ 26,460
1931—Cork v. Kilkenny (1st replay) .................................. 33,124
1931—Cork v. Kilkenny (2nd replay) .................................. 31,935
```
[Note: The new Hogan Stand was built in 1959 and, with the introduction of the seating under the Cusack Stand in 1966, it was officially estimated that the capacity attendance figure at Croke Park (in comfort) was 75,000.]

Note: Demolition of the existing Cusack Stand began immediately after the 1993 All-Ireland football final. It is envisaged that the new Cusack Stand with its ten-year club seats and 40 corporate boxes will be partially occupied by the time of the 1995 finals.

The capacity of the stadium will be 64,500 for the 1994 finals and 69,500 for the 1995 finals.

Ultimately, the capacity of Croke Park will be 79,500 after the Canal end has been redeveloped and the new Hogan Stand erected. Hill 16 will probably become a seated area in the final stage of the redevelopment programme.

For the record the old Cusack Stand was officially opened on Sunday, August 21, 1938, by then President of the GAA, Pádraig MacNamee of Belfast, the first Ulsterman to head the Association – the occasion of the Kerry v Laois All-Ireland senior football semi-final. Seating under the stand was introduced in 1966. The present Hogan Stand was built in 1959.

278

MUNSTER CHAMPIONSHIP ATTENDANCE
CORK v. TIPPERARY
(1949-1993)

1949—First round, Limerick 34,702
      Replay, also at Limerick .... (unofficial) 30,000
1950—Final, Killarney 38,733
1951—Final, Limerick 42,337
1952—Final, Limerick 43,236
1953—Final, Limerick 45,265
1954—Final, Limerick 52,449
1956—Semi-final, Limerick 36,949
1957—Semi-final, Limerick 40,847
1958—Semi-final, Limerick 45,662
1960—Final, Thurles 49,705
1961—Final, Limerick 60,177
1963—Semi-final, Limerick .... (unofficial) 30,000
1964—Final, Limerick 44,240
1965—Final, Limerick 39,687
1968—Final, Limerick .... (unofficial) 40,000
1969—Final, Limerick 43,569
1970—Final, Limerick 34,000
1972—Semi-final, Limerick (draw) 34,887
      Replay, also at Limerick 38,126
1976—Semi-final, Limerick 21,382
1979—Semi-final, Cork 40,690
1984—Final, Thurles 50,093
1985—Final, Cork 48,912
1987—Final, Thurles .... (official) 56,005
    (Note: The unofficial attendance was acknowledged as
reaching at least 59,000 to 60,000 as an entrance gate was
forced open and an estimated 3,000 to 4,000 spectators
gained admittance free.)
    Replay, Killarney 45,000

1988—Final, Limerick 50,000
    (Note: All-ticket game).
1990—Thurles: Cork v. Tipperary 45,000
1991—Pairc Ui Chaoimh: Tipperary v. Cork (draw) 47,500
    Thurles: Tipperary v. Cork (replay) 55,600
    (Note: All-ticket game.)

OTHER MUNSTER FINALS

1959—Thurles: Waterford v. Cork — 55,174
(New record that held to 1961)
1971—Killarney: Tipperary v. Limerick — 31,000.
1972—Thurles: Cork v. Clare — 25,648.
1973—Thurles: Limerick v. Tipperary — 41,722.
1974—Thurles: Limerick v. Clare — 36,446.
1975—Limerick: Cork v. Limerick — 46,851.
1976—Cork: Cork v. Limerick — 46,800.
1977—Thurles: Cork v. Clare — 44,586.
1978—Thurles: Cork v. Clare — 54,180.
1979—Thurles: Cork v. Limerick — 47,849.
1980—Thurles: Limerick v. Cork — 43,090.
1981—Thurles: Limerick v. Clare — 40,205.
1982—Thurles: Cork v. Waterford — 38,558
1983—Limerick: Cork v. Waterford — 35,000
1986—Killarney: Cork v. Clare — 39,975.
1989—-Pairc Ui Chaoimh: Tipperary v. Waterford — 30,241
1992—Pairc Ui Chaoimh: Cork v. Limerick — 48,036
1993—Limerick: Tipperary v. Clare – 41,557

LEINSTER FINALS

1957—Croke Park: Kilkenny v. Wexford (Record) — 52,272.
1971—Croke Park: Kilkenny v. Wexford — 19,344.
1972—Croke Park: Kilkenny v. Wexford (draw) — 18,611.
Croke Park: Kilkenny v. Wexford (replay) — 22,745.
1973—Croke Park: Kilkenny v. Wexford — 24,000.
1974—Croke Park: Kilkenny v. Wexford — 20,742.
1975—Croke Park: Kilkenny v. Wexford — 26,228.
1976—Croke Park: Wexford v. Kilkenny — 23,500.
1977—Croke Park: Wexford v. Kilkenny — 30,614.
1978—Croke Park: Kilkenny v. Wexford — 27,371.
1979—Croke Park: Kilkenny v. Wexford — 24,991.
1980—Croke Park: Offaly v. Kilkenny — 9,613.
1981—Croke Park: Offal v. Wexford — 29,053.
1982—Croke Park: Kilkenny v. Offaly — 32,093.
1983—Croke Park: Kilkenny v. Offaly — 35,707.
1984—Croke Park: Offaly v. Wexford — 30,016.
1985—Croke Park: Offaly v. Laois — 32,123.
1986—Croke Park: Kilkenny v. Offaly — 28,635.

1987—Croke Park: Kilkenny v. Offaly — 29,133.
1988—Croke Park: Offaly v. Wexford — 28,234.
1989—Croke Park: Offaly v. Kilkenny — 24,519.
1990—Croke Park: Offaly v. Dublin — 20,383.
1991—Croke Park: Kilkenny v. Dublin — 41,215.
         (S.F.C.: Meath v. Wicklow on same programme).
1992—Croke Park: Kilkenny v. Wexford — 41,097.
1993—Croke Park: Kilkenny v. Wexford (draw) – 37,715
         Croke Park: Kilkenny v. Wexford (replay) – 41,833

*ckie Power of Limerick, who wore the Green and White jersey with rare
nction from 1936 to 1949, is congratulated by President Mary Robinson
 receiving his All-Time All-Star Award in 1991. In centre is GAA Presi-
 Peter Quinn.*

ALL-IRELAND CLUB CHAMPIONSHIP (HURLING)

1971—Final, December 19, Birr: Roscrea (Tipperary) 4-5 (17); St. Rynagh's (Offaly) 2-5 (11).

1972—Final, May 14, at Waterford: Blackrock (Cork), 5-13 (28); Rathnure (Wexford), 6-9 (27).

1973—Final, December 9, Croke Park: Glen Rovers (Cork), 2-18 (24); St. Rynagh's (Offaly), 2-8 (14).

1974—Final (Replay), Dungarvan, April 28: Blackrock (Cork), 3-8 (18); Rathnure (Wexford), 1-9 (12).
Drawn Game: Croke Park, March 17: Blackrock, 2-14 (20); Rathnure, 3-11 (20).

1975—Final, March 16, Croke Park: St. Finbarr's (Cork) 3-8; The Fenians (Kilkenny) 1-6.

1976—Final, March 14, Thurles: James Stephens (Kilkenny) 2-10, Blackrock (Cork) 2-4.

1977—Thurles, March 27: Glen Rovers (Cork) 2-12; Camross (Laois) 0-8.

1978—Thurles, March 27: St. Finbarr's (Cork) 2-7; Rathnure (Wexford) 0-9.

1979—Thurles, March 25: Blackrock (Cork) 5-7; Shamrocks (Kilkenny) 5-5.

1980—Navan, June 1: Castlegar (Galway) 1-11; Ballycastle (Antrim) 1-8.

1981—Thurles, May 17: Ballyhale Shamrocks (Kilkenny) 1-15; St. Finbarr's (Cork) 1-11.

1982—Thurles, May 16: James Stephens (Kilkenny) 3-13, Mount Sion (Waterford) 3-8.

1983—Croke Park, April 18: Loughgiel Shamrocks (Antrim) 1-8, St. Rynaghs (Offaly) 2-5 (draw).
Casement Park, April 25: Loughgiel Shamrocks 2-12, St. Rynaghs 1-12 (replay).

1984—Birr, April 15: Ballyhale Shamrocks (Kilkenny) 1-10, Gort (Galway) 1-10 (draw).
Thurles, June 3: Ballyhale Shamrocks 1-10, Gort 0-7 (replay).

1985—Croke Park, March 17: St. Martins (Kilkenny) 2-9, Castlegar (Galway) 3-6 (draw).
Thurles, March 24: St. Martins 1-13, Castlegar 1-10 (replay).

1986—Croke Park, March 16: Kilruane McDonaghs (Tipperary) 1-15, Buffer's Alley (Wexford) 2-10.

1987—Croke Park, March 18: Borris-Illeigh (Tipperary) 2-9, Rathnure (Wexford) 0-9.

1988—Croke Park, March 17: Midleton (Cork) 3-8, Athenry (Galway) 0-9.

1989—Croke Park, March 17: Buffer's Alley (Wexford) 2-12, O'Donovan Rossa (Antrim) 0-12.

1990—Croke Park, March 17: Ballyhale Shamrocks (Kilkenny) 1-16, Ballybrown (Limerick) 0-16.

1991—Croke Park, March 17: Glenmore (Kilkenny) 1-13, Patrickswell (Limerick) 0-12.

1992—Thurles, March 29: Kiltormer (Galway) 0-15, Birr (Offaly) 1-8.

1993—Croke Park, March 17: Sarsfields (Galway) 1-17, Kilmallock (Limerick) 2-7.

Wing-back Donal Reid (left), a key figure in Donegal's first-ever All-and senior football title in in 1992.

ALL-IRELAND CLUB HURLING FINAL TEAMS
(1971-1993)

1971

Roscrea—T. Murphy, M. Hogan, K. Carey, B. Maher, P. Rowland, T. O'Connor, J. Crampton, M. Minogue, D. Moloney, F. Loughnane, J. Hannon, J. Cunningham, J. Tynan, M. Nolan, W. Stapleton.

St. Rynagh's—D. Martin, N. Gallagher, F. Whelehan, A. Horan, P. Moylan, P. Horan, S. Moylan, R. Horan, B. Johnson, B. Lyons, P. J. Whelehan, H. Dolan, G. Burke, B. Moylan, P. Mulhare.

1972

Blackrock—B. Hurley, P. Casey, P. Geary, J. Horgan, S. Murphy, F. Cummins, F. Norberg, M. Murphy, P. Kavanagh, D. Collins, R. Cummins, P. Moylan, B. Cummins, J. Rothwell, D. Prendergast.

Rathnure—M. Foley, J. Quigley, A. Somers, M. Mooney, J. O'Connor, T. O'Connor, J. Quigley, M. Byrne, J. Moore, J. Higgins, M. Quigley, J. Murphy, P. Flynn, J. English, D. Quigley. Sub.: S. Barron.

1973

Glen Rovers—F. O'Neill, D. O'Riordan, M. O'Doherty, P. Barry, J. O'Sullivan, D. Coughlan, M. O'Halloran, J. J. O'Neill, P. O'Doherty, P. Harte, R. Crowley, T. Buckley, M. Ryan, T. Collins, J. Young. Sub.: M. Corbett.

St. Rynagh's—D. Martin, J. Dooley, F. Whelehan, A. Horan, P. Moylan, P. Horan, H. Dolan, P. J. Whelehan, B. Johnson, B. Lyons, B. Moylan, J. Horan, R. Horan, P. Mulhare, S. Moylan.

1974

Blackrock—T. Murphy, J. Rothwell, P. Geary, J. Horgan, F. Cummins, C. O'Brien, F. Norberg, J. Russell, P. Moylan, P. Kavanagh, J. O'Halloran, D. Collins, D. Prendergast, R. Cummins, E. O' Donoghue. Subs.: S. Kearney, D. Buckley. (Note: B. Cummins played in drawn game.)

Rathnure—M. Foley, P. Quigley, Jim Quigley, M. Mooney, J. O'Connor, T. O'Connor, S. Murphy, M. Quigley, J. Higgins, P. Flynn, J. Murphy, M. Byrne, John Quigley, A. Somers, D. Quigley. (Note: J. Mooney, V. Fenlon played in draw, J. Higgins, A. Somers in replay.) Sub.: J. Higgins drawn game.

1975

St. Finbarr's—J. Power, T. Maher, S. Canty, C. Barrett, B. O'Brien, D. O'Grady, T. Butler, G. McCarthy, C. Roche, E. Fitpatrick, J. Barry Murphy, S. Gillen, C. McCarthy, S. Looney, J. O'Shea. Sub.: C. Cullinane.

The Fenians—P. J. Ryan, S. Delaney, N. Orr, M. Fitzpatrick, G. Murphy, P. Henderson, G. Henderson, F. Hawkes, M. Garrett, J. Moriarty, P. Delaney, J. Ryan, B. Fitzpatrick, B. Watson, P. Fitzpatrick. Sub.: P. Murphy.

1976

James Stephens—M. Moore, P. Neary, P. Larkin, N. Morrissey, T. McCormack, B. Cody, J. O'Brien, D. McCormack, M. Taylor, J. Hennessy, L. O'Brien, J. McCormack, M. Crotty, M. Leahy, G. Tyrell. Sub.: M. Neary.

Blackrock—T. Murphy, F. Norberg, C. O'Brien, D. McCurtain, A. Creagh, J. Horgan, J. Murphy, F. Cummins, T. Lyons, P. Moylan, D. Collins, P. Kavanagh, E. O'Sullivan, R. Cummins, E. O'Donoghue. Sub.: P. Butler.

1977

Glen Rovers—F. O'Neill, J. O'Sullivan, M. O'Doherty, T. O'Brien, F. O'Sullivan, D. Clifford, D. Coughlan, R. Crowley, J. J. O'Neill, P. Harte, P. Horgan, P. O'Doherty, M. Ryan, T. Collins, V. Marshall. Subs.: L. McAuliffe, T. O'Neill, F. Cunningham.

Camross—J. Carroll, J. Dooley, T. Cuddy, R. Maloney, J. Doran, J. Fitzpatrick, O. Cuddy, P. Dowling, P. J. Cuddy, Martin Cuddy, G. Cuddy, M. Carroll, Michael Cuddy, F. Keenan, S. Cuddy. Subs.: Tim Keenan, S. Bergin, S. Collier.

1978

St. Finbarr's—J. Power, C. Barrett, T. Maher, D. Burns, D. O'Grady, N. Kennefick, J. Murphy, G. McCarthy, J. Cremin, J. Allen, J. Barry Murphy, B. Wiley, E. Fitzpatrick, C. Ryan, C. McCarthy. Sub.: B. Meade.

Rathnure—M. Foley, A. Somers, D. Quigley, T. O'Connor, J. O'Connor, M. Codd, S. Murphy, J. Conran, J. Houlihan, D. O'Connor, M. Quigley, J. Murphy, P. Flynn, J. Quigley, P. Quigley. Sub.: L. Byrne.

1979

Blackrock—T. Murphy, F. Norberg, C. O'Brien, J. Horgan,

D. McCurtain, F. Cummins, A. Creagh, T. Cashman, J. O'Grady, P. Moylan, T. Lyons, D. Collins, E. O'Sullivan, R. Cummins, E. O'Donoghue. Sub.: D. Buckley.

Ballyhale Shamrocks—O. Harrington, D. Shefflin, L. Dalton, R. Reid, W. Phelan, M. Mason, F. Holohan, J. Walsh, S. Fennelly, M. Fennelly, P. Holden, G. Fennelly, L. Fennelly, B. Fennelly, K. Fennelly. Sub.: M. Healy.

1980

Castlegar—T. Grogan, Ted Murphy, Padraic Connolly, J. Coady, G. Glynn, John Connolly, M. Glynn, T. Murphy, S. Fahy, J. Francis, Joe Connolly, P. O'Connor, Gerry Connolly, Michael Connolly, L. Mulryan. Sub.: P. Burke.

Ballycastle — P. Smith, K. Boyle, K. Donnelly, G. McAuley, S. Donnelly, T. Donnelly, D. Donnelly, T. Barton, S. Boyle, B. Donnelly, P. Watson, P. Boyle, P. Dallat, E. Donnelly, O. Laverty.

1981

Ballyhale Shamrocks—K. Fennelly, W. Phelan, L. Dalton, R. Reid, F. Holohan, M. Mason, D. Connolly, J. Walsh, S. Fennelly, M. Fennelly, P. Holden, G. Fennelly, B. Fennelly, L. Fennelly, M. Kelly. Sub.: D. Fennelly.

Saint Finbarr's—G. Cunningham, A. Maher, D. O'Grady, J. Blake, D. Burns, B. O'Brien, N. Kennefick, J. Cremin, J. Meyler, C. Ryan, T. Maher, E. Fitzpatrick, J. Barry Murphy, C. McCarthy, J. Allen. Subs.: J. O'Shea, F. Scannell.

1982

James Stephens—M. Moore, P. Neary, B. Cody, P. Larkin, J. Hennessy, M. Hennessy, J. O'Brien, T. McCormack, D. McCormack, A. Egan, E. Kelly, B . Walton, J. McCormack, M. Crotty,J. J. Cullen. Sub.: D. Collins.

Mount Sion—S. Greene, B. Knox, E. Keogh, D. Shefflin, P. O'Grady, P. McGrath, P. Ryan, L. Slevin, D. Connolly, A. Cooney, T. Butler, K. Heffernan, M. Geary, P. Kelly, J. Greene. Subs.: J. Dalton, K. Ryan.

1983

Loughgiel Shamrocks—N. Patterson, M. Carey, P. J. Mullen, S. Carey, E. Connolly, P. McIlhatton, A. McNaughton, M. O'Connell, G. McGinley, P. Carey (junior), D. McGinley, B. Laverty, P. Carey (senior), A. McGarry, S. McNaughton. (Note:

M. Coyle and B. McGarry played in drawn game; P. Carey (senior) and (junior) subs in drawn match. Retained for replay.

St. Rynagh's—D. Martin, M. Whelehan, J. Dooley, W. Keane, T. White, A. Fogarty, T. Conneely, A. Horan, S. White, J. Kirwan, P. Horan, D. Devery, J. Horan, F. Kenny, H. Dolan. Sub.: G. O'Mahony (draw). J. Cannon and G. Dolan (replay).

1984

Ballyhale Shamrocks—O. Harrington, F. Holohan, L. Dalton, W. Phelan, M. Fennelly, M. Mason, S. Fennelly, J. Walsh, T. Phelan, B. Fennelly, G. Fennelly, M. Kelly, D. Fennelly, K. Fennelly, L. Fennelly. Sub.: L. Long.
(**Note:** L. Long, D. Connolly played in drawn game. Subs in drawn match, L. Fennelly, R. Keneally.)

Gort—J. Commins, S. Linnane, J. Nolan, J. Regan, J. Harte, P. Piggott, P. Neylon, C. Rock, M. Cahill, P. Hehir, B. Brennan, G. Lally, G. Linnane, K. Fahy, J. Crehan. Subs.: M. Murphy, M. Linnane, M. Mulkern. M. Brennan played in draw. J. Regan came on for replay. Subs in replay, M. Murphy, M. Mulcair.

1985

St. Martin's—B. Shore, J. Kelly, T. Maher, J. J. Dowling, T. Walsh, J. Moran, M. Maher, P. Lawlor, J. Moran, J. Morrissey, J. Brennan, P. Moran, D. Coonan, T. Moran, R. Moloney. Sub.: E. Morrissey draw and replay.

Castlegar—T. Grogan, P. Connolly, Ted Murphy, M. Glynn, T. McCormack, S. Murphy, G. Glynn, Tom Murphy, M. Connolly, M. O'Shea, S. Fahy, M. Costelloe, M. Murphy, John Connolly, G. Connolly. (Note: J. O'Connor and J. Coyne played in drawn game. M. Costelloe and M. Glynn came on as subs in drawn match and retained their places for replay.)

1986

Kilruane McDonaghs—T. Sheppard, J. Cahill, D. O'Meara, S. Gibson, J. Banaghan, J. O'Meara, G. Williams, E. Hogan, D. Cahill, Jerry Williams, Jim Williams, E. O'Shea, Pat Quinlan, P. Williams, Philip Quinlan. Sub.: S. Hennessy.

Buffers Alley—H. Butler, B. Murphy, P. Kenny, C. Doran, J. Donohue, P. Gahan, S. Whelan, M. Casey, G. Sweeney,T. Dempsey, T. Dwyer, M. Foley, M. Butler, T. Doran, S. O'Leary. Subs.: P. Donohue, E. Sinnott.

1987

Borris-Ileigh—N. Maher, F. Spillane, T. Stapleton,M. Ryan,

R. Stakelum, G. Stapleton, B. Ryan, T. Ryan, F. Collins, C. Stakelum, N. O'Dwyer, J. McGrath, M. Coen, P. Kenny, A. Ryan. Sub.: B. Kenny.

Rathnure—T. Morrissey, M. Codd, M. Quigley, J. Doyle, D. Sheehan, J. O'Connell, J. Conran, J. Holohan, L. Ronan, J. Codd, J. Redmond, N. Hearne, P. Codd, J. Morrissey, M. Morrissey. Sub.: J. Quigley.

1988

Midleton—G. Power, D. Mulcahy, M. Boylan, S. O'Mahony, E. Cleary, S. O'Brien, P. Hartnett, Tadhg McCarthy, M. Crotty, J. Fenton, J. Hartnett, J. Boylan, G. Fitzgerald, C. O'Neill, K. Hennessy. Subs.: G. Galvin, C. O'Neill, A. Smyth.

Athenry—M. Gannon, D. Monaghan, B. Caulfield, A. Jennings, P. Hardiman, M. Cahill, J. Keane, J. Hardiman, P. Healy, G. Dempsey, S. Keane, P. J. Molloy, S. Keane, P. Higgins, D. Higgins. Subs.: M. Donoghue, B. Feeney, J. Rabbitte.

1989

Buffer's Alley—H. Butler, B. Murphy, P. Kenny, J. O'Leary, P. Gahan, M. Foley, C. Whelan, E. Sinnott, S. Whelan, T. Dempsey, M. Casey, P. Donoghue, M. Butler, T. Doran, S. O'Laoire.

O'Donovan Rossa—P. Quinn, G. Rogan, D. Murray, M. Barr, A. Murray, M. Reynolds, S. Collins, J. Fagan, J. Close, D. Armstrong, C. Barr, P. Ward, N. Murray, J. Reilly, C. Murphy. Subs.: S. Shannon for Ward, P. Rogan for Close, C. Condon for Collins.

1990

Ballyhale Shamrocks—K. Fennelly, M. Fennelly, F. Holohan, W. Phelan, R. Walsh, P. Phelan, S. Fennelly, G. Fennelly, T. Shefflin, T. Phelan, J. Lawlor, D. Fennelly, B. Fennelly, L. Fennelly, B. Mason.

Ballybrown—F. O'Reilly, J. Coughlan, J. Kenny, S. Adams, P. O'Connor, J. O'Connor, A. Hall, J. Mann, C. Coughlan, O. O'Connor, P. Mulqueen, P. Davoren, C. Keyes, T. Kenny, S. Hayes. Subs.: E. Cliff for Hayes, G. O'Reilly for Mann.

1991

Glenmore—M. Deady, E. O'Connor, E. Aylward, P. J. O'Connor, L. Walsh, W. O'Connor, D. Ennett, R. Heffernan, D. Heffernan, D. Mullally, M. Phelan, P. Barron, J. Heffernan, C. Heffernan, J. Flynn. Subs.: S. Dollard for Ennett, M. "Foxy" Phelan for Flynn, M. Aylward for P. J. O'Connor.

Patrickswell—J. Murphy, Philip Foley, Paul Foley, E. Kelleher,

David Punch, P. Carey, Pa Foley, S. Carey, A. Carmody, C. Carey, G. Kirby, S. Kirby, N. Carey, S. Foley, L. Enright. Sub.: Dom Punch for Kelleher.

1992

Kiltormer—S. McKeigue, B. McManus, C. Hayes, K. Tierney, F. Curley, P. Dervan, G. Kelly, T. Larkin, A. Staunton, J. Campbell, T. Kilkenny, D. Curley, D. Cox, M. Staunton, S. Kelly. Subs.: T. Furey for Dervan, T. Hanrahan for McManus.

Birr—P. Kirwan, M. Hogan, D. Geoghegan, B. Hennessy, B. Whelehan, J. Errity, G. Cahill, J. Pilkington, M. Finnane, D. Regan, P. Murphy, D. Pilkington, M. Errity, R. Landy, O. O'Neill. Subs.: N. Hogan for M. Errity, J. Carroll for Finnane.

1993

Sarsfields—T. Kenny, Pakie Cooney, B. Cooney, M. Cooney, Padraic Kelly, D. Keane, W. Earls, N. Morrissey, J. Cooney, M. McGrath, J. McGrath, A. Donohue, Peter Kelly, M. Kenny, Peter Cooney.

Kilmallock—G. Hanly, S. Burchill, J. J. O'Riordan, S. O'Grady, D. Barry, D. Clarke, G. O'Riordan, M. Houlihan, S. Barrett, P. Barrett, M. Nelligan, P. Kelly, P. Tobin, B. Hanley, D. Hanley. Sub.: T. Nelligan for M. Nelligan.

CAPTAINS OF WINNING ALL-IRELAND CLUB HURLING TEAMS

1971—D. Moloney (Roscrea)
1972—J. Horgan (Blackrock)
1973—D. Coughlan (Glen Rovers)
1974—J. Horgan (Blackrock)
1975—J. Power (St. Finbarr
1976—P. Larkin (James Stephen's)
1977—M. Doherty (Glen Rovers)
1978—D. Burns (St. Finbarr's)
1979—J. Horgan (Blackrock)
1980—M. Connolly (Castlegar)
1981—R. Reid (Ballyhale Shamrocks)
1982—J. O'Brien (James Stephen's)
1983—N. Patterson (Loughgiel Shamrocks)
1984—K. Fennelly (Ballyhale Shamrocks)
1985—J. Brennan (St. Martin's)
1986—T. Sheppard (Kiluane McDonagh's)
1987—M. Ryan (Borris-Illigh)
1988—G. Power (Midleton)
1989—P. Kenny (Buffer's Alley)
1990—W. Phelan (Ballyhale Shamrocks)
1991—R. Heffernan (Glenmore)
1992—A. Staunton (Kiltormer)
1993—P. Cooney (Sarsfields)

BANK OF IRELAND ALL-STARS HURLING TEAMS

1971—D. Martin (Offaly), T. Maher (Cork), P. Hartigan (Limerick), J. Treacy (Kilkenny), T. O'Connor (Tipperary), M. Roche (Tipperary), M. Coogan (Kilkenny), F. Cummins (Kilkenny), J. Connolly (Galway). F. Loughnane (Tipperary), M. Keating (Tipperary), E. Keher (Kilkenny), M. Bermingham (Dublin), R. Cummins (Cork), E. Cregan (Limerick).

1972—N. Skehan (Kilkenny), T. Maher (Cork), P. Hartigan (Limerick), J. Treacy (Kilkenny), P. Lawlor (Kilkenny), M. Jacob (Wexford), C. Roche (Cork), F. Cummins (Kilkenny). D. Coughlan (Cork), F. Loughnane (Tipperary), P. Delaney (Kilkenny), E. Keher (Kilkenny), C. McCarthy (Cork), R. Cummins (Cork), E. Cregan (Limerick).

1973—N. Skehan (Kilkenny), F. Larkin (Kilkenny), P. Hartigan (Limerick), J. O'Brien (Limerick), C. Doran (Wexford), P. Henderson (Kilkenny), S. Foley (Limerick), R. Bennis (Limerick), L. O'Brien (Kilkenny), F. Loughnane (Tipperary), P. Delaney (Kilkenny), E. Grimes (Limerick), M. Quigley (Wexford), K. Purcell (Kilkenny), E. Keher (Kilkenny).

1974—N. Skehan (Kilkenny), P. Larkin (Kilkenny), P. Hartigan (Limerick), J. Horgan (Cork), G. Loughnane (Clare), P. Henderson (Kilkenny), C. Roche (Cork), L. O'Brien, (Kilkenny), J. Galvin (Waterford), J. McKenna (Limerick), M. Quigley (Wexford), M. Crotty (Kilkenny); J. Quigley (Wexford), K. Purcell (Kilkenny), E. Keher (Kilkenny).

1975—N. Skehan (Kilkenny), N. McInerney (Galway), P. Hartigan (Limerick), B. Cody (Kilkenny), T. O'Connor (Tipperary), S. Silke (Galway), I. Clarke (Galway), L. O'Brien (Kilkenny), G. McCarthy (Cork), M. Quigley (Wexford), J. McKenna (Limerick), E. Grimes (Limerick), M. Brennan (Kilkenny), K. Purcell (Kilkenny), E. Keher (Kilkenny).

1976—N. Skehan (Kilkenny), P. Larkin (Kilkenny), W. Murphy (Wexford), J. McMahon (Clare), J. McDonagh (Galway), M. Jacob (Wexford), D. Coughlan (Cork), F. Burke (Galway), P. Moylan (Cork), M. Malone (Cork), M. Quigley (Wexford), J. Barry Murphy (Cork), M. Brennan (Kilkenny), T. Doran (Wexford), S. O'Leary (Cork).

1977—S. Durack (Clare), J. McMahon (Clare), M. O'Doherty (Cork), J. Horgan (Cork), G. Loughnane (Clare), M. Jacob (Wexford), D. Coughlan (Cork), T. Cashman (Cork), M. Moroney (Clare), C. Keogh (Wexford), J. Barry Murphy (Cork), P. J. Molloy (Galway), C. McCarthy (Cork), R. Cummins (Cork), S. O'Leary (Cork).

1978—S. Durack (Clare), P. Larkin (Kilkenny), M. O'Doherty (Cork), J. Horgan (Cork), J. Hennessy (Kilkenny), G. Henderson (Kilkenny), D. Coughlan (Cork), T. Cashman (Cork), I. Clarke (Galway), J. Barry Murphy (Cork), N. Casey (Clare), C. Honan (Clare), C. McCarthy (Cork), J. McKenna (Limerick), T. Butler (Tipperary).

1979—P. McLoughney (Tipperary), B. Murphy (Cork), M. O'Doherty (Cork), T. O'Connor (Tipperary), D. McCurtain (Cork), G. Henderson (Kilkenny), I. Clarke (Galway); John Connolly (Galway), J. Hennessy (Kilkenny), J. Callinan (Clare), F. Burke (Galway), L. O'Brien (Kilkenny), M. Brennan (Kilkenny), J. McKenna (Limerick), N. Buggy (Wexford).

1980—P. McLoughney (Tipperary), N. McInerney (Galway), L. Enright (Limerick), J. Cooney (Galway), D. McCurtain (Cork), S. Silke (Galway), I. Clarke (Galway); J. Kelly (Offaly), M. Walsh (Waterford), Joe Connolly (Galway), P. Horgan (Cork), P. Carroll (Offaly), B. Forde (Galway), J. McKenna (Limerick), E. Cregan (Limerick).

1981—S. Durack (Clare), B. Murphy (Cork), L. Enright (Limerick), J. Cooney (Galway), L. O'Donoghue (Limerick), S. Stack (Clare), G. Coughlan (Offaly), S. Mahon (Galway), L. Currams (Offaly), J. Callinan (Clare), G. O'Connor (Wexford), M. Corrigan (Offaly), P. Carroll (Offaly), J. McKenna (Limerick), J. Flaherty (Offaly).

1982—N. Skehan (Kilkenny), J. Galvin (Waterford), B. Cody (Kilkenny), P. Fleury (Offaly), A. Fogarty (Offaly), G. Henderson (Kilkenny), P. Prendergast (Kilkenny), T. Crowley (Cork), F. Cummins (Kilkenny), T. O'Sullivan (Cork), P. Horgan (Cork), R. Power (Kilkenny), B. Fitzpatrick (Kilkenny), C. Heffernan (Kilkenny), J Greene (Waterford).

1983—N. Skehan (Kilkenny), J. Henderson (Kilkenny), L. Enright (Limerick), D. O'Hara (Kilkenny), J. Henessy (Kilkenny), G. Henderson (Kilkenny), T. Cashman (Cork), F. Cummins (Kilkenny), J. Fenton (Cork), N. English (Tipperary), G. Fennelly (Kilkenny), N. Lane (Galway), B. Fitzpatrick (Kilkenny), J. Barry Murphy (Cork), L. Fennelly (Kilkenny).

1984—G. Cunningham (Cork), P. Fitzmaurice (Limerick), E. Coughlan (Offaly), P. Fleury (Offaly), J. Hennessy (Kilkenny), J. Crowley (Cork), D. MacCurtain (Cork), J. Fenton (Cork), J. Kelly (Offaly), N. English (Tipperary), K. Brennan (Kilkenny), P. Kelly (Limerick), T. Mulcahy (Cork), N. Lane (Galway), S. O'Leary (Cork).

1985—G. Cunningham (Cork), S. Coen (Galway), E.

Coughlan (Offaly), S. Linnane (Galway), P. Finnerty (Galway),
P. Delaney (Offaly), G. Coughlan (Offaly), P. Critchley (Laois),
J. Fenton (Cork), N. English (Tipperary), B. Lynskey (Galway),
J. Cooney (Galway), P. Cleary (Offaly), P. Horan (Offaly), L.
Fennelly (Kilkenny).

1986—G. Cunningham (Cork), D. Mulcahy (Cork), C. Hayes
(Galway), S. Linnane (Galway), P. Finnerty (Galway), T. Keady
(Galway), B. Ryan (Tipperary), R. Power (Kilkenny), J. Fenton
(Cork), T. O'Sullivan (Cork), T. Mulcahy (Cork), J. Cooney
(Galway), D. Kilcoyne (Westmeath), J. Barry Murphy (Cork), K.
Hennessy (Cork).

1987—K. Hogan (Tipperary), J. Hennessy (Kilkenny), C.
Hayes (Galway), O. Kilkenny (Galway), P. Finnerty (Galway), G.
Henderson (Kilkenny), J. Conran (Wexford), S. Mahon
(Galway), J. Fenton (Cork), M. McGrath (Galway), Joe Cooney
(Galway), A. Ryan (Tipperary), P. Fox (Tipperary), N. English
(Tipperary), L. Fennelly (Kilkenny).

1988—J. Commins (Galway), S. Linnane (Galway), C. Hayes
(Galway),, M. Hanamy (Offaly), P. Finnerty (Galway), T. Keady
(Galway), B. Ryan (Tipperary), Colm Bonnar (Tipperary), G.
O'Connor (Wexford), D. Ryan (Tipperary), C. Barr (Antrim), M.
Naughton (Galway), M. McGrath (Galway), N. English (Tipperary),
T. O'Sullivan (Cork).

1989—J. Commins (Galway), A. Fogarty (Offaly), E. Cleary (Wex-
ford), D. Donnelly (Antrim), Conal Bonnar (Tipperary), B. Ryan
(Tipperary), S. Treacy (Galway), M. Coleman (Galway), D. Carr
(Tipperary), E. Ryan (Galway), J. Cooney (Galway), O. McFetridge
(Antrim), P. Fox (Tipperary), Cormac Bonnar (Tipperary), N.
English (Tipperary).

1990—G. Cunningham (Cork), J. Considine (Cork), N. Sheehy
(Tipperary), S. O'Gorman (Cork), P. Finnerty (Galway), J. Cashman
(Cork), L. Dunne (Wexford), M. Coleman (Galway), J. Pilkington
(Offaly), M. Cleary (Tipperary), J. Cooney (Galway), T. O'Sullivan
(Cork), E. Morrissey (Kilkenny), B. McMahon (Dublin), J. Fitzgib-
bon (Cork).

1991—M. Walsh (Kilkenny), P. Delaney (Tipperary), N. Sheehy
(Tipperary), S. Treacy (Galway), Conal Bonnar (Tipperary), J.
Cashman (Cork), C. Casey (Cork), T. McNaughten (Antrim), J.
Leahy (Tipperary), M. Cleary (Tipperary), G. Kirby (Limerick), D.
J. Carey (Kilkenny), P. Fox (Tipperary), Cormac Bonnar (Tip-
perary), J. Fitzgibbon (Cork).

1992—T. Quaid (Limerick), B. Corcoran (Cork), P. Dwyer
(Kilkenny), L. Simpson (Kilkenny), B. Whelehan (Offaly), C. Carey
(Limerick), W. O'Connor (Kilkenny), M. Phelan (Kilkenny), S.

McCarthy (Cork), G. McGrattan (Down), J. Power (Kilkenny), T.
O'Sullivan (Cork), M. Cleary (Tipperary), L. Fennelly (Kilkenny), D.
(Kilkenny), D. J. Carey (Kilkenny).

LEADING AWARD WINNERS

Noel Skehan (Kilkenny) 7 – 1972-'76, 1982, 1983.
Joe McKenna (Limerick) 6 – 1974, 1975, 1978, 1979, 1980, 1981.
Nicholas English (Tipperary) 6 – 1983-'85, 1987-'89.

ALL-TIME ALL-STAR AWARD WINNERS

HURLING

1980—Mick Mackey (Limerick)
1981—Jack Lynch (Cork)
1982—Garrett Howard (Limerick)
1983—Fowler McInerney (Clare)
1984—Jim Langton (Kilkenny)
1985—Eudie Coughlan (Cork)
1986—Tommy Doyle (Tipperary)
1987—Christy Moylan (Waterford)
1988—Paddy "Fox" Collins (Cork)
1989—M. J. "Inky" Flaherty (Galway)
1990—John Joe Doyle (Clare)
1991—Jackie Power (Limerick)
1992—Bobby and Billy Rackard (Wexford)

TEXACO HURLER OF THE YEAR AWARD

The following are the Hurling stars who have been awarded
Texaco Trophies by the Sports Editors since the inauguration of
the award in 1958. Also listed are the Hall of Fame winners in
hurling since the introduction of this category in 1960.

HURLING
1958—Tony Wall, Tipperary.
1959—Christy Ring, Cork.
1960—Nick O'Donnell, Wexford.
1961—Liam Devaney, Tipperary.
1962—Donie Nealon, Tipperary.

1963—Seamus Cleare, Kilkenny.
1964—John Doyle, Tipperary.
1965—Jimmy Doyle, Tipperary.
1966—Justin McCarthy, Cork.
1967—Ollie Walsh, Kilkenny.
1968—Dan Quigley, Wexford.
1969—Ted Carroll, Kilkenny.
1970—Pat McDonnell, Cork.
1971—Michael Keating, Tipperary.
1972—Eddie Keher, Kilkenny.
1973—Eamonn Grimes, Limerick.
1974—Pat Henderson, Kilkenny.
1975—Liam O'Brien, Kilkenny.
1976—Tony Doran, Wexford.
1977—Denis Coughlan, Cork.
1978—John Horgan, Cork.
1979—Ger Henderson, Kilkenny.
1980—John Connolly, Galway.
1981—Pat Delaney, Offaly.
1982—Noel Skehan, Kilkenny.
1983—Frank Cummins, Kilkenny.
1984—John Fenton, Cork.
1985—Eugene Coughlan, Offaly.
1986—Ger Cunningham, Cork.
1987—Joe Cooney (Galway)
1988—Tony Keady (Galway)
1989—Nicholas English (Tipperary)
1990—Tony O'Sullivan (Cork)
1991—Pat Fox (Tipperary)
1992—Brian Corcoran (Cork)

HALL OF FAME

1961—Mick Mackey, Limerick.
1971—Christy Ring, Cork.
1992—John Doyle (Tipperary)

●SOARING HIGH ... Colman Corrigan (Cork) and Colm O'Rourke (Meath) demonstrate perfectly the classic art of high fielding in this duel the Cork goalmouth. (Picture: Ray McManus)

G.A.A.

FOOTBALL

RECORDS

RESULTS AND TEAMS

ALL-IRELAND CHAMPIONSHIPS

1887-1993

Micheál Ó Muircheartaigh
A member of our winning team
every week in the

G.A.A. FOOTBALL RECORDS

RESULTS AND TEAMS

ALL-IRELAND CHAMPIONSHIPS
1887 – 1993

The distribution of Championship Honours to date is as follows:

ROLL OF HONOUR
SENIOR FOOTBALL

Kerry (30)—1903, 1904, 1909, 1913, 1914, 1924, 1926, 1929, 1930, 1931, 1932, 1937, 1939, 1940, 1941, 1946, 1953, 1955, 1959, 1962, 1969, 1970, 1975, 1978, 1979, 1980, 1981, 1984, 1985, 1986.

Dublin (21)—1891, 1892, 1894, 1897, 1898, 1899, 1901, 1902, 1906, 1907, 1908, 1921, 1922, 1923, 1942, 1958, 1963, 1974, 1976, 1977, 1983.

Galway (7)—1925, 1934, 1938, 1956, 1964, 1965, 1966.

Cork (6)—1890, 1911, 1945, 1973, 1989, 1990.

Meath (5)—1949, 1954, 1967, 1987, 1988.

Wexford (5)—1893, 1915, 1916, 1917, 1918.

Cavan (5)—1933, 1935, 1947, 1948, 1952.

Tipperary (4)—1889, 1895, 1900, 1920.

Kildare (4)—1905, 1919, 1927, 1928.

Down (4)—1960, 1961, 1968, 1991.

Louth (3)—1910, 1912, 1957.

Mayo (3)—1936, 1950, 1951.

Offaly (3)—1971, 1972, 1982.

Limerick (2)—1887, 1896.

Roscommon (2)—1943, 1944.

Donegal (1)—1992.

Derry (1)—1993

Note: No Championship in 1888.

MINOR FOOTBALL

Dublin (10)—1930, 1945, 1954, 1955, 1956, 1958, 1959, 1979, 1982, 1984.

Kerry (10)—1931, 1932, 1933, 1946, 1950, 1962, 1963, 1975, 1980, 1988.

Cork (9)—1961, 1967, 1968, 1969, 1972, 1974, 1981, 1991, 1993.

Mayo (6)—1935, 1953, 1966, 1971, 1978, 1985.

Galway (5)—1952, 1960, 1970, 1976, 1986.

UNDER-21 FOOTBALL

Cork (8)—1970, 1971, 1980, 1981, 1984, 1985, 1986, 1989.
Kerry (6)—1964, 1973, 1975, 1976, 1977, 1990.
Mayo (3)—1967, 1974, 1983.
Donegal (2)—1982, 1987.

Roscommon (2)—1966, 1978.
Tyrone (2)—1991, 1992.
Derry (1)—1968.
Kildare (1)—1965.
Down (1)—1979.

Antrim (1)—1969.
Galway (1)—1972.
Offaly (1)—1988.
Meath (1)—1993.

JUNIOR FOOTBALL

Kerry (12)—1913, 1915, 1924, 1928, 1930, 1941, 1949, 1954, 1963, 1967, 1983, 1991.
Cork (10)—1951, 1953, 1955, 1964, 1972, 1984, 1987, 1988, 1990, 1993.
London (6)—1938, 1966, 1969, 1970, 1971, 1986.
Dublin (5)—1914, 1916, 1939, 1948, 1960.
Louth (4)—1925, 1932, 1934, 1961.
Galway (4)—1931, 1958, 1965, 1985.
Meath (4)—1947, 1952, 1962, 1988.
Mayo (3)—1933, 1950, 1957.
Tipperary (2)—1912, 1923.
Armagh (1)—1926. *Cavan* (1)—1927. *Down* (1)—1946. *Longford* (1)—1937. *Roscommon* (1)—1940. *Sligo* (1)—1935. *Westmeath* (1)—1929. *Wicklow* (1)—1936. *Monaghan* (1)—1956. *Fermanagh* (1)—1959. *Tyrone* (1)—1968. *Laois* (1)—1973. *Wexford* (1)—1992.

Note: Junior football suspended in 1917-'22 and 1974-'82 (inclusive).

ALL-IRELAND SENIOR FINALS

1887—Clonskeagh, April 29, 1888. *Limerick* (Commercials), 1-4; Louth (Young Irelands), 0-3.

1888—Unfinished owing to U.S.A. invasion by G.A.A. athletes.

1889—Inchicore, October 20, 1889. *Tipperary* (Bohercrowe), 3-6; Laois (Maryboro'), nil.

1890—Clonturk, June 26, 1892. *Cork* (Midleton), 2-4; Wexford (Blues and Whites), 0-1.

1891—Clonturk, February 28, 1892. *Dublin* (Young Irelands), 2-1; Cork (Clondrohid), 1-9.

(At this time a goal outweighed any number of points).

1892—Clonturk, March 26, 1893. *Dublin* (Young Irelands), 1-4; Kerry (Laune Rangers), 0-3.

1893—Phoenix Park, June 24, 1894. *Wexford* (Young Irelands), 1-1; Cork (Dromtariffe), 0-2. Match unfinished.

1894—Clonturk, March 24, 1895. *Dublin* (Young Irelands), 0-6; Cork (Nils), 1-1. Draw.

(Goal equalled five points).

Replay—Thurles, April 21, 1895. Cork 1-2; Dublin 0-5. Unfinished. Dublin awarded championship.

1895—Jones's Road, March 15, 1896. *Tipperary* (Arravale Rovers), 0-4; Meath (Pierce Mahony's), 0-3.

1896—Jones's Road, February 6, 1898. *Limerick* (Commercials), 1-5; Dublin (Young Irelands), 0-7.

1897—Jones's Road, February 5, 1899. *Dublin* (Kickhams), 2-6; Cork (Dunmanway), 0-2.

1898—Tipperary, April 8, 1900. *Dublin* (Geraldines), 2-8; Waterford (Erin's Hope), 0-4.

1899—Jones's Road, February 10, 1901. *Dublin* (Geraldines), 1-10; Cork (Nils), 0-6.

1900—Jones's Road, October 26, 1902. *Tipperary* (Clonmel Shamrocks), 3-7; London (Hibernians), 0-2.

Home Final—Terenure, September 21, 1902. Tipperary, 2-17; Galway Krugers (Tuam), 0-1.

1901—Jones's Road, August 2, 1903. *Dublin* (Isles of the Sea), 0-14; London (Hibernians), 0-2.

Home Final—Tipperary, July 5, 1903. Dublin, 1-2; Cork (Nils), 0-4.

1902—Cork, September 11, 1904. *Dublin* (Bray Emmets), 2-8; London (Hibernians), 0-4.

Home Final—Kilkenny, July 24, 1904. Dublin, 0-6; Tipperary, 0-5.

1903—Jones's Road, November 12, 1905. *Kerry* (Tralee Mitchels), 0-11; London (Hibernians), 0-3.

Home Final—Tipperary, July 23, 1905. Kerry, 1-4; Kildare (Clane), 1-3. (Goal disputed).
Replay—Cork, August 27, 1905. Kerry, 0-7; Kildare, 1-4.
Replay—Cork, October 15, 1905. Kerry, 0-8; Kildare, 0-2.

1904—Cork, July 1, 1906. *Kerry* (Tralee Mitchels), 0-5; Dublin (Kickhams), 0-2.

1905—Thurles, June 16, 1907. *Kildare* (Roseberry), 1-7; Kerry (Tralee Mitchels), 0-5.

1906—Athy, October 20, 1907. *Dublin* (Kickhams), 0-5; Cork (Fermoy), 0-4.

1907—Tipperary, July 5, 1908. *Dublin* (Kickhams), 0-6; Cork (Lees), 0-2.

1908—Jones's Road, October 3, 1909, *Dublin* (Geraldines), 1-10; London (Hibernians),0-4.

Home Final—Thurles, May 9, 1909. Dublin, 0-10; Kerry (Mitchels), 0-3.

1909—Jones's Road, December 5, 1909. *Kerry* (Tralee Mitchels), 1-9; Louth (Trodaghs), 0-6.

1910—Fixed for Jones's Road. *Louth* (Tredaghs), w.o. Kerry (Tralee Mitchels) refused to travel.

1911—Jones's Road, January 14, 1912. *Cork* (Lees), 6-6; Antrim (Shauns), 1-2.

1912—Jones's Road, November 3, 1912. *Louth* (Tredaghs), 1-7; Antrim (Mitchels), 1-2.

1913—Croke Park, December 14, 1913. *Kerry* (Killarney), 2-2; Wexford (Raparees), 0-3.

1914—Croke Park, November 29, 1914 *Kerry* (Killarney), 2-3; Wexford (Blues and Whites), 0-6. Played a draw, 1-3 to 2-0, Dublin, November 1, 1914.

1915—Croke Park, November 7, 1915. *Wexford* (Blues and Whites), 2-4; Kerry (Selection), 2-1.

1916—Croke Park, December 17, 1916. *Wexford* (Blues and Whites), 2-4; Mayo (Stephenites, Ballina), 1-2.

1917—Croke Park, December 9, 1917. *Wexford* (Blues and Whites), 0-9; Clare (Selection), 0-5.

1918—Croke Park, February 16, 1919. *Wexford* (Blue and Whites), 0-5; Tipperary (Fethard), 0-4.

1919—Croke Park, September 29, 1919. *Kildare* (Caragh), 2-5; Galway (Selection), 0-1.

1920—Croke Park, June 11, 1922. *Tipperary*, 1-6; Dublin (O'Tooles), 1-2.

1921—Croke Park, June 17, 1923. *Dublin* (St. Mary's), 1-9; Mayo (Stephenites, Ballina), 0-2.

1922—Croke Park, October 7, 1923. *Dublin* (O'Tooles), 0-6; Galway (Ballinasloe), 0-4.

1923—Croke Park, April 27, 1924. Semi-final: Kerry, 1-3; Cavan, 1-2.
Croke Park, May 18, 1924. Semi-final: Dublin, 1-6; Mayo, 1-2.
Croke Park, Sept. 28, 1924. Final: *Dublin*, 1-5; Kerry, 1-3.

1924—Croke Park, December 7. Semi-final: Kerry, 1-4; Mayo, 0-1.
Croke Park, January 18, 1925. Semi-final: Dublin, 0-6; Cavan, 1-1.
Croke Park, April 26, 1925. Final: *Kerry*, 0-4; Dublin 0-3.

1925—*Galway* declared champions. Games in lieu of Championship:
Croke Park, December 6, 1925. Galway, 3-4; Wexford, 1-1.
Croke Park, January 10, 1926. Galway, 3-2; Cavan, 1-2. (Kerry, Munster Champions, refused to compete).
The results of the Championship semi-finals were: Tralee, August 23: Kerry, 1-7; Cavan, 2-3. Croke Park, August 23: Mayo, 2-4; Wexford, 1-4.

1926—Croke Park, August 8. Semi-final: Kerry, 1-6; Cavan, 0-1.
Croke Park, August 22. Semi-final: Kildare, 2-5; Galway, 0-2.
Croke Park, September 5. Final: Kerry, 1-3; Kildare, 0-6.
October 17. Replay: *Kerry*, 1-4; Kildare, 0-4.

1927—Tuam, August 28. Semi-final: Kerry, 0-4; Leitrim, 0-2.
Drogheda, August 28. Semi-final: Kildare, 1-7; Monaghan, 0-2.
Croke Park, September 25. Final: *Kildare*, 0-5; Kerry, 0-3.

1928—Cavan, August 26. Semi-final: Cavan, 2-5; Sligo, 0-4.
Cork, September 2. Semi-final: Kildare, 3-7; Cork, 0-2.
Croke Park, September 30. Final: *Kildare*, 2-6; Cavan, 2-5.

1929—Roscommon, August 18. Semi-final: Kerry, 3-8; Mayo, 1-1.
Croke Park, August 25. Semi-final: Kildare, 0-9; Monaghan, 0-1.
Croke Park, September 22. Final: *Kerry*, 1-8; Kildare, 1-5.

1930—Croke Park, August 24. Semi-final: Monaghan, 1-6; Kildare, 1-4.

Roscommon, August 24. Semi-final: Kerry, 1-9; Mayo, 0-4.

Croke Park, September 28. Final: *Kerry*, 3-11; Monaghan, 0-2.

1931—Tuam, August 30. Semi-final: Kerry, 1-6; Mayo, 1-4.

Cavan, August 30. Semi-final: Kildare, 0-10; Cavan, 1-5.

Croke Park, September 27. Final: *Kerry*, 1-11; Kildare, 0-8.

1932—Croke Park, August 21. Semi-final: Mayo, 2-4; Cavan, 0-8.

Croke Park, August 21. Semi-final: Kerry, 1-3; Dublin, 1-1.

Croke Park, September 25. Final: *Kerry*, 2-7; Mayo, 2-4.

1933—Mullingar, August 20. Semi-final: Galway, 0-8; Dublin, 1-4.

Cavan, August 27. Semi-final: Cavan, 1-5; Kerry, 0-5.

Croke Park, September 24. Final: *Cavan*, 2-5; Galway, 1-4.

1934—Tuam, August 12. Semi-final: Galway, 1-8; Cavan, 0-8.

Tralee, September 9. Semi-final: Dublin, 3-8; Kerry 0-6.

Croke Park, September 23. Final: *Galway*, 3-5; Dublin, 1-9.

1935—Croke Park, August 18. Semi-final: Cavan, 1-7; Tipperary, 0-8.

Croke Park, August 25. Semi-final: Kildare, 2-6; Mayo, 0-7.

Croke Park, September 22. Final: *Cavan*, 3-6; Kildare, 2-5.

1936—Roscommon, August 9. Semi-final: Mayo, 1-5; Kerry, 0-6.

Croke Park, August 23. Semi-final: Laois, 2-6; Cavan, 1-5.

Croke Park, September 27. Final: *Mayo*, 4-11; Laois, 0-5.

1937—Cork, August 15. Semi-final: Kerry, 2-3; Laois, 1-6.

Mullingar, August 22. Semi-final: Cavan, 2-5; Mayo, 1-7.

Waterford, August 29. Replay: Kerry, 2-2; Laois, 1-4.

Croke Park, September 26. Final: Kerry, 2-5; Cavan, 1-8.

Croke Park, October 17. Replay: *Kerry*, 4-4; Cavan, 1-7.

1938—Mullingar, August 14. Semi-final: Galway, 2-10; Monaghan, 2-3.

Croke Park, August 21. Semi-final: Kerry, 2-6; Laois, 2-4.
Croke Park, September 25. Final: Galway, 3-3; Kerry, 2-6.
Croke Park, October 23. Replay: *Galway,* 2-4; Kerry, 0-7.

1939—Croke Park, August 13. Semi-final: Kerry, 0-4; Mayo, 0-4.
Croke Park, August 20. Semi-final: Meath, 1-9; Cavan 1-1.
Croke Park, September 10. Replay: Kerry, 3-8; Mayo, 1-4.
Croke Park, September 24. Final: *Kerry,* 2-5; Meath, 2-3.

1940—Croke Park, August 18. Semi-final: Galway, 3-8; Meath, 2-5.
Croke Park, August 18. Semi-final: Kerry, 3-4; Cavan, 0-8.
Croke Park, September 22. Final: *Kerry,* 0-7; Galway, 1-3.

1941—Croke Park, August 10. Semi-final: Kerry, 0-4; Dublin, 0-4.
Tralee, August 17. Replay: Kerry, 2-9; Dublin, 0-3.
Croke Park, August 17. Semi-final: Galway 1-12; Cavan 1-4.
Croke Park, September 7. Final: *Kerry,* 1-8; Galway, 0-7.

1942—Croke Park, August 2. Semi-final: Dublin, 1-6; Cavan, 1-3.
Croke Park, August 9. Semi-final: Galway, 1-3; Kerry, 0-3.
Croke Park, September 20. Final: *Dublin,* 1-10; Galway, 1-8.

1943—Croke Park, August 8. Semi-final: Roscommon, 3-10; Louth, 3-6.
Croke Park, August 15. Semi-final: Cavan, 1-8; Cork, 1-7.
Croke Park, September 26. Final: Roscommon, 1-6; Cavan, 1-6.
Croke Park, October 10. Replay: *Roscommon,* 2-7; Cavan, 2-2.

1944—Croke Park, August 20, Semi-final: Roscommon, 5-8; Cavan, 1-3.
Croke Park, August 27. Semi-final; Kerry 3-3; Carlow, 0-10.
Croke Park, September 24. Final: *Roscommon,* 1-9; Kerry, 2-4.

1945—Croke Park, August 12. Semi-final: Cork, 2-12; Galway, 2-8.

Croke Park, August 19. Semi-final: Cavan, 1-4; Wexford, 0-5.

Croke Park, September 23. Final: *Cork,* 2-5; Cavan, 0-7.

1946—Croke Park, August 18. Semi-final: Kerry, 2-7; Antrim, 0-10.

Croke Park, August 25. Semi-final: Roscommon, 3-5; Laois, 2-6.

Croke Park, October 6. Final: Kerry, 2-4; Roscommon, 1-7.

Croke Park, October 27. Replay: *Kerry,* 2-8; Roscommon, 0-10.

1947—Croke Park August 3. Semi-final: Cavan, 2-4; Roscommon, 0-6.

Croke Park, August 10, Semi-final: Kerry, 1-11; Meath, 0-5.

Polo Grounds, New York, September 14. Final: *Cavan,* 2-11; Kerry, 2-7.

1948—Croke Park, August 22. Semi-final: Cavan, 1-14; Louth, 4-2.

Croke Park, August 29. Semi-final: Mayo, 0-13; Kerry, 0-3.

Croke Park, September 26. Final: *Cavan,* 4-5; Mayo, 4-4.

1949—Croke Park, August 14, Semi-final: Meath, 3-10; Mayo, 1-10.

Croke Park, August 21. Semi-final: Cavan, 1-9; Cork, 2-3.

Croke Park, September 25. Final: *Meath,* 1-10; Cavan, 1-6.

1950—Croke Park, August 13. Semi-final: Mayo, 3-9; Armagh, 0-6.

Croke Park, August 20. Semi-final: Louth, 1-7; Kerry, 0-8.

Croke Park, September 24. Final: *Mayo,* 2-5; Louth, 1-6.

1951—Croke Park, August 12. Semi-final: Kerry, 1-5; Mayo, 1-5.

Croke Park, August 19. Semi-final: Meath, 2-6; Antrim, 1-7.

Croke Park, September 9. Replay: Mayo, 2-4; Kerry, 1-5.

Croke Park, September 23. Final: *Mayo.* 2-8; Meath, 0-9.

1952—Croke Park, August 3. Semi-final: Meath, 1-6; Roscommon, 0-7.

Croke Park, August 17. Semi-final: Cavan, 0-10; Cork, 2-3.

Croke Park, September 28. Final: Cavan, 2-4; Meath, 1-7.

Croke Park, October 12, Replay: *Cavan,* 0-9; Meath, 0-5.

1953—Croke Park, August 9. Semi-final: Armagh, 0-8; Roscommon, 0-7.

Croke Park, August 23. Semi-final: Kerry, 3-6; Louth, 0-10.

Croke Park, September 27. Final: *Kerry,* 0-13; Armagh, 1-6.

1954—Croke Park, August 1. Semi-final: Meath, 1-5; Cavan, 0-7.

Croke Park, August 15. Semi-final: Kerry, 2-6; Galway, 1-6.

Croke Park, September 26. Final: *Meath,* 1-13; Kerry, 1-7.

1955—Croke Park, August 14. Semi-final: Kerry, 2-10; Cavan, 1-13.

Croke Park, August 21. Semi-final: Dublin, 0-7; Mayo, 1-4.

Croke Park, September 11. Replays: Kerry, 4-7; Cavan, 0-5; Dublin, 1-8; Mayo, 1-7.

Croke Park, September 25. Final: *Kerry,* 0-12; Dublin, 1-6.

1956—Croke Park, August 5. Semi-final: Cork, 0-9; Kildare, 0-5.

Croke Park, August 12. Semi-final: Galway, 0-8; Tyrone, 0-6.

Croke Park, October 7. Final: *Galway,* 2-13; Cork, 3-7.

1957—Croke Park, August 11. Semi-final: Cork, 2-4; Galway, 0-9.

Croke Park, August 18. Semi-final: Louth, 0-13; Tyrone, 0-7.

Croke Park, September 22. Final: *Louth,* 1-9; Cork, 1-7.

1958—Croke Park, August 17. Semi-final: Dublin, 2-7; Galway, 1-9.

Croke Park, August 24, Semi-final: Derry, 2-6; Kerry, 2-5.

Croke Park, September 28. Final: *Dublin,* 2-12; Derry, 1-9.

1959—Croke Park, August 16. Semi-final: Kerry, 1-10; Dublin, 2-5.

Croke Park, August 23, Semi-final: Galway, 1-11; Down, 1-4.

Croke Park, September 27. Final: *Kerry,* 3-7; Galway, 1-4.

1960—Croke Park, August 7. Semi-final: Kerry, 1-8; Galway, 0-8.

Croke Park, August 21. Semi-final, Down 1-10; Offaly, 2-7.

Croke Park, September 11. Replay: Down, 1-7; Offaly. 1-5.

Croke Park, September 25. Final: *Down,* 2-10; Kerry, 0-8.

307

1961—Croke Park, August 6. Semi-final: Down, 1-12; Kerry, 0-9.

Croke Park. August 20. Semi-final: Offaly, 3-6; Roscommon, 0-6.

Croke Park, September 24. Final: *Down,* 3-6; Offaly, 2-8.

1962—Croke Park, August 5. Semi-final: Kerry, 2-12; Dublin, 0-10.

Croke Park, August 19. Semi-final: Roscommon, 1-8; Cavan, 1-6.

Croke Park, September 23. Final: *Kerry,* 1-12; Roscommon, 1-6.

1963—Croke Park, August 4. Semi-final: Galway, 1-7; Kerry, 0-8.

Croke Park, August 18. Semi-final: Dublin, 2-11; Down, 0-7.

Croke Park, September 22: Final: *Dublin,* 1-9; Galway, 0-10.

1964—Croke Park, August 9. Semi-final: Galway, 1-8; Meath, 0-9.

Croke Park, August 23. Semi-final: Kerry. 2-12; Cavan, 0-6.

Croke Park, September 27. Final: *Galway,* 0-15; Kerry, 0-10.

1965—Croke Park, August 8. Semi-final: Kerry. 4-8; Dublin, 2-6.

Croke Park, August 22. Semi-final: Galway, 0-10; Down, 0-7.

Croke Park, September 26. Final: *Galway,* 0-12; Kerry, 0-9.

1966—Croke Park, August 7. Semi-final: Galway, 1-11; Cork, 1-9.

Croke Park, August 21. Semi-final: Meath, 2-16; Down, 1-9.

Croke Park, September 25. Final: *Galway.* 1-10; Meath, 0-7.

1967—Croke Park, August 6. Semi-final: Cork, 2-7; Cavan, 0-12.

Croke Park, August 20. Semi-final: Meath, 3-14; Mayo, 1-14.

Croke Park, September 24. Final: *Meath,* 1-9; Cork, 0-9.

1968—Croke Park, August 4. Semi-final: Kerry, 2-13; Longford, 2-11.

Croke Park, August 18. Semi-final: Down, 2-10; Galway, 2-8.

Croke Park, September 22. Final: *Down*. 2-12; Kerry,
1-13.
1969—Croke Park, August 10. Semi-final: Kerry. 0-14; Mayo,
1-10.
Croke Park, August 24. Semi-final: Cavan, 1-9; Offaly,
0-12.
Croke Park, September 14. Replay: Offaly, 3-8; Cavan,
1-10.
Croke Park, September 28. Final: *Kerry,* 0-10; Offaly.
0-7.
1970—Croke Park, August 9. Semi-final: Meath, 0-15; Galway.
0-11.
Croke Park, August 23. Semi-final: Kerry, 0-23; Derry,
0-10.
Croke Park, September 27. Final: *Kerry,* 2-19; Meatn,
0-18 (First 80-minute Final).

1971—Croke Park, August 8. Galway, 3-11; Down, 2-7.
Croke Park, August 22. Offaly, 1-16; Cork 1-11.
Croke Park, September 26. Final: *Offaly,* 1-14; Galway,
2-8.
1972—Croke Park, August 13. Semi-final: Kerry, 1-22; Roscommon, 1-12.
Croke Park, August 20. Semi-final: Offaly, 1-17;
Donegal, 2-10.
Croke Park, September 24. Final: Offaly, 1-13; Kerry,
1-13.
Croke Park, October 15. Replay: *Offaly,* 1-19; Kerry,
0-13.
1973—Croke Park, August 12. Semi-final: Galway, 0-16; Offaly,
2-8.
Croke Park, August 19. Semi-final: Cork, 5-10; Tyrone,
2-4.
Croke Park, September 23. Final: *Cork,* 3-17; Galway
2-13.
1974—Croke Park, August 11. Semi-final: Dublin, 2-11; Cork,
1-8.
Croke Park, August 18. Semi-final: Galway, 3-13;
Donegal, 1-14.
Croke Park, September 22. Final: *Dublin,* 0-14; Galway,
1-6.
1975—Croke Park, August 10. Semi-final: Kerry, 3-13; Sligo,
0-5.

Croke Park, August 24. Semi-final: Dublin, 3-13; Derry, 3-8.

Croke Park, September 28. Final: *Kerry,* 2-12; Dublin, 0-11.

[Note: The 70-minute Final was introduced in 1975]

1976—Croke Park, August 8. Semi-final: Kerry, 5-14; Derry, 1-10.

Croke Park, August 29. Semi-final: Dublin, 1-8; Galway, 0-8.

Croke Park, September 26. Final: *Dublin,* 3-8; Kerry, 0-10.

1977—Croke Park, August 14. Semi-final: Armagh, 3-9; Roscommon, 2-12 (draw).

Croke Park, August 28. Replay: Armagh, 0-15; Roscommon, 0-14.

Croke Park, August 21. Semi-final: Dublin, 3-12; Kerry, 1-13.

Croke Park, September 25. Final: *Dublin,* 5-12; Armagh, 3-6.

1978—Croke Park, August 13. Semi-final: Kerry, 3-11; Roscommon, 0-8.

Croke Park, August 20. Semi-final: Dublin, 1-16; Down, 0-8.

Croke Park, September 24. Final: *Kerry,* 5-11; Dublin, 0-9.

1979—Croke Park, August 12. Semi-final: Kerry, 5-14; Monaghan, 0-7.

Croke Park, August 19. Semi-final: Dublin, 0-14; Roscommon, 1-10.

Croke Park, September 16. Final: *Kerry,* 3-13; Dublin, 1-8.

1980—Croke Park, August 10. Semi-final: Roscommon, 2-20; Armagh, 3-11.

Croke Park, August 24. Semi-final: Kerry, 4-15; Offaly, 4-10.

Croke Park, September 21. Final: *Kerry,* 1-9; Roscommon, 1-6.

1981—Croke Park, August 9. Semi-final: Kerry, 2-19; Mayo, 1-6.

Croke Park, August 23. Semi-final: Offaly, 0-12; Down, 0-6.

Croke Park, September 20. Final: *Kerry,* 1-12; Offaly, 0-8.

1982—Croke Park, August 15. Semi-final: Kerry, 3-15; Armagh, 1-11.

Croke Park, August 22. Semi-final: Offaly, 1-12, Galway, 1-11.

Croke Park, September 19. Final: *Offaly,* 1-15; Kerry, 0-17.

1983—Croke Park, August 14. Semi-final: Galway, 1-12; Donegal, 1-11.

Croke Park, August 21. Semi-final: Dublin, 2-11; Cork, 2-11.

Páirc Uí Chaoimh, August 28. Replay: Dublin, 4-15; Cork, 2-10.

Croke Park, September 18. Final: *Dublin,* 1-10; Galway, 1-8.

1984—Croke Park, August 12. Semi-final: Kerry, 2-17; Galway, 0-11.

Croke Park, August 19. Semi-final: Dublin, 2-11; Tyrone, 0-8.

Croke Park, September 23. Final: *Kerry,* 0-14; Dublin, 1-6.

1985—Croke Park, August 11. Semi-final: Kerry, 1-12; Monaghan, 2-9 (draw).

Croke Park, August 18. Semi-final: Dublin, 1-13; Mayo, 1-13.

Croke Park, August 25. Replay: Kerry, 2-9; Monaghan, 0-10.

Croke Park, September 8. replay; Dublin, 2-12; Mayo, 1-7.

Croke Park, September 22. Final: *Kerry,* 2-12; Dublin, 2-8.

1986—Croke Park, August 17. Semi-final: Tyrone, 1-12; Galway, 1-9.

Croke Park, August 24. Semi-final: Kerry, 2-13; Meath, 0-12.

Croke Park, September 21. Final: *Kerry,* 2-15; Tyrone, 1-10.

1987—Croke Park, August 16. Semi-final: Cork, 1-11; Galway, 1-11 (draw).

Croke Park, August 23. Semi-final: Meath, 0-15; Derry, 0-8.

Croke Park, August 30. Replay: Cork, 0-18; Galway, 1-4.
Croke Park, September 20. Final: *Meath,* 1-14; Cork, 0-11.

311

1988—Croke Park, August 14. Semi-final: Cork, 1-14; Monaghan, 0-6.

Croke Park, August 21, Semi-final: Meath, 0-16; Mayo, 2-5.

Croke Park, September 18, Final: Cork, 1-9; Meath, 0-12 (draw).

Croke Park, October 9, Replay: *Meath,* 0-13; Cork, 0-12.

1989—Croke Park, August 13. Semi-final: Mayo 0-12, Tyrone 1-6.

Croke Park, August 20. Semi-final: Cork 2-10, Dublin 1-9.

Croke Park, September 17. Final: Cork 0-17, Mayo 1-11.

1990—Croke Park, August 12. Semi-final: Cork 0-17, Roscommon 0-10.

Croke Park, August 19. Semi-final: Meath 3-9, Donegal 1-7.

Croke Park, September 16. Final: Cork 0-11, Meath 0-9.

1991—Croke Park, August 11. Semi-final: Down 2-9, Kerry 0-8.

Croke Park, August 18. Semi-final: Meath 0-15, Roscommon 1-11.

Croke Park, September 15. Final: Down 1-16, Meath 1-14.

1992—Croke Park, August 16. Semi-final: Donegal 0-13, Mayo 0-9.

Croke Park, August 23. Semi-final: Dublin 3-14, Clare 2-12.

Croke Park, September 20. Final: Donegal 0-18, Dublin 0-14.

1993—Croke Park, August 15. Semi-final: Cork 5-15, Mayo 0-10.

Croke Park, August 22. Semi-final: Derry 0-15, Dublin 0-14.

Croke Park, September 19. Final: Derry 1-14, Cork 2-8.

ALL-IRELAND TEAMS

Author's Note: Despite checking with a number of sources, allowance must still be made for possible errors in early teams, as records are not reliable from these times. It must be noted too that teams were not given in line-out order until the thirties.

1887

Limerick—Denis Corbett (captain), P. Reeves, J. Mulqueen, M. Slattery, T. McNamara, T. Fitzgibbon, P. Kelly, P. J. Corbett, T. Kennedy, T. McMahon, J. Hyland, M. O'Brien, E. Casey, R. Normoyle, T. Keeting, W. J. Spain, J. R. Kennedy, W. Gunning, P. Keating, W. Cleery, R. Breen.

Louth—M. J. Carroll (capt.), E. Goodman, J. Dowdall, N. Fagan, R. Clarke, T. McGrane, T. O'Connor, P. McGuinness, J. McGuire, A. O'Hagan, T. Campbell, R. Morgan, P. Jackson, J. Keating, T. Murphy, E. Murphy, W. Wheetley, P. McGuinn, E. Fealy, T. O'Rourke, T. Lowry.

1888

No final played owing to visit of hurlers and athletes to the U.S.A., known as " The American Invasion."

1889

Tipperary—Gil Kavanagh (capt.), J. Cranley, P. Glasheen, T. Dwyer, P. Finn, W. O'Shea, P. Buckley, D. Whelan, J. Daly, J. Ronan, P. Hall, J. Carey, M. Wade, B. O'Brien, L. Fox, W. Ryan, Joe Ryan, Jack Ryan, Wm. Ryan, P. Ryan, J. Keating.

Laois—J. Delaney (capt.), J. Whelan, J. Fleming, J. Walsh, J. Murphy, N. Maher, P. Brady, D. Drennan, T. McDonnell, M. Culleton, J. Troy, D. Teehan, J. Conroy, J. Dunne, J. Teehan, J. O'Connor, Tom Cushion, Tim Cushion, P. Cushion, D. Cushion, M. Cushion.

1890

Cork—Jim Power (capt.), J. Downey, P. Moore, J. Leahy, R. Kelleher, M. Coleman, T. Lucey, Jack Fitzgerald, Jim Fitzgerald, M. Riordan, T. Downey, R. Power, J. D. O'Brien, M. Hennessy, M. Egan, J. Aherne, M. Murphy, M. Buckley, W. Buckley, W. Hennessy, P. O'Sullivan.

Wexford—P. Keating (capt.), J. McGrath, J. French, J. Meyler, D. Phillips, T. Gaffney, P. Byrne, T. Byrne, A. Furlong, T. Hayes, J. Kenny, M. Clancy, M. Murphy, J. Monaghan, M. Neill, J. Keegan, J. Doyle, P. Curran, J. O'Connor, J. Hayes, N. Meyler.

1891

Dublin—John Kenendy (capt.), G. Charlemont (gl.), G. Roche, J. Scully, T. Lyons, J. Roche, J. Silke. P. Heslin, J. Mahony, A. O'Hagan, P. O'Hagan, Dick Curtis, S. Hughes, S. Flood, T. Murphy, J. Geraghty, T. Halpin, M. Cooney, P. Kelly. R. Flood, M. Condon.

Cork—Con O'Leary (capt.), Denis O'Leary, J. O'Leary, Dan O'Leary, D. J. Kelleher, J. Kelleher, Con Kelleher, Jer. Kelleher, C. Duggan. J. Duggan, A. Desmond, P. Desmond, T O'Riordan, M. O'Riodan, M. Quill, J. O'Sullivan, J. Murphy, D. O'Sullivan, T. O'Shea, J. Ahern, M. Kelleher.

1892

Dublin—John Kennedy (capt.), G. Roche, G. Charlemont (gl.), J. Roche, J. Geraghty, R. Flood, S. Flood, S. Hughes, F. O'Malley, T. Doran, L. Kelly, P. Kelly, P. Heslin, M. Byrne, J. Silke T. ('Darby') Errity, R. Curtis.

Kerry—J. P. O'Sullivan (capt.), J. J. O'Sullivan, J. Curran, T. Curran, J. Murphy, P. Sugrue, F. Doherty, D. P. Murphy, M. O'Brien, W. O'Sullivan, M. Flynn, W. Fleming, M. Hayes, J. O'Reilly, P. O'Regan, D. Clifford, P. Teahan.

1893

Wexford—Thomas Hayes (capt.), James Maloney Redmond, T. ('Hoey') Redmond, P. Curran, M. Curran, J. McGinn, J. Doyle, N. Leecy, J. Bolger, J. O'Neill, W. O'Leary, A. Furlong, T. O'Connor, J. O'Connor, P. O'Connor, F. Boggan, J. Phelan.

Cork—Jack ('Fox') O'Keeffe (capt.), D. O'Hanlon, T. Burton, T. Forrest, D. Doherty, T. Irwin, J. O'Leary, J. Mulcahy, M. Buckley, M. O'Keeffe, T. Healy, J. Vaughan, J. Riordan, J. Cantillon, J. O'Sullivan, R. Mulcahy, W. Riordan.

1894

Dublin—John Kennedy (capt.), G. Charlemont (gl.), Dick Curtis, G. Roche, P. Heslin, T. Lyons, J. Geraghty, L. Kelly, P. Kelly, T. Hughes, T. O'Mahony, M. Condon, M. Byrne, T. ('Darby') Errity, P. O'Toole, J. Kirwan, F. O'Malley.

Cork—J. O'Leary (capt.), J. Mulcahy, P. J. Walsh, D. Kelleher, T. Houlihan, D. McSweeney, M. Coleman, M. McCarthy, W. Coughlan, D. Coughlan, F. Joyce, W. Burgess, P. Coughlan, D. O'Connell, M. Downey, T. Irwin, J. Riordan.

1895

Tipperary—Paddy Finn (capt.), Willie Ryan, B. Quane, J. Riordan, M. Finn, P. Glasheen, M. ('Terry') McInerney, J. Carew,

314

M. Conroy, J. Carey, D. Butler, W. P. Ryan, J. Heffernan, P. Daly, J. O'Brien, B. Finn, P. Dwyer.

Meath—M. Murray (capt.), H. Pendleton, P. Clarke, J. Hegarty, J. Russell, J. W. Toombe, J. A. Shaw, M. McCabe, P. Fox, J. Elliott, M. Rogers, C. Curtis, J. Sharkey, P. Daly, J. Quinn, V. McDermott, J. Fitzpatrick.

1896

Limerick—Con Fitzgerald (capt.), D. Birrane (gl.), W. Guiry, J. O'Riordan, L. Roche, J. O'Riordan, L. Sheehan, P. Roche, A. Quillinan, J. Buttimer, T. Campion, J. Dalton, B. Murphy, W. McNamara, J. Murphy, J. Nash, M. Ryan. Sub.: J. Griffin.

Dublin—George Roche (capt.), J. Kirwan, L. Kelly, W. Conlon, J. Teeling, T. Hession, J. Gannon, Dick Curtis, S. Mooney, R. Graham, P. O'Toole, J. Brady, T. Doran, T. ('Darby') Errity, P. Heslin, M. Byrne, J. Ledwidge.

1897

Dublin—P. J. Walsh (capt.), W. Guiry, R. Scanlon, L. Kelly, W. Callaghan, E. Downey, Dick Curtis, D. O'Donnell, M. Chambers, V. Kelly, C. Cannon, P. O'Donoghue, R. O'Brien, P. Redmond, J. Matthews, W. Flynn, J. O'Brien.

Cork—D. O'Donovan (capt.), T. J. Crowley, J. Fuller, J. O'Kelly-Lynch, D. Crowley, T. Lordan, P. Lordan, T. Coughlan, C. Coughlan, D. Bernard, F. Searles, T. Twohill, T. Crowley, T. Mullane, D. Coughlan, J. Murphy, J. Aherne.

1898

Dublin—Matt Rea (capt.), J. J. Keane, J. Lane, T. H. Redmond, W. Sherry, J. Heslin, D. O'Callaghan, P. Levey, C. Sargent, P. Redmond, P. McCann, T. Norton, T. ('Darby') Errity, P. Fitzsimmons, P. Smith, J. Ryan, J. Ledwidge.

Waterford—M. Cullinan, J. Nagle, W. Meade, P. Sullivan, J. Nestor, J. C. Heelan, P. Kirwan, J. Hogan, J. F. Flynn, J. Power, T. Power, J. Kennedy, R. Rockett, D. F. Flynn, S. Curran, M. Dunworth, G. Cummin.

1899

Dublin—Matt Rea (capt.), J. Lane, P. McCann, D. Smith, W. Sherry, T. ('Darby') Errity, G. Brady, John Ryan, J. Norton, J. J. Keane, J. Farrelly, P. Leary, P. Fitzsimmons, D. O'Callaghan, J. Heslin, J. Ledwidge, T. H. Redmond.

Cork—R. Coughlan (capt.), W. Mackessy, S. Murphy, J. Clifford, P. Coughlan, W. O'Neill, J. Long, J. Cronin, M. Howard, Tom

Irwin, M. Aherne, M. Sullivan, J. Collins, C. Walsh, J. Murphy, J. Kelleher, M. Barrett.

1900

Tipperary—J. Tobin (capt.), P. Moloney, W. McRell, J. Dwan, D. Myers, M. Walsh, J. O'Brien, R. Quane, R. Hourigan, P. Wall, W. O'Toole, D. Harney, J. O'Shea, J. Cooney, D. Smyth, P. Cox, J. Hayes.

London—M. J. Hayes, S. Maguire, J. Maguire, J. Hooper, D. Donovan, M. Reidy, T. Corcoran, J. Gaffney, T. J. ,Quilter J. Crowley, P. J. Crotty, F. Collins, M. J. O'Grady, T. Lyons, D. Cronin, J. Hayes, T. Brown.

Home Final: Tipperary—J. Tobin (capt.), P. Moloney, J. Long, R. Hourigan, M. Kelly, D. Smith, P. Cox, J. Hayes, P. Sweeny, M. Alyward, J. Dwan, D. Myers, M. Walsh, J. O'Brien, R. Quane, L. Tobin, P. Moroney.

Galway—J. Hosty, W. Kennedy, S. Bourke, T. Hannon, F. Walsh (capt.), M. Farrell, J. Kilkenny, T. Handlebury, M. Connor, J. O'Brien, C. Whyte, D. Hession, S. Barry, M. (Tom) Connolly, J. Ridge, J. O'Brien, M. Muldowney.

1901

Dublin—J. Darcy (capt.), J. McCullagh, J. Fahy, D. Holland, T. Doyle, J. O'Brien, B. Connor, P. Daly, M. Madigan, L. Kelly, J. Grace, P. Redmond, M. O'Brien, P. McCann, J. Whelan. T. Lawless, V. Harris.

London—S. Maguire (capt.), J. Maguire, D. Donovan, J. Hooper, M. J. Hayes, J. O'Driscoll, W. Morrissey, T. Corcoran, J. O'Dwyer, J. Griffin, M. Roddy, J. Scanlon, J. Fitzgerald, T. Twomey, M. J. O'Grady, D. Cronin, J. Shouldice.

Home Final: Dublin—J. Darcy (capt.), – McCullough, D. Brady, P. McCann, J. Fahy, J. O'Brien, M. Madigan, J. Grace, T. Doyle, J. Whelan, T. Lawless, M. O'Brien, L. Kelly, V. Harris, C. McCann, P. Redmond, P. Daly.

Cork—J. Murphy (capt.), J. Groegor, T. Hartigan, S. Murphy, J. McCarthy, J. Long, C. Walsh, J. Morrissey, W. Mackessy, C. McCarthy, W. McCarthy, W. O'Neill, P. Spillane, P. Daly, M. O'Connor, J. Desmond, T. Mahony.

1902

Dublin—J. Dempsey (capt.), S. Mulvey, D. Brady, W. Casey, W. Sherry, A. Wall, J. Brennan, P. Weymess, P, D. Breen, J.

McCann, T. Errity, J. Fahy, J. Grace, M. King, P. Brady, E. Brady, P. Daly.

London—J. Maguire, M. Hayes, D. Donovan, J. O'Driscoll, J. Fitzpatrick, P. Sheehan, J. Heffernan, J. O'S. Heffernan, M. Roddy, J. Shouldice, C. Shine, J. Kavanagh, J. Dwyer, J. Griffin, D. O'Leary, J. O'Grady, J. Fitzgerald.

Home Final: Dublin—J. Dempsey, S. Mulvey, D. Brady, M. Casey, W. Sherry, J. McCann, T. Errity, J. Keane, J. Grace, C. Brady, P. Daly, J. Brennan, P. Weymess, – Archdeacon, P. D. Breen, – Dunne.

Tipperary—R. Quane (capt.), W. P. Ryan, R. Butler, D. Quane, J. Noonan, J. Wyse, J. Butler, J. Bohan, J. Ryan, D. Smith, P. Myers, W. Barrett, P. Moloney, E. Kelly, T. Wall, J. O'Shea, J. Hayes, E. Brady.

1903

Kerry—T. O'Gorman (capt.), J. O'Gorman, D. Curran, Mce. McCarthy, J. Buckley, C. Healy, A. Stack, R. Fitzgerald, P. Dillon, W. Lynch, D. McCarthy, J. Myers, D. Kissane, F. O'Sullivan, R. Kirwan, D. Breen, J. T. Fitzgerald.

London—S. Maguire (capt.), D. Donovan, J. O'Driscoll, A. Leary, T. Doody, T. Quilter, J. Griffin, J. Shouldice, M. J. Collins, J. Heffernan, J. Walsh, J. P. McKeever, C. Shine, J. Dwyer, T. O'Neill, M. Sheehan, J. Scanlan.

Home Final: Kerry—(Third Match)—Same as above, except that E. O'Neill played instead of F. O'Sullivan. C. Duggan played instead of F. O'Sullivan in just two games.

Kildare—Jos. Rafferty (capt.), W. Merriman, L. Cribben, W. Losty, J. Wright, J. Dunne, W. Bracken, J. Murray, M. Murray, M. Kennedy, J. Scott, M. Donnelly, F. "Joyce" Conlon, J. Gorman, M. Fitzgerald, J. Fitzgerald, E. Kennedy.

1904

Kerry—A. Stack (capt.), M. McCarthy, J. T. Fitzgerald, J. O'Gorman, T. O'Gorman, C. Healy, P. J. Cahill, J. Buckley, D. Curran, J. O'Sullivan, P. Dillon, J. Myers, D. McCarthy, R. Fitzgerald, W. Lynch, F. O'Sullivan, D. Breen.

Dublin—J. Lynch (capt.), P. McCann, M. Kelly, P. Daly, J. Brennan, J. Dempsey, D. Brady, J. Grace, M. Kane, P. O'Callaghan, T. Murphy, M. Barry, J. Chadwick, L. Sheehan, T. Walsh, P. Casey, J. Fahy.

1905

Kildare—J. Murray (capt.), M. Murray, J. Fitzgerald, M. Kennedy, J. Rafferty, J. Gorman, T. Keogh, F. "Joyce" Conlon, J.

Scott, W. Merriman, L. Cribben, W. Bracken, W. Losty, J. Connolly, E. Kennedy, T. Kelly, M. Fitzgerald.

Kerry—M. McCarthy (capt.), P. J. Cahill, J. T. Fitzgerald, T. O'Gorman, J. O'Gorman, J. O'Sullivan, C. Healy, T. Costello, D. Curran, R. Fitzgerald, P. Dillon, J. Myers, C. Murphy, J. Spillane, R. Kirwan, D. Breen, J. Wrenn.

1906

Dublin—J. Grace (capt.), D. Brady, J. Dempsey, D. Kelleher, J. Brennan, M. Kelly, M. Keane, M. Curry, M. Barry, P. O'Callaghan, P. Casey, H. Hilliard, M. Madigan, T. Quane, T. Walsh, P. Grace, L. Sheehan.

Cork—M. O'Connor (capt.), P. Daly, P. Lenihan, C. Paye, J. Kent, R. O'Sullivan, W. Mackessy, M. Mehigan, M. Twomey, T. Breen, T. O'Donoghue, J. McCarthy, J. Morrissey, C. McCarthy, J. Murphy, F. Searle, R. Flavin.

1907

Dublin—D. Kelleher, D. Brady, J. Brennan, J. Grace (capt.), J. Lynch, H. Hilliard, T. Quane, J. Dempsey, P. Casey, M. Curry, M. Barry, M. Madigan, P. O'Callaghan, T. Walsh, M. Kelly, D. Kavanagh, P. Grace.

Cork—W. Mackessy, J. McCarthy, J. Morrissey, M. Mehigan, P. O'Neill, J. Ryan, T. Breen, J. Beckett, J. Shorten, C. O'Shea, J. Driscoll, J. Lehane, J. Kelleher, J. Kent, R. O'Sullivan, M. Murphy, R. Flavin.

1908

Dublin—D. Kelleher (capt.), J. Grace, H. Hilliard, T. Walsh, J. Lynch, D. Cavanagh, J. S. Brennan, T. Healy, F. Cooney, J. Brennan, P. Daly, T. McCauley, P. Whelan, P. Fallon, M. Collins, M. Power, J. Shouldice.

London—E. O'Sullivan (capt.), J. Kerin, D. Daly, J. B. Kavanagh, D. P. Cremin, M. Hickey, W. O'Brien, S. Black, T. Ambrose, C. Shine, J. Griffin, J. Walsh, J. Maguire, E. O'Leary, P. M. Attridge, C. Tobin, M. O'Donoghue.

Home Final: Dublin—Same as in final.

Kerry—J. T. Fitzgerald (capt.), P. Dillon, R. Fitzgerald, J. Sullivan, J. O'Riordan, J. Lawlor, M. Mahony, P. Mullane, B. O'Connor, C. Murphy, F. Cronin, E. Spillane, J. McCarthy, C. Healy, T. Costelloe, D. Breen, J. Casey. Sub.—J. Condon.

1909

Kerry—T. Costelloe (capt.), M. McCarthy, C. Healy, T. Rice, J. O'Sullivan, D. Breen, M. J. Quinlan, R. Fitzgerald, C. Murphy,

E. Spillane, J. Skinner, P. Mullane, J. Kennelly, B. O'Connor, J. McCarthy, F. J. Cronin, P. Dillon.

Louth—J. Carvin (capt.), W. Byrne, Joe Quinn, L. Clarke, Joe Donnelly, Jim Clarke, E. Burke, Joe Mulligan, J. Brennan, J. Hanlon, Joe Matthews, O. Markey, J. Bannon, L. McCormack, J. Hand, J. Donegan, J. Morgan.

1910

No Final: *Louth* awarded walk-over from Kerry.

1911

Cork—M. Mehigan (capt.), M. O'Shea, E. Barrett, J. A. Beckett, J. Shorten, J. Donovan, W. Mackessy, M. Cotter, T. Murphy, J. Lehane, W. Lehane, J. Lynch, C. Kelleher, J. Young, P. Connell, C. Paye, J. O'Neill. Subs.—P. McSweeney, T. Breen.

Antrim—H. Sheehan (capt.), H. Kane, J. Murphy, P. Barnes, J. Mulvihill, P. Moylan, P. D. Kelly, J. M. Darby, C. McCurry, J. Fegan, J. Mullen, E. Gorman, J. Healy, J. Coburn, W. Manning, P. Meany, W. Williams.

1912

Louth—J. Smith (capt.), M. Byrne, J. Clarke, J. Quinn, J. Fitzsimmons, J. Mulligan, E. Burke, L. McCormack, J. Reilly, J. Bannon, D. Warren, J. Johnstone, O. Markey, T. Matthews, J. Campbell, J Brennan, S. Fitzsimmons.

Antrim—J. Coburn (capt.), J. Monaghan, P. Moylan, T. Meany, H. Sheehan, P. L. Kelly, W. Manning, J. Murphy. M. Goggan, L. Waters, J. Mulvihill, E. Ward, J. Mullen, J. Gorman, P. Barnes, M. Maguire, J. Gallagher.

1913

Kerry—R. Fitzgerald (capt.), J. Skinner, D. Doyle, C. Murphy, P. Healy, J. O'Mahony, C. Clifford, T. Rice, J. J. Rice, M. McCarthy, T. Costelloe, J. Lawlor, D. Mullins, P. O'Shea, P. Kennelly.

Wexford—T. Doyle (capt.), T. Mernagh, A. Doyle, J. Cullen (goal), E. Black, T. Murphy, J. Doyle, J. Kennedy, P. Mackey, G. Kennedy, J. Mullally, R. Reynolds, F. Furlong, J. Byrne, J. Rossiter.

1914 REPLAY

Kerry—R. Fitzgerald (capt.), M. McCarthy, D. Doyle, J. Skinner, J. Mahony, C. Murphy, P. Healy, C. Clifford, P. Breen, T. Rice, J. J. Rice, J. Lawlor, D. Mullins (goal), T. Costelloe, P. O'Shea.

[J. Murphy and W. Keating played in drawn game. M. McCarthy and J. J. Rice came in for replay.]

319

Wexford—Sean Kennedy (capt.), T. McGrath (goal), T. Murphy, P. Mackey, J. Byrne, P. D. Breen, T. Doyle, T. Mernagh, P. Murphy, J. Doyle, J. Mullally, R. Reynolds, A. Doyle, G. Kennedy, J. Rossiter.

1915

Wexford—Sean Kennedy (capt.), Gus Kennedy, P. Mackey, T. Murphy, F. Furlong, J. Wall, Fr. E. Wheeler, T. Mernagh, T. Doyle, E. Black, A. Doyle, James Byrne, M. Howlett, R. Reynolds, T. McGrath (goal).

Kerry—R. Fitzgerald (capt.), M. McCarthy, J. Lawlor, T. Costelloe, T. Rice, H. Murphy, P. Healy, C. Clifford, Con Murphy, P. O'Shea, M. Donovan, J. Rice, D. Doyle, M. Carroll, D. Mullins (goal).

1916

Wexford—Sean Kennedy (capt.), T. McGrath (goal), P. Mackey, Fr. E. Wheeler, Jas. Byrne, T. Murphy, T. Mernagh, M. Howlett, F. Furlong, Tom Doyle, J. Crowley, R. Reynolds, J. Wall, A. Doyle, Gus Kennedy.

Mayo—P. Loftus, T. Gibson, J. Waldron, J. E. McEllin, T. Ruane, P. Robinson, J. Lyden, H. Hession, F. Courell, M. Murray, T. Boshell, M. Franklin, J. Reilly, T. Forde, T. Smith.

1917

Wexford—Sean Kennedy (capt.), G. Kennedy, P. Mackey, A. Doyle, T. Mernagh, T. McGrath (goal), T. Murphy, W. Hodgins, J. Quinn, J. Byrne, J. Crowley, F. Furlong, M. Howlett, T. Doyle, R. Reynolds. Sub.—R. Reilly, T. Forde, T. Smith.

Clare—M. Conole, P. Hennessy, J. Foran, E. McNamara, P. O'Brien, M. McMahon, J. Fitzgerald, M. McNamara, J. Marrinan, P. O'Donoghue, J. Spellissy, E. Carroll, M. Malone, E. Roche, T. Considine.

1918

Wexford—T. McGrath (goal), N. Stuart, P. Mackey, J. Byrne (capt.), T. Murphy, T. Doyle, M. Howlett, W. Hodgins, J. Doran, J. Crowley, R. Reynolds, T. Pierse, A. Doyle, G. Kennedy, J. Redmond.

Tipperary—A. Carroll, J. McNamara, E. O'Shea, J. Shelley, W. Ryan, E. Egan, T. Powell, J. Quinlan, J. Ryan, T. Ryan, W. Grant, J. Skinner, R. Heffernan, G. McCarthy, J. O'Shea.

1919

Kildare—L. Stanley (capt.), L. Cribben, J. Conlon, J. Moran,

T. Goulding, M. Buckley, J. O'Connor, P. Doyle, M. Sammon, G. Magan, J. Stanley, C. Flynn, B. McGlade, James O'Connor, F. "Joyce" Conlon.

Galway—T. Egan (capt.), D. Egan, J. Egan, Peter Higgins, M. "Knacker" Walsh, P. Roche, J. Hanniffy, G. Jennings, L. Raftery, M. Flannelly, H. Burke, G. Feeney, M. Walsh, T. McDonnell, M. Cawley.

1920

Tipperary—A. Carroll (goal), J. McNamara, Edwd. O'Shea, G. Lanigan, Bill Ryan, J. Shelly (capt.), W. Grant, W. Barrett, M. Tobin, J. Ryan, J. Doran, G. McCarthy, V. Vaughan, M. Arrigan, T. Powell.

Dublin—J. McDonnell (goal), W. Robbins, Joe Joyce, P. Carey, Joe Synnott, Joe Norris, John Reilly, J. Murphy, W. Donovan, J. Carey, P. McDonnell, Ger. Doyle, John Synnott, F. Burke, S. Synnott.

1921

Dublin—E. Carroll (capt.), John Reilly, Joe Norris, P. Carey, John Synnott, P. Kirwan, W. Donovan, P. Fallon (goal), John Murphy, Thomas Pierse, F. Burke, C. McDonald, A. Belmain, J. O'Grady, W. Fitzsimons.

Mayo—B. Durkin (capt.), J. White, Geo. Delaney, M. Barrett, J. Boshill, J. Leyden, J. Lavin, T. Mulderrig, F. Doherty, J. E. McEllin, P. O'Beirne, Dr. Mongey, K. Dillon (goal), B. Farrell, P. Colleran.

1922

Dublin—P. Carey (capt.), J. McDonnell (goal), P. McDonnell, W. Robbins, A. Gibbons, Joe Synnott, John Synnott, Joe Norris, John Reilly, W. Rooney, C. McDonald, Wm. Donovan, P. Kirwan, F. Burke, Tom Pierse.

Galway—M. Walshe (capt.), W. Flanagan (goal), D. Egan, J. Egan, T. Molloy, T. Hessian, J. Haniffy, L. McGrath, J. Kirwan, P. Roche, G. Jennings, P. Jennings, Wm. Walsh, M. Donnellan, P. Kilroy.

1923

Dublin—John Reilly, P. McDonnell (capt.), John Murphy, Joseph Norris, Joe Synnott, Patk. Carey, P. Kirwan, J. Stynes, Frank Burke, John McDonnell (goal), John Synnott, M. Shanahan, J. Sherlock, P. O'Beirne, L. Stanley.

Kerry—J. Sheehy (goal), J. Barrett, P. Sullivan, E. Moriarty,

P. Russell, T. Kelleher, J. Moriarty (capt.), C. Brosnan, P. McKenna, John Ryan, John J. Sheehy, D. O'Donoghue, John Baily, Jas. Baily, W. Landers.

1924

Kerry—J. Moriarty, John Sheehy (goal), Phil Sullivan (capt.), Joe Barrett, John Murphy, Paul Russell, Jack Walsh, Con Brosnan, R. Stack, John Ryan, John J. Sheehy, R. Prendeville, John Baily, Jas. Baily, W. Landers.

Dublin—P. McDonnell (capt.), J. McDonnell (goal), P. Carey, W. O'Reilly, Joe Synnott, Joe Norris, John Reilly, Peter Synnott, M. O'Brien, P. O'Beirne, John Murphy, M. Shanahan, F. Burke, G. Madigan, P. J. Kirwan.

1925

N.B.—No Football Final played. Kerry and Cavan being declared illegal, Mayo, nominated by Connacht Council, beat Wexford. and then lost the Connacht Final to *Galway*, who were declared champions. The Galway team which beat Mayo was: M. Walsh (capt.), T. Molloy, J. Egan, D. Egan, H. Burke, F. Benson, W. Smyth, T. Leetch, M. Bannerton, Leonard McGrath, P. Roche, G. Jennings, P. Ganley, Lar. McGrath, M. Donnellan.

1926

Kerry—John J. Sheehy (capt.), John Riordan (goal), P. Clifford, Joe Barrett, Jack Walsh, Paul Russell, J. Moriarty, John Slattery, Con Brosnan, Robt. Stack, John Ryan, Des. O'Connell, Tom Mahony, Jas. Baily, Wm. Gorman.

Kildare — Jos. Loughlin (capt.), Jas. Cummins (goal), Ml. Buckley, Matt. Goff, B. Graham, F. Malone, Jack Higgins, John Hayes, P. Martin, Gus. Fitzpatrick, L. Stanley, Paul Doyle, Wm. Gannon. T. Donoghue, Joe Curtis.

The Kerry and Kildare players given are those who did duty in the replay. D. O'Connell, J. Slattery and P. Clifford replaced J. Murphy, Joe O'Sullivan and Phil O'Sullivan on the Kerry side, while T. Donoghue and Gus. Fitzpatrick replaced A. O'Neill and G. Higgins on the Kildare side.

J. Slattery and P. Clifford came on as subs in drawn game.

1927

Kildare—M. Buckley (capt.), M. Walsh (goal), Gus Fitzpatrick, F. Malone, J. Higgins. J. Hayes, J. Loughlin, W. Gannon, J.

Curtis, P. Martin, P. Doyle, W. Mangan, P. Loughlin, T. Keogh, M. Goff. Subs.: P. Ryan, M. Connor.

Kerry—J. J. Sheehy (capt.), J. O'Riordan (goal), D. O'Connor, J. Barrett, J. Walsh, D. O'Connell, P. O'Sullivan, J. Slattery, C. Brosnan, R. Stack, J. Ryan, E. Fitzgerald, T. Mahony, Jas. Baily, J. J. Landers.

1928

Kildare—W. ("Squires") Gannon (capt.), M. Walshe, M. Buckley, M. Goff, Gus Fitzpatrick, F. Malone, J. Higgins, J. Hayes, Joe Loughlin, P. Martin, P. Loughlin, P. Doyle, W. Mangan, J. Curtis, T. Keogh. Sub.: D. Ryan.

Cavan—J. Smith (capt.), J. Morgan, T. Campbell, H. Clegg, J. J. Clarke, H. Mulvany, P. Lynch, H. O'Reilly, P. Devlin, Jas. Murphy, A. Condon, J. Farrell, W. Young, W. A. Higgins, G. Malcolmson. Sub.—T. Crowe.

1929

Kerry—J. Riordan (goal), D. O'Connor, Joe Barrett (capt.), Jack Walsh, Paul Russell, Joe O'Sullivan, T. O'Donnell, Con Brosnan, R. Stack, J. Ryan, M. Doyle, J. J. Landers, E. Sweeney, Jas. Baily, J. J. Sheehy.

Kildare—J. Higgins (capt.), J. O'Reilly (goal), J. Hayes, M. Goff, Gus. Fitzpatrick, M. Fenerall, F. Malone, P. Loughlin, Joe Loughlin, P. Martin, Wm. Hynam, Paul Doyle, T. Wheeler, P. Pringle, W. Gannon.

1930

Kerry—J. J. Sheehy (capt.), J. Riordan (goal), D. O'Connor, J. Barrett, Jack Walsh, P. Russell, J. O'Sullivan, T. O'Donnell, C. Brosnan, R. Stack, J. Ryan, M. Doyle, E. Fitzgerald, E. Sweeney, J. J. Landers.

Monaghan—P. Kilroy (capt.), T. Bradley (goal), T. Slevin, J. Farrell, P. Duffy, P. Heeran, J. Duffy, P. Lambe, W. Mason, M. McAleer, C. Fisher, J. O'Carroll, P. McCannon, J. Sexton, H. Brannigan. Sub.—P. J. Duffy.

1931

Kerry—Con Brosnan (capt.), D. O'Keeffe (goal), D. O'Connor, J. Barrett, Jock Walsh, P. Russell, J. O'Sullivan, T. Landers, R. Stack, J. J. Landers, M. Doyle, E. Fitzgerald, J. Ryan, P. Whitty, M. Regan.

Kildare—M. Walsh (capt.) (goal), J. Meaney, M. Goff, F.

Malone, P. Miles, J. Higgins, W. Hynam, P. Watters, P. Loughlin, J. Maguire, P. Martin, P. Byrne, H. Burke, D. Burke, P. Doyle.

1932

Kerry—D. O'Keeffe, D. O'Connor, Joe Barrett (capt.), Jack Walsh, P. Russell, Joe O'Sullivan, P. Whitty, R. Stack, J. Walsh, C. Geaney, M. Doyle, T. Landers, J. Ryan, C. Brosnan, J. J. Landers. Sub.—W. Landers.

Mayo—T. Burke, J. Gannon, P. Quinn, P. Kelly, T. Tunney, J. O'Malley, G. Ormsby, M. Mulderrig, M. Ormsby, P. Munnelly, T. Hanley, P. Flannelly, G. Courell, P. Moclair, J. Forde.

1933

Cavan—J. Smith (capt.), W. Young (goal), M. Denneny, P. Phair, T. O'Reilly, P. Lynch, H. O'Reilly, W. Connolly, T. Coyle, L. Blessing, P. Devlin, D. Morgan, J. Smallhorn, V. McGovern, M. J. Magee. Subs.—T. Crowe, P. W. Connolly, T. O'Reilly (Mullahoran).

Galway—M. Donnellan (capt.), F. Fox, B. Nestor, M. Brennan (goal), H. Carey, M. Connaire, J. Dunne, J. Kelleher, M. Kelly, T. McCarthy, F. Burke, M. Higgins, D. O'Sullivan, T. Hughes, D. Mitchell.

1934

Galway—M. Higgins (capt.), M. Brennan (goal), P. J. McDonnell, M. Ferriter, H. Carey, D. O'Sullivan, T. Hughes, T. McCarthy, F. Fox, J. Dunne, M. Connaire, R. Griffin, M. Kelly, D. Mitchell, B. Nestor.

Dublin—J. McDonnell (goal), G. Comerford, M. O'Brien, D. Brennan, M. Casey, F. Cavanagh, P. Cavanagh, P. Hickey, W. Dowling, R. Beggs, M. Wellington, G. Fitzgerald. M. Kelly, M. Keating (capt.), E. McCann.

1935

Cavan—W. Young (goal), J. Smith, W. Connolly, M. Denneny, T. Dolan, T. O'Reilly, P. Phair, H. O'Reilly (capt.), T. O'Reilly, D. Morgan, P. Devlin, J. Smallhorn, P. Boylan, L. Blessing, M. J. Magee.

Kildare—J. Maguire (goal), W. Mangan, M. Goff, J. Byrne, P. Watters, J. Higgins, F. Dowling, P. Matthews, C. Higgins, T. Mulhall, P. Byrne, P. Martin, J. Dowling, M. Geraghty, T. Keogh. Sub.—J. Dalton.

1936

Mayo—T. Burke (goal), P. Quinn, J. McGowan, "Purty"

Kelly, T. Regan, S. O'Malley (capt.), G. Ormsby, P. Flannelly, H. Kenny, J. Carney, P. Laffey, T. Grier, J. Munnelly, P. Moclair, P. Munnelly.

Laois—J. McDonnell (capt.), T. Delaney (goal), T. Delaney, J. Brennan, T. O'Brien, P. Swayne, D. Walsh, C. Delaney, W. Delaney, D. Douglas, J. Delaney, M. Delaney, T. Keogh, J. Keating, J. O'Reilly. Sub.—J. Moran.

`1937 REPLAY

Kerry—D. O'Keeffe (goal), W. Kinnerk, J. Keohane, W. Myers, T. O'Donnell, W. Dillon, T. Healy, J. Walsh, S. Brosnan, J. Flavin, C. O'Sullivan, T. Landers, J. J. Landers, M. Doyle (capt.), T. O'Leary. Sub.—T. O'Connor. Gearóid Fitzgerald played in drawn game.

Cavan—W. Young (goal), E. Finnegan, J. Smith, M. Denneny, D. Kerrigan, T. O'Reilly (capt.), J. J. O'Reilly, V. White, P. Smith, D. Morgan, P. Devlin, J. Smallhorn, P. Boylan, L. Blessing, M. Magee. Subs.—T. O'Reilly (Mullahorn), J. White, W. Carroll, J. Mitchell.

1938 REPLAY

Galway—J. McGauran (goal), M. Connaire, M. Raftery, D. O'Sullivan, R. Beggs, F. Cunniffe, C. Connolly, J. Burke, J. Dunne (capt.), J. Flavin, M. Higgins, R. Griffin, M. Kelly, E. Mulholland, B. Nestor. Subs.—M. Ryder, P. McDonagh.

Kerry—W. Kinnerk (capt.), D. O'Keeffe, P. Brosnan, W. Myers, W. Dillon, W. Casey, T. O'Connor, J. Walsh, S. Brosnan, P. Kennedy, A. McAuliffe, C. O'Sullivan, M. Regan, M. Doyle, T. O'Leary. Sub.—J. J. Landers.

J. J. Landers and Joe Keohane played in drawn game.

1939

Kerry—D. O'Keeffe, W. Myers, J. Keohane, T. Healy, W. Dillon, W. Casey, E. Walsh, P. Kennedy, J. O'Gorman, M. Kelly, T. O'Connor (capt.), J. Walsh, C. O'Sullivan, D. Spring, T. Landers.

Meath—H. McEnroe, P. Beggan, T. McGuinness, P. Donnelly, T. Meade, C. O'Reilly, J. Kearney, M. O'Toole, J. Loughran, M. Gilsenan (capt.), T. Donnelly, J. Clarke, W. Brien, J. Cummins, K. Devin. Subs.—H. Lynch, M. Clinton.

1940

Kerry—D. O'Keeffe, W. Myers, J. Keohane, T. Healy, W. Dillon, W. Casey, E. Walsh, S. Brosnan, J. Walsh, J. O'Gorman, T. O'Connor, P. Kennedy, M. Kelly, D. Spring (capt.), C. O'Sullivan. Sub.—P. Brosnan.

Galway—J. McGauran, M. Raftery, M. Connaire, D. O'Sullivan, F. Cunniffe, R. Beggs, C. Connolly, J. Dunne (capt.), J. Duggan, J. Flavin, J. Burke, J. Canavan, M. Higgins, E. Mulholland. B. Nestor.

1941

Kerry—D. O'Keeffe, W. Myers, Joe Keohane, T. Healy, W. Dillon (capt.), W. Casey, E. Walsh, S. Brosnan, P. Kennedy, J. Walsh, T. O'Connor, P. B. Brosnan, J. O'Gorman, M. Kelly, C. O'Sullivan. Subs.—T. Landers, M. Lyne.

Galway—J. McGauran, M. Raftery, P. McDonagh, D. O'Sullivan (capt.), F. Cunniffe, R. Beggs, J. Duggan, C. Connolly, D. Kavanagh, J. Hanniffy, J. Dunne, J. Canavan, E. Mulholland, P. McDonagh, J. Burke. Sub.—P. Thornton.

1942

Dublin—C. Kelly, R. Beggs, P. Kennedy, C. Crone, P. Henry, P. O'Reily, B. Quinn, M. Falvey, Joe Fitzgerald (capt.), J. Joy, P. Bermingham, Gerry Fitzgerald, M. Fletcher, P. O'Connor, T. Banks.

Galway—J. McGauran, F. Cunniffe, M. Connaire, P. McDonagh, J. Duggan, J. Casey, Tom O'Sullivan, D. Kavanagh, C. Connolly (capt.), J. Clifford, M. Fallon, J. Canavan, J. Flavin, P. Thornton, Sean Thornton. Subs.—E. Mulholland (for Clifford), Sean Walsh (for J. Flavin).

1943 REPLAY

Roscommon—F. Glynn, L. Cummins, J. P. O'Callaghan, W. Jackson, B. Lynch, W. Carlos, O. Hoare, E. Boland, L. Gilmartin, P. Murray, J. Murray (capt.), D. Keenan, D. McDermott, J. McQuillan, F. Kinlough.

Cavan—J. D. Benson, E. Finnegan, B. Cully, P. P. Galligan, G. Smith, T. O'Reilly (capt.), J. J. O'Reilly, S. Deignan, T. P. O'Reilly, D. Morgan, P. Smith, M. Higgins, P. Boylan, Joe Stafford, H. Rogers. Sub.—J. Keegan for H. Rogers.

W. Heavey, Roscommon, who played in the drawn game, was replaced by O. Hoare for replay. J. Maguire, Cavan who played in drawn game was replaced by H. Rogers for replay.

1944

Roscommon—O. Hoare, W. Jackson, J. P. O'Callaghan, J. Casserly, B. Lynch, W. Carlos, P. Murray, E. Boland, L. Gilmartin, F. Kinlough, J. Murray (capt.), D. Keenan, H. Gibbons, J. McQuillan, J. J. Nerney. Sub.—D. McDermott.

Kerry—D. O'Keeffe, T. Healy, J. Keohane, T. Brosnan, W.

Dillon, M. McCarthy, E. Walsh, P. Kennedy, S. Brosnan, J. Clifford, J. Lyne, P. B. Brosnan (capt.), D. Lyne, M. Kelly, E. Dunne. Subs.—D. Kavanagh for P. Kennedy, J. Walsh for P. B. Brosnan.

1945

Cork—M. O'Driscoll, D. Magnier, P. Murphy, C. Crone, P. Cronin, T. Crowley (capt.), D. O'Connor, F. O'Donavan, E. Young, E. Casey, H. O'Neill, M. Tubridy, J. Lynch, J. Cronin, D. Beckett. Sub.—J. Ahern for E. Casey.

Cavan—B. Kelly, T. O'Reilly (capt.), B. Cully, P. P. Galligan, J. Wilson, J. J. O'Reilly, P. Smith, A. Tighe, S. Deignan, A. Commiskey, J. Boylan, T. P. O'Reilly, J. Stafford, P. Donohue, P. J. Duke.

1946 REPLAY

Kerry—D. O'Keeffe, D. Lyne, J. Keohane, P. B. Brosnan, J. Lyne, W. Casey, E. Walsh, Teddy O'Connor, P. Kennedy (capt.), J. Falvey, Tom O'Connor, B. Garvey, F. O'Keeffe, P. Burke, D. Kavanagh.
Note: Gus Cremins (capt.) and Willie O'Donnell played in drawn game. F. O'Keeffe and J. Falvey came on for replay. Gus Cremin replaced J. Falvey as sub during replay.

Roscommon—G. Dolan, W. Jackson, J. Casserley, O. Hoare, B. Lynch, W. Carlos, T. Collins, P. Murray, E. Boland, F. Kinlough, J. Murray (capt.), D. Keenan, J. McQuillan, J. J. Fallon, J. J. Nerney. [Vincent Beirne came on as a sub in drawn game.]

1947

Cavan—V. Gannon, W. Doonan, B. O'Reilly, P. Smith, J. Wilson, J. J. O'Reilly (capt.), S. Deignan, P. J. Duke, P. Brady, A. Tighe, M. Higgins, C. McDyer, J. Stafford, P. Donohoe, T. P. O'Reilly.

Kerry—D. O'Keeffe, D. Lyne (capt.), J. Keohane, P. Brosnan, J. Lyne, W. Casey, E. Walsh, E. Dowling, E. O'Connor, E. O'Sullivan, D. Kavanagh, B. Garvey, F. O'Keeffe, T. O'Connor, P. Kennedy. Subs.—W. O'Donnell for E. Dowling, M. Finucane for E. Walsh, T. Brosnan for W. O'Donnell, G. Teehan for P. Kennedy.

1948

Cavan—J. D. Benson, W. Doonan, B. O'Reilly, P. Smith, P. J. Duke, J. J. O'Reilly (capt.), S. Deignan, P. Brady, V. Sherlock, A. Tighe, M. Higgins, J. J. Cassidy, J. Stafford, P. Donohoe, E. Carolan. Subs.—O. R. McGovern, for J. J. O'Reilly.

Mayo—T. Byrne, P. Quinn, P. Prendergast, S. Flanagan, J.

Forde, P. McAndrew, Jn. Gilvarry, E. Mongey, P. Carney, W. Kenny, T. Langan, Joe Gilvarry, T. Acton, P. Solon, S. Mulderrig.

1949

Meath—K. Smyth, M. O'Brien, P. O'Brien, K. McConnell, S. Heery, P. Dixon, C. Hand, P. O'Connell, J. Kearney, F. Byrne, B. Smyth (capt.), M. McDonnell, P. Meegan, W. Halfpenny, P. McDermott. Sub.—P. Carolan for F. Byrne.

Cavan—J. Morris, J. McCabe, P. Smith, O. R. McGovern, P. J. Duke, J. J. O'Reilly (capt.), S. Deignan, P. Brady, V. Sherlock, A. Tighe, M. Higgins, J. J. Cassidy, J. Stafford, P. Donohoe, E. Carolan.

1950

Mayo—W. Durkin, J. Forde, P. Prendergast, S. Flanagan (capt.), P. Quinn, H. Dixon, J. McAndrew, P. Carney, E. Mongey, M. Flanagan, W. Kenny, J. Gilvarry, M. Mulderrig, T. Langan, P. Solon. Subs.—S. Wynne for W. Durkin, M. Caulfield for W. Kenny, S. Mulderrig for M. Caulfield.

Louth—S. Thornton, M. Byrne, T. Conlon, J. Tuft, S. Boyle, P. Markey, P. McArdle, J. Regan, J. Reid, J. McDonnell, N. Roe, S. White, R. Lynch, H. Reynolds, M. Reynolds. Subs,—R. Mooney for N. Roe, M. McDonnell for P. McArdle.

1951

Mayo—S. Wynne, J. Forde, P. Prendergast, S. Flanagan (capt.), J. Staunton, H. Dixon, P. Quinn, E. Mongey, J. McAndrew, P. Irwin, P. Carney, S. Mulderrig, M. Flanagan, T. Langan, J. Gilvarry. Sub.—L. Hastings for H. Dixon.

Meath—K. Smyth, M. O'Brien, P. O'Brien, K. McConnell, S. Heery (capt.), C. Kelly, C. Hand, D. Taaffe, P. Connell, F. Byrne, M. McDonnell, P. Meegan, B. Smyth, J. Reilly, P. McDermott. Subs.—P. Dixon for C. Hand, C. Hand for S. Heery.

1952 REPLAY

Cavan—S. Morris, J. McCabe, P. Brady, D. Maguire, P. Carolan, L. Maguire, B. O'Reilly, V. Sherlock, T. Hardy, S. Hetherton, M. Higgins (capt.), E. Carolan, J. J. Cassidy, A. Tighe, J. Cusack.
Note: P. Fitzsimons played in drawn game. J. Cusack came on for replay. P. Fitzsimons was introduced as sub for J. J. Cassidy in replay.

Meath—K. Smyth, M. O'Brien, P. O'Brien, K. McConnell, T. O'Brien, C. Kelly, C. Hand, B. Maguire, D. Taaffe, D. Brennan, B. Smith, P. Meegan (capt.), M. McDonnell, J. Reilly, P. McDermott.

Note: P. McGearty and P. Connell played in drawn game. T. O'Brien and D. Brennan came on for replay.

1953

Kerry—J. Foley, J. Murphy (capt.), E. Roche, D. Murphy, C. Kennelly, J. Cronin, J. M. Palmer, S. Murphy, D. Hannifin, J. Brosnan, J. J. Sheehan, T. Lyne, T. Ashe. S. Kelly, J. Lyne. Sub. —G. O'Sullivan for Hannifin.

Armagh—E. McMahon, E. Morgan, J. Bratten, J. McKnight, F. Kernan, P. O'Neill, S. Quinn (capt.), M. O'Hanlon, M. McEvoy, J. Cunningham, B. Seeley, W. McCorry, P. Campbell, A. O'Hagan, G. O'Neill. Subs.—G. Wilson for McMahon, G. Murphy for Wilson. J. O'Hare for Quinn.

1954

Meath—P. McGearty, M. O'Brien, P. O'Brien, K. McConnell, K. Lenehan, J. O'Reilly, E. Durnin, P. Connell, T. O'Brien, M. Grace, B. Smyth, M. McDonnell, P. Meegan, T. Moriarty, P. McDermott (capt.).

Kerry—G. O'Mahoney, J. M. Palmer, E. Roche, D. Murphy, S. Murphy, J. Cronin, C. Kennelly, J. Dowling (capt.), T. Moriarty, R. Buckley, J. J. Sheehan, P. Sheehy, J. Brosnan, S. Kelly, T. Lyne.

1955

Kerry—G. Mahony, J. O'Shea, E. Roche, J. M. Palmer, S. Murphy, J. Cronin, T. Moriarty, J. Dowling (capt.), D. O'Shea, P. Sheehy, T. Costello, T. Lyne, J. Culloty, M. Murphy, J. Brosnan. Sub.—J. J. Sheehan for Moriarty.

Dublin—P. O'Flaherty, D. Mahony (capt.), J. Lavin, M. Moylan, M. Whelan, J. Crowley, N. Maher, J. McGuinness, C. O'Leary, D. Ferguson, O. Freaney, J. Boyle, P. Haughey, K. Heffernan, C. Freaney. Subs.—T. Jennings for McGuinness, W. Monks for Jennings.

1956

Galway—J. Mangan (capt.), J. Keeley, G. Daly, T. Dillon, J. Kissane, J. Mahon, M. Greally, F. Evers, M. McDonagh, J. Coyle, S. Purcell, W. O'Neill, J. Young, F. Stockwell, G. Kirwan. Sub. —A. Swords for Young.

Cork—P. Tyres, P. Driscoll, D. O'Sullivan (capt.), D. Murray, P. Harrington, D. Bernard, M. Gould, S. Moore, E. Ryan, D. Kelleher, C. Duggan, P. Murphy, T. Furlong, N. Fitzgerald, J. Creedon. Sub.—E. Goulding for Murphy.

NOBODY OFFERS YOU A BETTER COACH SERVICE

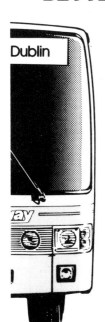

Return fares from Dublin

WATERFORD	£8.00
ROSSLARE	£10.00
BALLINA	£11.00
SLIGO	£11.00
BELFAST	£12.00
ENNIS	£12.00
GALWAY	£12.00
LIMERICK	£12.00
DONEGAL	£13.00
LETTERKENNY	£13.00
CORK	£15.00
TRALEE	£17.00

Travel mid-week at bargain return fares. Ask for details.

Something for Everyone

Take a Day Tour From as Little as £10
Take the family out for a great day on one of our day tours. Choose from over 60 tours nationwide. From as little as £10 per person. Ask for our DAY TOURS brochure.

Mini Breaks for £33
Our BREAKAWAY brochure shows you how to get away from it all. A choice of 24 locations. Terrific value at £33 per night sharing. Includes overnight accommodation, full Irish breakfast and return coach fare to your choice of destination.

Travel in Style. You'll enjoy the comfort and luxury of our award winning coaches. They're superb.

For travel information ring:
Central Bus Station (Busaras), Store Street, Dublin 1. (01) 366111.
Parnell Place Bus Station, Cork. (021) 508188.
Colbert Station, Limerick. (061) 313333.
Ceannt Station, Galway. (091) 62000.
Plunkett Station, Waterford. (051) 79000.
Casement Station, Tralee. (066) 23566.

Or your local Bus Éireann Office, Tourist Office, or Travel Agent.

Prices correct at time of going to press.

BUS ÉIREANN
we're on the move

330

Louth—S. Flood, O. Reilly, T. Conlon, J. Meehan, P. Coleman, P. Smith, S. White, K. Beahan, D. O'Neill, S. O'Donnell, D. O'Brien (capt.), F. Lynch, S. Cunningham, J. McDonnell, J. Roe.

Cork—L. Power, M. Gould, D. Bernard, D. Murray, P. Harrington, P. O'Driscoll, J. J. Henchion, E. Ryan, S. Moore, J. O'Sullivan, N. Fitzgerald, T. Furlong, E. Goulding, C. Duggan (capt.), D. Kelleher. Sub.—F. McAuliffe for O'Sullivan.

Dublin—P. O'Flaherty, L. Foley, M. Wilson, Joe Timmons, C. O'Leary, J. Crowley, J. Boyle, John Timmons, S. Murray, P. Haughey, O. Freaney, D. Ferguson, P. Farnan, J. Joyce, K. Heffernan (capt.). Subs.—Maurice Whelan for Murray, P. Downey for John Timmons.

Derry—P. Gormley. P. McLarnon, H. F. Gribben, T. Doherty, P. Breen, C. Mulholland, P. Smith, J. McKeever (capt.), P. Stuart, S. O'Connell, B. Murray, D. McKeever, B. Mullan, O. Gribben, C. Higgins. Subs.—R. Gribben for Higgins, L. O'Neill for Mullan, C. O'Neill for Breen.

Kerry—J. Culloty, J. O'Shea, N. Sheehy, T. Lyons, Sean Murphy, K. Coffey, M. O'Dwyer, M. O'Connell (capt.), Seamus Murphy, D. McAuliffe, T. Long, P. Sheehy, D. Geaney, J. Dowling, T. Lyne. Subs.—Jack Dowling for Lyons, Moss O'Connell for Mick O'Connell, G. McMahon for Geaney.

Galway—J. Farrell, J. Kissane, S. Meade, M. Greally, M. Garrett, J. Mahon, S. Colleran, F. Evers, Mattie McDonagh, J. Young, S. Purcell (capt.), Ml. McDonagh, M. Laide, F. Stockwell, J. Nallen. Subs.—J. Keeley for Nallen, P. Dunne for Greally.

Down—E. McKay, G. Lavery, L. Murphy, P. Rice, K. Mussen (capt.), D. McCartan, K. O'Neill, J. Lennon, J. Carey, S. O'Neill. J. McCartan, P. Doherty, A. Hadden, P. O'Hagan, B. Morgan. Sub.—K. Denvir for Lennon.

Kerry—J. Culloty, J. O'Shea, N. Sheehy, T. Lyons, Sean Murphy, K. Coffey, M. O'Dwyer, M. O'Connell, J. D. O'Connor, Seamus Murphy, T. Long, P. Sheehy (capt.), G. McMahon, John Dowling, T. Lyne. Subs.—Jack Dowling for John Dowling, J. Brosnan for McMahon, D. McAuliffe for Lyne.

1961

Down—E. McKay, G. Lavery, L. Murphy, P. Rice, P. O'Hagan, D. McCartan, J. Smith, J. Carey, J. Lennon, S. O'Neill, J. McCartan, P. Doherty (capt.), A. Hadden, P. J. McIlroy, B. Morgan. Subs.—K. O'Neill for P. Rice; Rice for G. Lavery.

Offaly—W. Nolan (capt.), P. McCormack, G. Hughes, J. Egan, P. O'Reilly, M. Brady, C. Wrenn, S. Brereton, S. Ryan, T. Cullen, P. Daly, T. Greene, M. Casey, D. O'Hanlon, H. Donnelly. Subs.—F. Weir, S. Foran, F. Higgins.

1962

Kerry—J. Culloty, S. Murphy, N. Sheehy, T. Lyons, S. Óg Sheehy, (capt.), N. Lucey, M. O'Dwyer, M. O'Connell, J. Lucey, D. McAuliffe, T. O'Sullivan, J. O'Riordan, G. McMahon, T. Long, P. Sheehy. Subs.— J. Barrett, K. Coffey.

Roscommon—A. Brady, J. J. Breslin, J. Lynch, J. O. Moran, R. Creaven, G. O'Malley (capt.), G. Reilly, B. Kyne, J. Kelly, G. Geraghty, E. Curley, A. Whyte, Don Feely, C. Mahon, Des Feely. Subs.—T. Turley, A. Kenny.

1963

Dublin—P. Flynn, L. Hickey, L. Foley, W. Casey, D. McKane, P. Holden, M. Kissane, D. Foley (capt.), J. Timmons, B. McDonald, M. Whelan, G. Davey, S. Behan, D. Ferguson, N. Fox. Sub.—P. Downey.

Galway—M. Moore, E. Colleran, N. Tierney, S. Meade, J. B. McDermott, J. Donnellan, M. Newell, M. Garrett (capt.), M. Reynolds, C. Dunne, M. McDonagh, P. Donnellan, J. Keenan, S. Cleary, S. Leydon. Sub.—B. Geraghty.

1964

Galway—J. Geraghty, E. Colleran, N. Tierney, J. B. McDermott, J. Donnellan (capt.), S. Meade, M. Newell, M. Garrett, M. Reynolds, C. Dunne, M. McDonagh, S. Leydon, C. Tyrrell, S. Cleary, J. Keenan.

Kerry—J. Culloty, M. Morris, N. Sheehy (capt.), P. Donoghue, Denis O'Sullivan, S. Murphy, J. O'Connor, M. Fleming, Donie O'Sullivan, P. Griffin, M. O'Dwyer, M. O'Connell, F. O'Leary, T. Long, J. J. Barrett. Subs.—J. McCarthy, B. O'Callaghan, K. Coffey.

1965

Galway—J. Geraghty, E. Colleran (capt.), N. Tierney, J. B. McDermott, J. Donnellan, S. Meade, M. Newell, P. Donnellan, M. Garrett, C. Dunne, M. McDonagh, S. Leydon, C. Tyrrell, S. Cleary, J. Keenan. Sub.—M. Reynolds.

Kerry J. Culloty, Donie O'Sullivan, N. Sheehy, M. Morris, Seamus Murphy, P. O'Donoghue, J. D. O'Connor (capt.), Denis O'Sullivan, M. O'Connell, V. Lucey, P. Griffin, D. O'Shea, B. O'Callaghan, M. O'Dwyer, J. J. Barret. Subs.—D. Geaney, J. O'Shea.

1966

Galway—J. Geraghty, E. Colleran (capt.), N. Tierney, J. B. McDermott, C. McDonagh, S. Meade, M. Newell, J. Duggan, P. Donnellan, C. Dunne, M. McDonagh, S. Leydon, L. Sammon, S. Cleary, J. Keenan. Sub.—J. Donnellan.

Meath—S. McCormack, D. Donnelly, J. Quinn, P. Darby, P. Collier, B. Cunningham, P. Reynolds, P. Moore, T. Brown, A. Brennan, M. O'Sullivan, D. Carty (capt.), G. Quinn, N. Curran, O. Shanley. Subs.—M. White, J. Fagan, M. Quinn.

1967

Meath—S. McCormack, M. White, J. Quinn, P. Darby (capt.), P. Collier, B. Cunningham, P. Reynolds, P. Moore, T. Kearns, T. Brennan, M. Kerrigan, M. Mellett, P. Mulvaney, N. Curran, O. Shanley.

Cork—W. Morgan, B. Murphy, J. Lucey, J. O'Mahony, F. Cogan, D. Coughlan, K. Dillon, M. Burke, M. O'Loughlin, E. Philpott, E. McCarthy, B. O'Neill, E. Ryan, C. O'Sullivan, F. Hayes. Subs.—J. Carroll, J. Downing, J. J. Murphy.

1968

Down—D. Kelly, B. Sloan, D. McCartan, T. O'Hare, R. McConville, W. Doyle, J. Lennon (capt.), J. Milligan, C. McAlarney, M. Cole, P. Doherty, J. Murphy, P. Rooney, S. O'Neill, J. Purdy. Subs.—L. Powell, G. Glynn.

Kerry—J. Culloty, S. Murphy, P. O'Donoghue, S. Burrows, Denis O'Sullivan, M. Morris, D. O'Sullivan, M. O'Connell, M. Fleming, B. Lynch, P. Griffin (capt.), E. O'Donoghue, T. Prendergast, D. J. Crowley, M. O'Dwyer. Subs.—P. Moynihan, S. Fitzgerald.

Referee: M. Loftus (Mayo).

1969

Kerry—J. Culloty (capt.), S. Murphy, P. O'Donoghue, S. Fitzgerald, T. Prendergast, M. Morris, M. O'Shea, M. O'Connell, D. J. Crowley, B. Lynch, P. Griffin, E. O'Donoghue, M. Gleeson, L. Higgins, M. O'Dwyer.

Offaly—M. Furlong, P. McCormack, G. Hughes, J. Egan

333

(capt.), E. Mulligan, N. Clavin, M. Ryan, L. Coughlan, W. Bryan, P. Keenan, A. Hickey, T. McTague, S. Kilroy, S. Evans, J. Cooney. Subs.—F. Costelloe, K. Kilmurray, P. Monaghan.

Referee: J. Moloney (Tipperary).

1970

Kerry—J. Culloty, S. Murphy, P. O'Donoghue, D. O'Sullivan (capt.), T. Prendergast, J. O'Keeffe, M. O'Shea, M. O'Connell, D. J. Crowley, B. Lynch, P. Griffin, E. O'Donoghue, M. Gleeson, L. Higgins, M. O'Dwyer. Sub.—S. Fitzgerald.

Meath—S. McCormack, M. White, J. Quinn (capt.), B. Cunningham. O. Shanley, T. Kearns, P. Reynolds, V. Foley, V. Lynch, A. Brennan, M. Kerrigan, M. Mellett, K. Rennicks, J. Murphy, M. Fay. Subs.—P. Moore, W. Bligh.

Referee: P. Kelly (Dublin).

1971

Offaly—M. Furlong, M. Ryan, P. McCormack, M. O'Rourke, E. Mulligan, N. Clavin, M. Heavey, W. Bryan (capt.), K. Claffey, J. Cooney, K. Kilmurray, A. McTague, J. Gunning, S. Evans, M. Connor. Subs.—J. Smith for Claffey, P. Fenning for Gunning.

Galway—P. J. Smyth, B. Colleran, J. Cosgrove, N. Colleran, L. O'Neill, T. J. Gilmore, C. McDonagh, L. Sammon (capt.), W. Joyce, P. Burke, J. Duggan, M. Rooney, E. Farrell, F. Canavan, S. Laydon. Subs.-T. Divilly for Rooney, M. Feerick for Burke.

Referee—P. Kelly (Dublin).

1972 (Replay)

Offaly—M. Furlong, M. Ryan, P. McCormack, L. Coughlan, E. Mulligan, S. Lowry, M. Heavey, W. Bryan, S. Evans, J. Cooney, K. Kilmurray, A. McTague (capt.), S. Darby, J. Smith, P. Fenning. Subs.—Murt Connor for Cooney, N. Clavin for Mulligan, M. Wright for Coughlan.

Note: Murt Connor played in drawn game. Seamus Darby came on for replay. Jody Gunning came on as a sub in drawn game.

Kerry—E. Fitzgerald, D. O'Sullivan, P. O'Donoghue, S. Fitzgerald, T. Prendergast (capt.), M. O'Shea, P. Lynch, M. O'Connell, J. O'Keeffe, B. Lynch, D. Kavanagh, E. O'Donoghue, M. Gleeson, L. Higgins, M. O'Dwyer. Subs.—D. Crowley for S. Fitzgerald, P. Griffin for Gleeson, J. Walsh for B. Lynch.

Referee—P. Devlin (Tyrone).

Note: Kerry fielded same team in both games Derry Crowley and Pat Griffin came on as subs in drawn game, refereed by F. Tierney (Wicklow).

334

1973

Cork—B. Morgan (capt.), F. Cogan, H. Kelleher, B. Murphy, K. J. O'Sullivan, J. Coleman, C. Hartnett, D. Long, D. Coughlan, N. Kirby, D. Barron, D. McCarthy, J. Barry Murphy, R. Cummins, J. Barrett. Subs.—S. Coughlan for Coleman; D. Hunt for McCarthy; M. Scannell for Kelleher.

Galway—G. Mitchell, J. Waldron, J. Cosgrove, B. Colleran, L. O'Neill, J. Gilmore, J. Hughes, W. Joyce, J. Duggan, M. Burke, L. Sammon (capt.), M. Rooney, J. Coughlan, T. Naughton, M. Hughes. Subs.—F. Canavan for Coughlan, C. McDonagh for Burke.

Referee—J. Moloney (Tipperary).

1974

Dublin—P. Cullen, G. O'Driscoll, S. Doherty (capt.), R. Kelleher, P. Reilly, A. Larkin, G. Wilson, S. Rooney, B. Mullins, B. Doyle, T. Hanahoe, D. Hickey, J. McCarthy, J. Keaveney, A. O'Toole.

Galway—G. Mitchell (capt.), J. Waldron, J. Cosgrove, B. Colleran, L. O'Neill, T. J. Gilmore, J. Hughes, W. Joyce, M. Rooney, T. Naughton, J. Duggan, P. Sands, C. McDonagh, L. Sammon, J. Tobin. Sub.—J. Burke for McDonagh.

Referee—P. Devlin (Tyrone).

1975

Kerry—P. O'Mahony, G. O'Keeffe, J. O'Keeffe, J. Deenihan, P. O'Shea, T. Kennelly, G. Power, P. Lynch, P. McCarthy, B. Lynch, D. "Ogie" Moran, M. O'Sullivan (capt.), J. Egan, M. Sheehy, P. Spillane. Subs.—G. O'Driscoll for O'Sullivan.

Dublin—P. Cullen, G. O'Driscoll, S. Doherty (capt.), R. Kelleher, P. Reilly, A. Larkin, G. Wilson, B. Mullins, B. Brogan, A. O'Toole, T. Hanahoe, D. Hickey, J. McCarthy, J. Keaveney, P. Gogarty. Subs.—B. Doyle for Brogan, P. O'Neill for McCarthy, B. Pocock for Reilly.

Referee—John Moloney (Tipperary).

1976

Dublin—P. Cullen, G. O'Driscoll, S. Doherty, R. Kelleher, T. Drumm, K. Moran, P. O'Neill, B. Mullins, B. Brogan, A. O'Toole, T. Hanahoe (capt.), D. Hickey, B. Doyle, J. Keaveney, J. McCarthy. Subs.—F. Ryder for Hanahoe, P. Gogarty for Doyle.

Kerry—P. O'Mahoney, G. O'Keeffe (capt.), J. O'Keeffe, J. Deenihan, P. O'Shea, T. Kennelly, G. Power, P. Lynch, P.

McCarthy, D. "Ogie" Moran, M. Sheehy, M. O'Sullivan, B. Lynch, J. Egan, P. Spillane. Subs.—C. Nelligan for O'Mahoney, S. Walsh for McCarthy, G. O'Driscoll for O'Sullivan.

Referee—P. Collins (Westmeath).

1977

Dublin—P. Cullen, G. O'Driscoll, S. Doherty, R. Kelleher, T. Drumm, K. Moran, P. O'Neill, B. Mullins, B. Brogan, A. O'Toole, T. Hanahoe (capt.), D. Hickey, B. Doyle, J. Keaveney, J. McCarthy. Subs.—P. Reilly for O'Neilly, A. Larkin for Brogan, J. Brogan for Kelleher.

Armagh—B. McAlinden, D. Stevenson, T. McCreesh, J. McKerr, K. Rafferty, P. Moriarty, J. Donnelly, J. Kernan, C. McKinistry, L. Kearns, J. Smyth (capt.), N. Marley, S. Devlin, P. Trainor, P. Loughran. Subs.—J. Loughran for Donnelly, S. Daly for Marley, F. Toman for McKerr.

Referee—J. Moloney (Tipperary).

1978

Kerry—C. Nelligan, J. Deenihan, J. O'Keeffe, M. Spillane, P. O'Shea, T. Kennelly, P. Lynch, J. O'Shea, S. Walsh, G. Power, D. "Ogie" Moran (capt.), P. Spillane, M. Sheehy, E. Liston, J. Egan. Sub.—P. O'Mahoney for J. Deenihan.

Dublin—P. Cullen, G. O'Driscoll, S. Doherty, R. Kelleher, T. Drumm, K. Moran, P. O'Neill, B. Mullins, B. Brogan, A. O'Toole, T. Hanahoe (capt.), D. Hickey, B. Doyle, J. Keaveney, J. McCarthy.

Referee—S. Aldridge (Kildare).

1979

Kerry—C. Nelligan, J. Deenihan, J. O'Keeffe, M. Spillane, P. O'Shea, T. Kennelly (capt.), P. Lynch, J. O'Shea, S. Walsh, T. Doyle, D. "Ogie" Moran, P. Spillane, M. Sheehy, E. Liston, J. Egan. Subs.—V. O'Connor for O'Keeffe.

Dublin—P. Cullen, M. Kennedy, M. Holden, D. Foran, T. Drumm, F. Ryder, P. O'Neill, B. Mullins, B. Brogan, A. O'Toole, T. Hanahoe (capt.), D. Hickey, M. Hickey, B. Doyle, J. McCarthy. Subs.—J. Ronayne for M. Hickey, G. O'Driscoll for McCarthy, B. Pocock for O'Toole.

Referee—H. Duggan (Armagh).

1980

Kerry—C. Nelligan, J. Deenihan, J. O'Keeffe, P. Lynch, P. O'Shea, T. Kennelly, G. O'Keeffe, J. O'Shea, S. Walsh, G. Power (capt.), D. "Ogie" Moran, P. Spillane, M. Sheehy, T. Doyle, J. Egan. Subs.—G. O'Driscoll for Power.

Roscommon—G. Sheerin, H. Keegan, P. Lindsay, G. Connellan, G. Fitzmaurice, T. Donlon, D. Murray (capt.), D. Earley, S. Hayden, J. O'Connor, J. O'Gara, A. Dooley, M. Finneran, T. McManus, E. McManus. Subs.—M. Dolphin for Dooley, M. McDermott for Hayden.

Referee—S. Murray (Monaghan).

1981

Kerry—C. Nelligan, J. Deenihan (capt.), J. O'Keeffe, P. Lynch, P. O'Shea, T. Kennelly, M. Spillane, S. Walsh, J. O'Shea, G. Power, D. "Ogie" Moran, T. Doyle, M. Sheehy, E. Liston, J. Egan. Subs.—P. Spillane for Egan, G. O'Keeffe for M. Spillane.

Offaly—M. Furlong, M. Fitzgerald, L. Connor, C. Conroy, P. Fitzgerald, R. Connor (capt.), L. Currams, T. Connor, P. Dunne, V. Henry, G. Carroll, A. O'Halloran, Matt Connor, S. Lowry, B. Lowry.

Subs.—J. Mooney for T. Connor, J. Moran for Henry.

Referee—P. Collins (Westmeath).

1982

Offaly—M. Furlong, M. Lowry, L. Connor, M. Fitzgerald, P. Fitzgerald, S. Lowry, L. Currams, T. Connor, P. Dunne, J. Guinan, R. Connor (capt.), G. Carroll, J. Mooney, Matt Connor, B. Lowry. Subs.—Stephen Darby for M. Lowry, Seamus Darby for Guinan.

Kerry—C. Nelligan, G. O'Keeffe, J. O'Keeffe, P. Lynch, P. O'Shea, T. Kennelly, T. Doyle, J. O'Shea, S. Walsh, G. Power, T. Spillane, D. "Ogie" Moran, M. Sheehy, E. Liston, J. Egan (capt.). Subs.—P. Spillane for Moran.

Referee—P. J. McGrath (Mayo).

1983

Dublin—J. O'Leary, M. Holden, G. Hargan, R. Hazley, P. Canavan, T. Drumm (capt.), P. J. Buckley, J. Ronayne, B. Mullins, B. Rock, T. Conroy, C. Duff, J. Caffrey, A. O'Toole, J. McNally. Subs.—J. Kearns for T. Conroy; K. Maher for J. Caffrey.

Galway—P. Coyne, J. Hughes, S. Kinneavy, M. Coleman, P. O'Neill, P. Lee, S. McHugh (capt.), B. Talty, R. Lee, B. Brennan, V. Daly, B. O'Donnell, T. Tierney, G. McManus, S. Joyce.

Subs.—M. Brennan for B. Talty; W. Joyce for P. Lee; J. Tobin for J. Hughes.

Referee—J. Gough (Antrim).

337

1984
Kerry—C. Nelligan, P. O'Shea, S. Walsh, M. Spillane, T. Doyle, T. Spillane, G. Lynch, J. O'Shea, A. O'Donovan (capt.), J. Kennedy, D. "Ogie" Moran, P. Spillane, G. Power, E. Liston, J. Egan. Sub: T. O'Dowd for Egan.

Dublin—J. O'Leary, M. Holden, G. Hargan, M. Kennedy, P. Canavan, T. Drumm (capt.), P. J. Buckley, J. Ronayne, B. Mullins, B. Rock, T. Conroy, K. Duff, J. Kearns, A. O'Toole, J. McNally. Subs: M. O'Callaghan for McNally, C. Sutton for Ronayne.

Referee—Paddy Collins (Westmeath).
1985
Kerry—C. Nelligan, P. O'Shea (capt.), S. Walsh, M. Spillane, T. Doyle, T. Spillane, G. Lynch, J. O'Shea, A. O'Donovan, T. O'Dowd, D. "Ogie" Moran, P Spillane, M. Sheehy, E. Liston, G. Power. Sub: J. Kennedy for Power.

Dublin—J. O'Leary, M. Kennedy, G. Hargan, R. Hazley, P. Canavan, N. McCaffrey, D. Synnott, J. Roynane, B. Mullins (capt.), B. Rock, T. Conroy, C. Redmond, J. Kearns, J. McNally, K. Duff. Subs: T. Carr for Redmond, P. J. Buckley for Mullins.   Referee—Paddy Kavanagh (Meath).

1986
Kerry—C. Nelligan, P. O'Shea, S. Walsh, M. Spillane, T. Doyle (capt.), T. Spillane, G. Lynch, J. O'Shea, A. O'Donovan, W. Maher, D. "Ogie" Moran, P. Spillane, M. Sheehy, E. Liston, G. Power. Sub: T. O'Dowd for O'Donovan.

Tyrone—A. Skelton, J. Mallon, C. MaGarvey, J. Lynch, K. McCabe, N. McGinn, P. Ball, P. Donaghy, H. McClure, M. McClure, E. McKenna (capt.), S. McNally, M. Mallon, D. O'Hagan, P. Quinn. Subs: S. Conway for Lynch, S. Rice for McKenna, A. O'Hagan for McKenna.

Referee—Jim Dennigan (Cork).
1987
Meath—M. McQuillan, R. O'Malley, M. Lyons (capt.), T. Ferguson, K. Foley, L. Harnan, M. O'Connell, L. Hayes, G. McEntee, D. Beggy, J. Cassells, P. J. Gillic, C. O'Rourke, B. Stafford, B. Flynn. Subs: C. Coyle for Cassells, P. Lyons for O'Connell.

Cork—J. Kerins, A. Davis, C. Corrigan, D. Walsh, T. Nation, C. Counihan (capt.), N. Cahalane, S. Fahy, T. McCarthy, J. O'Driscoll, L. Tompkins, J. Kerrigan, C. O'Neill, C. Ryan, J. Cleary. Subs: J. Evans for Corrigan, T. Leahy for Fahy, P. Hayes for Ryan.   Referee—Pat Lane (Limerick).

1988 (Replay)

Meath—M. McQuillan, R. O'Malley, M. Lyons, T. Ferguson, C. Coyle, L. Harnan, M. O'Connell, L. Hayes, G. McEntee, D. Beggy, J. Cassells (capt.), P. J. Gillic, C. O'Rourke, B. Stafford, B. Flynn. Sub.: M. McCabe for Gillic.

Note: Paraic Lyons, Kevin Foley and Mattie McCabe played in drawn game when Colm Coyle, Terry Ferguson and Joe Cassells came on as subs and were on the team for the replay. Mick Lyons was captain in the drawn game.

Cork—J. Kerins, N. Cahalane, C. Corrigan, S. O'Brien, A. Davis, C. Counihan, T. Nation (Capt.), S. Fahy, T. McCarthy, P. McGrath, L. Tompkins, B. Coffey, D. Allen, D. Barry, M. McCarthy. Subs.: C. O'Neill for McCarthy; J. O'Driscoll for McGrath.

Note: Stephen O'Brien, who came on as a sub for Denis Walsh in the first half of the drawn game retained his place for the replay.   **Referee—Tommy Sugrue (Kerry).**

1989

Cork—J. Kerins, N. Cahalane, S. O'Brien, J. Kerrigan, M. Slocum, C. Counihan, T. Davis, T. McCarthy, S. Fahy, D. Barry, L. Tompkins, B. Coffey, P. McGrath, D. Allen (Capt.), J. Cleary. Subs.: J. O'Driscoll for Coffey, M. McCarthy for Fahy, J. Culloty for Cleary.

Mayo—G. Irwin, J. Browne (Capt.), P. Forde, D. Flanagan, M. Collins, T. J. Kilgallon, J. Finn, S. Maher, L. McHale, G. Maher, W. J. Padden, N. Durkin, M. Fitzmaurice, J. Burke, K. McStay. Subs.: A. Finnerty for Burke, R. Dempsey for S. Maher, B. Kilkelly for G. Maher.

Referee: P. Collins (Westmeath).

1990

Cork—J. Kerins, T. Nation, S. O'Brien, N. Cahalane, M. Slocum, C. Counihan, B. Coffey, S. Fahy, D. Culloty, D. Barry, L. Tompkins (Capt.), T. McCarthy, P. McGrath, C. O'Neill, M. McCarthy. Subs.: J. O'Driscoll for M. McCarthy, P. Hayes for Barry, J. Cleary for McGrath.

Meath—D. Smyth, B. O'Malley, M. Lyons, T. Ferguson, B. Reilly, K. Foley, M. O'Connell, L. Hayes, G. McEntee, D. Beggy, P. J. Gillic, C. Brady, C. O'Rourke (Capt.), B. Stafford, B. Flynn. Subs.: C. Coyle for Brady, J. Cassells for McEntee, T. Dowd for Beggy.

Referee: P. Russell (Tipperary).

Down—N. Collins, B. McKernan, C. Deegan, P. Higgins, P. O'Rourke (Capt.), J. Kelly, D. J. Kane, B. Breen, E. Burns, R. Carr, G. Blaney, G. Mason, M. Linden, P. Withnell, J. McCartan. Subs.: L. Austin for Breen, A. Rodgers for Withnell.

Meath—M. McQuillan, B. Reilly, M. Lyons, T. Ferguson, K. Foley, L. Harnan, M. O'Connell, L. Hayes (Capt.), G. McEntee, D. Beggy, T. Dowd, C. Coyle, P. J. Gillic, B. Stafford, B. Flynn. Subs.: C. O'Rourke for Coyle, A. Browne for Lyons, M. McCabe for Gillic.

Referee: S. Prior (Leitrim).

Donegal—G. Walsh, B. McGowan, M. Gallagher, N. Hegarty, D. Reid, M. Gavigan, J. J. Doherty, A. Molloy (Capt.), B. Murray, J. McHugh, M. McHugh, J. McMullan, D. Bonner, T. Boyle, M. Boyle, Sub.: B. Cunningham for Murray.

Dublin—J. O'Leary, M. Deegan, G. Hargan, T. Carr (Capt.), P. Curran, K. Barr, E. Heery, P. Clarke, D. Foran, C. Redmond, J. Sheedy, N. Guiden, D. Farrell, V. Murphy, M. Galvin. Sub.: P. Bealan for Foran.

Referee: T. Sugrue (Kerry).

Derry—D. McCusker, K. McKeever, T. Scullion, F. McCusker, J. McGurk, H. Downey (Capt.), G. Coleman, A. Tohill, B. McGilligan, D. Heaney, D. Barton, D. Cassidy, J. Brolly, S. Downey, E. Gormley. Subs.: D. McNicholl for Cassidy, E. Burns for S. Downey.

Cork—J. Kerins, N. Cahalane, M. O'Connor, B. Corcoran, C. O'Sullivan, S. O'Brien, T. Davis, S. Fahy, T. McCarthy, D. Davis, J. Kavanagh, B. Coffey, C. Corkery, J. O'Driscoll, M. McCarthy (Capt.). Subs.: D. Culloty for T. McCarthy, J. Cleary for M. McCarthy, C. Counihan for C. Corkery.

1888—Tipperary, w.o., Limerick (scratched)
1889—Tipperary 1-2, Cork 0-3
1890—Cork 1-4, Kerry 0-1
    Cork 0-1, Kerry 0-0 (abandoned after 57 minutes when football burst)
1891—Cork 3-2, Waterford 1-1
1892—Kerry 3-6, Cork 0-5
1893—Cork, w.o., Kerry
1894—Cork 2-4, Tipperary 0-1 (refixture)
    Cork 0-6, Tipperary 0-2 (objection)
1895—Tipperary 0-5, Limerick 0-2
1896—Limerick 0-4, Waterford 0-1
    (unfinished. Title awarded to Limerick)
1897—Cork 0-5, Limerick 0-3
1898—Waterford 1-11, Cork 1-3
1899—Cork 3-11, Tipperary 0-1 (third match)
    Cork 1-2, Tipperary 0-1 (refixture, abandoned half-time, dispute over score)
    Tipperary 2-1, Cork 0-1 (first game, abandoned half-time no ball available)
1900—Tipperary 1-14, Kerry 1-4
1901—Cork 1-9, Limerick 1-6
1902—Tipperary 1-6, Kerry 1-5
    Tipperary 1-4, Kerry 1-4 (draw)
1903—Kerry 1-7, Cork 0-3
1904—Kerry 2-3, Waterford 0-2 (replay)
    Kerry 0-3, Waterford 0-3 (draw)
1905—Kerry 2-10, Limerick 1-6
1906—Cork 1-10, Kerry 0-3
1907—Cork 1-7, Tipperary 0-1
1908—Kerry 0-7, Waterford 0-2
1909—Kerry 1-6, Cork 0-6 (replay)
    Cork 2-8, Kerry 1-7 (objection)
1910—Kerry 0-4, Cork 0-2
1911—Cork 2-5, Waterford 0-1
1912—Kerry 0-3, Clare 0-1
1913—Kerry 1-6, Cork 0-1
1914—Kerry 0-5, Cork 0-1
1915—Kerry 4-3, Clare 0-1
1916—Cork 2-2, Clare 1-4
1917—Clare 5-4, Cork 0-1

1918—Tipperary 1-1, Kerry 0-1
1919—Kerry 6-11, Clare 2-0
1920—Tipperary 2-2, Kerry 0-2
1921—No. S.F. Champinship in Munster
1922—Tipperary 1-7, Limerick 0-1
1923—Kerry 0-5, Tipperary 0-3
1924—Kerry 5-8, Clare 2-2
1925—Kerry 5-5, Clare 0-0
1926—Kerry 0-11, Tipperary 1-4
1927—Kerry 4-4, Clare 1-3
1928—Cork 4-3, Tipperary, 0-4
1929—Kerry 1-14, Clare 1-2
1930—Kerry 3-4, Tipperary 1-2
1931—Kerry 5-8, Tipperary 0-2
1932—Kerry 3-10, Tipperary 1-4
1933—Kerry 2-8, Tipperary 1-4
1934—Kerry 1-14, Limerick 1-2
1935—Tipperary 2-8, Cork 1-2
1936—Kerry 1-11, Clare 2-2
1937—Kerry 4-9, Clare 1-1
1938—Kerry 4-14, Cork 0-6
1939—Kerry 2-11, Tipperary 0-4
1940—Kerry 1-10, Waterford 0-6
1941—Kerry 2-9, Clare 0-6
1942—Kerry 3-7, Cork 0-8
1943—Cork 1-7, Tipperary 1-4
1944—Kerry 1-6, Tipperary 0-5
1945—Cork 1-11, Kerry 1-6
1946—Kerry 2-16, Waterford 2-1
1947—Kerry 3-8, Cork 2-6
1948—Kerry 2-9, Cork 2-6
1949—Cork 3-6, Clare 0-7
1950—Kerry 2-5, Cork 1-5
1951—Kerry 1-6, Cork 0-4
1952—Cork 0-11, Kerry 0-2
1953—Kerry 2-7, Cork 2-3
1954—Kerry 4-9, Cork 2-3
1955—Kerry 0-14, Cork 2-6
1956—Cork 1-8, Kerry 1-7 (replay)
         Cork 0-8, Kerry 2-2 (draw)
1957—Cork 0-16, Waterford 1-2
1958—Kerry 2-7, Cork 0-3
1959—Kerry 2-15, Cork 2-8

1960—Kerry 3-15, Waterford 0-8
1961—Kerry 2-13, Cork 1-4 (replay)
      Kerry 0-10, Cork 1-7 (draw)
1962—Kerry4-8, Cork 0-4
1963—Kerry 1-18, Cork 3-7
1964—Kerry 2-11, Cork 1-8
1965—Kerry 2-16, Limerick 2-7
1966—Cork 2-7, Kerry 1-7
1967—Cork 0-8, Kerry 0-7
1968—Kerry 1-21, Cork 3-8
1969—Kerry 0-16, Cork 1-4
1970—Kerry 2-22, Cork 2-9
1971—Cork 0-25, Kerry 0-14
1972—Kerry 2-21, Cork 2-15
1973—Cork 5-12, Kerry 1-15
1974—Cork 1-11, Kerry 0-7
1975—Kerry 1-14, Cork 0-7
1976—Kerry 3-20, Cork 2-19 (replay) (after extra time)
      Kerry 0-10, Cork 0-10 (draw)
1977—Kerry 3-15, Cork 0-9
1978—Kerry 3-14, Cork 3-7
1979—Kerry 2-14, Cork 2-4
1980—Kerry 3-13, Cork 0-12
1981—Kerry 1-11, Cork 0-3
1982—Kerry 2-18, Cork 0-12 (replay)
      Kerry 0-9, Cork 0-9 (draw)
1983—Cork 3-10, Kerry 3-9
1984—Kerry 3-14, Cork 2-10
1985—Kerry 2-11, Cork 0-11
1986—Kerry 0-12, Cork 0-8
1987—Cork 0-13, Kerry 1-5 (replay)
      Cork 1-10, Kerry 2-7 (draw)
1988—Cork 1-14, Kerry 0-16
1989—Cork 1-12, Kerry 1-9
1990—Cork 2-23, Kerry 1-11
1991—Kerry 0-23, Limerick 3-12
1992—Clare 2-10, Kerry 0-12
1993—Cork 1-16, Tipperary 1-8

CONNACHT SENIOR FINALS

1900—Galway, unopposed
1901—Mayo 2-4, Galway 0-3
1902—Mayo 2-2, Galway 0-6
1903—Awarded Galway

1904—Mayo 3-6, Roscommon 0-1
1905—Roscommon 0-7, Mayo 0-5
1906—Mayo 2-13, Roscommon 0-5
1907—Mayo 3-9, Galway 0-1
1908—Mayo 1-4, Galway 0-3
1909—Mayo 1-4, Galway 0-5
1910—Galway 1-3, Roscommon 1-2
1911—Awarded to Galway
1912—Roscommon 0-2, Galway 0-0
1913—Galway 1-2, Mayo 0-3
1914—Roscommon 1-2, Leitrim 0-1
1915—Mayo 3-1, Roscommon 1-3
1916—Mayo 1-5, Roscommon 0-3
1917—Galway 1-4, Mayo 1-1
1918—Mayo 0-4, Galway 0-1
1919—Galway 1-6, Roscommon 0-5
1920—Mayo 2-3, Sligo 1-4
1921—Mayo 1-4, Roscommon 0-1
1922—Galway 2-4, Sligo 1-5 (replay)
        Sligo 3-2, Galway 1-7 (objection, replay ordered)
1923—Mayo 0-3, Galway 0-2
1924—Mayo 2-6, Galway 0-5 (replay)
        Mayo 0-1, Galway 0-1 (draw)
1925—Galway 1-5, Mayo 1-3
1926—Galway 3-2, Mayo 1-2
1927—Leitrim 2-4, Galway 0-3
1928—Sligo 1-4, Mayo 0-6
1929—Mayo 1-6, Galway 0-4
1930—Mayo 1-7, Sligo 1-2
1931—Mayo 2-10, Roscommon 3-2
1932—Mayo 2-6, Sligo 0-7
1933—Galway 1-7, Mayo 1-5
1934—Galway 2-4, Mayo 0-5
1935—Mayo 0-12, Galway 0-5
1936—Mayo 2-7, Galway 1-4 (replay)
        Mayo 2-4, Galway 1-7 (draw)
1937—Mayo 3-5, Galway 0-8
1938—Galway 0-8, Mayo 0-5
1939—Awarded to Mayo (Mayo 2-6, Galway 0-3)
1940—Galway 1-7, Mayo 0-5
1941—Galway 0-8, Roscommon 1-4
1942—Galway 2-6, Roscommon 3-2
1943—Roscommon 2-6, Galway 0-8

1944—Roscommon 2-11, Mayo 1-6
1945—Galway 2-6, Mayo 1-7
1946—Roscommon 1-9, Mayo 1-2 (replay)
       Roscommon 1-4, Mayo 0-6 (objection, replay ordered)
1947—Roscommon 2-12, Sligo 1-8
1948—Mayo 2-10, Galway 2-7 (replay) (after extra time)
       Mayo 2-4, Galway 1-7 (draw)
1949—Mayo 4-6, Leitrim 0-3
1950—Mayo 1-7, Roscommon 0-4
1951—Mayo 4-13, Galway 2-3
1952—Roscommon 3-5, Mayo 0-6
1953—Roscommon 1-6, Mayo 0-6
1954—Galway 2-10, Sligo 3-4
1955—Mayo 3-11, Roscommon 1-3
1956—Galway 3-12, Sligo 1-5
1957—Galway 4-8, Leitrim 0-4
1958—Galway 2-10, Leitrim 1-11
1959—Galway 5-8, Leitrim 0-12
1960—Galway 2-5, Leitrim 0-5
1961—Roscommon 1-11, Galway 2-7
1962—Roscommon 3-7, Galway 2-9
1963—Galway 4-11, Leitrim 1-6
1964—Galway 2-12, Mayo 1-5
1965—Galway 1-12, Sligo 2-6
1966—Galway 0-12, Mayo 1-8
1967—Mayo 4-15, Leitrim 0-7
1968—Galway 2-10, Mayo 2-9
1969—Mayo 1-11, Galway 1-8 (replay)
       Mayo 0-11, Galway 1-8 (draw)
1970—Galway 2-15, Roscommon 1-8
1971—Galway 1-17, Sligo 3-10 (replay)
       Galway 2-15, Sligo 2-15 (draw)
1972—Roscommon 5-8, Mayo 3-10
1973—Galway 1-17, Mayo 2-12
1974—Galway 2-14, Roscommon 0-8
1975—Sligo 2-10, Mayo 0-15 (replay)
       Sligo 2-10, Mayo 1-13 (draw)
1976—Galway 1-14, Roscommon 0-9 (replay)
       Galway 1-8, Roscommon 1-8
1977—Roscommon 1-12, Galway 2-8
1978—Roscommon 2-7, Galway 0-9
1979—Roscommon 3-15, Mayo 2-10
1980—Roscommon 3-13, Mayo 0-8

FOR CRYING OUT LOUD...

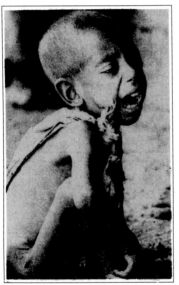

In Africa, millions have died of starvation. Millions more will follow . . . unless we help them to become self sufficient. By providing seeds, irrigation and tools, the Self Help Grow Fund helps African farmers. So if you support the Self Help Grow Fund today, there will be less hunger in the world tomorrow.

**PLEASE SUPPORT
SELF HELP**

1981—Mayo 0-12, Sligo 0-4
1982—Galway 3-17, Mayo 0-10
1983—Galway 1-13, Mayo 1-10
1984—Galway 2-13, Mayo 2-9
1985—Mayo 2-11, Roscommon 0-8
1986—Galway 1-8, Roscommon 1-5
1987—Galway 0-8, Mayo 0-7.
1988—Mayo 1-12, Roscommon 0-8
1989—Mayo 0-12, Roscommon 1-9 (draw)
        Mayo 3-14, Roscommon 2-13 (replay)
1990—Roscommon 0-16, Galway 1-11
1991—Roscommon 0-14, Mayo 0-14 (draw)
        Roscommon 0-13, Mayo 1-9 (replay)
1992—Mayo 1-14, Roscommon 0-10
1993—Mayo 1-5, Roscommon 0-7

ULSTER SENIOR FINALS

1887—No Ulster championship
1888—Monaghan 0-3, Cavan 0-1 (replay)
        Monaghan 0-2, Cavan 0-2 (draw)
1889—No Ulster championship
1890—Armagh 2-8, Tyrone 1-2
1891—Cavan 1-11, Armagh 0-0 (replay)
        (*Note:* First game unfinished, disputed goal.)
1892-'99—No Ulster championship
    (*Note:* Cavan played in Leinster in 1895.)
1900—Antrim walk over
1901—Antrim 3-5, Armagh 2-5
1902—Armagh 0-8, Antrim 0-7
1903—Cavan 0-8, Armagh 0-4 (second replay)
        Cavan 0-5, Armagh 0-5 (replay)
        Cavan 0-5, Armagh 0-5 (draw)
1904—
1905—Cavan 0-7, Monaghan 0-3
1906—Monaghan 2-10, Antrim 1-2
1907—No Final result in records.
1908—Antrim 1-8, Cavan 0-4
1909—Antrim 1-9, Cavan 0-5
1910—Antrim 3-4, Cavan 0-1
1911—Antrim 2-8, Cavan 0-4

347

1912—Antrim 2-2, Armagh 0-1
1913—Antrim 2-1, Monaghan 1-2
1914—Monaghan 2-4, Fermanagh 0-2
1915—Cavan 0-4, Monaghan 0-3 (replay)
      Cavan 3-2, Monaghan 2-5 (draw)
1916—Monaghan 3-1, Cavan 0-2
1917—Monaghan 4-2, Armagh 0-4
1918—Cavan 3-2, Antrim 0-0
1919—Cavan 5-6, Antrim 0-2
1920—Cavan 4-6, Armagh 1-4
1921—Monaghan 2-2, Derry 0-1
1922—Cavan 3-4, Monaghan 3-3 (replay)
      Cavan 2-3, Monaghan 2-3 (draw)
1923—Cavan 5-10, Monaghan 1-1
1924—Cavan 2-3, Monaghan 1-3 (replay)
      Cavan 1-3, Monaghan 0-6
1925—Cavan 3-6, Antrim 0-1 (replay)
      Cavan 2-3, Antrim 3-0 (draw)
1926—Cavan 5-3, Antrim 0-6
1927—Monaghan 3-5, Armagh 2-5
1928—Cavan 2-6, Armagh 1-4
1929—Monaghan 1-10, Cavan 0-7 (replay)
      Monaghan 1-4, Cavan 1-4 (draw)
1930—Monaghan 4-3, Cavan 1-5
1931—Cavan 0-8, Armagh 2-1
1932—Cavan 2-4, Armagh 0-1
1933—Cavan 6-13, Tyrone 1-2
1934—Cavan 3-8, Armagh 0-2
1935—Cavan 2-6, Fermanagh 2-1
1936—Cavan 1-7, Monaghan 0-7
1937—Cavan 0-13, Armagh 0-3
1938—Monaghan 2-5, Armagh 2-2
1939—Cavan 2-3, Armagh 1-4 (replay)
      Cavan 2-3, Armagh 1-3 (first game)
      (*Note:* Replay ordered, game unfinished.)

1940—Cavan 4-10, Down 1-5
1941—Cavan 3-9, Tyrone 0-5
1942—Cavan 5-11, Down 1-3
1943—Cavan 2-3, Monaghan 0-5
1944—Cavan 1-9, Monaghan 0-5
1945—Cavan 4-10, Fermanagh 1-4
1946—Antrim 2-8, Cavan 1-7

1947—Cavan 3-4, Antrim 1-6
1948—Cavan 2-12, Antrim 2-4
1949—Cavan 1-7, Armagh 1-6
1950—Armagh 1-11, Cavan 1-7
1951—Antrim 1-7, Cavan 2-3
1952—Cavan 1-8, Monaghan 0-8
1953—Armagh 1-6, Cavan 0-5
1954—Cavan 2-10, Armagh 2-5
1955—Cavan 0-11, Derry 0-8
1956—Tyrone 3-5, Cavan 0-4
1957—Tyrone 1-9, Derry 0-10
1958—Derry 1-11, Down 2-4
1959—Down 2-16, Cavan 0-7
1960—Down 3-7, Cavan 1-8
1961—Down 2-10, Armagh 1-10
1962—Cavan 3-6, Down 0-5
1963—Down 2-11, Donegal 1-4
1964—Cavan 2-10, Down 1-10
1965—Down 3-5, Cavan 1-8
1966—Down 1-7, Donegal 0-8
1967—Cavan 2-12, Down 0-8
1968—Down 0-16, Cavan 1-8
1969—Cavan 2-13, Down 2-6
1970—Derry 2-13, Antrim 1-12
1971—Down 4-15, Derry 4-11
1972—Donegal 2-13, Tyrone 1-11
1973—Tyrone 3-13, Down 1-11
1974—Donegal 3-9, Down 1-12 (replay)
      Donegal 1-14, Down 2-11 (draw)
1975—Derry 1-16, Down 2-6
1976—Derry 0-22, Cavan 1-16 (replay) (after extra time)
      Derry 1-8, Cavan 1-8 (draw)
1977—Armagh 3-10, Derry 1-5
1978—Down 2-19, Cavan 2-12
1979—Monaghan 1-15, Donegal 0-11
1980—Armagh 4-10, Tyrone 4-7
1981—Down 3-12, Armagh 1-10
1982—Armagh 0-10, Fermanagh 1-4
1983—Donegal 1-14, Cavan 1-11
1984—Tyrone 0-15, Armagh 1-7
1985—Monaghan 2-9, Derry 0-8
1986—Tyrone 1-11, Down 0-10

1987—Derry 0-11, Armagh 0-9
1988—Monaghan 1-10, Tyrone 0-11
1989—Tyrone 0-11, Donegal 0-11 (draw)
      Tyrone 2-13, Donegal 0-7 (replay)
1990—Donegal 0-15, Armagh 0-14
1991—Down 1-15, Donegal 0-10
1992—Donegal 0-14, Derry 1-9
1993—Derry 0-8, Donegal 0-6

LEINSTER SENIOR FINALS

1887—No Final, open draw.
1888—Kilkenny 1-4, Wexford 0-2
1889—Laois 0-3, Louth 0-2
1890—Wexford 1-3, Dublin 1-2
1981—Dublin w.o. Kildare (scratched)
1892—Dublin w.o. Louth (scratched)
1893—Kilkenny 0-5, Wexford 0-1 (unfinished – Wexford
      awarded title)
1894—Dublin 1-8, Meath 1-2 (second replay)
      Dublin 0-2, Meath 0-2 (replay)
      Dublin 0-4, Meath 0-4 (draw)
1895—Meath 0-6, Dublin 0-2
1896—Dublin 2-4, Meath 1-5
1897—Dublin 1-9, Wicklow 0-3
1898—Dublin 2-6, Wexford 0-0
1899—Dublin 1-7, Wexford 0-3
1900—Kilkenny 0-12, Louth 0-0
1901— Dublin 1-9, Wexford 0-1
1902—Dublin 1-5, Wexford 0-5 (replay)
      Dublin 2-4, Wexford 0-2 (unfinished, replay ordered)
1903—Kildare 0-9, Kilkenny 0-1 (second replay)
      Kildare 1-6, Kilkenny 1-5 (point disputed)
      Kildare 1-2, Kilkenny 0-5 (draw)
1904—Dublin 0-5, Kilkenny 0-1
1905—Kildare 1-8, Louth 1-7
1906—Dublin 1-9, Kildare 0-8
1907—Dublin 1-11, Offaly 0-4
1908—Dublin 1-7, Kildare 0-3
1909—Louth 2-9, Kilkenny 0-4
1910—Louth 0-3, Dublin 0-0
1911—Kilkenny 2-4, Meath 1-1

1912—Louth 1-2, Dublin 1-1
1913—Wexford 3-6, Louth 0-1
1914—Wexford 0-3, Louth 0-1
1915—Wexford 3-5, Dublin 1-3 (replay)
      Wexford 2-2, Dublin 2-2 (draw)
1916—Wexford 1-7, Kildare 1-0
1917—Wexford 1-3, Dublin 1-1
1918—Wexford 2-5, Louth 1-4
1919—Kildare 1-3, Dublin 1-2
1920—Dublin 1-3, Kildare 0-3
1921—Dublin 3-3, Kildare 1-2 (replay)
      Dublin 0-6, Kildare 1-3 (draw)
1922—Dublin 1-7, Kilkenny 0-2
1923—Dublin 3-5, Meath 0-0
1924—Dublin 3-5, Wexford 2-3 (replay)
      Dublin 1-4, Wexford 1-4 (draw)
1925—Wexford 2-7, Kildare 0-3
1926—Kildare 2-8, Wexford 1-5
1927—Kildare 0-5, Dublin 0-3
1928—Kildare 0-10, Dublin 1-6
1929—Kildare 2-3, Laois 0-6
1930—Kildare 2-6, Meath 1-2 (replay)
      Kildare 0-6, Meath 1-3 (draw)
1931—Kildare 2-9, Westmeath 1-6
1932—Dublin 4-6, Wexford 1-5 (replay)
      Dublin 0-8, Wexford 1-5 (draw)
1933—Dublin 0-9, Wexford 1-4
1934—Dublin 2-9, Louth 1-10 (second replay)
      Dublin 3-2, Louth 2-5 (replay)
      Dublin 1-2, Louth 0-5 (draw)
1935—Kildare 0-8, Louth 0-6
1936—Laois 3-3, Kildare 0-8
1937—Laois 0-12, Louth 0-4
1938—Laois 2-8, Kildare 1-3
1939—Meath 2-7, Wexford 2-3
1940—Meath 2-7, Laois 1-7
1941—Dublin 4-6, Carlow 1-4
1942—Dublin 0-8, Carlow 0-6
1943—Louth 3-16, Laois 2-4
1944—Carlow 2-6, Dublin 1-6
1945—Wexford 1-9, Offaly 1-4
1946—Laois 0-11, Kildare 1-6
1947—Meath 3-7, Laois 1-7

351

Shop catalogue available from
Séamus Ó Midheach at

Cumann Lúthchleas Gael
Páirc an Chrócaigh, Baile Átha Cliath 3
Telefón (01) 363222

1948—Louth 2-10, Wexford 2-5
1949—Meath 4-5, Westmeath 0-6
1950—Louth 3-5, Meath 0-13 (replay)
      Louth 1-3, Meath 1-3 (draw)
1951—Meath 4-9, Laois 0-3
1952—Meath 1-6, Louth 0-8
1953—Louth 1-7, Wexford 0-7
1954—Meath 4-7, Offaly 2-10
1955—Dublin 5-12, Meath 0-7
1956—Kildare 2-11, Wexford 1-8
1957—Louth 2-9, Dublin 1-7
1958—Dublin 1-11, Louth 1-6
1959—Dublin 1-18, Laois 2-8
1960—Offaly 0-10, Louth 1-6
1961—Offaly 1-13, Dublin 1-8
1962—Dublin 2-8, Offaly 1-7
1963—Dublin 2-11, Laois 2-9
1964—Meath 2-12, Dublin 1-7
1965—Dublin 3-6, Longford 0-9
1966—Meath 1-9, KIldare 1-8
1967—Meath 0-8, Offaly 0-6
1968—Longford 3-9, Laois 1-4
1969—Offaly 3-7, Kildare 1-8.
1970—Meath 2-22, Offaly 5-12
1971—Offaly 2-14, Kildare 0-6
1972—Offaly 1-18, Kildare 2-8
1973—Offaly 3-21, Meath 2-12
1974—Dublin 1-14, Meath 1-9
1975—Dublin 3-13, Kildare 0-8
1976—Dublin 2-8, Meath 1-9
1977—Dublin 1-9, Meath 0-8
1978—Dublin 1-17, Kildare 1-6
1979—Dublin 1-8, Offaly 0-9
1980—Offaly 1-10, Dublin 1-8
1981—Offaly 1-18, Laois 3-9
1982—Offaly 1-16, Dublin 1-7
1983—Dublin 2-13, Offaly 1-11
1984—Dublin 2-10, Meath 1-9
1985—Dublin 0-10, Laois 0-4
1986—Meath 0-9, Dublin 0-7
1987—Meath 1-13, Dublin 0-12
1988—Meath 2-5, Dublin 0-9
1989—Dublin 2-12, Meath 1-10

1990—Meath 1-14, Dublin 0-14
1991—Meath 1-11, Laois 0-8
1992—Dublin 1-13, Kildare 0-10
1993—Dublin 0-11, Kildare 0-7

ALL-IRELAND MINOR FOOTBALL FINALS

1929—Clare 5-3, Longford 3-5.
1930—Dublin 1-3, Mayo 0-5.
1931—Kerry 3-4, Louth 0-4.
1932—Kerry 3-8, Laois 1-3.
1933—Kerry 4-1, Mayo 0-9.
1934—Tipperary awarded title.
1935—Mayo 1-6, Tipperary 1-1.
1936—Louth 5-1, Kerry 1-8.
1937—Cavan 1-11, Wexford 1-5.
1938—Cavan 3-3, Kerry 0-8.
1939—Roscommon 1-9, Monaghan 1-7.
1940—Louth 5-5, Mayo 2-7.
1941—Roscommon 3-6, Louth 0-7.
1942—No competition.
1943—No competition.
1944—No competition.
1945—Dublin 4-7, Leitrim 0-4.
1946—Kerry 3-7, Dublin 2-3.
1947—Tyrone 4-4, Mayo 4-3.
1948—Tyrone 0-11, Dublin 1-5.
1949—Armagh 1-7, Kerry 1-5.
1950—Kerry 3-6, Wexford 1-4.
1951—Roscommon 2-7, Armagh 1-5.
1952—Galway 2-9, Cavan 1-6.
1953—Mayo 2-11, Clare 1-6.
1954—Dublin 3-3, Kerry 1-8.
1955—Dublin 5-4, Tipperary 2-7.
1956—Dublin 5-14, Leitrim 2-2.
1957—Meath 3-9, Armagh 0-4.
1958—Dublin 2-10, Mayo 0-8.
1959—Dublin 0-11, Cavan 1-4.
1960—Galway 4-9, Cork 1-5.
1961—Cork 3-7, Mayo 0-5.

1962—Kerry 6-5, Mayo 0-7.
1963—Kerry 1-10, Westmeath 0-2.
1964—Offaly 0-15, Cork 1-11.
1965—Derry 2-8, Kerry 2-4.
1966—Mayo 1-12, Down 1-8.
1967—Cork 5-14, Laois 2-3.
1968—Cork 3-5, Sligo 1-10.
1969—Cork 2-7, Derry 0-11.
1970—Galway 1-8, Kerry 2-5 (draw).
        Galway 1-11, Kerry 1-10
        (replay).
1971—Mayo 2-15, Cork 2-7.
1972—Cork 3-11, Tyrone 2-11.
1973—Tyrone 2-11, Kildare 1-6.
1974—Cork 1-10, Mayo 1-6.
1975—Kerry 1-10, Tyrone 0-4.
1976—Galway 1-10, Cork 0-6.
1977—Down 2-6, Meath 0-4.
1978—Mayo 4-9, Dublin 3-8.
1979—Dublin 0-10, Kerry 1-6.
1980—Kerry 3-12, Derry 0-11.
1981—Cork 4-9, Derry 2-7.
1982—Dublin 1-11, Kerry 1-5.
1983—Derry 0-8, Cork 1-3.
1984—Dublin 1-9, Tipperary 0-4.
1985—Mayo 3-3, Cork 0-9.
1986—Galway 3-8, Cork 2-7.
1987—Down 1-12, Cork 1-5.
1988—Kerry 2-5, Dublin 0-5
1989—Derry 3-9, Offaly 1-6
1990—Meath 2-11, Kerry 2-9
1991—Cork 1-9, Mayo 1-7
1992—Meath 2-5, Armagh 0-10
1993—Cork 2-7, Meath 0-9

ALL-IRELAND MINOR FOOTBALL FINAL TEAMS
(1929-1993)
1929

Clare—T. Crowe, J. O'Leary, G. Comerford, E. Kelly, J. McMahon, D. Twomey, J. Keane, L. Conlon, J. Morgan, J. Kilmartin, J. Lucey, P. Keane, P. Lucey, P. Stack, J. Brown.

Longford—B. Phipps, A. Vaughan, J. Mulvey, J. Lyons, J. Quinn, J. Sheridan, P. Keenan, P. Farrell, J. Barden, W. Clarke, T. McHale, P. McLoughlin, M. Barden, W. Farrell, J. Smith.

1930

Dublin—B. Synott, G. McLoughlin, T. Sharkey, K. Barry, S. O'Toole, T. Markham, T. Lawless, J. Scott, P. Diffney, W. Fallon, W. Baston, B. Murphy, M. Grimes, J. Pearse, P. Castian, F. Williams, J. Brady, P. Crummey.

Mayo—John O'Gara, C. Gannon, C. Ward, G. Ormsby, C. McHale, John Acton, J. O'Donoghue, M. Flannery, C. O'Boyle, Jas. McGowan, T. Burke, W. Dever, P. McGoff, B. Scanlon, Martin O'Connor.

1931

Kerry—B. Reidy, F. O'Neill, P. Walsh, E. Mahony, D. J. McCarthy, J. O'Keeffe, T. O'Sullivan, J. O'Gorman, P. McMahon, T. Murphy, P. O'Sullivan, M. Buckley, T. Chute, C. O'Sullivan, B. Healy.

Louth—P. McDonnell, J. Tiernan, J. Hearty, J. Beirne, L. Dyas, G. Marley, J. Kelly, J. Caffrey, K. McArdle, P. Collier, - Fearon, A. Dempsey, G. Watters, J. Harlin, A. Bradley.

1932

Kerry—B. Reidy, F. O'Neill, E. Healy, J. P. Doyle, P. McMahon, P. Ronan, S. McCarthy, J. O'Sullivan, T. Weir, P. McMahon (Listowel), T. Wrenn, P. Ferriter, M. Brosnan, T. Leary, C. O'Sullivan.

Laois—E. Roche, P. Hinchion, J. Hyland, W. Troy, J. Nolan, M. Fanning, J. Shortt, S. Harkins, P. Mulhall, W. Delaney, J. J. Delaney, J. J. Reilly, J. Meehan, M. Cahill, T. Kehoe.

1933

Kerry—B. Reidy, M. O'Gorman, M. McCarthy, L. Crowley, S. Sullivan, W. Myers, T. O'Leary, W. Dillon, S. Brosnan, E. Buckley, B. Cronin, D. Griffin, W. Fitzgibbon, P. Kennedy, J. Counihan.

Mayo—W. McHale, Joe Murphy, J. O'Neill, J. O'Donoghue, B. Duggan, J. Munnelly, J. Wright, P. Murphy, W. Mongey, M. Gallagher, J. Bracken, R. Winters, J. J. Kilroy, T Hoban, M. Griffin.

1934

Tipperary—A. Greensmith, J. O'Connor, W. Power, M. Byrne, H. O'Donnell, J. Hickey, M. Lawlor, H. McGrath, T. Kenny, C. Dillon, M. Gavin, J. Maher, M. Power, P. Blanchfield, B. Kissane.
DUBLIN/TYRONE Disqualified.

1935

Mayo—T. Hannon, P. J. Irwin, D. Egan, M. J. Kearney, D. McNamara, W. Durkin, P. O'Malley, P. J. Judge, J. Galvin, J. McLoughlin, P. J. Roche, M. O'Malley, P. McNicholls, J. Keane, P. Quinn.

Tipperary—M. Gavin, E. O'Meara, W. Treacy, H. Greensmith, E. Smith, P. Quinn, M. Flynn, W. McCarthy, P. Dillon, J. Hickey, P. Rafferty, T. Kenny, W. Hennessy, W. O'Donoghue, W. Power.

1936

Louth—F. Rock, A. Lynn, P. Tuite, B. O'Dowda, L. Byrne, M. Cunningham, L. McEntee, L. Waller, J. O'Reilly, G. Hall, E. McGrath, D. Brady, K. O'Dowda, G. Cunningham, M. McArdle.

Kerry—G. Teahan, P. Dowling, P. Kennedy, T. Healy, J. Keohane, S. O'Sullivan, T. Lyne, T. O'Connor, T. Healy, T. O'Sullivan, P. Breen, P. Sexton, B. Scannell, T. Brosnan, W. Casey.

1937

Cavan—J. J. Brady, M. Argue, B. Cully, T. Cully, P. Clarke, M. O'Reilly, T. P. O'Reilly, P. O'Reilly, D. Brady, P. Conaty, H. Bouchier, P. McDonald, J. McCormack, P. Farrell, P. Fay.

Wexford—M. Keogh, J. Dwyer, M. Butler, H. Kenny, D. Hall, T. Hurley, J. Morris, J. Murphy, P. Foley, P. Dunbar, T. Redmond, W. Howlin, J. Williams, S. Rice, S. Thorpe.

1938

Cavan—J. D. Benson, W. Doonan, B. Cully, P. P. Galligan, M. Reilly, P. Coyle, S. Deignan, J. Maguire, J. McCormack, K.

O'Reilly, P. Conaty, M. Fitzsimons, F. Coyle, J. Johnson, P. Doyle.
Kerry—O. Brien, P. Burke, E. Dunne, T. Long, P. O'Donnell, M. Farrell, D. Kavanagh, T. O'Connor, J. Flavin, D. Rice, M. O'Shea, J. Bailey, T. Lyne, M. Fitzgerald, M. Kennedy.

1939

Roscommon—S. Naughton, L. Cummins, W. Carlos, D. Boyd, P. Sweeney, L. Gilmartin, A. Murray, T. Lynch, S. Lavin, C. O'Beirne, J. Tiernan, J. McDermott, J. Bambrick, G. Kilduff, H. Winston.
Monaghan—P. Farrell, D. Hughes, Phill Donoghue, D. Marron, J. McKeogh, O. King, V. Flanagan, P. Ruttledge, D. Rice, F. McCormack, J. McGeogh, P. McCartney, J. Woods, P. McKenna, J. McHugh.

1940

Louth—C. Brown, D. Breen, B. Burke, M. Flanagan, B. Fretwell, E. Reay, O. Mahon, L. Murphy, P. J. Kelly, A. Cahill, S. McGovern, P. Corr, P. McCourt, J. Kiernan, J. G. Brennan,
Mayo—A. Breslin, M. Galvin, C. Long, J. McLaughlin, T. Acton, F. Mongey, S. Durkin, M. Langan, J. Forkin, J. Ralph, J. J. McGowan, A. O'Malley, J. Jennings, T. Byrne, D. Loughrey. Sub.: P. Browne.

1941

Roscommon: G. Dolan, T. F. Bannon, T. J. Lynch, L. Kelly, P. Donnelly, B. Lynch, P. Hoare, W. Carlos, E. Curran, B. O'Gara, P. Duignan, B. O'Rourke, C. Murray, G. Kilduff, P. Hanley.
Louth—J. Allen, J. P. Grist, J. Mulligan, W. Pigott, J. Larkin, M. O'Grady, J. Clarke, B. O'Dowda, P. McCourt, P. Corr, J. McArlan, A. Cahill, E. Boyle, M. Hardy, J. O'Reilly. Sub.: P. Kelly

1945

Dublin—C. Freeney, D. O'Mahony, J. Sharry, G. Jennings, N. Maher, D. Healy, T. Nolan, S. McEntaggert, S. Guinan, L. Donnelly, O. Freeney, J. Nugent, J. Copeland, P. McCarthy, L. Dignam.

Leitrim—F. Heeran, T. P. Reynolds, J. Bohan, M. Dolan, J. Brennan, S. Mulvey, T. Cryan, J. Heslin, H. O'Beirne, P. Donlan, M. Fallon, B. McTiernan, M. J. McKeown, K. Hanratty, C. Cassidy. Subs.: P. Canning, L. de Loin.

1946

Kerry: J. Ryan, S. McCarthy, B. O'Sullivan, D. Murphy, S. O'Sullivan, D. Sheehan, J. Fenton, T. Moriarty, T. Ashe, M. Lynch, D. O'Regan, P. O'Sullivan, J. O'Brien, J. Madden, P. Godley.

Dublin—C. Freeney, D. O'Mahony, P. Lawlor, P. Cloonan, J. Butler, J. Lavin, B. Clancy, N. Fingleton, N. Maher, L. Donnelly, O. Freeney, D. Stanley, K. Heffernan, N. Clohessy, C. Mehigan.

1947

Tyrone—M. Bradley, L. Campbell, R. McNulty, V. Cullen, M. Vaughan, E. Devlin, M. Cushenan, S. McGrath, J. Poyntz, H. Hartop, M. Dargan, J. McConnell, D. McCafferty, T. Sullivan, P. Donnelly.

Mayo—A. O'Toole, M. Kinnane, P. Flanagan, M. Jordan, A. McMorris, P. Doherty, N. Keane, M. McDonnell, T. Walsh, M. Loughnane, P. Carroll, C. McHale, L. Flynn, P. Solan, M. O'Connell.

1948

Tyrone—J. McGoughran, D. Donnelly, Mal Connolly, E. Knox, Louis Campbell, E. Devlin, P. O'Hanlon, S. McGrath, H. Hartop, J. O'Reilly, M. Dargan, B. Eastwood, Leo Devlin, J. J. O'Hagan, J. Twomey. Sub.: S. Donnelly.

Dublin—P. King, P. Connolly, K. Lougheed, G. Brogan, W. Fleming, S. Page, P. McGahan, T. Jennings, C. Freaney, B. Conboy, D. Ferguson, J. Kelly, P. Ryan, D. Carney, B. Redmond. Sub.: J. Guidon.

1949

Armagh—L. McCorry, E. McCann, J. Bratton, J. McKnight, F. Kernan, B. O'Neill, T. McConville, E. Mee, S. Collins, T. Connolly, S. Blaney, J. Cunningham, S. Smith, P. J. McKeever, B. McGrane. Sub.: M. McKnight.

Kerry—J. Foley, J. O'Shea, P. Colgan, M. Galway, M. Kerins, J. Moriarty, P. Costello, J. Murphy, D. Falvey, P. Coleman, P. O'Donnell, P. Sheehy, B. Galvin, T. Lawlor, P. Fitzgerald.

1950

Kerry—D. O'Neill, M. Galway, M. Brosnan, J. Collins,T. Murphy, P. O'Donnell, J. Kerins, S. Murphy, P. Sheehy, R. Millar, C. Kennelly, C. O'Riordan, B. Galvin, T. Lawlor, P. Fitzgerald.

Wexford: T. O'Sullivan, M. O'Donoghue, R. McCabe, M. Hyde, M. Culliton, A. Doyle, J. Synott, P. O'Kennedy, B. McGuinness, W. Bennett, L. Larkin, P. Sheehan, J. O'Sullivan, P. Jordan, J. Doran.

1951

Roscommon—P. Muldoon, O. Murray, J. Lynch, E. O'Connor, B. Molloy, T. Finnegan, G. Healy, H. Connolly, J. Rafferty, J. O'Brien, J. Campbell, E. Duignan, L. Duffy, M. Shivnan, H. Penny.

Armagh—G. Murphy, G. Donnelly, B. Seeley, P. Moore, D. Skelton, E. Quinn, M. Grimley, B. O'Neill, S. McCresh, A. Dilllon, S. Hanratty, S. Crossey, P. Kickham, P. McArdle, D. McCorry. Sub.: S. McMahon.

1952

Galway—M. Ryan, B. Naughton, S. Kyne, S. Hoban, M. Lohan, E. Dunleavy, M. Hawkshaw, M. Kelly, B. Mahon, T. Brosnan, S. Mitchell, L. Manning, B. Waldron, G. Kirwan, M. Geraghty.

Cavan—S. Frawley, P. O'Hare, S. Farrelly, P. A. Farrell, D. Kelly, B. Brady, S. Keoghan, T. Maguire, G. Keyes, S. Farrelly, G. Smythe, V. Blythe, G. Fitzpatrick, M. McKenna, S. McDonald.

1953

Mayo—S. Stewart, P. Gavin, S. Veldon, F. Fahy, W. Joyce, J. Jennings, B. Keane, D. Keane, M. Stewart, E. Neilan, T. Treacy, V. Blyth, V. Kilcullen, C. McDonnell, E. Walsh. Sub.: M. Tuohy.

Clare—M. Garry, J. Carmody, T. Griffin, D. Fitzgerald, J. Power, T. Mangan, S. Barrett, P. O'Dea, M. Greene, P. Griffin, F. Cassidy, J. Drury, T. Flynn, C. Comer, M. McGrath. Subs.: P. Daly, A. Slattery.

1954

Dublin—R. Brady, M. Bohan, B. O'Boyle, D. Sweeney, M. Bracken, N. Boylan, M. Cronin, B. McLaughlin, P. Heron, V.

Bell, P. Farnan, A. Kavanagh, G. O'Reilly, P. Feeney, C. Waters. Subs.: E. Gilbert, V. Lyons.

Kerry—M. Cournane, T. Barrett, J. Dowling, L. Cloghlan, B. Kennelly, P. Shea, F. O'Leary, T. Long, J. Foley, T. O'Dowd, J. Cullotty, F. Lynch, T. Garvey, B. Sheehy, G. White. Sub.: T. Foley.

1955

Dublin—S. Denigan, V. Murphy, D. Sweeney, D. Hearns, R. Doherty, S. Graham, C. Jones, P. Heron, L. Foley, E. Burgess, S. Linehan, C. McSweeney, J. Joyce, G. Wolfe, C. Leaney. Sub.: Boyle.

Tipperary—S. Ryan, G. King, S. Condon, P. Burke, S. Connolly, T. Walsh, D. Stapleton, P. Tobin, L. Boland, A. Danagher, E. Casey, M. Moroney, M. Ryan, S. Ferris, S. Brennan. Sub.: P. Nolan.

1956

Dublin—D. Creed, A. Talbot, P. Lacey, D. Hearns, R. Doherty, D. Cashel, V. Kavanagh, L. Foley, S. Lenihan, J. Brogan, D. Foley, N. Fox, R. McCrea, G. Wolfe, C. Leaney. Sub. P. Dennis.

Leitrim—L. Feehily, S. Bredin, T. Fallon, P. McGloin, W. McWeeney, P. McGowan, S. Fallon, P. Heslin, J. Murray, L. Foran, J. O'Donnell, P. Dolan, P. McIntyre, F. Canning, P. Conboy. Sub.: S. Clyne.

1957

Meath—P. J. O'Reilly, T. Gibney, J. Kelleher, B. Cunningham, J. Fagan, T. Fitzsimons, M. Clerkin, J. Halpin, S. Clinch, P. Hanley, J. Grey, B. Cahill, T. Monaghan, M. Greville, L. Drumm.

Armagh—J. Finnegan, S. McConville, A. Bennett, B. Connolly, F. Toal, B. Donaghy, A. Casey, O. Agnew, R. Dowds, S. Mallon, S. Murphy, H. Loughran, B. McGeary, K. Halpenny, S. Toner. Subs.: N. Greene, C. McNiece.

1958

Dublin—K. Donnelly, N. Joyce, P. Holden, D. Mulligan, D. Jones, A. Whelan, M. Kissane, D. Foley, A. O'Reilly, P. Taylor, N. Fox, B. McDonald, J. Sweeney, A. Gilroy, B. Beggs. Sub.: S. Behan.

Mayo—K. Doherty, M. O'Boyle, M. Sweeney, M. Tighe, J.

Rowe, L. Doherty, C. Maguire, T. Rochford, J. Rowe, J. Corcoran, T. Gibbons, J. Cosgrove, M. Lyons, J. Langan, P. Sheridan. Sub.: A. O'Connell, P. Griffin.

1959

Dublin—P. Talbot, E. Grainger, A. Doran, F. McCourt, M. Campion, M. Kissane, F. Byrne, S. Behan, J. Levins, P. Delaney, B. McDonald, J. Dowling, J. McKettrick, G. McCabe, S. Coen. Subs.: B. Cooney, P. Taylor.

Cavan—S. Boyle, F. Cafferty, F. McKiernan, F. O'Reilly, P. Flood, T. Morris, F. Kennedy, B. Morris, P. McCluskey, B. Sherlock, D. Brady, K. Blessing, L. McCluskey,K. McCormack, P. Murray. Subs.: T. McTiernan, G. O'Reilly.

1960

Galway—M. King, G. Lohan, N. Tierney, L. O'Brien, E. Colleran, A. Ryan, S. Smith, A. Anderson, S. Cleary, C. Tyrell, G. Prendergast, S. Leydon, S. Gavin, E. Slattery, A. Donnelly.

Cork—T. Hegarty, J. Burke, J. McGrath, V. Cronin, P. Pyne, E. O'Connor, G. Harrington, M. O'Brien, P. Curely, J. Travers, B. Coughlan, B. Larkin, T. Burke, E. Coughlan, T. Monaghan. Subs.: D. Buckley, D. Nangle.

1961

Cork—R. Cawley, D. Nangle, J. McGrath, V. Cronin, G. Harrington, B. Larkin, J. O'Donoghue, F. Cogan, E. Coughlan, F. Hayes, D. Barrett, D. Philpott, T. Burke, M. Archer, T. Monaghan.

Mayo—H. O'Brien, C. Hanley, B. Reape, S. Murphy, E. Carroll, G. Nicholson, V. Nally, J. Langan, J. Madden, D. McSweeney, M. Connaughton, P. J. McLoughlin, J. Nealon, E. Maguire, J. Warde. Subs.: D. Carroll, M. O'Malley.

1962

Kerry—S. Fitzgerald, D. Lovett, C. O'Connor, S. Burrowes, T. Fitzgerald, P. O'Donoghue, A. Burrowes, D. O'Sullivan, T. Doyle, S. O'Mahony, A. Barrett, D. O'Shea, S. Flavin, R. O'Donnell, T. Mulvihill. Subs.: S. Corridon, T. Kenneally.

Mayo—L. McEllin, A. Brett, J. Early, D. O'Leary, N. Golden, M. Brennan, E. Carroll, M. Connaughton, M. O'Malley, F. McDonald, P. Costello, C. Dolan, N. Maguire, D. McSweeney, J. J. Cribben. Sub.: T. Staunton.

1963

Kerry—S. Fitzgerald, A. Behan, J. McCarthy, S. Burrowes, T. O'Shea, B. Burrowes, C. O'Riordan, D. O'Sullivan, G. Curran, T. O'Hanlon, A. Spring, J. Saunders, T. Kelleher, H. McKinney, C. Donnelly. Subs.: M. O'Sullivan, S. O'Shea.

Westmeath—K. Higgins, B. Glynn, P. Malone, T. King, S. Murray, P. Bradley, R. Cornally, G. Frawley, R. Niland, P. Buckley, F. Connaughton, C. Kelly, J. V. Costello, C. Coffey, M. Fagan. Subs: T. Reeves, D. Hamm.

1964

Offaly—M. Furlong, S. Coughlan, S. Smith, M. Ryan, E. Mulligan, S. Grogan, L. Duffy, O. Kilmurray, F. Greene, W. Bryan, A. McTeague, J. Gunning, E. Kennedy, P. McIntyre, M. Byrne. Sub.: M. O'Rourke.

Cork—T. Murphy, R. Kelly, J. Cawley, P. Lyne, B. O'Brien, N. O'Donovan, Coleman McCarthy, J. Cogan, J. Downing, E. Philpott, T. F. Hayes, C. Roche, B. O'Leary, L. McAuliffe, Charlie McCarthy. Sub.: D. Bermingham.

1965

Derry—E. McCaul, A. Burke, T. Quinn, M. Kelly, C. Mullen, M. McAfee, A. McGuckian, T. Diamond, S. Lagan, B. Mullen, M. Niblock, E. Coleman, S. Kearney, S. McCluskey, P. Friel.

Kerry—B. Lynch, J. O'Sullivan, J. Coughlan, T. Crean, P. O'Donovan, M. Aherne, P. Scanlon, P. O'Connell, F. Moroney, R. Geaney, D. Moriarty, B. McCarthy, K. Griffin, G. O'Donnell, T. Kelleher. Sub.: S. O'Connor.

1966

Mayo—E. Rooney, S. Hughes, T. Snee, B. Meenehan, G. Nevin, T. McCafferky, B. McHale, S. O'Dowd, A. Joyce, J. Timoney, T. Fitzgerald, D. Griffith, P. Glavey, J. Smyth, A. Kelly. Sub.: S. Kilbride.

Down—J. Harte, S. Brennan, L. Sloan, H. Smith, B. Sloan, C. McAlarney, D. Curan, J. Murphy, D. Mooney, J. Purdy, N. Millar, M. Cole. M. Lavery, P. Rooney, J. Morgan. Sub.: H. McGrath.

1967

Cork—M. Cotter, S. Looney, Ted Murphy, J. Fahy, Der Cogan, S. Murphy, K. Kehilly, Donal Aherne, D. Long, Jerry Horgan, D. Hunt, J. Barrett, D. Morley, N. Kirby, Ted O'Brien. Sub.: David Aherne.

Laois—A. Burke, M. Murphy, P. Fingleton, J. Mangan, J. Kavanagh, W. Monaghan, C. Murphy, S. Fleming, I. Houlihan, S. Furey, R. Millar, S. Allen, E. Condron, J. Lawlor, T. Keane. Sub.: C. McEvoy.

1968

Cork—D. O'Mahony, Jerry Coleman, F. Cronin, S. Looney, D. Cogan, R. O'Sullivan, C. Hartnett, Donal Aherne, Barry Murphy, Tony Murphy, John Coleman, H. O'Sullivan, F. Twomey, M. O'Doherty, B. Cummins. Sub.: D. McCarthy.

Sligo: P. McLoughlin, R. Lipsett, J. Brennan, N. Kellegher, J. Kilgallon, J. Gilmartin, K. Conway, G. Hegarty, A. Richardson, D. Kerins, R. Henry, H. Quinn, R. Sherlock, R. Boland, P. Kearins. Sub.: J. Kilgannon.

1969

Cork—B. O'Brien, P. Barry, G. B. O'Sullivan, D. Moloney, Brian Murphy, M. O'Doherty, C. Hartnett, E. Hallinan, J. Coleman, D. Curran, E. Fitzparick, H. O'Sullivan, J. Courtney, D. Barron, P. Lonergan.

Derry—K. McGahon, P. Burke, L. Murphy, P. McGuckian, B. Kearney, M. Moran, R. Hasson, E. Laverty, H. McGoldrick, S. Mullan, B. Ward, T. McWilliams, M. O'Neill, S. McGeehan, G. O'Neill. Subs.: M. Bradley, S. Coyle.

1970

Galway—J. Higgins, S. Cloonan, A. Marren, J. Kemple, P. J. Burke, M. Geraghty, J. Corcoran, T. O'Connor, P. Silke, J. Barrett, M. Rooney, J. Lardner, M. Burke, J. Meehan, J. Tobin. Sub.: M. Walsh who played in drawn game. J. Meehan came on as sub in drawn game.

Kerry—P. O'Mahony, B. O'Shea, S. Clifford, J. Deenihan, D. Healy, M. O'Sullivan, G. O'Keeffe, P. Lynch, J. Long, C. O'Connell, J. Egan, G. Power, P. B. Brosnan, S. Fitzgerald, D. Moore. Subs.: M. O'Connor, R. Casey. T. McEllistrim and A. Morris came on as subs in drawn game. J. Murphy played in draw.

1971

Mayo—M. Griffin, J. O'Mahony, S. Reilly, A. Durkan, G. Feeney, C. Moynihan, J. Culkin, J. Quinn, R. McNicholas, M. Gannon, J. P. Kean, M. Higgins, G. Farragher, F. Harty, M. Maloney. Sub.: M. Fahy.

Cork: G. Stanton, K. Collins, J. O'Shea, K. Murphy, M. Corbett, C. Kelleher, R. Wilmot, J. Lynch, S. Fitzgerald, D. Crowley, S. Coughlan, S. Murphy, D. Philpott, J. Barry Murphy, A. Fahy. Subs.: V. Twomey, D. O'Sullivan, G. Aherne.

1972

Cork—T. O'Sullivan, D. Keohane, Conor Barrett, T. Creedon, S. O'Farrell, S. O'Sullivan, R. Wilmot, K. Murphy, K. Collins, L. Gould, D. O'Hare, G. Aherne, Liam Good, J. Barry Murphy, S. O'Shea. Sub.: B. Óg Murphy.

Tyrone—P. Kerlin, G. Goodwin, H. Mooney, D. Daly, P. O'Neill, C. McAleer, J. Doherty, F. McGuigan, D. McKenna, M. Quinn, J. Hughes, B. O'Neill, T. Campbell, M. Harte, P. Quinn. Subs.: D. Kennedy, M. Coyle.

1973

Tyrone—B. Campbell, G. Goodwin, M. Lennon, H. Mooney, S. Gormley, C. McAleer, J. O'Doherty, P. Kerlin, D. McKenna, S. O'Kane, E. McKenna, J. Cunningham, M. Quinn, B. O'Neill, K. Currie. Sub.: S. Coyne.

Kildare—A. Dunne, J. Clery, J. Grehan, S. Ryan, J. Jacob, P. Archibald, T. Browne, N. Fennelly, P. Winders, P. Mulhearn, J. Geoghegan, J. Delaney, E. Delahunt, N. Fahy, B. Whelan. Subs.: P. Lyons, J. Dooley.

1974

Cork—F. Delaney, W. Lynch, J. Slattery, E. Desmond, B. Twomey, J. Crowley, T. Cashman, D. Good, R. Kenny, Declan Murphy, Diarmuid McCarthy, Don McCarthy, G. O'Sullivan, M. O'Regan, T. Murphy. Subs.: M. Carey, D. McCurtain, W. O'Driscoll.

Mayo—J. Cuddy, S. Sweeney, D. Conway, J. Gallagher, E. Brett, V. Ryan, J. Brennan, P. Mahan, W. Nally, K. Geraghty, M. Burke, S. Moran, G. Hennigan, J. Burke, M. Mannion. Subs.: J. Nally, G. Reilly, T. McCormack.

1975

Kerry—C. Nelligan, V. O'Connor, M. O'Sullivan, M. Colgan, J. J. O'Connor, M. Spillane, G. Casey, S. Walsh, N. O'Donovan, F. Scannell, J. Mulvihill, R. Bunyan, C. O'Connor, J. O'Shea, P. Sheehan.

Tyrone—A. Skelton, B. Campbell, K. McGarvey, P. McCallan, P. J. Trainor, K. McCabe, J. J. Campbell, T. O'Rourke, G. McCallan, P. Teague, M. McCoy, P. Donnelly, D. O'Hagan, M. McAnneny, S. Daly. Subs.: S. Donnelly, E. McCann.

Galway—P. Coyne, M. Coleman, O. Burke, C. Flaherty, J. Kelly, R. Bermingham, G. Forde, G. Burke, L. Higgins, B. Brennan, S. Ruane, P. Conroy, K. O'Sullivan, G. McManus, F. Rooney. Sub.: K. Donnellan.

Cork—S. Martin, T. Healy, J. Murphy, M. Moloney, D. Buckley, J. Cremin, J. Nolan, P. McCarthy, B. McSweeney, T. Dalton, M. Mullins, P. Smith, K. O'Leary, G. Mulcahy, J. O'Sullivan. Subs.: M. Shinnick, J. Wilmot.

Down—P. Donnan, S. McNulty, A. McAulfield, Seán Brunker, P. O'Rourke, M. Sands, B. McGovern, John McCartan, P. Kennedy, E. Toner, A. Rogers, M. McCann, T. Bradley, B. Loughran, J. Digney. Subs.: E. McGivern, F. Rooney.

Meath—M. McQuillan, L. Harnan, B. Cullen, C. O'Reilly, G. Gough, C. Brazil, M. Sheilds, A. Tormey, J. Butler, G. Cooney, N. O'Sullivan, P. Finnerty, J. McCluskey, F. O'Sullivan, B. Reddy. Sub.: J. Tallon.

Mayo—S. Warde, M. Maloney, G. Golden, M. Walsh, N. Heffernan, A. Garvey, E. Melvin, M. Joyce, T. J. Kilgallon, S. Clarke, J. Maughan, A. McNicholas, K. O'Malley, J. Lyons, E. Griffin. Subs.: L. Lyons, T. Byrne, C. Gilmartin.

Dublin—P. O'Toole, F. Walsh, P. Canavan, C. Finnegan, K. Byrne, S. Fleming, T. Mannion, J. Kelly, A. White, C. Duff, M. Loftus, C. Griffin, N. Gaffney, B. Rock, K. Barry. Sub.: D. Deasy.

Dublin—J. O'Leary, J. Grace, V. Conroy, S. Wade, C. Euastace, C. Finnegan, D. Murphy, B. Kavanagh, P. Boylan, B. Jordan, M. Loftus, C. Duff, D. Murphy, B. Rock, K. Barry. Subs.: T. Kelly, P. McCabe.

Kerry—N. Cronin, J. Keane, B. Ladden, C. Bambury, D. Keane, P. Sheehan, A. Shannon, A. O'Donovan, T. Dee, J. Chute, L. Kearns, D. Kennelly, W. O'Connor, T. Spillane, G. O'Donnell.

Kerry—R. O'Brien, D. Keane, M. Crowley, M. Counihan, J. O'Sullivan, T. Sheehy, J. T. O'Sullivan, P. O'Donoghue, A.

O'Donovan, T. Dee, J. Shannon, L. Kearns, T. Parker, W. Maher, M. McAuliffe. Sub.: T. Spillane.

Derry—J. Mackle, B. McNabb, M. O'Brien, M. Tully, M. Convery, O. McKee, D. McCluskey, D. Barton, D. O'Kane, L. McIlhenny, B. McErlean, J. McErlean, P. McKiernan, T. McGuckian, R. McCusker. Subs.: M. Bradley, D. McNicholl.

1981

Cork—M. Maguire, D. O'Brien, J. Murphy, N. Cahalane, C. Hannon, V. Hedderman, A. Davis, A. Leahy, T. Mannix, Tony O'Sullivan, E. O'Mahony, P. Fitzgerald, P. Healy, C. O'Neill, J. Cleary. Sub.: T. Cole.

Derry—L. Peoples, B. McNabb, K. Rafferty, E. Reilly, C. Kelly, B. McPeake, M. Tully, L. McIlhenny, M. Bradley, Eunan Rafferty, D. O'Kane, T. McGuckian, Dermot McNicholl, J. McErlean, J. A. Mullen. Subs.: J. McGrath, P. McCormack.

1982

Dublin—J. McNally, C. Sage, F. McGrath, L. O'Rourke, E. Heary, T. Delaney, M. Deegan, D. Sheehan, B. Cooke, M. Coffey, M. Egan, S. O'Brien, P. O'Carroll, T. McCormack, B. Redmond. Sub.: T. Murphy.

Kerry—D. O'Neill, D. Cremin, J. Keane, J. O'Connell, J. Moriarty, J. O'Donnell, J. Rice, T. Brosnan, S. Wight, D. O'Donoghue, M. Keating, P. Galvin, B. Keane, E. Fitzgerald, M. McAuliffe. Sub.: P. J. O'Leary.

1983

Derry—D. Kelly, P. O'Donnell, P. Bradley, J. McGurk, R. Conway, B. Kealy, N. Mullan, P. Young, C. Barton, C. McNicholl, D. McNicholl, E. McIlhenny, E. Lynch, D. Cassidy, Tony McKiernan.

Cork—R. Duffy, M. Maguire, T. Minihane, K. Scanlon, M. Slocum, B. Searles, J. Moynihan, B. Coffey, B. Stack, M. McCarthy, Teddy McCarthy, D. Kennedy, J. Cashman, M. Kelleher; P. Harrington. Subs.: I. Breen, E. Kenneally, T. Power.

1984

Dublin—M. Broderick, G. Walsh, J. Barry, Ciarain Walsh, A. Martin, J. Power, B. McKeon, J. Stynes, P. Clarke, D. de Lappe, A. McClean, J. Fahy, N. Clancy, M. Crowley, C. Crowley. Subs.: P. Daly, D. Whelan.

Tipperary—G. Enright, D. Walsh, R. Quirke, D. Williams, J.

Owens, F. Howlin, M. Holland, B. Burke, G. Ryan, M. Goonan, J. O'Meara, K. Farrelly, T. Sheehan, A. Crosse, S. Brett. Subs.: D. Pyke, J. Hackett.

1985

Mayo—J. Cummins, K. Beirne, E. Gilvarry, M. Coyle, D. Burke, D. Fitzgerald, J. French, M. Fitzmaurice, G. Maher, Tony Munnelly, P. Walsh, T. O'Grady, M. Mullaghy, M. J. Mullen, J. Gallagher. Subs.: P. McCarthy, P. Kirrane.

Cork—J. O'Mahony, M. Murphy, D. Duggan, J. Allen, N. Creedon, B. Murphy, T. Griffin, K. Kiely, J. O'Driscoll, B. Harte, D. O'Connell, G. O'Regan, P. Cahill, P. Collins, R. Sheehan. Sub.: K. Nagle.

1986

Galway—A. Brennan, B. Silke, F. McWalter, G. Farrell, P. Fallon, A. Mulholland, M. Tarpey, J. Joyce, K. Walsh, T. Kilcommins, F. O'Neill, M. McDonagh, T. Mannion, P. Maher, T. Finnerty. Subs.: B. Walsh, N. Costelloe, J. Mitchell.

Cork—P. Hayes, S. O'Brien, M. O'Connor, S. O'Rourke, N. Murphy, M. Crowley, D. Burke, F. Corrigan, G. Lally, P. Davis, M. Mullins, P. Coleman, N. Twomey, D. Larkin, I. Aherne. Subs.: M. Farr, R. Sheehan.

1987

Down—D. Hawkins, N. Caulfield, L. Duggan, M. McGivern, M. Quinn, C. Deegan, C. Mason, B. McCartan, P. Hannaway, C. Murray, R. Haughean, G. Breen, R. Fitzpatrick, T. Fagan, J. McCartan.

Cork—J. J. Sweeney, D. O'Callaghan, B. Cooney, M. Lyons, S. Coughlan, S. O'Brien, D. Burke, L. Honohan, S. Dineen, G. McPolin, M. Burke, D. Davis, J. J. Barrett, D. O'Sullivan, N. Twomey. Subs.: F. Fitzgerald, J. Corcoran, S. Calnan.

1988

Kerry—P. O'Leary, P. Lenihan, N. Savage, J. B. O'Brien, L. Flaherty, V. Knightly, S. Walsh, E. Stack. F. Ashe, P. Laide, D. Cahill, S. O'Sullivan, C. Geeney, D. Farrell, B. O'Sullivan. Sub.: F. Doherty.

Dublin—D. O'Farrell, P. McManus, J. Jordan, C. Kavanagh, T. O'Boyle, B. Murray, G. O'Regan, D. Quinlivan, P. Cassells, D. Howard, B. Stynes, T. Keogh, D. Farrell, S. Moylan, B. Barnes. Subs.: S. Cahill for Cassells, T. Gavigan for O'Boyle.

1989

Derry—M. O'Connor, J. Martin, P. McAllister, G. Simpson, B. McGonigle, G. Coleman, R. Skelly, J. Mulholland, A. Tohill, R. McEldowney, J. Lynn, E. Burns, E. O'Kane, D. Heaney, D. Bateson. Subs.: K. Diamond for Martin, R. Murphy for Lynn.

Offaly—D. Scully, K. Flynn, C. Maher, P. Dunne, B. Daly, F. Cullen, P. Moran, S. Grennan, B. O'Brien, A. Hogan, N. Hand, D. McKeon, W. Reynolds, S. Kellaghan, C. McTeague. Subs.: F. Kinnally for Daly, J. Hiney for Reynolds, P. Carroll for Dunne.

1990

Meath—C. Martin, V. Ryan, E. McManus, N. Collier, R. McGrath, G. Geraghty, T. Hanley, J. Hendrick, J. McCarthy, T. Byrne, D. Martin, B. Kealy, H. Carolan, T. O'Connor, C. Sheridan. Sub.: C. Macken for Ryan.

Kerry—D. O'Keeffe, F. Stack, J. Cronin, J. O'Driscoll, O. Joy, S. Moynihan, B. O'Shea, C. Kennedy, S. O'Driscoll, J. Bowler, W. O'Donnell, K. O'Shea, C. O'Grady, J. Wieboldt, G. Farrell. Sub.: S. Curtin for S. O'Driscoll.

1991

Cork—K. O'Dwyer, D. O'Callaghan, B. Corcoran, B. Murphy, G. McCullagh, T. Lynch, A. McCarthy, F. Collins, P. Hegarty, S. Barrett, M. O'Sullivan, P. O'Mahony, K. Harrington, J. Kavanagh, P. O'Rourke. Subs.: F. O'Mahony for O'Rourke, D. O'Neill for Barrett.

Mayo—B. Heffernan, T. Burke, J. McSharry, K. Mortimer, P. Cunney, D. Leyden, F. Costello, M. Smith, P. McNamara, T. J. McHugh, K. O'Neill, R. Golding, D. Burke, T. Walkin, D. McDonagh. Subs.: S. Brady for McDonagh, C. Deacy for McHugh

1992

Meath—B. Murphy, K. Cantwell, J. Brady, J. Smith, P. Shankey, J. Tighe, B. Sheridan, D. Hunt, N. Dunne, K. Harten, C. Hall, G. Bell, P. Duff, P. O'Sullivan, T. Giles. Subs.: P. Nestor for Duff, M. Farrelly for Harten.

Armagh—D. Whitmarsh, E. Fearon, E. Martin, E. Bratten, C. Wilson, M. Hanratty, K. O'Hagan, B. O'Hagan, P. McGrane, B. Hughes, D. Marsden, P. McNulty, D. Toner, D. Mackin, N. McGleenan. Subs.: J. Rafferty for McGleenan, A. McCann for Fearon, K. Mallie for Bratten.

Cork—D. McAuley, T. O'Mahony, K. O'Connell, J. Kingston, A. O'Shea, E. Sexton, S. Prendeville, J. O'Connell, D. Dempsey, M. Cronin, A. O'Regan, J. Buckley, S. Collins, P. O'Flynn, B. Cuthbert. Sub.: J. McCarthy for Dempsey.

Meath—N. Craven, N. Kearney, C. Woods, H. Traynor, P. Reynolds, D. Fay, B. Sheridan, T. Giles, A. Finnegan, N. Farrelly, J. Lacy, N. Walsh, O. Murphy, B. Callaghan, P. Nestor. Subs.: P. Duff for Nestor, N. Regan for Walsh, J. Farrelly for Finnegan.

CAPTAINS OF WINNING ALL-IRELAND
MINOR FOOTBALL TEAMS

1929—G. Comerford (Clare)
1930—B. Synott (Dublin)
1931—J. O'Gorman (Kerry)
1932—C. O'Sullivan (Kerry)
1933—T. O'Leary (Kerry)
1934—A. Greensmith (Tipperary)
1935—W. Durkin (Mayo)
1936—L. McEntee (Louth)
1937—J. J. McCormack (Cavan)
1938—P. Conaty (Cavan)
1939—L. Gilmartin (Roscommon)
1940—B. Burke (Louth)
1941—W. Carlos (Roscommon)
1942-'44—Abandoned
1945—S. McEntaggart (Dublin)
1946—T. Moriarty (Kerry)
1947—E. Devlin (Tyrone)
1948—E. Devlin (Tyrone)
1949—S. Blaney (Armagh)
1950—M. Brosnan (Kerry)
1951—B. Molloy (Roscommon)
1952—B. Mahon (Galway)
1953—E. Walsh (Mayo)
1954—V. Bell (Dublin)
1955—P. Heron (Dublin)
1956—L. Foley (Dublin)
1957—B. Cahill (Meath)
1958—D. Foley (Dublin)
1959—M. Kissane (Dublin)
1960—S. Cleary (Galway)
1961—E. Coughlan (Cork)
1962—S. O'Mahony (Kerry)

1963—T. O'Hanlon (Kerry)
1964—S. Grogan (Offaly)
1965—T. Diamond (Derry)
1966—S. O'Dowd (Mayo)
1967—D. Aherne (Cork)
1968—D. Aherne (Cork)
1969—E. Fitzpatrick (Cork)
1970—J. Corcoran (Galway)
1971—J. P. Keane (Mayo)
1972—G. Aherne (Cork)
1973—D. McKenna (Tyrone)
1974—E. Desmond (Cork)
1975—R. Bunyan (Kerry)
1976—G. Burke (Galway)
1977—J. McCartan (Down)
1978—A. Garvey (Mayo)
1979—M. Loftus (Dublin)
1980—T. Dee (Kerry)
1981—V. Hedderman (Cork)
1982—L. O'Rourke (Dublin)
1983—D. McNicholl (Derry)
1984—P. Clarke (Dublin)
1985—M. Fitzmaurice (Mayo)
1986—J. Joyce (Galway)
1987—M. Quinn (Down)
1988—D. Cahill (Kerry)
1989—G. Coleman (Derry)
1990—E. McManus (Meath)
1991—A. McCarthy (Cork)
1992—P. O'Sullivan (Meath)
1993—Brian Cuthbert (Cork)

1929—Longford 3-4, Dublin 1-4
1930—Dublin 1-6, Longford 0-4
1931—Louth 3-2, Wexford 0-3
1932—Laois 3-2, Louth 1-7
1933—Dublin 3-7, Laois 0-6
1934—Dublin 0-5, Kildare 0-2.
1935—Louth 1-7, Dublin 1-6
1936—Louth 3-6, Wexford 2-1
1937—Wexford 2-7, Louth 2-5
1938—Longford 3-6, Louth 2-8
1939—Westmeath 1-2, Louth 0-2
1940—Louth 3-5, Kildare 1-6
1941—Louth 4-4, Wexford 1-6
1942—Louth 5-10, Kildare 0-6
1943-1944 Championships suspended.
1945—Dublin 3-5, Wexford 1-0
1946—Dublin 4-6, Meath 0-3
1947—Offaly 1-7, Dublin 1-7
      Offaly 1-7, Dublin 1-5 (Replay)
1948—Dublin 2-5, Offaly 1-6
1949—Dublin 3-10, Kildare 1-5
1950—Wexford 3-6, Dublin 2-8
1951—Louth 3-9, Westmeath 2-5
1952—Westmeath 3-14, Wicklow 3-3
1953—Louth 1-6, Kildare 0-6
1954—Dublin 2-7, Meath 0-11
1955—Dublin 2-11, Meath 1-4
1956—Dublin 1-10, Meath 1-9
1957—Meath 0-8, Offaly 0-5
1958—Dublin 2-10, Louth 1-6
1959—Dublin 3-13, Offaly 1-7
1960—Offaly 1-12, Louth 1-5
1961—Dublin 2-8, Offaly 1-8
1962—Offaly 2-8, Dublin 1-4
1963—Westmeath 2-14, Dublin 3-7
1964—Offaly 1-7, Laois 1-6
1965—Offaly 2-11, Kildare 1-5
1966—Laois 1-10, Offaly 0-7
1967—Laois 1-8, Dublin 2-4
1968—Dublin 1-11, Laois 0-8
1969—Wexford 0-11, Dublin 0-7

1970—Dublin 2-8, Meath 0-13
1971—Dublin 2-7, Louth 0-4
1972—Meath 3-8, Dublin 1-10
1973—Kildare 4-11, Laois 0-10
1974—Wicklow 5-6, Longford 1-9
1975—Kildare 2-9, Meath 3-5
1976—Dublin 2-8, Offaly 0-13
1977—Meath 1-7, Dublin 0-9
1978—Dublin 3-12, Wexford 0-11
1979—Dublin 2-13, Meath 0-8
1980—Meath 1-12, Kildare 1-9
1981—Dublin 1-8, Meath 0-9
1982—Dublin 0-10, Westmeath 0-4
1983—Kildare 1-11, Meath 1-6
1984—Dublin 0-12, Westmeath 1-6
1985—Meath 0-11, Offaly 1-4
1986—Dublin 2-16, Meath 0-6
1987—Kildare 0-13, Dublin 2-5.
1988—Dublin 4-6, Meath 0-8
1989—Offaly 2-11, Kildare 0-7
1990—Meath 1-19, Kildare 1-6
1991—Kildare 2-8, Dublin 0-12
1992—Meath 1-8, Westmeath 1-5
1993—Meath 1-16, Wicklow 3-3

ULSTER MINOR FOOTBALL FINALS

1930—Armagh 3-4, Monaghan 0-10
1931—Tyrone 0-7, Armagh 0-4
1932—Antrim 2-7, Tyrone 1-2
1933—Antrim 2-7, Armagh 1-2
1934—Tyrone 1-4, Down 1-3
1935—Tyrone 2-2, Donegal 2-1
    Objection and counter-objection – Competition declared
    null and void.
1936—Antrim 2-7, Tyrone 2-4
1937—Cavan 1-10, Armagh 0-3
1938—Cavan 2-7, Antrim 2-4
1939—Monaghan 1-8, Cavan 1-7 (replay)
    Monaghan 0-5, Cavan 0-5 (draw)
1940—Monaghan 0-8, Antrim 0-4
1941—Antrim 4-7, Cavan 1-8
1942-1944—Abandoned.
1945—Monaghan 1-7, Down 0-7
1946—Tyrone 1-4, Monaghan 0-5

DOWNEY'S DAY OF DELIGHT

● *HISTORIC MOMENT . . . Henry Downey holds the Sam Maguire high* *❍ triumph after leading Derry to the county's first-ever All-Ireland senior* *❍otball championship title in 1993.*

● *Joe Brolly epitomises the overflowing joy of the Derry players after the final whistle had sounded in Croke Park on Sunday, September 19, 1993.*

● *Derry All-Ireland Senior Football Champions 1993: Back row (from left): Joe Brolly, Dermot Heaney, Anthony Tohill, Damien McCusker, Seamus Downey, Tony Scullion, Damien Barton, Brian McGilligan. Front row (from left): Enda Gormley, John McGurk, Henry Downey, Kieran McKeever, Gary Coleman, Fergal McCusker, Damien Cassidy. (Pictures INPHO)*

● *Anthony Tohill, the brilliant Derry midfielder, whose performances contributed so much to the All-Ireland title win and who was named in the "Football Team of the Championship" in the Sunday Independent for the '93 season.*

● *The Cork defence at full stretch in the 1993 All-Ireland final as Joe Brolly (13) and Damien Barton (11) lead the attack. Brian Corcoran is at left.*

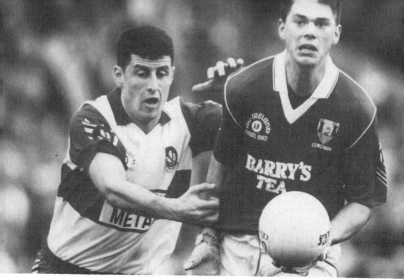

● *Cork wing forward Don Davis about to pass the ball as he is tackled by Fergal McCusker.*

● *What the future Croke Park will be like on All-Ireland Day . . . a model of the redeveloped stadium viewed from behind the new Cusack Stand. It will accommodate 79,500 spectators.*

● *Micheál Ó Muirheartaigh, the "Voice of RTE Radio", receives the acclaim of Dan McGing, Chairman of ACCBANK, and John Meagher, Deputy Chairman Independent Newspapers plc, after being presented with a special award for his services as a commentator to the national games.*

● *Kerry's Pat Spillane, winner of a Sunday Independent/ACCBANK Personality of the Year award, in conversation with John McCloskey, Chief Executive ACCBANK, and Joe Hayes, Managing Director of Independent Newspapers Ireland Ltd.*

● *Meath's brilliant corner-back, Bobby O'Malley, in relaxed mood with Aengus Fanning, Editor of the Sunday Independent (left) and John Meagher, Deputy Chairman Independent Newspapers plc, after receiving his Sunday Independent/ACCBANK Football Personality of the Year award.*

● *The legendary Jimmy Murray (left) who led Roscommon to victory in successive All-Irelands in 1943-'44, with John McCluskey, Chief Executive of the ACCBANK, after receiving his Sunday Independent/ACCBANK Captain of the Decade award and (right) Liam McHale, the stylish Mayo midfielder, winner of a Personality of the Year award for 1989, when he starred against Cork in the All-Ireland final.*

● Kilkenny forward, P. J. Delaney, son of Paddy Delaney of the 1969-'75 team, receives his Evening Herald/ACCBANK Personality of the Month award from Jim Skelly, General Manager Retail Banking ACCBANK.

● Tipperary's Nicky English (with trophy) with the members of the Lattin-Cullen squad after they had won the St Jude's/ACCBANK All-Ireland Junior Hurling Sevens played on the eve of the 1993 All-Ireland Hurling Final at Tymon Park, Templeogue. Twenty clubs from as far apart as Cork and Antrim took part.

O'CONNOR THE PROUD CAPTAIN

● *TWO BACK TO BACK . . . Eddie O'Connor with the Liam McCarthy Cup after Kilkenny had made it two All-Ireland titles back to back by defeating Galway in the 1993 final. (Picture: Sportsfile)*

1947—Tyrone 3-6, Armagh 2-8
1948—Tyrone 5-7, Monaghan 2-3
1949—Armagh 4-6, Donegal 1-4
1950—Antrim 1-9, Armagh 1-1 (replay)
      Antrim 1-8, Armagh 1-8 (draw)
1951—Armagh 3-1, Cavan 1-4
1952—Cavan 1-5, Down 1-3
1953—Armagh 2-15, Tyrone 3-2
1954—Armagh 2-8, Down 0-9
1955—Antrim 4-3, Cavan 2-6
1956—Donegal 2-5, Armagh 0-6
1957—Armagh 3-6, Donegal 0-10
1958—Down 3-9, Cavan 3-1
1959—Cavan 2-11, Antrim 2-7
1960—Down 2-7, Monaghan 1-4
1961—Armagh 3-8, Monaghan 1-4
1962—Down 2-5, Armagh 0-8
1963—Down 4-6, Donegal 2-11
1964—Antrim 2-10, Cavan 0-6
1965—Derry 3-11, Cavan 2-4
1966—Down 1-12, Derry 1-9
1967—Tyrone 0-16, Fermanagh 2-5
1968—Armagh 4-8, Derry 1-7
1969—Derry 1-9, Tyrone 0-5
1970—Derry 1-14, Fermanagh 0-11
1971—Tyrone 0-19, Fermanagh 0-7
1972—Tyrone 3-6, Cavan 1-6
1973—Tyrone 1-13, Down 0-9
1974—Cavan 3-9, Derry 1-4
1975—Tyrone 0-10, Cavan 0-7
1976—Tyrone 5-7, Cavan 1-9
1977—Down 0-11, Armagh 1-6 (replay)
      Down 0-8, Armagh 1-5 (draw)
1978—Tyrone 3-11, Monaghan 2-9
1979—Down 1-7, Tyrone 0-6
1980—Derry 3-14, Armagh 1-2
1981—Derry 0-11, Armagh 1-2
1982—Antrim 2-10, Down 3-5
1983—Derry 3-9, Monaghan 0-4
1984—Derry 1-4, Armagh 0-3
1985—Donegal 2-11, Cavan 1-3
1986—Down 1-12, Derry 0-10
1987—Down 1-7, Armagh 0-4.

1988—Tyrone 2-7, Cavan 0-3
1989—Derry 2-15, Armagh 2-3
1990—Derry 2-10, Down 2-8
1991—Donegal 1-10, Tyrone 1-9
1992—Armagh 0-13, Donegal 0-9
1993—Tyrone 1-9, Derry 1-5

MUNSTER MINOR FOOTBALL FINALS

1929—Clare 1-6, Waterford 0-4
1930—Clare 2-3, Tipperary 1-3
1931—Kerry 3-6, Tipperary 0-7
1932—Kerry 4-5, Cork 2-5
1933—Kerry 2-9, Cork 3-4
1934—Tipperary 3-10, Waterford 0-5
1935—Tipperary 3-5, Cork 0-4
1936—Kerry 1-5, Tipperary 1-2
1937—Kerry 3-8, Clare 1-2
1938—Kerry 8-9, Cork 1-2
1939—Cork 3-3, Kerry 3-2
1940—Kerry 1-3, Clare 1-2
1941—Kerry 7-5, Waterford 2-1
1942-'44—Championship abandoned
1945—Kerry 2-4, Cork 2-3.
1946—Kerry 4-17, Tipperary 0-2
1947—Kerry 0-7, Cork 1-3
1948—Kerry 3-4, Cork 1-5
1949—Kerry 0-7, Cork 0-5
1950—Kerry 4-10, Limerick 1-5
1951—Kerry 0-7, Cork 1-3
1952—Cork 3-9, Clare 1-1
1953—Clare 0-7, Cork 0-2
1954—Kerry 4-10, Cork 1-3

1955—Tipperary 0-9, Kerry 1-5 (replay)
        Tipperary 0-9, Kerry 1-6 (draw)
1956—Limerick 1-7, Kerry 1-5
1957—Kerry 1-5, Cork 0-5
1958—Kerry 3-11, Waterford 0-4
1959—Cork 2-7, Kerry 0-7
1960—Cork 3-8, Kerry 0-7
1961—Cork 2-12, Clare 0-2
1962—Kerry 2-9, Cork 0-9
1963—Kerry 0-11, Cork 0-4 (replay)
        Kerry 0-8, Cork 0-8 (draw)

1964—Cork 4-11, Clare 0-5
1965—Kerry 3-11, Cork 1-5
1966—Cork 5-12, Kerry 1-7
1967—Cork 2-8, Kerry 0-3
1968—Cork 2-13, Kerry 0-2
1969—Cork 3-11, Kerry 0-12
1970—Kerry 4-9, Cork 1-11
1971—Cork 2-13, Kerry 1-2
1972—Cork 2-14, Kerry 1-14
1973—Cork 1-13, Kerry 3-5
1974—Cork 0-13, Kerry 1-6
1975—Kerry 3-7, Cork 1-11
1976—Cork 0-10, Kerry 1-5
1977—Cork 1-7, Kerry 1-3
1978—Kerry 1-4, Cork 0-6
1979—Kerry 1-11, Cork 1-5 (replay
      Kerry 3-6, Cork 2-9 (draw)
1980—Kerry 1-12, Cork 1-10
1981—Cork 0-9, Kerry 1-5
1982—Kerry 1-11, Cork 0-5
1983—Cork 1-11, Tipperary 1-5
1984—Tipperary 2-3, Kerry 0-8
1985—Cork 1-8, Kerry 0-4
1986—Cork 2-12, Kerry 0-4
1987—Cork 0-12, Kerry 1-8 (replay)
      Cork 0-8, Kerry 0-8 (draw)
1988—Kerry 1-8, Cork 0-10
1989—Kerry 2-10, Cork 2-9
1990—Kerry 1-10, Cork 0-3
1991—Cork 0-10, Kerry 0-8
1992—Cork 0-11, Kerry 2-5 (draw)
      Cork 3-6, Kerry 2-7 (replay)
1993—Cork 2-15, Tipperary 2-7

CONNACHT MINOR FOOTBALL FINALS

1930—May 3-4, Sligo 1-1
1931—Mayo 2-10, Roscommon 3-2
1932—Galway 3-5, Mayo 1-4
1933—Mayo 5-7, Roscommon 0-6
1934—Mayo 2-13, Galway 0-5

1935—Mayo 2-2, Sligo 1-3
1936—Mayo 4-9, Sligo 1-8
1937—Galway 2-8. Mayo 1-3
1938—Galway 6-5, Leitrim 1-6
1939—Roscommon 1-10, Mayo1-3
1940—Mayo 8-5, Leitrim 1-6
1941—Roscommon 2-6, Galway 0-6
1942-'44—Competition suspended in war years
1945—Leitrim 2-6, Sligo 1-5 (replay)
       Leitrim 1-5, Sligo 2-2 (draw)
1946—Mayo 4-9, Galway 1-5
1947—Mayo 3-6, Sligo 2-5
1948—Galway 3-4, Leitrim 0-5
1949—Roscommon 2-4, Sligo 1-7
       Replay—Roscommon 3-10, Sligo 2-7
       (Sligo awarded title on objection)
1950—Mayo 3-7, Roscommon 1-4
1951—Galway 1-8, Roscommon 2-4
       (Roscommon awarded title on objection).
1952—Galway 4-11, Sligo 0-3
1953—Mayo 1-9, Roscommon 1-3
1954—Mayo 9-16, Sligo 0-4
1955—Mayo 2-5, Galway 1-5
1956—Leitrim 2-7, Roscommon 1-6
1957—Mayo 4-4, Leitrim 2-5
1958—Mayo 1-8, Roscommon 1-4
1959—Galway 3-9, Mayo 1-8
1960—Galway 4-11, Roscommon 0-3
1961—Mayo 5-8, Sligo 0-5
1962—Mayo 7-8, Galway 0-10
1963—Mayo 3-5, Roscommon 1-5
1964—Mayo 2-7, Galway 1-3
1965—Roscommon 2-10, Mayo 1-10
1966—Mayo 1-9, Roscommon 0-7
1967—Roscommon 2-5, Mayo 1-5
1968—Sligo 1-8, Galway 0-7
1969—Galway 3-3, Mayo 0-8
1970—Galway 2-11, Mayo 1-6
1971—Mayo 2-12, Roscommon 1-8
1972—Galway 4-11, Roscommon 1-11
1973—Mayo 3-7, Galway 0-3
1974—Mayo 4-12, Roscommon 2-3

1975—Roscommon 1-15, Galway 0-5
1976—Galway 6-16, Sligo 3-3
1977—Mayo 2-20, Leitrim 0-7
1978—Mayo 2-6, Galway 0-4
1979—Mayo 5-11, Galway 3-7
1980—Mayo 3-8, Roscommon 2-9
1981—Roscommon 2-8, Mayo 3-4
1982—Galway 1-7, Leitrim 0-7
1983—Galway 2-10, Roscommon 2-5
1984—Roscommon 3-9, Mayo 2-8 (replay)
        Roscommon 1-11, Mayo 2-8 (draw)
1985—Mayo 0-6, Galway 1-1
1986—Galway 1-9, Mayo 2-1
1987—Galway 2-8, Mayo 2-4
1988—Galway 2-9, Mayo 3-4
1989—Galway 2-8, Roscommon 0-13
        (Provincial Council decides to replay: disputed penalty
        goal)
Roscommon 2-11, Galway 0-15 (after extra time)
1990—Galway 1-18, Roscommon 2-3
1991—Mayo 4-9, Leitrim 0-6
1992—Roscommon 0-10, Mayo 0-9
1993—Galway 3-8, Mayo 1-10 (replay)
        Galway 0-11, Mayo 1-8 (draw)

The High Rollers of The Turf

ONLY a limited number of copies of the autographed hardback edition of Raymond Smith's best-selling book, *The High Rollers of The Turf* are now available. It represents an ideal gift for all lovers of good racing yarns.

J. P. (The Sundance Kid) McManus, Barney Curley, Paddy Sleator, Mick O'Toole, Tommy (The Coalminer) O'Brien, Robert Sangster and John Magnier are among those featured.

Available at £16 (including packaging and postage) from Sporting Books Publishers, 4 Sycamore Road, Mount Merrion, Co. Dublin.

ALL-IRELAND UNDER-21 FOOTBALL FINALS

1964—Kerry 1-10, Laois 1-3
1965—Kildare 2-11, Cork 1-7
1966—Roscommon 2-10, Kildare 1-12
1967—Mayo 4-9, Kerry 1-7 (replay)
       Mayo 2-10, Kerry 2-10 (draw)
1968—Derry 3-9, Offaly 1-9
1969—Antrim 1-8, Roscommon 0-10
1970—Cork, 2-11, Fermanagh 0-9
1971—Cork 3-10, Fermanagh 0-3
1972—Galway 2-6, Kerry 0-7
1973—Kerry 2-13, Mayo 0-13
1974—Mayo 2-10, Antrim 2-8 (replay)
       Mayo 0-9, Antrim 0-9 (draw)
1975—Kerry 1-15, Dublin 0-12
1976—Kerry 0-14, Kildare 1-3
1977—Kerry 1-11, Down 1-5
1978—Roscommon 1-9, Kerry 1-8
1979—Down 1-9, Cork 0-7
1980—Cork 2-8, Dublin 1-5
1981—Cork 2-9, Galway 1-6 (replay)
       Cork 0-14, Galway 2-8 (draw)
1982—Donegal 0-8, Roscommon 0-5
1983—Mayo 1-8, Derry 1-5 (replay)
       Mayo 2-5, Derry 1-8 (draw)
1984—Cork 0-9, Mayo 0-6
1985—Cork 0-14, Derry 1-8
1986—Cork 3-16, Offaly 0-12
1987—Donegal 1-12, Kerry 2-4 (replay)
       Donegal 1-7, Kerry 0-10 (draw)
1988—Offaly 0-11, Cavan 0-9.
1989—Cork 2-8, Galway 1-10
1990—Kerry 5-12, Tyrone 2-11
1991—Tyrone 4-16, Kerry 1-5
1992—Tyrone 1-10, Galway 1-7
1993—Meath 1-8, Kerry 0-10

ALL-IRELAND UNDER-21 FOOTBALL FINAL TEAMS
(1964-1993)

1964

Kerry—S. Fitzgerald, M. Morris, P. O'Donoghue, D. Lovett, S. McCarthy, V. Lucey, Donie O'Sullivan, Denis O'Sullivan, P. Griffin, H. McKinney, A. Barrett, D. O'Shea, D. O'Donnell, J. J. Barrett, S. Burrowes. Subs.: P. Cahill, T. Fitzgerald.

Laois—T. Miller, E. Finlay, A. Maher,J. Conway, G. Lawlor,J. Leonard, S. Harkins, G. Brennan, E. Mulhall, J. Fennelly, M. Fennelly, D. Brennan, C. O'Connor, P. Delaney, B. Delaney. Subs.: D. Miller, J. Heenan.

1965

Kildare—O. Crinnigan, D. Wynne, S. Cash, J. McTeague, S. Reilly, P. Nally, J. Millar, J. Donnelly, P. Mangan, T. Carew, P. Dunne, K. Kelly, T. Walsh, P. Newins, M. Behan. Subs.: T. Keogh, P. Harman.

Cork—W. Morgan, D. Kehilly, J. Lucey, J. Crowley, D. Dineen, F. Cogan, J. Dunlea, D. Couglan, J. Dowling, E. Philpott, M. O'Loughlin, J. Cogan, Batt O'Keeffe, B. O'Neill, Brendan O'Keeffe. Sub.: C. Roche.

1966

Roscommon—P. Reynolds, P. Clarke, P. Nicholson, C. Shine, G. Mannion, P. Moclair, T. Heneghan, M. J. Keane, J. O'Connor, J. Finnegan, D. Earley, J. Cox, M. Cummins, J. Keane, J. Kelly. Sub.: M. O'Gara.

Kildare—O. Crinnigan, D. Wynne, S. Cash, J. McTeague, J. O'Reilly, P. Nally, T. Keogh, P. Mangan, L. Casey, T. Carew, P. Dunny, T. Walsh, K. Kelly, M. Mullins, N. Behan. Sub.: M. Mannion.

1967

Mayo—E. Rooney, J. Earley, C. Loftus, N. McDonald, J. Ryan, T. Cafferkey, M. Flatley, W. Loftus, T. Keane, S. O'Dowd, J. Gibbons, W. McGee, T. Fitzgerald, D. Griffith, J. Smith. Sub.: J. Clark. (Note: M. Nally played in drawn game.)

Kerry—J. O'Brien, P. Sweeney, G. McCarthy, C. O'Sullivan, D. Crowley, S. Burrowes, T. O'Callaghan, P. O'Connell, M. Aherne, B. McCarthy, P. Finnegan, P. O'Connor, E. O'Donoghue, W. Kennedy, B. Lynch. Subs.: P. Joy, V. McDyer.

1968

Derry—J. Somers, M. Trolan, T. Quinn, M. P. Kelly, T. Diamond, M. McAfee, G. O'Loughlin, T. McGuinness, S. Lagan, E. Coleman, M. Niblock, J. J. Kearney, A. McGuickan, S. McCloskey, K. Teague. Subs.: A. McGurk, C. O'Donnell.

Offaly—N. Kinnarney, L. Pender, J. Smith, P. Byrne, E. Mulligan, N. Clavin, P. Monaghan, W. Bryan, S. Evans, C. Daly, L. Flynn, G. Grehan, M. Feehan, S. Kilroy, P. Keegan. Subs.: J. Dunne, P. Fenning.

1969

Antrim—R. McIlroy, D. Burns, S. Killough, M. McGranaghan, J. Mullan, L. Millar, M. Colbert, L. Boyle, T. Dunlop, A. Hamill, G. McCann, G. Mellis, A. McCallin, G. Dillon, D. McGrogan. Sub.: G. Pollock.

Roscommon—W. Gallagher, T. Mahon, T. Mahon, E. Beades, W. Feeley, P. Tiernan, A. O'Sullivan, J. Kirrane, D. Earley, M. Cox, J. Kelly, T. Hunt, M. Freyne, J. Cox, M. O'Gara.

1970

Cork—D. O'Mahony, M. O'Doherty, M. Scannell, S. Looney, S. Murphy, K. Kehilly, C. Hartnett, D. Hunt, D. Long, Tony Murphy, E. Kirby, John Coleman, J. Barrett, D. Barron, T. O'Brien. Subs.: F. Twomey, Donal Aherne.

Fermanagh—P. Sheridan, P. Reilly, C. Campbell, J. Courtney, M. McGarrity, S. Sheridan, S. Flanagan, D. Campbell, D. McKenna, T. McGrath, A. Campbell, E. McPartland, E. Treacy, G. Gallagher, P. McGinnitty. Sub.: T. Boyle.

1971

Cork—D. O'Mahony, P. Barry, M. O'Doherty, S. Looney, D. Cogan, B. Murphy, C. Hartnett, J. Coleman, D. Aherne, T. Murphy, B. Daly, F. Twomey, B. Cogan, D. Barron, D. Curran. Sub.: J. Lynch.

Fermanagh—P. Sheridan, P. O'Reilly, C. Campbell, P. Burne, B. McGovern, S. Flanagan, G. Lynch, D. McKenna, C. Gallagher, P. McGinnitty, A. Campbell, M. Cassidy, E. Treacy, T. McGrath, B. O'Reilly. Subs.: H. Kelly, M. McGarritty.

1972

Galway—M. Noonan, J. Waldron, J. Dillon, B. Costelloe, P. J. Burke, M. Geraghty, S. Stephens, M. Walsh, M. Rooney, P. Burke, T. Naughton, M. Burke, J. Lardner, F. Rush, J. Tobin.

Kerry—J. Crean, S. O'Donovan, J. Deenihan, D. O'Keeffe, M. Murphy, P. Lynch, G. O'Keeffe, N. O'Sullivan, J. O'Keeffe, M. McEllistrim, M. O'Sullivan, J. Walsh, P. Horan, M. Ferris, G. Power. Subs.: J. Egan, M. O'Connor.

1973
Kerry—P. O'Mahony, B. Harman, J. Deenihan, B. O'Shea, G. O'Keeffe, G. Power, K. O'Donoghue, J. Long, P. Lynch, J. Coffey, M. O'Sullivan, P. O'Shea, M. O'Shea, J. Egan, M. Sheehy. Subs.: M. Ferris, N. Brosnan.
Mayo—S. Langan, P. Cunningham, S. Reilly, J. O'Mahony, G. Feeney, C. Moynihan, J. Culkin, R. McNicholas, G. Farragher, M. Gannon, T. Webb, R. Bell, E. Ralph, S. McGrath, E. Flannery. Subs.: S. Barrett, S. Weir.

1974
Mayo—I. Heffernan, A. Durkin, S. Reilly, J. O'Mahony, G. Feeney, C. Moynihan, J. Culkin, R. Bell, G. Farragher, M. Flannery, J. P. Kean, T. Webb, M. Moloney, D. McGrath, M. Higgins. Subs.: D. McGrath draw; J. Burke replay; J. Burke played in drawn game.
Antrim—C. Moore, N. Madden, P. McKiernan, J. McAllister, G. McHugh, J. P. O'Kane, C. Smith, L. Jennings, J. McKiernan, K. Gough, P. Armstrong, B. Growcott, H. McRory, J. O'Hare, D. Cormican. Subs.: J. McAllister, K. Young draw; K. Young replay; R. Carlin played in drawn game.

1975
Kerry—C. Nelligan, K. O'Donoghue, P. O'Shea, G. Leahy, M. Spillane, T. Kennelly, D. (Ogie) Moran, G. O'Driscoll, S. Walsh, B. Walsh, M. Sheehy, D. Murphy, T. Doyle, J. O'Shea, P. Spillane.
Dublin—A. Fayne, B. Fitzpatrick, L. Egan, G. McCaul, K. Bruton, J. Thompson, M. Holden, F. Ryder, J. Corcoran, P. Connellan, B. Mullins, P. J. Buckley, P. Reaney, C. Fitzpatrick, S. McCarthy. Subs.: D. O'Reilly, A. Cunningham, P. Rooney.

1976
Kerry—C. Nelligan, M. Colgan, P. O'Shea, G. Leahy, M. Spillane, D. Moran, V. O'Connor, S. Walsh, J. O'Shea, N. O'Donovan, P. Spillane, G. Murphy, B. Walsh, G. O'Sullivan, P. Foley.
Kildare—A. Dunne, C. Farrell, P. O'Donoghue, F. Mulligan,

THE RAILWAY END

We've been bringing spectators by the thousand to all the big games in Croke Park le Blianta Fada. Expectant on the upward journey. Exultant, sad or perhaps philosophical on the return. The train for many is an integral part of the day for the chat, the food and perhaps, the few jorums.

And we're getting closer! The new development plans for Croke Park include a station 'under the stand'! so that in the next century we'll be bringing you right to the grounds.

Contact us to carry any GAA group no matter how small. We will be delighted to talk terms with you.

RING: Tony Cassidy, Connolly Station at (01) 363333
Andrew Roche, Cork at (021) 504888
Greg Mullen, Sligo at (071) 69888
Frank Hogan, Waterford at (051) 73401
Jack Frahill, Limerick at (061) 418666
Seamus Collins, Galway at (091) 64222

IIF inter City

D. O'Reilly, J. Crofton, P. Kenny, J. Geoghegan, M. Fennelly, T. Shaw, M. Condon, P. Mulhern, N. Fahy, M. O'Gorman, B. Whelan. Subs.: S. Ryan, P. Lyons, P. Carr.

1977

Kerry—C. Nelligan, M. Keane, V. O'Connor, M. Spillane, D. (Ogie) Moran, J. Mulvihill, G. Casey, J. O'Shea, O. Liston, T. Doyle, S. Walsh, P. Foley, D. Moran, T. Bridgman, D. Coffey. Sub.: G. O'Sullivan.

Down—J. Carr, M. Sands, D. Carey, H. Trainor, J. McCartan, T. McGovern, P. O'Rourke, J. Wright, L. Austin, D. Watson, R. Matthews, V. McGovern, B. Loughran, J. McCartan, M. McCann. Subs.: E. McGivern, A. McAulfield.

1978

Roscommon—B. Kenny, D. Newton, P. Dolan, S. Tighe, G. Connellan, R. O'Beirne, E. Egan, S. Hayden, G. Fitzmaurice, M. Finneran, G. Emmett, C. Reynolds, A. McHugh, H. Crowley, T. McManus. Sub.: A. Dooley.

Kerry—C. Nelligan, M. Keane, V. O'Connor, M. Spillane, G. Lynch, J. Mulvihill, G. Casey, J. O'Shea, S. Walsh, T. Bridgman, D. Higgins, J. L. McElligot, P. Foley, E. Liston, P. Sheehan. Sub.: D. Coffey.

1979

Down—Pat Donnan, E. King, A. McAulfield, M. Sands, G. Murdock, P. O'Rourke, B. McGovern, P. Kennedy, L. Austin, J. McCartan, M. Burns, G. Blaney, Peter Donnan, G. O'Hare, J. Digney. Sub.: M McCann.

Cork—B. O'Driscoll, T. Healy, M. Healy, J. Murphy, L. Forde, M. Moloney, J. Kerrigan, B. Lotty, D. O'Mahony, T. Dalton, M. Mullins, B. McSweeney, S. Hayes, G. Mulcahy, F. O'Mahony. Subs.: D. Kelleher, D. Philpott, J. Nolan.

1980

Cork—M. Creedon, J. Fouhy, M. Healy, C. Counihan, B. McSweeney, T. Hennebry, J. Kerrigan, D. Philpott, B. Lotty, D. Barry, S. Hayes, T. Dalton, E. Fitzgerald, N. O'Connor, F. O'Mahony. Sub.: M. Burns.

Dublin—J. O'Leary, F. Walsh, V. Conroy, D. Foran, P. Canavan, S. Wade, C. Eustace, J. Ronayne, P. Boylan, D. O'Brien, M. Loftus, C. Duff, W. Hughes, B. Rock, A. McCaul. Subs.: S. Fleming, V. Kearney, G. O'Neill.

1981

Cork—M. Creedon, J. Fouhy, M. Healy, P. Buckley, M. Hannon, M. Burns, C. Corrigan, B. Lotty, D. Murphy, D. Barry, S. Hayes, M. Connolly, T. O'Sullivan, N. O'Connor, E. Fitzgerald. (Note: C. Hartnett and D. Kelleher played in drawn game. P. Buckley and A. O'Sullivan came on for replay.) Subs.: P. Buckley, T. Ross drawn match; D. Kelleher, T. Ross replay.

Galway—P. Coyne, S. Cronin, P. Connolly, S. Rattigan, H. Heskin, T. Tierney, M. Gleeson, A. Murphy, P. Kelly, V. Daly, M. McDonagh, M Brennan, P. O'Dea, C. O'Dea, C. Gibbons. (Note: S. Kelly, P. Clancy, H. Blehein, B. O'Donnell played in drawn game. S. Rhatigan, G. Gibbons, P. Kelly and H. Heskin came on for replay.) Subs.: H. Heskin, P. Kelly drawn game; M. Sweeney replay.

1982

Donegal—M. Kelly, M. McBrearty, S. Bonnar, N. Gallagher, E. McIntyre, T. McDermott, B. Tuohy, A. Molloy, D. Reid, M. McHugh, C. Mulgrew, J. McMullen, S. Meehan, P. Carr, P. McGroarty. Subs.: P. Gallagher, S. Maguire.

Roscommon—G. Cunniffe, G. Wynne, G. Collins, M. Shanaghan, P. McNeill, M. Tiernan, P. Rogers, E. Glancy, T. Corcoran, E. McManus, P. Hickey, J. Connellan, P. Earley, R. McPhillips, P. Doorey. Subs.: J. Kelly, S. Killoran.

1983

Mayo—G. Irwin, P. Forde, J. Maughan, E. Gibbons, J. McNabb, M. Feeney, J. Finn, G. Geraghty, S. Maher, P. Brogan, J. Lindsay, N. Durkin, B. Kilkelly, T. Grogan, P. Duffy. (Note: M. Kerins played in draw and substituted in replay; K. McStay sub in both games.)

Derry—J. Mackle, K. Rafferty, F. Burke, T. Scullion, J. McErlean, B. McPeake, C. Keenan, C. Quinn, D. Barton, L. McIlhenny, D. McNicholl, P. McCann, T. McGuinness, R. McCusker, T. McGuckian. (Note: E. Cassidy, B. McErlean played in drawn game.) Subs.: R. McCusker, P. McCann draw (they regained their places for the replay). D. O'Kane, M. Tully, E. Cassidy replay.

1984

Cork—M. Maguire, John Murphy (Passage), N. Cahalane, A. Davis, D. Cleary, M. Slocum, T. Nation, D. Cullotty, T. Leahy, B. Coffey, T. Mannix, M. McCarthy, K. McCarthy, C. O'Neill, T. O'Sullivan. Subs.: T. McCarthy, J. Cleary, B. Stack.

Mayo—G. Irwin, C. Dever, J. Gilmore, E. Gibbons, A.

McGarry, J. McNabb, J. Finn, P. Brogan,S. Maher, J. Dooley, P. Duffy, N. Durkin, B. Kilkelly, L. McHale, P. O'Reilly. Sub.: T. Morgan.

1985

Cork—J. O'Mahony, K. Scanlon, A. Davis, D. Walsh, D. Cleary, B. Stack, M. Slocum, D. Cullotty,P. Hayes, M. McCarthy, T. McCarthy, B. Coffey, S. O'Donovan, C. O'Neill, P. McGrath. Sub.: B. Lane.

Derry—D. McCusker, B. Young, F. Bourke, P. McCann, J. McGurk, B. McPeake, N. Mullan, D. O'Kane, D. Healy, Declan McNicholl, D. Cassidy, M. McGurk, Dermot McNicholl, Cathal McNicholl, T. McKiernan. Subs.: P. Bradley, C. Barton, J. Mulholland.

1986

Cork—J. O'Mahony, K. Scanlon, J. Murphy (Glanmire), D. Walsh, M. Slocum, B. Stack, A. Griffin, P. Hayes, T. McCarthy, C. O'Connell, M. McCarthy, B. Coffey, P. Harrington, J. O'Driscoll, P. McGrath. Subs.: J. O'Brien, A. McCarthy.

Offaly—A. Daly, J. Owens, C. Higgins, K. Corcoran, A. Stewart, K. Rigney, B. Scully, G. O'Brien, P. Brady, V. Claffey, D. Claffey, C. Ryan, R. Scully, M. Casey, V. Brady. Subs.: G. Blong, K. Brasil, G. Galvin.

1987

Donegal—D. Gallagher, J. J. Doherty, J. Connors, T. Maguire, P. Carr, J. Cunningham, D. Keon, B. Cunningham, J. Gallagher, P. Hegarty, T. Ryan, B. McGowan, D. Ward, M. Boyle, L. Gavigan. Sub.: S. Ward replay.

Kerry—C. Moran, K. Savage, M. Brosnan, M. Nix, S. Stack, N. O'Leary, P. Coughlan, M. Galway, J. Brosnan, P. J. Gaine, G. Looney, D. McEvoy, G. Murphy, P. Hoare, M. Dennehy. (Note: M. Downey played in draw.) Subs.: G. Murphy draw (he retained his place for replay); M. Downey, T. Walsh, replay.

1988

Offaly—D. O'Neill, P. Moran, G. O'Brien, T. Coffey, J. Stewart, A. Bracken, P. O'Reilly, M. Plunkett, K. Kelleghan, G. Daly, D. Claffey, N. O'Shea, M. Casey, J. Mullan, B. Flynn. Subs.: B. Scully, V. Daly.

Cavan—J. Reilly, G. Smith, D. O'Reilly, B. Sweeney, J. Donnellan, J. Brady, P. Sharkey, L. Brady, M. Fegan, F. Cahill, S. Donoghue, D. Brady, V. Kelly, V. Dowd, F. Mooney. Sub.: C. Murtagh.

1989

Cork—A. Cawley, M. Lyons, M. O'Connor, D. Burke, S. Coughlan, S. O'Brien, N. Murphy, D. Fitzgerald, L. Honohan, I. Ahearne, M. Mullins, D. Davis, J. Barrett, D. O'Sullivan, N. Twomey. Subs.: S. Calnan for Ahearne, C. Corkerry for Barrett.

Galway—A. Brennan, J. Kilraine, F. McWalter, B. Walsh, P. Fallon, A. Mulholland, N. Ó Neachtain, B. Moylan, A. O'Connor, S. De Paor, T. Mannion, F. O'Neill, T. Kilcommins, K. Walsh, T. Finnerty. Subs.: B. Silke, for Kilraine, J. Joyce for de Paor, E. Geraghty for Mannion.

1990

Kerry—P. O'Leary, J. B. O'Brien, S. Burke, L. Flaherty, P. Slattery, V. Knightley, E. Breen, M. Fitzgerald, N. O'Mahony, P. Laide, P. McKenna, G. O'Driscoll, P. Dennehy, D. Farrell, W. O'Sullivan. Sub.: P. Griffin for Dennehy.

Tyrone—C. Blee, F. Devlin. A. McGinn, P. Devlin, P. Donnelly, B. McGinn, A. Morris, A. Kilpatrick, D. Barr, A. Cush, M. Cummings, P. Canavan, L. Strain, C. McElduff, C. Loughran, Sub.: E. McCaffrey for Cummings.

1991

Tyrone—C. Blee, D. Hagan, C. Lawn, F. Devlin, P. Donnelly, B. McGinn, T. O'Neill, A. Kilpatrick, D. Barr, A. Cush, E. McCaffrey, P. Canavan, C. Loughran, C. McBride, B. Gormley. Subs.: S. Lawn for Donnelly, J. Cassidy for Blee.

Kerry—P. O'Leary, J. O'Brien, N. Savage, J. Cronin, L. Flaherty, V. Knightley, S. Walsh, F. Ashe, C. Kearney, P. Laide, G. O'Driscoll, S. O'Sullivan, G. Farrell, D. Farrell, W. O'Sullivan. Subs.: E. Stack for Kearney, D. Cahill for Walsh, T. Byrnes for Laide.

1992

Tyrone—B. McConnell, E. Martin, C. Lawn, F. Devlin, S. Lawn, J. Gormley, C. Hughes, A. Kilpatrick, S. McCallan, E. McCaffrey, C. Donnelly, P. Canavan, K. Loughran, C. McBride, B. Gormley. Sub.: M. Slevin for C. Lawn.

Galway—D. Ó Flaharta, K. Fallon, G. Fahy, E. Godwin, I. O'Donoghue, P. Crowley, D. Cronin, F. Gavin, P. Boyce, J. Wilson, C. McGauran, T. Wilson, B. Forde, J. Fallon, N. Finnegan. Subs.: F. Keenan for Crowley, A. Feerick for Forde.

Meath—C. Martin, V. Ryan, E. McManus, R. McGrath, J. McCarthy, G. Geraghty, T. Hanley, J. Hendrick, J. McGuinness, T. Shine, H. Carolan, T. Byrne, P. O'Sullivan, T. O'Connor, C. Sheridan. Subs.: B. Kealy for Hendrick, T. Giles for O'Connor, N. Collier for McCarthy.

Kerry—D. O'Keeffe, M. Hassett, G. McGrath, N. Mangan, S. Curtin, F. Stack, J. O'Connell, S. Moynihan, J. Quirke, C. O'Grady, B. O'Shea, P. O'Driscoll, E. Hennessy, J. O'Shea, S. Culloty. Subs.: D. O'Shea for Quirke, K. Scanlon for McGrath, S. O'Driscoll for J. O'Shea.

The Vincent O'Brien Story

VINCENT O'BRIEN was according to his peers "a good hurler" in his school-going days in local matches between Clasganniff and Churchtown in County Cork. "He had a great eye and a great shot", said Jack Murphy of Churchtown.

Who knows but that if Vincent had concentrated on hurling rather than on horses he might have taken the path of a Christy Ring and worn the Red and White of Cork with distinction in the inter-county field. But he went on to become Ireland's most world-renowned trainer.

Vincent O'Brien – The Master of Ballydoyle, by Raymond Smith, is the absorbing biography of the man who trained six Epsom Derby winners, three successive Aintree Grand National winners, won the Gold Cup four times and the Champion Hurdle with Hatton's Grace three years running.

Autographed copies of the hardback edition can be obtained for £15 (including postage and packaging) from Sporting Books Publishers, 4 Sycamore Road, Mount Merrion, County Dublin.

CAPTAINS OF WINNING ALL-IRELAND UNDER-21 FOOTBALL TEAMS

1964—D. O'Donnell (Kerry)
1965—P. Dunny (Kildare)
1966—C. Shine (Roscommon)
1967—W. Loftus (Mayo)
1968—T. Diamond (Derry)
1969—L. Boyle (Antrim)
1970—D. Hunt (Cork)
1971—S. Looney (Cork)
1972—J. Waldron (Galway)
1973—J. Coffey (Kerry)
1974—J. Culkin (Mayo)
1975—K. O'Donoghue (Kerry)
1976—G. Murphy (Kerry)
1977—D. "Ogie" Moran (Kerry).
1978—S. Hayden (Roscommon)
1979—J. McCartan (Down)
1980—T. Dalton (Cork)
1981—S. Hayes (COrk)
1982—B. Tuohy (Donegal)
1983—E. Gibbons (Mayo)
1984—N. Cahalane (Cork)
1985—A. Davis (Cork)
1986—M. Slocum (Cork)
1987—J. Cunningham (Donegal)
1988—G. O'Brien (Offaly)
1989—S. O'Brien (Cork)
1990—V. Knightley (Kerry)
1991—Peter Canavan (Tyrone)
1992—Peter Canavan (Tyrone)
1993—Thomas Hanley (Meath)

LEINSTER UNDER-21 FOOTBALL FINALS

1964—Laois 1-8, Offaly 0-8
1965—Kildare 1-11, Offaly 0-10
1966—Kildare 4-14, Longford 2-5
1967—Kildare 3-11, Wicklow 0-4
1968—Offaly 2-13, Wexford 0-7
1969—Laois 2-7, Wicklow 2-6
1970—Louth 2-13, Offaly 3-9
1971—Offaly 1-9, Meath 0-11
1972—Kildare 2-9, Offaly 0-6 (replay)
         Kildare 0-14, Offaly 2-8 (draw)
1973—Offaly 3-8, Kildare 3-6
1974—Dublin 1-10, Wexford 0-8
1975—Dublin 0-12, Laois 1-6
1976—Kildare 1-12, Dublin 0-9
1977—Offaly 0-12, Kildare 0-4
1978—Louth 2-8, Offaly 2-7
1979—Offaly 4-14, Louth 5-4
1980—Dublin 0-10, Kildare 0-8 (replay)
         Dublin 2-7, Kildare 1-10 (draw)
1981—Louth 2-8, Longford 0-6
1982—Laois 2-11, Longford 0-3
1983—Kildare 1-13, Louth 1-8
1984—Dublin 0-9, Carlow 1-5
1985—Meath 2-7, Kildare 0-12
1986—Offaly 1-10, Laois 0-9 (replay)
         Offaly 1-11, Laois 2-8 (draw)
1987—Laois 1-12, Meath 1-8
1988—Offaly 2-7, Wexford 2-5 (third replay)
         Offaly 1-12, Wexford 1-12 (second replay) after extra time
         Offaly 0-12, Wexford 2-6 (first replay) after extra time
         Offaly 0-8, Wexford 1-5 (draw)
1989—Meath 2-5, Kildare 0-9
1990—Meath 1-14, Wicklow 0-6
1991—Meath 0-9, Wicklow 1-5
1992—Kildare 2-12, Dublin 0-9
1993—Meath 2-11, Dublin 2-9

ULSTER UNDER-21 FOOTBALL FINALS

1963—Donegal 3-6, Cavan 1-3
1964—Donegal 2-14, Monaghan 0-4
1965—Down 0-9, Cavan 1-2

1966—Donegal 2-12, Down 1-6
1967—Derry 1-11, Monaghan 1-4
1968—Derry 4-9, Monaghan 2-4
1969—Antrim 2-8, Down 1-9
1970—Fermanagh 0-13, Cavan 0-8
1971—Fermanagh 2-12, Tyrone 1-8
1972—Derry 1-7, Tyrone 1-7
      Tyrone 3-13, Derry 1-6 (replay)
1973—Tyrone 2-14, Monaghan 2-5
1974—Antrim 2-6, Tyrone 1-8
1975—Antrim 2-7, Tyrone 0-7
1976—Derry 1-6, Down 1-4
1977—Down 3-5, Cavan 0-10
1978—Down 0-11, Cavan 1-6
1979—Down 1-9, Tyrone 0-5
1980—Tyrone 4-4, Down 2-5
1981—Monaghan 0-8, Donegal 0-6
1982—Donegal 0-10, Derry 1-5
1983—Derry 3-13, Donegal 1-3
1984—Down 1-10, Antrim 1-8
1985—Down 3-7, Tyrone 0-7
1986—Derry 4-7, Donegal 0-6
1987—Donegal 0-7, Monaghan 1-4
      Donegal 1-11, Monaghan 0-8 (replay)
1988—Cavan 3-10, Antrim 0-6
1989—Antrim 1-6, Down 1-5
1990—Tyrone 2-8, Down 0-11
1991—Tyrone 3-10, Dwn 0-8
1992—Tyrone 0-14, Monaghan 2-6
1993—Derry 1-9, Down 1-8

MUNSTER UNDER-21 FOOTBALL FINALS

1962—Kerry 2-7, Cork 1-4
1963—Cork 2-3, Kerry 1-4
1964—Kerry 0-15, Tipperary 1-2
1965—Cork 2-14, Tipperary 1-6
1966—Kerry 3-8, Cork 0-14
1967—Kerry 2-12, Clare 1-7
1968—Kerry 5-7, Clare 2-9
1969—Cork 1-14, Kerry 1-11
1970—Cork 5-12, Clare 1-7
1971—Cork 1-10, Waterford 2-5

1972—Kerry 1.11, Cork 2-7
1973—Kerry 2-12, Cork 1-12
1974—Cork 3-5, Kerry 1-10
1975—Kerry 0-17, Waterford 1-5
1976—Kerry 2-16, Cork 1-6
1977—Kerry 2-8, Cork 0-8
1978—Kerry 0-14, Cork 0-9
1979—Cork 1-11, Clare 1-9
1980—Cork 3-15, Clare 0-4
1981—Cork 0-11, Kerry 0-6
1982—Cork 2-12, Kerry 0-4
1983—Kerry 1-10, Cork 0-12
1984—Cork 1-18, Limerick 0-4
1985—Cork 1-18, Clare 1-7
1986— Cork 0-7, Tipperary 0-6
1987—Kerry 0-15, Tipperary 1-11 (replay after extra time)
        Kerry 0-7, Tipperary 0-7 (draw)
1988—Kerry 0-14, Clare 2-6
1989—Cork 3-15, Clare 1-7
1990—Kerry 2-9, Cork 0-9
1991—Kerry 1-8, Cork 0-10
1992—Kerry 3-12, Cork 1-8
1993—Kerry 1-21, Waterford 3-5

CONNACHT UNDER-21 FOOTBALL FINALS

1964—Galway 3-6, Mayo 3-5
1965—Galway 3-9, Mayo 1-13
1966—Roscommon 1-15, Mayo 0-9
1967—Mayo 3-11, Roscommon 2-8
1968—Mayo 1-13, Roscommon 2-3
1969—Roscommon 1-10, Galway 2-3 (replay after extra time)
        Roscommon 1-9, Galway 0-12 (draw)
1970—Mayo 0-14, Roscommon 1-10
1971—Mayo 5-10, Roscommon 0-8
1972—Galway 0-16, Roscommon 0-5
1973—Mayo 1-7, Galway 0-5
1974—Mayo 1-12, Roscommon 0-9
1975—Mayo 2-10, Galway 0-9
1976—Mayo 1-8, Galway 0-2
1977—Leitrim 1-3, Roscommon 0-5

1978—Roscommon 3-9, Galway 2-11
1979—Galway 0-12, Sligo 0-9
1980—Mayo 4-11, Galway 1-5
1981—Galway 0-9, Mayo 0-8
1982—Roscommon 1-10, Galway 0-5
1983—Mayo 1-19, Roscommon 1-6
1984—Mayo 2-7, Galway 2-4
1985—Mayo 2-6, Galway 0-7
1986—Mayo 0-12, Leitrim 0-5
1987—Galway 1-10, Roscommon 0-10
1988—Galway 0-10, Roscommon 0-6
1989—Galway 1-13, Roscommon 0-3
1990—Galway 0-9, Leitrim 0-5
1991—Leitrim 1-7, Galway 0-9
1992—Galway 1-12, Mayo 0-12
1993—Galway 0-14, Roscommon 0-9

THE SON OF OLLIE

● *Michael Walsh, son of Ollie Walsh, the Kilkenny manager and forme brilliant goalie, makes a fine save against Galway in the 1993 All-Irelan final.*

ALL-IRELAND JUNIOR FOOTBALL FINALS
1912-1993

1912—Tipperary 1-4, Louth 1-3
1913—Kerry 0-7, Carlow 1-2
1914—Dublin 5-4, Mayo 1-6
1915—Kerry 0-6, Westmeath 1-2
1916—Dublin 6-4, Limerick 0-3 (replay)
      Dublin 1-2, Limerick 1-2 (draw)
1917-1922—Suspended
1923—Tipperary 2-6, Carlow 1-1
1924—Kerry 1-6, Longford 0-4
1925—Louth 2-6, Mayo 2-5
1926—Armagh 4-11, Dublin 0-4
1927—Cavan 4-1, Britain 1-1
1928—Kerry 2-8, Louth 2-3
1929—Westmeath 0-9, London 1-2
1930—Kerry 2-2, Dublin 1-4
1931—Galway 3.3, London 1-5
1932—Louth 0-6; London 0-4
1933—Mayo 3-7, London 2-4
1934—Louth 1-3, London 0-3
1935—Sligo 5-8; London 0-3
1936—Wicklow 3-3, Mayo 2-5
1937—Longford 0-9, London 0-4
1938—London 5-7, Leitrim 2-9
1939—Dublin 2-14, London 0-4
1940—Roscommon 2-9, Westmeath 0-5
1941—Kerry 0-9, Cavan 0-4
1942—45—Suspended
1946—Down 2-10, Warwickshire 1-9
1947—Meath 2-11, London 2-6
1948—Dublin 2-11, London 1-5
1949—Kerry 2-11, Lancashire 0-6
1950—Mayo 2-4, London 0-3
1951—Cork 5-11, Warwickshire 1-3
1952—Meath 3-9, London 0-4
1953—Cork 1-11, Lancashire 1-4
1954—Kerry 1-7, London 1-5
1955—Cork 3-9, Warwickshire 1-5
1956—Monaghan 3-7, London 2-6
1957—Mayo 2-7, Warwickshire 2-5

1958—Galway 4-5, Lancashire 3-1
1959—Fermanagh 1-11, London 2-4
1960—Dublin 2-5, London 0-5
1961—Louth 1-13, Yorkshire 1-10
1962—Meath 1-13, London 3-5
1963—Kerry 3-5, Lancashire 2-5
1964—Cork 1-8, London 2-4
1965—Galway 1-8, Hertfordshire 0-4
1966—London 1-6, Cork 0-8
1967—Kerry 0-9, London 0-4
1968—Tyrone 3-8, London 0-7.
1969—London 3-9, Wicklow 1-12
1970—London 1-12, Kildare 0-11
1971—London 1-9, Dublin 0-9
1972—Cork 5-16, Hertfordshire 0-3
1973—Laois 0-12, London 1-8
1974-1982—Suspended.
1983—Kerry 0-15, Yorkshire 0-2
1984—Cork 3-20, Warwickshire 0-7
1985—Galway 4-17; Warwickshire 0-4
1986—London 1-9, Cork 0-7
1987—Cork 0-14, Warwickshire 0-3
      Home Final: Cork 2-4, Dublin 0-8
1988—Meath 1-10, London 0-3
      Home Final: Meath 1-9, Cork 1-5
1989—Cork 0-18, Warwickshire 0-3
      Home Final: Cork 1-11, Kildare 0-3
1990—Cork 3-16, Warwickshire 0-8
      Home Final: Cork 1-12, Meath 1-10
1991—Kerry 2-14, London 0-5
      Home Final: Kerry 1-15, Meath 0-12
1992—Wexford 1-9, Cork 0-11
      Semi-finals:
      Cork 1-19, London 1-4
      Wexford 1-13, Mayo 0-12
1993—Semi-finals:
      Laois 1-19, Lancashire 2-6
      Cork 0-15, Mayo 0-7
      Final: Cork 0-11, Laois 2-3

1993—Cork 0-11, Laois 2-3

NATIONAL FOOTBALL LEAGUE RESULTS
(1927-1993 (inclusive)

1926-27—*Laois* beat Sligo (repiay, 4-6 to 1-4) and Kerry (1-6 to 1-5), and Dublin (2-1 to 1-0) in Final.

1927-28—Deciders: Kildare (0-8 to 0-5) and Kerry (0-6 to 0-4) beat Mayo, and *Kerry* beat Kildare (2-4 to 1-6) in Final.

1928-1929—Deciders. Kildare (4-5) beat Monaghan (0-5); Sligo (1-5) beat Westmeath (0-4); *Kerry* (1-5) beat Sligo (1-2) and in Final, Kildare (1-7 to 2-3).

1930-31—Final: *Kerry* (1-3) beat Cavan (1-2). *Division II*— Northern Donegal. Midland A — Kilkenny. Midland B — Westmeath.

1931-32—Semi-final: Kerry, 2-5; Mayo, 1-6. Meath refused to meet Cork (at home). Final: *Kerry,* 5-2; Cork, 3-3.

1932-33—Final at Croke Park: *Meath,* 0-10; Cavan, 1-6. (Special Division—Final). Wexford, 3-5; Cork, 1-8.

1933-34—Division I—Inter-Group Test, May 13, 1934, at Castlebar: Mayo, 2-3; Dublin, 1-6. Replay, October 15, Croke Park. Mayo, 2-4; Dublin, 1-5. (Division II—Inter-Group Test, October 14, 1934, at Tuam: *Offaly,* 3-6; Sligo, 1-6).

1934-35—Division I—Inter-Group Tests, June 9, 1935, Clonmel: Mayo, 6-8; Tipperary, 2-5. August 4, 1935, Castlebar: Mayo, 5-8; Fermanagh, 0-2. Tipperary were winners of McGrath Cup in Munster, and Fermanagh in Ulster tournaments. Division II— Final at Armagh, October 27, 1935: *Armagh,* 3-1, Westmeath, 0-9.

1935-36—Division I—*Mayo* (12 points from eight games). Runners-up: Dublin and Cavan (with 10 points). (Division II—Final at Mullingar, March 29, 1936: *Offaly,* 3-3, Longford 1-6.)

1936-37—Division I—Decider, April 11, 1937. Croke Park: Mayo, 5-4; Meath, 1-8. D'vision II—Decider, March 7, 1937, Ardara: *Longford,* 1-7; Donegal, 1-3.

1937-38—Division I—Decider, Castlebar, July 3, 1938: *Mayo,* 3-9; Wexford, 1-3. Division II—*Tipperary.* (Connacht League— Sligo).

1938-39—Final, at Ballina: *Mayo,* 5-9; Meath, 0-6. (Twenty-seven counties took part in this season's League).

1939-40—Final. at Croke Park: *Galway,* 2-5; Meath, 1-5. (Mayo (holders) did not compete. Twenty-three counties participated).

1940-41—Group Winners: Mayo and Dublin. Final, at Croke Park: *Mayo,* 3-7; Dublin, 0-7.

1941-42—National Leagues suspended. Substitute Competitions — South Leinster — Laois. Connacht — Roscommon. Ulster — Antrim. North Leinster—Dublin.

1943-44—Leinster League—Meath.
1944-45—Leinster League—Meath.
1944—Ulster Minor League—Armagh. Connacht League—Galway.
1945—Connacht League—Sligo.
1945-46—Final: *Meath,* 2-2; Wexford, 0-6.
1946-47—Final: *Derry,* 2-9; Clare, 2-5.
1947-48—Final: *Cavan,* 5-9; Cork, 2-8 in replay (Draw: Cavan, 2-11; Cork, 3-8).
1948-49—Final: *Mayo,* 1-8; Louth, 1-6.
1949-50—Final: *New York,* 2-8; Cavan, 0-12 (In Croke Park). Home Final: Cavan, 2-8; Meath, 1-6.
1950-51—Final. *Meath,* 1-10; New York, 0-10 (n New York). Home Final: Meath. 0-6; Mayo, 0-3.
1951-52—Final: *Cork,* 1-12; New York, 0-3 (in Croke Park). Home Final: Cork, 2-3; Dublin, 1-5.
1952-53—Final: *Dublin,* 4-6; Cavan, 0-9.
1953-54—Final: *Mayo,* 2-10; Carlow, 0-3.
1954-55—Final. *Dublin,* 2-12; Meath, 1-3.
1955-56—Final: *Cork,* 0-8; Meath, 0-7.
1956-57—Final: *Galway,* 1-8; Kerry, 0-7.
1957-58—Final: *Dublin,* 3-13; Kildare, 3-8.
1958-59—Final: *Kerry,* 2-8; Derry, 1-8.
1959-60—Final: *Down,* 0-12; Cavan, 0-9.
1960-61—Final. *Kerry,* 4-16; Derry, 1-5.
1962—Final: *Down,* 2-5; Dublin, 1-7.
1963—Final: *Kerry,* 1-18; New York, 0-10 (in Croke Park).
       Home Final: Kerry, 0-9; Down, 1-5.
1964—Final: *New York,* 2-12; Dublin, 1-13 (in New York).
       Home Final: Dublin, 2-9; Down, 0-7.
1965—27/6/'65. Galway, 1-4; New York, 0-8 (in New York).
       4/7/'65: Galway, 3-8; New York, 0-9 (in New York).
       Aggregate: *Galway,* 4-12; New York, 0-17.
       Home Final. Galway, 1-7; Kerry, 0-8.
1966—2/10/'66: Longford, 1-9; New York, 0-7 (in Longford).
       9/10'66: Longford, 0-9; New York, 0-10 (at Croke Park).
       Aggregate: *Longford,* 1-18; New York, 0-17.
       Home Final: Longford, 0-9; Galway, 0-8.
1967—14/5/'67: New York, 3-5; Galway, 1-6 (in New York).
       21/5/'67: New York, 4-3; Galway, 0-10 (in New York).
       Aggregate: *New York,* 7-8; Galway, 1-16.
       Home Final: Galway, 0-12; Dublin, 1-7.

1968—26/5/'68. Down, 2-14; Kildare, 2-11 (at Croke Park).
1969—22/6/'69: Kerry, 0-12; New York, 0-12 (in New York).
29/6/'69: Kerry, 2-21; New York, 2-12 (after extra time).
Aggregate: Kerry, 2-33; New York, 2-24.
Home Final: 18/5/'69: Kerry, 3-11; Offaly, 0-8.
1970—10/5/'70: Mayo, 4-7; Down, 0-10 (at Croke Park).
1971—20/6/'71: Kerry, 0-11; Mayo, 0-8 (at Croke Park).
1972—*Kerry*, 2-11; Mayo, 1-9 (at Croke Park).
1973—*Kerry*, 2-12; Offaly, 0-14 (at Croke Park).
1974—Kerry, 1-6; Roscommon, 0-9 (draw, at Croke Park).
Kerry, 0-14; Roscommon, 0-8 (replay, also at Croke
1975—*Meath*, 0-16; Dublin, 1-9 (at Croke Park).
1976—*Dublin*, 2-10; Derry, 0-15 (at Croke Park).
1977—*Kerry*, 1-8; Dublin, 1-6 (at Croke Park).
1978—*Dublin*, 2-18; Mayo, 2-13 (at Croke Park).
1979—*Roscommon*, 0-15; Cork, 1-3 (at Croke Park).
1980—*Cork*, 0-11; Kerry, 0-10 (at Pairc Ui Chaoimh).
1981—*Galway*, 1-11; Roscommon, 1-2 (at Croke Park).
1982—Kerry, 0-11; Cork, 0-11 (draw, at Killarney). *Kerry*, 1-9;
Cork. 0-5 (replay, Pairc Ui Chaoimh).
1983—*Down*, 1-8; Armagh, 0-8 (at Croke Park).
1983-'84 — Semi-finals: April 1, Croke Park — Kerry, 0-12;
Down, 1-6. Galway, 1-10; Meath, 0-13 (Draw). April 15, Croke
Park — Galway, 0-10; Meath, 0-9 (Replay).
Final: April 29, Limerick — Kerry, 1-11; Galway, 0-11.
1984-'85 — Semi-finals: March 24, Croke Park — Armagh,
1-9; Down 0-6. Monaghan, 1-6; Tyrone 0-9 (Draw). March 31,
Armagh – Monaghan. 1-8; Tyrone 0-8 (Replay, after extra time).
Final: April 7, Croke Park — Monaghan, 1-11; Armagh 0-9.
1985-'86 — Semi-finals: April 20, Croke Park — Laois, 0-12;
Dublin, 1-7. Monaghan, 0-10; Mayo 1-6.
Final: May 4, Croke Park — Laois, 2-6; Monaghan, 2-5.
1986-'87—Semi-finals: April 12, Croke Park — Kerry, 2-11;
Monaghan, 2-9. April 19, Croke Park — Dublin 1-8, Galway 0-8.
Final: April 26, Croke Park — Dublin 1-11, Kerry 0-11.
1987-'88—Semi-finals: April 3, Croke Park — Dublin, 4-12;
Monaghan, 1-8; Meath 0-13, Down, 1-9.
Final: April 17, Croke Park — Meath 0-11, Dublin 1-8.
Replay: May 22, Croke Park — Meath 2-13, Dublin 0-11.
1988-'89—Semi-finals: April 9, 1989: Croke Park — Dublin 1-10,
Cavan 1-9; April 9, 1989: Pairc Ui Chaoimh—Cork 0-10, Kerry
0-4.
Home Final: April 23, 1989: Croke Park — Cork 0-15, Dublin
0-12. 396

Final: May 7, 1989: Gaelic Park (New York) — 1st leg — Cork 1-12, New York 1-5; May 14, 1989: Gaelic Park (New York) — 2nd leg — Cork 2-9, New York 1-9.

Aggregate — Cork 3-21, New York 2-14.

1989-'90—Semi-finals: April 15, 1990: Croke Park — Meath 0-14, Cork 0-10: Down 4-8, Roscommon 0-11.

Final: April 29, 1990: Croke Park — Meath 2-7, Down 0-11.

1990-'91—Semi-finals: April 21, 1991: Croke Park — Kildare 0-14, Donegal 0-10; Dublin 1-18, Roscommon 0-11.

Final: May 5, 1991: Croke Park — Dublin 1-9, Kildare 0-10.

1991-'92—Semi-finals: April 19, 1992: Croke Park — Derry 0-12, Meath 1-8; Tyrone 0-13, Dublin 1-9.

Final: May 3, 1992: Croke Park — Derry 1-10, Tyrone 1-8.

1992-'93—Semi-finals: April 18, 1993: Croke Park — Donegal 1-12, Clare 1-7; Dublin 1-10, Kerry 0-11.

Final: May 2, 1993: Croke Park — Dublin 0-9, Donegal 0-9 (draw). May 9, 1993: Croke Park — Dublin 0-10, Donegal 0-6 (replay).'

Roll of Honour: Kerry (15), Mayo (10), Dublin (8), Meath (6), Cork (4), Down (4), Galway (4), New York (3), Derry (2), Laois (2), Cavan (1), Longford (1), Monaghan (1), Roscommon (1).

Dublin's Keith Barr in action against Meath with, on left, the ageless veteran, Colm O'Rourke and (right) Mick Kennedy.

397

ALL-IRELAND "B" FOOTBALL FINALS

1990—Roscommon, November 11. Leitrim 2-11, Sligo 0-2.

1991—Ballinasloe, November 17. Clare 1-12, Longford 0-9 (extra time).

1992—Navan, December 6. Wicklow 1-5, Antrim 0-4.

[Note: 1993 competition not finished at time of going to press.]

A GREAT DUAL STAR

● *Cork's Teddy McCarthy breaks clear from Gerry McCarvi (Monaghan) in the 1988 All-Ireland semi-final. He went on to create a spec niche for himself in GAA history by winning All-Ireland senior hurling a football medals in the same year – with his county in 1990.*

RAILWAY CUP FOOTBALL
INTERPROVINCIAL CHAMPIONSHIP
1927-1992

ROLL OF HONOUR

Leinster (22)—1928, 1929, 1930, 1932, 1933, 1935, 1939, 1940, 1944, 1945, 1952, 1953, 1954, 1955, 1959, 1961, 1962, 1974, 1985, 1986, 1987, 1988.

Ulster (20)—1942, 1943, 1947, 1950, 1956, 1960, 1963, 1964, 1965, 1966, 1968, 1970, 1971, 1979, 1980, 1983, 1984, 1989, 1991, 1992.

Munster (13)—1927, 1931, 1941, 1946, 1948, 1949, 1972, 1975, 1976, 1977, 1978, 1981, 1982.

Connacht (9)—1934, 1936, 1937, 1938, 1951, 1957, 1958, 1967, 1969.

Universities (1)—1973.

1927—November 14, 1926, Cavan: Munster 1-8; Ulster 3-1.
November 14, 1926, Ballinasloe: Connacht 1-4; Leinster 1-3.
Final, March 17, Croke Park: *Munster* 2-3; Connacht 0-5.

1928—February 19, Portlaoise: Leinster 1-9; Connacht 1-5.
February 26, Croke Park: Ulster 2-8; Munster 2-6. (Unfinished).
Final, March 17, Croke Park: *Leinster* 1-8; Ulster 2-4.

1929—February 10, Cavan: Leinster 2-3; Ulster 1-2.
(Connacht was struck out and Munster got a bye.)
Final, March 17, Croke Park: *Leinster* 1-7; Munster 1-3.

1930—February 23, Croke Park: Leinster 0-8; Connacht 0-3.
Munster 2-13; Ulster 1-3.
Final, March 17, Croke Park: *Leinster* 2-3; Munster 0-6.

1931—February 1, Athlone: Munster 4-5; Connacht 1-7.
February 8, Navan: Leinster 1-8; Ulster 1-2.
Final, March 17, Croke Park: *Munster* 2-2; Leinster 0-6.

1932—February 14, Cork: Munster 1-9; Connacht 0-5.
February 14, Drogheda: Leinster 4-11; Ulster 1-3.
Final, March 17, Croke Park: *Leinster* 2-10; Munster 3-5.

1933—February 12, Cork: Leinster 2-4; Munster 1-2.
February 12, Monaghan: Connacht 1-5; Ulster 0-5.
Final, March 17, Croke Park. *Leinster* 0-12; Connacht 2-5.

1934—February 11, Cork: Leinster 2-6; Munster 1-5.
February 18, Castlebar: Connacht 0-8; Ulster 0-6.
Final, March 17, Croke Park: *Connacht* 2-9; Leinster 2-8.

399

1935—February 17, Mullingar: Leinster 1-6; Connacht 1-5.
February 24, Croke Park: Munster 0-10; Ulster 1-5.
Final, March 17, Croke Park: *Leinster* 2-9; Munster 0-7.
1936—February 9, Dundalk: Leinster 0-2; Ulster 0-2.
February 9, Castlebar: Connacht 1-7; Munster 2-2.
Replay, March 1, Cavan: Ulster 1-7; Leinster 1-5.
Final, March 17, Croke Park: *Connacht* 3-11; Ulster 2-3.
1937—February 7, Carrick-on-Shannon: Connacht 4-6; Ulster 1-4.
February 21, Portlaoise: Munster 5-6; Leinster 1-1.
Final, March 17, Croke Park: *Connacht* 2-4; Munster 0-5.
1938—February 13, Croke Park: Munster 0-8; Leinster 1-4.
February 13, Cavan: Connacht 2-8; Ulster 0-3.
Final, March 17, Croke Park: *Connacht* 2-6; Munster 1-5.
1939—February 19, Croke Park: Ulster 2-8; Munster 1-6.
February 19, Ballinasloe: Leinster 3-4; Connacht 2-5.
Final, March 17, Croke Park: *Leinster* 3-8; Ulster 3-3.
1940—February 11, Ballinasloe: Munster 3-4; Connacht 2-5.
February 11, Dundalk: Leinster 2-4; Ulster 0-6.
Final, March 17, Croke Park: *Leinster* 3-7; Munster 0-2.
1941—February 9, Killarney: Munster 1-9; Connacht 0-6.
February 9, Cavan: Ulster 1-9; Leinster 2-5.
Final, March 16, Croke Park: Munster 1-8; Ulster 1-8.
Replay, April 14, Croke Park: *Munster* 2-6; Ulster 1-6.
1942—February 21, Wexford: Munster 2-7; Leinster 0-6.
February 21, Longford: Ulster 3-7; Connacht 2-6.
Final, March 17, Croke Park: *Ulster* 1-10; Munster 1-5.
1943—February 21, Croke Park: Ulster 3-8; Connacht 0-8.
February 28, Tralee: Leinster 1-3; Munster 0-4.
Final, March 17, Croke Park: *Ulster* 3-7; Leinster 2-9.
1944—February 20, Croke Park: Ulster 2-10; Munster 1-7.
February 27, Croke Park: Leinster 2-11; Connacht 1-8.
Final, March 17, Croke Park: *Leinster* 1-10; Ulster 1-3.
1945—February 18, Ballinasloe: Connacht 2-8; Munster 1-6.
February 25, Croke Park: Leinster 4-3; Ulster 2-9.
Replay, March 4, Croke Park: Leinster 4-9; Ulster 3-6.
Final, March 17, Croke Park. *Leinster* 2-5; Connacht 0-6.
1946—February 24, Cork: Munster 1-6; Connacht 0-5.
February 24, Cavan: Leinster 2-5; Ulster 1-5.
Final, March 17, Croke Park: *Munster* 3-5; Leinster 1-9.
1947—February 16, Croke Park: Ulster 0-11; Munster 1-3.

March 9, Croke Park: Leinster 3-7; Connacht 1-7.
Final, March 17, Croke Park: *Ulster* 1-6; Leinster 0-3.

1948—February 22, Tralee: Munster 3-5; Connacht 2-6.
February 29, Croke Park: Ulster 2-10; Leinster 1-12.
Final, March 17, Croke Park: *Munster* 4-5; Ulster 2-6.

1949—February 20, Ballinasloe: Munster 4-7; Connacht 1-11.
February 20, Clones: Leinster 3-5; Ulster 2-2.
Final, March 17, Croke Park: Munster 2-7; Leinster 2-7.
Replay, March 20, Croke Park: *Munster* 4-9; Leinster 1-4.

1950—February 12, Croke Park: Ulster 2-9; Connacht 2-6.
February 19, An Uaimh: Leinster 2-6; Munster 1-5.
Final, March 17. Croke Park: *Ulster* 4-11; Leinster 1-7.

1951—February 25, Tralee: Munster 2-8; Leinster 1-9.
February 25, Croke Park: Connacht 3-6; Ulster 2-8.
Final, March 17, Croke Park: *Connacht* 1-9; Munster 1-8.

1952—February 24, Croke Park: Munster 1-7; Ulster 0-3.
February 24, Ballinasloe: Leinster 1-8; COnnacht 1-7.
Final, March 17, Croke Park: *Leinster* 0-5; Munster 0-3.

1953—February 8, Croke Park: Leinster 2-11; Connacht 2-7.
February 15, Croke Park: Munster 2-5; Ulster 2-5. (Draw).
Replay, February 22, Croke Park: Munster 1-12; Ulster 2-7.

Final, March 17, Croke Park: *Leinster* 2-9; Munster 0-6.

1954—February 14, Croke Park: Leinster 3-14; Ulster 3-6.
February 14, Tralee: Connacht 2-9; Munster 2-8.
Final, March 17, Croke Park: *Leinster* 1-7; Connacht 1-5.

1955—February 13, Cavan: Leinster 2-9; Ulster 2-4.
February 13, Castlebar: Connacht 1-6; Munster 1-5.
Final, March 17, Crcke Park: *Leinster* 1-14; Connacht 1-10.

1956—February 19, Casement Park: Ulster 3-8; Connacht 1-4.
March 4, Croke Park: Munster 3-4; Leinster 0-9.
Final, March 17, Croke Park: *Ulster* 0-12; Munster 0-4.

1957—February 10, Cork: Munster 2-5; Leinster 0-9.
February 10, Markievicz Park: Connacht 2-8; Ulster 0-8.
Final, March 17, Croke Park: *Connacht* 2-9; Munster 1-6.

1958—February 16, Ballinasloe. Connacht 1-11; Leinster 0-7.
February 23, Cavan: Munster 1-6; Ulster 0-8.
Final, March 17, Croke Park: *Connacht* 2-7; Munster 0-8.
1959—February 15, Tullamore: Leinster 0-10; Connacht 0-8.
March 8, Tralee: Munster 2-12; Ulster 0-7.

Hackett Bookmakers

Turf and Football Accountants

Head Office:

79 DAME STREET, DUBLIN 2

Phone 6775101 :: Fax 6777938

BRANCHES CITY AND COUNTY

DUBLIN BRANCHES

79 Dame Street	151 Crumlin Road
26 Parliament Street	200 Whitehall Road, Trenure
87 North King Street	59 Lower Clanbrassil Street
107 Marlborough Street	106A Tyrconnel Road, Inchicore
360 N.C.R., Phibsboro	Old Naas Road, Bluebell
46 Brookwood Rise, Artane	2A Seafort Avenue, Sandymount
402 Collins Avenue	72 Upper George's Street,
34A Parkgate Street	Dun Laoghaire
4 Whitehall Road, W. Crumlin	Woodpark, Sallynoggin

COUNTRY BRANCHES

Market Square, Tullamore	Patrick Street, Mountmellick
J.K.L. Street, Edenderry	Main Street, Portarlington
Market Square, Birr	Castle Street, Carlow
Westgate, Clonmel	John Street, Kilkenny
Parnell Street, Thurles	Parliament Street, Kilkenny
Mitchell Street, Nenagh	Leinster Street, Athy
Bank Place, Tipperary	Charlotte Street, Newbridge
Friary Street, Cashel	94 Lower Main Street, Portlaoise
Main Street, Roscrea	2 Bank Street, Templemore

Final, March 17, Croke Park: *Leinster* 2-7; Munster 0-7.

1960—February 21, Croke Park: Ulster 2-9; Leinster 1-5.
February 28, Tralee: Munster 4-9; Connacht 2-3.
Final, March 17, Croke Park: *Ulster* 2-12; Munster 3-8.

1961—February 19, Belfast: Leinster 2-5; Ulster 1-7.
February 26, Tuam: Munster 0-6; Connacht 1-3.
Replay, March 12, Croke Park: Munster 4-7; Connacht 1-6.
Final, March 17, Croke Park: *Leinster* 4-5; Munster 0-4.

1962—February 18, Tullamore: Leinster 2-17; Munster 0-6.
February 25, Cavan: Ulster 5-6; Connacht 1-7. (Jim McCartan scored 3-1).
Final, March 17, Croke Park: *Leinster* 1-11; Ulster 0-11.

1963—February 17, Tralee: Leinster 2-6; Munster 1-8. (Des Foley, Leinster captain, scored winning goal two minutes from the end).
February 17, Sligo: Ulster 2-8; Connacht 1-5.
Final, March 17, Croke Park: *Ulster* 2-8; Leinster 1-9.

1964—February 16, Croke Park: Ulster 3-6; Munster 0-11.
February 23, Ballinasloe: Leinster 3-7; Connacht 0-9.
Final, March 17, Croke Park: *Ulster* 0-12; Leinster 1-6.

1965—Febuary 21, Croke Park: Ulster 0-14; Munster 0-9.
February 28, Navan: Connacht 1-7; Leinster 0-8.
Final, March 17, Croke Park: *Ulster* 0-19; Connacht 0-15. (Paddy Doherty scored 0-11 for Ulster, four from play and Cyril Dunne 0-10, all from frees. Neither missed a shot at the posts from a free. A crowd of 30,734 saw Ulster record their first treble).

1966—February 27, Tralee: Munster 0-11; Connacht 0-11.
Replay, March 13, Nenagh: Munster 2-8; Connacht 2-6.
February 27, Croke Park: Ulster 1-8; Leinster 1-4.
(Paddy Doherty 0-8, seven from frees and the eighth when he collected a rebound from the upright to send the ball over at the second attempt).
Final, March 17, Croke Park: *Ulster* 2-5; Munster 1-5.
(Ulster recorded four-in-a-row before 24,312 attendance).

1967—February 26, Galway: Connacht 0-11; Munster 0-6.
March 3, Belfast: Ulster 0-9; Leinster 0-8. (Seán O'Connell, Derry, 0-6, five from frees.)
Final, March 17, Croke Park: *Connacht* 1-9; Ulster 0-11. (Ulster's five-in-a-row bid failed before 22,054 attendance. Vital Connacht goal scored by Mickey Kearins,

403

Sligo, just before interval).

1968—February 25, Navan: Leinster 0-11; Munster 0-6.
   February 25, Cavan: Ulster 4-8; Connacht 1-10. (Sean
   O'Neill 3-0; Sean O'Connell 1-2).
   Final, March 17, Croke Park: *Ulster* 1-10; Leinster, 0-8.
   (Before an attendance of 11,158, the lowest on record,
   Ulster won their fifth title in six years).

1969—February 23, Tuam: Connacht 1-11; Ulster 2-4.
   February 23, Killarney, Munster 2-11; Leinster 1-9.
   Final, March 17, Croke Park: *Connacht* 1-12; Munster
   0-6.

1970—February 22, Croke Park: Ulster 2-12; Munster 0-6.
   Februray 22, Crossmalina: Connacht 1-11; Leinster 1-4.
   Final, March 17, Croke Park: *Ulster* 2-11; Connacht 0-10.

1971—February, Navan: Connacht 1-9; Leinster 0-9.
   February 28, Croke Park: Ulster 2-7; Munster 1-7.
   Final, March 17, Croke Park: *Ulster* 3-11; Connacht 2-11.
   (Before an attendance of 20,306, almost 4,000 more than
   in 1970, Ulster won their seventh title in nine years and
   Sean O'Neill set a record by winning his eighth Railway
   Cup medal and gave a classic display in the process).

1972—Roscommon, February 13. Preliminary Round: Connacht
   1-15, Combined Universities 1-9.

1972—February 20, Cork: Munster 1-9; Connacht 0-9.
   February 20, Croke Park: Leinster 0-13; Ulster 1-9.
   Final: March 17, Croke Park: Munster 1-15; Leinster
   1-15.
   Replay in Cork, April 23: *Munster* 2-14; Leinster 0-10.

1973—Cavan, January 27. Preliminary Round: Combined
   Universities 2-7, Ulster 0-12.

1973—February 18, Roscommon: Connacht 3-10; Munster 2-10.
   February 18, Croke Park: Universities 0-11; Leinster 0-8.
   Final, March 17, Croke Park: Universities 2-12 (18);
   Connacht 0-18.
   Replay, April 23, Athlone: *Universities* 4-9; Connacht 1-11.

1974—Mardyke, January 26. Preliminary Round: Combined
   Universities 1-7, Munster 1-4.

1974—February 10, Tullamore: Leinster 0-12; Universities 0-9.
   February 10, Ballybay: Connacht 2-11; Ulster 4-4.
   Final, March 17, Croke Park: *Leinster* 2-10; Connacht 1-7.

1975 —February 16, Cork (Mardyke): Munster 1-9; Leinster 0-8.
February 16, Carrick-on-Shannon: Ulster 5-13; Connacht 1-12.
Final, March 17, Croke Park: *Munster* 6-7; Ulster 0-15.
1976 —February 15, Ballina: Leinster 2-9; Connacht 1-10.
February 15, Croke Park: Munster 3-7; Ulster 0-9.
Final, March 17, Croke Park: *Munster* 2-15; Leinster 2-8.
1977—February 13, Croke Park: Munster 0-14; Ulster 0-8.
February 13, Navan: Connacht 2-13; Leinster 1-8.

Final, March 17, Croke Park: *Munster* 1-14; Connacht 1-9.
1978 —March 19, Sligo: Munster 2-6; Connacht 0-7.
March 19, Cavan: Ulster 1-7; Leinster 0-7.

Final (Replay), April 6, Croke Park: *Munster* 4-12; Ulster 0-19 (after extra time).
March 27, Croke Park: Munster 2-7; Ulster 2-7 (draw).
Final, March 27, Croke Park: *Munster* 4-12; Ulster 0-19 (after extra time).
1979 —March 11, Croke Park: Ulster 5-8; Leinster 1-13.
March 11, Tralee: Munster 4-7; Connacht 1-6.
Final, March 18, Croke Park: *Ulster* 1-7; Munster 0-6.
1980 —March 2, Newbridge: Munster 2-10; Leinster 1-11.
March 2, Cavan: Ulster 0-17; Connacht 1-3.
Final, March 17, Croke Park: *Ulster* 2-10; Munster 1-9.
1981—March 8, Roscommon: Connacht 2-19; Ulster 2-14 (after extra time).
March 8, Killarney: Munster 2-12; Leinster 0-10.
Final, March 17, Ennis: *Munster* 3-10; Connacht 1-9.
1982—February 14, Croke Park: Munster 4-5; Ulster 0-10.
February 14, Galway: Connacht 0-8; Leinster 0-2.
Final, March 17, Tullamore: *Munster* 1-8; Connacht 0-10.
1983 —February 6, Tullamore: Leinster 1-9; Connacht 0-7.
February 6, Croke Park: Ulster 2-10; Munster 2-4.
Final, March 17, Cavan: *Ulster* 0-24; Leinster 2-10 (after extra time).
1984—March 17, Ballinasloe: Connacht 0-15, Leinster 1-9.
March 17, Limerick: Ulster 0-12, Munster 0-9.
Final, March 18, Ennis: *Ulster* 1-12, Connacht 1-7.
1985—January 27, Croke Park: Leinster 2-8, Ulster 2-7.
January 27, Roscommon: Munster 3-7, Connacht 0-12.
Final, March 17, Croke Park: *Leinster* 0-9, Munster 0-5.
1986—February 16, Tralee: Connacht 2-6, Munster 0-7.
February 16, Cavan: Leinster 3-7, Ulster 1-9.

Final, March 17, Ballinasloe: *Leinster* 2-8, Connacht 2-5.
1987—October 3, Newbridge: Munster 3-12, Ulster 1-9.
Leinster 2-10, Connacht 1-9.
Final, October 4, Newbridge: *Leinster* 1-13, Munster 0-9.
1988—October 15, Ballina: Leinster 2-11, Munster 0-8.
Ulster 3-12, Connacht 1-10.
Final, October 16, Ballina: Leinster 2-9, Ulster 0-12.
1989—October 7, Macroom: *Munster* 0-8, Leinster 0-7.
October 7, Mitchelstown: *Ulster* 4-8, Connacht 0-7.
Final, October 8, Pairc Uì Chaoimh: *Ulster* 1-11,
Munster 1-8.
1990—No competition
1991—March 24, Ballybofey: *Ulster* 1-15, Connacht 1-13
(after extra time).
March 24, Navan: *Munster* 1-10, Leinster 0-11.
Final, April 7, Croke Park: *Ulster* 1-11, Munster 1-8.
1992—March 1, Tralee: *Munster* 2-7, Leinster 1-9.
March 1, Carrick-on-Shannon: *Ulster* 0-11, Connacht 0-7.
Final, March 15, Newry: *Ulster* 2-7, Munster 0-8.

● *The Winning Goal ... despite the attention of Kildare's John Crofton,*
Dublin's Vinny Murphy gets in the angled kick at the Canal end that brough
the fortuitous goal after just five-and-a-half minutes play that killed the Lily
Whites' hopes of victory in the 1991 League final.

RAILWAY CUP FOOTBALL TEAMS

1927

Munster—J. Riordan (goal), John J. Sheehy, Joe Barrett, J. Walsh, Paul Russell, E. Fitzgerald, J. Slattery, C. Brosnan, R. Stack, J. Ryan, Joe Sullivan, T. Mahony, James Baily, Frank Sheehy, P. Clifford (all Kerry).

Connacht—T. Molloy, M. Walsh, M. Bannerton, T. Leech, T. Hegarty (Galway), P. O'Beirne, R. Creagh, John Forde, M. Mulderrig (Mayo), G. Higgins (goal), Thos. Shevlin, M. Murphy (Roscommon), P. Colleran (Sligo), W. Martin, M. Dolan (Leitrim).

1928

Leinster—M. Walsh (goal), M. Goff, J. Higgins, F. Malone, P. Martin, P. Doyle (Kildare), P. Russell, P. McDonnell (Dublin), M. O'Neill, N. Walsh (Wexford), M. McKeown, W. Lawless (Louth), P. Bates, W. Whelan (Laois), M. Keoghan (Meath). Sub.: J. Delaney (Laois).

Paul Russell selected for both Munster and Leinster, Central Council ruled that he play for Leinster.

Ulster—P. Kilroy, T. Bradley (goal), F. Farrell, J. Brannigan, J. Duffy, J. Treanor (Monaghan), G. Hanratty, J. Maguire, P. Fearon, J. McCusker (Armagh), J. P. Murphy, J. Smith (Cavan), P. Cunning, J. C. McDonnell (Antrim), T. J. Weymes (Monaghan).

1929

Leinster—W. Gannon, M. Goff, A. Fitzpatrick, J. Higgins, P. Doyle, P. Martin (Kildare), J. McDonnell (goal), J. Norris, M. O'Brien, P. McDonnell (Dublin), P. Bates, J. Delaney (Laois), M. McKeown (Louth), N. Walsh, M. O'Neill (Wexford).

Munster—Dr. J. Kearney, M. Donegan (Cork), J. Riordan (goal), M. Murphy, J. Barrett, J. Walsh, P. Russell, J. O'Sullivan, C. Brosnan, E. Fitzgerald, J. J. Sheehy, J. Landers (Kerry), M. Keating (Limerick), T. Lee, C. Keane (Tipperary).

1930

Leinster—John Higgins, M. Goff, W. Hynan, F. Malone, P. Loughlin, P. Doyle, P. Martin (Kildare), John McDonnell (goal), P. McDonnell, M. O'Brien (Dublin), D. Walsh, D.

Douglas, J. Delaney (Laois), P. Byrne (Wexford), M. Rogers (Meath). Sub.: M. O'Neill (Wexford).

Munster—J. Barrett, J. Riordan (goal), J. Walsh, J. O'Sullivan, P. Russell, T. O'Donnell, C. Brosnan, R. Stack, J. Ryan, M. Doyle, E. Sweeney, J. J. Sheehy, M. O'Rourke, T. Barrett (Kerry), M. Donegan (Cork).

1931

Munster—J. O'Riordan, D. O'Connor, J. Barrett, J. Walsh, P. Russell, J. O'Sullivan, T. O'Donnell, C. Brosnan, R. Stack, E. Fitzgerald, M. Doyle, J. J. Landers, E. Sweeney, T. Landers, J. J. Sheehy (all Kerry).

Leinster—M. Goff, J. Hayes, F. Malone, J. Higgins, W. Ryan, P. Loughlin, P. Martin (Kildare), John McDonnell, M. O'Brien, T. O'Dowd (Dublin), T. Nulty, M. Rogers (Meath), D. Walsh, D. Douglas, J. Delaney (Laois).

1932

Leinster—J. Higgins, M. Goff, P. Martin, P. Byrne, D. Burke (Kildare), J. McDonnell (goal), P. Hickey, T. O'Dowd (Dublin), M. Nulty, T. Meade, M. Rogers, T. McGuinness (Meath), D. Walsh, J. Delaney, D. Douglas (Laois).

Munster—D. O'Keeffe (goal), D. O'Connor, P. Whitty, John Walsh, P. Russell, T. Landers, C. Brosnan, R. Stack, M. Doyle, J. Landers, J. Ryan, C. Gainey (Kerry), G. Comerford (Clare), J. Duggan (Limerick), P. Arragan (Tipperary).

1933

Leinster—J. McDonnell, P. Hickey, C. McLoughlin, D. Brennan, E. McCann, T. O'Dowd (Dublin), T. Meade, W. Shaw (Meath), J. Higgins, P. Martin, P. Byrne (Kildare), N. Walsh, P. Spillane (Wexford), D. Douglas, J. Delaney (Laois).

Connacht—T. Burke, P. Kelly, P. Quinn, S. O'Malley, G. Courell, P. Moclair, F. O'Fuartharn (Mayo), H. Carey, Ml. Donnellan, Ml. Higgins, F. Fox, Mar. Donellan (Galway), L. Colleran, M. Kilcoyne (Sligo), J. Creighton (Roscommon).

1934

Connacht—T. Burke (goal), P. Quinn, P. Kelly, P. Flannelly, G. Ormsby, J. Carney, G. Courell, P. Moclair (Mayo), H. Carey, M. Connaire, F. Fox, J. Dunne, M. Donnellan, M. Higgins, B. Nestor (Galway).

Leinster—J. McDonnell (goal), D. Brennan, P. Synnott, M. Kelly (Dublin), T. Meade, J. Loughran (Meath), M. McKeown (Louth), P. Fane, P. Mythen, N. Walsh (Wexford), J. Higgins, P. Martin, P. Byrne (Kildare), D. Douglas, J. Delaney (Laois).

1935

Leinster—J. McDonnell (goal), R. Beggs, P. Cavanagh, G. Comerford (Dublin), E. Boyle, J. Coyle (Louth), T. McGuinness, W. Shaw, A. Donnelly (Meath), J. Byrne, P. Watters, P. Byrne (Kildare), W. Delaney, John Delaney, D. Douglas (Laois).

Munster—P. Russell, T. O'Donnell, P. Whitty, D. O'Connor (Kerry), M. O'Sullivan (goal), J. Lonergan, T. O'Keeffe, R. Power, R. Allen B. McGann (Tipperary), M. Studdert (Calre), T. Greany, P. O'Donnell (Waterford), T. Culhane (Limerick), T. Cotter (Cork).

1936

Connacht—T. Burke (goal), P. Kelly, T. Regan, G. Ormsby, H. Kenny, P. Flannelly, J. Carney, P. Moclair (Mayo), M. Connaire, F. Fox, B. Beggs, M. Higgins, R. Griffin, B. Nestor (Galway), P. Kavanagh (Sligo). Sub.: F. Cunniffe (Galway).

Ulster—W. Young (goal), T. Dolan, M. Denneny, T. O'Reilly, P. Phair, H. O'Reilly, T. O'Reilly, D. Morgan, P. Devlin, J. Smallhorn, P. Boylan, L. Blessing, M. J. Magee (Cavan), J. Vallely, J. McCullagh (Armagh).

1937

Connacht—T. Burke (goal), T. Regan, P. Quinn, P. Kelly, P. Flannelly, H. Kenny, J. Carney, P. Laffey, J. Munnelly, P. Moclair (Mayo), M. Connaire, J. Dunne, D. O'Sullivan, B. Nestor, B. Beggs (Galway). Sub.: J. McGowan (Mayo).

Munster—D. O'Keeffe (goal), J. O'Gorman, J. Walsh, P. Kennedy, M. Doyle, G. Fitzgerald, T. Landers, M. Kelly (Kerry), W. McMahon, M. Casey, G. Comerford, J. Burke (Clare), W. Scott, R. Power (Tipperary), T. Culhane (Limerick). Sub.: A. Slattery (Clare).

1938

Connacht—P. Moclair, T. Burke (goal), J. McGowan, T. Regan, H. Kenny, J. Carney, P. Laffey, J. Munnelly, P. Kelly (Mayo), M. Connaire, C. Connolly, D. O'Sullivan, J. Dunne, M. Higgins, B. Nestor (Galway). Sub.: P. Flannelly (Mayo).

Munster—J. Keohane, D. O'Keeffe (goal), W. Casey, W. Myers, W. Kinnerk, W. Dillon, T. Healy, J. Walsh, P. Kennedy, J. J. Landers, C. O'Sullivan (Kerry), T. Culhane (Limerick), C. Comerford, J. Burke (Clare), T. Cotter (Cork). Sub.: J. Slattery (Clare).

1939

Leinster—M. Farrell, D. Walsh, M. Delaney, J. Slator, W. Delaney, C. Delaney (Laois), E. Boyle, E. Callan, J. Coyle (Louth), T. McEvoy (Offaly), J. Loughran, A. Donnelly (Meath), P. Bermingham (Dublin), P. O'Sullivan (Wicklow), T. Mulhall (Kildare). Sub.: J. Delaney (Laois).

Ulster—A. Lynn, R. Keelaghan, J. Crawley, V. Duffy (Monaghan), E. McMahon, E. McLoughlin, J. McCullagh, A. Murray, J. Fitzpatrick (Armagh), P. Smith, T. O'Reilly, J. J. O'Reilly, V. White (Cavan), J. Doherty (Donegal), E. Thornbury (Antrim).

1940

Leinster—P. Dowling (goal), P. Bermingham (Dublin), E. Boyle (Louth), T. McEvoy, W. Mulhall (Offaly), D. Walsh, M. Delaney, W. Delaney, T. Murphy, C. Delaney (Laois), J. Kearney, M. Gilsenan, A. Donnelly (Meath), P. O'Sullivan (Wicklow), T. Mulhall (Kildare).

Munster—D. O'Keeffe (goal), W. Myers, J. Keohane, T. Healy, W. Dillon, W. Casey, E. Walsh, P. Kennedy, T. O'Connor, M. Kelly, Seán Brosnan, J. Walsh, J. Gorman, D. Spring, T. Landers. Subs.: P. Brosnan, C. O'Sullivan (all Kerry).

1941 REPLAY

Munster—D. O'Keeffe, W. Myers, Joe Keohane, T. Healy (Kerry), R. Harnedy (Cork), W. Casey, E. Walsh, S. Brosnan, P. Kennedy, J. Walsh, T. O'Connor (Kerry), E. Young (Cork), M. Kelly, P. Brosnan, J. O'Gorman (Kerry).

Ulster—B. Kelly (Cavan), E. McLoughlin, E. McMahon (Armagh), J. McGlory (Down), G. Smith (Cavan), J. McCullagh (Armagh), T. O'Reilly, J. J. O'Reilly, P. Smith, D. Morgan (Cavan), A. Murray (Armagh), T. P. O'Reilly (Cavan), J. Carr, M. Lynch (Down), V. Duffy (Monaghan). Sub.: B. Cully (Cavan) for E. Mahon.

P. B. Brosnan (Kerry) replaced C. O'Sullivan (Kerry) on the Munster team, while T. P. O'Reilly (Cavan) and M. Lynch

(Down) replaced P. Conaty (Cavan) and J. Gallagher (Donegal) on the Ulster team which played in the drawn game.

1942

Ulster—B. Kelly (Cavan), E. McLoughlin (Armagh), B. Cully, T. O'Reilly, G. Smith (Cavan), J. McCullagh (Armagh), V. Duffy (Monaghan), C. McDyer (Donegal), J. J. O'Reilly (Cavan), K. Armstrong (Antrim), A. Murray (Armagh), T. P. O'Reilly (Cavan), B. Cullen (Tyrone), S. Deignan (Cavan), H. Gallagher (Donegal).

Munster—D. O'Keeffe, W. Myers, J. Keohane, T. Healy, W. Dillon, W. Casey, E. Walsh, S. Brosnan, P. Kennedy, John Walsh, T. O'Connor (Kerry), E. Young (Cork), J. O'Gorman, M. Kelly, P. B. Brosnan (Kerry). Sub.: R. Harnedy (Cork) for E. Walsh.

1943

Ulster—J. D. Benson (Cavan), E. McLoughlin (Armagh), B. Cully, T. O'Reilly, G. Smith (Cavan), J. McCullagh (Armagh), V. Duffy (Monaghan), J. J. O'Reilly (Cavan), C. McDyer (Donegal), K. Armstrong (Antrim). A. Murray (Armagh), P. Maguire (Derry), T. McCarney (Monaghan), S. Deignan (Cavan), H. Gallagher (Donegal).

Leinster—P. Lynch (Wexford), J. Murphy, P. Kennedy, C. Crone, P. Henry, P. O'Reilly (Dublin), J. Clarke (Meath), J. Fitzgerald (Dublin), T. Murphy (Laois), J. Joy (Dublin), W. Delaney (Laois), P. Bermingham (Dublin), M. Gilsenan (Meath), P. O'Connor, T. Banks (Dublin).

1944

Leinster—P. Larkin (Louth), J. Archbold (Carlow), E. Boyle (Louth), C. Crone, P. O'Reilly (Dublin), J. Quigley (Louth), M. Geraghty (Kildare), W. Delaney (Laois), J. Thornton (Louth), D. O'Neill (Wicklow), O. Halpin (Louth), P. McDermott (Meath), P. Bermingham (Dublin), C. Delaney (Laois), J. Rea (Carlow).

Ulster—H. Vernon (Antrim), E. McLoughlin, J. McCullagh (Armagh), E. Finnegan, G. Smith (Cavan), E. McDonald (Monaghan), J. J. O'Reilly, L. McAlinden (Armagh), S. Deignan (Cavan), K. Armstrong (Antrim), A. Murray (Armagh), P. Maguire (Derry), P. McCarney (Monaghan), B. McAteer (Antrim), H. Gallagher (Donegal). Sub.: F. Hamill (Antrim) for E. Finnegan.

1945

Leinster—P. Larkin, S. Boyle, E. Boyle (Louth), P. McIntyre (Dublin), P. Whelan (Carlow), P. O'Reilly (Dublin), M. Geraghty (Kildare), J. Morris (Carlow), J. Hanniffy (Longford), F. Byrne (Meath), W. Delaney (Laois), D. O'Neill (Wicklow), P. Meegan (Meath), C. Delaney (Laois), J. Rea (Carlow). Sub.: T. Murphy (Laois) for J. Hanniffy.

Connacht—T. Byrne (Mayo), W. Jackson (Roscommon), T. Dunleavy (Sligo), C. Connolly (Galway), B. Lynch, W. Carlos (Roscommon), T. O'Sullivan (Galway), E. Boland (Roscommon), C. McDyer (Sligo), M. Fallon (Galway), J. Murray, D. Keenan, P. Murray, J. McQuillan (Roscommon), T. Hoban (Mayo). Subs.: L. McAlinden (Leitrim) for C. McDyer, J. Munnelly (Mayo) for E. Boland.

1946

Munster—J. Williams (Tipperary), D. Magnier, P. Murphy, C. Crone, P. Cronin, T. Crowley (Cork), E. Walsh, P. Kennedy (Kerry), M. Cahill (Tipperary), M. Tubridy (Cork), W. O'Donnell (Kerry), E. Young (Cork), D. Kavanagh (Kerry), J. Cronin (Cork), J. Lyne (Kerry).

Leinster—P. Larkin, S. Boyle, E. Boyle (Louth), J. Cody, J. Culleton, W. Goodison (Wexford), M. Geraghty (Kildare), M. O'Brien (Wicklow), J. Morris (Carlow), F. Byrne (Meath), W. Delaney (Laois), D. O'Neill (Wexford), P. Meegan (Meath), N. Rackard (Wexford), J. Rea (Carlow).

1947

Ulster—J. O'Hare (Down), W. Feeney, G. Watterson (Antrim), J. McCullagh (Armagh), E. McDonnell (Monaghan), J. J. O'Reilly,S. Deignan (Cavan), H. O'Neill, S. Gallagher, K. Armstrong (Antrim), M. Higgins (Cavan), F. Niblock (Derry), S. Gibson, B. McAteer, S. McCallin (Antrim).

Leinster—K. Smyth (Meath), M. O'Brien (Kildare), E. Boyle (Louth), J. Cody (Wexford), P. O'Reilly (Dublin), W. Goodison (Wexford), M. Geraghty (Kildare), M. Haughney, D. Connolly (Laois), F. Byrne, P. McDermott (Meath), D. O'Neill (Wexford), P. Meegan (Meath), P. Lennon, R. Byrne (Wicklow).

1948

Munster—D. O'Keeffe (Kerry), P. A. Murphy (Cork), J. Keohane, P. B. Brosnan, J. Lyne (Kerry), T. Crowley (Cork), E.

O'Connor, T. Spillane (Kerry), M. Cahill (Tipperary), C. McGrath (Cork), W. O'Donnell, B. Garvey (Kerry), N. Crowley (Clare), J. Cronin, J. Aherne (Cork). Subs.: T. O'Sullivan (Kerry) for T. Crowley and F. O'Keeffe (Kerry) for W. O'Donnell.

Ulster—J. O'Hare (Down), W. Doonan (Cavan), G. Watterson (Antrim), P. Smith, P. J. Duke, J. J. O'Reilly, S. Deignan (Cavan), E. McDonnell (Monaghan), S. Gallagher, K. Armstrong (Antrim), M. Higgins (Cavan), S. Gallagher (Donegal), S. Gibson (Antrim), P. Donohoe, A. Tighe (Cavan). Subs.: H. O'Neill (Antrim) for M. Higgins and M. Higgins later for W. Doonan.

1949 REPLAY

Munster—M. O'Driscoll (Cork), E. O'Connor (Kerry), P. A. Murphy (Cork), P. B. Brosnan, M. Finucane, J. Lyne (Kerry), M. Cahill (Tipperary), C. McGrath (Cork), E. Dowling (Kerry), D. O'Donovan, C. Duggan (Cork), B. Garvey (Kerry), N. Crowley (Clare), J. Cronin (Cork), P. Brennan (Tipperary). Sub.: T. Spillane (Kerry) for T. O'Connor.

Tom O'Connor (Kerry) played in drawn game. Packie Brennan (Tipperary) came on for replay.

Leinster—K. Smith (Meath), J. Bell (Louth), A. Murphy (Carlow), J. Coady (Wexford), S. Boyle, P. Markey (Louth), S. Brennan (Kildare), J. Dunican (Offaly), P. O'Brien (Meath), F. Fegan (Louth), P. White (Kildare), D. Connolly (Laois), W. Halpenny (Meath), W. Kelly (Wexford), P. McDermott (Meath). Subs.: A. Burke (Kildare), S. White (Louth) and J. Quigley (Louth) for A. Murphy, J. Dunican and W. Halpenny.

Des Connolly (Laois) who came on as sub in first game for Kevin Heffernan (Dublin) retained his place for the replay.

1950

Ulster— J. O'Hare (Down), J. J. O'Reilly (Cavan), M. Moyna (Monaghan), P. Smith, P. J. Duke (Cavan), P. O'Neill, S. Quinn (Armagh), P. Brady (Cavan), W. McCorry (Armagh), A. Tighe, M. Higgins, V. Sherlock (Cavan), K. Armstrong (Antrim), P. Donohue (Cavan), H. McKearney (Monaghan). Sub.: S. Gallagher (Antrim) for V. Sherlock.

Leinster—K, Smith (Meath), J. Bell (Louth), N. Redmond (Wexford), K. McConnell (Meath), W. Geraghty (Kildare), W. Goodison (Wexford), C. Hand, P. Connell (Meath), J. McDonnell (Louth), F. Byrne, B. Smyth (Meath), S. White (Louth), W. Kelly, N. Rackard (Wexford), P. McDermott (Meath). Sub.: S. Brennan (Kildare) for W. Geraghty.

1951

Connacht—J. Mangan (Galway), W. McQuillan (Roscommon), P. Prendergast, S. Flanagan (Mayo), E. Boland (Roscommon), H. Dixon, E. Mongey (Mayo), S. Purcell (Galway), G. O'Malley (Roscommon), E. Keogh (Galway), P. Carney, J. Gilvarry, M. Mulderrig, T. Langan, P. Solon (Mayo). Subs.: M. Flanagan (Mayo), F. White (Sligo).

Munster—L. Fitzgerald, J. Murphy (Kerry), P. A. Murphy (Cork), P. B. Brosnan (Kerry), P. Driscoll (Cork), J. Lyne (Kerry), S. Cronin (Cork), S. Connolly (Clare), C. Duggan (Cork), T. McGrath (Waterford), C. McGrath (Cork), P. J. O'Dea (Clare), P. Brennan (Tipperary), J. M. Palmer (Kerry), D. O'Donovan (Cork). Sub.: D. Murphy (Kerry) for S. Connolly.

1952

Leinster—T. Malone (Kildare), M. O'Brien (Meath), T. Conlon, J. Tuft (Louth), G. O'Reilly (Wicklow), P. Dunne (Laois), S. Brennan (Kildare), D. Taaffe (Meath), J. Rogers (Wicklow), P. Meegan (Meath), O. Freaney (Dublin), S. White (Louth), M. McDonnell (Meath), H. Reynolds (Louth), K. Heffernan (Dublin). Subs.: K. McConnell (Meath) for Tuft; J. Crowley (Dublin) for Taaffe and C. O'Leary (Dublin) for McDonnell.

Munster—D. O'Keeffe (Cork), J. Murphy (Kerry), P. A. Murphy (Cork), P. B. Brosnan, S. Murphy (Kerry), J. Cronin (Cork), J. M. Palmer (Kerry), C. McGrath, C. Duggan (Cork), J. Brosnan (Kerry), E. Young (Cork), Pakie Brennan (Tipperary), T. Ashe (Kerry), M. Cahill (Cork), P. J. O'Dea (Clare). Sub.: P. Sheehy (Kerry) for M. Cahill.

1953

Leinster—T. Malone (Kildare), M. O'Brien, P. O'Brien, K. McConnell (Meath), G. O'Reilly (Wicklow), P. Dunne (Laois), A. Murphy (Carlow), S. Brennan (Kildare), J. Rogers (Wicklow), P. Meegan (Meath), V. Tierney (Longford), S. White (Louth), O. Freaney (Dublin), J. McDonnell (Louth), K. Heffernan (Dublin).

Munster—D. Roche (Cork), J. Murphy, E. Roche, J. O'Shea (Kerry), P. O'Driscoll (Cork), J. Cronin, C. Kennelly, B. O'Shea (Kerry), D. Kelleher, D. O'Donovan (Cork), T. Lyne (Kerry), W. Kirwan (Waterford), M. Cahill (Cork), S. Kelly (Kerry), P. Brennan (Tipperary). Sub.: F. Meeny (Clare) for B. O'Shea.

1954

Leinster—J. O'Neill (Wexford), M. O'Brien, P. O'Brien, K. McConnell (Meath), G. O'Reilly (Wicklow), P. Dunne (Laois),

414

A. Murphy (Carlow), J. Rogers (Wicklow), S. White (Louth), J. Reilly (Meath), O. Freaney, C. O'Leary (Dublin), P. Meegan (Meath), J. McDonnell (Louth), K. Heffernan (Dublin).

Connacht—A. Brady, P. English (Roscommon), P. Prendergast, S. Flanagan (Mayo), B. Lynch (Roscommon), T. Dillon (Galway), F. Kelly, G. O'Malley (Roscommon), J. Nallen (Mayo), I. O'Dowd (Sligo), S. Purcell (Galway), E. O'Donohue (Roscommon), T. Hayden (Leitrim), T. Langan (Mayo), P. McGarty (Leitrim).

1955

Leinster—P. McGearty, M. O'Brien, P. O'Brien, K. McConnell (Meath), A. Murphy (Carlow), J. Fitzparick (Wicklow), S. White (Louth), J. Rogers (Wicklow), P. Casey (Offaly), J. McDonnell (Louth), O. Freaney, C. O'Leary (Dublin), M. McDonnell, T. Moriarty (Meath), K. Heffernan (Dublin).

Connacht—A. Brady (Roscommon), F. White (Sligo), P. Prendergast, S. Flanagan (Mayo), J. Mahon, T. Dillon (Galway), F. Kelly, G. O'Malley (Roscommon), I. O'Dowd (Sligo), P. Irwin (Mayo), S. Purcell, W. O'Neill (Galway), E. O'Donohue (Roscommon), M. Gaffney (Sligo), P. McGarty (Leitrim). Sub.: T. Langan (Mayo) for O'Donohue.

1956

Ulster—S. Morris, N. O'Reilly (Cavan), J. Bratten, J. McKnight (Armagh), K. Mussen (Down), J. Rice (Monaghan), J. McDonnell (Cavan), J. McKeever (Derry), T. Maguire (Cavan), K. Denvir (Down), J. Taggart (Tyrone), J. Cunningham, P. Campbell (Armagh), V. Sherlock (Cavan), Rody Gribben (Derry).

Munster—P. Tyers (Cork), J. O'Shea (Kerry), D. O'Sullivan, P. Driscoll (Cork), T. Moriarty (Kerry), D. Bernard, D. Murray (Cork), J. Dowling (Kerry), E. Ryan (Cork), P. Sheehy (Kerry), C. Duggan (Cork), T. Lyne, J. Culloty, M. Murphy (Kerry), T. Cunningham (Waterford). Sub.: S. Murphy (Kerry) for Culloty.

1957

Connacht—J. Mangan (Galway), W. Casey (Mayo), I. O'Dowd (Sligo), T. Dillon (Galway), G. O'Malley (Roscommon), J. Mahon (Galway), E. Moriarty (Mayo), N. Blessing (Leitrim), J. Nallen (Mayo), F. Evers, S. Purcell (Galway), P.

McGarty (Leitrim), J. Young, F. Stockwell (Galway), M. Christie (Sligo).

Munster—D. O'Neill (Kerry), P. O'Driscoll (Cork), E. Roche, J. O'Shea, S. Murphy (Kerry), D. Bernard, D. Murray, S. Moore (Cork), T. Long (Kerry), E. Ryan, C. Duggan (Cork), T. Lyne, J. Brosnan, M. Murphy (Kerry), D. Kelleher (Cork), Subs.: N. Fitzgerald (Cork) for Brosnan, T. Moriarty (Kerry) for Long.

1958

Connacht—A. Brady (Roscommon), W. Casey (Mayo), I. O'Dowd (Sligo), T. Dillon, J. Mahon (Galway), G. O'Malley (Roscommon), M. Greally (Galway), J. Nallen (Mayo), F. Evers, M. McDonagh, S. Purcell (Galway), P. McGarty (Leitrim), G. Kirwan, F. Stockwell (Galway), C. Flynn (Leitrim).

Munster—L. Power (Cork), J. O'Shea, T. Lyons (Kerry), P. Driscoll, P. Harrington (Cork), T. Cunningham (Waterford), D. Murray (Cork), M. O'Connell (Kerry), S. Moore, N. Fitzgerald (Cork), J. Dowling (Kerry), E. Ryan (Cork), P. Sheehy, M. Murphy (Kerry), D. Kelleher (Cork).

1959

Leinster—S. Flood (Louth), G. Hughes (Offaly), A. Doyle (Wexford), J. Timmons, J. Boyle (Dublin), P. Nolan (Offaly), M. Grace (Meath), F. Walsh (Laois), C. O'Leary (Dublin), S. Brereton (Offaly), O. Freaney (Dublin), J. Kenna (Laois), P. Farnan, J. Joyce, K. Keffernan (Dublin).

Munster—L. Power (Cork), Jack Dowling, T. Lyons (Kerry), D. Murray (Cork), Seán Murphy, J. O'Shea, M. O'Dwyer (Kerry), P. Harrington (Cork), Seamus Murphy (Kerry), T. Mangan (Clare), N. Fitzgerald (Cork), P. Sheehy (Kerry), T. Furlong (Cork), John Dowling, T. Long (Kerry). Subs.: E. Ryan (Cork) for Seamus Murphy.

1960

Ulster—T. Turbett (Tyrone), G. Kelly (Cavan), H. F. Gribben (Derry), P. Rice (Down), P. Breen (Derry), T. Maguire (Cavan), J. McDonnell (Cavan), J. Lennon (Down), J. O'Neill (Tyrone), S. O'Neill (Down), J. McKeever (Derry), P. Doherty (Down), J. Whan (Armagh), J. Brady (Cavan), A. Hadden (Down). Sub.: K. Mussen (down) for Breen.

Munster—L. Power (Cork), J. O'Shea (Kerry), C. O'Sullivan (Cork), N. Sheehy (Kerry), P.Harrington (Cork), K. Coffey, M.

O'Dwyer, M. O'Connell, S. Murphy, D. McAuliffe (Kerry), E. Ryan (Cork), T. Long (Kerry), J. O'Sullivan (Cork), J. Dowling (Kerry), E. McCarthy (Cork).

1961

Leinster—W. Nolan, P. McCormack, G. Hughes, J. Egan, M. Brady (Offaly), P. Holden (Dublin), C. Wrenn (Offaly), M. Carley (Westmeath), S. Foran (Offaly), K. Beahan, F. Lynch (Louth), J. Kenna (Laois), S. Brereton (Offaly), J. Joyce, K. Heffernan (Dublin).

Munster—J. Culloty (Kerry), P. Harrington (Cork), T. Lyons, N. Sheehy, K. Coffey, T. Long, M. O'Dwyer, S. Murphy (Kerry), C. O'Sullivan, E. McCarthy (Cork), J. Keating (Tipperary), P. Sheehy (Kerry), T. Power (Waterford), J. Dowling, G. McMahon (Kerry). Subs.: D. McAuliffe (Kerry) for Power, J. O'Sullivan (Cork) for Keating.

1962

Leinster—A. Phillips (Wicklow), P. McCormack, G. Hughes (Offaly), M. Carolan (Kildare), B. Barden (Longford), P. Holden (Dublin), C. Wrenn (Offaly), D. Foley (Dublin), M. Carley (Westmeath), S. Brereton (Offaly), M. Whelan (Dublin), T. Greene (Offaly), P. Gearty (Longford), J. Timmons, K. Heffernan (Dublin). Sub.: F. Lynch (Louth).

Ulster—T. McArdle (Monaghan), G. Kelly (Cavan), L. Murphy, P. Rice (Down), B. Mone (Monaghan), D. McCartan (Down), J. McDonnell (Cavan), J. Carey (Down), E. Larkin (Armagh), S. O'Neill, J. McCartan, P. Doherty (Down), S. O'Connell (Derry), J. Whan (Armagh), B. Morgan (Down). Subs.: T. Hadden (Down), M. Donaghy (Tyrone).

1963

Ulster—T. Turbett (Tyrone), G. Kelly (Cavan), L. Murphy, P. Rice (Down), P. J. Flood (Donegal), T. Maguire, J. McDonnell (Cavan), S. Ferriter (Donegal), R. Carolan (Cavan), S. O'Neill (Down), F. McFeeley (Donegal), P. Doherty (Down), J. Whan (Armagh), P. T. Treacy (Fermanagh), B. Morgan (Down). Subs.: J. O'Neill (Tyrone), J. McCartan (Down).

Leinster—A. Phillips (Wicklow), P. McCormack, G. Hughes (Offaly), P. Connolly (Kildare), W. Casey, P. Holden (Dublin), C. Wrenn (Offaly), M. Carley (Westmeath), M. Carolan (Kildare), F. Walsh (Laois), D. Foley, M. Whelan (Dublin), P. Cum-

mins (Kildare), N. Delaney (Laois), S. Brereton (Offaly). Subs.:
L. Foley (Dublin), F. Lynch (Louth), T. Browne (Laois).

1964

Ulster—S. Hoare (Donegal), G. Kelly (Cavan), L. Murphy
(Down), B. Brady (Donegal), D. McCartan (Down), T. Maguire,
J. McDonnell (Cavan), J. Lennon (Down), S. Ferriter (Donegal),
S. O'Neill, J. McCartan, P. Doherty (Down), J. Whan
(Armagh), P. Treacy (Fermanagh), F. Donnelly (Tyrone). Subs.:
C. Gallagher (Cavan), J. O'Neill (Tyrone).

Leinster—A. Phillips (Wicklow), P. McCormack, G. Hughes
(Offaly), W. Casey, M. Kissane, P. Holden (Dublin), F. Lynch
(Louth), D. Foley (Dublin), T. Browne (Laois), J. Mulroy
(Louth), J. Timmons, M. Whelan (Dublin), S. Murray, B. Burns
(Longford), G. Kane (Westmeath). Subs.: L. Foley (Dublin), M.
Carley (Westmeath), B. McDonald (Dublin).

1965

Ulster—S. Hoare (Donegal), G. Kelly (Cavan), B. Brady
(Donegal), A. Morris (Cavan), D. McCartan (Down), T. Maguire
(Cavan), P. Kelly, S. Ferriter (Donegal), R. Carolan (Cavan), S.
O'Connell (Derry), J. O'Neill (Tyrone), P. Doherty (Down), C.
Gallagher (Cavan), S. O'Neill (Down), P. T. Treacy (Fer-
managh). Sub.: J. Carroll (Monaghan).

Connacht—J. Geraghty, E. Colleran, S. Meade (Galway), J.
Murray (Leitrim), J. Donnellan (Galway), C. Cawley (Sligo), M.
Newell (Galway), J. Langan (Mayo), M. Reynolds, C. Dunne
(Galway), P. McGarty (Leitrim), M. Kearins (Sligo), M.
McDonagh, S. Cleary, S. Leydon (Galway).

1966

Ulster—S. Hoare, P. Kelly (Donegal), T. McCreesh (Armagh),
T. O'Hare, P. O'Hagan, D. McCartan (Down), P. J. Flood
(Donegal), R. Carolan (Cavan), J. O'Neill (Tyrone), J. Lennon,
J. McCartan, P. Doherty (Down), C. Gallagher (Cavan), S.
O'Neill (Down), P. T. Treacy (Fermanagh). Subs.: A. Morris
(Cavan), S. O'Connell (Derry).

Munster—J. Culloty, Donie O'Sullivan (Kerry). S.; Downes
(Clare), M. Morris, Denis O'Sullivan (Kerry), A. Fitzgerald
(Limerick) J. D. O'Connor, M. Fleming (Kerry), M. Burke
(Cork), P. McMahon (Clare), P. Moynihan, D. Geaney, B.

O'Callaghan (Kerry), C. O'Sullivan (Cork), M. Keating (Tipperary). Subs.: M. Tynan (Limerick), J. Lucey (Cork).

1967

Connacht—J. Geraghty, E. Colleran, N. Tierney, J. B. McDermott, J. Donnellan (Galway), J. Morley (Mayo), R. Craven (Roscommon), P. Donnellan (Galway), J. Langan (Mayo), C. Dunne, J. Duggan (Galway), M. Kearins (Sligo), J. Keenan (Galway), J. Corcoran (Mayo), S. Leydon (Galway). Sub.: D. Earley (Roscommon).

Ulster—S. Hoare (Donegal), G. Kelly (Cavan), B. Brady (Donegal), T. O'Hare, D. McCartan (Down), P. J. Flood (Donegal), J. Lennon (Down), R. Carolan (Cavan), C. McAlarney (Down), M. Brewster (Fermanagh) J. McCartan (Down), S. O'Connell (Derry), M. McLoone (Donegal), S. O'Neill (Down), M. Griffin (Donegal). Subs.: J. O'Neill (Tyrone), S. Ferriter (Donegal).

1968

Ulster—S. Hoare (Donegal), G. Kelly (Cavan), B. Brady (Donegal), T. O'Hare, J. Lennon, D. McCartan (Down), P. Pritchard, R. Carolan (Cavan), C. McAlarney (Down), M. Niblock (Derry), J. J. O'Reilly (Cavan), N. Gallagher (Donegal), S. O'Connell (Derry), S. O'Neill (Down), C. Gallagher (Cavan). Sub.: D. O'Carroll (Donegal).

Leinster—M. Furlong (Offaly), P. Cole (Westmeath), L. Gillen (Longford), J. Smith (Offaly), J. Donlon (Longford), L. Toal (Louth), G. Davey (Dublin), J. Donnelly (Kildare), L. Coughlan (Offaly), B. Gaughran (Louth), J. Hannify (Longford), A. McTague (Offaly), D. Dolan (Westmeath), M. Whelan (Dublin), S. Donnolly (Longford). Subs.: J. Conway (Laois), W. Bryan (Offaly).

1969

Connacht—P. Brennan (Sligo), N. Colleran, N. Tierney (Galway), R. Craven (Roscommon), J. Morley, J. Carey (Mayo, L. Caffrey (Sligo), J. Duggan (Galway), D. Earley (Roscommon), H. O'Carroll (Leitrim), J. Colleary, M. Kearins (Sligo), J. Corcoran, W. McGee (Mayo), J. Keenan (Galway). Sub.: S. Leydon (Galway).

Munster—W. Morgan, B. Murphy (Cork), S. Downes (Clare), Donie O'Sullivan (Kerry), F. Cogan (Cork), M. Morris (Kerry),

B. Hartigan (Limerick), M. Fleming (Kerry), B. O'Neill (Cork), B. Lynch, P. Griffin (Kerry), M. Haugh (Clare), M. O'Connell (Kerry), R. Cummins (Cork), E. O'Donoghue (Kerry). Sub.: F. McMahon (Clare).

1970

Ulster—A. Gallagher (Tyrone), A. McCabe (Cavan), T. McCreesh (Armagh), T. O'Hare (Down), B. McEniff (Donegal), M. McAfee (Derry), E. McGowan, R. Carolan (Cavan), A. McAtamney (Antrim), J. Murphy (Down), M. Niblock (Derry), S. Duggan, G. Cusack (Cavan), S. O'Neill (Down), S. O'Connell (Derry).

Connacht—E. Rooney, J. Carey, R. Prendergast (Mayo), N. Colleran (Galway), G. Mannion (Roscommon), J. Morley (Mayo), L. Caffrey (Sligo), D. Earley (Roscommon), J. Duggan (Galway), H. O'Carroll (Leitrim, J. Colleary, M. Kearins (Sligo), J. Kelly (Roscommon), W. McGee (Mayo). J. Keenan (Galway).

1971

Ulster—P. McCarthy (Monaghan), J. Burns (Antrim), H. Diamond (Derry), A. McCabe (Cavan), B. McEniff (Donegal), M. McAfee (Derry), E. McGowan, R. Carolan (Cavan), F. Fitzsimmons (Antrim), S. O'Connell (Derry), C. McAlarney (Down), M. Niblock (Derry), G. Cusack (Cavan), S. O'Neill (Down), A. McCallin (Antrim). Subs.: E. Coleman (Derry), J. Murphy (Down).

Connacht—E. Rooney, J. Carey (Mayo), N. Colleran (Galway), T. Colleary (Sligo), G. Mannion (Roscommon), J. Morley (Mayo), L. O'Neill, J. Duggan (Galway), D. Earley (Roscommon), B. Wynne (Leitrim), J. Colleary, M. Kearins (Sligo), L. Sammon (Galway), W. McGee (Mayo), J. Corcoran (Mayo).

1972 REPLAY

Munster—B. Morgan (Cork), D. O'Sullivan (Kerry), J. Wall (Waterford), S. Fitzgerald, T. Prendergast, J. O'Keeffe (Kerry), K. J. O'Sullivan (Cork), M. O'Connell (Kerry), F. Cogan, D. Hunt, D. Coughlan (Cork), E. O'Donoghue (Kerry), M. Keating (Tipperary), R. Cummins (Cork), M. O'Dwyer (Kerry). Sub.: J. Barrett (Cork) for O'Donoghue.

Leinster—M. Furlong, M. Ryan, P. McCormack (Offaly), J. Conway (Laois), E. Mulligan, N. Clavin (Offaly), P. Mangan

(Kildare), W. Bryan (Offaly), B. Millar (Laois), K. Rennicks (Meath), K. Kilmurray, A. McTague, J. Cooney (Offaly), T. Carew (Kildare), M. Fay (Meath). Subs.: Murt Connor (Offaly) for Fay. P. Reynolds (Meath) for Millar.

Mick Scannell (Cork) came on as a sub in drawn game. Murt Connor (Offaly) played in drawn game. Mick Fay was selected for replay. Jim Mulroy (Louth) and John Smith (Offaly) came on as subs in drawn game.

1973 REPLAY

Universities–N. Murphy (U.C.C. & Cork), J. Waldron (U.C.D. & Galway), S. Killough (Queens & Antrim), J. Stafford (U.C.D. & Cavan), G. McHugh (Queens & Antrim), P. O'Neill (U.C.D. & Dublin), T. Regan (U.C.G. & Roscommon), J. O'Keeffe (U.C.D. & Kerry), K. Kilmurray (U.C.D. & Offaly), B. Lynch (U.C.C. & Kerry), D. McCarthy (U.C.D. & Cork), M. Carney (U.C.G. & Donegal), P. Moriarty (Queens & Armagh), D. Kavanagh (U.C.C. & Kerry), A. McGuirk (Queens & Derry).

P. Lynch (U.C.C. and Kerry), J. Rainey (Queens and Antrim) and C. Hughes (Maynooth and Carlow) played in drawn game. J. Stafford, P. O'Neill and M. Carney came on for replay. Sub (drawn game): J. P. Kane (U.C.D. and Mayo).

Connacht—J. Neill, T. Heneghan (Roscommon), J. Brennan (Sligo), J. Morley (Mayo), B. Murphy (Sligo), T. J. Gilmore, L. O'Neill (Galway), D. Earley (Roscommon), S. Kilbride (Mayo), B. Wynne (Leitrim), L. Sammon (Galway), M. Kearins (Sligo), M. Burke (Galway), M. Freyne (Roscommon), J. Duggan (Galway). Subs.: J. Kelly (Roscommon) for Burke; J. Gibbons (Mayo) for Wynne.

Matty Brennan (Sligo) and John Kelly (Roscommon) played in drawn game. T. J. Gilmore and Jimmy Duggan came on for replay. Sub (drawn game): Jimmy Duggan.

1974

Leinster—M. Furlong (Offaly), D. Dalton (Kildare), M. Ryan, M. O'Rourke, E. Mulligan, S. Lowry (Offaly), G. Wilson (Dublin), P. Mangan (Kildare), R. Millar (Laois), P. Fenning (Offaly), S. Allen (Laois), K. Rennicks (Meath), J. Cooney, W. Bryan (Offaly), B. Gaughran (Louth). Subs.: D. Nugent (Louth) for Wilson, P. Dunny (Kildare) for Gaughran.

Connacht—N. Crossan (Leitrim), J. Waldron (Galway), J. Brennan (Sligo), H. Keegan, J. Kerrane (Roscommon), T. J. Gilmore (Galway), P. Henry (Sligo), D. Earley (Roscommon), S. Kilbride (Mayo), L. Sammon, J. Duggan (Galway), M. Kearins

421

(Sligo), T. O'Malley (Mayo), M. Freyne (Roscommon), J. Tobin (Galway). Subs.: M. Brennan (Sligo) for Henry, J. Morley (Mayo for Kilbride, M. Burke (Galway) for Tobin.

1975

Munster—W. Morgan (Cork), E. Webster (Tipperary), H. Kelleher (Cork), J. Deenihan (Kerry), K. J. O'Sullivan (Cork), J. O'Keeffe, G. Power (Kerry), D. Long, D. McCarthy (Cork), B. Lynch (Kerry), J. Barrett (Cork), M. O'Sullivan (Kerry), J. Barry-Murphy (Cork), S. Kearney (Tipperary), J. Egan (Kerry). Sub.- D. Hunt (Cork) for Long.

Ulster—L. Turbett (Tyrone), D. Monaghan, P. McShea (Donegal), P. Mulgrew (Tyrone), P. Kerr (Monaghan), J. P. O'Kane (Antrim), E. Tavey (Monaghan), T. McGuinness (Derry), P. McGinnity (Fermanagh), F. McGuigan (Tyrone), C. McAlarney (Down), M. Carney (Donegal), P. Rooney (Down), S. Bonner (Donegal), S. O'Neill (Down). Subs.: A. Curran (Donegal) for Mulgrew, M. Slevin (Down) for Kerr, B. Donnelly (Tyrone) for Rooney.

1976

Munster—P. O'Mahoney (Kerry), E. Webster (Tipperary), B. Murphy (Cork), J. Deenihan, P. O'Shea (Kerry), K. Kehily (Cork), G. Power (Kerry), D. Long (Cork), D. Moran (Kerry), D. Allen (Cork), M. Sheehy, M. O'Sullivan, J. Egan (Kerry), J. Barry-Murphy (Cork), P. Spillane (Kerry). Sub.: G. O'Keeffe (Kerry) for Webster.

Leinster—P. Cullen, G. O'Driscoll (Dublin), J. Conway (Laois), R. Kelleher (Dublin), J. Balfe (Kildare), S. Lowry (Offaly), K. Brennan (Laois), B. Mullins (Dublin), K. Rennicks (Meath), R. Doyle, A. Hanahoe, D. Hickey (Dublin) P. Fenning (Offaly), J. Keaveney, A. O'Toole (Dublin). Subs.: M. O'Rourke (Offaly) for Balfe. S. Doherty (Dublin) for O'Rourke.

1977

Munster—B. Morgan, K. Kehily (Cork), J. O'Keeffe (Kerry), B. Murphy (Cork), D. Moran, T. Kennelly, G. Power (Kerry), D. Long, D. McCarthy, S. O'Shea (Cork), M. Sheehy, P. Spillane (Kerry), J. Barry-Murphy (Cork), S. Walsh, J. Egan (Kerry). Subs.: J. O'Shea (Kerry) for D. McCarthy (Cork). D. Allen (Cork) for S. O'Shea.

Connacht—G. Mitchell (Galway), G. Kirrane (Mayo), M. J. Judge, S. McHugh (Galway), G. Feeney (Mayo), J. Hughes (Galway), P. Henry (Sligo), T. J. Gilmore, W. Joyce (Galway),

R. Bell, J. P. Kean (Mayo), M. Martin (Leitrim), T. O'Malley (Mayo), J. Duggan, L. Sammon (Galway). Subs.: T. Naughton (Galway) for Gilmore. H. Keegan (Roscommon) for McHugh.

1978

Munster—B. Morgan, B. Murphy (Cork), J. O'Keeffe, J. Deenihan, P. O'Shea, T. Kennelly (Kerry), M. Murphy (Clare), G. McGrath (Tipperary), M. Quish (Limerick), P. Spillane, M. Sheehy, G. Power (Kerry), J. Barry-Murphy (Cork), S. Walsh (Kerry), J. Hennessy (Waterford). Subs.: J. O'Shea (Kerry) for Quish. G. O'Driscoll (Kerry) for Spillane. D. Moran (Kerry) for Hennessy.

K. Kehilly, D. Allen, D. McCarthy (all Cork) and Ger O'Driscoll (Kerry) played in drawn game. B. Murphy, M. Quish, J. B. Murphy and M. Sheehy came on for replay.

Ulster—J. Somers (Derry), D. Stevenson (Armagh), P. Mulgrew (Tyrone), E. McGowan (Cavan), P. Moriarty (Armagh), A. McGurk, M. Moran (Derry), C. McAlarney (Down), P. McGinnity (Fermanagh), L. Austin (Down), E. McKenna (Tyrone), J. Kernan (Armagh), J. Byrne (Down), P. Rooney (Down), P. Traynor (Armagh). Sub.: K. McCabe (Tyrone) for Moriarty. N. Marley (Armagh) for Traynor. B. Kelly (Derry) for Byrne, J. Smith (Armagh) for Austin. The game went to extra time. C. Digney (Down), Ger McGowen, Kevin McCabe (Tyrone) and J. Smith (Armagh) played in drawn game. P. Moriarty and Joe Kernan came on for replay. Subs (drawn game): N. Marley (Armagh), D. Watson (Down) and J. Kernan (Armagh).

1979

Ulster—B. McAlinden, D. Stevenson (Armagh), T. McGovern (Down), F. Ward (Donegal), K. McCabe (Tyrone), P. Moriarty (Armagh), M. Moran (Derry), P. McGinnity (Fermanagh). L. Austin, C. McAlarney (Down), J. Kernan (Armagh), B. Donnelly (Tyrone), P. Loughran (Armagh), P. Rooney (Down), S. Devlin (Armagh). Subs.: C. Digney (Down) for Moran, P. McNamee (Cavan) for Loughran. J. Smyth (Armagh) for Donnelly.

Munster—C. Nelligan (Kerry), K. Kehily (Cork), J. O'Keeffe (Kerry), T. Creedon (Cork), P. O'Shea, T. Kennelly, P. Lynch, J. O'Shea, S. Walsh (Kerry), P. Leahy (Limerick), M. Sheehy, G. Power (Kerry), J. Barry-Murphy (Cork), E. Liston, J. Egan (Kerry). Subs.: P. Spillane (Kerry) for Leahy, D. Moran (Kerry) for Egan.

1980

Ulster—B. McAlinden (Armagh), E. Hughes (Monaghan), T. McGovern (Down), F. Ward (Donegal), K. McCabe (Tyrone), P. Moriarty (Armagh), S. McCarville (Monaghan), P. McGinnity (Fermanagh), L. Austin, C. McAlarney (Down), J. Kernan (Armagh), E. Young (Derry), P. McNamee (Cavan), P. Rooney (Down), P. Loughran (Armagh). Sub.: M. Moran (Derry) for Loughran.

Munster—C. Nelligan, J. Deenihan, J. O'Keeffe (Kerry) K. Kehily (Cork), P. O'Shea, T. Kennelly (Kerry), T. Creedon (Cork), S. Walsh (Kerry), C. Ryan (Cork), G. Power, M. Sheehy, P. Spillane (Kerry), D. Allen (Cork), E. Liston, J. Egan (Kerry). Sub.: J. Barry-Murphy (Cork) for Power.

1981

Munster—C. Nelligan, J. Deenihan, J. O'Keeffe (Kerry), K. Kehily (Cork), P. O'Shea, T. Kennelly, D. Moran, S. Walsh, J. O'Shea, G. Power (Kerry), D. Allen (Cork), P. Spillane, M. Sheehy, E. Liston, J. Egan (Kerry).

Connacht—M. Webb (Mayo), J. Hughes (Galway), P. Lindsay, J. McManus (Roscommon), S. McHugh (Galway), T. Donnellan, D. Murray, S. Hayden (Roscommon), M. McCarrick (Sligo), B. Brennan (Galway), J. Kent (Sligo), D. Earley, M. Finneran, T. McManus (Roscommon), M. Carney (Mayo). Subs.: H. Gavin (Mayo) for Hughes, G. McManus (Galway) for Finneran.

1982

Munster—C. Nelligan (Kerry), J. Evans (Cork), J. O'Keeffe (Kerry), K. Kehily (Cork), P. O'Shea, T. Kennelly (Kerry), M. Moloney (Cork), J. O'Shea, S. Walsh, G. Power (Kerry), C. Ryan (Cork), D. Moran (Kerry), S. Moloney (Clare), E. Liston (Kerry), D. Allen (Cork). Subs.: J. Kerrigan (Cork) for M. Moloney. N. Normoyle (Clare) for Power.

Connacht—M. Webb, M. Gavin (Mayo) P. Lindsay (Roscommon), M. O'Toole (Mayo), P. O'Neill, M. Coleman, S. McHugh, B. Talty (Galway), J. Lyons (Mayo), D. Earley, T. McManus (Roscommon), J. Kent (Sligo). B. Brennan (Galway), J. Burke (Mayo). G. McManus (Galway). Subs.: S. Hayden (Roscommon) for Lyons. M. Carney (Mayo) for Brennan.

1983

Ulster—B. McAlinden (Armagh), P. Kennedy (Down), G. McCarville (Monaghan), J. Irwin (Derry), E. Hughes (Monaghan), P. Moriarty (Armagh), J. Reilly (Cavan), L. Austin (Down), F. McMahon (Armagh), P. McGinnity (Fermanagh), G. Blaney, J. McCartan (Down), J. Corvan (Armagh), E. McKenna (Tyrone), M. McHugh (Donegal). Subs.: P. O'Rourke (Down) for McCarville, P. McNamee (Cavan) for McCartan, D. Stevenson (Armagh) for Hughes. McCarville for McHugh.

Leinster—M. Furlong (Offaly), T. Foley (Wexford), L. O'Connor, M. Fitzgerald, P. Fitzgerald (Offaly), P. O'Donoghue (Kildare), M. Casey (Longford), T. Connor (Offaly), T. O'Dwyer (Carlow), P. Dunne, R. Connor, G. Carroll (Offaly), C. O'Rourke (Meath), M. Connor (Offaly), S. Fahy (Kildare). Subs.: L. Tompkins (Kildare) for O'Dwyer. G. McEntee (Meath) for T. Connor, B. Rock (Dublin) for O'Rourke, A. Wiseman (Louth) for O'Donoghue, T. Connor for McEntee. J. Crofton (Kildare) for P. Fitzgerald. This final went to extra time.

1984

Ulster—B. McAlinden (Armagh), P. Kennedy (Down), G. McCarville (Monaghan), J. Irwin (Derry), M. Carr, M. Lafferty (Donegal), J. Reilly (Cavan), L. Austin (Down), E. McKenna (Tyrone), P. McGinnity (Fermanagh), J. Kernan (Armagh), G. Blaney (Down), M. McHugh (Donegal), F. McGuigan (Tyrone), E. Hughes (Monaghan). Subs.: T. McDermott (Donegal) for Irwin. F. McMahon (Armagh) for Austin. P. O'Rourke (Down) for Carr.

Connacht—P. Coyne (Galway), H. Keegan (Roscommon), S. Kinneavy, S. McHugh, P. O'Neill, T. Tierney (Galway), D. Flanagan (Mayo), M. Quinn (Leitrim), M. McCarrick (Sligo), B. Talty (Galway), D. Earley (Roscommon), M. Martin (Leitrim), J. Kent (Sligo), S. Mulhern (Leitrim), S. Joyce (Galway). Subs.: T. J. Kilgallon (Mayo) for Quinn. B. O'Donnell (Galway) for McCarrick.

1985

Leinster—J. O'Leary, M. Holden (Dublin), M. Lyons (Meath), M. Drennan (Laois), P. Canavan (Dublin), J. Cassells (Meath), C. Brown (Laois), B. Mullins (Dublin), P. Dunne (Offaly), L. Tompkins (Kildare), T. Conroy, C. Duff, B. Rock

(Dublin), C. O'Rourke (Meath), J. Mooney (Offaly). Sub.: S. Fitzhenry (Wexford).

Munster—C. Nelligan, P. O'Shea, T. Spillane, M. Spillane (Kerry), N. Roche (Clare), J. Kerrigan (Cork), G. Lynch, J. O'Shea, A. O'Donovan, J. Kennedy, G. Power (Kerry), C. O'Neill, E. O'Mahony (Cork), E. Liston (Kerry), F. Kelly (Tipperary). Subs.: G. McGrath (Tipperary), E. O'Brien (Waterford).

1986

Leinster—J. O'Leary (Dubin), P. Dunne (Laois), G. Hargan (Dublin), P. Lyons (Meath), C. Browne (Laois), N. McCaffrey, D. Synnott (Dublin), L. Hayes, J. Cassells (Meath), B. Rock (Dublin), K. O'Brien (Wicklow), G. Brown (Laois), J. Mooney (Offaly), T. Conroy, C. Duff (Dublin).

Connacht—G. Sheerin (Roscommon), M. Carney (Mayo), H. Keegan (Roscommon), S. McHugh (Galway), F. Noone (Mayo), V. Daly (Galway), D. Flanagan (Mayo), T. Tierney (Galway), T. J. Kilgallon (Mayo), P. Kelly (Galway), J. Kent (Sligo), N. Durkin, J. Burke (Mayo), P. Earley (Roscommon), M. Martin (Leitrim). Subs.: K. McStay (Mayo), P. Brogan (Mayo), M. McCarrick (Sligo).

1987

Leinster—J. O'Leary (Dublin), R. O'Malley (Meath), G. Hargan (Dublin), S. Dowling (Kildare), C. Brown (Laois), L. Harnan (Meath), N. McCaffrey (Dublin), G. McEntee (Meath), L. Hayes (Meath), P. J. Gillic (Meath), J. McNally (Dublin), K. Duff (Dublin), B. Lowry (Offaly), B. Stafford (Meath), B. Flynn (Meath). Subs.: G. Brown (Laois) for McNally; Mick Lyons (Meath) for G. Brown.

Munster—J. Kearns (Cork), A. Davis (Cork), A. Moloney (Clare), N. Roche (Clare), N. Cahalane (Cork), C. Counihan (Cork), G. Lynch (Kerry), A. Leahy (Cork), L. O'Connor (Waterford), T. Brown (Limerick), D. Fitzgerald (Limerick), F. Griffin (Clare), J. Cleary (Cork), F. Ryan (Limerick), J. McGrath (Waterford). Subs.: M. McAuliffe (Kerry for McGrath; D. Culloty (Cork) for Brown; P. Ivers (Limerick) for Cahalane.

1988

Leinster—M. McQuillan (Meath), D. Sinnott (Dublin), J. O'Gorman (Wexford), M. Kennedy (Dublin), D. Kelly (Offaly),

426

L. Harnan (Meath), K. Foley (Meath), D. Kavanagh (Offaly), D. Bolger (Dublin), C. Coyle (Meath), V. Murphy (Dublin), C. Duff (Dublin), P. Brady (Offaly), B. Stafford (Meath), D. Barry (Longford). Subs.: E. Heery (Dublin) for Sinnott and M. McCabe (Meath) for Murphy.

Ulster—P. Linden (Monaghan), J. Lynch (Tyrone), E. Sherry (Monaghan), A. Scullion (Derry), C. Murray (Monaghan), D. Loughman (Monaghan), J. Reilly (Cavan), B. McGilligan (Derry), P. Donaghy (Tyrone), K. McCabe (Tyrone), G. Blaney (Down), D. McNicholl (Derry), N. Hughes (Monaghan), E. Murphy (Monaghan). M. McHugh (Donegal). Subs.: F. Cahill (Cavan) for McNicholl.

1989

Ulster—P. Linden (Monaghan), C. Hamill (Antrim), E. Sherry (Monaghan), T. Scullion (Derry), M. McQuillan (Armagh), D. Loughman (Monaghan), J. Reilly (Cavan), M. Grimley (Armagh), P. Donaghy (Tyrone), J. McMullan (Donegal), D. O'Hagan (Tyrone), G. Blaney (Down), M. McHugh (Donegal), E. McKenna (Tyrone), J. McConville (Armagh). Subs.: P. McErlean (Antrim) for McMullan, A. Molloy (Donegal) for Donaghy.

Munster—C. Nelligan (Kerry), C. Murphy (Kerry), M. O'Connor (Cork), N. Roche (Clare), J. Costello (Tipperary), C. Counihan (Cork), A. Davis (Cork), T. McCarthy (Cork), A. O'Donovan (Kerry), P. McGrath (Cork), M. McCarthy (Cork), B. Coffey (Cork), C. O'Neill (Cork), J. O'Driscoll (Cork), M. McAuliffe (Kerry). Subs.: M. Fitzgerald (Kerry) for McAuliffe, D. Culloty (Cork) for McCarthy, D. Fitzgibbon (Limerick) for McGrath.

1990
No competition

1991

Ulster—G. Walsh (Donegal), J. J. Doherty (Donegal), C. Deegan (Down), T. Scullion (Derry), M. McQuillan (Armagh), D. Loughman (Monaghan), M. Shovlin (Donegal), B. McGilligan (Derry), P. Donaghy (Tyrone), A. Cush (Tyrone), N. Smith (Armagh), D Bonner (Donegal), P. Canavan (Tyrone), G. Blaney (Down), J. McCartan (Down). Subs.: D. McNicholl (Derry) for Cush, E. Kilpatrick (Tyrone) for Deegan, K. McGurk (Armagh) for Bonner.

Munster—J. Kerins (Cork), N. Roche (Clare), N. Cahalane (Cork), C. Murphy (Kerry), M. Slocum (Cork), C. Counihan (Cork), A. Davis (Cork), D. Culloty (Cork), N. O'Mahony (Kerry), D. Barry (Cork), J. Costello (Tipperary), S. O'Brien (Cork), C. O'Neill (Cork), F. McInerney (Clare), E. O'Brien (Waterford). Subs.: D. Fitzgibbon (Limerick) for Costello, P. Vaughan (Clare) for O'Mahony.

1992

Ulster—N. Collins (Down), M. Gallagher (Donegal), C. Deegan (Down), T. Scullion (Derry), M. McQuillan (Armagh), E. Kilpatrick (Tyrone), B. Breen (Down), S. King (Cavan), P. Brogan (Donegal), R. Carr (Down), N. Smith (Armagh), A. Cush (Tyrone), M. Linden (Down), M. Boyle (Donegal), R. Carolan (Cavan). Subs.: B. McGilligan (Derry) for Brogan M. McHugh (Donegal) for Cush.

Munster—P. O'Leary (Kerry), N. Roche (Clare), P. Coleman (Cork), A. Davis (Cork), E. Breen (Kerry), C. Counihan (Cork), L. Flaherty (Kerry), D. Culloty (Cork), A. O'Donovan (Kerry), J. O'Driscoll (Cork), T. Fleming (Kerry), G. Killeen (Clare), J. Cronin (Kerry), D. Fitzgerald (Limerick), F. Kelly (Tipperary). Subs.: D. Fitzgibbon (Limerick) for Killeen, A. Moloney (Clare) for Counihan, M. McCarthy (Cork) for Fitzgerald.

CAPTAINS OF WINNING RAILWAY CUP
FOOTBALL TEAMS

1927—John Joe Sheehy (Kerry)
1928—Matt Goff (Kildre)
1929—Bill Gannon (Kildare)
1930—John Higgins (Kildare)
1931—Joe Barrett (Kerry)
1932—John Higgins (Kildare)
1933—John McDonnell (Dublin)
1934—Mick Donnellan (Galway)
1935—John McDonnell Dublin)
1936—Paddy Moclair (Mayo)
1937—Purty Kelly (Mayo)
1938—Paddy Moclair (Mayo)
1939—Bill Delaney (Laois)
1940—Matty Gilsenan (Meath)
1941—Danno Keeffe (Kerry)
1942—John J. O'Reilly (Cavan)
1943—John J. O'Reilly (Cavan)
1944—Jim Thornton (Louth)
1945—Peeny Whelan (Carlow)
1946—Tadgh Crowley (Cork)
1947—Kevin Armstrong (Antrim)
1948—Jackie Lyne (Kerry)
1949—Batt Garvey (Kerry)
1950—John J. O'Reilly (Cavan)
1951—Seán Flanagan (Mayo)
1952—Paddy Meegan (Meath)
1953—Paddy Meegan (Meath)
1954—Stephen White (Louth)
1955—Paddy O'Brien (Meth)
1956—Tom Maguire (Cavan)
1957—Jack Mangan (Galway)
1958—Seán Purcell (Galway)
1959—Kevin Heffernan (Dublin)
1960—Seán O'Neill (Down)
1961—Willie Nolan (Offaly)
1962—Greg Hughes (Offaly)
1963—Jim McDonnell (Cavan)
1964—Paddy Doherty (Down)
1965—Charlie Gallagher (Cavan)

1966—Jim McCartan (Down)
1967—Enda Colleran (Galway)
1968—Joe Lennon (Down)
1969—Noel Tierney (Galway)
1970—Ray Carolan (Cavan)
1971—Seán O'Connell (Derry)
1972—Donal Hunt (Cork)
1973—Brendan Lynch (U.C.C. and Kerry)
1974—Martin Furlong (Offaly)
1975—Billy Morgan (Cork)
1976—Michael O'Sullivan (Kerry)
1977—John O'Keeffe (Kerry)
1978—John O'Keeffe (Kerry)
1979—Colm McAlarney (Down)
1980—Peter McGinnity (Fermanagh)
1981—Ger Power (Kerry)
1982—Tim Kennelly (Kerry)
1983—Peter McGinnitty (Fermanagh)
1984—Eugene McKenna (Tyrone)
1985—Brian Mullins (Dublin)
1986—John O'Leary (Dublin)
1987—Ger McEntee (Meath)
1988—Michael McQuillan (Meath)
1989—Jim Reilly (Cavan)
1990—No competition
1991—Tony Scullion (Derry)
1992—Greg Blaney (Down).

ATTENDANCE FIGURES—ALL-IRELAND FINALS

1993—Cork v. Derry ....
1992—Donegal v. Dublin...........64,547
1991—Down v. Meath;;;;;;;;;;;;;;;64,500
1990—Cork v. Meath.................65,723
1989—Cork v. Mayo.................65,519
1988—Meath v. Cork (replay)...64,067
1988—Meath v. Cork (drawn game)
65,000 (all-ticket)
1987—Meath v. Cork.............68.431
1986—Kerry v. Tyrone...........68,628
1985—Kerry v. Dublin...........69,389
1984—Kerry v. Dublin...........68,365
1983—Dublin v. Galway...........71,988
1882—Offaly v. Kerry.............62,309
1981—Kerry v. Offaly.............61,489
1980—Kerry v. Roscommon......63,854
1979—Kerry v. Dublin.............72,185
1978—Kerry v. Dublin.............71,503
1977—Dublin v. Armagh (all ticket)
66,542
1976—Dublin v. Kerry (new record)
73,588
1975—Dublin v. Kerry.............66,346
1974—Dublin v. Galway...........71,898
1973—Cork v. Galway.............73,309
1972—Offaly v. Kerry
(record for replay).........66,136
1972—Offaly v. Kerry
(drawn game)...............72,032
1971—Offaly v. Galway..........70,798
1970—Kerry v. Meath...........71,775
1969—Kerry v. Offaly...........67,828
1969—Down v. Kerry 71,294
1967—Meath v. Cork............70,343
1966—Galway v. Meath 71,569
1965—Galway v. Kerry...........77,735
1964—Galway v. Kerry.........76,498
1963—Dublin v. Galway........87,106
1962—Kerry v. Roscommon .. 75,771

1961—Down v. Offaly...........90,556
1960—Down v. Kerry 87,768
1959—Kerry v. Galway.........85,897
1958—Dublin v. Derry 73,371
1957—Louth v. Cork 72,732
1956—Galway v. Cork...........70.772
1955—Kerry v. Dublin 87,102
1954—Meath v. Kerry...........72,276
1953—Kerry v. Armagh 86,155
1952—Cavan v. Meath..........62,515
(Replay)
1951—Mayo v. Meath...........78,201
1950—Mayo v. Louth 76,174
1949—Meath v. Cavan...........79,460
1948—Cavan v. Mayo...........74,645
*1947—Cavan v. Kerry.........34,941
1946—Kerry v. Roscommon .. 75,771
1945—Cork v. Cavan...........67,329
1944—Roscommon v. Kerry .. 79,245
943—Roscommon v. Cavan . 68,023
1943—Roscommon v. Cavan....47,193
(Replay)
1942—Dublin v. Galway........37,105
1941—Kerry v. Galway.........45,512
1940—Kerry v. Galway.........60,824
1939—Kerry v. Meath...........46,828
1938—Galway v. Kerry.........68,950
1938—Galway v. Kerry.........47,581
(Replay)
1937—Kerry v. Cavan 52,325
1937—Kerry v. Cavan 51,234
(Replay)
1936—Mayo v. Laois...........50,168
1935—Cavan v. Kildare 50,380
1934—Galway v. Dublin 36,143
*1933—Galway v. Cavan 45,188

* The 1933 figures set up a new record, the previous highest being an attendance of 43,839 at the 1929 final, in which Kerry defeated Kildare. The 1947 football final between Cavan and Kerry, was played in the Polo Grounds New York.

The attendance of 73,588 at the Dublin-Kerry game in 1976 was the highest at a final since the capacity of Croke Park was reduced with the installation of the seats under the Cusack Stand in 1966 (the previous best for the altered Croke Park was set in 1973 when 73,308 saw the Cork-Galway final).

When the full redevelopment programme in Croke Park (which started with the demolition of the old Cusack Stand after the 1993 All-Ireland Final) has been completed, the capacity will be 79,500.

ALL-IRELAND CLUB FINALS (Football)

1971—Croke Park, November 21: East Kerry 5-9, Bryansford (Down) 2-7.

1972—Croke Park, May 12: Bellaghy (Derry) 0-15, U.C.D. 1-11.

1973—Portlaoise, June 4: Nemo Rangers (Cork) 2-11, St. Vincent's (Dublin) 2-11 (draw): Thurles, June 24: Nemo Rangers 4-6, St. Vincent's 0-10 (replay).

1974—Croke Park, March 18: U.C.D. 1-6, Clan na Gael (Armagh) 1-6 (draw): Croke Park, April 28: U.C.D. 0-14, Clan na Gael 1-4.

1975—Croke Park, March 16: U.C.D. 1-11, Nemo Rangers (Cork) 0-12.

1976—Portlaoise, March 14: St. Vincent's (Dublin) 4-10, Roscommon Gaels 0-5.

1977—Croke Park, March 13: Austin Stacks (Kerry) 1-13, Ballerin (Derry) 2-7.

1978—Croke Park, March 26: Thomond College (Limerick) 2-14, St. John's (Antrim) 1-3.

1979—Croke Park, March 17: Nemo Rangers (Cork) 2-9, Scotstown (Monaghan) 1-3.

1980—Tipperary, May 25: St. Finbarr's (Cork) 3-9, St. Grellan's (Galway) 0-8.

1981—Croke Park, May 31: St. Finbarr's (Cork) 1-9, Walterstown (Meath) 0-6.

1982—Ennis, May 16: Nemo Rangers (Cork) 6-11, Garrymore (Mayo) 1-8.

1983—Cloughjordan, March 20: Portlaoise 0-12, Clan na Gael (Roscommon) 2-0.

1984—Athlone, February 12: Nemo Rangers (Cork), 2-10, Walterstown (Meath) 0-5.

1985—Tipperary, March 24: Castleisland Desmonds (Kerry) 2-2, St. Vincent's (Dublin) 0-7.

1986—Croke Park, March 16: Burren (Down) 1-10, Castleisland Desmonds (Kerry) 1-6.

1987—Croke Park, March 17: St. Finbarr's (Cork) 0-10, Clan na Gael (Roscommon) 0-7.

1988—Croke Park, March 17: Burren (Down) 1-9, Clan na Gael (Roscommon) 0-8.

1989—Croke Park, March 17: Nemo Rangers (Cork) 1-13, Clan na Gael (Roscommon) 1-3.

1990—Croke Park, March 17: Baltinglass (Wicklow) 2-7, Clan na Gael (Roscommon) 0-7.

1991—Croke Park, March 17: Lavey (Derry) 2-9, Salthill (Galway) 0-10.
1992—Croke Park, March 17: Dr. Croke's (Kerry) 1-11, Thomas Davis (Dublin) 0-13.
1993—Croke Park, March 17: O'Donovan Rossa (Cork) 1-12, Éire Óg (Carlow) 3-6 (draw): Limerick, March 28: O'Donovan Rossa 1-7, Eire Og 0-8 (replay).

Linda Mellerick proudly displays the winning trophy after leading Cork to tory over Galway in the 1993 All-Ireland Camogie Senior Championship al. (Picture: Sportsfile).

ALL-IRELAND CLUB FOOTBALL FINAL TEAMS
1971-1993

1971

East Kerry—E. Fitzgerald, D. O'Sullivan, D. Crowley, J. Gleeson, G. Cullinane, N. Power, J. O'Donoghue, P. Moynihan, P. Casey, P. O'Donoghue, D. O'Keeffe, D. Healy, D. Coffey, M. Gleeson, D. Kavanagh. Sub.: T. Looney.

Bryansford—J. Boden, B. Cunningham, O. Burns, J. Neeson, D. McNamara, P. Cunningham, S. Cunningham, B. Ward, P. Neeson, W. Kane, M. Cunningham, K. Bailie, S. O'Hara, B. Neeson, E. Grant. Subs.: McGinn J. McGinn.

1972

Bellaghy—P. McTaggart, T. Scullion, A. Mulholland, F. Cassidy, T. Diamond, H. McGoldrick, C. Browne, L. Diamond, P. Doherty, F. Downey, B. Cassidy, F. O'Loane, H Donnelly, T. Quinn, K. Cassidy.

U.C.C.—N. Murphy, J. Gleeson, M. Keane, J. Coughlan, J. O'Grady, S. Looney, T. Looney, N. O'Sullivan, P. Lynch, B. Lynch, R. Bambury, D. Murray, D. Coffey, D. Kavanagh, N. Brosnan. Sub.: S. Murphy.

1973

Nemo Rangers—B. Morgan, J. Corcoran, E. Brophy, B. Murphy, R. Twomey, F. Cogan, D. O'Driscoll, D. Barrett, M. O'Donoghue, K. Collins, S. Coughlan, B. Cogan, L. Good, J. Barrett, C. Murphy. (Note: D. Cogan played in drawn game.)

St. Vincent's—T. O'Byrne, L. Ferguson, G. O'Driscoll, M. Hannick, M. Behan, D. Billings, E. Brady, P. Hallinan, P. J. Reid, B. Doyle, T. Hanahoe, B. Mullins, C. Keaney, D. Foley, J. Keaveney. (Note: G. Keavey, S. Mullins played in drawn game.) Subs.: L. Foley, D. Redmond drawn game. L. Foley, D Redmond, S. Mullins replay.

1974

U.C.D.—I. Heffernan, M. Judge, G. O'Reilly, P. Gilroy, F. O'Donoghue, E. O'Donoghue, P. Kerr, K. Kilmurray, B. Gaughran, E. Condron, O. Leddy, J. Walsh, J. P. Keane, D. O'Connor, P. Duggan. (Note: J. Waldron, P. J. O'Halloran, J. O'Keeffe played in drawn game.) Sub.: D. O'Connor in drawn match.

Clann na Gael—P. Scullion, K. France, J. O'Hagan, T.

Moore, O. Crewe, J. Greene, S. Lavelle, S. O'Hagan, C. McKinstry, M. O'Neill, J. Smyth, T. McCaughey, G. Hamill, N. O. Hagan, P. McGuinness. (Note: J. McKenna and J. Byrne played in drawn game.) Subs.: J. McKenna and J. Moore in replay.

1975

U.C.D.—I. Heffernan, M. Judge, G. O'Reilly, C. Moynihan, P. J. O'Halloran, E. O'Donoghue, F. O'Donoghue, M. Carty, P. O'Neill, B. Dunleavy, J. P. Keane, J. Walsh, B. Walsh, P. Duggan, B. Heneghan. Subs.: E. Condron.

Nemo Rangers—W. Morgan, J. Corcoran, E. Brophy, D. O'Sullivan, D. Cogan, B. Murphy, D. O'Driscoll, K. Collins, K. Murphy, L. Goode, S. Coughlan, S. Leydon, N. Morgan, J. Barrett, C. Murphy. Subs.: Declan Murphy, M. O'Donoghue.

1976

St. Vincent's—N. Bernard, D. Billings, G. O'Driscoll, M. Hannick, M. Behan, V. Lambe, B. Pocock, B. Mullins, F. Ryder, B. Reddy, T. Hanahoe, M. Whelan, L. Deegan, J. Keaveney, B. Doyle. Sub.: P. Reid.

Roscommon Gales—T. O'Connor, P. Kelly, P. Doran, S. Hunt, M. Menton, M. McNeela, A. de Paoli, J. O'Gara, J. Donnellan, J. Martin, M. McNamara, H. Griffin, F. Daly, L. O'Gara, P. Shaughnessy. Sub.: M. Moloney.

1977

Austin Stacks—T. Brick, G. Scollard, N. Power, P. Lucey, F. Lawlor, A. O'Keeffe, G. Power, G. O'Keeffe, J. O'Keeffe, F. Ryan, D. Long, T. Sheehan, J. Power, P. McCarthy, M. Sheehy. Sub.: C. Mangan.

Ballerin—S. Deighan, E. Moloney, S. McGahan, G. Forrest, V. Moloney, P. Stevenson, B. O'Kane, M. McAfee, J. Scullion, G. O'Connell, G. Keane, J. McAfee, C. Faulkner, S. O'Connell, P. M. Deighan.

1978

Thomond College—L. Murphy, M. Heuston, S. O'Shea, E. Mahon, M. Spillane, B. McSweeney, M. Connolly, T. Harkin, B. Talty, J. Dunne, R. Bell, D. Smyth, M. Kilcoyne, P. Spillane, J. O'Connell. Sub.: D. O'Boyle.

Saint John's—P. McCann, D. McNeill, K. McFerran, G. McCann, J. Rainey, J. McGuinness, J. Donnelly, L. Jennings, P.

McGinnitty, K. Gough, H. McRory, A. McCallin, M. Darragh, S. McFerran, P. McFaul. Subs.: J. McGranaghan, J. Cunningham.

1979

Nemo Rangers—W. Morgan, F. Cogan, F. Stone, K. Murphy, J. Kerrigan, B. Murphy, D. O'Driscoll, K. Brady, D. Linehan, J. Barrett, D. Allen, T. Dalton, N. Morgan, K. Collins, C. Murphy. Sub.: D. Murphy.

Scottstown—E. Keenan, M. McCarville, G. McCarville, F. Caulfield, D. Stirratt, S. McCarville, J. Treanor, B. Lillis, S. McCrudden, B. Morgan, Seamus McCarville, C. Morgan, J. McCabe, J. Moyna, B. Rice. Sub.: R. McDermott.

1980

St. Finbarr's—B. O'Brien, D. O'Grady, E. Desmond, N. Aherne, D. Brosnan, M. Lynch, M. Carey, C. Ryan, D. Philpott, F. Twomey, R. Kenny, F. O'Mahony, J. Barry Murphy, J. Allen, J. O'Callaghan. Sub.: D. Barry.

St Grellan's—W. Devlin, N. Jennings, J. Kelly, J. Boswell, P. Cunningham, E. Flanagan, K. Mitchell, B. Brennan, P. McGettigan, M. Cunningham, J. Manton, G. Gibbons, J. Whelan, C. Loftus, S. Riddell. Subs.: P. Ryan, L. White.

1981

St. Finbarr's—B. O'Brien, J. Cremin, M. Healy, E. Desmond, M. Carey, C. Ryan, D. O'Grady, T. Holland, M. Lynch, D. Barry, R. Kenny, F. O'Mahony, J. Barry Murphy, J. Allen, J. O'Callaghan. Sub.: J. Barry.

Walterstown—S. Reilly, P. Smith, W. Clarke, M. Sheils, E. Ward, C. Bowens, G. Reynolds, C. Reynolds, N. O'Sullivan, E. O'Brien, E. Barry, G. McLaughlin, G. Cooney, O. O'Brien, F. O'Sullivan. Subs.: M. Barry, T. Clarke.

1982

Nemo Rangers—D. Bevan, F. Cogan, B. Murphy, A. Keane, D. O'Driscoll, T. Hennebry, J. Kerrigan, M. Niblock, T. Dalton, S. Coughlan, D. Allen, S. Hayes, C. Murphy, E. Fitzgerald, M. Dorgan. Subs.: Charlie Murphy, K. Murphy, D. Linehan.

Garrymore—M. J. Connolly, P. Nally, D. Conway, J. Nally, P. Flannery, D. Mellett, G. Farraghter, J. Monaghan, P. Mohan, T. Walsh, P. Dixon, D. Dolan, T. Connolly, L. Dolan, B. Fitzpatrick. Subs.: P. Monaghan, M. Walsh.

1983

Portlaoise—M. Mulhall, J. Bohane, J. Bergin, M. Kavanagh, C. Browne, M. Lillis, B. Conroy, E. Whelan, M. Dooley, N. Prendergast, L. Scully, P. Critchley, T. Prendergast, J. Keenan, G. Browne. Sub.: W. Bohane.

Clan na Gael—J. O'Neill, W. Harney, L. O'Neill, C. Deignan, G. Pettit, M. Keegan, J. McManus, E. McManus, F. Nicholson, E. McManus (junior), M. McManus, O. McManus, P. J. Glynn, T. McManus, D. Shine. Subs.: L. Dunne, V. Harney.

1984

Nemo Rangers—D. Bevan, A. Keane, B. Murphy, K. Murphy, J. Kerrigan, M. Lynch, T. Nation, M. Niblock, T. Dalton, S. Coughlan, S. Hayes, C. Murphy, E. Fitzgerald, D. Allen, M. Dorgan. Sub.: Charlie Murphy.

Walterstown—C. Bowen, G. McLaughlin, W. Clarke, P. SMith, P. Carr, E. O'Brien, G. Reynolds, C. Reynolds, N. O'Sullivan, J. Barry, E. Barry, M. Barry, F. O'Sullivan, O. O'Brien, G. Cooney. Subs.: O. Clynch, K. McLoughlin.

1985

Castleisland Desmond's—C. Nelligan, D. Ciarubhain, B. Lyons, W. King, D. Lyons, M. J. Kearney, P. Callaghan, M. O'Connor, D. Hannafin, W. O'Connor, C. Kearney, D. Lyne, J. O'Connor, D. Buckley, P. Horan. Subs.: M. Downey, J. Lyons.

St. Vincent's—N. Bernard, T. Diamond, V. Conroy, S. Wade, R. Hazley, S. Fleming, A. Devlin, P. Canavan, B. Mullins, T. Conroy, B. Jordan, S. McDermott, C. Bufini, M. Loftus, P. McLoughlin. Sub.: E. Heery.

1986

Burren—D. Murdock, B. McKernan, A. Murdock, M. Murdock, K, McConville, W. McMahon, B. McGovern, T. McGovern, P. O'Rourke, L. Fitzpatrick, J. Treanor, P. McKay, J. McGreevy, V. McGovern, T. McArdle. Sub.: C. Doyle.

Castleisland Desmond's—C. Nelligan, D. O'Ciarubhain, B. Lyons, W. King, J. O'Connor, M. J. Kearney, P. O'Callaghan, M. O'Connor, D. Hannafin, W. O'Connor, C. Kearney, D. Lyne, P. Horan, D. Buckley, J. Lordan. Sub.: M. Downey.

St. Finbarr's—J. Kerins, J. Cremin, J. Meyler, E. Desmond, M. Carey, K. Scanlon, B. O'Connell, P. Hayes, T. Leahy, K. McCarthy, C. Ryan, M. Slocum, T. Power, D. O'Mahony, J. Allen. Sub.: M. Barry.

Clan na Gael—T. Seery, J. Dowling, M. Keegnan, J. McManus, O. McManus, F. Nicholson, A. McManus, P. McManus, E. McManus (senior), K. Pettit, P. Naughton, E. McManus (junior), T. Lennon, T. McManus, E. Durney. Subs.: H. Moody, J. Connaughton.

Burran—D. Murdock, B. McKernan, A. Murdock, M. Murdock, K. McConville, L. Fitzpatrick, B. McGovern, B. Laverty, T. McGovern, T. McArdle, J. Traenor, P. McKay, R. Fitzpatrick, V. McGovern, T. Fegan. Sub.: P. Fegan.

Clan na Gael—T. Seery, J. Dowling, M. Keegan, V. Harney, O. McManus, F. Nicholson, A. McManus, P. McManus, J. McManus, J. Connaughton, S. Lennon, E. McManus (junr.), P. Naughton, T. Lennon, J. McManus. Subs. E. McManus (senr.), E. Durney.

Nemo Rangers—J. O'Mahoney, A. Keane, N. Creedon, M. Lynch, J. Kerrigan, T. Griffin, D. Creedon, D. O'Sullivan, T. Dalton, S. O'Brien, E. O'Mahoney, T. Nation, S. Calnan, D. Allen, M. Dargan. Subs.: P. O'Donovan for Dalton, S. Hayes for Calnan.

Clan na Gael—P. Naughton, J. Dowling, J. McManus, D. Rock. O. McManus, J. Lennon, A. McManus, P. McManus, G. Lennon, J. Connaughton, E. McManus (Sen.), E. McManus (Junr.), P. Naughton, T. McManus, E. Durney. Sub.: L. Dunne for Durney.

Baltinglass—D. Leigh, S. O'Brien, H. Kenny, T. Donohue, B. Fitzpatrick, P. Murphy, B. Kilcoyne, R. Danne, B. Kenny, P. Kenny, R. McHugh, L. Horgan, C. Murphy, K. O'Brien, T. Murphy. Sub.: B. Timmons for P. Kenny.

Clan na Gael—Paul Naughton, D. Rock, M. Keegan, F. Nicholson, J. Connaughton, J. McManus, A. McManus, P. McManus, Eamonn McManus, Eoin McManus, Eamonn McManus (Junr.), E. Durney, Pauric Naughton, T. Lennon, T.

McManus. Subs.: D. Kenny for Pauric Naughton, D. Nolan for Durney.

1991

Lavey—B. Regan, D. Doherty, A. Scullion, B. Scullion, J. McGurk, H. Downey, Ciaran McGurk, D. O'Boyle, J. Chivers, F. Rafferty, B. McCormack, H. M. McGurk, D. Mulholland, S. Downey, Colm McGurk. Sub.: A. McGurk for Colm McGurk.

Salthill—C. McGinley, J. Kilraine, E. O'Donnellan, G. O'Farrell, F. Mitchell, I. O'Donoghue, M. Tarpey, A. Mulholland, M. Gibbs, P. J. Kelly, M. Butler, J. McDonagh, N. Costelloe, P. Comer, N. Finnegan, Subs.: C. McGauran for Kelly, M. Ruane for McDonagh.

1992

Dr. Crokes—P. O'Brien, D. Keogh, L. Hartnett, S. Clarke, J. Clifford, J. Galvin, C. O'Shea, C. Murphy, N. O'Leary, C. Doherty, D. Cooper, S. O'Shea, P. O'Shea, V. Casey, G. O'Shea.

Thomas Davis—F. Troy, D. Nugent, J. J. Martin, E. O'Toole; J. Fadian, P. Curran, G. Kilmartin, D. Foran, P. Godson, P. Waldron, P. Nugent, S. Grealis, P. Joyce, L. Adamson, V. Carney. Subs.: K. O'Donovan for O'Toole, P. Dwane for Joyce.

1993

O'Donovan Rossa—K. O'Dwyer, J. Evans, J. O'Donovan, F. McCarthy, G. O'Driscoll, A. Davis, I. Breen, D. O'Driscoll, B. O'Donovan, B. Carmody, J. O'Driscoll, D. Davis, N. Murphy, M. McCarthy, P. Davis. Sub.: M. McCarthy for G. O'Driscoll. (In drawn game, sub.: D. Whooley for Murphy).

Éire Óg—J. Kearns, J. Wynne, R. Moore, J. Dooley, B. Hayden, A. Callinan, N. Fallon, G. Ware, H. Brennan, J. Hayden, J. Morrissey, T. Nolan, J. Murphy, C. Hayden, A. Keating. Sub.: D. Moore for Nolan. (In drawn game, D. Wynne at full-back, D. Walker centre half-back.)

CAPTAINS OF WINNING ALL-IRELAND
CLUB FOOTBALL TEAMS

1971—M. Gleeson (East Kerry)
1972—T. Scullion (Ballaghy)
1973—W. Morgan (Nemo Rangers)
1974—P. Kerr (U.C.D.)
1975—M. Carty (U.C.D.)
1976—T. Hanahoe (St. Vincent's)
1977—J. O'Keeffe (Austin Stacks)
1978—R. Bell (Thomond College)
1979—B. Murphy (Nemo Rangers)
1980—N. Aherne (St. Finbarr's)
1981—B. O'Brien (St. Finbarr's)
1982—C. Murphy (Nemo Rangers)
1983—L. Scully (Portlaoise)
1984—J. Kerrigan (Nemo Rangers)
1985—B. Lyons (Castleisland Desmonds)
1986—T. McGovern (Burren)
1987—J. Meyler (St. Finbarr's)
1988—V. McGovern (Burren)
1989—Tony Nation (Nemo Rangers).
1990—Brian Fitzpatrick (Baltinglass).
1991—John McGurk (Lavey).
1992—Seán O'Shea (Dr. Crokes).
1993—Mick McCarthy (O'Donovan Rossa).

BANK OF IRELAND ALL-STAR FOOTBALL TEAMS

1971—P. J. Smyth (Galway); Johnny Carey (Mayo), Jack Cosgrove (Galway), Donie O'Sullivan (Kerry); Eugene Mulligan (Offaly), Nicholas Clavin (Offaly), Pat Reynolds (Meath); Liam Sammon (Galway), Willie Bryan (Offaly); Tony McTague (Offaly), Ray Cummins (Cork), Mickey Kearns (Sligo); Andy McCallin (Antrim), Seán O'Neill (Down), Seamus Leydon (Galway).

1972—Martin Furlong (Offaly); Mick Ryan (Offaly), Paddy McCormack (Offaly), Donie O'Sullivan (Kerry); Brian McEniff (Donegal), Tommy Joe Gilmore (Galway), Kevin Jer O'Sullivan (Cork); Willie Bryan (Offaly), Mick O'Connell (Kerry); Johnny Cooney (Offaly), Kevin Kilmurray (Offaly), Tony McTague (Offaly); Mickey Freyne (Roscommon), Seán O'Neill (Down), Paddy Moriarty (Armagh).

1973—Billy Morgan (Cork); Frank Cogan (Cork), Mick Ryan (Offaly), Brian Murphy (Cork); Liam O'Neill (Galway), Tommy Joe Gilmore (Galway), Kevin Jer O'Sullivan (Cork); John O'Keeffe (Kerry), Denis Long (Cork); Johnny Cooney (Offaly), Kevin Kilmurray (Offaly), Liam Sammon (Galway); Jimmy Barry Murphy (Cork), Ray Cummins (Cork), Anthony McGurk (Derry).

1974—Paddy Cullen (Dublin); Donal Monaghan (Donegal), Seán Doherty (Dublin), Robbie Kelleher (Dublin); Paddy Reilly (Dublin), Barnes Murphy (Sligo), Johnny Hughes (Galway); Dermot Earley (Roscommon), Paud Lynch (Kerry); Tom Naughton (Galway), Declan Barron (Cork), David Hickey (Dublin); Jimmy Barry Murphy (Cork), Jimmy Keaveney (Dublin), Johnny Tobin (Galway).

1975—Paud O'Mahony (Kerry); Gay O'Driscoll (Dublin), John O'Keeffe (Kerry), Robbie Kelleher (Dublin); Peter Stevenson (Derry), Anthony McGurk (Derry), Ger Power (Kerry); Denis Long (Cork), Colm McAlarney (Down); Gerry McElhinney (Derry), Ken Rennicks (Meath), Mickey O'Sullivan (Kerry); John Egan (Kerry), Matt Kerrigan (Meath), Anton O'Toole (Dublin).

1976—Paddy Cullen (Dublin); Ger O'Keeffe (Kerry), John O'Keeffe (Kerry), Brian Murphy (Cork); Johnny Hughes (Galway), Kevin Moran (Dublin), Ger Power (Kerry); Brian Mullins (Dublin), Dave McCarthy (Cork); Anton O'Toole (Dublin), Tony Hanahoe (Dublin), David Hickey (Dublin); Bobby Doyle (Dublin), Mike Sheehy (Kerry), Pat Spillane (Kerry).

1977—Paddy Cullen (Dublin); Gay O'Driscoll (Dublin), Pat Lindsay (Roscommon), Robbie Kelleher (Dublin); Tommy Drumm (Dublin), Paddy Moriarty (Armagh), Pat O'Neill (Dublin); Brian Mullins (Dublin), Joe Kernan (Armagh); Anton O'Toole (Dublin),

Jimmy Smyth (Armagh), Pat Spillane (Kerry); Bobby Doyle (Dublin), Jimmy Keaveney (Dublin), John Egan (Kerry).

1978—Ollie Crinnigan (Kildare); Harry Keegan (Roscommon), John O'Keeffe (Kerry), Robbie Kelleher (Dublin); Tommy Drumm (Dublin), Ollie Brady (Cavan), Paud Lynch (Kerry); Colm McAlarney (Down), Tomás Connor (Offaly); Ger Power (Kerry), Declan Barron (Cork), Pat Spillane (Kerry); Mike Sheehy (Kerry), Jimmy Keaveney (Dublin), John Egan (Kerry).

1979—Paddy Cullen (Dublin); Eugene Hughes (Monaghan), John O'Keeffe (Kerry), Tom Heneghan (Roscommon); Tommy Drumm (Dublin), Tim Kennelly (Kerry), Danny Murray (Roscommon); Dermot Earley (Roscommon), Bernard Brogan (Dublin); Ger Power (Kerry), Seán Walsh (Kerry), Pat Spillane (Kerry); Mike Sheehy (Kerry), Seán Lowry (Offaly), Joe McGrath (Mayo).

1980—Charlie Nelligan (Kerry); Harry Keegan (Roscommon), Kevin Kehily (Cork), Gerry Connellan (Roscommon); Kevin McCabe (Tyrone), Tim Kennelly (Kerry), Danny Murray (Roscommon); Jack O'Shea (Kerry), Colm McKinstry (Armagh); Ger Power (Kerry), Denis Allen (Cork), Pat Spillane (Kerry); Matt Connor (Offaly), Eoin Liston (Kerry), John Egan (Kerry).

1981—Martin Furlong (Offaly); Jimmy Deenihan (Kerry), Paddy Kennedy (Down), Paud Lynch (Kerry); Paud O'Shea (Kerry), Richie Connor (Offaly), Seamus McHugh (Galway); Jack O'Shea (Kerry), Seán Walsh (Kerry); Barry Brennan (Galway), Denis "Ogie" Moran (Kerry), Pat Spillane (Kerry); Mike Sheehy (Kerry), Eoin Liston (Kerry), Brendan Lowry (Offaly).

1982—Martin Furlong (Offaly); Mick Fitzgerald (Offaly), Liam Connor (Offaly), Kevin Kehily (Cork); Paud O'Shea (Kerry), Seán Lowry (Offaly), Liam Currams (Offaly); Jack O'Shea (Kerry), Pádraig Dunne (Offaly); Peter McGinnity (Fermanagh), Joe Kernan (Armagh), Matt Connor (Offaly); Mike Sheehy (Kerry), Eoin Liston (Kerry), John Egan (Kerry).

1983—M. Furlong (Offaly), P. O'Shea (Kerry), S. Kinneavy (Galway), J. Evans (Cork), P. Canavan (Dublin) T. Drumm (Dublin), J. Kerrigan (Cork), J. O'Shea (Kerry), L. Austin (Down), B. Rock (Dublin), M. Connor (Offaly), G. Blaney (Down), M. McHugh (Donegal), C. O'Rourke (Meath), J. McNally (Dublin).

1984—J. O'Leary (Dublin), P. O'Shea (Kerry), M. Lyons (Meath), S. McHugh (Galway), T. Doyle (Kerry), T. Spillane (Kerry), P. J. Buckley (Dublin), J. O'Shea (Kerry), E. McKenna (Tyrone), B. Rock (Dublin), E. Liston (Kerry), P. Spillane

(Kerry), M. Sheehy (Kerry), F. McGuigan (Tyrone), D. McNicholl (Derry).

1985—J. O'Leary (Dublin), P. O'Shea (Kerry), G. Hargan (Dublin), M. Spillane (Kerry), T. Doyle (Kerry), C. Murray (Monaghan), D. Flanagan (Mayo), J. O'Shea (Kerry), W. J. Padden (Mayo), B. Rock (Dublin), T. Conroy (Dublin), P. Spillane (Kerry), K. McStay (Mayo), P. Early (Roscommon), E. Hughes (Monaghan).

1986—C. Nelligan (Kerry), H. Keegan (Roscommon), M. Lyons (Meath), J. Lynch (Tyrone), T. Doyle (Kerry), T. Spillane (Kerry), C. Browne (Laois), P. Donaghy (Tyrone), L. Irwin (Laois), R. McCarron (Monaghan), E. McKenna (Tyrone), P. Spillane (Kerry), M. Sheehy (Kerry), D. O'Hagan (Tyrone), G. Power (Kerry).

1987—J. Kearns (Cork), R. O'Malley (Meath), C. Corrigan (Cork), T. Scullian (Derry), N. Cahlane (Cork), T. Spillane (Kerry), G. Lynch (Kerry), G. McEntee (Meath), B. McGilligan (Derry), D. Beggy (Meath), L. Tompkins (Cork), K. Duff (Dublin), V. Daly (Galway), B. Stafford (Meath), B. Flynn (Meath).

1988—Paddy Linden (Monaghan), Bobby O'Malley (Meath), Colman Corrigan (Cork), Mick Kennedy (Dublin), Niall Cahalane (Cork), Noel McCaffrey (Dublin), Martin O'Connell (Meath), Shea Fahy (Cork), Liam Hayes (Meath), Maurice Fitzgerald (Kerry), Larry Tompkins (Cork), Kieran Duff (Dublin), Colm O'Rourke (Meath), Brian Stafford (Meath), Eugene Hughes (Monaghan).

1989—Gabriel Irwin (Mayo), Jimmy Browne (Mayo), Gerry Hargan (Dublin), Dermot Flanagan (Mayo), Connie Murphy (Kerry), Conor Counihan (Cork), Anthony Davis (Cork), Teddy McCarthy (Cork), Willie Joe Padden (Mayo), Dave Barry (Cork), Larry Tompkins (Cork), Noel Durkin (Mayo), Paul McGrath (Cork), Eugene McKenna (Tyrone), Tony McManus (Roscommon).

1990—John Kerins (Cork), Bobby O'Malley (Meath), Stephen O'Brien (Cork), Terry Ferguson (Meath), Michael Slocum (Cork), Conor Counihan (Cork), Martin O'Connell (Meath), Shea Fahy (Cork), Mickey Quinn (Leitrim), David Beggy (Meath), Val Daly (Galway), Joyce McMullan (Donegal), Paul McGrath (Cork), Kevin O'Brien (Wicklow), James McCartan (Down).

1991—Michael McQuillan (Meath), Mick Deegan (Dublin), Conor Deegan (Down), Enon Gavin (Roscommon), Tommy Carr

INTERNATIONAL SERIES
(Under Compromise Rules)

1984

First International — Cork:
 Australia 70 pts, Ireland 57 pts.
Second International — Croke Park:
 Ireland 80 pts, Australia 76 pts.
Third International — Croke Park:
Australia 76 pts, Ireland 71 pts.

1986

First International — Perth:
 Australia 64 pts, Ireland 57 pts.
Second International — Melbourne:
 Ireland 62 pts, Australia 46 pts.
Third International — Adelaide:
 Ireland 55 pts, Australia 32 pts.

1987

First International — Croke Park:
 Ireland 53 pts, Australia 51 pts.
Second International — Croke Park:
 Australia 72 pts, Ireland 47 pts.
Third International — Croke Park:
 Australia 59 pts, Ireland 55.

1990

First International — Melbourne
 Ireland 47 pts, Australia 38 pts
Second International — Canberra
 Ireland 52 pts, Australia 31 pts
Third International — Perth
 Australia 50 pts, Ireland 44 pts

Note: The international links with Australia were first established in October, 1967 when an Australian party visited this country and played two matches, defeating Meath (3-16 to 1-10) and Mayo (2-12 to 2-5), both games at Croke Park. Then Meath became the trail-blazers Down Under in March 1968 and played five games in all, embracing Perth, Melbourne, Sydney, Adelaide and Melbourne again. They won all five.

(Dublin), Keith Barr (Dublin), Martin O'Connell (Meath), Barry Breen (Down), Martin Lynch (Kildare), Ross Carr (Down), Greg Blaney (Down), Tommy Dowd (Meath), Colm O'Rourke (Meath), Brian Stafford (Meath), Bernard Flynn (Meath).

1992—Gary Walsh (Donegal), Seamus Clancy (Clare), Matt Gallagher (Donegal), Tony Scullion (Derry), Paul Curran (Dublin), Martin Gavigan (Donegal), Eamonn Heery (Dublin), Anthony Molloy (Donegal), T. J. Kilgallon (Mayo), Anthony Tohill (Derry), Martin McHugh (Donegal), James McHugh (Donegal), Tony Boyle (Donegal), Vinny Murphy (Dublin), Enda Gormley (Derry).

LEADING AWARD WINNERS

Pat Spillane (Kerry) 9 – 1976-'81, 1984-'86.
Mike Sheehy (Kerry) 7 – 1976, 1978, 1979, 1981, 1982, 1984, 1986.
Jack O'Shea (Kerry) 6 – 1980-'85.
Ger Power (Kerry) 6 – 1975, 1976, 1978, 1979, 1980, 1986.

ALL-TIME ALL-STAR AWARD WINNERS
FOOTBALL

1980—Larry Stanley (Kildare).
1981—Tommy Murphy (Laois)
1982—Paddy Moclair (Mayo)
1983—Jim McCullogh (Armagh)
1984—John Dunne (Galway)
1985—J. J. (Purty) Landers and Tim (Roundy) Landers (Kerry)
1986—Alf Murray (Armagh)
1987—Mick Higgins (Cavan)
1988—Kevin Armstrong (Antrim).
1989—Peter McDermott (Meath).
1990—Eddie Boyle (Louth).
1991—Seán Purcell (Galway).
1992—Seán Flanagan (Mayo).

DUAL AWARD WINNERS

Ray Cummins (Cork): Hurling 1971, 1972, 1977. Football 1971, 1973.
Jimmy Barry Murphy (Cork): Hurling 1976, 1977, 1978, 1983, 1986. Football 1973, 1974.
Brian Murphy (Cork): Hurling 1978, 1981. Football 1973, 1976.
Liam Currams (Offaly): Hurling 1981. Football 1982.

The Australians returned to Ireland in October '68 and drew with Kerry in Killarney. Then they played two matches in Croke Park, beating the Combined Universities (3-9 to 1-11) and Down (1-11 to 2-7).

Kerry went on a World Tour in March 1970 and played five matches in Australia, wining all of them. The most interesting was that with the oval ball under lights in Adelaide (Kerry 10-14, South Australia 5-9) but it must be stressed that this was a gaelic football match and not under the compromise rules as at present.

Incidentally, Kerry's top scorer in that World Tour, which also took in Auckland and San Francisco, was Mick O'Dwyer with 9-30 (57 points) in seven games (average 8.14 points).

● *Kevin Heffernan and Tony Hanahoe who thwarted Mike Sheehy, Pat Spillane and the other greats of the Kerry 1975-'78 combinations of two more All-Ireland medals by playing such vital roles in Dublin's 1976-'77 victories over the Kingdom.*

LEADING ALL-IRELAND SENIOR MEDAL WINNERS

Football

Paidi O'Shea (Kerry) 8: 1975, 1978, 1979, 1980, 1981, 1984, 1985, 1986

Denis "Ogie" Moran (Kerry) 8: 1975, 1978, 1979, 1980, 1981, 1984, 1985, 1986

Pat Spillane (Kerry) 8: 1975, 1978, 1979, 1980, 1981 (in as sub), 1984, 1985, 1986

Ger Power (Kerry) 8: 1975, 1978, 1979 (sub), 1980, 1981, 1984, 1985, 1986.

Mike Sheehy (Kerry) 8: 1975, 1978, 1979, 1980, 1981, 1984 (sub), 1985, 1986

Dan O'Keeffe (Kerry) 7: 1931, 1932, 1937, 1939, 1940, 1941, 1946

John O'Keeffe (Kerry) 7: 1969 (sub), 1970, 1975, 1978, 1979, 1980, 1981

Charlie Nelligan (Kerry) 7: 1978, 1979, 1980, 1981, 1984, 1985, 1986

Seán Walsh (Kerry) 7: 1978, 1979, 1980, 1981, 1984, 1985, 1986

Hurling

Noel Skehan (Kilkenny) 9: 1963 (sub), 1967 (sub), 1969 (sub), 1972, 1974, 1975, 1979, 1982, 1983

Christy Ring (Cork) 8: 1941, 1942, 1943, 1944, 1946, 1952, 1953, 1954

John Doyle, Tipperary 8: 1949, 1950, 1951, 1958, 1961, 1962, 1964, 1965

Frank Cummins (Kilkenny) 8: 1967 (sub), 1969, 1972, 1974, 1975, 1979, 1982, 1983

Jimmy Doyle (Tipperary) 6: 1958, 1961, 1962, 1964, 1965, 1971 (in as sub).

Jack Lynch's Distinction

Jack Lynch (Cork) had the distinction of winning six All-Ireland senior championship medals in a row, five in hurling (1941-'44 and 1946) and one in football, 1945.

TEXACO FOOTBALLER OF THE YEAR AWARD

The following are the football stars who have been awarded Texaco Trophies by the Sports Editors since the inauguration of the award in 1958. Also listed are the Hall of Fame winners in football since the introduction of this category in 1960.

FOOTBALL

1958—Jim McKeever, Derry.
1959—Seán Murphy, Kerry.
1960—Jim McCartan, Down.
1961—Jim McCartan, Down.
1962—Mick O'Connell, Kerry.
1963—Lar Foley, Dublin.
1964—Noel Tierney, Galway.
1965—Martin Newell, Galway.
1966—Mattie McDonagh, Galway.
1967—Bertie Cunningham, Meath.
1968—Seán O'Neill, Down.
1969—Mick O'Dwyer, Kerry.
1970—Tom Prendergast, Kerry.
1971—Eugene Mulligan, Offaly.
1972—Willie Bryan, Offaly.
1973—Billy Morgan (Cork).
1974—Kevin Heffernan, Dublin (coach/manager).
1975—John O'Keeffe, Kerry.
1976—Jimmy Keaveney, Dublin.
1977—Jimmy Keaveney, Dublin.
1978—Pat Spillane, Kerry.
1979—Mike Sheehy, Kerry.
1980—Jack O'Shea, Kerry.
1981—Jack O'Shea, Kerry.
1982—Martin Furlong, Offaly.
1983—Tommy Drumm, Dublin.
1984—Jack O'Shea, Kerry.
1985—Jack O'Shea, Kerry.
1986—Pat Spillane, Kerry.
1987—Brian Stafford, Meath.
1988—Bobby O'Malley (Meath)
1989—Teddy McCarthy (Cork)
1990—Shay Fahy (Cork)
1991—Colm O'Rourke (Meath)
1992—Martin McHugh (Donegal)

449

HALL OF FAME

1963—John Joe Sheehy (Kerry)
1970—Larry Stanley (Kildare)
1989—Mick Higgins (Cavan)
1992—John Doyle (Tipperary)

In 1993 Jack Lynch (Cork) was given the Hall of Fame award under the heading Gaelic Sport as he had won five All-Ireland senior hurling medals with Cork (1941-'44 and '46) and one senior football medal in 1945.

HIGHEST SCORERS IN ALL-IRELAND FINALS

Hurling:

60 minute finals: Michael "Gah" Ahearne (Cork) 19 points (5-4 v Galway 1928).

70 minute finals: Nicholas English (Tipperary) 18 points (2-12 v Antrim 1989).

80 minute finals: Eddie Keher (Kilkenny) 17 points (2-11 v Tipperary 1971).

Football:

60 minute finals: Frank Stockwell (Galway) 11 points (2-5 v Cork 1956).

70 minute finals: Jimmy Keaveney (Dublin) 12 points (2-6 v Armagh 1977); Mike Sheehy (Kerry) 12 points (2-6 v Dublin 1979).

80 minute finals: Mick Fay (Meath) 10 points (0-10 v Kerry 1970); Brendan Lynch (Kerry) 10 points (1-7 v Offaly 1972 draw): Tony McTague (Offaly) 10 points (0-10 v Kerry 1972 replay).

TEAMS OF THE CENTURY AND CENTENARY TEAMS

In the Centenary ·Year of 1984 the *Sunday Independent*/Irish Nationwide/GAA Teams of the Century in Hurling and Football were selected by a special panel, after the *Sunday Independent* had carried out a national poll of its readers.

Hurling: Tony Reddan (Tipperary), Bobby Rackard (Wexford), Nick O'Donnell (Wexford), John Doyle (Tipperary), Jimmy Finn (Tipperary), John Keane (Waterford), Paddy Phelan (Kilkenny), Lory Meagher (Kilkenny), Jack Lynch (Cork), Christy Ring (Cork), Mick Mackey (Limerick), Jimmy Langton (Kilkenny), Jimmy Doyle (Tipperary), Nick Rackard (Wexford), Eddie Keher (Kilkenny).

Football: Danno Keefe (Kerry), Enda Colleran (Galway), Paddy O'Brien (Meath), Seán Flanagan (Mayo), Seán Murphy (Kerry), John Joe O'Reilly (Cavan), Stephen White (Louth), Mick O'Connell (Kerry), Jack O'Shea (Kerry), Seán O'Neill (Down), Seán Purcell (Galway), Pat Spillane (Kerry), Mike Sheehy (Kerry), Tom Langan (Mayo), Kevin Heffernan (Dublin).

Also in 1984 the *Sunday Independent*/Irish Nationwide/GAA Centenary Teams were selected by a special panel, comprising players who had never won an All-Ireland Senior Championship medal.

Hurling: Seán Duggan (Galway), Jim Fives (Waterford), Noel Drumgoole (Dublin), J. J. ("Goggles") Doyle (Clare), Seán Herbert (Limerick), Seán Stack (Clare), Colm Doran (Wexford), Joe Salmon (Galway), "Jobber" McGrath (Westmeath), Josie Gallagher (Galway), Martin Quigley (Wexford), Kevin Armstrong (Antrim), Jimmy Smith (Clare), Christy O'Brien (Laois), Mick Bermingham (Dublin).

Football: Aidan Brady (Roscommon), Willie Casey (Mayo), Eddie Boyle (Louth), John McKnight (Armagh), Gerry O'Reilly (Wicklow), Gerry O'Malley (Roscommon), Seán Quinn (Armagh), Jim McKeever (Derry), Tommy Murphy (Laois), Seán O'Connell (Derry), Pakie McGarty (Leitrim), Michael Kearns (Sligo), Charlie Gallagher (Cavan), Willie McGee (Mayo), Dinny Allen (Cork).

COLLEGES

ALL-IRELAND CHAMPIONSHIPS

HURLING

ROLL OF HONOUR 1944-1993

St. Kieran's, Kilkenny (12) – 1948, 1957, 1959, 1961, 1965, 1971, 1975, 1988, 1989, 1990, 1992, 1993.

St. Flannan's, Ennis (11) – 1944, 1945, 1946, 1947, 1958, 1976, 1979, 1982, 1983, 1987, 1991.

St. Finbarr's, Farranferris, Cork (5) — 1963, 1969, 1972, 1974, 1984.

St. Peter's, Wexford (4) — 1962, 1967, 1968, 1973.

North Monastery, Cork (4) — 1960, 1970, 1980, 1985.

Limerick C.B.S. (2) — 1964, 1966.

Kilkenny C.B.S. (1) — 1981.

St. Colman's, Fermoy (1) — 1977.

Templemore C.B.S. (1) — 1978.

Birr Community School (1) – 1986.

Only Leinster and Munster took part, 1944-'48

1944—Final—Thurles, April 23: *St. Flannan's* (Ennis) 5-5; St. Kieran's (Kilkenny) 3-3.

1945—Final—Croke Park, April 29: *St. Flannan's* (Ennis) 7-10; St. Joseph's (Marino) 2-3.

1946—Final—Croke Park, May 5: *St. Flannan's* (Ennis) 5-7; O'Connell Schools (Dublin) 5-2.

1947—Final—Thurles, May 4: *St. Flannan's* (Ennis) 6-8; St. Joseph's (Roscrea) 3-1.

1948—Final—Croke Park, May 2: *St. Kieran's* (Kilkenny) 2-12; St. Colman's (Fermoy) 2-2.

1949—1956—Suspended.

1957—Galway—April 7: St. Flannan's (Ennis) 7-4; St. Mary's (Galway) 1-6.
Final—Thurles, April 28: *St. Kieran's* (Kilkenny) 4-2; St. Flannan's (Ennis) 2-7.

1958—Ennis—March 30: Flannan's (Ennis) 6-8; St. Joseph's (Galway) 1-3.

1976—Nenagh—April 4: Presentation (Athenry) 2-11; Kilkenny C.B.S. 2-7.
Final—Nenagh—May 2: St. Flannan's (Ennis) 3-7; Presentation (Athenry) 4-4.
(Replay)—Nenagh—May 16: *St. Flannan's* (Ennis) 3-9; Presentatin (Athenry) 1-7.

1977—Nenagh—April 3rd: St. Colman's (Fermoy) 2-10; Presentation (Athenry) 2-3.
Final—Thurles—May 1: *St. Colman's* (Fermoy 2-13; St. Kieran's (Kilkenny) 1-9.

1978—Carlow—April 16: St. Peter's (Wexford) 1-9; Our Lady's (Gort) 0-4.
Final—Kilkenny—May 7: *Templemore C.B.S.* 2-11; St. Peter's 1-4.

1979—Nenagh—March 31: St. Flannan's (Ennis) 4-15; St. Mary's (Galway) 1-1.
Final—Thurles—April 29: *St. Flannan's* (Ennis) 3-15; Presentation (Birr) 2-3.

1980—Roscrea—March 30: Birr Community School 0-7; St. Joseph's (Garbally) 1-4.
(Replay)—Thurles—April 6: Birr Community School 2-15; St. Joseph's (Garbally) 3-4.
Final—Thurles—April 27: *North Mon.* (Cork) 5-11; Birr Community 3-7.

1981—Thurles—April 13; *North Mon.* (Cork) 1-9; Our Lady's (Gort) 0-4.
Final—Waterford—May 10: *Kilkenny C.B.S.* 3-5; North Mon. (Cork) 1-8.

1982—Thurles—April 25: St. Peter's (Wexford) 1-18; Our Lady's (Gort) 1-9.
Final—Thurles—May 9: St. Flannan's (Ennis) 1-4; St. Peter's 1-4.
(Replay)—Thurles—May 16: *St. Flannan's* (Ennis) 2-9; St. Peter's 0-10.

1983—Cloughjordan—April 24: St. Flannan's (Ennis) 4-7; St. Joseph's (Garbally) 0-11.
Final—Thurles—May 8: *St. Flannan's* (Ennis) 0-16; Kilkenny C.B.S. 2-4.

1984—Birr—April 15: St. Kieran's (Kilkenny) 3-8; Our Lady's (Gort) 1-5.
Final—Croke Park—May 6: *St. Finbarr's* (Farrenferris) 1-15; St. Kieran's 0-8.

1985—Limerick—April 22: North Mon. (Cork) 2-11; St.

Joseph's (Garbally) 0-7.

Final—Portlaoise—May 12: North Mon. 2-7; Birr Community School 3-4.

(Replay)—Limerick—May 19: *North Mon.* (Cork) 4-11; Birr Community School 1-5.

1986—Tynagh—April 13: Birr Community School 2-10; St. Joseph's (Garbally) 1-5.

Final—Portlaoise—April 27: *Birr C.S.* 5-8; North Mon. (Cork) 1-8.

1987—Athenry—April 12: St. Flannan's (Ennis) 2-15; St. Joseph's (Garbally) 1-5.

Final—Birr—May 10: *St. Flannan's* (Ennis) 4-11; St. Kieran's (Kilkenny) 1-7.

1988—Portumna—April 24: St. Kieran's (Kilkenny) 3-8; St. Mary's (Galway) 0-4.

Final—Waterford—May 8: *St. Kieran's* 3-10; Midleton C.B.S. 2-7.

1989—Ballinsaloe, April 23: St. Flannan's (Ennis) 1-16, St. Mary's (Galway) 0-5.

Final – Nenagh, May 7: St. Kieran's (Kilkenny) 3-5, St. Flannan's 1-9.

1990—Birr, April 15: St. Kieran's (Kilkenny) 4-7, St. Mary's (Galway) 2-3.

Final – Mitchelstown, May 6: St. Kieran's 2-10, St. Flannan's (Ennis) 0-7.

1991—Whitegate, April 13: St. Flannan's (Ennis) 1-7, St. Raphael's (Loughrea) 0-9.

Final – Thurles, April 27: St. Flannan's 1-15, St. Kieran's (Kilkenny) 1-9.

1992—Trim, April 5: St. Colman's (Fermoy) 1-12, St. Patrick's (Maghera) 0-3. Tullamore, April 12: St. Kieran's (Kilkenny) 4-13, St. Raphael's (loughrea) 3-3.

Final – Thurles, April 26: St. Kieran's 1-7, St. Colman's 0-8.

1993—Athboy, April 4: St. Kieran's (Kilkenny) 1-15, St. Patrick's (Maghera) 0-3. Ennis, April 4: Our Lady's (Gort) 1-9, St. Michael's CBS (Limerick) 2-5.

Final – Nenagh, April 25: St. Kieran's 3-15, Our Lady's 1-10.

COLLEGES

ALL-IRELAND CHAMPIONSHIPS

FOOTBALL

ROLL OF HONOUR 1946-1993

St. Jarlath's, Tuam (10) – 1947, 1958, 1960, 1961, 1964, 1966, 1974, 1978, 1982, 1984.
St. Colman's, Newry (5) – 1967, 1975, 1986, 1988, 1993.
St. Mel's, Longford (4) – 1948, 1962, 1963, 1987.
Coláiste Chríost Rí, Cork (4) – 1968, 1970, 1983, 1985.
Carmelite College, Moate (3) – 1976, 1980, 1981.
St. Brendan's, Killarney (2) 1969, 1992.
St. Patrick's, Maghera (2) – 1989, 1990.
Ard Scoil Rís, Dublin (1) – 1979.
Franciscan College, Gormanston (1) – 1973.
St. Columb's, Derry (1) – 1965.
St. Colman's, Claremorris (1) – 1977.
St. Joseph's, Fairview, Dublin (1) – 1959.
St. Mary's CBS, Belfast (1) – 1971.
St. Patrick's, Armagh (1) – 1946.
St. Patrick's, Cavan (1) – 1972.
St. Nathy's, Ballaghaderreen (1) – 1957.
St. Fachtna's, Skibbereen (1) – 1991.

1946—Killarney—April 8: St. Jarlath's (Tuam) 2-14; St. Brendan's (Killarney) 2-4.

Cavan—April 8: St. Patrick's (Armagh) 3-7; St. Mel's (Longford) 2-7.

Final—Croke Park—May 5: *St. Patrick's* (Armagh) 3-11; St. Jarlath's (Tuam) 4-7.

1947—Tuam—April 20: St. Jarlath's (Tuam) 5-12; St. Brendan's (Killarney) 1-0.

Cavan—April 27: St. Patrick's (Armagh) 3-12; St. Mel's (Longford) 2-6.

Final— Croke Park—May 11: *St. Jarlath's* (Tuam) 4-10; St. Patrick's (Armagh) 3-8.

1948—Longford—April 18: St. Mel's (Longford) 1-7; Tralee C.B.S. 2-2.

Longford—April 18: St. Patrick's (Cavan) 2-15; Roscommon C.B.S. 0-6.

Final—Croke Park—May 2: *St. Mel's* (Longford) 4-7; St. Patrick's (Cavan) 3-3.

1949–1956—Suspended.

1957—Navan—March 31: St. Colman's (Newry) 5-4; Presentation (Ballyfin) 1-4.

Killarney—March 31: St. Nathy's (Ballaghaderreen) 3-7; Colaiste Iosagain (Ballyvourney) 0-4.

Final—Croke Park—April 14: *St. Nathy's* (Ballaghaderreen) 1-7; St. Colman's (Newry) 0-4.

1958—Croke Park—March 30: Franciscan College (Gormanstown) 3-7; St. Colman's (Newry) 1-9.

Tuam—March 30: St. Jarlath's (Tuam) 0-9; De La Salle (Waterford) 1-4.

Final—Croke Park—April 27: *St. Jarlath's* (Tuam 1-7; Franciscan College, Gormanstown 2-3.

1959—Sligo—March 22: St. Nathy's (Ballaghaderreen) 2-10; Abbey C.B.S. (Newry) 1-7.

Roscrea—March 22: St. Joseph's (Fairview) 1-7; St. Flannan's (Ennis) 0-7.

Final—Croke Park—April 19: *St. Joseph's* (Fairview) 3-9; St. Nathy's (Ballaghaderreen) 2-8.

1960—Croke Park—April 10: St. Jarlath's (Tuam 2-10; St. Colman's (Newry) 1-2.

Portlaoise—April 10: St. Finian's (Mullingar) 0-8; Limerick C.B.S. 0-7.

Final—Athlone—May 1: *St. Jarlath's* (Tuam) 3-10; St. Finian's, Mullingar 3-7.

1961—Croke Park—March 19: St. Mel's (Longford) 1-10; De La
       Salle (Waterford) 2-7.
       (Replay)—Croke Park—March 26: St. Mel's (Longford)
       1-14; De La Salle (Waterford) 3-4.
       Longford—March 26: St. Jarlath's (Tuam) 5-9; St.
       Patrick's (Cavan) 1-8.
       Final—Athlone—April 16: *St. Jarlath's* (Tuam) 2-8;
       St.Mel's (Longford) 1-8.
1962—Croke Park—March 24: St. Mel's (Longford) 2-5; De La
       Salle (Waterford) 2-3.
       Athlone—March 24: St. Jarlath's (Tuam) 2-8; St.
       Patrick's (Cavan) 1-3.
       Final—Ballinasloe—April 8: *St. Mel's* (Longford) 3-11;
       St. Jarlath's (Tuam) 2-12.
1963—Limerick—April 7: St. Brendan's (Killarney) 1-7; St.
       Jarlath's (Tuam) 0-8.
       Kells—April 7: St. Mel's (Longford) 1-10; St. Colman's
       (Newry) 2-5.
       Final—Croke Park—April 28: *St. Mel's* (Longford) 1-6;
       St. Brendan's (Killarney) 2-2.
1964—Tullamore—March 22: St. Jarlath's (Tuam) 1-10; De La
       Salle (Waterford) 1-7.
       Clones—March 22: St. Mel's (Longford) 3-10; Newry
       C.B.S. 3-2.
       Final—Athlone—April 19: St. Jarlath's (Tuam) 0-11; St.
       Mel's (Longford) 1-8.
       (Replay)—Tullamore—May 3: *St. Jarlath's* (Tuam) 1-10;
       St. Mel's (Longford) 0-4.
1965—Ballybay—March 28: St. Columb's (Derry) 3-9; St.
       Jarlath's (Tuam) 1-11.
       Carlow—March 28: Belcamp O.M.I. (Dublin) 2-9; De La
       Salle (Waterford) 2-8.
       Final—Cavan—April 11: St. Columb's (Derry) 0-9;
       Belcamp O.M.I. (Dublin) 0-9.
       (Replay)—Ballybay—May 9: *St. Columb's* (Derry) 0-11;
       Belcamp O.M.I. (Dublin) 1-7.
1966—Nenagh—April 3: St. Finian's (Mullingar) 1-6; St. Bren-
       dan's (Killarney 0-9.
       (Replay)—Nenagh—April 17: St. Finian's (Mullingar)
       3-13; St. Brendan's (Killarney) 3-9.
       Cavan—April 3: St. Jarlath's (Tuam) 3-7; St. Columb's
       (Derry) 3-5.
       Final—Athlone—May 1: *St. Jarlath's* (Tuam) 1-10; St.

Finian's (Mullingar) 1-9.

1967—Drogheda—April 9: St. Colman's (Newry) 2-7; Belcamp O.M.I. (Dublin) 0-4).

Nenagh—April 9: St. Jarlath's (Tuam) 2-13; Col. Chriost Rí (Cork) 3-5.

Final—Mullingar—April 23: *St. Colman's* (Newry) 1-8; St. Jarlath's (Tuam) 1-7.

1968—Portlaoise—April 7: Col. Chriost Rí (Cork) 1-7; St. Nathy's (Ballaghaderreen) 1-7.

(Replay)—Limerick—April 28: Col. Chriost Rí (Cork) 2-11; St. Nathy's (Ballaghaderreen) 0-15.

Croke Park—April 7: Belcamp O.M.I. (Dublin) 2-7; St. Colman's (Newry) 0-11.

Final—Croke Park—May 5: *Col. Chriost Rí* (Cork) 3-11; Belcamp O.M.I. (Dublin) 1-10.

1969—Longford—March 30: St. Mary's (Galway) 1-6; St. Colman's (Newry) 0-4.

Thurles—April 20: St. Brendan's (Killarney) 2-6; St. Mel's (Longford) 1-9.

(Replay)—Thurles—April 27: St. Brendan's (Killarney) 2-8; St. Mel's (Longford) 1-10.

Final—Thurles—May 4: *St. Brendan's* (Killarney) 1-13; St. Mary's (Galway) 3-3.

1970—Cavan—May 22: St. Malachy's (Belfast) 4-9; St. Colman's (Claremorris) 2-6.

Thurles—May 22: Col. Chriost Rí (Cork) 1-5; Franciscan College (Gormanstown) 0-6.

Final—Croke Park—April 19: *Col. Chriost Rí* (Cork) 4-5; St. Malachy's (Belfast) 1-13.

1971—Dundalk—April 4: St. Mary's C.B.S. (Belfast) 2-6; St. Mel's (Longford) 0-4.

Athlone—April 4: Col. Iosagain (Ballyvourney) 1-10; Summerhill (Sligo) 2-6.

Final—Croke Park—April 25: *St. Mary's C.B.S.* (Belfast) 1-13; Col. Iosagain (Ballyvourney) 1-7.

1972—Longford—March 26: St. Patrick's (Cavan) 4-6; St. Jarlath's (Tuam) 0-7.

Nenagh—March 26: St. Brendan's (Killarney) 1-12; Franciscan College (Gormanstown) 0-12.

Final—Croke Park—April 16: *St. Patrick's* (Cavan 2-11; St. Brendan's (Killarney) 1-5.

1973—Limerick—April 1: St. Jarlath's (Tuam) 2-13; St. Brendan's (Killarney) 2-10.

Ballybay—April 1: Franciscan College (Gormanstown) 1-8; St. Michael's (Enniskillen) 1-6.

Final—Athlone—April 15: *Franciscan College* (Gormanstown) 1-7; St. Jarlath's (Tuam) 0-8.

1974—Limerick—March 24: St. Jarlath's (Tuam) 1-11; St. Brendan's (Killarney) 0-8.

Cavan—March 31: Franciscan College (Gormanstown) 1-9; Omagh C.B.S. 1-7.

Final—Athlone—April 7: *St. Jarlath's* (Tuam) 4-11; Franciscan College (Gormanstown) 2-11.

1975—Clones—March 23: St. Colman's (Newry) 1-9; Summerhill (Sligo) 2-4.

Thurles—April 13: Carmelite College (Moate) 0-12; Col. Iognaid Ris (Cork) 1-9.

(Reply)—Thurles—April 27: Carmelite College (Moate) 1-16; Col. Iognaid Ris (Cork) 1-13.

Final—Croke Park—May 4: *St. Colman's* (Newry 1-7; Carmelite College (Moate) 2-3.

1976—Mullingar—April 4: St. Jarlath's (Tuam) 1-13; St. Colman's (Newry) 1-2.

Nenagh—April 4: Carmelite College (Moate 1-14; Tralee C.B.S. 1-3.

Final—Roscommon—May 2: *Carmelite College* (Moate) 1-10; St. Jarlath's (Tuam) 0-11.

1977—Clones—April 3: Carmelite College (Moate) 1-9; St. Patrick's (Maghera) 1-8.

Limerick—April 3: St. Colman's (Claremorris 1-11; St. Brendan's (Killarney) 3-4.

Final—Roscommon—April 24: *St. Colman's* (Claremorris) 1-11; Carmelite College (Moate) 1-10.

1978—Limerick—April 16: St. Jarlath's (Tuam) 5-10; Col. Chriost Rí (Cork) 1-6.

Croke Park—April 16: St. Colman's (Newry) 0-13; Carmelite College (Moate) 3-2.

Final—Croke Park—April 30: *St. Jarlath's* (Tuam) 2-11; St. Colman's (Newry) 2-4.

1979—Cavan—April 8: St. Jarlath's (Tuam) 2-4; St. Colman's (Newry) 1-2.

Cashel—April 8: Ard Scoil Ris (Dublin) 2-8; Col. Chriost Rí (Cork) 1-7.

Final—Tullamore—May 6: Ard Scoil Ris (Dublin) 0-10; St. Jarlath's (Tuam) 0-10.

(Replay)—Tullamore—May 13: *Ard Scoil Ris* (Dublin)

2-9; St. Jarlath's (Tuam) 1-10.

1980—Sligo—March 30: St. Patrick's (Maghera) 2.7; Tuam C.B.S. 1-9.

Carlow—March 30: Carmelite College (Moate) 0-10; Col. Chriost Rí (Cork) 0-6.

Final—Croke Park—April 20: *Carmelite College* (Moate) 0-12; St. Patrick's (Maghera) 1-8.

1981—Cloughjordan—April 5: St. Colman's (Claremorris) 3-5; Col. Iosagain (Ballyvourney) 0-10.

Cavan—April 5: Carmelite College (Moate) 1-5; St. Colman's (Newry) 0-6.

Final—Roscommon—May 3: *Carmelite College* (Moate) 2-2; St. Colman's (Claremorris) 1-4.

1982—Athlone—April 25: St. Jarlath's (Tuam) 2-7; St. Mel's (Longford) 1-8.

Croke Park: St. Fachna's (Skibbereen) 0-15; St. Patrick's (Maghera) 1-9.

Final—Thurles—May 9: St. Jarlath's (Tuam) 1-7; St. Fachtna's (Skibbereen) 1-7.

(Reply)—Limerick—May 16: *St. Jarlath's* (Tuam) 1-8; St. Fachtna's (Skibbereen) 0-7.

1983—Cavan—April 17: St. Jarlath's (Tuam) 1-9; St. Patrick's (Maghera) 0-9.

Cloughjordan—April 17: Col. Chriost Rí (Cork) 2-7; St. Mary's (Mullingar) 1-6.

Final—Croke Park—May 1: *Col. Chriost Rí* (Cork) 3-6; St. Jarlath's (Tuam) 2-5.

1984—Limerick—April 15: St. Jarlath's (Tuam) 1-14; Col. Chriost Rí (Cork) 1-6.

Cavan—April 15: St. Patrick's (Maghera) 1-5; Portarlington C.B.S. 0-8.

(Replay)—Cavan—April 21: St. Patrick's (Maghera) 0-15; Portarlington C.B.S. 1-5.

Final—Croke Park—*St. Jarlath's* (Tuam) 0-10; St. Patrick's (Maghera) 2-3.

1985—Mullingar—April 21: Summerhill (Sligo) 1-10; Dundalk C.B.S. 0-8.

Croke Park—April 21: Col. Chriost Rí 2-6; St. Patrick's (Maghera) 0-?.

Final—Portlaoise—May 12: *Col. Chriost Rí* 1-9; Summerhill 0-9.

1986—Nenagh—April 13: St. David's (Artane) 0-9; St. Brendan's (Killarney) 1-4.

Mullingar—April 13: St. Colman's (Newry) 1-6; St. Mary's (Galway) 1-5.

Final—Portlaoise—April 27: *St. Colman's* (Newry) 3-10; St. David's 0-7.

1987—Ennis—April 12: St. Mary's (Galway) 0-7; Col. Chriost Rí (Cork) 0-6.

Kells—April 19: St. Mel's (Longford) 0-7; Abbey C.B.S. (Newry) 1-2.

Final—Roscommon—May 3: *St. Mel's* (Longford) 0-8; St. Mary's (Galway) 1-4.

1988—Portlaoise—April 17: St. Colman's (Newry) 2-14; North Mon. (Cork) 1-5.

April 17: St. Mel's (Longford) 1-9; St. Mary's Galway) 0-8.

Final—Clones—May 1: *St. Colman's* (Newry) 1-11; St. Mel's (Longford) 1-7.

1989—Portlaoise, April 23: Col. Chríost Rí (Cork) 4-9, St. Mel's (Longford) 2-6. Cavan, April 23: St. Patrick's (Maghera) 1-9, Tuam CBS 0-7.

Final – Portlaoise, May 7: St. Patrick's 1-5, Col. Chríost Rí 0-8 (draw); Longford, May 14: St. Patrick's 2-15, Col. Chríost Rí 1-6 (replay).

1990—Castleblayney, April 22: St. Patrick's (Maghera) 5-12, St. Mel's (Longford) 1-5; Emly, April 22: St. Jarlath's (Tuam) 1-13, St. Fachtna's (Skiberreen) 1-18.

Final – Cavan, May 6: St. Patrick's (Maghera) 1-4, St. Jarlath's 0-7 (draw); Cavan, May 13: St. Patrick's 1-11, St. Jarlath's 0-13 (replay).

1991—Athlone, April 20: St. Patrick's (Navan) 1-14, St. Mary's (Galway) 2-9. Tullamore, April 21: St. Fachtna's (Skiberreen) 1-11, St. Patrick's (Dungannon) 1-7.

Final – Croke Park, April 28: St. Fachtna's 2-9, St. Patrick's 0-7.

1992—Clonmel, April 5: St. Brendan's (Killarney) 3-10, St. Peter's (Wexford) 3-8. Longford, April 12: St. Jarlath's (Tuam) 0-8, St. Michael's (Enniskillen) 0-5.

Final – Thurles, April 26: St. Brendan's 0-9, St. Jarlath's 0-5.

1993—Ballinsaloe, April 4: St. Jarlath's (Tuam) 4-12, St. Flannan's (Ennis) 1-3. Cavan, April 4: St. Colman's (Newry) 1-14, St. Patrick's (Navan) 0-7.

Final – Longford, April 25: St. Colman's 2-10, St. Jarlath's 1-9.

LEINSTER SENIOR HURLING

ROLL OF HONOUR

St. Kieran's, Kilkenny (41); St. Peter's, Wexford (8); Kilkenny CBS (5): Mount St Joseph's, Roscrea (4): Birr Community School, formerly Presentation College, Birr to 1980 (4); P.B.S., Ballyfin (4); Colaiste Caoimghin, Dublin (2); O'Connell School, Dublin (2); St. Joseph's, Marino, Dublin (1); Blackrock College, Dublin (1); Castleknock College, Dublin (1); Knockbeg College, Carlow (1).

1918—Castleknock College, Dublin
1919—No Competition
1920-'21— Mount St. Joseph's, Roscrea
1922—St. Kieran's, Kilkenny
1923— Mount St. Joseph's, Roscrea
1924— Mount St. Joseph's, Roscrea
1925—St. Kieran's, Kilkenny
1926—St. Kieran's, Kilkenny
1927—St. Kieran's, Kilkenny
1928—St. Kieran's, Kilkenny
1929—St. Kieran's, Kilkenny
1930—Col. Caoimhghin, Dublin
1931—St. Kieran's, Kilkenny
1932—St. Kieran's, Kilkenny
1933—St. Kieran's, Kilkenny
1934—Col. Caoimhghin, Dublin
1935—Blackrock College, Dublin
1936—Kilkenny C.B.S.
1937—St. Kieran's, Kilkenny
1938—St. Kieran's, Kilkenny
1939—St. Kieran's, Kilkenny
1940—St. Kieran's, Kilkenny
1941—St. Kieran's, Kilkenny
1942—P.B.S. Ballyfin
1943—St. Kieran's, Kilkenny
1944—St. Kieran's, Kilkenny
1945—St.Joseph's, Marino, Dublin
1946—O'Connell's School, Dublin
1947— Mount St. Joseph's, Roscrea
1948—St. Kieran's, Kilkenny
1949—St. Kieran's, Kilkenny
1950—St. Kieran's, Kilkenny
1951—St. Kieran's, Kilkenny
1952—P.B.S. Ballyfin

1953—St. Kieran's, Kilkenny
1954—O'Connell Schools, Dublin
1955—Knockbeg College, Carlow
1956—P.B.S. Ballyfin
1957—St. Kieran's, Kilkenny
1958—St. Kieran's, Kilkenny
1959—St. Kieran's, Kilkenny
1960—St. Peter's, Wexford
1961—St. Kieran's, Kilkenny
1962—St. Peter's, Wexford
1963—P.B.S. Ballyfin
1964—St. Peter's, Wexford
1965—St. Kieran's, Kilkenny
1966—St. Kieran's, Kilkenny
1967—St. Peter's, Wexford
1968—St. Peter's, Wexford
1969—St. Kieran's, Kilkenny
1970—Kilkenny C.B.S.
1971—St. Kieran's, Kilkenny
1972—St. Kieran's, Kilkenny
1973—St. Peter's, Wexford
1974—St. Kieran's, Kilkenny
1975—St. Kieran's, Kilkenny
1976—Kilkenny C.B.S.
1977—St. Kieran's, Kilkenny
1978—St. Peter's, Wexford
1979—Presentation, Birr
1980—Birr Community School
1981—Kilkenny C.B.S.
1982—St. Peter's, Wexford
1983—Kilkenny C.B.S.
1984—St. Kieran's, Kilkenny
1985—Birr Community School
1986—Birr Community School

1987—St. Kieran's, Kilkenny
1988—St. Kieran's, Kilkenny
1989—St. Kieran's, Kilkenny
1990—St. Kieran's, Kilkenny

1991—St. Kieran's, Kilkenny
1992—St. Kieran's, Kilkenny
1993—St. Kieran's, Kilkenny

LEINSTER SENIOR FOOTBALL

ROLL OF HONOUR

St. Mel's, Longford (28), St. Finian's, Mullingar (9); Carmelite College, Moate (6); Franciscan College, Gormanstown (6); Knockbeg College, Carlow (4); Belcamp College, Dublin (3); Coláiste Caoimhghin, Dublin (3); St. Conleth's, Newbridge (2); St. Joseph's, Fairview, Dublin (2); St. Patrick's, Navan (2); Ard Scoil Ris, Dublin (1); Franciscan College, Multyfarnham (1); St. Joseph's, Roscrea (1); St. Kieran's College, Kilkenny (1); St. Mary's CBS, Mullingar (1); St. Joseph's, Portarlington (1); Dundalk CBS (1); St. David's, Artane (1); P.B.S., Ballyfin (1); St. Peter's, Wexford (1).

1920—Knockbeg College, Carlow
1921—St. Conleth's, Newbridge
1922—St. Kieran's, Kilkenny
1923—St. Conleth's, Newbridge.
1924—St. Joseph's, Roscrea
1925—St. Finian's, Mullingar
1926—St. Finian's, Mullingar
1927—St. Finian's, Mullingar
1928—St. Mel's, Longford
1929—Col. Caoimhghin, Dublin
1930—Col. Caoimhghin, Dublin
1931—Col. Caoimhghin, Dublin
1932—Knockbeg College, Carlow
1933—St. Mel's, Longford
1934—St. Mel's, Longford
1935—St. Mel's, Longford
1936—St. Mel's, Longford
1937—St. Mel's, Longford
1938—St. Mel's, Longford
1939—St. Finian's, Mullingar
1940—St. Mel's, Longford
1941—St. Mel's, Longford
1942—St. Mel's, Longford
1943—St. Mel's, Longford
1944—St. Finian's, Mullingar

1945—St. Mel's, Longford
1946—St. Mel's, Longford
1947—St. Mel's, Longford
1948—St. Mel's, Longford
1949—St. Finian's, Mullingar
1950—St. Finian's, Mullingar
1951—St. Mel's, Longford
1952—Franciscan College,
        Multyfarnham
1953—St. Finian's, Mullingar
1954—Knockbeg College, Carlow
1955—Knockbeg College, Carlow
1956—St. Joseph's, Fariview
1957—P.B.S. Ballyfin
1958—Franciscan College,
        Gormanstown
1959—St. Joseph's, Fairview
1960—St. Finian's, Mullingar
1961—St. Mel's, Longford
1962—St. Mel's, Longford
1962—St. Mel's, Longford
1963—St. Mel's, Longford
1964—St. Mel's, Longford
1965—Belcamp O.M.I., Dublin
1966—Franciscan College,
        Gormanstown

1967—Belcamp O.M.I., Dublin
1968—Belcamp O.M.I., Dublin
1969—St. Mel's, Longford
1970—Franciscan College,
       Gormanstown
1971—St. Mel's, Longford
1972—Franciscan College,
       Gormanstown
1973—Franciscan College,
       Gormanstown
1974—Franciscan College,
       Gormanstown
1975—Carmelite College, Moate
1976—Carmelite College, Moate
1977—Carmelite College, Moate
1978—Carmelite College, Moate

1979—Ard Scoil Ris, Dublin
1980—Carmelite College, Moate
1981—Carmelite College, Moate
1982—St. Mel's, Longford
1983—St. Mary's, Mullingar
1984—Portarlington C.B.S.
1985—Dundalk C.B.S.
1986—St. David's, Artaine
1987—St. Mel's, Longford
1988—St. Mel's, Longford
1989—St. Mel's, Longford
1990—St. Mel's, Longford
1991—St. Patrick's, Navan
1992—St. Peter's, Wexford
1993—St. Patrick's, Navan

CONNACHT SENIOR HURLING

ROLL OF HONOUR

St. Mary's, Galway (24); Our Lady's, Gort (10); St. Joseph's, Garbally Park, Ballinsloe (7); Presentation, Athenry (4); St. Molaise's, Portumna (2); Roscommon CBS (2); St. Raphael's, Loughrea (2); De La Salle, Loughrea (1); St. Joseph's P.B.S., Galway (1).

1938—Roscommon C.B.S.
1939—Roscommon C.B.S.
1940—St. Mary's, Galway
1941—St. Mary's, Galway
1941—St. Mary's, Galway
1943-'45—None
1946—St. Mary's, Galway
1947—St. Mary's, Galway
1948—De La Salle, Loughrea
1949—St. Mary's, Galway
1950—St. Mary's, Galway
1951—St. Mary's, Galway
1952—St. Mary's, Galway
1953—St. Mary's, Galway
1954—St. Mary's, Galway
1955—St. Mary's, Galway
1956—St. Mary's, Galway
1957—St. Mary's, Galway
1958—St. Joseph's, Galway

1959—St. Joseph's, Garbally
1960—St. Mary's, Galway
1961—St. Molaises', Portumna
1962—St. Molaises', Portumna
1963—St. Mary's, Galway
1964—St. Mary's, Galway
1965—St. Mary's, Galway
1966—St. Mary's, Galway
1967—St. Mary's, Galway
1968—St. Joseph's, Garbally
1969—Our Lady's, Gort
1970—Presentation, Athenry
1971—Presentation, Athenry
1972—Our Lady's, Gort
1973—Our Lady's, Gort
1974—Our Lady's, Gort
1975—Our Lady's, Gort
1976—Presentation, Athenry
1977—Presentation, Athenry

1978—Our Lady's, Gort
1979—St. Mary's, Galway
1980—St. Joseph's, Garbally
1981—Our Lady's, Gort
1982—Our Lady's, Gort
1983—St. Joseph's, Garbally
1984—Our Lady's, Gort
1985—St. Joseph's, Garbally

1986—St. Joseph's, Garbally
1987—St. Joseph's, Garbally
1988—St. Mary's, Galway
1989—St. Mary's, Galway
1990—St. Mary's, Galway
1991—St. Raphael's, Loughrea
1992—St. Raphael's, Loughrea
1993—Our Lady's, Gort

CONNACHT SENIOR FOOTBALL

ROLL OF HONOUR

St. Jarlath's, Tuam (38), Summerhill College, Sligo (7); St. Mary's, Galway (6); Roscommon CBS (4); St. Nathy's, Ballaghaderreen (4); St. Colman's, Claremorris (3); Tuam CBS (2); St. Gerard's, Castlebar (1).

1929—St. Gerard's, Castlebar
1930—Summerhill, Sligo
1931—Summerhill, Sligo
1932—St. Jarlath's, Tuam
1933—St. Jarlath's, Tuam
1934—St. Jarlath's, Tuam
1935—St. Jarlath's, Tuam
1936—St. Jarlath's, Tuam
1937—St. Jarlath's, Tuam
1938—St. Jarlath's, Tuam
1939—St. Jarlath's, Tuam
1940—Roscommon C.B.S.
1941—Roscommon C.B.S
1942—Roscommon C.B.S.
1943—St. Jarlath's, Tuam
1944—St. Jarlath's, Tuam
1945—St. Jarlath's, Tuam
1946—St. Jarlath's, Tuam
1947—St. Jarlath's, Tuam
1948—Roscommon C.B.S.
1949—St. Nathy's, Ballaghaderreen
1950—St. Jarlath's Tuam
1951—St. Jarlath's, Tuam
1952—St. Mary's, Galway
1953—St. Jarlath's, Tuam
1954—Summerhill, Sligo
1955—Summerhill, Sligo
1956—St. Jarlath's, Tuam

1957—St. Nathy's, Ballaghaderreen
1958—St. Jarlath's, Tuam
1959—St. Nathy's, Ballaghaderreen
1960—St. Jarlath's, Tuam
1961—St. Jarlath's, Tuam
1962—St. Jarlath's, Tuam
1963—St. Jarlath's, Tuam
1964—St. Jarlath's, Tuam
1965—St. Jarlath's, Tuam
1966—St. Jarlath's, Tuam
1967—St. Jarlath's, Tuam
1968—St. Nathy's, Ballaghaderreen
1969—St. Mary's, Galway
1970—St. Colman's, Claremorris
1971—Summerhill, Sligo
1972—St. Jarlath's, Tuam
1973—St. Jarlath's, Tuam
1974—St. Jarlath's, Tuam
1975—Summerhill, Sligo
1976—St. Jarlath's, Tuam
1977—St. Colman's, Claremorris
1978—St. Jarlath's, Tuam
1979—St. Jarlath's, Tuam
1980—Tuam C.B.S.
1981—St. Colman's, Claremorris
1982—St. Jarlath's, Tuam
1983—St. Jarlath's, Tuam
1984—St. Jarlath's, Tuam

1985—Summerhill, Sligo
1986—St. Mary's, Galway
1987—St. Mary's, Galway
1988—St. Mary's, Galway
1989—Tuam CBS

1990—St. Jarlath's, Tuam
1991—St Mary's, Galway
1992—St. Jarlath's, Tuam
1993—St. Jarlath's, Tuam

MUNSTER SENIOR HURLING

Dr. Harty Cup

ROLL OF HONOUR 1918-1988

North Monastery, Cork (19); St. Flannan's, Ennis (16); Limerick CBS (9); St. Finbarr's, Farrenferris (7); Thurles CBS (6); Rockwell College (5); St. Colman's, Fermoy (4); Coláiste Chríost Rí, Cork (2); Coláiste Iognáid Rís, Cork (1); Ennis CBS (1); Mount Sion, Waterford (1); Midleton CBS (1); St. Munchin's, Limerick (1); Tipperary CBS (1); Templemore CBS (1); St. Michael's CBS, Limerick (1).

1918—Rockwell College
1919—North Monastery, Cork
1920—Limerick C.B.S.
1921—None
1922—St. Munchin's, Limerick
1923—Rockwell College
1924—Rockwell College
1925—Limerick C.B.S.
1926—Limerick C.B.S.
1927—Limerick C.B.S.
1928—No Competition
1929—North Monastery, Cork
1930—Rockwell College
1931—Rockwell College
1932—Limerick C.B.S.
1933—Thurles C.B.S.
1934—North Monastery, Cork
1935—North Monastery, Cork
1936—North Monastery, Cork
1937—North Monastery, Cork
1938—Thurles C.B.S.
1939—Thurles C.B.S.
1940—North Monastery, Cork
1941—North Monastery, Cork
1942—North Monastery, Cork
1943—North Monastery, Cork

1944—St. Flannan's, Ennis
1945—St. Flannan's, Ennis
1946—St. Flannan's, Ennis
1947—St. Flannan's, Ennis
1948—St. Colman's, Fermoy
1949—St. Colman's, Fermoy
1950—Thurles C.B.S.
1951—Thurles C.B.S.
1952—St. Flannan's, Ennis
1953—Mount Sion, Waterford
1954—St. Flannan's, Ennis
1955—North Monastery, Cork
1956—Thurles C.B.S.
1957—St. Flannan's, Ennis
1958—St. Flannan's, Ennis
1959—Tipperary C.B.S.
1960—North Monastery, Cork
1961—North Monastery, Cork
1962—Ennis C.B.S.
1963—St. Finbarr's, Farranferris
1964—Limerick C.B.S.
1965—Limerick C.B.S.
1966—Limerick C.B.S.
1967—Limerick C.B.S.
1968—Col. Chriost Rí, Cork
1969—St. Finbarr's, Farranferris

1970—North Monastery
1971—St. Finbarr's, Farranferris
1972—St. Finbarr's, Farranferris
1973—St. Finbarr's, Farranferris
1974—St. Finbarr's, Farranferris
1975—Col. Iognaid Ris, Cork
1976—St. Flannan's, Ennis
1977—St. Coleman's, Fermoy
1978—Templemore C.B.S.
1979—St. Flannan's, Ennis
1980—North Monastery, Cork
1981—North Monastery, Cork

1982—St. Flannan's, Ennis
1983—St. Flannan's, Ennis
1984—St. Finbarr's, Farranferris
1985—North Mon., Cork
1986—North Mon., Cork
1987—St. Flannan's, Ennis
1988—Midleton C.B.S.
1989—St. Flannan's, Ennis
1990—St. Flannan's, Ennis
1991—St. Flannan's, Ennis
1992—St. Colman's, Fermoy
1993—St. Michael's CBS, Limerick

MUNSTER SENIOR FOOTBALL

Corn Uí Mhuiri

ROLL OF HONOUR

St. Brendan's, Killarney (15); Tralee C.B.S. (13); Colaiste Chriost Rí, Cork (11); Colaiste Iosagain, Ballyvourney (7); De La Salle, Waterford (6); North Monastery, Cork (3); St. Fachtna's, Skibbereen (3); Limerick CBS (2); St. Flannan's, Ennis (2); Colaiste Iognaid Ris, Cork (1); Colaiste na Mumhan, Mallow (1); High School, Clonmel (1); Rochestown College, Cork (1).

1928—High School, Clonmel
1929—St. Brendan's, Killarney
1930—St. Brendan's, Killarney
1931—Tralee C.B.S.
1932—Tralee C.B.S.
1933—Tralee C.B.S.
1934—Tralee C.B.S.
1935—North Monastery, Cork
1936—North Monastery, Cork
1937—St. Brendan's, Killarney
1938—St. Brendan's, Killarney
1939—Col. na Mumhan, Mallow
1940—Tralee C.B.S.
1941—Tralee C.B.S.
1942—Tralee C.B.S.
1943—St. Brendan's, Killarney
1944—Tralee C.B.S.
1945—Tralee C.B.S.
1946—St. Brendan's, Killarney
1947—St. Brendan's, Killarney

1948—Tralee C.B.S.
1949—Col. Iosagain, Ballyvourney
1950—Rochestown College, Cork
1951—Col. Iosagain, Ballyvourney
1952—Col. Iosagain, Ballyvourney
1953—Tralee C.B.S.
1954—Col. Iosagain, Ballyvourney
1955—Tralee C.B.S.
1956—Limerick C.B.S.
1957—Col. Iosagain, Ballyvourney
1958—De La Salle, Waterford
1959—St. Flannan's, Ennis
1960—Limerick C.B.S.
1961—De La Salle, Waterford
1962—De La Salle, Waterford
1963—De La Salle, Waterford
1964—De La Salle, Waterford
1965—De La Salle, Waterford
1966—St. Brendan's, Killarney
1967—Col. Chriost Rí, Cork

1968—Col. Chriost Rí, Cork
1969—St. Brendan's, Killarney
1970—Col. Chriost Rí, Cork
1971—Col. Iosagain, Ballyvourney
1972—St. Brendan's, Killarney
1973—St. Brendan's, Killarney
1974—St. Brendan's, Killarney
1975—Col. Iogaid Ris, Cork
1976—Tralee C.B.S.
1977—St. Brendan's, Killarney
1978—Col. Chriost Rí, Cork
1979—Col. Chriost Rí, Cork
1980—Col. Chriost Rí, Cork

1981—Col. Iosagain, Ballyvourney
1982—St. Fachtna's, Skibbereen
1983—Col. Chriost Rí, Cork
1984—Col. Chriost Rí, Cork
1985—Col. Chriost Rí, Cork
1986—St. Brendan's, Killarney
1987—Col. Chriost Rí, Cork
1988—North Mon., Cork.
1989—Col. Chriost Rí, Cork
1990—St. Fachtna's, Skibbereen
1991—St. Fachtna's, Skibbereen
1992—St. Brendan's, Killarney
1993—St. Flannan's, Ennis

ULSTER SENIOR FOOTBALL

ROLL OF HONOUR

St. Colman's Newry (18); St. Patrick's, Armagh (12); St. Patrick's, Cavan (10); St. McCartan's, Monaghan (8); St. Patrick's, Maghera (8); Abbey CBS, Newry (4); St. Columb's, Derry (2); St. Malachy's, Belfast (2); St. Mary's, Dundalk (2); St. Michael's, Enniskillen (2); Omagh CBS (1); St. Mary's, Belfast (1); St. Patrick's, Dungannon (1).

Note: St. Patrick's, Armagh and St. McCartan's, Monaghan shared the 1934 title.

1919—St. Patrick's, Armagh
1920-'23—None
1924—St. Patrick's, Armagh
1925—Unfinished
1926—St. Patrick's, Armagh
1927—St. Patrick's, Armagh
1928—St. Patrick's, Armagh
1929—St. Malachy's, Belfast
1930—St. Macarten's, Monaghan
1931—St. Patrick's, Armagh
1932—St. Macarten's, Monaghan
1933—St. Macarten's, Monaghan
1934—St. Macarten's, Monaghan
　　　St. Patrick's, Armagh
　　　(joint holders)
1935—St. Patrick's, Cavan
1936—St. Patrick's, Cavan
1937—St. Patrick's, Cavan
1938—St. Mary's, Dundalk

1939—St. Patrick's, Cavan
1940—St. Macarten's, Monaghan
1941—St. Mary's, Dundalk
1942—St. Macarten's, Monaghan
1943—St. Patrick's, Cavan
1944—St. Patrick's, Armagh
1945—St. Patrick's, Armagh
1946—St. Patrick's, Armagh
1947—St. Patrick's, Armagh
1948—St. Patrick's, Cavan
1949—St. Colman's, Newry
1950—St. Colman's, Newry
1951—St. Patrick's, Cavan
1952—St. Macarten's, Monaghan
1953—St. Patrick's, Armagh
1954—Newry C.B.S.
1955—St. Patrick's, Cavan
1956—St. Macarten's, Monaghan
1957—St. Colman's, Newry

470

1958—St. Colman's, Newry
1959—Newry C.B.S.
1960—St. Coleman's, Newry
1961—St. Patrick's, Cavan
1962—St. Colman's, Newry
1963—St. Colman's, Newry
1964—Newry C.B.S.
1965—St. Columb's, Derry
1966—St. Columb's, Derry
1967—St. Colman's, Newry
1968—St. Colman's, Newry
1969—St. Colman's, Newry
1970—St. Malachy's, Belfast
1971—St. Mary's C.B.S., Belfast
1972—St. Patrick's, Cavan
1973—St. Michael's, Enniskillen
1974—Omagh C.B.S.
1975—St. Colman's, Newry

1976—St. Colman's, Newry
1977—St. Patrick's, Maghera
1978—St. Colman's, Newry
1979—St. Colman's, Newry
1980—St. Patrick's, Maghera
1981—St. Colman's, Newry
1982—St. Patrick's, Maghera
1983—St. Patrick's, Maghera
1984—St. Patrick's, Maghera
1985—St. Patrick's, Maghera
1986—St. Colman's, Newry
1987—Abbey C.B.S., Newry
1988—St. Colman's, Newry
1989—St. Patrick's, Maghera
1990—St. Patrick's, Maghera
1991—St. Patrick's, Dungannon
1992—St. Michael's, Enniskillen
1993—St. Colman's, Newry

Ollie Walsh, the former brilliant Kilkenny goalie, who as team manager helped guide the Noresiders to successive All-Ireland victories in 1992-'93.

471

SIGERSON CUP

Ulster Teams Make a Big Impact

By NOEL FALLON

THE Sigerson Cup, the trophy for the Higher Education gaelic football championship, was presented by Strabane man, Dr George Sigerson, a Professor in UCD in 1911 and has been played for ever since.

Initially, only UCD, UCC, UCG and Queens participated. UCD, who enjoyed a golden era in the 1970s when they won the competition six times in seven years along with two All-Ireland club titles, hold the record with 32 Cup victories.

UCG, who produced a great team in the early 1980s, are next in line with 22 triumphs.

In recent times Ulster teams have come to enjoy outstanding success in the Sigerson Cup. Up to 1986 the trophy had only gone north three times but Queens, Jordanstown and St Mary's have won six of the last eight Sigersons between them.

Queens captured the 1993 title when they beat St Mary's by eleven points in March with UUJ the hosts.

The Hurling and Football Annual

The *Hurling and Football Annual*, edited by Raymond Smith, incorporates special coverage of the Colleges and Universities scene.

It is normally available before Christmas and retails at £5.95.

ROLL OF HONOUR

UCD 32; UCG 22; UCC 17; QUB 6; UUJ Jordanstown 3; St Mary's 2.

1911—UCC	1940—UCG	1970—UCC
1912—UCG	1941—UCG	1971—QUB
1913—UCC	1942—UCG	1972—UCC
1914—UCC	1943—UCC	1973—UCD
1915—UCC	1944—UCD	1974—UCD
1916—UCD	1945—UCD	1975—UCD
1917—UCD	1946—UCD	1976—St Patrick's
1918—UCD	1947—UCD	Maynooth
1919—UCC	1948—UCG	1977—UCD
1920—UCD	1949—UCD	1978—UCD
1921—UCG	1950—UCG	1979—UCD
1922—UCC	1951—UCC	1980—UCG
1923—UCD	1952—UCC	1981—UCG
1924—UCC	1953—UCD	1982—QUB
1925—UCC	1954—UCG	1983—UCG
1926—UCD	1955—UCD	1984—UCG
1927—UCC	1956—UCD	1985—UCD
1928—UCD	1957—UCD	1986—UUJ
1929—UCD	1958—QUB	1987—UUJ
1930—UCD	1959—UCD	1988—St Mary's
1931—UCD	1960—UCG	1990—QUB
1932—UCD	1961—UCD	1991—UUJ
1933—UCG	1962—UCG	1992—UCG
1934—UCG	1963—UCG	1993—QUB
1935—UCD	1964—QUB	
1936—UCG	1965—UCC	
1937—UCG	1966—UCC	
1938—UCG	1967—No Competition*	
1939—UCG	1968—UCD	
	1969—UCC	

After the 1966 Sigerson Cup the timing of the event was changed from Autumn to Spring. Hence no Sigerson was held in 1967 calendar year.

VOCATIONAL SCHOOLS

ALL-IRELAND FOOTBALL FINALS (1961-1993)

1961—Cork City 7-5, Offaly 3-8
1962—Dublin City 3-6, Sligo 1-1
1963—Dublin City 4-8, Sligo 0-5
1964—Galway 0-7, Offaly 0-4
1965—Galway 1-9, Kerry 1-4
1966—Fermanagh 2-7, Kerry 2-2
1967—Tyrone 2-6, Kerry 1-7
1968—Antrim 6-7, Galway 1-4
1969—Tyrone 0-8, Dublin 1-4
1970—Tyrone 3-11, Clare 2-7
1971—Mayo 2-4, Antrim 0-9
1972—Carlow 3-9, Leitrim 1-5
1973—Kerry 3-8, Mayo 2-6
1974—Wicklow 2-7, Tyrone 1-7
1975—Mayo 1-15, Tyrone 0-11
1976—Galway 4-9, Longford 2-9
1977—Kerry 1-9, Kildare 0-11
1978—Kerry 0-12, Mayo 1-7
1979—Derry 2-3, Mayo 0-9
    (Replay) Derry 1-5, Mayo 0-6

1980—Derry 2-8, Wicklow 0-6
1981—Derry 1-11, Cork 2-6
1982—Mayo 1-9, Kerry 2-4
1983—Wicklow 0-8, Clare 0-4
1984—Donegal 3-9, Longford 2-3
1985—Donegal 3-8, Cork 1-4
1986—Kerry 2-7, Offaly 1-4
1987—Kerry 2-13, Donegal 2-9
1988—Tyrone 1-9, Mayo 1-4
1989—Tyrone 0-13, Mayo 1-6
1990—Kerry 0-11, Cavan 0-7
1991—Cork 2-13, Galway 1-6
1992—Kerry 4-15, Offaly 1-5
1993—Kerry 3-13, Wicklow 3-7

ROLL OF HONOUR

Kerry 8, Tyrone 5, Galway 3, Mayo 3, Derry 3, Dublin City 2, Wicklow 2, Donegal 2, Fermanagh 1, Antrim 1, Carlow 1, Cork City 1, Cork 1.

ALL-IRELAND HURLING FINALS (1961-1993)

1961—Limerick City 10-6, Kilkenny 7-9
1962—North Tipperary 6-11, Kilkenny 4-3
1963—Kilkenny 12-3, Cork City 3-4
1964—North Tipperary 9-3, Down 1-3
1965—North Tipperary 8-9, Kilkenny 2-4
1966—North Tipperary 5-11, Wexford 5-3
1967—North Tipperary 4-8, Offaly 3-6
1968—North Tipperary 7-15, Antrim 4-2
1969—North Tipperary 8-5, Offaly 3-2
1970—Cork County 3-6, Offaly 1-5
1971—Antrim 7-14, North Tipperary 5-4
1972—Kilkenny 3-9, Cork 3-7
1973—Kilkenny 3-11, North Tipperary 1-8
1974—North Tipperary 4-13, Offaly 3-4
1975—Kilkenny 3-8, North Tipperary 2-6
1976—Kilkenny 1-15, Galway 1-10

1977—Kilkenny 2-12, North Tipperary 1-10
1978—North Tipperary 1-7, Kilkenny 1-7
     (Replay) North Tipperary 8-11, Kilkenny 8-9
1979—Clare 1-8, Kilkenny 1-8
     (Replay) Clare 4-5, Kilkenny 1-8
1980—Galway 3-8, Down 2-7
1981—Galway 1-11, Offaly 1-5
1982—Galway 4-7, Offaly 1-8
1983—Galway 2-8, Kilkenny 2-8
     (Replay) Galway 2-10, Kilkenny 3-5
1984—Galway 4-9, Offaly 4-2
1985—Galway 3-8, Offaly 1-2
1986—Galway 3-12, North Tipperary 2-8
1987—Galway 5-7, Offaly 1-2
1988—Tipperary 5-3, Kilkenny 2-9
1989—Kilkenny 3-11, Offaly 1-14
1990—Tipperary 2-10, Kilkenny 0-11
1991—Kilkenny 2-10, Offaly 2-7
1992—Galway 3-13, Kilkenny 0-10
1993—Galway 5-7, Tipperary 1-10

ROLL OF HONOUR
Galway 10, North Tipperary 9, Kilkenny 8, Tipperary 2, Limerick City 1,
Cork County 1, Antrim 1, Clare 1.

INDIVIDUAL SCHOOLS SENIOR FOOTBALL

1975—Tralee 1-9, Virginia 1-6
1976—Newry 2-6, Rathmore 2-6 (draw)
     Newry 1-10, Rathmore 1-6 (replay)
1977—Newry 3-14, Achill 1-5
1978—Rathmore 1-6, Newry 0-3
1979—St Piux X Magherafelt 1-14, Tuam 2-8
1980—Tralee 1-8, La Salle Belfast 0-10
1981—Newry 4-8, Moneenageisha 1-5
1982—Newry 1-6, Tullow Com. 2-2
1983—Newry 5-12, Tuam 0-2
1984—Armagh Technical College 2-13, Carlow 1-3
1985—Edenderry 2-4, Tuam 1-7 (draw)
     Edenderry 2-8, Tuam 1-1 (replay)
1986—Newry Tech. 2-8, St David's, Greystones 1-7
1987—Rathmore CC 2-6, Moneenageisha CC 2-4
1988—Coláiste Gobnait 0-13, Dungannon CFE 0-8
1989—Dungannon CFE 1-9, Tullow 1-4

1990—Dungannon CFE 1-13, Moneenageisha CC 2-5
1991—Tralee CC 2-12, Dungannon CFE 2-12 (draw)
         Tralee CC 0-9, Dungannon CFE 1-5 (replay)
1992—Tullow CS 2-19, Boherbue CS 2-7
1993—Rathmore CC 3-5, Athlone CC 0-5

INDIVIDUAL SCHOOLS SENIOR HURLING

1978—Gort 5-5, Enniscorthy 3-5
1979—Ennis 2-5, Banagher 0-5
1980—Roscrea 3-6, Banagher 0-6
1981—New Inn 4-7, Ennis 2-6
1982—Johnstown 3-7, Bandon 2-3
1983—Portumna 2-19, Johnstown 2-9
1984—Nenagh 4-6, Enniscorthy 2-3
1985—Banagher 2-5, Loughrea 0-8
1986—Banagher 3-8, Borrisokane 1-5
1987—Thomastown 3-12, Borrisokane 1-5
1988—Moneenageisha 1-10, Banagher 0-12
1989—Banagher 1-12, Roscrea 2-6
1990—Banagher 3-15, Moneenageisha 1-13
         Moneenageisha awarded match after objection.
1991—Roscrea 1-13, Moneenageisha 1-9
1992—Athenry 3-9, Bandon 2-7
1993—Athenry 1-18, Kilcormac 1-9

INDIVIDUAL SCHOOLS UNDER 15 HURLING

1982—Rathdowney 1,12, Moneenageisha 1-5
1983—Borrisokane 3-5, Loughrea 2-8 (draw)
         Borrisokane 2-8, Loughrea 1-7 (replay)
1984—Banagher 2-4, Borrisokane 1-5
1985—Rathdowney 5-8, Loughrea 2-7
1986—Moneenageisha 2-4, Rathluirc 1-3
1987—Johnstown 2-6, Bandon 2-3
1988—Johnstown 2-13, New Inn 1-9
1989—Killenaule 4-7, Ballyhale 4-4
1990—Borrisokane 4-9, Thomastown 2-7
1991—Gort 3-5, Causeway 2-6
1992—Killenaule 3-4, Gort 2-4
1993—New Ross VS 4-8, Loughrea VS 3-10

INDIVIDUAL SCHOOLS UNDER-15 FOOTBALL

1974—Johnstown declared winners
1975—St Mark's, Warrenpoint 2-7, Tuam 2-4
1976—St Mark's, Warrenpoint 5-9, Swords 0-4
1977—St Mark's, Warrenpoint 3-10, Rathmore 1-4
1978—St Pius X, Magherafelt 2-12, Newcastlewest 0-6
1979—Tullow CC 3-7, Midleton 2-2
1980—St Paul's, Bessbrook 1-11, Newcastlewest 0-6
1981—Dungannon 1-12, Scoil Stiofain Naofa 2-7
1982—Castlewellan 4-4, Scoil Stiofain Naofa 1-4
1983—Clara 4-11, Tipperary Town 2-6
1984—Edenderry 1-4, Limavaddy 1-3
1985—St Pius X, Magherafelt 2-17, Scoil Stiofain Naofa 0-1
1986—St Pat's, Omagh 2-5, Ard Scoil Chiarain 0-9
1987—St Piux X, Magherafelt 6-11, Dunshaughlin VS 0-3
1988—St Mark's, Warrenpoint 5-14, Moneenageisha CC 0-6
1989—St Pius X, Magherafelt 3-5, Edenderry VS 0-6
1990—Killorglin CC 1-6, St Pat's, Dungiven 1-5
1991—Rathmore CC 4-16, Kilkeen, Down 3-2
1992—St Joseph's, Coalisland 2-4, Davitt College, Castlebar 0-9
1993—St Ciaran's HS, Ballygawley 0-16, Rathmore CC 2-8.

GAELIC GAMES AND
THE GARDA CONNECTION

by NOEL FALLON

THE Garda GAA Club was formed in Dublin in 1923 by Commissioner Eoin O'Duffy. Right from the beginning the Club attracted some of the greatest hurlers and footballers in the country.

The Club made an immediate impact in the Dublin hurling and football championships with the hurlers crowned County champions in 1924, 1926-29 and 1931 and the footballers victorious in 1927 and 1929 before winning three-in-a-row from 1933 to 1935.

Yet for all the footballers achievements it was the greatness of the hurlers which shone most luminously during this period. The team reached its Everest peak of greatness in 1927 when it provided nine members of the Dublin team which won the All-Ireland title that year.

The side which contained Mick Gill, Pat "Fowler" McInerney, Garret Howard, Matty Power and Ned Tobin from Garda is still considered one of the finest of McCarthy Cup winners.

The footballers of that era contained such players as the legendary Larry Stanley, Dick Creagh (Mayo) and Paddy Colloran (Sligo).

Inevitably the Garda Club became a victim of its success and it was disbanded because its sides were considered too strong and members were transferred to various parts of the country. However, the Club reformed in 1947 and as in the 1920s it made an immediate impact by winning the 1948 Dublin SFC with a memorable victory over St Vincent's.

That set the stage for a series of magnificent matches which culminated in 1952 with a then-record 25,000 spectators attending that year's County final. That Garda team included Paddy Kennedy, Bill Carlos, Brendan Lynch, Liam Gilmartin and Tom Langan. While the footballers never reached such heights for the rest of the 1950s and 1960s the Force continued to produce extraordinary talent.

In 1966 the Garda Recreation Club donated a cup for an interdivisional competition which has since become the premier competition. Cork East were the first winners while Garda hurlers and footballers have always played an integral part in the representative series with the Combined Universities and the Defence Forces.

After being briefly disbanded, Michael O'Connor and Jim Murphy were the driving forces behind the reformation of the Garda Club in 1969. Since winning the intermediate championship in 1986 the team has proved a major power in the Dublin Championship with the 1993 side containing such players as Dermot Deasy, Jack Sheedy (Dublin), John Newton (Roscommon) and Davy Byrne (Monaghan).

The last twenty years has been something of a golden era for the Garda with the Force producing some of the greatest players in the history of gaelic games. Matt Connor, John Egan, Paudie O'Shea, John McCarthy, Tom Prendergast, Seamus Bonner, Anthony Davis, Brian Murray and the late John Morley of Mayo embellished the reputation of the Force while Joachim Kelly, Ken Hogan, Frank Cummins, Mossie Walsh were among the best hurlers of their generation.

Another Garda, Brian Murphy of Cork, was among the most honoured dual-players in the history of gaelic games.

● *The power of Donegal's Tony Boyle is captured in this picture from the 1992 All-Ireland championship campaign.*

GAELIC GAMES AND THE ARMY CONNECTION

by NOEL FALLON

G AELIC games have figured prominently in the Army since the first championships were held in 1923 with some of the greatest hurlers and footballers of all time involved in Army competition, particularly in the halcyon days of the '40s and '50s.

The Defence Forces have distinguished themselves at representative level since the '30s with memorable games against the Combined Universities and Ireland selections. The matches versus Garda commenced in the early '60s and were enlarged to include the Combined Universities and Combined Colleges in the current quadrangular format.

In football the Army has had the services of such players as John Joe O'Reilly, Jack Gallagher, Jim Fives and Dermot Earley right down to John Maughan, Shea Fahy, Dermot Hanafin and Tommy Carr at the present time.

The Cork team which won the Sam Maguire Cup in 1945 contained seven Army players including Eamon Young, Mick Turbidy and Matt Driscoll while five members of the victorious 1956 side, including Billy O'Neill and Joe Young were Army men.

The standard of Army football weakened from the '60s onwards with less inter-county players appearing in the ranks of the Cadets and Units in the Army. However outstanding individual players such as Earley, Seamus Coughlan, Kevin McStay, Shea Fahy and Noel Roche still emerged.

The Southern Command and the Air Corps produced outstanding teams to dominate the All-Army Championships in the '50s and '60s respectively but dominance in that prestigious competition has swung decisively to the Western and Eastern Commands in the last two decades.

Mick Mackey is the most illustrious of the many great hurlers who have participated in Defence Forces competition. Many other great players have also left a profound impact on hurling in the Defence Forces. Four of the Tipperary team which won the 1945 All-Ireland were from the Army while Vin Baston was a prominent member of Waterford's breakthrough team of 1948.

Two Army men, Mick Kenny (1957) and Tony Wall (1958) captained their counties to All-Ireland success in successive years while Tipperary's Larry Kiely, who also attained excellence as an international showjumper, was one of the most gifted of the many fine hurlers that went through the Defence Forces in the '60s.

Ciaran Fitzgerald was another versatile sportsman who proved himself on the hurling field, helping Eastern Command to the All-Army championship in 1973. The Kilkenny connection has become prominent in recent years with the Brennan brothers Kieran, Gerard and Canice along with Frank Holohan and Brian Ryan the most prominent of many stars.

The Curragh Command have been the foremost power in the All-Army Hurling Championship in recent times.

● Jack Lynch pictured with Kitty Mackey (left) and Rita Ring (right) after they had received the Team of the Century trophies on behalf of their late husbands, the two incomparables, Mick Mackey and Christy Ring.

481

GAELIC GAMES IN THE UNIVERSITIES

FITZGIBBON CUP RECORDS

by NOEL FALLON

THE Fitzgibbon Cup, the trophy for the Higher Education hurling championship, is named after Dr. Edwin Fitzgibbon, a Capuchin priest who was Professor of Philosophy in University College Cork from 1911 to 1936.

In 1912 Dr. Edwin donated most of his annual salary to present the trophy that bears his name for the hurling championship between the constituent colleges of the NUI.

The competition was dominated in the early year by UCC, UCD and to a lesser extent UCG before Queens made the breakthrough in 1953.

Maynooth won two successive titles in the '70s before a major breakthrough took place in the late '80s when all teams in Division 1 of the Higher Education League were allowed to participate in the Fitzgibbon and its sister football championship, the Sigerson Cup.

Since the event went "open" University of Limerick and Waterford RTC have recorded memorable victories. UCC lead the Roll of Honour with 36 championships but UCD gained a magnificent 31st title in March 1993, when they defeated Cork in one of the greatest finals in the distinguished history of the competition.

ROLL OF HONOUR

UCC (35); UCD (31); UCG (10); St. Patrick's, Maynooth (2): Queens University Belfast (1); University of Limerick (1); Waterford RTC (1).

Continued on page 284

Top of the League for car and home insurance.

Church & General takes extra care to bring you
the best in home insurance and car insurance.
Call Church & General and discover the difference between
the best insurance team – and the runners-up.

Church & General

1912–UCD	1954–UCG
1913–UCC	1955–UCC
1914–UCC	1956–UCC
1915–UCD	1957–UCD
1916–UCD	1958–UCC
1917–UCD	1959–UCD
1918–UCC	1960–UCD
1919–UCG	1961–UCC
1920–UCC	1962–UCC
1921–NOT PLAYED	1963–UCD
1922–UCC	1964–UCD
1923–UCD	1965–UCD
1924–UCD	1966–UCC
1925–UCC	1967–UCC
1926–UCG	1968–UCD
1927–UCD	1969–UCD
1928–UCC	1970–UCG
1929–UCC	1971–UCC
1930–UCC	1972–UCC
1931–UCD	1973–St. Patrick's, Maynooth
1932–UCD	1974–St. Patrick's, Maynooth
1933–UCC	1975–UCD
1934–UCD	1976–UCC
1935–UCD	1977–UCG
1936–UCD	1978–UCD
1937–UCC	1979–UCD
1938–UCD	1980–UCG
1939–UCC	1981–UCC
1940–UCC	1982–UCC
1941–UCD	1983–UCC
1942–UCG	1984–UCC
1943–UCC	1985–UCC
1944–UCD	1986–UCC
1945–UCG	1987–UCC
1946–UCG	1988–UCC
1947–UCC	1989–University of Limerick
1948–UCD	1990–UCC
1949–UCG	1991–UCC
1950–UCD	1992–Waterford RTC
1951–UCD	1993–UCD
1952–UCD	
1953–QUB	

CAMOGIE

ROLL OF HONOUR

Dublin (26): 1932, 1933, 1937, 1938
1942, 1943, 1944, 1948, 1949,
1950, 1951, 1952, 1953, 1954,
1955, 1957, 1958, 1959, 1960,
1961, 1962, 1963, 1964, 1965,
1966, 1984.

Cork (16): 1934, 1935, 1936, 1939,
1940, 1941, 1970, 1971, 1972,
1973, 1978, 1980, 1982, 1983,
1992, 1993.

Kilkenny (11): 1974, 1976, 1977,
1981, 1985, 1986, 1987, 1988,
1989, 1990, 1991.

Antrim (6): 1945, 1946, 1947, 1956,
1967, 1979.

Wexford (3): 1968, 1969, 1975.

1932—Dublin 3-2 Galway 0-2
1933—Dublin 9-2; Galway 4-0
1934—Cork 4-3; Louth 1-4
1934—Cork 3-4; Dublin 4-0
1936—Cork 6-4; Louth 3-3
1937—Dublin 9-4; Galway 1-0
1938—Dublin 5-0; Cork 2-3
1939—Cork 6-1; Galway 1-1
1940—Cork 4-1; Galway 2-2
1941—Cork 7-5; Dublin 1-2
1942—Dublin 4-1; Cork 2-2 Replay
   Dublin 1-2; Cork 1-2 Draw
1943—Dublin 8-0; Cork 1-1
1944—Dublin 5-4; Antrim 0-0
1945—Antrim 5-2; Waterford 3-2
1946—Antrim 4-1; Galway 2-3
1947—Antrim 2-4; Dublin 2-1
1948—Dublin 11-4; Down 4-2
1949—Dublin 8-6; Tipperary 4-1
1950—Dublin 6-5; Antrim 4-1
1951—Dublin 8-6; Antrim 4-1
1952—Dublin 5-1; Antrim 4-2
1953—Dublin 8-4; Tipperary 1-3

1954—Dublin 10-4; Derry 4-2
1955—Dublin 9-2; Cork 5-6
1956—Antrim 5-3; Cork 4-2
1957—Dublin 3-3; Antrim 3-1
1958—Dublin 5-4; Tipperary 1-1
1959—Dublin 11-6; Mayo 1-3
1960—Dublin 6-2; Galway 2-0
1961—Dublin 7-2; Tipperary 4-1
1962—Dublin 5-5; Galway 2-0
1963—Dublin 7-3; Antrim 2-5
1964—Dublin 7-4; Antrim 3-1
1965—Dublin 10-1; Tipperary 5-3
1966—Dublin 2-2; Antrim 0-6
1967—Antrim 3-9; Dublin 4-2, Replay
   Antrim 4-2; Dublin 4-2, Draw
1968—Wexford 4-2; Cork 2-5
1969—Wexford 4-4; Antrim 4-2
1970—Cork 5-7; Kilkenny 3-2
1971—Cork 4-6; Wexford 1-2
1972—Cork 2-5; Kilkenny 1-4
1973—Cork 2-5; Antrim 3-1
1974—Kilkenny 3-3; Cork 1-5, Replay
   Kilkenny 3-8; Cork 4-5, Draw
1975—Wexford 4-3; Cork 1-2
1976—Kilkenny 0-6; Dublin 1-2
1977—Kilkenny 3-4; Wexford 1-3
1978—Cork 6-4; Dublin 1-2
1979—Antrim 2-3; Tipperary 1-3
1980—Cork 1-8; Limerick 2-2, Replay
   Cork 2-7; Limerick 3-4, Draw
1981—Kilkenny 1-9; Cork 0-7, Replay
   Kilkenny 3-9; Cork 3-9, Draw
1982—Cork 2-7; Dublin 2-6
1983—Cork 2-5; Dublin 1-6
1984—Dublin 5-8; Tipperary 2-5
1985—Kilkenny 0-13; Dublin 1-5
1986—Kilkenny 2-12; Dublin 2-3
1987—Kilkenny 3-10; Cork 1-7
1988—Kilkenny 4-11; Cork 3-8
1989—Kilkenny 3-10; Cork 2-6
1990—Kilkenny 1-14; Wexford 0-7
1991—Kilkenny 3-8; Cork 0-10
1992—Cork 1-20; Wexford 2-6
1993—Cork 3-15; Galway 2-8

ALL-IRELAND CHAMPIONSHIPS (Junior)

ROLL OF HONOUR

Cork (4): 1973, 1980, 1983, 1984.
Galway (4): 1972, 1979, 1985, 1988.
Dublin (3): 1970, 1971, 1975.
Clare (3): 1974, 1981, 1986.
Down (3): 1968, 1976, 1991.
Kildare (3): 1987, 1989, 1990.
Derry (2): 1969, 1978.
Limerick (1): 1977.
Louth (1): 1982.
Tipperary (1): 1992.

FINALS

1968—Down 2-3; Cork 1-1
1969—Derry 4-2; Cork 2-4
1970—Dublin 4-2; Armagh 3-3
1971—Dublin 2-2; Cork 1-2
1972—Galway 3-6; Werxford 2-1
1973—Cork 4-4; Galway 1-4
1974—Clare 3-2; Dublin 3-0
1975—Dublin 5-0; Down 0-3
1976—Down 3-4; Wexford 3-3
1977—Limerick 2-7; Wexford 3-1
1978—Derry 3-4; Coark 1-4
1979—Galway 4-3; Cork 3-2
1980—Cork 4-4; Tyrone 1-4
1981—Clare 3-2; Antrim 0-7
1982—Louth 1-7; Cork 1-6
1983—Cork 2-5; Dublin 2-3
1984—Cork 5-8; Cavan 2-2
1985—Galway 8-7; Armagh 3-7
1986—Clare 1-13; Kildare 3-4
1987—Kildare 2-10; Armagh 0-7
1988—Galway 3-4; Limerick 1-5
1989—Kildare 0-15; Galway 2-9 (draw)
      Kildare 3-11; Galway 1-3 (replay)
1990—Kildare 2-14; Tipperary 3-7
1991—Down 3-13; Tipperary 2-14
1992—Tipperary 6-13; Galway 2-7
1993—Clare 1-8; Dublin 1-5

INTERMEDIATE

1992—Dublin 4-11; Down 4-4
1993—Armagh 2-10; Galway 0-6 (replay)
      Armagh 3-9; Galway 3-9 (draw)

ALL-IRELAND CHAMPIONSHIPS (Minor)

ROLL OF HONOUR

Cork (8): 1975, 1976, 1978, 1979, 1980, 1983, 1984, 1985.
Galway (4): 1977, 1981, 1986, 1987.
Kilkenny (3): 1988, 1989, 1991.
Tipperary (3): 1990, 1992, 1993.
Down (1): 1974.
Dublin (1): 1982.

FINALS

1974—Down 3-0; Cork 0-1
1975—Cork 6-2; Galway 0-3
1976—Cork 4-6; Down 2-1
1977—Galway 5-4; Dublin 2-1
1978—Cork 5-1; Dublin 3-4
1979—Cork 5-3; Cavan 3-0
1980—Cork 5-5; Cavan 0-2
1981—Galway 3-4; Antrim 3-3
1982—Dublin 5-3; Galway 2-3
1983—Cork 3-3; Dublin 2-3
1984—Cork 2-12; Galway 5-0
1985—Cork 3-8; Galway 2-3
1986—Galway 2-8; Wexford 1-4
1987—Galway 1-11; Cork 3-3
1988—Kilkenny 5-6; Armagh 2-5
1989—Kilkenny 9-10; Tipperary 3-8
1990—Tipperary 2-11; Kilkenny 3-6
1991—Kilkenny 4-12; Galway 3-7
1992—Tipperary 4-9; Kilkenny 1-3
1993—Tipperary 3-10; Galway 2-9 (rep)
      Tipperary 1-5; Galway 1-5 (dra

NATIONAL LEAGUES (Senior)

ROLL OF HONOUR

Kilkenny (9): 1978, 1980, 1982, 1985, 1987, 1988, 1989, 1990, 1993.
Dublin (3): 1979, 1981, 1983.
Cork (4) 1984, 1986, 1991, 1992.
Wexford (1): 1978.
Tipperary (1): 1977.

FINALS

1977—Tipperary 4-2; Wexford 1-3
1978—Wexford 2-5; Cork 0-4
1978—Kilkenny 2-4; Limerick 1-5
1979—Dublin 0-6; Limerick 0-0
1980—Kilkenny 3-8; Tipperary 1-3
1981—Dublin 1-7; Cork 1-4
1982—Kilkenny 2-5; Cork 1-4
1983—Dublin 4-8; Wexford 1-6
1984—Cork 1-8; Dublin 0-4
1985—Kilkenny 4-7; Dublin 3-6
1986—Cork 3-8; Dublin 1-10
1987—Kilkenny 4-8; Dublin 1-6
1988—Kilkenny 3-10; Dublin 2-4
1989—Kilkenny 6-7; Cork 1-11
1990—Kilkenny 1-10; Wexford 2-4
1991—Cork 2-13; Kilkenny 2-6
1992—Cork 2-17; Wexford 0-11
1993—Kilkenny 4-7; Cork 1-13

NATIONAL LEAGUE
(Junior)

ROLL OF HONOUR

Dublin (4): 1982, 1983, 1984, 1987.
Armagh (3): 1980, 1988, 1993.
Kildare (3): 1986, 1989, 1990.
Limerick (2): 1991, 1992.
Cavan (1): 1981.
Galway (1): 1985.

1980—Armagh 2-5; Kildare 1-3
1981—Cavan 0-4; Louth O-2. Replay
    Cavan 2-4; Louth 1-7 Draw
1982—Dublin 6-9; Tyrone 0-2
1983—Dublin 3-9; Westmeath 2-5
1984—Dublin 2-4; Armagh 1-3
1985—Galway 3-10; Kildare 3-3
1986—Kildare 2-3; Dublin 1-4
1987—Dublin 6-4; Kildare 1-7
1988—Armagh 1-9; Dublin 0-6
1989—Kildare 2-14; Armagh 3-8
1990—Kildare 2-13; Kilkenny 2-8
1991—Limerick 3-13; Roscommon 3-4
1992—Limerick 4-13; Down 2-6
1993—Armagh 3-8; Dublin 2-1

GAEL LINN
SENIOR INTERPROVINCIAL CHAMPIONSHIPS
ROLL OF HONOUR

Leinster (23): 1956, 1957, 1958, 1959, 1960, 1962, 1965, 1968, 1969, 1970, 1971, 1972, 1978, 1979, 1981, 1983, 1984, 1985, 1986, 1987, 1988, 1989, 1991.

Munster (8): 1961, 1963, 1964, 1966, 1980, 1982, 1990, 1992.

Connacht (2): 1973, 1974.
Ulster (1): 1967.

FINALS

1956—Leinster 7-1; Ulster 3-1
1957—Leinster 5-1; Munster 3-1
1958—Leinster 8-2; Ulster 3-3
1959—Leinster 6-0; Ulster 1-3
1960—Leinster 4-9; Munster 3-1
1961—Munster 5-2; Connacht 1-0
1962—Leinster 7-2; Ulster 5-3
1963—Munster 3-2; Leinster 2-2
1964—Munster 2-6; Leinster 3-2
1965—Leinster 4-3; Ulster 4-1
1966—Munster 4-2; Leinster 1-3
1967—Ulster 5-4; Leinster 5-1
1968—Leinster 7-0; Ulster 2-5
1969—Leinster 5-4; Munster 2-2
1970—Leinster 12-2; Ulster 4-1
1971—Leinster 5-4; Ulster 0-5
1972—Leinster 7-7; Connacht 4-2
1973—Connacht 4-4; Leisnter 3-3
1974—Connacht 3-7; Munster 3-0
1975-'77—Suspended
1978—Leinster 4-9; Connacht 2-2
1979—Leinster 1-5; Munster 0-4
1980—Munster 2-5; Leinster 2-1
1981—Leinster 3-10; Ulster 2-4
1982—Munster 3-10; Leinster 2-12
1983—Leinster 2-7; Munster 1-7
1984—Leinster 3-9; Connacht 1-4
1985—Leinster 4-9; Munster 1-6
1986—Leinster 4-6; Munster 1-6
1987—Leinster 8-11; Connacht 0-5
1988—Leinster 2-9, Connacht 2-4

1989—Leinster 5-12; Munster 3-6
1990—Munster 10-10; Ulster 1-2
1991—Leinster 5-13; Munster 0-7
1992—Munster 1-18; Leinster 2-9

1989—Ulster 1-11; Leinster 2-3
1990—Ulster 5-11; Munster 5-3
1991—Ulster 4-5; Munster 0-6
1992—Munster 6-11; Connacht 3-3

GAEL LINN
JUNIOR INTERPROVINCIAL CHAMPIONSHIPS FINALS
ROLL OF HONOUR

Munster (9): 1975, 1977, 1978, 1980, 1983, 1985, 1987, 1988, 1992.
Leinster (4): 1976, 1982, 1984, 1986.
Ulster (4): 1979, 1989, 1990, 1992.
Connacht (1): 1981.

1975—Munster 5-1; Ulster 2-0
1976—Leinster 2-6; Munster 2-3
1977—Munster 3-7; Connacht 3-1
1978—Munster 3-2; Ulster 2-1
1979—Ulster 0-4; Munster 1-0
1980—Munster 1-9; Leinster 3-2
1981—Connacht 2-3; Munster 2-2
1982—Leinster 3-16; Connacht 2-8
1983—Munster 1-12; Leinster 1-11
1984—Leinster 3-6; Ulster 1-3
1985—Munster 1-7; Ulster 2-3
1986—Leinster 1-15; Munster 0-7
1987—Munster 2-6; Ulster 2-5
1988—Munster 4-3, Leinster 3-5

ALL-IRELAND CLUB CHAMPIONSHIPS

St. Paul's, Kilkenny (8): 1968, 1969, 1970, 1974, 1976, 1987, 1988, 1989.

Buffer's Alley, Wexford (5): 1979, 1981, 1982, 1983, 1984.

Glen Rovers, Cork (3): 1986, 1990, 1992.

Austin Stacks, Dublin (2): 1971, 1972.

St. Patrick's, Glengoole, Tipperary (2): 1965, 1966.

Ballyagran, Limerick (1): 1978.

Celtic, Dublin (1): 1964.

Croagh-Kilfinny, Limerick (1): 1975.

Eoghan Ruadh, Dublin (1): 1967.

Killeagh, Cork (1): 1980.

Oranmore, Galway (1): 1973.

Athenry, Galway (1): 1977.

Mullagh, Galway (1): 1991.

Crumlin, Dublin (1): 1985.

ALL-IRELAND CLUB FINALS

1964—Celtic, Dublin 5-2; Deirdre, Belfast 1-0
1965—St. Patrick's Glengoole, Tipperary 3-3; Deirdre, Belfast 2-3
1966—St. Patrick's, Glengoole, Tipperary 5-5; St. Paul's, Kilkenny 2-1
1967—Eoghan Ruadh, Dublin 7-3; Oranmore, Galway 1-0
1968—St. Paul's Kilkenny 7-2; Ahane, Limerick 1-2
1969—St. Paul's, Kilkenny 3-7; Ahane, Limerick 2-1
1970-'71—St. Paul's, Kilkenny 6-5; Bellaghy, Derry 2-0
1971-'72—Austin Stacks, Dublin 5-4; Thurles, Tipperary 2-1
1972-'73—Austin Stacks, Dublin 4-3; Portglenone, Antrim 2-0
1973-'74—Oranmore, Galway 3-2; St. Paul's, Kilkenny 2-3
1974-'75—St. Paul's Kilkenny 3-3; Oranmore, Galway 1-1
1975-'76—Croagh-Kilfinny, Limerick 4-6; Athenry, Galway 4-5
1976-'77—St. Paul's, Kilkenny 6-3; Athenry, Galway 1-3

1977-'78—Athenry, Galway 10-5; Portglenone, Antrim 1-1
1978—Ballyagran, Limerick 1-3; Buffer's Alley, Wexford 0-1
1979—Buffer's Alley, Wexford 2-6; Athenry, Galway 1-2
1980—Killeagh, Cork 4-2; Buffer's Alley, Wexford 1-7
1981—Buffer's Alley, Wexford 2-6; Killeagh, Cork 1-4
1982—Buffer's Alley, Wexford 3-2; Athenry, Galway 0-2
1983—Buffer's Alley, Wexford 3-7; St. Mary's, Kilkerrin-Glenamaddy,
        Galway 0-6
1984—Buffer's Alley, Wexford 3-7; Glenamaddy, Galway 0-6
1985—Crumlin, Dublin 4-8; Athenry, Galway 3-2
1986—Glen Rovers, Cork 4-11; St. Paul's, Kilkenny 5-7
1987—St. Paul's, Kilkenny 1-4; Glen Rovers, COrk 0-5
1988—St. Paul's, Kilkenny 4-5; St. Mary's, Glenamaddy 3-7
1989—St. Paul's, Kilkenny 6-10; Mullagh, Galway 4-2
1990—Glen Rovers, Cork 4-13; St. Paul's, Kilkenny 2-7
1991—Mullagh, Galway 4-13; Eglish, Tyrone 0-2
1992—Glen Rovers, Cork 1-9; St. Anne's, Rathnure, Wexford 0-2

LEADING ALL-IRELAND SENIOR MEDAL HOLDERS

The following are the leading All-Ireland Senior Medal holders:
Kathleen Mills, Dublin (15): 1942-1961
Una O'Connor, Dublin (13): 1953-1966
Angela Downey, Kilkenny (11): 1974-1991
Ann Downey, Kilkenny (11): 1974-1991
Gerry Hughes, Dublin (9): 1954-1963
Kay Ryder, Dublin (9): 1955-1966
Bridie McGarry, Kilkenny (9): 1974-1991
Jo Dunne, Kilkenny (8): 1974-1991
Sophie Brack, Dublin (8): 1948-1956
Eileen Duffy, Dublin (8): 1949-1957
Kay Lyons, Dublin (8): 1957-1966
Eithne Leech, Dublin (8): 1959-1966
Marion McCarthy, Cork (8): 1970-1983

HANDBALL

MAJOR DEVELOPMENTS OVER THE LAST 25 YEARS

KILKENNY'S "DUXIE" WALSH HAS WON A STRING OF TITLES

By MICK DUNNE

THREE very significant developments in Irish handball over the last quarter of a century changed the sport considerably, gave it a much more modern image and had far-reaching consequences.

Hectic building activity during this period, even in areas without previous handball tradition, saw the erection of numerous small, American-size alleys with measurements of 40 ft. by 20 ft. compared with the traditional 60×30 Irish standard. There are now over 300 of these small courts in a country where none existed 25 years ago.

Since the first one opened in Oldtown, Co. Dublin, in 1969 so many more have been built throughout the country that there are almost as many as there are 60×30s. All of them are indoors, many of them part of larger sports complexes and several contain one or more full glass walls, which provide greater spectator viewing space.

Secondly, greater, and welcome, emphasis has been placed on handball as "a lifetime sport" to be still played competitively – but, more important – for fun and health reasons into advanced years. From club tournaments up to All-Ireland championships there is now a wide range of activities for players aged 40 and over.

In 1967 All-Ireland championships were introduced for masters (over-40s) in doubles, a singles competition was added nine years later and in 1982 a golden masters (over-50s) category was launched in both singles and doubles. We saw a prime example of a player still hugely enjoying his sport, and successfully, in May 1993 when life-long Dublin handballer Joe Maxwell was one of the winning golden masters doubles 40×20 champions at the ripe age of 62.

INTERNATIONAL DIMENSION

The third major devleopment in latter times has been the avail-
ability of plenty of international competition for players of all
ages. Since 1981 Irish players have been entered annually in the
United States national championships for juveniles and Michael
"Duxie" Walsh set an example for many youngsters who followed
when he won the 15-and-under title at these championships in
Tucson, Arizona.

The Kilkenny super player went on to win the 17s and 19s (and
indeed the under-23s) in later years. Success soon followed for
Eamonn O'Neill (Limerick), Peter McAuley (Louth), Frank
Kavanagh (Westmeath), John Duggan (Clare) Walter O'Connor
(Meath), Ciaran Curran (Tyrone) who has also won the "teenage
treble", Michael Finnegan (Cavan) and Michael McHale
(Roscommon).

The revival of the World Championships by the I.H.C. in 1984
accelerated the growth in international competition for men and
boys, girls and women. The return of these championships to
Ireland in October '94 will give a new dimension to the sport here.

THE KIRBYS' FEAT

By 1975 enough 40×20s had been built in this country to enable
the I.H.C. inauguarate All-Ireland championships for the smaller
courts. These were monopolised at the start by Pat Kirby of Clare
who had returned from the U.S., and he was involved in winning
six singles titles and five doubles (with his brother Mick). Unquestionably Pat would have collected many more singles if he hadn't
gone back to live in America in 1980. His successive singles feat
was equalled in 1991 by Duxie Walsh, but the latter is still three
short of Kirby's five consecutive doubles

But in the 60×30 championships Walsh has been phenomenally
successful and without equal in modern times, winning a string of
singles and (with partner Eugene Downey) several doubles. In
1992 Duxie equalled the 55-year-old record of eight consecutive
singles established by the late Paddy Perry in 1930-'37.

And Walsh etched an indelible place for himself in the annals
of handball when he created a new record in mid-September. By
beating Walter O'Connor (Meath) again in the 60x30 senior
singles final he got his ninth consecutive singles championship
and topped the eight won by the late Paddy Perry (Roscommon).

HANDBALL RECORDS
ALL-IRELAND CHAMPIONSHIPS
(1925-1993)
SENIOR SOFTBALL SINGLES

1925—M. Joyce (Dublin)
1926—T. Behan (Kilkenny)
1927—W. McGuire (Dublin)
1928—J. McNally (Mayo)
1929—D. Brennan (Kilkenny)
1930—P. Perry (Roscommon)
1931—P. Perry (Roscommon)
1932—P. Perry (Roscommon)
1933—P. Perry (Roscommon)
1934—P. Perry (Roscommon)
1935—P. Perry (Roscommon)
1936—P. Perry (Roscommon)
1937—P. Perry (Roscommon)
1938—J. J. Gilmartin (Kilkenny)
1939—J. J. Gilmartin (Kilkenny)
1940—M. Walsh (Galway)
1941—J. Dunne (Kilkenny)
1942-45—Suspended due to
        scarcity of softballs
1946—J. J. Gilmartin (Kilkenny)
1947—L. Rowe (Dublin)
1948—J. Bergin (Tipperary)
1949—L. Rowe (Dublin)
1950—J. Bergin (Tipperary)
1951—L. Rowe (Dublin)
1952—J. Ryan (Wexford)
1953—M. Griffin (Cork)
1954—J. Ryan (Wexford)
1955—J. Ryan (Wexford)
1956—J. Ryan (Wexford)
1957—J. Ryan (Wexford)
1958—P. Downey (Kerry)
1959—F. Confrey (Louth)

1960—F. Confrey (Louth)
1961—P. Downey (Kerry)
1962—J. Delaney (Kilkenny)
1963—J. Maher (Louth)
1964—J. Maher (Louth)
1965—R. Lyng (Wexford)
1966—S. McCabe (Monaghan)
1967—S. McCabe (Monaghan)
1968—J. Maher (Louth)
1969—J. Maher (Louth)
1970—J. Maher (Louth)
1971—R. Lyng (Wexford)
1973—P. Murphy (Wexford)
1973—J. Maher (Louth)
*1974—P. Kirby (Clare)
1975—P. Kirby (Clare)
1976—P. Kirby (Clare)
1977—P. Kirby (Clare)
1978—R. Lyng (Wexford)
1979—T. O'Rourke (Kildare)
1980—P. Ryan (Dublin)
1981—P. Reilly (Kilkenny)
1982—O. Harold (Kilkenny)
1983—A. Ryan (Tipperary)
1984—T. O'Rourke (Kildare)
1985—M. Walsh (Kilkenny)
1986—M. Walsh (Kilkenny)
1987—M. Walsh (Kilkenny)
1988—M. Walsh (Kilkenny)
1989—M. Walsh (Kilkenny)
1990—M. Walsh (Kilkenny)
1991—M. Walsh (Kilkenny)
1992—M. Walsh (Kilkenny)
1993—M. Walsh (Kilkenny)

* This was the first open-draw championship.

SENIOR HARDBALL SINGLES

1925—W. Aldridge (Kildare)
1926—T. Soye (Dublin)
1927—T. Soye (Dublin)
1928—T. Soye (Dublin)
1929—T. Soye (Dublin)

1930—T. Soye (Dublin)
1931—T. Soye (Dublin)
1932—J. Lucas (Kilkenny)
1933—P. Bell (Meath)
1934—P. Reid (Carlow)

1935—S. Tormey (Meath)
1936—J. J. Gilmartin (Kilkenny)
1937—J. J. Gilmartin (Kilkenny)
1938—J. J. Gilmartin (Kilkenny)
1939—J. J. Gilmartin (Kilkenny)
1940—J. J. Gilmartin (Kilkenny)
1941—J. J. Gilmartin (Kilkenny)
1942—J. J. Gilmartin (Kilkenny)
1943—M. Dowling (Kildare)
1944—A. Clarke (Dublin)
1945—J. J. Gilmartin (Kilkenny)
1946—J. J. Gilmartin (Kilkenny)
1947—J. J. Gilmartin (Kilkenny)
1948—A. Clarke (Dublin)
1949—A. Clarke (Dublin)
1950—R. Grattan (Kildare)
1951—A. Clarke (Dublin)
1952—J. Ryan (Wexford)
1953—J. Ryan (Wexford)
1954—A. Clarke (Dublin)
1955—A. Clarke (Dublin)
1956—J. Ryan (Wexford)
1957—J. Ryan (Wexford)
1958—P. Downey (Kerry)
1959—P. Downey (Kerry)
1960—P. Downey (Kerry)
1961—J. Maher (Louth)
1962—P. Downey (Kerry)
1963—J. Maher (Louth)

1964—J. Maher (Louth)
1965—P. McGee (Mayo)
1966—P. Hickey (Tipperary)
1967—P. McGee (Mayo)
1968—J. Maher (Louth)
1969—J. Maher (Louth)
1970—J. Maher (Louth)
1971—P. Hickey (Tipperary)
1972—P. McGee (Mayo)
1973—P. McGee (Mayo)
1974—P. McGee (Mayo)
1975—P. McGee (Mayo)
1976—P. McGee (Mayo)
1977—P. McGee (Mayo)
1978—C. Winders (Kildare)
1979—P. McGarry (Limerick)
1980—P. McGarry (Limerick)
1981—P. Winders (Kildare)
1982—P. McGee (Mayo)
1983—P. McGee (Mayo)
1984—P. Winders (Kildare)
1985— T. O'Rourke (Kildare)
1986—W. Bourke (Kilkenny)
1987—M. Walsh (Kilkenny)
1988—T. O'Rourke (Kildare)
1989—T. O'Rourke (Kildare)
1990—T. O'Rourke (Kildare)
1991—P. McAuley (Louth)
1992—B. Bourke (Kilkenny)
1993—

SENIOR SOFTBALL DOUBLES

1926—T. Behan and J. Norton (Kilkenny)
1926—J. Whyte and G. Barrett (Galway)
1927—M. Joyce and C. Ryan (Dublin)
1928—J. Flavin and M. Battersby (Waterford)
1929—D. Brennan and J. Lucas (Kilkenny)
1930—M. O'Neill and L. Sherry (Wicklow)
1931—M. O'Neill and L. Sherry (Wicklow)
1932—P. Perry and A. Mullaney (Roscommon)
1933—P. Perry and A. Mullaney (Roscommon)
1934—J. Hassett and E. Hassett (Tipperary)
1935—J. Hassett and E. Hassett (Tipperary)
1936—J. Hassett and E. Hassett (Tipperary)
1937—J. Hassett and E. Hassett (Tipperary)
1938—J. Hassett and E. Hassett (Tipperary)
1939—J. J. Gilmartin and J. Dunne (Kilkenny)
1940—J. J. Gilmartin and J. Dunne (Kilkenny)
1941—J. J. Gilmartin and J. Dunne (Kilkenny)

1942—J. Collins and C. Collins (Tipperary)
1943-45—Suspended
1946—L. Rowe and G. Rowe (Dublin)
1947—J. Bergin and J. O'Rourke (Sligo)
1948—L. Rowe and G. Rowe (Dublin)
1949—J. Bergin and J. Sweeney (Tipperary)
1950—J. Bergin and J. Sweeney (Tipperary)
1951—J. Hassett and J. O'Brien (Kerry)
1952—J. Hassett and J. O'Brien (Kerry)
1953—M. Griffin and M. Walsh (Cork)
1954—C. Delaney and J. Dunne (Kilkenny)
1955—P. Downey and J. O'Brien (Kerry)
1956—P. Downey and J. O'Brien (Kerry)
1957—J. Ryan and J. Doyle (Wexford)
1958—T. McGarry and M. Mullins (Limerick)
1959—T. McGarry and M. Mullins (Limerick)
1960—P. Downey and J. O'Brien (Kerry)
1961—P. Downey and J. O'Brien (Kerry)
1962—P. Downey and J. O'Brien (Kerry)
1963—P. Downey and J. O'Brien (Kerry)
1964—P. Downey and J. O'Brien (Kerry)
1965—J. Delaney and T. Ryan (Kilkenny)
1966—M. Walsh and P. McGee (Mayo)
1967—L. Molloy and D. McGovern (Meath)
1968—T. McEllistrim and M. McEllistrim (Kerry)
1969—P. Lee and J. Cleary (Wicklow)
1970—R. Lyng and S. Buggy (Wexford)
1971—T. McEllistrim and M. McEllistrim (Kerry)
1972—P. Murphy and J. Quigley (Wexford)
1973—M. McEllistrim and N. Kerins (Kerry)
1974—P. Murphy and J. Quigley (Wexford)
1975—R. Lyng and P. Murphy (Wexford)
1976—M. Hogan and P. McGarry (Limerick)
1977—R. Lyng and S. Buggy (Wexford)
1978—D. Kirby and J. Kirby (Clare)
1979—R. Lyng and S. Buggy (Wexford)
1980—P. Reilly and O. Harold (Kilkenny)
1981—A. Greene and P. Hughes (Kilkenny)
1982—R. Lyng and J. Goggins (Wexford)
1983—Tom and John Quish (Limerick)
1984—Tom and John Quish (Limerick)
1985—M. Walsh and E. Downey (Kilkenny)
1986—Tom and John Quish (Limerick)
1987—M. Walsh and E. Downey (Kilkenny)
1988—M. Walsh and E. Downey (Kilkenny)
1989—M. Walsh and E. Downey (Kilkenny)
1990—M. Walsh and E. Downey (Kilkenny)
1991—M. Walsh and E. Downey (Kilkenny)
1992—T. Sheridan and J. McGovern (Meath)
1993—M. Walsh and E. Downey (Kilkenny)

SENIOR HARDBALL DOUBLES

1926—J. J. Bowles and S. Gleeson (Limerick)
1927—T. Soye and T. O'Reilly (Dublin)
1928—T. Soye and T. O'Reilly (Dublin)
1929—P. Ormonde and C. Maloney (Tipperary)
1930—T. Soye and G. Brown (Dublin)
1931—P. Ormonde and C. Maloney (Tipperary)
1932—P. Bell and J. Doyle (Meath)
1933—P. Bell and J. Doyle (Meath)
1934—J. Lucas and T. Cherry (Kilkenny)
1935—P. Bell and J. Doyle (Meath)
1936—P. Perry and P. Reid (Roscommon)
1937—J. J. Gilmartin and A. Cullen (Kilkenny)
1938—J. J. Gilmartin and T. Cherry (Kilkenny)
1939—J. J. Gilmartin and T. Jordan (Kilkenny)
1940—J. J. Gilmartin and P. Dalton (Kilkenny)
1941—J. J. Gilmartin and J. Dunne (Kilkenny)
1942—A. Clarke and J. Clarke (Dublin)
1943—W. Walsh and D. Keogh (Cork)
1944—W. Walsh and D. Keogh (Cork)
1945—J. J. Gilmartin and P. Dalton (Kilkenny)
1946—J. J. Gilmartin and P. Dalton (Kilkenny)
1947—J. J. Gilmartin and P. Dalton (Kilkenny)
1948—W. Walsh and T. Morrissey (Cork)
1949—R. Grattan and J. Bolger (Kildare)
1950—A. Clarke and G. Moran (Dublin)
1951—J. Hassett and J. O'Brien (Kerry)
1952—J. Ryan and J. Doyle (Wexford)
1953—J. Hassett and P. Downey (Kerry)
1954—J. Ryan and J. Doyle (Wexford)
1955—J. Ryan and J. Doyle (Wexford)
1956—J. Ryan and J. Doyle (Wexford)
1957—J. Ryan and J. Doyle (Wexford)
1958—J. Ryan and J. Doyle (Wexford)
1959—P. Downey and J. O'Brien (Kerry)
1960—P. Downey and J. O'Brien (Kerry)
1961—J. Delaney and C. Delaney (Kilkenny)
1962—J. Ryan and M. Shanahan (Tipperary)
1963—P. Downey and J. O'Brien (Kerry)
1964—J. Maher and P. Reilly (Louth)
1965—P. McGee and P. Bolingbrook (Mayo)
1966—P. McGee and P. Bolingbrook (Mayo)
1967—P. McGee and P. Bolingbrook (Mayo)
1968—P. Hickey and C. Cleere (Tipperary)
1969—W. Doran and G. Lawlor (Kildare)
1970—S. McCabe and L. Gilmore (Monaghan)
1971—M. Sullivan and J. Doyle (Dublin)

1972—P. Hickey and C. Cleere (Tipperary)
1973—A. Byrne and W. Mullins (Westmeath)
1974—P. McGee and B. Colleran (Mayo)
1974—P. Hickey and J. Cleere (Tipperary)
1976—P. McGee and P. McCormack (Mayo)
1977—G. Lawlor and C. Winders (Kidare)
1978—P. McGarry and J. Bennis (Limerick)
1979—P. McGarry and J. Bennis (Limerick)
1980—P. McGarry and J. Bennis (Limerick)
1981—P. Winders and M. Purcell (Kildare)
1982—Cecil and Pius Winders (Kildare)
1983—Pius and Cecil Winders (Kildare)
1984—Tom and John Quish (Limerick)
1985—Tom and John Quish (Limerick)
1986—Tom and John Quish (Limerick)
1987—Tom and John Quish (Limerick)
1988—T. O'Rourke and P. McCormack (Kildare)
1989—B. McCarthy and N. Ryan (Tipperary)
1990—T. O'Rourke and M. Dowling (Kildare)
1991—B. Bourke and W. Pratt (Kilkenny)
1992—T. Sheridan and W. O'Connor (Meath)

MINOR SOFTBALL SINGLES

1949—J. O'Brien (Kerry)
1950—L. Egan (Kilkenny)
1951—R. Doherty (Roscommon)
1952—R. Doherty (Roscommon)
1953—J. Lyng (Wexford)
1954—E. Horan (Kerry)
1955—T. McGarry (Limerick)
1956—J. Murrary (Kilkenny)
1957—M. Mullins (Limerick)
1958—J. Clery (Wicklow)
1959—J. Clery (Wicklow)
1960—T. Ledwith (Westmeath)
1961—R. Lyng (Wexford)
1962—J. McElistrim (Kerry)
1963—M. Henry (Sligo)
1964—M. Henry (Sligo)
1965—P. Clarke (Roscommon)
1966—P. McCarthy (Limerick)
1967—P. Murphy (Dublin)
1968—P. Bennis (Limerick)
1969—M. Brady (Dublin)
1970—M. Walsh (Roscommon)
1971—S. McLoughlin (Wexford)

1972—S. McLoughlin (Wexford)
1973—T. O'Rourke (Kildare)
1974—D. Doolan (Roscommon)
1975—S. Wafer (Wexford)
1976—M. Maher (Louth)
1977—S. McGovern (Meath)
1978—A. Ryan (Tipperary)
1979—W. Bourke (Kilkenny)
1980—W. Bourke (Kilkenny)
1981—W. Bourke (Kilkenny)
1982—M. Walsh (Kilkenny)
1983—M. Walsh (Kilkenny)
1984—M. Walsh (Kilkenny)
1985—F. Kavanagh (Westmeath)
1986—T. Sheridan (Meath)
1987—P. McAuley (Louth)
1988—P. Galvin (Limerick)
1989—A. Heneghan (Roscommon)
1990—T. Hynes (Wexford)
1991—B. Gilhooly (Wexford)
1992—M. Finnegan (Cavan)
1993—M. Finnegan (Cavan)

MINOR HARDBALL SINGLES

1953—J. Redmond (Wexford)
1954—E. Horan (Kerry)
1955—J. Ryan (Tipperary)
1956—M. Sullivan (Kilkenny)
1957—P. Hickey (Tipperary)
1958—P. McGrath (Wexford)
1959—J. Clery (Wicklow)
1960—M. Purcell (Kildare)
1961—J. Brennan (Kilkenny)
1962—P. McLoughlin (Tipperary)
1963—T. Morrissey (Kilkenny)
1964—P. Cody (Cork)
1965—T. Geoghegan (Kildare)
1966—M. O'Gara (Roscommon)
1967—G. Lawlor (Kildare)
1968—J. Quigley (Wexford)
1969—J. Quigley (Wexford)
1970—M. Walsh (Roscommon)
1971—P. McCormack (Mayo)
1972—C. Quinn (Mayo)
1973—P. Hughes (Kilkenny)
1974—P. Hughes (Kilkenny)

1975—P. Finnerty (Galway)
1976—J. Dineen (Limerick)
1977—A. Ryan (Tipperary)
1978—A. Ryan (Tipperary)
1979—W. O'Donnell (Tipperary)
1980—W. Bourke (Kilkenny)
1981—W. Bourke (Kilkenny)
1982—J. O'Donoghue (Tipperary)
1983—J. O'Donoghue (Tipperary)
1984—M. Walsh (Kilkenny)
1985—T. Sheridan (Meath)
1986—W. O'Connor (Meath)
1987—P. McAuley (Louth)
1988—K. Lyons (Limerick)
1989—J. Connoly (Kilkenny)
1990—G. O'Brien (Kilkenny)
1991—D. Moloney (Tipperary)
1992—T. Winders (Kildare)

MINOR SOFTBALL DOUBLES

1938—J. Doran and G. Brogan (Dublin)
1939—A. Kelly and J. Goughran (Roscommon)
1940—P. Kennedy and J. Sweeney (Tipperary)
1941—P. Kennedy and J. Sweeney (Tipperary)
1942-45—Suspended
1946—J. Ryan and A. Power (Wexford)
1947—P. Doherty and M. Mulhern (Mayo)
1948—P. Somers and J. O'Keeffe (Kilkenny)
1949—P. Bolingbrook and K. Swords (Mayo)
1950—T. Hughes and J. O'Brien (Mayo)
1951—S. Commane and M. Dennehy (Kerry)
1952—R. Tunney and J. Swords (Mayo)
1953—M. O'Connor and E. Horan (Kerry)
1954—E. Horan and D. Downey (Kerry)
1955—T. McGarry and M. Mullins (Limerick)
1956—M. Sullivan and J. Murray (Kilkenny)
1957—M. Mullins and G. Mitchell (Limerick)
1958—W. Mullen and P. Geelan (Westmeath)
1959—J. Clery and M. Dwyer (Wicklow)
1960—N. Kerins and J. McMullan (Kerry)
1961—R. Lyng and P. Lennon (Wexford)

1962—D. Kirby and J. Kirby (Clare)
1963—H. Ryan and P. Kavanagh (Wexford)
1964—W. Myles and M. Fitzgibbon (Kerry)
1965—W. Myles and M. Fitzgibbon (Kerry)
1966—V. Grimes and C. Grimes (Meath)
1967—P. Murphy and P. Domigan (Dublin)
1968—J. Quigley and J. Sydney (Wexford)
1969—J. Quigley and N. Quigley (Wexford)
1970—M. Quigley and S. McLoughlin (Wexford)
1971—P. McCormack and C. Quinn (Mayo)
1972—D. Doolan and P. J. Moran (Roscommon)
1973—O. Harold and J. Barron (Kilkenny)
1974—P. Hughes and E. Mahon (Kilkenny)
1975—S. Wafer and S. Goggins (Wexford)
1976—J. McGovern and F. Carroll (Meath)
1977—J. and M. McGovern (Meath)
1978—J. and M. McGovern (Meath)
1979—B. Bourke and M. Cantwell (Kilkenny)
1980—W. Bourke and M. Lawlor (Kilkenny)
1981—E. Jensen and C. McGovern (Meath)
1982—M. Walsh and M. Lawlor (Kilkenny)
1983—Michael Walsh and Joe Walsh (Kilkenny)
1984—M. Walsh and P. O'Keeffe (Kilkenny)
1985—T. Sheridan and W. O'Connor (Meath)
1986—T. Sheridan and W. O'Connor (Meath)
1987—K. Lyons and P. Galvin (Limerick)
1988—K. Lyons and P. Galvin (Limerick)
1989—D. J. Carey and G. O'Brien (Kilkenny)
1990—A. and C. Heneghan (Roscommon)
1991—D. Moloney and N. Murphy (Tipperary)
1992—M. Finnegan and R. Cunningham (Cavan)
1993—M. Finnegan and R. Cunningham (Cavan)

MINOR HARDBALL DOUBLES

1953—J. Redmond and M. Redmond (Wexford)
1954—M. Sullivan and M. Hayes (Kilkenny)
1955—J. O'Neill and M. Keyes (Limerick)
1956—M. Sullivan and J. Murray (Kilkenny)
1957—M. Mullins and J. O'Connell (Limerick)
1958—M. Purcell and R. Winders (Kildare)
1959—C. Cleere and J. Cleary (Tipperary)
1960—M. Purcell and J. Byrne (Kildare)
1961—J. Byrne and J. Browne (Kildare)
1962—P. McLoughlin and A. Murphy (Tipperary)
1963—G. Lawlor and T. Geoghegan (Kildare)
1964—P. Cody and N. O'Brien (Cork)
1965—T. Curley and S. Lynch (Galway)
1966—G. Lawlor and A. Campbell (Kildare)

1967—G. Lawlor and C. Winders (Kildare)
1968—W. McCarthy and S. Halley (Tipperary)
1969—M. Brady and M. Williams (Dublin)
1970—M. Walsh and P. J. Moran (Roscommon)
1971—S. McLoughlin and C. Kehoe (Wexford)
1972—P. Hughes and J. Barron (Kilkenny)
1973—P. Hughes and J. Barron (Kilkenny)
1974—P. Hughes and E. Mahon (Kilkenny)
1975—A. McConnell and J. Reddy (Meath)
1976—F. McCann and M. Porter (Sligo)
1977—T. Ryan and W. O'Donnell (Tipperary)
1978—T. Ryan and W. O'Donnell (Tipperary)
1979—M. McGovern and J. Smith (Meath)
1980—W. Bourke and M. Lawlor (Kilkenny)
1981—W. Bourke and M. Lawlor (Kilkenny)
1982—E. Jensen and R. Morris (Meath)
1983—J. O'Donoghue and E. Corbett (Tipperary)
1984—M. Walsh and P. O'Keeffe (Kilkenny)
1985—T. Sheridan and W. O'Connor (Meath)
1986—T. Sheridan and W. O'Connor (Meath)
1987—P. McAuley and M. McAuley (Louth)
1988—K. Lyons and P. Galvin (Limerick)
1989—G. O'Brien and E. Law (Kilkenny)
1990—D. Moloney and N. Marshall (Tipperary)
1991—D. Moloney and N. Marshall (Tipperary)
1992—D. Moloney and n. Marshall (Tipperary)

JUNIOR SOFTBALL SINGLES

1928—M. Flannery (Waterford)
1929—P. Perry (Roscommon)
1930—J. Hassett (Tipperary)
1931—P. Delaney (Carlow)
1932—J. Smith (Wexford)
1933—P. Murray (Offaly)
1934—J. Dunne (Kilkenny)
1935—M. McMahon (Tipperary)
1936—P. Phelan (Kilkenny)
1937—W. Delaney (Wexford)
1938—L. Rowe (Dublin)
1939—M. Walsh (Galway)
1940—P. Molloy (Kilkenny)
1941—E. McMahon (Tipperary)
1942-45—Suspended
1946—P. Clarke (Mayo)
1947—J. Ryan (Wexford)

1948—H. Haddock (Armagh)
1949—V. Sherlock (Cavan)
1950—M. Griffin (Dublin)
1951—C. Delaney (Kilkenny)
1952—S. Commane (Kerry)
1953—P. McCarthy (Kerry)
1954—J. Delaney (Kilkenny
1955—J. Lyng (Wexford)·
1956—J. Maher (Louth)
1957—P. Kirby (Clare)
1958—F. Confrey (Louth)
1959—M. Kirby (Clare)
1960—M. O'Brien (Limerick)
1961—D. Walshe (Sligo)
1962—S. McCabe (Monaghan)
1963—R. Lyng (Wexford)
1964—W. Kearins (Kerry)

1965—P. Sheerin (Offaly)
1966—T. McEllistrim (Kerry)
1967—P. McGarry (Limerick)
1968—D. Kirby (Clare)
1969—P. Davin (Tipperary)
1970—M. Conway (Tyrone)
1971—B. Colleran (Mayo)
1972—P. Reilly (Kilkenny)
1973—J. Howlin (Wexford)
1974—P. Ryan (Dublin)
1975—O. Harrold (Kilkenny)
1976—T. O'Brien (Kerry)
1977—J. Roche (Limerick)
1978—J. Scully (Galway)

1979—A. Ryan (Tipperary)
1980—T. Quish (Limerick)
1981—P. Mullins (Tipperary)
1982—W. Bourke (Kilkenny)
1983—M. Sweeney (Sligo)
1984—J. Fleming (Wexford)
1985—D. Doolin (Roscommon)
1986—P. Delaney (Galway)
1987—E. Jensen (Meath)
1988—W. McCarthy (Tipperary)
1989—W. Fitzpatrick (Tipperary)
1980—R. McCarthy (Wesmeath)
1991—J. Rossiter (Carlow)
1992—J. Herlihy (Cork)
1993—S. O'Callaghan (Tipperary)

JUNIOR HARDBALL SINGLES

1928—J. Ryan (Tipperary)
1929—J. O'Mahoney (Cork)
1930—P. Bell (Meath)
1931—J. Foley (Kildare)
1932—J. O'Mahoney (Cork)
1933—T. Cherry (Kilkenny)
1934—A. Cullen (Kilkenny)
1935—J. J. Gilmartin (Kilkenny)
1936—P. Murray (Offaly)
1937— W. Butler (Dublin)
1938—T. Jordan (Kilkenny)
1939—M. Butler (Dublin)
1940—P. Molloy (Kilkenny)
1941—M. Dowling (Kildare)
1942—P. Murray (Offaly)
1943—James Gilmartin (Kilkenny)
1944—C. Drumgoole (Wexford)
1945—M. O'Gorman (Tipperary)
1946—G. Ryan (Kildare)
1947—R. Grattan (Kildare)
1948—J. Bolger (Kildare)
1949—P. Kennedy (Tipperary)
1950—M. O'Brien (Kildare)
1951—P. Downey (Kerry)
1952—C. O'Brien (Tipperary)
1953—W. Lawlor (Kildare)
1954—J. Delaney (Kilkenny)
1955—M. Redmond (Kildare)
1956—J. Maher (Louth)
1957—W. Doran (Kildare)

1958—J. Ryan (Tipperary)
1959—D. Downey (Kerry)
1960—J. Donovan (Kerry)
1961—J. Cleary (Tipperary)
1962—P. Hickey (Tipperary)
1963—T. Dowd (Wexford)
1964—P. Bolingbrook (Mayo)
1965—P. Sheerin (Offaly)
1966—T. McEllistrim (Kerry)
1967—M. O'Gara (Roscommon)
1968—A. Byrne (Dublin)
1969—A. McAuliffe (Limerick)
1970—J. Hartnett (Limerick)
1971—J. Quigley (Wexford)
1972—E. Sheeran (Offaly)
1973—M. Purcell (Kildare)
1974—P. McCormack (Mayo)
1975—P. Hughes (Kilkenny)
1976—M. Walsh (Roscommon)
1977—W. McCarthy (Tipperary)
1978—C. Quinn (Mayo)
1979—Noel Ryan (Tipperary)
1980—N. Quigley (Wexford)
1981—W. Pratt (Kilkenny)
1982—W. Bourke (Kilkenny)
1983—E. Lee (Dublin).
1984—N. O'Toole (Cork)
1985—M. Dowling (Kildare)'
1986—J. O'Donoghue (Tipperary)
1987—P. McAuley (Louth)

1988—W. O'Connor (Meath)
1989—P. O'Keeffe (Kilkenny)
1990—E. Jenson (Meath)

1991—M. Walsh (Kilkenny)
1992—D. Moloney (Tipperary)

JUNIOR SOFTBALL DOUBLES

1928—T. O'Keeffe and J. McCarthy (Tipperary)
1929—P. Perry and T. Gaughran (Roscommon)
1930—J. Molloy and H. Smith (Cavan)
1931—C. Darcy and J. Cahill (Kildare)
1932—W. Doyle and J. Fleming (Carlow)
1933—T. Cherry and J. O'Brien (Kilkenny)
1934—A. Cullen and P. Power (Kilkenny)
1935—A. Roe and H. Gallagher (Dublin)
1936—J. McDonald and J. Geraghty (Mayo)
1937—J. Bergin and M. O'Gorman (Tipperary)
1938—A. Collins and C. Collins (Tipperary)
1939—W. McDonald and R. Gibbons (Mayo)
1940—D. McDonald and P. Ryan (Carlow)
1941—S. Rice and E. McMahon (Tipperary)
1942—P. Kennedy and J. Gaughran (Roscommon)
1943-45—Suspended
1946—W. Buggy and T. Buggy (Kilkenny)
1947—G. Grogan and C. Donohoe (Dublin)
1948—J. O'Connell and M. O'Keeffe (Kilkenny)
1949—P. Kennedy and D. Carey (Tipperary)
1950—T. McCormack and P. McCormack (Mayo)
1951—P. Downey and T. Commane (Kerry)
1952—J. Byrne and P. Sutherland (Wexford)
1953—P. Munroe and M. Fahy (Dublin)
1954—P. Hackett and J. Moynihan (Limerick)
1955—T. Ryan and S. Lennon (Kilkenny)
1956—E. Connolly and S. Fleming (Mayo)
1957—T. McGarry and M. Mullins (Limerick)
1958—J. Clery and W. McKenna (Wicklow)
1959—T. Reilly and P. Reilly (Louth)
1960—M. O'Brien and S. Walsh (Limerick)
1961—J. Coughlan and G. Barry (Offaly)
1962—M. Walsh and P. McGee (Mayo)
1963—L. Gilmore and J. Gilmore (Cavan)
1964—W. Kerins and P. Moriarty (Kerry)
1965—L. Molloy and D. McGovern (Meath)
1966—T. McElisrim and M. McElistrim (Kerry)
1967—M. Henry and J. Gaffney (Sligo)
1968—R. Doherty and P. Clarke (Roscommon)
1969—N. Cahill and P. Masterson (Dublin)
1970—R. Walsh and J. O'Brien (Dublin)

1971—J. Kirby and M. Hogan (Clare)
1972—P. Reilly and P. Delaney (Kilkenny)
1973—J. Howlin and J. Goggins (Wexford)
1974—E. Hannon and P. Walsh (Sligo)
1975—O. Harold and B. Fitzpatrick (Kilkenny)
1976—G. and D. Sheridan (Cavan)
1977—P. Winders and T. O'Rourke (Kildare)
1978—N. O'Brien and T. Morrissey (Tipperary)
1979—J. B. Molloy and F. Carroll (Meath)
1980—T. and J. Quish (Limerick)
1981—F. McCann and M. Porter (Sligo)
1982—E. Farrell and B. Mullins (Tipperary)
1983— M. Walsh and E. Downey (Kilkenny)
1984—J. Fleming and P. Cleary (Wexford)
1985—P. Donagh and P. Hand (Cavan)
1986—P. Delaney and M. Connors (Galway)
1987—T. Sheridan and J. McGovern (Meath)
1988—W. O'Connor and J. Grant (Meath)
1989—E. Corbett and J. O'Donoghue (Tipperary)
1990—P. Kealey and B. Mullins (Offaly)
1991—J. Donlan and N. Breen (Clare)
1992—T. Derrig and P. McCormack (Mayo)
1993—N. Buggy and T. Hynes (Wexford)

JUNIOR HARDBALL DOUBLES

1928—S. Ryan and S. McInerney (Tipperary)
1929—J. O'Mahoney and D. O'Mahoney (Cork)
1930—N. Gorman and T. Maloney (Tipperary)
1931—J. McGrath and J. O'Connell (Kilkenny)
1932—A. Dalton and C. Baker (Kilkenny)
1933—S. Tormey and P. Bell, Junior (Meath)
1934—A. Cullen and J. Dunne (Kilkenny)
1935—P. Coyne and J. Purcell (Carlow)
1936—G. Ryan and J. Costello (Kildare)
1937—J. Hassett and M. O'Gorman (Tipperary)
1938— J. Hurley and T. Twohill (Cork)
1939—M. Butler and J. Roche (Dublin)
1940—W. Walsh and R. Ward (Cork)
1941—J. McGrath and D. Brennan (Kilkenny)
1942—P. Murray and J. McHugh (Offaly)
1943—James Gilmartin and J. O'Brien (Kilkenny)
1944—C. Drumgoole and J. Duggan (Wexford)
1945—W. Grace and C. Murphy (Kildare)
1946—M. Dalton and J. Dunne (Kilkenny)
1947—J. McGrath and J. Phelan (Kilkenny)
1948—W. McCabe and T. Tormey (Meath)
1949—J. Doyle and P. Doyle (Wexford)

1950—M. O'Brien and R. Maher (Kildare)
1951—S. Monahan and J. Doherty (Kilkenny)
1952—J. Kennedy and M. Heffernan (Tipperary)
1953—W. Lawlor and P. Monahan (Kildare)
1954—M. Gleeson and R. Doyle (Dublin)
1955—M. Redmond and J. Parle (Kildare)
1956—J. Maher and J. McArdle (Louth)
1957—W. Doran and J. Curran (Kildare)
1958—T. Doheny and M. Shanahan (Tipperary)
1959—A. Daly and P. Winders (Kildare)
1960—T. Cleere and C. Cleere (Tipperary)
1961—M. Kelly and G. Connolly (Galway)
1962—P. Hickey and T. Breedy (Tipperary)
1963—P. Supple and J. Murphy (Cork)
1964—G. Mahon and K. Fullard (Roscommon)
1965—M. Sullivan and J. Doyle (Dublin)
1966—T. McElistrim and M. McElistrim (Kerry)
1967—G. Lawlor and R. Winders (Kildare)
1968—N. Kerins and T. Fitzgerald (Kerry)
1969—E. Deegan and J. Browne (Kildare)
1970—J. Hartnett and P. Clancy (Limerick)
1971—P. Murphy and J. Quigley (Wexford)
1972—T. Geoghegan and C. Winders (Kildare)
1973—M. Purcell and J. Byrne (Kildare)

1974—M. Brady and T. Hurley (Dublin)
1975—P. Hughes and P. Kennedy (Kilkenny)
1976—G. and D. Sheridan (Cavan)
1977—J. Bennis and V. Moane (Limerick)
1978—E. Rabbitte and G. Scully (Galway)
1979—Tony and Noel Ryan (Tipperary)
1980—T. and J. Quish (Limerick)
1981—P. Cleary and S. McLoughlin (Wexford)
1982—W. Bourke and M. Lawlor (Kilkenny)
1983—E. Lee and R. Walsh (Dublin)

1984—M. Lorden and N. O'Toole (Cork)
1985—P. Hand and P. Donagh (Cavan)
1986—E. Corbett and J. O'Donoghue (Tipperary)
1987—F. McCann and S. Davey (Sligo)
1988—P. O'Connell and P. Quish (Limerick)
1989—C. McGovern and T. Sheridan (Meath)
1990—E. Jenson and D. Gough (Meath)
1991—M. Walsh and J. Connolly (Kilkenny)
1992—D. Moloney and J. O'Dwyer (Tipperary)

ALL-IRELAND 4×20 CHAMPIONSHIPS

SENIOR SINGLES

1975—P. Kirby (Clare)
1976—P. Kirby (Clare)
1977—P. Kirby (Clare)
1978—P. Kirby (Clare)
1979—P. Kirby (Clare)
1980—P. Kirby (Clare)
1981—T. Ryan (Tipperary)
1982—T. Ryan (Tipperary)
1983—T. Ryan (Tipperary)
1984—M. Hennigan (Mayo)
1985—M. Hennigan (Mayo)
1986—M. Walsh (Kilkenny)
1987—M. Walsh (Roscommon)
1988—M. Walsh (Kilkenny)
1989—M. Walsh (Kilkenny)
1990—M. Walsh (Kilkenny)
1991—M. Walsh (Kilkenny)
1992—W. O'Connor (Meath)
1993—E. Corbett (Tipperary)

SENIOR DOUBLES

1975—P. and M. Kirby (Clare)
1976—P. and M. Kirby (Clare)
1977—P. and M. Kirby (Clare)
1978—P. and M. Kirby (Clare)
1979—P. and M. Kirby (Clare)
1980—P. McGee and P. McCormack (Mayo)
1981—P. Delaney and W. Mullins (Offaly)
1982—J. Fleming and P. Cleary (Wexford)
1983—J. Fleming and P. Cleary (Wexford)
1984—J. Fleming and P. Cleary (Wexford)
1985—E. Rabbitt and P. Delaney (Galway)
1986—M. Walsh and M. Reade (Kilkenny)
1987—T. Sheridan and J. McGovern (Meath)
1988—T. Sheridan and J. McGovern (Meath)
1989—M. Walsh and M. Reade (Kilkenny)
1990—T. Sheridan and J. McGovern (Meath)
1991—E. Corbett and J. O'Donoghue (Tipperary)
1992—T. Sheridan and J. McGovern (Meath)
1993—T. Sheridan and J. McGovern (Meath)

JUNIOR SINGLES

1975—P. O'Keeffe (Tipperary)
1976—M. Walsh (Roscommon)
1977—P. Morris (Cork)
1978—P. Delaney (Offaly)
1979—Tony Ryan (Tipperary)
1980—G. O'Callaghan (Cork)
1981—J. Fleming (Wexford)
1982—G. Coughlan (Clare)
1983—E. Conneely (Galway)
1984—W. Bourke (Kilkenny)
1985—M. Walsh (Kilkenny)
1986—J. Herlihy (Cork)
1987—P. McAuley (Louth)
1988—W. Silcock (Antrim)
1989—E. Jenson (Meath)
1990—D. J. Carey (Kilkenny)
1991—F. McCann (Sligo)
1992—J. Donlan (Clare)
1993—P. Crothers (Antrim)

JUNIOR DOUBLES

1975—J. Morrissey and E. Farrell (Tipperary)
1976—P. Kealy and W. Mullins (Offaly)
1977—G. Scully and M. Ward (Galway)
1978—M. Aherne and B. O'Brien (Kerry)
1979—E. Rabbitte and J. Callinan (Galway)
1980—M. Hennigan and M. Sweeney (Mayo)
1981—J. Fleming and P. Cleary (Wexford)
1982—G. Coughlan and J. Duggan (Clare)
1983—J. McGovern and M. McGovern (Meath)
1984—W. Bourke and M. Reade (Kilkenny)
1985—P. Hall and D. O'Brien (Dublin)
1986—T. Quish and J. Quish (Limerick)
1987—P. McAuley and M. Maher (Louth)
1988—N. Breen and P. Devanney (RIP) (Clare)
1989—W. Pratt and W. O'Keeffe (Kilkenny)
1990—E. Corbett and J. O'Donoghue (Tipperary)
1991—R. McCarthy and J. Guilfoyle (Westmeath)
1992—J. Donlan and P. Walsh (Clare)
1993—P. Crothers and j. McGarry (Antrim)

MINOR SINGLES

1,975—M. Maher (Louth)
1976—M. Maher (Louth)
1977—T. Ryan (Tipperary)
1978—T. Ryan (Tipperary)

1979—W. O'Donnell (Tipperary)
1980—W. Bourke (Kilkenny)
1981—W. Bourke (Kilkenny)
1982—J. Duggan (Clare)

1983—M. Walsh (Kilkenny)
1984—M. Walsh (Kilkenny)
1985—W. O'Connor (Meath)
1986—P. McAuley (Louth)
1987—P. McAuley (Louth)
1988—D. J. Carey (Kilkenny)

1989—D. J. Carey (Kilkenny)
1990—P. Walsh (Clare)
1991—C. Curran (Tyrone)
1992—M. Finnegan (Cavan)
1993—M. Finnegan (Cavan)

MINOR DOUBLES

1975—P. Delaney and B. O'Connell (Offaly)
1976—P. Murphy and D. Neff (Cork)
1977—A. Ryan and W. O'Donnell (Tipperary)
1978—A. Ryan and N. McDonnell (Tipperary)
1979—M. Cantwell and W. Bourke (Kilkenny)
1980—W. Bourke and M. Lawlor (Kilkeeny)
1981—W. Bourke and M. Lawlor (Kilkenny)
1982—J. Duggan and P. Clavin (Clare)
1983—J. Duggan and P. Clavin (Clare)
1984—M. Walsh and P. O'Keeffe (Kilkenny)
1985—W. O'Connor and T. Sheridan (Meath)
1986—P. McAuley and J. McArdle (Louth)
1987—D. Gough and P. O'Rourke (Meath)
1988—D. J. Carey and E. Law (Kilkenny)
1989—D. J. Carey and E. Law (Kilkenny)
1990—D. King and S. Kavanagh (Carlow)
1991—D. Moloney and N. Murphy (Tipperary)
1992—M. Finnegan and D. Bartley (Cavan)
1993—M. Finnegan and R. Cunningham (Cavan)

IRISH OPEN

1992—W. O'Connor (Meath)
1993—M. Walsh (Kilkenny)

LADIES' FOOTBALL

THE Ladies' Gaelic Football Association (Cumann Peile Gael na mBan) was founded in Hayes's Hotel, Thurles, in 1974. Four counties – Offaly, Kerry, Galway and Tipperary – were represented at the meeting. The Association has built up steadily in the intervening years. Today there are 29 counties, including London and Manchester, playing ladies' football on an organised basis. The Association has a membership of approximately 25,000.

The structure of the Association exactly mirrors that of the GAA with clubs, County boards, Provincial Councils, Central Council and Annual Congress. The National President is elected for a three-year term of office.

The Ladies' Gaelic Football Association and the Camogie Association are sister organisations, but are not under the direct control of the GAA. However, the GAA recognises both Associations as catering for the playing needs of the fairer sex. This recognition was given to the Ladies' Association in 1982 after the GAA set up a Committee comprising its President, Dr Mick Loftus, Mick Spain, Tom Dowd, Marion O'Shea and Agnes Gorman.

ACCIDENT FUND

In 1984 the Ladies' Gaelic Football Association set up its own Accident Fund. This Fund is compulsory except for those taking part in official school competitions. The object of the Fund is to mitigate against hardship incurred by medical expenses and loss of wages or salary. It has proved to be a huge success as the injuries sustained have been few, due to the stringent rules that apply against over-robust play. The present rate of subscription to the injury fund is £4 per adult and £1.50 for members under 18.

In 1986 the big breakthrough was achieved when Ladies' football was played in Croke Park for the first time. Waterford was the first team to win at Croke Park when they captured the Junior title. Kerry took the Senior, their fifth in a row.

The Association organises inter-county competitions for senior, junior, minor, under-16 and under-14 teams as well as national competitions for senior club, third level colleges, post primary schools and an All-Ireland seven-a-side blitz. A ladies' Allstar team is selected each year and play the All-Ireland champions in an exhibition match shortly after the All-Ireland final.

By now the game has spread to London and Manchester. Emigration meant that many young people had moved across the Irish sea and clubs in London and Manchester provide football for these. In 1992 an Ontario ladies' select team came to Ireland on tour and played matches in Dublin, Westmeath and Cork.

PLAYING RULES

The playing rules of ladies' gaelic football are similar to that of men's gaelic football. There are some modifications which are designed mostly to speed up the game and to eliminate unnecessary physical contact which are outlined as follows:

1. A size four football is used in all grades of competition.
2. A player may pick the ball off the ground providing she is in a standing position. (The standing restriction does not apply to the goalkeeper inside the small parallelogram.)
3. A player while on the ground may play the ball away from her but cannot bring it into her possession.
4. All **deliberate** bodily contact is forbidden. When executing the tackle to dispossess an opponent it must be timed as the ball leaves the hands of the player in possession, i.e. while the ball is being hopped or in the act of soloing or kicking. It may also be knocked from an opponent's hands by flicking it with the open hand.
5. Deliberate use of the shoulder is forbidden.
6. When a free is awarded any player has the option to take it either from the hand or off the ground.
7. A team may use five substitutes during the game.

ALL-IRELAND SENIOR CHAMPIONSHIP

Winners	*Runners-up*
1989—Kerry	Wexford
1990—Kerry	Laois
1991—Waterford	Laois
1992—Waterford	Laois
1993—Kerry 4-8	Laois 2-6

JUNIOR CHAMPIONSHIP

1988—Leitrim	London
1989—Dublin	Clare
1990—Wicklow	London
1991—Clare	London
1992—Monaghan	London
1993—London 4-8	Donegal 0-3

UNDER-18 CHAMPIONSHIP

1988—Cork	Wexford
1989—Clare	Laois
1990—Clare	Dublin
1991—Waterford	Roscommon
1992—Laois	Waterford
1993—Waterford	Wexford

UNDER-16 CHAMPIONSHIP

1988—Laois	Kerry
1989—Dublin	Waterford
1990—Clare	Offaly
1991—Waterford	Roscommon
1992—Waterford	Wexford
1993—Wicklow	Kerry

INTERPROVINCIAL CHAMPIONSHIP

1989—Leinster	Connacht
1990—Leinster	Munster
1991—Munster	Leinster
1992—Leinster	Munster
1993—Munster	Leinster

SENIOR CLUB CHAMPIONSHIP

1988—Adamstown	Ballymacarbery
(Wexford)	(Waterford)
1989—Ballymacarbery	Rochfortsbridge
(Waterford)	(Westmeath)
1990—Ballymacarbery	St. Grellan's
	(Galway)
1991—Ballymacarbery	Rochfortbridge
1992—Ballymacarbery	Rochfortbridge

NATIONAL SENIOR LEAGUE

1988—Kerry	Waterford
1989—Kerry	Waterford
1990—Kerry	Waterford
1991—Kerry	Waterford
1992—Waterford	Laois

NATIONAL JUNIOR LEAGUE

1988—Cork	Dublin
1989—Dublin	Galway
1990—Clare	Kerry
1991—Clare	Mayo
1992—Cork	Monaghan
1993—Carlow	Roscommon

PRESIDENTS OF THE G.A.A.

1884—Maurice Davin (Tipperary)
1887—Eamonn Bennett (Clare)
1888—Maurice Davin (Tipperary)
1889—Peter J. Kelly (Galway)
1895—Frank B. Dineen (Limerick)
1898—Michael Deering (Cork)
1901—James Nowlan (Kilkenny)
1921—Daniel McCarthy (Dublin)
1924—Patrick D. Breen (Wexford)
1926—William P. Clifford (Limerick)
1928—Seán Ryan (Dublin)
1932—Seán McCarthy (Cork)
1935—Bob O'Keeffe (Laois)
1938—Pádraig McNamee (Antrim)
1943—Seamus Gardiner (Tipperary)
1946—Dan O'Rourke (Roscommon)
1949—Michael Kehoe (Wexford)
1952—Michael V. O'Donoghue (Waterford)
1955—Seamus McFerran (Antrim)
1958—Dr. J. J. Stuart (Dublin)
1961—Hugh Byrne (Wicklow)
1964—Alf Murray (Armagh)
1967—Seamus Ó Riain (Tipperary)
1970—Pat Fanning (Waterford)
1973—Dr Donal Keenan (Roscommon)
1976—Con Murphy (Cork)
1979—Paddy McFlynn (Down)
1982—Paddy Buggy (Kilkenny)
1985—Dr Mick Loftus (Mayo)
1988—John Dowling (Offaly)
1991—Peter Quinn (Fermanagh)

Note: In the Spring of 1994, Jack Boothman (Wicklow) is due to take over as President for the scheduled three-year term.

GENERAL SECRETARY/DIRECTOR GENERAL

1884-'85—Michael Cusack (Clare)
1884-'85—John McKay (Cork)
1884-'87—John Wyse Power (Kildare)
1885-'87—J. B. O'Reilly (Dublin)
1885-'89—Timothy O'Riordan (Cork)
1887-'88—James Moore (Louth)
1888-'89—William Prendergast (Tipperary)
1889-'90—P. R. Cleary (Limerick)
1890-'92—Maurice Moynihan (Kerry)
1891-'94—Patrick Tobin (Dublin)
1894-'95—David Walsh (Cork)
1895-'98—Richard T. C. Blake (Meath)
1898-'1901—Frank B. Dineen (Limerick)
1901-'09—Luke J. O'Toole (Dublin)
1929-'64—Pádraic Ó Caoimh (Cork)
1964-'79—Seán Ó Síocháin (Cork) Director General
1979   —Liam Mulvihill (Longford) Director-General

COUNTY COLOURS

Antrim: Saffron with white trim
Armagh: Orange with white trim
Carlow: Red, green and yellow
Cavan: Royal blue with white trim
Clare: Saffron with blue hoop
Cork: Red with white trim
Derry: White with red hoop and trim
Donegal: Gold, white, green trim
Down: Red with black trim
Dublin: Sky blue with navy trim
Fermanagh: Green with white trim
Galway: Maroon with white trim
Kerry: Green with gold hoop
Kildare: White with black numbers
Kilkenny: Black and amber vertical stripes
Laois: Royal blue with white hoop
Leitrim: Green with gold trim
Limerick: Green with white trim
Longford: Royal blue with gold trim
Louth: Red with white trim
Mayo: Green with red hoop
Meath: Green with gold trim
Monaghan: White with blue trim
Offaly: Green, white and gold thirds
Roscommon: Yellow with royal blue trim
Sligo: White with black trim
Tipperary: Royal blue with gold hoop
Tyrone: White with red trim
Waterford: White with blue trim
Westmeath: Maroon with white trim
Wexford: Purple with gold shoulders
Wicklow: Royal blue with gold trim

INDEX

Quick reference index to what is covered in Chapter 1 to Chapter 11 (inclusive):

FOOTBALL

Chapter 1: Pp. 3-16, Great teams of football history of the past half century (1943-'93). Pp. 10-13, Kerry and Dublin teams of the 1970s. Pp. 13-15, Meath team of 1986-'88.

Chapter 2: Pp. 17-32, Donegal's first ever All-Ireland title win and why Dublin lost 1993 All-Ireland final. Pp. 26-28, Donegal's defeat by Dublin in 1993 League final replay. Pp. 28-30, Donegal's defeat by Derry in 1993 Ulster Championship. Pp. 30-32, Donegal v Armagh in 1993 Ulster Championship.

Chapter 3: Pp. 33-43, Epic Meath v Dublin series of four games in 1991. Pp. 39-41, Meath lose to Dublin in 1993 Leinster Championship. Pp. 41-43, Dublin beat Kildare in 1993 Leinster final.

Chapter 4: Pp. 44-54, Down's 1991 All-Ireland triumph. Pp. 53-54, Down fail to Derry in Newry in 1993 Ulster Championship.

Chapter 5: Pp. 55-65, Clare beat Kerry in 1992 Munster final. Pp. 60-61, Clare lose to Dublin in 1992 All-Ireland semi-final. Pp. 61-63, Banner County loses to Donegal in 1993 League semi-final. Pp. 63-65, Cork beat Clare in Ennis in 1993 Munster semi-final.

Chapter 6: Pp. 66-80, Cork's tough battles with Meath in 1987 and 1988, All-Ireland victories in 1989 and 1990. Pp. 74-77, Galway lose to Leitrim in 1993 Connacht Championship. Pp. 79-80, Mayo lose to Cork in 1993 All-Ireland semi-final.

Chapter 7: Pp. 81-91, Derry's first ever All-Ireland title win. Victory over Cork in 1993 All-Ireland final and over Dublin in semi-final.

HURLING

Chapter 8: Pp. 95-107, The All-Ireland victories of Galway (1980) and Offaly (1981) at outset of 1980s. Pp. 100-106, Galway's outstanding 1987-'90 team and other great sides in the "Top Ten" of the past fifty years.

Chapter 9: Pp. 108-120, Tipperary win 1991 All-Ireland crown. Pp. 109-117, The 1990, '91 and '92 Cork v Tipperary classic Munster battles. Pp. 117-120, Defeats of Galway and Kilkenny by Tipperary in 1991. Pp. 118-120, Kilkenny defeat Cork in 1992 All-Ireland final.

Chapter 10: Pp. 121-136, The 1984 Cork v Tipperary epic Centenary Munster Final. Pp. 122-127, 1987 drawn game between Tipperary and Cork and marathon replay in Killarney. Pp. 127-129, Tipperary v Cork in 1993 National Hurling League semi-final. Cork win 1993 National League title after three tremendous games with Wexford. Cork fail to Clare in 1993 Munster semi-final. Pp. 130-131, Kerry's sensational defeat of Waterford in Munster Championship. Pp. 131-133, Kilkenny beat Offaly in classic in the rain in Leinster. Pp. 133-136, Kilkenny overcome Wexford in Leinster final replay.

Chapter 11: Pp. 137-142, Kilkenny make it two All-Ireland titles back to back in 1993. Pp. 142-144, Tipperary lose to Galway in 1993 All-Ireland semi-final.

RECORDS SECTION
Quick reference Index to what is covered in the Records Section

HURLING

P. 149, Roll of Honour of Championship Titles Won. Pp. 150-160, All-Ireland Senior Championship Results. Pp. 161-192, All-Ireland Final Teams. Pp. 193-195, Munster Senior Finals. Pp. 196-198, Leinster Senior Finals. Pp. 199-200, All-Ireland Minor Finals. Pp. 201-216, All-Ireland Minor Final Teams. Pp. 217-218, Captains of All-Ireland Minor Final Winning Teams. Pp. 219-220, Leinster Minor Finals. Pp. 220-222 Munster Minor Finals. Pp. 222-223, All-Ireland Under-21 Finals. Pp. 224-232, All-Ireland Under-21 Final Teams. P. 236, "B" Championship Finals and All-Ireland Intermediate Finals. P. 237, All-Ireland Junior Hurling Finals. Pp. 238-242, National Hurling League Records. Pp. 245-251, Railway Cup Records. Pp. 252-275, Railway Cup Final Teams. Pp. 275-276, Captains of Winning Railway Cup Teams. Pp. 277-278, Attendance Figures All-Ireland Finals. Pp. 279-281, Attendance Figures Munster and Leinster Finals. Pp. 282-289, All-Ireland Club Hurling Final Results and Teams. P. 290, Captains of Winning All-Ireland Club Teams. Pp. 291-294, Bank of Ireland All-Stars Hurling Teams.

FOOTBALL

Pp. 299-312, Roll of Honour of Championship Titles Won. Pp. 313-340, All-Ireland Senior Championship Teams. Pp. 341-343, Munster Senior Finals. Pp. 343-347, Connacht Senior Finals. Pp. 347-350, Ulster Senior Finals. Pp. 350-354, Leinster Senior Finals. P. 354, All-Ireland Minor Finals. Pp. 355-369, All-Ireland

Minor Final Teams. P. 370, Captains of All-Ireland Minor Finals. Pp. 371-372, Leinster Minor Finals. Pp. 372-374, Ulster Minor Finals. Pp. 374-375, Munster Minor Finals. Pp. 375-377, Connacht Minor Finals. P. 378, All-Ireland Under-21 Football Finals. Pp. 379-387, All-Ireland Under-21 Football Final Teams. P. 388, Captains of All-Ireland Under-21 Winning Teams. P. 389, Leinster Under-21 Finals. Pp. 389-390, Ulster Under-21 Finals. Pp. 390-391, Munster Under-21 Finals. Pp. 391-392, Connacht Under-21 Finals. P. 393, All-Ireland Junior Finals. Pp. 394-397, National Football League Results. Pp. 399-406, Railway Cup Football Records. Pp. 407-428, Railway Cup Football Teams. Pp. 429-430, Captains of Winning Railway Cup Teams. P. 431, Attendance Figures at All-Ireland Finals. Pp. 432-440, All-Ireland Club Finals Results, Teams and Winning Captains. Pp. 441-445, Bank of Ireland All-Star Football Teams. Pp. 446-447, International Series. P. 448, Leading All-Ireland Senior Medal Winners. Pp. 449-450, Texaco Footballer of the Year Awards and Hall of Fame. P. 451, Teams of the Century and Centenary Teams.

Pp. 452-471, Colleges Records.

Pp. 472-473, Sigerson Cup.

Pp. 474-477, Vocational Schools Records.

Pp. 478-479, Gaelic Games and the Garda Connection.

Pp. 480-481, Gaelic Games and the Army Connection.

Pp. 482-484, Gaelic Games in the Universities.

Pp. 485-489, Camogie.

Pp. 490-506, Handball Review and Records.

Pp. 507-510, Ladies Football.

P. 511, Presidents of the GAA.

P. 512, General Secretary/Director General.

P. 513, County Colours.

P. 514. Quick Reference Index to Editorial Chapters and Hurling and Football Records.